How Finkelstein Broke the Trauma Bond and Beat the Holocaust:

Traumatic Memory and the Struggle Against Systemic Evil

Books by Lawrence Swaim

Novels

Waiting for the Earthquake
The Killing
Dangerous Pilgrims

Non-Fiction

(Genesis Trilogy)

The Death of Judeo-Christianity: Religious Aggression and Systemic Evil in the Modern World

Trauma Bond: An Inquiry into the Nature of Evil

How Finkelstein Broke the Trauma Bond, and Beat the Holocaust: Traumatic Memory and the Struggle against Systemic Evil

How Finkelstein Broke the Trauma Bond and Beat the Holocaust:

Traumatic Memory and the Struggle Against Systemic Evil

Lawrence Swaim

**PSYCHE
BOOKS**

Winchester, UK
Washington, USA

First published by Psyche Books, 2015
Psyche Books is an imprint of John Hunt Publishing Ltd., Laurel House, Station Approach,
Alresford, Hants, SO24 9JH, UK
office1@jhpbooks.net
www.johnhuntpublishing.com
www.psyche-books.com

For distributor details and how to order please visit the 'Ordering' section on our website.

ISBN: 978 1 78535 020 7
Library of Congress Control Number: 2015933778

A CIP catalogue record for this book is available from the British Library.

Design: Stuart Davies

Printed and bound by CPI Group (UK) Ltd, Croydon, CR0 4YY, UK

We operate a distinctive and ethical publishing philosophy in all
areas of our business, from our global network of authors to
production and worldwide distribution.

CONTENTS

Preface

For most of my adult life—as vice-president of a San Francisco postal union, a journalist in Europe and Latin America, a college professor, a novelist and a counselor at a residential crisis program—I have been fascinated by aggression and systemic evil. About ten years ago I began work on a trilogy of books (the 'Genesis Trilogy') about the ways in which aggression is disseminated in society, and how aggression ends up becoming systemic evil in certain situations. In *The Death of Judeo-Christianity: Religious Aggression and Systemic Evil in the Modern World*, I wrote about the way in which American religion unconsciously disseminates aggression as part of the believer's worldview.

The second book of the trilogy, *Trauma Bond: an Inquiry into the Nature of Evil*, contains in detail my basic theory of aggression and systemic evil. It explains the manner in which aggression is disseminated from person to person, and from institutions to individuals. Violence causes psychological trauma, and traumatic memory, I discovered, is the medium through which aggression is disseminated. Victims of human violence internalize the aggression of those that harm them, and act it out against others (or, as often happens, against themselves). Past trauma often bonds people to a violent worldview, and to aggression as a way of life. Victims internalize the violence of the aggressor because it is the only way they can survive psychologically; and it is usually to this that we refer when we speak of a "cycle of violence" in those parts of the world plagued by organized conflict.

"Ah, but everybody knows that!" exclaim the psychological establishment. "The influence of past trauma on behavior has been around since the days of Sigmund Freud." But if that is so, why does society not apply this lesson to its social problems—

1

war, exploitation and racism, among other forms of aggression that affect human behavior? Psychotherapists try to correct personal pathologies, but ignore the social ones; social justice activists flail away at unjust institutions, but changing institutions is never enough. The human personality itself has to change at the same time that corrupt social institutions do, and when possible they should change as part of the same struggle. That would be the goal and message of the moral psychology I advocate.

I've written two books about trauma bonding; this book is about people who have broken free of its malevolent influence. This third and last book of the 'Genesis Trilogy,' *How Finkelstein Broke the Trauma Bond, and Beat the Holocaust: Traumatic Memory and the Struggle against Systemic Evil,* tells the illuminating and sometimes mind-boggling stories of courageous individuals who broke free of traumatic memory, often at the same time that they broke free of oppressive social situations that kept those traumatic memories alive. Their insights gave to them—and now to you, reader—the tools to understand how the internalized aggression of traumatic memory is used by those that seek to do harm.

Sometimes traumatic memory is widely shared within an aggrieved group; other times, it is intergenerational. Sometimes it is society-wide, making it especially easy for psychopathic leaders to invoke past trauma to prepare people psychologically for war, torture, extrajudicial execution, rape, genocide, ethnic cleansing and other atrocities. The aggression embedded in traumatic memory is the wheelhouse of systemic evil committed by the state, and is used by tyrants everywhere. At its worst, the use of past trauma to justify present oppression by aggrieved groups becomes a form of 'traumatic privilege,' which when institutionalized becomes an extremely dangerous form of destructive entitlement.

This book's 'recovery dualism' does not banish all internalized aggression, nor does it defeat all the systemic evil in particular societies. But clearly it is an effective way for individuals to manage whatever aggression they may have internalized, and to anticipate the toxic appeals to traumatic memory by demagogues in particular settings.

Aggressors are *always* aggrieved, and always posture themselves as pitiful victims; that is one of the observable constants in the economy of human aggression. Likewise aggressive ideologies *always* encourage adherents to embrace victim status, preparatory to acting out their internalized aggression. Understanding the calamitous triumvirate of traumatic memory, aggression and systemic evil—and the gutter politics by which demagogues and violent governments use the first to strengthen the second and third—is probably the single most important insight for those seeking peace and human rights in the 21st century.

Lawrence Swaim
Napa Valley
November 2014

There are a thousand hacking at the branches of evil to one who is striking at the root.
—Henry David Thoreau

Chapter One

What Causes Human Aggression, and How it is Disseminated in Society

1.

This book does *not* promise the reader money, power or happiness, and it is not an inspirational book. On the other hand, it *does* offer an important kind of self-help—it contains a comprehensive theory of aggression and evil, and shows how certain courageous people have broken free of the cycle of violence in which our world is enmeshed. It explains how aggression replicates itself in human interactions, how victims become aggressors, and how aggression becomes systemic evil—all important insights, to be sure; but more importantly, it also examines how certain individuals were able to break free of this ugly cycle.

It is true that humankind is caught in a cycle of violence, coercion and deceit, but it is the conviction of this author that every individual can find a good way to manage the effects of this omnipresent aggression, and to a great extent break free of its influence. In a great many cases this starts by developing a thoughtful moral code, one that is cognizant of the values of honesty, cooperation rather than domination, and a thoughtful win-win negotiating strategy.

But these are easy things to say, and hard to do. Aggression and deceit have a powerful hold on humanity's imagination, and on the world's most powerful institutions. Why is aggression so powerful in human affairs? Where does aggression come from, and what's the difference between aggression and systemic evil? This book addresses these questions from the micro and macro viewpoints, both the individual and societal points of view. One is able to adopt both viewpoints because the manner in which societies fall under the spell of aggression is essentially the individual case writ large.

Aggression is something we all know when we see it, but it arises from the seemingly unknowable emotional orientations of individuals. How are these aggressive emotional orientations disseminated in society? Victims of human violence tend to internalize the aggression they have endured, and afterwards act out that internalized aggression against others, or against themselves. In other words, the abused child grows up to become an abuser—this insight has become part of the vernacular wisdom of humankind. But what causes that to happen, and what are the implications of it?

Why, in other words, don't people learn from their violent experiences, and chose a different way? A few do, but more don't, because the manner in which they become bonded to aggression is a process that is largely unconscious. So, what exactly is the relationship between psychological trauma, human aggression and the problem of systemic evil? It is precisely this malevolent triumvirate that this book interrogates, ultimately concluding that psychological trauma and traumatic memory is the medium by which aggression is most often internalized, and then acted out.

How does that happen? Victims of human brutality can quickly become trauma-bonded to aggression as the highest and most authentic emotional state, and for that reason seek to rationalize its brutal effects; but unacceptable human aggression— when hidden, rationalized, covered-up or romanticized— becomes a form of evil. When the state or other powerful institutions systematically use this kind of evil it becomes a form of systemic evil. (Think Hitler, Stalin and the six major genocides that broke out in the 20th century. All were all examples of systemic evil.) The key to understanding systemic evil is understanding the way traumatic memory is manipulated by sociopathic tyrants in order to start wars, persecute minorities or cause violence generally—and the way this mass process tends to bond people to aggression on a mass level.

That, in outline form, is the cycle of destruction in which humankind is caught. The pivotal issue is the way aggression changes people, making them more violent, or at least more aggressive, as they internalize the aggression they have endured, witnessed or perpetrated. On the face of it, that part of this book's theory seems simple; but when taken as part of a comprehensive theory of aggression, it threatens popular ideas regarding cognition and behavior. One popular belief is that victims of violence ought to be able to learn from—or even become ennobled by—the violence they endure; people cling to this idea, it seems, partly in order to justify their belief in the progress, ethical and otherwise, of the societies in which they live. (One is reminded of Dostoyevsky's belief, one quite reminiscent of medieval Christianity, that suffering "purifies the soul," whereas in reality suffering tends to corrode the soul and disorient personal agency.)

This book insists that the truth is simple but hard: victims of violent oppression are precisely the ones that seek to oppress others. On some level this is a truth of which we are all aware, but it is also a truth we wish to ignore or suppress. A few individual victims of violence and oppression learn from their experience, and since they are able to escape the cycle of aggression they were previously caught in, these individuals become the teachers of humankind. (One thinks of Gandhi and Martin Luther King.) But many more victims of violence and oppression can hardly wait to start oppressing someone else; and if they are not able to do so personally, they identify with—and support—people who do.

Again: this happens when people are traumatized by human aggression, because they tend to internalize the aggression they endure, and become bonded to it as the centralizing principle of life, wholly or in part. And since that kind of aggressive emotional orientation demands to be expressed, they either seek out new victims, or end up acting out—in a process far more common than people realize—their internalized aggression against themselves. Women very often tend to take out their internalized aggression against themselves, in the form of depression, self-harm, substance abuse, sleep disturbance and self-doubt; men tend to act it out against others. That's how the cycle of violence works.

Of course, there are aggressive people whose particular brand of aggression did not come from being personally victimized by aggression, but those who were so victimized are often the most active—and vocal—in acting out the aggression they have internalized. Find leaders of violent social movements, find the most racist and xenophobic and hateful among them (especially those who demand the right to hurt the weak and vulnerable) and you will usually find people who have themselves suffered great abuse, and who have internalized that aggression. The trauma bond is the electrical charge that holds the entire malignant cycle of societal aggression together.

That being the case, understanding the trauma bond—and then doing something about it—could tip the scales toward survival of the species. The hopeful reality is this: the aggression that victims internalize, and the aggressive worldview to which they become bonded, can be deconstructed over time. This can be accomplished, first, when victims of violence talk about what happened to them with someone whom they trust; and secondly, by participating in some form of socially-beneficial behavior that specifically has to do with the aggression that originally caused the trauma. (For example, victims of rape and violence against women recover more quickly by working with other victims to change the laws to better protect women in the future, and by raising consciousness in general about crimes against women.) In that way victims seek to reverse-engineer the psychological damage they've experienced, by deconstructing the aggression that was internalized, making both it and the traumatic memory manageable.

Traumatic memory is by definition a wound that cannot heal—but it can be managed, and it can be managed well. What is different about this book is its insistence that psychological trauma resulting from human aggression is different from trauma resulting from the earthquake, the tornado or the house fire.[1] Traumata from man-made violence—war, genocide, rape and criminal assaults—create traumatic memories in the form of overwhelming emotions, first experienced during the violence; but they also have the capacity to influence later thought and behavior, because traumatic memory as a result of human violence is a remnant of the violence itself, emotions that are frozen in time in the victim's memory. The result is an aggressive emotional orientation of which the victim may be mainly unaware.

It is because human actors engage in war, genocide, rape and criminal violence that traumatic memories from these experiences influence attitudes toward humanity and society in general. Traumata from natural disasters, on the other hand, tend to trigger chaotic memories and feelings, but not necessarily aggression. It is at the time of the original human violence that the aggression is internalized, so to overcome the after-effects the individual must strive to deconstruct aggressive emotional orientations that were internalized *during the traumatizing events*. Those same aggressive emotional orientations tend to remain, and can develop a life of their own as part of a traumatic memory. Needless to say, the victim may be completely unaware of the cause of the aggression she is now feeling, especially if she is directing that aggression against herself.

Aggression can be caused in many ways, but trauma bonding is important to understand, this writer insists, because it happens unconsciously, because it is so common, and because its malevolent after-effects can be deconstructed. It also appears to be the main way that aggression is unconsciously disseminated in society, from parent to child, person to person, and institution to individual. The experience of violence, of human aggression, enters the personality in a particularly powerful and behavior-altering way. But it should go without saying, of course, that aggression in societies arises for other reasons than the internalization of aggression during a psychologically traumatizing event. Therefore, before we look further at traumatic memory and aggression, it would probably be a good idea to take a brief look at some other causes of human aggression.

2.

Inherent Aggression. Males tend to be more aggressive than females from a very early age, at least according to specialists in early childhood development; there is a significant relativity between testosterone and aggression, which requires the learning of coping mechanisms and social skills on the part of males. But can we honestly say that testosterone is the problem? No, because that same testosterone can be used to become a superb ballet dancer, a gifted scientist, or a loving husband and father. Testosterone is no more the cause of aggression than alcohol is the cause of alcoholism.

Whether testosterone leads to violence or not depends entirely on how one learns to sublimate one's aggression, and to channel it into socially-acceptable goals. Those who can control and channel their aggressive impulses thrive; those who can't go to prison, or waste their lives in a highly unromantic pursuit of self-destruction. Sublimating aggression is a process that is learned. Some people never get the hang of it, but most do.

But whence comes all this inherent human aggression? From the fact that humans are descendants of violent animals, animals that fought and killed each other, who hunted and ate the flesh of other creatures. Once people developed societies, they sought power and developed empires by engaging incessantly in wars with each other, seeking also to reduce women to sexual slavery, and ritually killing animals and each other to propitiate a variety of angry gods. This violence we inherit in our biological DNA, and in various cultural influences. (Of all the cultural influences that make us more violent, those of patriarchy, nationalism and militarism are probably the strongest.)

At the time of the Neolithic Revolution, humans built huge slave empires of a surpassing brutality, and during the Industrial Revolution approximately ten thousand years later Europeans developed weapons to further enslave vast sections of the earth (what we today call 'the developing world') in order to steal their natural resources, employ cheap labor, and acquire new markets. We inherited the emotional remnants of European wars and imperialism in our cultural DNA, not to mention several centuries of incredibly brutal religious wars, and the European penchant for solving social problems by dominating others. But there's little doubt that the original source of human aggression comes from our collective past as violent animals 'red in tooth and claw' in the forest primeval.

Even right-wing Christian evangelicals who don't believe in evolution of organisms unknowingly acknowledge this fact in their imagery. If you ask them where aggression comes from, they say it came from the Fall in the Garden of Eden. But what lured Adam and Eve into eating the forbidden fruit in the first place? A lowly serpent, that's what. And look at the pictorial representations of the Devil in both religious and popular culture—check out the tail, the hooves, the horns and that hairy body!

This is a creature that is half human and half animal, a ferocious beast that is trying to become a human—which in metaphoric terms is exactly what humanity is doing right now. The struggle with our inherent aggression is what drives the question of human good and evil, partly because it is a funda-mental problem that underlies all human thought and culture;

but more immediately, if we can't get a handle on it, humankind seems destined to destroy itself. We're violent animals that have somehow acquired the gift of reason, and are going through an especially tumultuous adolescence, in which we're all struggling to make sense of the weird combination of reason and raw aggression that makes up the human personality. The scariest part is that what we believe to be rational decision-making is too often driven by aggressive emotional orientations that are more likely to push us in the direction of self-destruction than enable us to find rational answers to problems. This struggle with human aggression—a fair amount of which is inherent—is the great dilemma of our time.

Situational Aggression. The remarkable documentary film *Blackfish* tells the disconcerting story of killer whales that are held in captivity in order to participate in carefully choreographed shows aimed at entertaining human spectators. Specifically the film is about Tilicum, a killer whale that was involved in the deaths of three trainers at two facilities owned by SeaWorld. (SeaWorld is a chain of animal-theme parks that feature performances by captive orca, sea lions and dolphins.) Tilicum was captured near Iceland in 1983, and was first taken to 'Sealand of the Pacific' in British Columbia.

Two older killer whales behaved with extreme aggression toward Tilicum in captivity, which the management responded to by putting him in an inappropriately small tank; food deprivation was also used as a training method, which means that Tilicum was first given food and then deprived of it in order to sustain particular behaviors. Tilicum exhibited extreme agitation and aggression throughout his captivity, at times cooperating with and then attacking training staff. *Blackfish* argues convincingly that orcas—killer whales—should not be in captivity, as captivity makes them profoundly aggressive.

On 20 February 1991, Keltie Byrne, a 20-year-old competitive swimmer and marine biology student, slipped into a pool containing Tilicum and the two older orcas, and was dragged underwater by Tillicum and drowned. Shortly after that tragic incident, in early 1992, Tilicum was moved to SeaWorld Orlando, in Florida. ('Sealand of the Pacific' closed down shortly afterwards.) It was at Orlando, on July 6, 1999, that a homeless man who snuck into the pool after hours was killed by Tilicum, who tore off his swim trucks along with his testicles; the homeless man died of drowning and hyperthermia. On February 24, 2010, 40-year-old trainer Dawn Brancheau was grabbed as she was rubbing down Tilicam as part of their usual post-show routine, and was dragged underwater and mutilated in a particularly horrible way. (SeaWorld Orlando released public statements that Tilicum grabbed her by her ponytail, but witnesses say that he grabbed her by the arm.)

On August 23, 2010, SeaWorld Orlando was fined $75,000 by the Occupational Safety and Health Administration (OSHA) for safety violations. The film *Blackfish* features numerous interviews with trainers and experts who testified that keeping killer whales penned in small spaces makes them extremely aggressive. We may conclude, then, that the aggression exhibited by Tilicum—and by other orcas held in captivity and trained to perform for the entertainment of human spectators—are the result of the captivity and training itself, rather than inherent aggression, and are therefore examples of situational aggression.

Dangerous neighborhoods where shots fired are regularly heard at night, where children are killed by gunfire in the turf wars of drug lords—neighborhoods where one's child cannot safely walk to school—are likely to cause people to feel aggression that they wouldn't feel if they lived in a gated community full of rich people with political clout. Likewise the Palestinians that live in Gaza, whose children are regularly shot if they mistakenly get too close to the wire barriers maintained by the Israelis, might also feel aggression that they wouldn't feel if there was a peace agreement that guaranteed security for both sides. (I'm sure that Israelis living in Sderot, which is regularly targeted by Qassam rockets from Gaza, endure the same kind of gut-wrenching emotions as the Gazans.)

Situational aggression is generated by a particular social arrangement, as a result of which the level of aggression can presumably be altered by changing the arrangement or situation. Situational aggression generated by violent environments is often turned inward against oneself, causing drug addictions, depression, high-risk behavior, miscarriages, anxiety disorders and Post-Traumatic Stress Disorder, among many other problems and conditions.

Biologically-Based Aggression and Hyper-Aggression. On 1 August 1966, Charles Whitman, a former Marine and an engineering student at the University of Texas, went on a deadly shooting rampage from the University Tower, in which 16 people were killed and 32 were wounded. The rampage ended with his death at the hands of the police; subsequent investigation revealed that he had also killed his wife and his mother earlier that morning. Growing up, Charles had experienced many problems with his father, who was reportedly abusive, and Charles had also been bothered by a gambling addiction when in the Marines. He had struck his wife three times, and suffered enormous remorse as a result, which he documented in a journal. On the day of the killings, he left several notes that indicated that he did not expect to survive the massacre.

Whitman had been aware for some time that something was wrong, and sought help from at least five doctors, the last one a psychiatrist. He acknowledged being confused and frightened by violent urges he did not understand, and which he had difficulty controlling. He visited the staff psychiatrist at the health center at the University of Texas, who found him "oozing with hostility," with "periods of hostility with a very minimum of provocation." In one of his suicide notes, Whitman wrote of his experience with the psychiatrist: "I talked with a Doctor once for about two hours and tried to convey to him my fears that I felt [overcome by] overwhelming violent impulses. After one visit, I never saw the Doctor again, and have been fighting my mental turmoil alone, and seemingly to no avail." According to the psychiatrist's notes, Whitman said that he had fantasies of going up in the campus tower to kill people with a deer rifle. Whitman wrote in one of several suicide notes: "I am supposed to be an average reasonable and intelligent young man. However, lately (I cannot recall when it started) I have been a victim of many unusual and irrational thoughts."

Interestingly, Whitman asked for an autopsy in his suicide notes. (He also asked that any insurance money go to a "mental health foundation," writing that "[m]aybe research can prevent further tragedies of this type.") The first autopsy found nothing remarkable. But Texas Governor John Connally created a high-level commission to conduct a more thorough investigation. This second commission, which included psychologists and psychiatrists as well as pathologists and neurosurgeons, found a significant and growing glioblastoma tumor next to the amygdalae region of the brain; and concluded—based on malformations near the tumor—that it had started growing after long being dormant. The tumor was in a position to press against the amygdalae area, which affects fight-or-flight impulses. Therefore, the commission concluded, it "could have contributed to his inability to control his emotions and actions."

This is a dramatic example of aggression (in this case irrational and very destructive aggression) being caused, partially or wholly, by a biological change in one's body. There are many other such examples. People suffering from bipolar disorder can become uncharacteristically aggressive, even violent, when manic; schizophrenics hearing command voices can also do harmful things, although most schizophrenics are not violent. And we can all think of situations in which we were fatigued, overworked or physically stressed when we snapped at workmates, spouses or friends. In general, aggression that occurs because of a physical problem or anomaly could be addressed by correcting the physical problem.

Drug-Induced Aggression. During the Battle of the Bulge, the largest battle ever fought by American armed forces, allied soldiers were astonished at the unlimited energy and audacity of the German soldiers. They fought with a seemingly deranged vigor in all types of weather, at all times of the day and night, and simply didn't seem to know when they were beaten. This was no accident. To begin with, these were fresh troops, brought up to the front with the specific intention of breaking through the American lines. But there was another and even more important reason. The top command of the Wehrmacht was giving their frontline troops large amounts of amphetamines, which enabled those soldiers to fight for long periods without sleep, and with a seemingly uncanny amount of physical resilience. They literally fought until they dropped, and they dropped only when they were killed or wounded.

It may have been partly for this reason that General Dwight Eisenhower used his superior numbers to form a long, curving but uniform front to steadily push the Germans back, instead of engaging in the strategic and tactical pyrotechnics advocated by General George Patton. The long front was intended not to defeat the Wehrmacht with brilliant tactics, but to convince them that despite their high energy they could not regain the momentum— there were simply too many allied troops there to stop them. In time Eisenhower was successful, and the allies won the Battle of the Bulge. After a period of time amphetamines were no longer enough to sustain momentum, and it became clear to all that the tide had turned, and that this last desperate effort by the Nazi high command had failed

This is but one instance of the manner in which particular drugs can reinforce or generate significant amounts of human aggression. Another example—one that many Americans have unfortunately become familiar with—is the threatening and harmful side effects of steroid use by athletes and performers. Use of steroids to enhance athletic performance can generate the sudden onset of extreme feelings of aggression, which—because the individual has not had time to develop coping strategies— can be disruptive at best, and at worst result in suicide and/or homicide.

Steroid use is particularly common among teenage males in high school; yet such is the celebrity status of professional athletes, and so desperate is the economic situation of so many young people, that many will unhesitatingly make a Faustian bargain with steroids to improve their performance, very often because they hope to win a sports scholarship. It is likely that steroid use by young males—estimated to be as high as five percent of the youthful male demographic—has exceeded heroin and methamphetamine use.

Anabolic steroids—more properly called anabolic-androgenic steroids, or AAS—are synthetic variants of male testosterone. When teenage boys take them it can interfere in the normal processes of adolescence in alarming ways. One of the more well-known (and dangerous) side effects of steroid use are the episodes of so-called "'roid rage"—the sudden onset of intense, and sometimes uncontrollable, aggressive impulses and emotions. A surprisingly high percentage of boys take out these aggressive emotional orientations on themselves, committing suicide rather than asking for help.

In the case of Charles Whitman examined above, it is worth noting that many of the doctors he saw gave him drugs in an attempt to help him control his over-the-top aggressive impulses. One gave him Valium, which could have calmed his nervous system, but which could not treat the source of his problem—a growing tumor in an area that could stimulate aggressive impulses. He was also given Dexadrine, which he had in his possession at the time he was killed by the police. It is hard to see how giving such a young man Dexadrine—a very strong psycho-stimulant and amphetamine stereoisomer usually prescribed for ADHD in children—could in any way help him with his aggressive impulses, since amphetamine abuse can itself cause inappropriate aggression.

Concerning Valium, it should be noted that in the late 1960s and early 1970s many Vietnam Veterans were given Valium by the Veterans Administration upon being discharged from the military (and told to take three 10 MG tabs a day) immediately upon arriving back in civilian life, to help them deal with any "re-entry problems" they might be having. In reality, young vets tended to use the Valium to suppress aggressive impulses, anxiety, nightmares and other symptoms of PTSD. The upshot was that they often became addicted to 'downers' such as Valium, especially when potentiated with alcohol. For that reason, the Valium given by the Veterans Administration, far from helping most returning Vietnam Veterans, often became the gateway drug to a lifetime of addictions.

Having looked briefly at these examples of human aggression, let's move on to the subject of this book, which is the examination of aggression—or aggressive emotional orientations—that occur as a direct result of psychological trauma resulting from human violence.

3.

Traumatic Memory and Trauma Bonding. We're all born with some aggression. But this book insists that experiencing human violence as a victim (or even a witness to violence) is most likely the main way aggression is disseminated in society, and is likely to greatly enhance whatever inherent or innate aggression one already possesses. As we've already seen, victims of human aggression tend to internalize the aggression they endure—it's an automatic function of the victim's personality, to ensure its own survival during a traumatizing event. All those violent, aggressive emotions then get stuck in the victim's memory, and create an aggressive emotional orientation that affects everything in the personality. The traumatic memory of the victim can also cause him or her to become bonded to aggression as a lifestyle or fundamental attitude, with men usually acting out their internalized aggression against other people, and women taking it out against themselves.

This is a fascinating and rather alarming aspect of human nature, one that few people understand wholly, and one that a great many people don't *want* to understand, because it suggests that the human capacity for aggression and evil is much greater than most people want to admit. And there's another and even more dangerous social aspect to this process. Traumatic memory, and the internalized aggression that usually accompanies it, can be endlessly manipulated by demagogic politicians and dictators to stir up racism, religious wars, ethnic cleansing and persecution of racial and religious minorities. Furthermore, aggressive ideologies invariably play on victim status as a justification of aggression against others. When these things are done by the state, it becomes a form of systemic evil.

Being victimized by human violence is the usual way by which human beings become aggressive, a truism we acknowledge when we say, "The abused child grows up to be an abuser." But let us examine that idea for a moment. Why doesn't the physically and emotionally abused child simply shake off his traumatic memories once he reaches adulthood, and rationally choose a non-violent, humane parenting style? Why don't people learn from the violence they have experienced? Some do, but many more don't. The reality is, there is a very powerful force that causes most people who have suffered violence to re-enact the violence they have endured, either against themselves or others.

Again: *victims of human aggression tend to internalize the violence they have experienced, in the form of an aggressive emotional orien-*

tation. That orientation will stay inside them unless they find some way to deconstruct it, or otherwise manage it. This brings us to a discussion of the central thesis of this book, which is about the way aggression is acquired or enhanced through psychological trauma, in which aggression is internalized and remains in the personality as part of a traumatic memory. Over time this is likely to cause the victim to act out the aggression he has previously internalized.

But this isn't just a generalized philosophical idea—it's actually a predictable psychological process that can be observed and quantified. When psychologists Donald C. Dutton and Susan Painter began to study traumatic bonding in the early 1980s, they did so in the context of abusive relationships between men and women. They concentrated on the powerful (but life-threatening and extremely pathological) bond that transpires between an abusive man and his female victim or victims. Family courts and attorneys specializing in family law likewise have noted the trauma bond that regularly develops between abusive parents and their children. Both abused spouses and abused children have a dangerous tendency to identify with their abusers, and often adopt the aggressor's reasoning, values and worldview. It's paradoxical, it makes no sense, but it happens.

Adults that are exposed to human aggression—combat in war, sexual assault, criminal assaults, whatever—also very often internalize the violence they endure, but the kind of trauma bonding they experience happens differently than with children or abused spouses. Whereas abused children tend to bond *personally* to the abusive parent, and abused spouses bond *personally* to the abusive spouse, adults tend to develop a bond *to aggression itself,* rather than to the aggressor. This is not necessarily a sign of character weakness—traumatized victims of human violence internalize the aggression they endure as a way of psychologically surviving it. The manner in which this occurs is taken up at length in my book *Trauma Bond: an Inquiry into the Nature of Evil.*

It starts at the moment the aggression itself occurs, such as in an ambush in war, a rape, a criminal attack, or what have you. The victim momentarily identifies with the world of the aggressor in order to outsmart or defeat that same aggressor, then begins to internalize the aggression inherent to the violent situation as he or she fights back and struggles to out-maneuver the aggressor.

In *Trauma Bond* the momentary identification is characterized thus: "The world of the victim is completely overwhelmed by the attacker's aggression, as that same aggression quickly becomes the victim's world. The victim is in a strange terrain, but must somehow master it quickly to survive. Thus he has no choice except to identify totally with the world of the aggressor, because only total alertness to the danger that is upon him is going to help him survive the danger." The victim isn't identifying with the aggressor, but with his aggression, so that he—the victim— can figure out how to defeat, deflect or escape it. And because all personal barriers come down during human violence, the victim's personality is changing during the violent and traumatizing event, as the victim begins to internalize the attacker's aggression.

"The personality is overwhelmed by so much stimulation that cognition closes down. The victim is running totally on adrenaline, nervous energy and something close to hysteria. The soldier reverts to the training he has internalized, but is no longer making conscious decisions. A woman being raped may disassociate cognitively. The mind and emotions are totally out of whack, which is why part of post-traumatic treatment is helping the victim get his or her thoughts and feelings back, afterwards, into some kind of workable juxtaposition to each other." That happens because long after the traumatizing event is over, the emotions associated with that event will continue to exist in the personality as a traumatic memory.

But it will be a very special kind of memory, a memory consisting of strong feelings of fear and aggression. The traumatic memory tells the victim that the threat is still there, long after the threat is gone. The traumatic memory will cause him to go on red alert even when there is objectively no danger, because it will tell him that he is still in danger long after the threat has past. While natural disasters (tornadoes, tsunamis and earthquakes) create traumatic memories that can haunt victims for a lifetime, they are qualitatively different than traumatic memories from war, rape or criminal attacks. Traumatic memories from human violence destroy trust, create fears of human unpredictability, and may make it difficult for victims to participate in social contracts.

The really difficult part of this process is that the aggression is likely to stay in the unconscious part of the victim's personality for a very long time, until the traumatized individual decides to do something about it. We know that aggression is a part of most traumatic memories from human violence because, for one thing, victims of past aggression often report feelings of extreme aggression in response to present, real-world stimuli: noises, circumstances, feelings or thoughts that by themselves are harmless, but nonetheless trigger powerful aggressive feelings, often accompanied by unreasoning fear. The embedded aggression may also result in a worldview in which violence is seen as the best and most honorable response to human problems, and in which human conflict is the fundamental standard by which everything else is to be measured. In men, such a worldview can become an intense form of patriarchy, resulting in a profound conviction that force is the proper way to deal with a variety of complex human problems, rather than compromise and consensus.

And it's not just that traumatic memories are acts of extreme violence, frozen in time in the memory of the victim. It *changes the personality* of the victim, and almost surely the brain as well. "The logical mind is so overwhelmed and at such a disadvantage that it can no longer process events very well, since the victim is functioning mainly on instinct, adrenaline and intuition. But the unconscious mind of the victim knows the danger, and turns the tables on the attacker. It responds to the aggression with a gambit used in judo—it accepts the aggression, using the hostile energy of the attack to pull the aggression in. It is trying desperately to control the situation by internalizing it. This mental flip-flop is the mind's way of trying to ensure the survival of the victim." Evolutionary biologists believe that this tendency to internalize the aggression of an aggressor may have been selected into the panoply of human responses a long, long time ago, perhaps in pre-historic times.

"By internalizing the aggression attacking it, the personality of the victim can now bend instead of break. Instead of resisting the aggression, the unconscious mind welcomes it into the personality, making the victim feel that he has gained some control and making the attack a little less overwhelming." But that internalized aggression stays in the personality of the victim long after the attack is over. "This aggressive orientation is likely to grow stronger if the conscious mind cannot retrospectively make sense of the violence endured—and it usually can't, if the victim cannot create some kind of moral context for what he has been through."

Of course, the best way to put one's traumatized emotions and the traumatizing events into some kind of perspective is to talk about them as soon as possible afterwards, with professionals if possible. But talk therapy alone may not be enough to deconstruct the aggression once it has been internalized. It may also require action, as we will explain.

"When one speaks of internalizing the aggression of an attacker, a threatening figure, or a battlefield enemy, it sounds more like a physical than an emotional process, like an exchange of blood-borne pathogens. But it isn't a physical transfer. It's a sharp, violent and emotional response to aggression, in which the victim's emotions violently reorient themselves and take on an aggressive emotional orientation that the victim didn't have before. The unconscious mind isn't just accommodating the aggression it is experiencing—it is unconsciously imitating and conforming to the aggression being visited against it, in a desperate bid to survive it. The longer the aggression goes on, and the longer the victim is in a threatening or violent environment, the more these changes are likely to occur, and to affect the victim's personality later."

"When US soldiers went out on patrol in Iraq, as they tended to do almost daily, similar changes in the soldier's personality were extremely likely to happen, because a constant state of aggressive alertness was the only way the American soldier could compensate for the familiarity of the enemy with the terrain, the culture and the prevailing tribal alignments. Again, it was an effort to imitate the readiness that the insurgents already possessed, simply because they were Iraqis, and the Americans weren't. The Iraqi insurgents were, in other words, playing on their home field; and the Americans had to adopt a hyper-vigilant and aggressive attitude to compensate for the advantage." And that attitude would stay in place, in the soldier's personality, long after the soldier left the combat zone.

"Without the agency of moral choice, without conscious decision-making, the entire unconscious linkage of emotion, instinct and sensory awareness coheres to fit the pattern of the attacker's aggression. The personality of the combat soldier is understandably affected by a powerful aggressive emotional orientation—and it becomes very difficult to turn the spigot off. A specific crime, attack or threatening situation may end, but its effects on the victim's personality may remain for a very long time—and affect the victim's behavior in strange and unexpected ways in the future."

"Some people, of course, are able to very quickly figure out a way to deconstruct the aggression they've internalized, and to sublimate it or channel it in positive ways; but unless people are

24

willing to talk about the things that traumatized them, internalized aggression can become so volatile and so uncomfortable that it is intrinsically difficult to control."

Some people, however, seem to be born with an innate ability to deconstruct aggression they have internalized—either that, or they are deeply motivated to find such a way. Most of the people whose stories appear in this book found ways to deconstruct the traumatic memories that haunted them, while at the same time deconstructing the intense aggression that was at the heart of those memories. These people became, in this writer's opinion, the spiritual teachers and heroes of a world desperate to find a way out of the spiral of aggression in which we're all unfortunately caught.

People who have internalized aggression aren't usually aware of it. "Since this aggressive emotional orientation ends up in the unconscious part of the victim's personality, over a long period of time it is likely to influence the victim's behavior in ways he or she may not be consciously aware of. It is also likely to affect the victim's worldview. Men traumatized by human aggression (either because they were victims of it, or were perpetrators of it, or both) are prone to identify with aggression in the larger society by supporting patriarchy, nationalism or a coercive attitude toward the resolution of social problems. The male victim may bond with other people, usually males, who engage in violence together. (Think paramilitary militias, biker gangs, Serbian nationalists, fraternities that haze student pledges, and so forth.)"

For many men, participating with other men in group violence may be the only form of intimacy they've ever known. Over a period of time, people who have internalized a great deal of violence—such as men that were physically abused as children—may become victim-aggressors, people whose behavior is extremely violent but who think each act of violence is somebody else's fault. Such a person may feel like a victim even as he is lying to, stealing from, raping or killing others.

"The unconscious mind does not seek cognitive answers, but emotional ones—and if cognitive reasons for behavior are also lacking, that exponentially increases the need for emotional answers. What the traumatized person seeks, on one level, is an answer to the riddle of evil. The traumatized person longs to go back to the original place of violence, as though an emotional Eden lies waiting to be discovered in the instant right before the ambush, IED explosion, domestic violence or gunshot wound, the instant before the violence created a new person and a new world inside the victim. So traumatized men must cash in their spiritual IOUs, and Bogart their way back, back to the Garden, back through the violence to the safety and innocence encapsulated in the moment before the aggression. Or is it the violence itself that contains the answer they are longing for?"

"Traumatized men can never be completely sure, until they start dealing with the aggression they've internalized. Traumatized women—rape victims in particular—spend an enormous amount of time blaming themselves, trying to figure out what they did wrong, when it is actually rape that is wrong. Trauma-bonded people never really know what they're searching for—all they know is that they want to examine the agency of violence that transformed them, and in that way get back the innocence they lost, and in the process find out once and for all what the hell happened to them."

But once the person has endured the aggression, it does not lend itself easily to logical analysis. "Reason does not understand aggression, and aggression does not understand reason. The victim of psychological trauma is often trapped in this discontinuity between cognition and aggression, which plays out in an existential borderland in which the conscious and unconscious minds have not only parted company, but are no longer on speaking terms. Try as it may, the self can find no logical answers about the past in these emotional badlands. Out of this radically unknowable quality of human aggression rises the trauma bond: it organizes and focuses violent emotions in ways that neither reason nor emotion could ever do alone." But it does so by bonding people to aggression as the dominant, inevitable and underlying dynamic of human life.

Of course not all people want to get rid of their aggression, either the aggression they've internalized or the latent aggression they were born with. "Some people make such a good adjustment to their own aggression that they have no reason to become less violent. They are people who know how to lie convincingly about the aggression they are acting out, and to seamlessly rationalize their own brutality. Sometimes whole societies do it—the infamous Joseph Goebbels, for example, created an alternative national narrative in Nazi Germany that justified everything that Hitler and the Nazi regime did, which was almost completely bogus but which a great many people wanted to believe. Stalin's minions, likewise, adopted a complicated ideology that promised the ultimate eradication of aggression and exploitation if only people would look the other way when the Soviet state engaged in its own massive aggression."

"When people dissemble, cover up, or rationalize human aggression against the innocent, it is at that point that aggression becomes a form of evil. That is in fact this book's working definition of evil: *Unacceptable aggression plus deceit equals evil.* And aggression that is successfully concealed is far more likely to become systemic evil (a coordinated system of aggression accompanied by government lying to rationalize or cover it up) which is used by the state to oppress large numbers of people."[2]

4.

So there it is. Victims or witnesses to violence internalize the aggression, but can later deconstruct it. No single part of this book's theory is completely unknown, but mainstream

27

psychology seems often hesitant to generalize about the powerful ways aggression affects the personality. Nor does it feel particularly comfortable with these insights when presented as part of a comprehensive theory of human evil. That is probably because mainstream psychology does not experience human aggression as a moral problem, even though victims of aggression experience it in that way. It may be partly because institutional psychology is uncomfortable with such terms as "systemic evil," or that psychologists are afraid that acknowledging a moral dimension in the study of human behavior might cause them to lose their scientific objectivity. But since morality is a human phenomenon, why should psychology and science shy away from the opportunity to describe—and study—morality itself?

Psychology in America is particularly concerned with encouraging people to adjust to various social realities, rather than encouraging them to question whether those social realities are good or bad, and perhaps even the cause of many of their problems. Sadly, many Americans live in a Disney world in which the capacity for evil is never present; American psychology is at pains to be marketable in that world. Other people do not wish to understand aggression and evil because they do not understand—or do not wish to understand—the severity of the crisis humanity is passing through. (Reminding one of Bertolt Brecht's famous quip, "He who smiles has not yet heard the bad news.")

Perhaps some are afraid to consider the evidence for personal reasons, or are frightened by the worldly vocabulary a moral psychology might conjure up. It is, for example, an astonishing fact that many educated people in the 21st century do not acknowledge the existence of human evil—which perhaps should not surprise us, since we all tend to deny, to some extent, the presence of aggression when it arises in our own behavior. There is, in other words, an inbuilt human queasiness regarding the question of good and evil, especially evil, which this book defines as unacceptable aggression that is hidden, covered-up, romanticized or rationalized.

But we are at a time when people are increasingly forced to see the reality of human evil, including their own capacity for it; and when that happens people are likely to look for practical, applied methods for dealing with it in their own lives (while also dealing with systemic evil in society). This is precisely the task of the moral psychology implicit in this book, the categorical imperative of which is that human aggression must be managed or sublimated, and that internalized aggression must be deconstructed, starting with the individual. If not, it is very likely that humanity will destroy itself. Interestingly, the methods for dealing with internalized aggression, although quite varied, are surprisingly direct, especially when compared to the seemingly paradoxical manner in which human aggression originally enters and changes the personality.

Although much psychoanalytic thought has now become irrelevant, one aspect of it is more important today than ever before. Most people do not comprehend the actual motives that drive their behavior, nor do they generally understand the underlying emotional orientations that drive their attitudes and articulated beliefs. Of course, Freud was mainly wrong—humanity's greatest problem is not repressed sexual impulses, but aggression. Still, in identifying aggression as humankind's major problem, this book is in the same tradition that arose with psychoanalysis, and later the many schools of applied psychotherapy, because it identifies unseen but powerful emotions as the wheelhouse of the personality. But there are differences. Throughout the twentieth century psychotherapy—and especially psychoanalysis—noted the presence of aggression only in passing ("without moralizing," as psychoanalysts were wont to say) whilst concentrating on helping the client or patient make a good adjustment to society, or helping them in their quest for "happiness."

Moral psychology, on the other hand, believes that internalized aggression is the real underlying problem of many people seeking help, and that systemic evil is the central problem of civilization. It values personal integrity and the formation of a life-affirming moral code as its foremost goal, and the idea of finding happiness by making an adjustment to society as fundamentally contemptible, especially if the society is moving toward exploitation, war and corruption.

Moral psychology intervenes in the cycle of violence by helping those with traumatic memories deconstruct whatever aggressive emotional orientations they have internalized, believing that happiness, if it happens at all, will occur as a by-product. Thus moral psychology sees the development of a personal morality, or moral code, as central to the individual's integrity, and the source of meaning in that person's life; it sees learning to sublimate aggression as the gateway to the formation and empowerment of one's moral code, and therefore also the key to integrity.

Happiness is a feeling, often a transitory or even illusory one; whereas integrity is a dialectical experience of self and the world, a dance of life that is capable, when we make the best choices, of giving enormous pleasure. It is in that dance that we discover love, and learn how to act it out. But that in turn has everything to do with deconstructing or managing aggression, and then making choices that serve the best interests of self and society. We cannot escape the centrality of aggression because its presence defines the essential dilemma of human life. It is the individual management of aggression, in fact, that gives individuals and governments the freedom to make moral choices. Without that, people and institutions are driven by emotional orientations they don't understand, and can't control.

The stories in this book illustrate what people can do when they have internalized extreme forms of aggression and find themselves bonded to it, very often bonded to aggression they are acting out against themselves. Of course, not everybody who experiences aggression internalizes it; furthermore, there are those gifted persons who see through the cycle of violence and subterfuge, and strive to avoid internalizing the aggression they instinctively perceive as unhealthy. And finally, it is not enough simply to understand how aggression and evil replicate themselves. We must do something about it if humankind is not to destroy itself. But the place to start is always with oneself — then, and only then, can one move on to confront injustice in the world.

Sometimes people become involved in powerful conflicts during times of radical social changes, but are able to avoid internalizing violence because they adopt techniques that are deliberately calibrated to interfere with the cycle of violence within which they are operating. For example: the way Gandhi got his followers to promise not to strike back at those who attacked them, and the way Martin Luther King did the same with his followers. In those cases the cycle of violence was greatly reduced, and societies benefited from the changes Gandhi and King brought about. Gandhi and Dr. King teach us that conflict is not the same as violence, if we are willing to follow nonviolent techniques for social change.

This book, on the other hand, is not for extraordinary individuals like Dr. King and Gandhi, but for the rest of us. The people in this book were seemingly ordinary folk who undertook extraordinary challenges. Their great victory was that they broke the bonding effect of traumatic memory, by deconstructing the aggression they had internalized. They did this through what this book refers to as a 'recovery dualism.' **First**, they talked or wrote about the source of their traumatic memory, sometimes engaging with counselors, psychologists and psychiatrists in a clinical setting, learning to access and experience traumatic memories of human violence without being overwhelmed by them. **Secondly**, they engaged in socially-beneficial *and relevant* activities and behaviors that helped them challenge those forces in society that kept their traumatic memories alive. This combination of activities was effective in helping them to deconstruct the aggression that was embedded in their traumatic memories.

They generally needed talk therapy to put their experiences in perspective; but they also needed to actively participate in socially-beneficial activities, in that manner to replace aggressive emotional orientations rooted in the past with better orientations rooted in the present. All but one of the individuals whose stories are told in this book succeeded in doing this. These are courageous people who not only sought to remake themselves, but whose narratives are representative—and quite frequently archetypical—examples of humankind's unquenchable desire to know itself. Finally, the people in this book sought to fundamentally challenge society while transfiguring their own personalities, and in so doing decisively confronted the problem of good and evil in our time.

Chapter Two

How Finkelstein Broke the Trauma Bond, and Beat the Holocaust

Who can deny the irony of the contrast between the careful study of human 'aggressiveness' in our socio-psychological sciences, and our encounter with a form of aggressiveness in actual life which is informed by such manias, illusions, historical aberrations and confusions, as could possible come under the microscope of the scientific procedures used in some of these studies?
Reinhold Niebuhr
The Irony of American History

1.

We begin with the story of Norman Finkelstein, the brilliant, irascible political scientist whose searing books vividly dissect the mistakes and chicanery of an entire generation of America's cultural and political elites. Although nobody questions his facts, Finkelstein was unceremoniously kicked out of American academia and permanently blacklisted from teaching because of the inconvenient and dramatic nature of those facts. A political scholar with a popular following whose writings bear a strong family resemblance to the muckraking authors of a century ago, he also revealed, in his shocking book-length exposé *The Holocaust Industry: Reflections on the Exploitation of Jewish Suffering*, astonishing examples of corruption in his own community, which were enabled and aided by no less than President Bill Clinton. Among other things, Finkelstein sought to expose the frantic machinations of a variety of shady hustlers, greedy attorneys and bottom-feeding political operatives that sought to cash in on the suffering of Jewish victims of the Nazi Holocaust.

Few living Holocaust survivors ever saw any of the billions of dollars that these swindlers managed to lay their hands on. As we'll see, despite the consistency with which the Likud government of Israel talks about the Holocaust, survivors of the Holocaust living in Israel receive almost nothing. This exploitation of Jewish suffering by faceless bureaucrats, along with the suffering of Palestinians under Israeli occupation, became Finkelstein's burning issues. These were issues that almost all Americans were afraid to discuss, to a great extent because of the traumatic memory that underlay them; and also because of the predictably histrionic attacks by billionaire donors and political operatives on anybody who sought to systematically investigate them. The venom with which Finkelstein is attacked suggests that there's more to these efforts to stigmatize him than a simple political disagreement or two.

For stubbornly insisting on his right to explore these issues in his books, Finkelstein suffered the near-hysterical and ongoing condemnation of the US Israel Lobby, but he also became the target, as we will see, of almost the entire US political and cultural elite. In connecting the traumatic memory of the Holocaust and the suffering of Palestinians, two subjects that most Americans are afraid even to think about, Finkelstein sought to act out the values of his parents, both of whom were Holocaust survivors. It is one of the most telling ironies of our time that leading figures in the American cultural establishment sought to accuse Finkelstein of being a Holocaust denier, when both his mother and father were Holocaust survivors. Amazingly, Finkelstein was able to partially avoid—and eventually deconstruct—those aspects of intergenerational Holocaust trauma in his family that most affected him.

This happened, I believe, because of the positive example of his mother, who daily struggled to make sense of her own traumatic Holocaust memories. She sought to do so by constantly referencing experiences in the Nazi camps, comparing them to current events, and going out of her way to denounce any attitude or behavior in the present that she associated with the Nazi madness. (Including extremist attitudes internalized and acted out by the political class in Israel.) This was a lesson Finkelstein learned from his mother, and acted out in his life: ultimately, he discovered, you defeat the Holocaust by refusing to internalize its violence, then by creating and living out an alternative to it, first in your own personality and then in the world.

Finkelstein's mother, Maryla Husyt Finkelstein, struggled with the traumatic memory of her years in the Nazi camps by relentlessly opposing injustice in the world around her, and by acting out strong personal alternatives to that injustice. In copying this simple but very effective method, Finkelstein found a way out of the intergenerational trauma of the Holocaust, most powerfully by writing about those who sought to profit from the suffering of its victims. Because the violence of the Holocaust was so deeply internalized by survivors, breaking free of its influence is harder than most people would imagine—indeed, we are to some extent all haunted by the Holocaust, because it forces us to confront the existence of systemic evil. But although it is a hard school, learning to manage that magnitude of traumatic memory is exactly the kind of personal and social transformation necessary to break out of the world's cycle of violence. It means coming to terms with the internalized aggression in one's own personality; but it also means struggling to change a world in which something as horrible as the Holocaust could happen.

For about 25 years, beginning in early 1980s and ending in 2007, when he was unceremoniously kicked out of American academia and blacklisted forever, Norman Finkelstein was probably the most controversial public intellectual in America. Noam Chomsky, a former academic advisor of Finkelstein—also a well-known public intellectual—has written books that are every bit as radical in his exploration of inconvenient American truths as Finkelstein's, but the extent to which Norman Finkelstein has publicly criticized leaders of his own Jewish community—and the violent way he is denounced by that community's advocacy organizations—are unique in modern American history. Since Finkelstein's scathing investigatory scholarship almost invariably has to do with the two most controversial subjects in the modern world (the Nazi Holocaust and Israel/Palestine), the hysterical uproar that greeted virtually everything he wrote is a tip-off to the depth, ferocity and diabolical intensity of the issues he seeks to illuminate.

These same burning issues are finally not only about power and systemic evil, but the equally timeless themes of guilty knowledge and self-delusion. Regarding Israel/Palestine, Finkelstein's presentation is that of a man who has, for some time now, been patiently engaged in pointing out that the Titanic is sinking, while his critics tend to be those on the upper decks who prefer to drown whilst loudly blaming everybody else for their predicament. His books are exposés of the ways in which some people derive money and power from secrets, but they're also about the way people keep secrets from themselves.

At its core, much of Finkelstein's personal philosophy arises from the innate moral sense of his mother, which was humanistic, universal and intensely Jewish. By copying her method for interrogating history in the present moment, he was led to bear witness to the irreducible connection between the Holocaust and the Israeli/Palestinian conflict, and the techniques of those who use the traumatic memory of the Holocaust to make money, generate conflict, and advance their corrupt institutional interests. In this manner, he was true to the values of his parents, the same values that helped them survive Hitler's camps. As we will see, deconstructing the traumatic memory of the Holocaust may be the necessary precursor—the key, one might say—to deconstructing the trauma and aggression at the heart of the

36

Israeli/Palestinian conflict. And that can be just as simple, and just as difficult, as taking a good look in the mirror.

2.

Although both Norman Finkelstein's mother and father were Holocaust survivors, Maryla Husyt Finkelstein, Norman's mother, was without question the greatest influence in his life. She was a native of Warsaw, Poland, and grew up during the dissolution of Polish life and culture that occurred during and after the Pilsudski dictatorship, in which everything was increasingly defined by the growing inevitability of world war. Although anti-Semitism had long run deep in Polish society, nobody could have predicted the madness that would follow Hitler's invasion of Poland on September 1st, 1939 (and the invasion by the Soviet Union on the 17th of that same month.). Poland capitulated on September 28th of that year, and Maryla Husyt Finkelstein was caught up in the accelerating horrors of the Second World War. Like many other Jews of that time and place, she ended up in the Warsaw Ghetto, and later in the Majdanek concentration camp. Finally she was sent to two slave labor camps. She had married before the war; but her first husband—about whom little is known—did not survive the death camps.

Maryla said in an interview that the worst day of her life was the day on which she was liberated from the Nazi camp where she had been incarcerated. Why such despair at the very moment that she was liberated? The reason, quite simply, was her sudden realization that all who were dear to her, including her parents, husband and siblings, were all dead—and that she was completely alone in the world. The shock of loneliness and grief was compounded in her consciousness with a lacerating survival guilt, which together formed much of her attitude toward the world from that moment forward. She expressed more than once an irrational shame that she had survived the Holocaust, and also a recurring, bone-deep idea, typical of survival guilt, that those who perished in the camps were noble and compassionate, and those that survived were in some way tainted with evil. This survival guilt is all but universal in the narratives of Holocaust survivors; but in Maryla's case it was appropriately combined with deep, unremitting anger at the incomprehensible nature of the experience itself.

In recordings made after the War, Maryla described her life just after liberation from the Nazi labor camp: she spoke of working at a school for Jewish orphans who had been living in the Polish forests, children who had somehow survived the Nazi occupation. They were, she said, avid to be taught—"there was no way you could keep them from learning," she says on these recordings. Apparently at some point Zionists came to take the children to Israel, she relates, remarking that they were taken there "to build, but unfortunately not only to build. They also destroyed."

In this same recorded interview, she expresses her distrust of Jewish leaders, a trait inherited in multiples by her son Norman. This is easier to understand if one considers the mistakes of Jewish leaders in Eastern Europe, leaders who found it difficult, as did the rest of the world, to believe in the genocidal intentions of the Nazis; as a consequence, they frequently attempted to strike bargains with the Nazis, or their local representatives, regarding the defense of their communities. In reality, however, no strategy, no matter how well-considered, could have kept the Jewish communities in Eastern Europe safe. Jews that opted to join guerilla bands fighting the Nazis very often lost their lives in combat against the German Wehrmacht, and some were killed by anti-Semitic Polish nationalists. In Maryla Husyt Finkelstein's opinion, many leaders of the various Jewish communities were opportunists because they tried to bargain with the Nazis. But few people of that time, regardless of their ethnicity or religion, understood the total depravity of the Nazis.

Zacharias Finkelstein, Maryla's second husband and Norman's father, was a survivor of both the Warsaw Ghetto and Auschwitz. After he married Maryla, he immigrated to the US with her, where he became a factory worker. Interestingly, according to a 2001 article in the progressive Israeli newspaper *Haaretz*, Norman's father Zacharias, while in the Warsaw Ghetto, developed a strong friendship with Israel Guttman, who would someday become chief historian at Yad Vashem in Jerusalem.

From the Warsaw Ghetto, Zacharias and Guttman were sent to the Auschwitz extermination camp, which the two young men somehow managed to survive. They planned to immigrate to Palestine, but were separated by unforeseen events in postwar Europe; Zacharias ended up marrying Maryla and going to the US. Israel Guttman went to Palestine; and although disappointed in Zacharias' decision, Guttman remained friends with him. Until late in life, Zacharias welcomed Guttman into his home when the latter was visiting in the US; but toward the end of Zacharias' life the two men had a falling out.

"With bitter disappointment," Finkelstein wrote, "my father eventually admitted that [Guttman] had also been corrupted by the Holocaust industry, selling his beliefs for power and profit." (Finkelstein does not mention Guttman by name, but there seems little doubt that he is referring to him.) Does Finkelstein's disapproval arise from Guttman's role at Yad Vashem in indoctrinating young Israelis into the fashionable worship of victim status? Surely Yad Vashem has some cultural value apart from its obvious political function. What role did Norman's scholarship and strong opinions play in his father Zacharias' alleged disillusionment with Guttman's work in Israel? Whatever the truth of this may be, Guttman became a bitter critic of Zachrias' son Norman Finkelstein, and like most Zionists referred to him as either an anti-Semite or a self-hating Jew.

According to several accounts, the conversation of Norman Finkelstein's mother Maryla often included references to the

Holocaust, remarking that certain things that merited her disapproval were "worse than Hitler," which become the standard denunciation for everything disgusting and evil. (Including, at times, her children's misbehavior.) In fact Maryla Finkelstein's frequent references to the Holocaust, expressed in a way many would find arbitrary, clearly had the function of coming to terms on a daily basis with memories of her time in the Majdanek camps and the slave labor camps. She had a horror of images and footage of war and exploitation on TV, comparing what the US was doing in Vietnam to what the Nazis had done in Europe: "Every night as we watched the news on television my mother would avert her eyes and raise her hand to block the screen when scenes from Vietnam flashed across it," Norman Finkelstein wrote. "After a few moments the question would invariably come: 'Is it over yet?'"

Both Maryla and her husband Zacharias were on the left politically, and Maryla was in addition a passionate pacifist; her opposition to the Vietnam War was based on an instinctive horror of destruction of the weak by the powerful. One friend reportedly experienced Maryla's passionate belief in human rights as "bordering on hysteria,"[1] and that word was also used in his memoir-in-progress by Finkelstein himself, as we will see. Norman has written that there was something about the immediacy of his mother's furious denunciations of aggression that greatly appealed to him; but it must have also caused him some anxiety, because it was so clearly driven by the demons of traumatic memory.

In any case, he learned with some relief later—upon reading the work of Noam Chomsky, in fact—that he could combine his mother's furious hatred of injustice with a certain scholarly judiciousness. To this was compounded Finkelstein's natural-born gift for edgy wit and excoriating sarcasm, which was aimed particularly at the professional hypocrites, inside his community and out of it, who posture themselves as benefactors of humanity when they were simply opportunists out to make good careers, or—in some cases—to make money.

Maryla's distrust of Jewish elites was based on her European experiences, but also on a perception that leaders of the organized Jewish community in the US were traveling rapidly to the right; as well as a sense that they—like other religious elites—had a tendency to rule certain things out of bounds for open discussion within their own communities. This led to another factor in Finkelstein's books, a talent for prophetic negatives—that is, he had a gift for deconstructing elements of group ideology that caused people to believe in things that are factually untrue. Above all, Finkelstein was able to show that a great many of the most popular beliefs about Israel in America are based on half-truth and distortions, and not just in the Jewish community; a great deal of journalism and so-called scholarship about Israel/Palestine is actually rather shoddy propaganda.

But it was a peculiar kind of propaganda for which people seemed to have a deep psychic need. Although Finkelstein did not articulate this insight in the beginning of his career, he may have sensed—because of his close association with this mother— the connection between this dangerous emotional need for soothing falsehoods regarding Israel/Palestine, and the Holocaust. We are now becoming all too familiar with this same phenomenon in conservative-evangelical Christian circles, in which the lust for power and money—and the open appeals to violent religious nationalism—are regularly justified by pious and often nauseating appeals to scripture, and the rabid promotion of novel theologies that portray religious war, torture and oppression as God's will at the end of history.

Growing up in Maryla's house, Finkelstein has written that he wondered at times what she might have been forced to do to survive life in the camps. But there was no question of Maryla's belief in universal human rights, because it was at the heart of her Jewish identity. Norman inherited—along with many other

Jews raised in Left, liberal and non-Zionist homes—this under-standing of Jewish culture based on critical thought (the search for truth), as well as a commitment to personal liberty and the quest for social justice. At its heart the central dream and expec-tation of cultural Judaism in Europe was always the idea of universal human rights, including freedom of religion and full civil rights for Jews. Indeed, to the extent to which most Jews believed in God, it was understood that God worked in human history on the side of social justice, which they also believed would ultimately bring about civil rights for Jews.

That was the heart of Jewish identity, not just for Maryla Husyt Finkelstein and her son Norman, but also most liberal, non-Orthodox or non-Chassidic Jews in the US and in Europe prior to the foundation of Israel in 1948. At the same time the dream of universal human rights was also Maryla's core identity as a human being, because it was her only hope for the eventual realization of a better world. And that dream was fundamental to her daily struggle to defeat the pain of traumatic memory, which began in Hitler's camps and continued to beset her.

Maryla's passion for human rights came partly from Left ideas picked up as a young student in Poland, and partly from the worldview of Jewish liberals and leftists in her milieu. There is also every indication, alas, that it also harks back to that traumatic moment of Maryla's awful realization, in the first few hours of being released from a slave labor camp, that she was alone in the world—that she had lost all her family members, even her young husband, to the Nazis. The radical injustice and horror of it—the very anomaly of such a thing happening in the 20th century—would never completely leave her consciousness. If one understands it as the last part of the long agony she experi-enced in the death camps (as a moment of culminating horror) it would probably not be inaccurate to say that much of the traumatic horror of that moment was buried deep in the non-conscious part of her personality, and drove her most vocal and important values.

But even if that terrible moment defined the emotional and spiritual problem with which she would struggle every day for a lifetime, it did not define her. She spent her life working to define her life apart from and in resistance to that moment—to remember it, but to resist it every day (indeed, every moment) afterwards. In short, she fought on a daily basis to deconstruct the traumatic effects of the moment of maximum loss and horror—the moment in which that she realized that everything and everyone she loved had been taken from her and reduced to ashes and smoke.

And that is what she did, as an immigrant homemaker and parent in the US, by daring to imagine a new kind of world, and to talk about the kind of universal human rights that would be necessary for a truly just society in that new world. In short, she was a witness to the loss of everybody she loved, but she also never stopped witnessing to her vision of a better world, in which such horrors would not be allowed. And to her it simply made sense to start with the injustices in her own community, especially since they so radically contradicted all the Jewish values she had internalized before the Nazi deluge.

In her home there was evidently a kind of division of labor in which her husband Zacharias almost never talked about the Holocaust, while she talked about it on a daily basis. (Norman admitted that he was afraid to talk to his father about the Holocaust, for fear the floodgates would open—and that neither of them could live with what came out.) But isn't it possible that Zacharias married Maryla for just that reason, because she was a fearless and unstoppable daily witness to the Holocaust's devastation, something that he also felt on a daily basis, even if he didn't talk about it? If she talked incessantly about it, Zacharias did not have to; and although he did not—and probably could not—talk about it, this writer's guess is that he listened, and took satisfaction in what Maryla Finkelstein said. He knew that she witnessed to a truth, humanity's profound capacity for evil; and witnessing to a truth is always healthier that suppressing it, especially if the truth in question concerns a traumatizing past that influences the truth-teller's present.

The traumatic memory of Maryla Husyt Finkelstein consisted of very concrete and lacerating images and thoughts about her experiences in the Nazi concentration camps; we know that because she mentioned them often. Therefore we take it as a given that the horror that had destroyed an entire people was to some extent always with her. Yet although her traumatic memories never left her, this was a woman who absolutely refused to let the Holocaust's aggression into her personality, much less identify with it. She was constantly engaged in clawing her way past the traumatizing events that she remembered, past her acknowledgement of humanity's fundamental evil, past self-pity, past self-justification and past victimhood. She was never for one moment, ever, a victim—she was too busy denouncing the world's injustice to claim victim status. It was her private vocation to confront, on a daily basis, the horrible events that had changed everything; and although she could not banish them, she never stopped fighting them, and by so doing kept the most toxic material from unconsciously influencing her behavior.

Seeing that other survivors let in too much of the Nazi violence through the portal of their memories, she became a woman who absolutely refused to let the aggression into her spirit and soul, much less identify with, and internalize, its aggression. *The key was her unremitting anger that such crimes could be committed against the weak and innocent.* Maryla Husyt Finkelstein was not a victim, but ultimately she was also a lot more than a survivor. She was a protagonist and a fighter, who never forgot for a moment what the Nazis had done; and as a direct result, also never forgot that it was one's responsibility to resist evil by opposing it in the present.

She demanded—however furiously and sometimes intrusively—a better world than the one that had taken away her family. Her vision of a better world began with a furious denunciation of the world as it was, which to a great extent put her in a great tradition of immigrants to America, where the damaged and the challenged re-invent themselves. She was not completely successful; but the strong American emphasis on re-invention of the Self almost surely helped her detach somewhat from the broken dreams of her European youth.

These are my impressions and my theory as to what they mean, about which I could be wrong in some important points. But there seems no doubt whatsoever that Maryla Husyt Finkelstein carried on a remarkable and heroic daily struggle against the existence of human evil, the presence of which lingered in her memory. She was defined by the trauma of the Holocaust, but not bonded to it, because she spent her life refusing to give in to those dynamics that make trauma bonding possible, even when—or especially when—she recognized them in her own community. She cannot be faulted for her dark view of human nature, as well as her disgust for the leaders—whether Jewish or Christian—that seized power in the 20th century; she saw them as self-serving opportunists and scoundrels, for the most part, and had no trouble communicating the disgust their lies and self-delusions generated. Maryla's comprehension of the errors of her American community's leaders was not a deficit associated with her traumatic past, in this writer's opinion, but rather best evidence for her moral clarity of vision in the present.

And here is where she sets an example for all of us: she saw the evil in humankind, yet never gave up fighting it, and struggling to imagine—and work for—a better world based on universal human rights. That is the supreme task of our time. Maryla Husyt Finkelstein was socially awkward and somewhat unpredictable—even in her own home she could be difficult and demanding—but she was also heroic, because her story is of a Holocaust victim who refused, on a daily basis, to act on the dark nihilism of her traumatic memories. She perfectly defines, in other words, a particularly heroic kind of Holocaust survivor, who refuses to internalize the aggression of the Holocaust into the unconscious mind. In so doing, she teaches us a valuable lesson: the best way for victims of traumatic memory to deconstruct the aggression they've internalized is to talk about it. It will lose its uniqueness, and furthermore if one talks enough about it, the traumatic memories will lose the ability to destroy one's personality. The whole of psychoanalysis and psychotherapy is based on that premise—the 'talking cure.'

Of course, if you talk too much about those past experiences that traumatized you, and you make your own losses the center of the story, you're liable to start defining yourself by the trauma itself, and that can be dangerous on its own account: one can get stuck in the past, and for that reason some victims have found it hard to leave victim status behind, and operate as a survivor in the present moment. But Maryla Funkelstein had, in fact, discovered by far the best way to keep from getting stuck in the past: she talked about what happened to her, but in the context of comparing the evil things she saw in the Nazi camps to the evil she saw *in the present moment*. It was all about identifying the evil in the present, then finding a better way.

Above all, Maryla Finkelstein refused to repress her memories into a separate part of her mind. This has been called 'splitting,' and appears quite memorably in a book by French Resistance and Communist leader Charlotte Delbo, who was sent to Auschwitz by the Nazis. Repressing one's memories, or treating them as though they belong to a different part of the personality, is at best a short-term strategy, and usually doesn't work very well. (Even Delbo was eventually compelled to write about Auschwitz to fully manage her memories of it.) Maryla Husyt Finkelstein adopted a strategy that was exactly the opposite of repression— she talked about her traumatic memories constantly, but with a specific purpose in mind: to identify aspects of evil, systemic and individual, in the world around her.

In her frequent conversations with her son Norman, she used her Auschwitz experiences as a vivid cautionary metaphor, pointing to specific evils she'd experienced during the Holocaust, and warning that this was where certain injustices in American and Israeli life would inevitably lead, if there were not constituencies (or 'countervailing forces,' as the sociologists would say) brave enough or smart enough to oppose them. She was absolutely right about that, this writer would argue—the test of any democratic society is the way it can learn from the past, so that good people are able to organize constituencies that can stop systemic evil in the present. (A current example is the debate between those Americans who wish to stop torture, those conservatives that defend it, and those who prefer not to talk about it.) The reality is, democracy—and human decency itself— is always in danger from those who see the rule of law as an impediment to their pursuit of power and profit. That is arguably a tragic view of the social behavior of human beings, but it is a correct one.

Maryla Husyt Finkselstein's traumatic memory of the Holocaust probably never left her, but because of her constant struggle with it, she did not internalize its aggression—and for just that reason was far from being bonded to it. She empowered herself with her frequent denunciations of injustice, which were not only an expression of her indomitable spirit but a defense against the influence of traumatic memory. She deconstructed the aggression encoded in those same memories by comparing them to the evil, mendacity and mediocrity she saw around her, which she communicated at length to her family members.

Maryla Finkelstein never stopped remembering the apocalyptic moment after her liberation from the slave labor camps, the moment when she realized that everyone she loved was dead. It was, she said later, the worst moment of her life. Yet she refused to let that moment own her, neutralizing its diabolical charge by talking about it sufficiently that it lost its potential ability to destroy her. If she never succeeded in freeing herself from her traumatic memories, she succeeded spectacularly in being the protagonist of her own life, by virtue of her determination to fight the same kind of aggression in the modern world that drove Hitler's madness in the past. Is it any wonder, then, that her son, who was almost surely affected by what we now call intergenerational trauma, spent his career as a political scientist searching for, and eventually finding, effective ways to continue the recovery from traumatic memory that his mother began?

3.

The young Norman Finkelstein attended James Madison High school in New York, and was for a time a friend of Chuck Schumer, who would later become a Democratic Senator from New York. (No doubt Schumer would go to great lengths to avoid being seen with Finkelstein today, because of the fear and loathing of Finkelstein in the New York political and Jewish establishments.) As a precocious teenager, it could be said that Finkelstein came of age during the Vietnam War (he was sixteen in 1969) and was deeply affected by it, mainly because of his mother's furious objection to it. "My mother's whole being revolted against it," Finkelstein has written in a memoir. "I wouldn't say she was emotional about the war; she was hysterical. Although knowledgeable about the facts, she detested any intellectualizing of it. Even to engage in debate about Vietnam constituted a moral travesty."

Finkelstein read a description of atrocities being committed by the US in Vietnam to a high school class, and was amazed that the other students were not as shocked and horrified as he was. Later, in college, he suffered a complete emotional meltdown during a teach-in on the Vietnam War, an experience that made him cringe when he thought about it later. There were times when his mother actually worried about this fervor for social justice, wondering if he had perhaps internalized too much of her fury at injustice; and there were times when Norman had his own doubts as well. But as he matured, Finkelstein was relieved to discover that a passionate love of justice and scholarly intelligence actually worked rather well together. "It was only many years later," Finkelstein wrote, "after reading Noam Chomsky, that I learned it was possible to unite exacting scholarly rigor with scathing moral outrage; that an intelligent argument didn't have to be an intellectualizing one." Indeed—and to that potent stylistic mix he would add his own gift for sarcasm.

Although Finkelstein's mother Maryla referred to the Holocaust on an almost daily basis, it was not to reinforce her own victim status, but to move away from that status by understanding its relation to the historical moment she was in. Her isolation as an immigrant, her lack of formal education, and her occasional misreading of American nuances kept her from making common cause with others in social justice movements. But she never stopped trying to relate the Holocaust to the world around her—the war of the strong against the weak, the uses of racism and economic exploitation, all were extensions of the same systemic evil that she had witnessed in a pure form. She never stopped making the connections between what had once broken her heart, and what was going on in the present moment.

Norman Finkelstein wrote about this: "Much later in life I came across a passage in Primo Levi contrasting two kinds of survivors: those who experienced the Nazi holocaust as a traumatic but nonetheless meaningless blow, and those able to make out, beyond the sheer horror and brutality, its darker truths. My mother's mind was sufficiently capacious that she could mentally encompass the Nazi holocaust; and, certain of the profundity of what she had experienced, my mother never ceased trying to penetrate its meaning."

He was right—she didn't stop trying to penetrate its meaning. And he, in turn, would simply continue this same process in his own way, by examining those great social evils that arose directly from the Holocaust. The Holocaust destroyed not one people, but two: it destroyed European Jewry, its primary target, but ironically it also destroyed Palestinian society as it had existed before 1948, because of the displacement of the Palestinians by the Zionists. It was precisely Finkelstein's great enterprise as a prophetic intellectual to make the connection between the systemic evil of the Holocaust, on the one hand, and on the other to identify and illuminate the aggression it generated. But it was probably a connection that he to some extent learned from his mother.

Finkelstein's relationship with his father was more nuanced, and in one area completely different: his father never discussed what he experienced in Auschwitz. Perhaps even more significantly, Norman never asked his father about it. As pointed out earlier, Zacharias and Maryla had a division of labor not uncommon in burdened families, in which one spouse talks often of a psychic horror that has befallen them, while the partner legitimizes the other's burden by listening and perhaps nodding occasionally, in that manner not merely witnessing, but silently validating, the shocking events the more verbal partner is relating. Finkelstein was loath to upset this finely-tuned emotional ecology; but in addition he had a second—and highly personal—reason for not encouraging his father to talk about his Holocaust experiences. "The simple answer is I was terrified at opening the floodgates. Once I became privy to the horrors he'd personally endured, I would relinquish the right ever again to be angry at him, which I'd often been: in the face of this knowledge, guilt over being angry would always get the better of the anger itself."

Smart teenage boys need a father to rebel against, and in families with a high level of cultural literacy the rebellion is often disguised as (or rather, takes the form of) fervent discussions about politics, religion, art and social justice. Once Finkelstein had seen the vulnerability of his father, he was afraid of the spiritual destruction such discussion might visit upon him. Zacharias may have felt this as well, since he did not himself seek to discuss his experiences in the death camps.

Finkelstein had already gotten an idea of the tragedy that Zacharias carried inside him. His mother Maryla claimed that she had once glimpsed Zacharias' sister being transported into one of the camps. Was this brief glimpse a false or distorted memory, as many memories relating to psychological trauma might tend to be, or had Maryla really glimpsed her husband's sister for a moment? Evidently Zacharias also strained to remember his sister, comparing his more comprehensive collection of memories to his wife's momentary one. "Every so often during their marriage my father, standing stiff and forlorn, would yet again ask my mother to describe exactly how his sister looked at that moment." It is in poignant incidents like this that one begins to comprehend fully the destructive horror of the human catastrophe we call the Nazi Holocaust.

Can we blame Finkelstein, having witnessed the pathos of this moment, for not "opening the floodgates," as he put it, and by inquiring further, perhaps causing his father to lose his composure, or break down completely? (On an unconscious level he may have feared that some traumatic memories had the strength to kill his father—that Auschwitz might still possess, in the timeless world of the unconscious mind, the ability to kill both of them.) Maryla, on the other hand, seemed to challenge the traumatic memory directly. "Whenever 'Yesterday' came on the radio, my mother, drifting off into herself, would emphatically sing along, 'Oh, I believe in yesterday.' A close friend of hers from Warsaw once lamented how totally the war had shattered my mother: 'She used to be always laughing and joking.'"

But what was the underlying purpose of her daily struggles? A big part of it was to penetrate the meaning of what had happened so long ago, by comparing it to more recent kinds of evil that she witnessed on TV news or read in the newspapers; but as I've already indicated, there was probably a subsidiary reason as well. Her constant rumination over her experiences in the Warsaw Ghetto and in the camps, her near-constant invocation of traumatic memories that crowded into her waking and dreaming life, she intentionally made into a conscious obsession, to keep them from becoming an unconscious obsession. By talking obsessively about her Holocaust experiences each day, and by identifying other examples of social and systemic evils in her world, she struggled to keep her memories in her moment-to-moment consciousness. Once they sank into her unconscious mind, they would begin to influence her attitudes and behavior. She had seen it happen to others.

And so had Norman. At one point, Maryla traveled to Germany to testify at the trials of several people who had been guards at death camps, taking her son Norman with her. (It is emblematic of his learning curve and their closeness that she allowed him to witness this testimony.) On that trip she stopped off with her son at the house of M———, a German Jew, also a Holocaust survivor. "Somehow we got on the subject of the Israel-Palestine conflict. M———- said some pretty disgusting things. 'The only thing Arabs ever invented was camel shit.' My mother and I looked at each other knowingly: He had obviously learned a lot from the Nazi holocaust." That is, he had internalized much of the aggression that had been directed against him by the Nazis.

Maryla's outraged monologues about the Holocaust happened precisely to keep that from happening to her. It was her prophylaxis against internalization of the aggression that haunted her—once it was internalized she might make some subtle adjustment to it, and she might end up acting it out. She would not yield control to her whatever aggression she had internalized, and her method for preventing that from happening was by keeping her traumatic memories firmly fixed in the present moment, where she could monitor them and keep them, as best she could, from affecting both her personality and her behavior.

This does not mean she could not engage in anger—but she when she did so, she did it in such a spontaneous manner that she quickly discharged her aggression. She knew well that her memories could make her cruel—but she wasn't about to let that happen, by the simple expedient of talking about her memories with sufficient frequency they never had the chance to embed themselves in her unconscious mind. She also had an almost talismanic intuition for Holocaustic evil in her own world, habitually blocking it out—such as by refusing to watch TV footage of American troops fighting Viet Cong and North Vietnamese soldiers—keeping out the images before she could internalize them. Yet she never stopped denouncing their presence in her world.

Norman Finkelstein immortalized a representative example of his mother's rage by documenting an incident from his mother's testimony to the German court: "When the judge asked my mother to identify the guards from up close, she refused, saying that, if she got any nearer, she would beat them. Exasperated, the judge then asked my mother to identify them from an album collecting contemporary photographs from Maijdanek of the guards. She again refused. 'I won't look at them alive in the camp. If you give me pictures of them dead, not only will I look at them, I'll do a dance for the courtroom.'"

But this appreciation of evil did not turn her into a Jewish nationalist or a right-wing Zionist—or a Zionist of any kind—because she had become convinced of the potential for evil in all people, including Jews. She often gave that as a reason why she didn't immigrate to Israel after the war ("I had enough of Jewish leaders") citing the example of the ghetto police who collaborated with the Nazis.

When in Germany to testify at the trial of death camp guards, she ran into a woman she had known. "As it happened,"

Finkelstein wrote, "my mother knew this woman from the Warsaw ghetto. I expected that their seeing each other again would be an occasion replete with pathos, but they only exchanged a few cursory words and swiftly parted ways, never to meet again. The woman was nervous, my mother subsequently explained, because the ghetto resistance had targeted her in leaflets for death as a collaborator. She apparently guessed that my mother knew."

Maryla Finkelstein was obsessed by the Holocaust, but she sought no unified field theory of genocide to encompass and explain the tragedy, because to a woman of her sensibilities that would surely have sounded too much like a rationalization. She simply saw and denounced the Holocaust when she was reminded of it by the evils of everyday life, and by the glimpses of gratuitous aggression and systemic evil she saw in America; and she used this awareness of systemic evil as the subject matter for her endless talking points and cautionary tales. "Exaggerated as it might sound, almost every conversation I had with my mother eventually did come back to the war," Norman Finkelstein wrote. "It's not as if she systematically lectured me. On the contrary, except during the rare interview or public presentation, I don't recall any sustained reflections by her on the Nazi Holocaust. Rather, incidents from the war served as parables to illustrate this or that point in our conversations."

In fact the present writer believes that Maryla Husyt Finkelstein's reaction to the Nazi Holocaust was correct. For humanity to survive, we ought to denounce systemic evil continually and unremittingly, and if others do not like it, and if some think it boorish or unnecessary, too bad for them. (Of course, courtesy and good timing are always desirable, particularly where effective social advocacy are concerned, but some have better social skills than others; the important point to remember is that there is always an intrinsic value in the recognition and denunciation of evil, regardless of the tone with which it is done.)

In any case, such an expedient keeps the toxic emotional material from sinking to the lowest parts of the unconscious mind, where it can influence the individual person's behavior and continue to harm the world.

It was not a private form of evil that had imprisoned and brutalized Maryla Finkelstein, but a particularly malevolent form of systemic evil run by a criminal state. Therefore she was right to talk about it; and indeed she believed it her vocation to witness to the presence of evil in the present moment. Furthermore, she was quite acute in her perceptions of evil in the world, especially in the Israeli treatment of the Palestinians, and therefore acted as a teacher to those who would listen. The Holocaust had not simply traumatized her, it had taught her something about the real nature of humanity, something that most people never know; and she was determined to tell all who would listen about what she had learned about human nature and the real nature of human society.

One recent study of intergenerational trauma summarized the dilemma of the children of Holocaust survivors in this manner:

For their parents, CHSs [Children of Holocaust Survivors] were a source of reassurance and confirmation of survival. They were submitted to a role reversal, becoming parents of their parents, and to an intense emotional overinvestment. They represented a narcissistic extension of the family. HSs [Holocaust Survivors] viewed their children's development only through a dichotomous assessment of their performance: Were they doing well in school, or were they dunces? Were they neat and polite or did they cause their parents shame? CHSs learned to neglect their own feelings, to regard their own problems and anxieties as unimportant compared to those of their parents. They rapidly realized that their most important task was to be a "good son" or a "good daughter."

However, they soon realized that no matter how hard they tried to achieve this goal, they would never fully satisfy their traumatized caregivers. They were vulnerable, therefore, to feelings of helplessness.[2]

While there are some ways in which Norman Finkelstein fits this profile, there are other ways in which he most definitely does not. Above all he was not emotionally paralyzed—at least not for long—by the feelings of emotional helplessness mentioned in the last sentence of the paragraph above. He did not feel helpless because he learned from his mother that people who have been deeply traumatized need to talk about what happened to them— and Maryla Husyt Finkelstein certainly talked about her experiences in the Nazi camps. At bottom she seemed to believe quite simply that if enough people accepted the existence of evil in human affairs—and that if enough people accepted that they, too, have a capacity for it—people might learn to control it.

Maryla Finklestein did not care who knew that she had been in Hitler's slave-labor camps, she did not care if people approved of her talking about her experiences or not. From her, Norman Finkelstein learned the first rule of shared traumatic memory: you must talk about those things that happened to you, even if it is about a magnitude of evil that others—including others in the aggrieved group—tell you should never be discussed. There is no doubt that Norman internalized a great deal of his mother's traumatic memory, but he also learned from his mother the personal traits that would allow him to break free from it.

From his mother Norman Finkelstein also learned a second great lesson about recovering from traumatic memory, which is that to deconstruct the aggression ensconced in traumatic memory one must, in addition to talking about it, engage in socially-beneficial activity that in some way opposes or seeks to reform the social forces that first caused the original trauma. Maryla Finkelstein used her traumatic memories of the

Holocaust as talking points for her political opposition to the Vietnam War; but she used those same memories as a point of departure for her criticisms of the Israeli state. She was able to see the universality of evil, which a great many people are unable to do, and that allowed her to perceive that some people in her own aggrieved group were acting out the same kind of aggression they had once endured in Europe.

She used her traumatic memory to witness to the presence of evil in the present moment, both in her adopted country of America, and also regarding Israeli mistreatment of the Palestinians (and wherever else she encountered it). She also made a shrewd connection between her own trauma and the way the right-wing parties in Israel were able to use traumatic memories. Her vision was so tragic, so true to the painful home truths that humanity tries to conceal from itself, that ultimately there was—and is—an exhilarating freedom about it. It worked for her, and ultimately also for her son, who used something very close to that same method in his work as an investigative scholar. It was precisely the forbidden truths that Norman Finkelstein articulated, demanding that evil, both past and present, must be opposed with special vigor in one's own tribe. But he sought not just to expose evil in his own community, but also in the cultural and political elites of America.

4.

In college Norman Finkelstein plunged almost immediately into the anti-Vietnam War movement, taking with him—as most people do when leaving home at that age—the internalized premises of his family's private theater of emotional orientations, ideas and values. It was a burden he probably did not understand particularly well, partly because intergenerational trauma was not well understood as a psychological dynamic in the 1970s and 1980s. In any case, Finkelstein did not, as we have seen, completely fit the profile of the average child of Holocaust survivors, although there is little doubt that he was affected by a certain level of intergenerational trauma. Americans were generally not aware of the extent to which the Holocaust impacted the children of survivors, and would continue to impact humanity culturally and psychologically in the future. To most Americans, it would probably be fair to say, the Nazi Holocaust was to be considered as simply a horrific crime that had been committed in the past, and belonged to the past. But traumatic memory, while rooted in the past, affects people in the present.

Finkelstein, because of what he had learned from his mother, was extremely sensitive to social justice issues, and was developing his own unrelenting (if overly-intellectualized) moral code regarding social justice issues. As a result he had, as a young adult, no difficulty in recognizing the ongoing importance of the antiwar movement to his generation, and he became an active and enthusiastic participant. During this time he considered himself a dedicated Maoist, although his politics consisted of little more than talk, typical of the juvenile posturing typical of a great many middleclass youth in the late 1960s and early 1970s.

Despite what must have been many cringe-worthy memories of Maoist adventuring, Finkelstein succeeded in graduating from Binghamton University in New York in 1974, and went to Paris for an interlude studying at the Ecole Practique des Hautes Etudes. Finkelstein got his Master's Degree at Princeton in 1980, where he would later receive his PhD under highly unusual and disturbing circumstances. The fact that he was accepted at Princeton indicates the extent to which he had already impressed his elders in academia with his work ethic, his curiosity, and his highly polemical talent as a writer. And so far, he had not studied or written about anything that was taboo—his antiwar sentiments were shared by almost all academics of that time, especially in the Ivy League universities.

So it was not by crossing the Atlantic that Norman Finkelstein would pass the great meridian that was destined to change his world. What changed his world was the reading of the writings of Noam Chomsky—not Chomsky's writings on linguistics, but his books about America's increasingly imperialistic foreign policy, and about social justice and American power generally; Finkelstein saw that underneath Chomsky's scholarly prose there burned an incandescent fire of compassion for the exploited and oppressed, which happily reinforced Finkelstein's idea that one could be both an exacting scholar and a passionate advocate. Chomsky was never a particularly acute stylist, and he had little interest in the psychological orientations that drive human behavior. But the political contents of Chomsky's books, the subjects he undertook to write about, were unusual and quite explosive.

After World War Two, the US became the powerful center for a new imperialism, based on anti-Communism, on the one hand, and on the other hand on the economic exploitation of countries in the so-called Third World by the US corporate upper class. In the Third World—or the 'developing world,' as we are more likely to call it today—the US gave men, material and vast amounts of money to support extreme right-wing dictatorships, from Iran to Guatemala, police states based on torture, imprisonment of dissenters, systematic sexual abuse of women and political murder. Noam Chomsky made it his job to write about this massive network of murder and exploitation, and he did so systematically.

This was a huge shock to the political class of America—it was a shock, to begin with, that anyone cared enough for people in the developing world to write something about their exploitation. It was generally assumed by Americans during the Cold War that the US could do almost anything it wanted in the Third World in the name of anti-Communism; but Chomsky was often able to demonstrate that black, brown and yellow people had very much the same aspirations and characteristics as people in Europe and America, and that there were many instances in which US-exported repression served no one but a corporate ability to make greater profits. And those same corporations did not hesitate to destroy democratic institutions in poor countries when they thought it would make it easier for them to make money.

The political class of America never forgave him for this, because one of the great American Cold War myths was that capitalism, and the operation of the marketplace, was sacred — that if left to operate alone and free of regulation, the marketplace could solve all the problems to which humankind was heir. Chomsky showed that the marketplace could be used for corrupt reasons just like any other system, and furthermore demonstrated that without internalized moral restraints or powerful government regulation the marketplace tended to corrupt people through greed, commercialism and consumerism. Significantly, Chomsky's revelations about American foreign policy demonstrated that greed could also cause America to support some of the world's most brutal dictatorships, and destroy democratic institutions in other countries whenever that might lead to greater profits.

This suggested that there was — and is — a tragic flaw in the American character, a childlike tendency to believe that making money is always a virtuous and good thing, and has a personally redemptive effect on those that accumulate it. To the ideologues of the corporate upper class, Chomsky's critique of the American worship of profit came across as a hideous attack on capitalism, the real religion — or True Church — of secular America during the Cold War; but Chomsky couldn't be fired from his job as a professor because he had tenure, as well as an international reputation as a linguist and cognitive scientist.

Noam Chomsky did something else that cleared the way for Finkelstein. He wrote about Israel and its effects on American culture and political discourse, and he also wrote about what the

Israelis had done to the Palestinians. He wrote about this even before the so-called New Historians in Israel had gone into the military archives to find out what really happened in 1948, and despite the hysterical attacks upon him by the nascent Israel Lobby—indeed, by leaders of almost every major Jewish organization except A Jewish Voice for Peace—Chomsky continued to write the truth as he found it. The prophetic dimension to Chomsky's writings was something that Finkelstein intuitively understood. This led to a meeting between Finkelstein and Chomsky, as Finkelstein contemplated a subject for his PhD at Princeton.

Finkelstein wanted to write a critique of Joan Peters' *From Time Immemorial: the Origins of the Arab-Jewish Conflict over Palestine*, a book published in 1984 that sought to dissemble the tragic ethnic cleansing of Palestinians in 1947-49. This supposedly scholarly work had quickly been understood in other countries, including Israel, as a deliberately falsified exercise in propaganda with no historical or literary value whatsoever. (The Israeli historian Yehoshua Porath called the book a "sheer forgery," stating also that in Israel "the book was almost universally dismissed as sheer rubbish except maybe as a propaganda weapon," an opinion typical of reviewers everywher except America.) In the US, on the other hand, *From Time Immemorial* became the great literary discovery of the publishing season of 1984, and praise was lavished upon it from every quarter.

Finkelstein was preparing to do his PhD at Princeton, and had the bright idea of writing an exposé of the Peters book as a thesis, especially since he wanted to specialize as a political scientist in scholarship about Israel/Palestine. In his essay "The Fate of an Honest Intellectual," in *Understanding Power*, Noam Chomsky picks up his side of the unfolding story. I quote Chomsky's account word for word, because of what it tells us about the true nature of American academia, and American power generally:

"[*From Time Immemorial*] was the big intellectual hit for that year: Saul Bellow, Barbara Tuchman, everybody was talking about it as the greatest thing since chocolate cake. Well, one graduate student at Princeton, a guy named Norman Finkelstein, started reading through the book. He was interested in the history of Zionism, and as he read the book he was kind of surprised by some of the things it said. He's a very careful student, and he started checking the references—and it turned out that the whole thing was a hoax, it was completely faked: probably it had been put together by some intelligence agency or something like that. Well, Finkelstein wrote up a short paper of just preliminary findings, it was about twenty-five pages or so, and he sent it around to I think thirty people who were interested in the topic, scholars in the field and so on, saying: "Here's what I've found in this book, do you think it's worth pursuing?"

"Well, he got back one answer, from me. I told him, yeah, I think it's an interesting topic, but I warned him, if you follow this, you're going to get in trouble—because you're going to expose the American intellectual community as a gang of frauds, and they are not going to like it, and they're going to destroy you. So I said: if you want to do it, go ahead, but be aware of what you're getting into. It's an important issue, it makes a big difference whether you eliminate the moral basis for driving out a population—it's preparing the basis for some real horrors—so a lot of people's lives could be at stake. But your life is at stake too, I told him, because if you pursue this, your career is going to be ruined."

"Well, he didn't believe me. We became very close friends after this, I didn't know him before. He went ahead and wrote up an article, and he started submitting it to journals. Nothing: they didn't even bother responding. I finally managed to place a piece of it in *In These Times*, a tiny left-wing journal published in Illinois, where some of you may have seen it. Otherwise nothing, no response. Meanwhile his professors—this is Princeton

University, supposed to be a serious place—stopped talking to him: they wouldn't make appointments with him, they wouldn't read his papers, he basically had to quit the program."

Chomsky suggested that Finkelstein move to another department within Princeton, hoping that maybe he'd get a better deal there. (Chomsky knew some people in that department, and recommended Finkelstein.) "Unfortunately, Finkelstein's new professors were also fearful of what he was writing about, so fearful that, like before, he couldn't get them to read his thesis. Finally, out of embarrassment, they granted him a Ph.D.—he's very smart, incidentally—but they will not even write a letter for him saying that he was a student at Princeton University. I mean, sometimes you have students for whom it's hard to write good letters of recommendation, because you really didn't think they were very good—but you can write something, there are ways of doing these things. This guy was good, but he literally cannot get a letter."

Chomsky remarks that it's not as bad as dying from a death squad, but it serves the same purpose as a death squad, because both censorship and a death squad are about social control. He continues his story of Finkelstein's challenge to the Joan Peters book, and how it changed American intellectual history—in indirect ways, of course, since nobody could talk directly about why they were afraid of the Peters book.

"Finkelstein's very persistent: he took a summer off and sat in the New York Public Library, where he went through every single reference in the book—and he found a record of fraud that you cannot believe. Well, the New York intellectual community is a pretty small place, and pretty soon everybody knew about this, everybody knew the book was a fraud and it was going to be exposed sooner or later. The one journal that was smart enough to react intelligently was the *New York Review of Books*— they knew that the thing was a sham, but the editor didn't want to offend his friends, so he just didn't run a review at all. That was the one journal that didn't run a review."

"Meanwhile, Finkelstein was being called in by big professors in the field who were telling him, 'Look, call off your crusade; you drop this and we'll take care of you, we'll make sure you get a job,' all this kind of stuff. But he kept doing it—he kept on and on. Every time there was a unfavorable review, he'd write a letter to the editor which wouldn't get printed; he was doing whatever he could do. We approached the publishers and asked them if they were going to respond to any of this, and they said no—and they were right. Why should they respond? They had the whole system buttoned up, there was never going to be a critical word about this in the United States. But then they made a technical error: they allowed the book to appear in England, where you can't control the intellectual community quite as easily."

"Well, as soon as I heard that the book was going to come out in England, I immediately sent copies of Finkelstein's work to a number of British scholars and journalists who are interested in the Middle East—and they were ready. As soon as the book appeared, it was just demolished; it was blown out of the water. Every major journal, the *Times Literary Supplement*, the *London Review*, the *Observer*, everybody had a review saying, this doesn't even reach the level of nonsense, of idiocy. A lot of the criticism used Finkelstein's work without any acknowledgment, I should say—but about the kindest word anybody said about the [Joan Peters] book was 'ludicrous,' or 'preposterous.'"

"Well, people here read British reviews—if you're in the American intellectual community, you read the *Times Literary Supplement* and the *London Review*, so it began to get a little embarrassing. You started getting back-tracking: people started saying, 'Well, look, I didn't really say the book was good, I just said it's an interesting topic,' things like that. At that point, the *New York Review* swung into action, and they did what they always do in these circumstances. See, there's like a routine that you go through—if a book gets blown out of the water in England in places people here will see, or if a book gets praised in England, you have to react. And if it's a book on Israel, there's a standard way of doing it: you get an Israeli scholar to review it. That's called covering your ass—because whatever an Israeli scholar says, you're pretty safe: no one can accuse the journal of anti-Semitism, none of the usual stuff works."

"So after the Peters book got blown out of the water in England, the *New York Review* assigned it to a good person actually, in fact Israel's leading specialist on Palestinian nationalism [Yehoshua Porath], someone who knows a lot about the subject. And he wrote a review, which they then didn't publish—it went on for almost a year without the thing being published; nobody knows exactly what was going on, but you can guess that there must have been a lot of pressure not to publish it. Eventually it was even written up in the *New York Times* that this review wasn't getting published, so finally some version of it did appear. It was critical, it said the book is nonsense and so on, but it cut corners, the guy didn't say what he knew."

"Actually, the Israeli reviews in general were extremely critical: the reaction of the Israeli press was that they hoped the book would not be widely read, because ultimately it would be harmful to the Jews—sooner or later it would get exposed, and then it would just look like a fraud and a hoax, and it would reflect badly on Israel. They underestimated the American intellectual community, I should say. Anyhow, by that point the American intellectual community realized that the Peters book was an embarrassment, and [the book] sort of disappeared—nobody talks about it anymore. I mean, you still find it at newsstands in the airport and so on, but the best and the brightest know that they are not supposed to talk about it anymore: because it was exposed and they were exposed."[3]

Just how far this fear goes among intellectuals can be seen in Chomsky's remark that none of Finkelstein's academic advisors had the courage to even *read* his thesis—so the brave academics of Princeton (the same ones Chomsky called a "gang of frauds") simply graduated Finkelstein to get rid of him. If that is not a perfect example of social promotion arising from the failure of educators to do their job, what exactly is it? In this writer's experience, there is practically no limit to the cowardice to be found concerning Israel/Palestine within academia, and the closer one gets to the Ivy League—the "better" universities—the greater the hypocrisy around this issue is likely to be. Liberals in academia don't hate America, as Fox News would have it, they simply don't have the backbone to tell the truth where doing so might involve some risk to their careers. And then, because of guilt at their own cowardice, they will immediately attack anybody who *does* tell the truth.

5.

The adulatory American reception of Joan Peters' *From Time Immemorial: the Origins of the Arab-Jewish Conflict over Palestine* should have tipped off Norman Finkelstein to the fact that he was not dealing with historical or political science, but with a social pathology. The proximate causes of this pathology arose in large part simply from the desire of individuals to avoid knowing uncomfortable or inconvenient truths, and who therefore sought to suppress them. It was aided by the American tendency to mythologize history, to reduce morally challenging scenarios to simple narratives—that is, to soap operas and fairy tales—and it was also aided by an unmistakable gullibility among Americans generally, not to mention a certain gutlessness common to American intellectuals. But there was an added factor that made it particularly volatile.

Influencing and partly driving these rather juvenile American tendencies was the traumatic memory of the Holocaust, which had become intractably (although often unconsciously) interwoven with attitudes toward Israel in America and the West generally. This expressed itself as the fanatical conviction of many uncritical supporters of Israel that nobody should ever be allowed to criticize the Jewish state, even when—or especially when—it makes mistakes or does bad things. This was enforced by the political power of the Israel Lobby, the political movement known as neo-conservatism, and the most irrational and dangerous kind of religious nationalism. Nonetheless, Finkelstein set out to deconstruct Peters' falsehoods, treating it as something that could be dealt with logically, as with any other book. It would be nowhere near that easy, of course, because the emotional needs of those intellectuals who praised the book were essentially irrational.

Joan Peters' *From Time Immemorial* came out in the spring of 1984, and Finkelstein's decision to write his PhD thesis criticizing it was apparently made that summer. It was in September of that year that Noam Chomsky succeeded in getting some of Finkelstein's arguments critical of the Peters book into *In These Times*, the small left-wing newspaper in Chicago. Other than that, however, nobody wanted to hear Finkelstein's findings. Not only would his academic advisors refuse to read his PhD thesis, intellectual leaders and academics competed with each other to see who could shout the loudest hosannas in honor of the Peters book. The publication of Joan Peters' book *From Time Immemorial: the Origins of the Arab-Jewish Conflict over Palestine* became a huge publishing event in America, greeted with euphoria by the reviewers who clamored to praise the book.

There was a generalized feeling, especially among those who hadn't read the Peters book, that the thorny Israeli/Palestinian conflict, which had befuddled the world and evaded all attempts at resolution, had suddenly been resolved with a single book. How could this happen? Joan Peters, a writer without any special qualifications in writing about the Middle East, had discovered that the Palestinians didn't really exist. Instead of a thriving, well-established culture of over a million Arabic-speaking people in Palestine which other historians had written about at length, Peters insisted that there was, in reality, only a ragtag miscellany of job-hungry wanderers who were in effect simply passing through.

This ghostly rabble of indigents constituted a "hidden immigration" of Arabic-speakers inexplicably pouring into, and through, that part of Palestine that eventually became Israel, a phenomenon that had somehow been missed by everybody else, including people who actually lived in Palestine and the Middle East. So how could anybody take the claims of the Palestinians seriously, Peters asked, when they were hardly respectable burghers, like the much more likeable and affluent Jewish settlers, when they weren't even indigenous to the area, when they were just traveling about, hat in hand, looking for jobs?

Norman Finkelstein, like everybody else who possessed some modicum of actual expertise regarding the Middle East, knew that this was not even remotely true. Finkelstein had also discovered that the great majority of Peters' references were brazenly, systematically and purposely falsified, in the sense that a substantial majority of quotations were deliberately doctored. (That is, changed to something different from what the people quoted had intended them to mean.) *From Time Immemorial* was, in other words, a deliberate attempt at propaganda posing as scholarship, and an especially offensive one at that, because it was done so poorly.

But almost the entire cultural US establishment—not merely that part of it centered around New York and the East Coast generally, but extending even to California's Left Coast—had been led to believe (or had talked themselves into believing) that the book was brilliant, original and destined to permanently alter the Middle Eastern debate. Intellectuals love nothing more than the image of an author who single-handedly changes history in some way (think Zola, think Upton Sinclair) to the chagrin of politicians who have likewise tried to do so but ingloriously failed; and no doubt this was part of the book's appeal, at least to those that had not read it.

The idea that the book was going to have an impact of historical proportions wasn't just a rallying cry among Jewish organizations, leaders and intellectuals, many of whom might be expected to have an interest in the Middle East; *everybody* seemed to believe that the book was a kind of turning point, after which it would never be possible to think about Israel and the Middle East in the same way as they had before. With famous writers and editors singing the praises of *From Time Immemorial* to the skies, it apparently never occurred to anyone, in the face of such organized hyperbole, that the book might be a scam. Peters' claim that there was a "hidden immigration" of Arabic-speaking people into Palestine was enough to cause skepticism, at the very least, especially since she couldn't document it—but unfortunately nobody wanted to discuss specifics. It is doubtful, in retrospect, that very many people even read the book.

Here Finkelstein summarizes the incredible hoopla that accompanied the book's publication in spring of 1984, and the fraudulent nature of the book itself:

"Virtually every important journal of opinion printed one or more reviews within weeks of the book's release. Harper and Row reported that scarcely eight months after publication, *From Time Immemorial* went into its seventh printing. Author Joan Peters reportedly had two hundred and fifty speaking engagements scheduled during 1985."

"Reviewers had differed in their overall assessment of the book. But they have almost uniformly hailed the research and the demographic finds that are at the core of Peters' study. Jehuda Reinharz, the distinguished biographer of Chaim Weizmann, acclaimed Peters's 'valuable synthesis' and "convincing... new analysis' in the *Library Journal* (15 April 1984). Walter Reich, in his *Atlantic* review (July 1984), wrote that if Peters' 'arguments, especially the demographic one, are confirmed, they will certainly change [our] assumptions about the Arab-Israeli conflict'. Ronald Sanders, author of a monumental study of the Balfour Declaration, likewise opined in *The New Republic* (23 April 1984) that Peters' demographics 'could change the entire Arab-Jewish polemic over Palestine.'"

"In *Commentary* (July 1984), the Islamophobe and right-wing Zionist Daniel Pipes threw all caution to the wind in his appraisal of Peters' findings—her 'historical detective work has produced startling results which should materially influence the future course of the debate about the Palestinian problem'. Martin Peretz, in the *The New Republic* (23 July 1984), suggested that there wasn't a single factual error in the book, and that, if widely read, it 'will change the mind of the generation. If understood, it could also affect the history of the future.' Timothy Foote, in the *Washington Post* (24 June 1984) acclaimed *From Time Immemorial* as 'part historical primer, part polemic, part revelation, and a remarkable document in itself.'"

"The accolades continued. Nazi Holocaust scholar Lucy Dawidowicz congratulated Peters for having 'brought into the light the historical truth about the Mideast'. Barbara Probst Solomon called *From Time Immemorial* 'brilliant, provocative and enlightened.' Barbara Tuchman ventured that the book was a 'historical event in itself'. Saul Bellow predicted: 'Millions of people the world over, smothered by false history and propaganda, would be grateful for this clear account of the origins of the Palestinians.' Moralist Elie Wiesel promised that Peters's 'insight and analysis' would shed new light on our understanding of the Mideast conflict. Arthur Goldberg, Paul Cowan and others added their voices—and names—to the chorus of praise."

"That a scholarly work meets with critical acclaim would hardly be news were it not for the fact that *From Time Immemorial* is among the most spectacular frauds every published on the Arab-Israeli conflict. In a field littered with crass propaganda, forgeries and fakes, this is no mean distinction. But Peters's book has thoroughly earned it."

"The fraud in Peters's book is so pervasive and systematic that it is hard to pluck out a single thread without getting entangled in the whole unraveling fabric. To being with, the fraud falls into two basic categories. First, the evidence Peters adduces to document massive illegal Arab immigration into Palestine is almost entirely falsified. Second, the conclusions Peters draws from the demographic study of Palestine's indigenous Arab population are not borne out by the data she presents. To confound the reader further, Peters resorts to plagiarism."

Finkelstein has related that in late 1984, rumors began to circulate that he was writing the definitive exposure of Peters' book—aided, perhaps, by the author's own claims in discussions with friends; and to be sure, Finkelstein tried repeatedly to get articles and even letters published in various publications, but his research was systematically suppressed in all of them. (*The New Republic*, the *Atlantic Monthly* and *Commentary* all refused to run letters and the *Village Voice*, *Dissent* and the *New York Review of Books* all refused his articles commenting on Peters' book.) But when manuscripts and letters are sent, they are often read all the way through by editors, even those who suppress the material they receive on political grounds; and regarding such a sensitive issue word gets around, especially in New York, and successful editors know exactly what kind of political thought needs to be suppressed. There was no doubt a fair amount of concern at Harper and Row, since if Finkelstein's charges were correct, a major scandal was in the offing. But there was no slowing down the sales, which continued to climb.

There was a further aspect of the Peters hoopla, one that had to do with certain events then ongoing in Israel. The Israelis opened their military archives in the 1980s, and a group generally referred to as the New Historians—all Israeli Jews—were busily writing about events leading to the foundation of the Israeli state. Since they based their writing on original sources, they told the real story of how Israel came to be, not the inspiring Disney version disseminated in America. Instead of Palestinians leaving Israel voluntarily, the original sources revealed that they had either been ordered to leave at gunpoint, or were frightened away by massacres of Palestinian civilians. Around 750,000 of them had crossed over the borders into neighboring countries, intending to come back when it was safe to do so, but had then been prevented from returning. Saddest of all, the Israelis then destroyed the network of villages (around 500 to 600 of them) that constituted the heart and soul of Palestinian communal life. This was done so that if by chance any Palestinian succeeded in getting back to his or her village, no houses would be left standing. The Israelis then coolly took over the farms, orchards, homes and other property of the departed Palestinians. That was what the New Historians were finding out and writing about.

Joan Peters' book came just in time, a comforting fantasy that many Americans greatly preferred to the emerging truth about Israel's origins. Peters' narrative, albeit a fictional one, was balm to the anxious Western conscience, still troubled by the inexplicable nature of systemic evil in the Holocaust, but doggedly unwilling to explore systematically those dynamics in Christianity that brought about anti-Semitism in the first place. Peters' main audience would be people who had started to have doubts about what they'd heard concerning Israel's treatment of the Palestinians, and would pay top dollar to read a book that would exonerate Israelis as guiltless victims of circumstances. Above all, the West desired a "happy ending" to the Holocaust, in the form of an inspiring story of Jewish nation-building. Thus the West wouldn't have to look very deeply into why the Holocaust happened, or whether the claims of Palestinians were true or not. If Christians in the West started thinking critically about such issues, they might start wondering exactly why, for all those centuries, anti-Semitism had been such an important part of Christianity.

As recounted above by Noam Chomsky, Finkelstein's work was sent to interested parties in Britain, and when the British edition of *From Time Immemorial* came out, it received a thorough drubbing from British historians and public intellectuals, who immediately perceived it for the fraud it was. There was now a generalized awareness, at least partly due to Chomsky's mentoring, that Finkelstein had written a comprehensive and magnificent deconstruction of the Peters book in his PhD thesis—and that the Princeton mandarins had refused to read it for precisely that reason. Finkelstein did not get the opportunity to completely set out his entire argument for a wider audience until 1988, when *Blaming the Victims: Spurious Scholarship and the Palestine Question* was published. This was an elegant series of well-documented and scholarly essays edited by Christopher Hitchens and the Palestinian-American scholar Edward W. Said, which included a powerful essay by Finkelstein, in which he sets out his case in full against the Joan Peters book, recapitulating and enhancing material from the PhD thesis his Princeton instructors had been too corrupt and too fearful to read.

To begin with, Finkelstein was aware, as were most scholars, that immigration to Mandate Palestine—and those areas that would become Israel—had been quite low. But Peters' book claimed that there had been *massive* immigration. How was it that no historians were aware of this? Peters solved this problem by claiming that this massive immigration was "hidden." But if it was hidden, how could Peters even prove that it existed? How such a massive undertaking as a "hidden migration" could occur, without being noticed by reputable scholars, Peters did not say.

As Finkelstein notes, Peters comments "almost exclusively on the standard official documents of the period," which are the 1930 Hope Simpson Report, the 1937 Peel Commission Report, the 1945-46 Anglo-American Survey of Palestine, and the annual British reports to the League of Nations. All these reports say the same thing: immigration to Palestine was at a very *low* level. Since Peters writes that it was at a very *high* level, she either claims that these reports are wrong, or quotes them as saying the opposite of what they actually say. (Peters will appear to quote from an authoritative source to back up her point—but when one checks the source, one finds that it says exactly the opposite of what Peters claims.) Finally, Peters falls back on the favorite gambit of charlatans: there was, she says, a malevolent but massive cover-up by people unwilling to accept her bizarre findings.

Now, you cannot make this many mistakes by accident, references don't doctor themselves, and neither can quotations alter themselves. The point here is not so much about shoddy scholarship, but rather deliberate dishonesty disguised as serious history, which is to say, fraud. The author Joan Peters knowingly and deliberately manipulated sources to make them support things they didn't actually support, or say things they didn't really say. Joan Peters' thesis that there was a massive "hidden immigration" into (or within) Palestine prior to the foundations of Israel is simply not true. Peters' intent was clearly to mislead readers for political purposes, and for that reason her book was (first) wildly successful in America, and (secondly) a deliberate fraud.

But if this kind of propagandizing seems primitive, consider the fact that Peters' business instincts were quite sophisticated. She never wrote another book, and she didn't have to. Early sales for *From Time Immemorial: the Origins of the Arab-Jewish Conflict over Palestine* exceeded even the publisher's expectations, and Peters got on the lecture circuit before scholars revealed the fraud in her research. (The massive cover-up by corrupt American intellectuals certainly helped her in this regard.) She knew exactly what her audience was aching to hear, and she created a book that gave it to them, marketed as scholarship that was both popular and groundbreaking. Some British critics (as well as

Chomsky himself) have suggested that because it so closely matched what certain readers wanted to hear, that it might be in part the product of an intelligence agency. But Joan Peters may simply be an opportunist, one of many such shady individuals found at any given time in the publishing business. From a literary and editorial point of view, what is important is that her "scholarship" was bogus, to begin with; and secondly, hundreds of thousands of highly educated people wanted to believe it was true, and therefore paid good money to reward her fraudulence.

Why? Why did Joan Peters' book fare so well? Because it contained fabrications that people in the US cultural and political elites desperately wanted to believe, and to promote for purposes of social control. And Joan Peters was quite aware of their desperation. Most calculated of all was Joan Peters' assessment of the willingness of American intellectuals to accept fantasy rather than a form of systemic evil in which they had been, and continued to be, complicit. Such an audience would be terribly anxious to exonerate Israel of any wrongdoing, and would be likely to overlook even the most gauche fabrications, in the same way that Communist Party members in the 1930s had a built-in incentive to believe that the Stalinist show trials in the Soviet Union didn't really happen, but were fabrications invented by professional liars paid by rich capitalists. It didn't mean that such people were evil, necessarily. It simply meant that they didn't want to be troubled by uncomfortable truths about certain kinds of systemic evil in the historical moment in which they lived and acted; so they accepted a particularly deceitful form of deliberate propaganda rather than think and investigate for themselves.

People longed to believe Peters not just because of what Israel had done in the past, but because of the negotiating positions of Palestinians in the future. If most Palestinians were not indigenous to Palestine, their territorial claims became substantially less important. And if they were, as Peters claimed, simply hopeful job-seekers attracted to opportunities created by Jewish settlers, their rights would seem much less impressive than the rights of all those industrious European Jews. As a matter of historical fact, however, there were many more Palestinians than Jews, Palestinians owned more property, and the only massive immigration that occurred during the first half of the 20th century was when 750,000 Palestinians were ethnically cleansed by Zionists. But Americans, both Jews and Christian evangelicals, were desperate to believe the worst about Palestinians: that they were simply vagabonds, without a real communal life in mandate Palestine, and hence people who were not respectable enough— indeed, not quite human enough—to have or deserve human rights.

What is notable, finally, about this kind of dissembling is its intentionality. You cannot fake, doctor, or misrepresent scores of footnoted sources without intending to do so. That is unmistakable evidence of Peters' bad faith, in the sense that the author knowingly falsified things that were actually known about the time and place she writes about. Ultimately Peters' weird theory of a "hidden immigration," without any evidence to substantiate it, takes on the nature of a paranormal event. It also crosses, at several points, into the psychic territory reserved for the *reductio ad absurdum* argumentation of the self-deluded fanatic. Since the Arab immigration Peters writes about was so completely "invisible," there can be but very little tangible proof for it, and since there is so little proof, that is further evidence of its invisibility.

Let it suffice simply to say that Peters' book is full of deliberate lies and distortions; her main thesis—that there was a huge migration of Arabs to areas in Palestine settled by Jews, and that this migration was "hidden"—is so silly that it is an insult to the educated reader; and the rest of her book, an attempt to prove her thesis, includes cooked figures and thoroughly bogus charts that ended up giving this writer a bad headache. In short, Peters' book was not only propaganda, but very bad propaganda. Yet it was this silly book, which Finkelstein characterized as a "monumental hoax," that was praised to the skies by the entire American intellectual and academic elite.

But since critics of this supposedly groundbreaking book were systematically prevented, in the US, from publishing criticism of it, Peters' fortunes seemed to gain momentum in America at exactly the same time that it was denounced as a fraud everywhere else. But this façade of ecstatic consensus was soon to crumble. Here I quote from Finkelstein's *Image and Reality of the Israel-Palestine Conflict* on the meteoritic rise and gradual disintegration of the consensus that had been artificially created around Joan Peters' book:

"Joan Peters, via her publisher, peremptorily dismissed the finding of fraud as 'without merit' and Harper and Row senior editor Aaron Asher defended Peters' right to ignore, and to refuse to reply to, 'published attacks on her work, regardless of the nature or provenance'." [It seems exceedingly odd that any publisher would announce, as part of a successful publishing strategy, that it was an author's "right" not to reply to questions about the verisimilitude of her facts. One would think that a publisher might instead welcome controversy and debate, to better publicize the book.] "The periodicals in which *From Time Immemorial* had already been favorably reviewed refused to run any critical correspondence (e.g. *The New Republic, The Atlantic, Commentary*). Periodicals that had yet to review the book rejected a manuscript on the subject as of little or no consequence (e.g. *The Village Voice, Dissent, The New York Review of Books*)."

"In April 1985, *From Time Immemorial* was awarded the prestigious National Jewish Book Award in the 'Israel' category. Chairing the committee that honored Peters was the renowned authority on the 'Arab mind', Raphael Patai. Mr. Patai and his fellow judges discounted without explanation the copious documentation of fraud. Reaffirming that it was 'very happy' with the Peters selection, the Jewish Book Council declared the matter 'closed'." But why would a Book Council, set up ostensibly to explore books and ideas, seek to declare any controversy "closed?"

"Yet in early 1985, the disinformation effort began to unravel as Peters' book went into a British edition. The reviews in Britain were devastating. Oxford's great orientalist, Albert Hourani, denounced *From Time Immemorial* in *The Observer* as 'ludicrous and worthless'. (Privately, Hourani called it 'a grotesque work', noting that every quotation checked 'proved to be wrong in one way or another'.) Ian and David Gilmour, in the *London Review of Books*, concluded an exhaustive 8000-word dissection of the book by calling it 'preposterous'. *The Spectator* likened it to the Clifford Irving 'autobiography' of Howard Hughes. *Time Out* reported it as a 'piece of disinformation roughly the size and weight of a dried cowpat'. The Israelis also got into the act, even before a Hebrew edition of the book had appeared. The Israeli Labor Party daily Davar compared *From Time Immemorial* to Israel's more ignoble past propaganda exercises; the liberal weekly *Koteret Rashit* published a detailed expose of the cover-up by the US media; and the chair of the philosophy department at the Hebrew University, Avishai Margalit, derided Peters' 'web of deceit.'"

"Back in the United States *l'affaire* Peters was fast becoming a singular embarrassment as word began to circulate that a major literary-political scandal was being suppressed. In February 1985, *The New York Review of Books* finally commissioned and in early March received a lengthy piece on *From Time Immemorial* by the noted Israeli scholar Yehoshua Porath. For fully nine months it kept it under wraps." [Strong circumstantial evidence, I would say, that the issues under consideration were neither literary nor historical, but political.] "Published only after a barrage of critical commentary, the Porath essay dismissed out of hand Peters' 'theses', yet scrupulously avoided any mention of her fraudulent scholarship; every effort to raise this obviously crucial issue in the *Review*'s correspondence columns proved unavailing. In October, Edward Said delivered a stunning and eloquent riposte to Peters and her acolytes in the pages of *The Nation*."

The New York Times finessed the scandal in a typically duplicitous manner. It engaged in the many starts and stops typical of editors when they are collectively trying to conceal something. "Faced with escalating accusations of censorship leveled mainly by the British press, the *Times* finally ran a piece in November 1985. It was placed in the Thanksgiving Day (non)-issue, on the theater page, without even a listing in the index. Indeed, all the painstakingly assembled documentation of the hoax was cut from the published version. Porath was quoted to the effect that *From Time Immemorial* 'is a sheer forgery', and that 'In Israel, at least, the book was almost universally dismissed as sheer rubbish, except maybe as a propaganda weapon', while historian Barbara Tuchman continued to insist that the Palestinian people were 'a fairy tale.' Martin Peretz, editor-in-chief of *The New Republic*, alleged that the attack on Peters was part of a calculated leftist plot and Peters herself refused, for the nth time, to be interviewed."

"*Haaretz* reported in June [apparently in 1986] that, at an international conference on Palestinian demography at Haifa University, virtually all the participants ridiculed Peters' demographic 'thesis' and the most authoritative scholar in attendance, Professor Yehoshua Ben-Arieh of the Hebrew University, condemned the Peters enterprise for discrediting the 'Zionist cause'."

When the *eminence grise* of organized Zionism denounces your propaganda as harming the cause, you know the jig is probably up. Although most intellectuals in Israel were now becoming aware that *From Time Immemorial* was a deliberate fraud, that didn't stop certain intellectuals in the West from conducting a rear-guard defense, relying finally on what was now becoming the standard personal attack. Barbara Tuchman ascribed criticism of *From Time Immemorial* to 'growing anti-Semitism' and to certain 'committed and long-term apologists of the Palestine Liberation Organization.' Bernard Lewis, the famous historian of Islam and supporter of the US invasion of Iraq, refused to comment on his previous support for Peters; Saul Bellow likewise tap-danced away from any meaningful comment regarding his praise for Peters' book. Leo Wieseltier, literary editor of *The New Republic*, heaped scorn on Peters' book at scholarly conferences, yet continued to run articles praising it, and refusing articles critical of it. The American intellectual class dealt with the scandal in the dishonorable way that it usually does, by being both for and against the book in question, depending on the audience, and then moving briskly on to other interests and in effect denying that the scandal ever happened.

As for Joan Peters herself, she went from well over two hundred appearances a year on the lecture circuit to being no longer welcome in polite company. In 1995, Finkelstein remarked that she "has not been seen or heard from in nearly a decade." There was an attempt to rehabilitate her book after 9/11, and vague talk about a movie, but nothing came of it. Joan Peters died on January 6, 2015.

A brief check of the internet in late 2013, as this book was being written, revealed that Joan Peters, author of *From Time Immemorial: the Origins of the Arab-Jewish Conflict over Palestine*, had profiles at both the Harry Walker Speakers' Agency, a respectable agency serving today's languishing lecture circuit, and the somewhat less respectable Grabow Entertainment Booking Agency, which represents musicians, corporate comedians and magicians. The latter agency, which is dedicated to "putting show big into your biz," according to its website, advises the reader that in order "to get information about booking Joan Peters for a corporate event, private performance, wedding or meeting," they should submit a 'Questions or

Comments' form, which the Agency kindly supplies.

This rather sad echo of the 'At Liberty' ads famously used by vaudevillians of yesteryear, is apparently all that was left of the career of Joan Peters, although it is hard to imagine how an author, especially a discredited one, could credibly perform at a "corporate event, private performance, wedding or meeting," unless she had radically altered her solo billing to include standup comedy or musical entertainment.

6.

But what led Norman Finkelstein to write about the Israel/Palestine conflict in the first place? What was the connection between the Holocaust—which Finkelstein would also write extensively about—and what the Palestinians have endured, and are still enduring? Historically, the connection is simple. It was the Holocaust that caused a large plurality of Jews to accept the perceived need for a Jewish state. Before that time, the vast majority of Jews living in Europe wanted nothing to do with the idea. But after the Holocaust, the trauma was so great among Holocaust survivors that Zionism seemed to make sense. Jews had to protect themselves, and for that they needed their own state, and their own army to defend them. That would be the final resolution of the problem of anti-Semitism, according to Zionists. If a few Palestinians got hurt in the process, that was just too bad—thus the ethnic cleansing of Palestinians in 1947-1949. The Holocaust not only destroyed the Jewish community in Europe, it destroyed the Palestinian community in the Middle East. The Palestinians were the victims in an international cycle of violence that began with European anti-Semitism and progressed through the founding of Israel and the ethnic cleansing of Palestinians.

The aggression of the Zionists didn't appear out of nowhere—it was a response to the Holocaust, and came out of the internalized aggression embedded in the shared traumatic memory of

Jews in Europe. Indeed, there was a tremendous emphasis in the writing of Zionists at that time on the necessity of being ruthless, adopting a military posture, and learning to be as aggressive as — well, as aggressive as the European Christians who had so recently killed six million of them. In other words, the Zionists had to a large extent internalized the most aggressive attitudes of the Europeans, and have been acting them out against the Palestinians ever since, including those Zionists that consider themselves socialists, social democrats and liberals.[4]

Finkelstein doesn't write about the connection between the Holocaust and Israeli behavior as a psychological phenomenon, because his discipline is historical science and not psychology. But he regularly denounced — and still denounces — certain Israeli behaviors as Nazi-like, and Israeli ruthlessness as being similar to European racism, imperialism and fascism; and in so doing he is clearly making the connection, one that seems historically self-evident to him. Because of his personal experience with intergenerational trauma, Finkelstein seems unusually sensitive to the way traumatic memory affects other people, although he prefers to discuss it in the contest of political behavior. In the summer of 2014, as the Likud government was slaughtering Palestinians in Gaza, Finkelstein continued this comparison, referring on his website at the Likud government of Israel as behaving like Nazis. Certainly the Israeli propaganda Finkelstein deconstructs sounds very much like the dissimulations of Christian society as it once tried to hide or rationalize anti-Semitic violence against Jews.

As is usual in such cases, Finkelstein the prophet is hated, denounced, demonized and marginalized by his community — and he returns the favor by amplifying his rhetorical fury. But it is not the anger in his voice that hurts, but rather the truth of his facts. Tiny inconsistencies in his argument are magnified by Finkelstein's enemies to prove that he is an agent of the devil; phrases are taken out of context and beaten to death, until they can no longer threaten those they describe. And this is done, as it is always done to prophetic figures, because to look in the mirror—to inquire if there is some truth to what the prophet says—invites a pandemonium of the soul.

That partially explains why there was so much animosity against Finkelstein as an individual. But that does not completely explain the hysteria invoked by the Joan Peters literary and publishing scandal. The Peters brouhaha arguably had a larger function. As I have already suggested, it was in great part a distraction from something that was happening in Israel, something that threatened to become public in the US. The Israeli military, as we have already seen, had decided to open up their extensive military archives; and a group of Israeli historians jumped at the chance to explore them, intent on finding out what really happened during 1947-1949.

They discovered rather conclusively that there had been an ethnic cleansing of Palestinians, and that most Palestinians had fled because of some 20 to 25 massacres conducted by the Jewish militias. After most Palestinians had fled, the borders had been sealed, preventing them from returning. The Israelis had then taken over their homes, farms, vineyards and other properties. (See *The Ethnic Cleansing of Palestine*, by the Jewish-Israeli historian Ilan Pappe.)

So why was that such a big deal in the US? Because certain American Jewish leaders had repeatedly—I am tempted to say ritually—denied that such an ethnic cleansing had ever occurred at all, and declaimed that such reports were lies by anti-Semites, self-hating Jews and Arabs. But as the New Historians in Israel demonstrated with unflagging verisimilitude, there *had* been an ethnic cleansing of Palestinians, which meant that those of the Jewish rabbis and leaders in the US who had denied it had been lying all along, or were at best victims of their own wishful thinking.

Here are the facts as discovered by the New Historians in Israel: before the foundation of the state of Israel, Arabic-speaking people in Palestine (what we would today call Palestinians) handily outnumbered Jews in Palestine. The Jewish armed forces, including the Jewish militias, got rid of 750,000 of them by "encouraging" them to leave, and then closed the border so they couldn't come home. Furthermore, the Jewish forces blew up and then plowed under some 500 to 600 villages where these people had lived, in what had previously been Palestine, ensuring that the people that had lived in them would never have homes to return to. This gave the Jews a majority; and since the Palestinians would not be allowed to return, they would be forced to have their children in foreign lands, separate forever from what was, for many, ancestral lands. (That very often means simply the land—specifically, the village graveyards—where their ancestors are buried.) That, in turn, gave the victors a Jewish majority and allowed them to found a Jewish state.

That explains the appeal of *From Time Immemorial*. If you can somehow convince everybody that the Arabic-speaking people in Palestine were recent arrivals, ethnically cleansing them wouldn't seem so bad. This is what a great many Americans, Jews and Christians alike, desperately wanted to believe. And it was they who paid top dollar for this deceit du jour, which for some Americans came just in time. *From Time Immemorial: the Origins of the Arab-Jewish Conflict over Palestine* was black propaganda disguised as scholarship, black in the sense that its author systematically doctored original sources and repeatedly attempted to dissemble historical facts specifically for the purpose of political disinformation.

Jews quite naturally find it very hard—for some, impossible—to acknowledge that Israelis are behaving toward the Palestinians much like the Christian anti-Semites in Europe behaved toward Jews. But they have an even harder time admitting that it is *because* Jews were persecuted that they feel so inclined to despise Palestinians and inflict pain on them in the name of a sterile ideology. That is not surprising. The hardest thing for the victim-aggressor to do is to admit that he has internalized his aggressor's violence, and is now acting out that aggression against new victims of his own. But the central thesis of this book is that victims and witnesses to systemic evil *do* tend to internalize it and *do* tend to act it out later, either against themselves or against others. In other words, the Holocaust and Israeli ethnic cleansing of the Palestinians are not coincidental, but are cause and effect.

That kind of insight is hard to live with, because once you see it clearly, once you understand where the internalized aggression came from, you must deconstruct your own aggression, which means talking about it, and working for a different and better world. Or you can hang onto your aggressive emotional orientation, and learn how to enjoy the pain of other people—which the American evangelicals that support torture have long since learned—or adopt some self-exculpatory ideology to justify it. Or you can simply use bullying tactics, as the US Israel Lobby does, in order to suppress as many of the facts as possible, and punish those that disseminate those facts.

Above all, you must somehow justify to yourself your own proximity to, and complicity in, systemic evil. The method of the Likud leadership in Israel is to frenetically and repeatedly appeal to the shared traumatic memory of the Holocaust, to stir up and enhance, on an almost daily basis, fear and aggression toward the Palestinians. The Likudniks do this by hinting—or declaring outright—that another Holocaust is coming, if Jews do not shut up and obediently support the aggression of the Holy State. Sadly, until people in Israel actively seek to deconstruct their internalized aggression—arising from the shared traumatic memory of the Holocaust and their complicity in the ethnic cleansing of the Palestinians—it will get worse. And that aggression will be directed against the Palestinians, including those whose weapons are only words and ideas, growing more intense with each year. The Palestinians must be hated, because they know Israel's secret—they know how undemocratic Israel really is, and how aggressive the Israelis really are.

A difficult but much more rewarding alternative is to become a different kind of person, and work with others to change Israel, and help it reach a better future. To accomplish this, the world must find a way to force Israel to stop oppressing Palestinians, because its political class will never give up that kind of corrupt and addictive power without substantial economic, social and political pressure. At the same time, the world must create incentives for a new Jewish leadership class that can begin the work of conciliation—and ultimately comprehensive settlement—with the Palestinians. That is hard work, to be sure; it is a lot easier to suppress difficult truths, or torture or shoot people that embody them.

It is far easier to tout people like Joan Peters, who would happily tell Israel's uncritical supporters the lies they want to hear, as long as they will buy them—that systemic evil really doesn't exist in Israel, and that nobody is really complicit with anything bad and that therefore nobody has to make any changes or do anything. There's a big market for it. Just look at the way Christians have historically sought to justify their own cruelty toward Jews for the last thousand years. They developed an entire theology to explain everything from The Fall in the Garden of Eden to the Apocalypse, not to mention the theory of salvation by blood atonement—a classic if unconscious argument for redemptive violence—and a fair amount of these frantic cogitations existed mainly, I would suggest, to hide from Christians the worst and cruelest aspects of their own religion. Jews saw the hypocrisy in European Christianity right from the beginning, but for precisely that reason many leaders of the Ashkanazim ultimately internalized Christianity's worst and most brutal features.

The difference between the will to seek truth, and the will to embrace lies, is fundamental to the operation of systemic evil.

The way that aggression becomes evil—and how evil becomes systemic—is important to this book's thesis, so let me reiterate it. Aggression becomes evil when the aggressor conceals, rationalizes, romanticizes or dissembles that aggression; when used or encouraged by the state this process becomes *systemic evil*. Furthermore, the more acute the aggression becomes, the more likely the aggressor is to seek impunity for his crimes, in order to commit more crimes once the heat is off. This drives the aggressor to seek a propaganda system in which criminal acts can be endlessly rationalized or denied. This is precisely the kind of propaganda system that Finkelstein was uncovering when he exposed the chicanery in the Joan Peters fiasco.

Finkelstein's experience with the Peters scandal succeeded in bringing into sharp focus the two inter-connected subjects he would spend the next fifteen years of his life writing about—the Nazi Holocaust and the Israeli/Palestinian conflict. What he had been forced to confront in the Peters case was the astonishing capacity of the Holocaust to disorient and corrupt virtually all who use it to make money, gain political power, or generate aggression. His second great subject would be the manner in which crimes against the Palestinians, and the frantic need of US intellectuals to lie about it, were fundamentally corrupting Jews in Israel and in the Diaspora, as well as Christians, Palestinians, the Arabic-speaking Middle East and the world at large.

By his choice of subject matter he seemed, however, to be signaling that identification with the Palestinians was, for him, the key to coming to terms with the Holocaust. Why Palestinians? Because they were simply the latest victims of the Holocaust, victims of the same evil that drove Jews from Europe and frightened them into accepting Zionism—and in the process adopting the worst and most imperial kind of European cruelty. The Holocaust caused European Jews to accept Zionism, the False Messiah that would in one fell swoop corrupt Judaism and bring disaster to the Palestinians.

What Finkelstein discovered, however, really had more to do with America than Israel. What Finkelstein exposed was a profound form of systemic evil, in which Americans gleefully threw away their own agency (that is, their own capacity to experience verifiable truth) while instead accepting the most ridiculous kind of political fantasy. This is not new in America, since the ability to ignore unjustifiable and brutal systems of bondage goes all the way back to slavery, and the fact that southern segregation up to the Civil Rights and Voting Rights Acts of 1964 and 1965 was slavery in all but name. Furthermore in dealing with the Israelis—and the Americans in the Israel Lobby—Finkelstein was encountering a prime example of *traumatic privilege*, a state of mind in which aggrieved people act out, or become complicit in covering up or rationalizing, the aggression inherent in the aggrieved group's traumatic memory. *Traumatic privilege* creates a state of mind roughly similar to that of the sociopath. If it is not challenged and eradicated, traumatic privilege can become institutionalized as a form of *destructive entitlement*, a shared orientation that both causes and rationalizes systemic evil by the state.

Finkelstein was already discovering a way out of this conundrum, however, which is why he is so important to this book. His ideological and emotional key to deconstructing the power of traumatic memory—as well as its concomitant aggression—was an intense identification with universal human rights, an identification that he inherited from his mother. First, he dedicated himself to telling those truths about Israel/Palestine that Americans didn't want to hear; and secondly, he committed himself to working for human rights for Palestinians. That commitment to human rights for Palestinians constitutes a form of socially-beneficial behavior that empowered him to break free of the tyranny of intergenerational trauma, and in so doing to choose and act out a better future.

7.

Finkelstein's next project would be a thoroughgoing deconstruction of *Hitler's Willing Executioners: Ordinary Germans and the Holocaust*, a highly speculative book about the Holocaust by Daniel Jonah Goldhagen. If Joan Peters' book was over-the-top propaganda regarding Israel/Palestine, Goldhagen's controversial book could be seen as staking out a similarly extreme position regarding the history, the psychological underpinnings, and the ultimate meaning of the Nazi Holocaust. Needless to say, Finkelstein was not about to be left out of *that* controversy.

Daniel Goldhagen's book almost immediately attracted the vehement opposition of most established historians, including the dean of Holocaust historians Raul Hilberg, who testily denounced Goldhagen's book as "totally wrong about everything" and "worthless."[5] In his book Goldhagen offers a comprehensive, if wildly simplistic and supremely biased, explanation for the Holocaust. The Holocaust wasn't a secret from most Germans, Goldhagen alleges—on the contrary, everybody knew about it, and furthermore the average German couldn't wait to start killing Jews. The reason they all jumped at the chance to kill Jews was because of a uniquely murderous "eliminationist" form of anti-Semitism among German-speaking people. The reason that Nazis pulled off the Holocaust wasn't because they were evil, but because they were Germans.

Alone among historians Goldhagen even took the position that Hitler and his brigands were able to rule "without massive coercion or violence" because the German people were thrilled to at long last have a leader who was as anti-Semitic as they were. Of course, one does not have to be a trained historian to know that Hitler began using concentration camps as early as 1933 precisely because he had so many active opponents that they had to be incarcerated by the hundreds of thousands, and eventually the millions. And although Hitler eventually got a very high level of compliance from those Germans he hadn't killed or incarcerated, the fact that the Nazis ran a totalitarian government based on torture and murder was not incidental to their success—in fact it was unmistakably the biggest factor in achieving it.

Although German historians were generally aware that Goldhagen had his facts wrong, the German translation of his book arguably had a positive effect in Germany, because it sparked widespread discussion of the *Hitlerzeit* and its victims. Because of the extraordinary sensitivity of Germans to the Holocaust, Goldhagen became the darling of the German reading public, and was thereafter kept busy traveling to various destinations in Germany to receive historical and literary prizes; but his thesis had the disadvantages of all arguments that verge on collective guilt: if all Germans were equally guilty, all Germans were equally innocent. But that is not the way the world works. Even under totalitarian governments some people are guiltier than others, some are less guilty, and some are innocent. In order for Germany to reconstitute itself as a society based on law and representative government (and for humanity at large to bring justice to the Nazi murderers), it was necessary, beginning with the Nuremberg Trials, to establish accountability for the systemic evil committed under Nazi rule; and that process consisted in finding individual guilt in specific cases of mass evil, and separating out the guilty from both the less guilty and the innocent.

How does one establish individual guilt? One begins with the underlings who did the actual dirty work of murdering and torturing; then the higher-ups, the officers in the military and paramilitary and police organizations that gave the kill orders; and finally those who, from a position of power, designed the murderous ideologies that justified the crimes that they wanted their underlings to commit, killing those who wouldn't do as they say, and profiting, in terms of power and prestige, from the whole criminal shebang. Find those three groups—the most egregious perpetrators, the officer corps of the most murderous organizations, and politicians and top leaders most involved in designing, guiding and encouraging crimes against humanity— and you will have the guilty parties.

Furthermore, to say that the entire German nation was crazy with anti-Semitism actually amounts to a kind of excuse for the Nazis, as Finkelstein points out. How can you say that a man is guilty if he is so crazy that he cannot tell the difference between right and wrong? All the evidence indicates that many Germans knew very well that Hitler was engaged in evil, but followed orders anyway, because they were afraid of being killed or tortured, or because they were swept along by the hypnotic influence of German nationalism. But there is nothing uniquely German about those things; cowardice, sadism and ultra-nationalism are universal.

What was unique was the peculiar psychopathology of Adolph Hitler; the trauma of Versailles; depression and hyper-inflation; the trauma of daily pitched street battles during the Weimer years; and the divisions in the German Left between Social Democrats and Communists. All of these things contributed to the ascension of a band of criminals to power in a highly organized, highly educated, highly industrialized nation, the centralization of which gave Hitler's henchmen extraordinary powers to kill or imprison those who opposed him. I mention the causal factors above because they are usually mentioned by almost all historians who write about Germany and the rise of Nazism. The reader should note, also, that almost all of the causal factors mentioned above—with the possible exception of the split in the Left—involve profound and widespread emotional trauma. Weimer Germany was a society convulsed by violence and repeated social dislocation and its traumatic emotional effects.

But Daniel Goldhagen did not believe any of these causal factors were important. Goldhagen in particular disliked Christopher Browning's 1992 book *Ordinary Men: Reserve Police*

Battalion 101 and the Final Solution in Poland, one of the most rewarding and detailed books ever written about the evolution of systemic evil in a paramilitary organization. Browning emphasized the way in which ordinary people could be indoctrinated into a particularly brutal form of systemic evil. Browning especially concentrates on the importance of the 'first day'—that is, the first day of active service in the Reserve Battalion—in which recruits discovered the exact nature of the murderous crimes against innocent civilians they were to commit, first witnessed what the killing of men, women and children was really like, and finally engaged in their first mass killing. After that, after the trauma had started to bond them to the aggression that was the whole reason for the Reserve Battalion's existence, the mass murdering became progressively easier.

All these things involved in the recruits' indoctrination into systematic mass criminality is very much like the manner in which criminal organizations around the world typically 'initiate' new recruits. New recruits are commonly forced to kill someone in full view of the others, sometimes they are required to kill a friend, or are sometimes required to publicly torture people or even to be tortured themselves. The leaders of criminal organizations intuitively understand that violence has a collective bonding effect on men regularly engaged in it, and the leaders use it for that reason.

Germans had already been exposed to the trauma of daily violence during Weimer, which included some 500 reported assassinations by right-wing extremists during the 1920s, not to mention the extreme emphasis on violence in the rhetoric and behavior of Hitler's inner circle, a violence that reached its highest domestic expression in the horrific mass government pogrom in 1938 known as *Kristallnacht*. It seems almost a certainty that the Nazi aggression was systematically accompanied—or at the very least encouraged—by the criminal state's creation of mass emotional trauma, creating over time a trauma bond, which was experienced by many as an unbreakable addiction to aggression organized by the state. Accompanied by intense patriarchy, nationalism and a sense of Germans as victims, these violent events predisposed and prepared men to act out the internalized aggression that accompanies widespread social trauma. This bondage to aggression—consisting of nothing less than mass traumatic bonding—resulted not just in incredibly violent social behavior, but produced by way of justification an irrational but transcendent conviction that aggression on behalf of the Fatherland was the highest, noblest and most authentic activity to which any German could possibly aspire.

But if Browning's data was correct, virtually anybody might be slowly but surely induced to commit evil acts. Browning's data tended to validate the findings of Stanley Milgram's 'Obedience Study,' an extremely controversial but revealing laboratory experiment in which unsuspecting subjects were induced to murder what they believed to be an innocent stranger in an adjoining room, using gradually ascending electric shocks. Milgram likewise concluded that virtually anybody would do terrible things to their fellow human beings, by being ordered to do so by someone who seemed to possess ultimate authority, and facilitated this by placing subjects in a strange and traumatizing situation. That truth Goldhagen could not accept. In his mind, the source of the evil was not something in the human personality, but in being German.

Norman Finkelstein wrote a book-length essay pointing out the main flaws of Goldhagen's book, "Daniel Jonah Hagen's 'Crazy' Thesis." Another critic was Canadian historian Ruth Bettina Birn, who was an archivist at a facility that supplied primary sources to Goldhagen. Birn's and Finkselstein's essays were eventually combined in a single volume, *A Nation on Trial: The Goldhagen Thesis and Historical Truth*. In response to it, Goldhagen characteristically dismissed Finkelstein with a personal attack as "a supporter of Hamas," also writing to Birn's employers demanding an investigation of her because he believed her to be "a member of the perpetrator race" (Birn was born in Germany).

Goldhagen's weird response to Birn is indicative of the main problem with his thesis, and with Goldhagen himself: an intense, unhealthy and obsessive Germanophobia, which often verges on racism, pure and simple. As more than one critic has pointed out, Goldhagen adopted the Nazi concept of race-as-identity in order to use it against the Germans. It also ignored the fact that fascism—with varying degrees of anti-Semitism—swept Spain, Italy and most of Eastern Europe, creating a ready-made network of anti-Semitic dictatorships that aided in the rounding up of Jews by Hitler's minions. (And what about the genocides of the Armenians and the Roma, not to mention the later genocides in Cambodia, Bangladesh, Bosnia and Rwanda?) Goldhagen's thesis denies the universality of evil, systemic or otherwise, in human affairs, locating the source of evil not in human psychology, but in race. The Germans under Hitler engaged in systemic evil, according to Goldhagen, not because of any particular historical causes, not because of unusual emotional states, not because of the after-effect of emotional trauma, but because they were Germans.

There was an add-on benefit adhering to the Goldhagen thesis for the well-funded neo-conservative movement in the US, which was and still is obsessively focused on Zionism and Israel. One reason the neo-cons plugged for the Goldhagen view of the Nazi Holocaust as unique in human history, is that it can be used to defend aggressive Israeli military practices. (Because if Nazi aggression was both extreme and anomalous, the Israelis can also use brutality that is extreme and anomalous.) In terms of numbers, the Holocaust is unique, but to understand why and how it happened one must locate the Nazi genocide on the full spectrum of genocidal events in the 20th century. The neo-cons refuse to do that, sometimes insisting that it is anti-Semitic to even compare the Holocaust to other genocides.

Nevertheless the Nazi Holocaust must be compared to other genocides, especially of the Armenians, and later the Cambodians and the Rwandans. In the case of Rwanda, the Hutu Power militants were preparing for the final genocide of Tutus for decades before the 1990s; furthermore, they engaged in considerable street violence just like the Nazis, and their beliefs strongly resembled those of fascists everywhere. The Turks who conducted the Armenian genocide were enraged at having lost the First World War and by the collapse of the Ottoman Empire, and the Cambodian Khmer Rouge was led by psychopathic murderers who engaged from the beginning in daily murder rituals as a pathological political ceremony. It seems clear that genocide arises from discernible psychological states (the most important of which is psychological trauma) and is enhanced by describable historical circumstances (the most important of which is probably early impunity for the violent acts of the aggressor).

Goldhagen's neo-con fans couldn't be more mistaken about the racial basis for evil. Every human society—including Israel—is capable of systemic evil, because evil is universal and not unique to one nation, race or language group. And Israel has in fact created a particularly brutal form of systemic evil by setting up an apartheid system in the Occupied Palestinian Territories. America itself engages in systemic evil when it supports these Israeli monstrosities, including the mass use of torture, extrajudicial executions and collective punishment of Palestinians. Although Israeli apartheid is *at this time* nowhere near as evil as Nazi anti-Semitism, the religious conflicts spawned by its fanaticism could become just as destructive if there are no countervailing forces imposing accountability on the Israelis, instead of the impunity they currently enjoy as a client state of the US. Indeed, the increasing irrationality of Israel's religious parties, Israel's accelerating drift into neo-fascism and religious fanaticism, along with the US tendency to rationalize or dissemble everything Israel does, are one of the biggest sources of international danger in the Middle East at present.[6]

However controversial Finkelstein's previous books may have been, they were nothing compared to the hysteria ignited by Finkelstein's next book, which would explore the extent to which the Holocaust was used by a group of powerful, shady operatives to shake down the entire continent of Europe for billions of dollars, money that was supposed to be distributed to Holocaust survivors but mostly never was. His book would do so in a manner so shocking that Finkelstein, already declared a pariah by almost all the Jewish organizations in America, would ultimately be kicked out of American academia, the culmination of a process that began when professors and administrators at Princeton graduated him while refusing to read his PhD thesis. As usual, his critics generally didn't challenge his facts, but rather attacked him for the crime of revealing those facts.

8.

Finkelstein's next book *The Holocaust Industry: Reflections on the Exploitation of Jewish Suffering*, which came out in 2000 (with a second edition in 2003), tells a story that is almost as mind-boggling, and as difficult to comprehend and believe, as the Holocaust itself.[7] In 1995 a group of rich, powerful and politically-connected individuals, led by the late multi-billionaire Edgar Miles Bronfman, Sr., set up a consortium that demanded that European banks contribute to a fund for Jewish Holocaust survivors. The reason for this, they said, was that many wealthy Jews had left their money in Swiss bank accounts only to later perish in the Nazi gas chambers; therefore, said Bronfman and his friends, Swiss banks should take the money in those abandoned accounts and put it into a fund to be distributed to still-living Holocaust survivors, who often lived in deplorable poverty.

Nobody knew if money left in abandoned accounts really existed, or—if it did—how much of it belonged to Holocaust victims, or even how much money might be involved. Nor did they know where it was located, or where interested parties should start searching for it. Stories about bank accounts of Holocaust victims abandoned in the 1930s and early 1940s had been circulating for decades, but there was little in the way of reliable information about it, and nothing that might substantiate Bronfman's claims. What probably won most people over— as it did this writer in 1995—was the proposal by Bronfman and his deputy Rabbi Israel Singer to distribute all the money they located to destitute Holocaust survivors. What could possibly go wrong with that?

The problem, however—one that was not obvious to people who had no day-to-day contact with Bronfman and his team— was that he refused to discuss the obvious problems that would be involved in disbursing the recovered money, which would, among other things, involve the creation of an international data bank of Holocaust survivors. Instead Bronfman's people consistently found ways to change the subject when questions of oversight over the eventual disbursement of funds came up. In retrospect, it seems clear that from the very beginning Bronfman was grooming his Swiss contacts to accept the idea that he alone had the right to disburse any recovered funds.

But Bronfman and everybody else associated with him did promise, repeatedly and in the most heartfelt language, to disburse whatever funds they recovered to needy Holocaust survivors; and in time this became their biggest selling point. Few doubted this because it was hard, at that time, to imagine that any group of people would participate in a scam based on the economic needs of Holocaust survivors. Meanwhile, Bronfman not only insisted that the abandoned money existed, but that Swiss banks knew more about it than they were telling. Very often Bronfman and his team sounded like they had proprietary information that nobody else had; other times they simply declared that the money existed, without adducing any evidence that might support that assertion. When people expressed doubts, Edgar Bronfman would often respond by accusing them of disrespecting Jews that had perished in the Holocaust, hinting that they were anti-Semitic. But while making these charges, Bronfman cited no evidence for the existence of the money, or reasons why anybody should trust him with it, if it did exist.

Edgar Miles Bronfman, Sr., was an extremely wealthy and well-connected heir to the Seagram liquor fortune, and a scion of the colorful Canadian-American Bronfman family, a tribe well known in the world of Jewish philanthropy and political gamesmanship. Edgar and other family members have, at one time or another, been major political donors for the Democratic Party. Edgar Bronfman was elected President of the World Jewish Congress in 1981, which according to Norman Finkelstein was a relatively unknown organization until Bronfman started using it for his various European machinations; he kept his position there until 2007. As early as 1992, Bronfman created the World Jewish Restitution Organization (WJRO), which, from its earliest beginnings, claimed legal jurisdiction over the assets of all Holocaust survivors, including those that were still living. (But how can any organization claim legal jurisdiction over money belonging to a living person? That was the first big red flag, which everybody chose to ignore.)

Bronfman's long-time deputy in these machinations was Rabbi Israel Singer, whose wealth—while not comparable to Edgar Bronfman's—came from real estate, and was not inconsiderable. It was Bronfman and Singer who opened negotiations with the Swiss banking industry. When informed in 1995 by Swiss bankers that they were able to come up with only a mere $32 million in accounts that could be proven to be of Holocaust victims, Bronfman was furious; his response was to reach out to Senator Alphonse D'Amato of New York for the wielding of

American political influence. This consortium of advocates added several new faces during the late 1990s; but at no time did Bronfman or any or his shifting band of associates offer any proof regarding the abandoned bank accounts, but simply made repeated assertions that they were there.

If Bronfman had been on the level, the first order of business should have been for him to organize an international group of banking experts, and ask European governments to appoint observers to monitor its activities. The job of this high-level group would be to investigate Bronfman's claim that there were abandoned bank accounts of Holocaust victims. If significant amounts of money were found, the group would also provide close oversight for dispersal of funds. The response of Bronfman and the WJRO when the issue of oversight was brought up was to become accusatory and sometimes hysterical, especially if it was brought up by Swiss banks or politicians; Bronfman's position at this point was that anybody who questioned the WJRO's proposals were either part of a conspiracy of Swiss banking interests, or intent on insulting dead Holocaust victims.

Anyone who has studied the ways of criminals will probably recognize a distinct family resemblance between the claims made by Bronfman and his consortium, and certain well-know confidence games. There is an entire genre of con games (the famous 'pigeon drop' being probably the best-known) that involves the existence of money that cannot be verified, usually because it is physically concealed in an envelope, a suitcase or a locker in an airport. The entire hustle depends on talking about the purloined money so much that everybody comes to assume that it actually exists. Alas, when the victim finally gets around to opening the envelope, suitcase or locker, the money has fled.

Perhaps because of the more slippery aspects of the demands being made by Bronfman, Singer and the World Jewish Restitution Organization (WJRO), and the fact that nobody could prove that money of Holocaust victims in abandoned accounts really existed—or where it was or anything else about it—the Bronfman/Singer team began over a period of time to shy away from attempts to systematically investigate the matter. Instead they began to present their scheme as a kind of late 20th-century European reparations scheme for Holocaust victims. But why should Bronfman and his teammates be in charge of receiving the money from such a scheme? Shouldn't that be the job of democratically-elected governments, or commissions? The complete absence of any plan for oversight was already enough, in this writer's opinion, to qualify the whole thing as a scam. Legitimate charities do not object to oversight. (The fact that a great many charities *do* object to oversight is evidence of their illegitimacy, and the abominable ethics currently prevailing in the world of organized charitable giving.)

The main sticking point regarding Bronfman's claims was—and would continue to be throughout—whether there really was money of Holocaust victims in abandoned accounts at all, or not; and if there was, how much. There either were bank accounts abandoned by Jews that perished in the Holocaust, or there weren't. But Bronfman and Singer increasingly shied away from that question, which could, after all, be resolved only through a thorough investigation, one that might take a fair amount of time. But as we will see, the last thing Bronfman and Singer were interested in was finding out whether such abandoned accounts really existed. Indeed, the power of their allegations rested on the fact that nobody knew if there really *were* abandoned accounts, and how much money might be in them.

If there were abandoned accounts, the Swiss asked, exactly which principle of law or custom made the Swiss responsible for that abandoned money, and why would such an idea even come up, since that same abandonment—if it happened on the mass basis that Bronfman claimed it had—was caused not by the Swiss but by the Nazis, and since the Third Reich had been located not in Switzerland, but in Germany?

Bronfman, Singer, the World Jewish Congress and its offspring the World Jewish Restitution Committee (WJRC) seemed unperturbed by these early salvos of doubt and incredulity, and responded by rolling out their big guns. Virtually every word the Swiss bankers uttered was a lie, Bronfman, Singer and the WJRC informed an attentive world. In reality, they said, the Swiss knew very well that money had been left by Holocaust victims, and since those same bankers had kept impeccable records of it, they knew exactly where it was located. And the total amount of money left in abandoned accounts by Holocaust survivors, Bronfman managed to hint at several junctures, was of such a colossal amount as to stagger the imagination. But Bronfman's cohorts were never able to say exactly how much it might be, nor did they explain where their information came from. They simply accused the Swiss of having all the relevant information, and shamelessly lying about it.

Furthermore, Bronfman and Singer insisted, the Swiss banking industry was still profiting from their possession of this vast capital. That's why the Swiss bankers were lying, according to the Bronfman team—not only had the heartless Swiss bankers originally taken advantage of Holocaust victims, even now they continued to leech the last drops of profit out of the lost fortunes of Hitler's victims! The entire situation, quite simply, was a criminal conspiracy of the Swiss banks! First, the Swiss had profited from the money of the Holocaust dead; second, they had concealed this fact and were now lying about it; and third, they continued to profit from it. In short, they had not only stolen from the dead, they had gotten rich from the abandoned money they had stolen.

These astonishing and completely unsubstantiated charges, made in various press releases and conferences, rapidly gained traction. To begin with, Bronfman and the WJRO had tapped into a certain resentment of banks in general, and Swiss banks in particular. (Characterized by jealousy on the part of those too poor to have a secret Swiss bank account, and guilt on the part of those that had.) Secondly, as mentioned above, rumors about abandoned Swiss banks accounts of Holocaust victims had been rattling around Europe for years, with one such story appearing in a recent Paris edition of the *New York Herald Tribune*. And the Singer/Bronfman twosome were so confident, and so full of righteous indignation regarding their allegations, that it was difficult for many people to imagine that they were bluffing. But unless Bronfman had secret information that he wasn't making public—and why *wouldn't* he make it public?—that is exactly what he and his associates were doing.

Since it is impossible to prove a negative, the constant and sensational reiterations of the Bronfman confreres—that vast amounts of purloined money was being concealed by the Swiss, and that they were deliberately lying about it—began to create, in Europe and the US, a de facto public sense that the Swiss were hiding something. And it wasn't clear to most independent observers at that time how and why anyone would benefit from Bronfman's charges, which added to the verisimilitude of their accusations. Bronfman and Singer appeared to the public as idealistic advocates of social justice who, at great risk to themselves (and apparently at their own expense) had taken upon themselves the job of standing up for the continued exploitations of Holocaust victims who had trustingly placed their life savings in numbered Swiss accounts, only to die hideously in the gas chambers. And Bronfman and Singer would not personally benefit from any monies discovered, would they, since they were going to give it all to the needy Holocaust survivors?

The Bronfman team now revealed their endgame to a fascinated world. They intended to sue the Swiss bankers as a group, they said, in order to recover the money left by Jews that had perished in the Holocaust; and then they would *personally* distribute the funds so recovered to needy Holocaust survivors, wherever they happened to live! Never mind all that blather about oversight—Bronfman and his group had it all covered, they would do it personally! Bronfman's team was well on its way to becoming folk heroes, an unaffiliated philanthropic David against the villainous Goliath of the Swiss banking system; and they had nothing to gain but the satisfaction of achieving some justice for those who died in Hitler's gas chambers!

Legally, since hardly a day went by that Bronfman's associates didn't make an unpleasant charge both verbally and in print about banking functions they had no proprietary knowledge of, and since they presented no proof to back up their assertions, their accusations were technically, if they could be proven false, both libelous and slanderous. But the Swiss banking system couldn't prove that they were, because—astonishingly enough—they apparently didn't know themselves whether they had abandoned bank accounts, or how many there were, or what the total amount of money in them might be.

Clearly, then, they couldn't sue Bronfman and his minions using truth as best evidence, because they did not themselves know what the truth was. This may have been incompetence, or it may simply have been a very old-fashioned way of doing things in a vast banking system; nevertheless, their vacillation, the fact that the left hand of the Swiss banking enterprises didn't seem to know what their right hand was doing—not to mention the vastness of their system—created the impression that they knew much more than they were revealing. The truth, this writer now believes, is that they knew next to nothing about their own operations, to the extent that they did not even have—and may still not have—a legal or practical definition of what makes an account abandoned, instead of merely unused for a long period.

Many Holocaust survivors, the Bronfman consortium kept reiterating again and again, were living in deplorable conditions, were sick, and in some cases literally starving. Could not Europe reach out to do something for these poor folks? This was the perfect opportunity for a rare bit of poetic justice—the abandoned accounts of the Holocaust dead, so long hidden by the ruthless Swiss, would be given to Holocaust survivors! The mental image of starving Holocaust survivors was so dramatic that everybody had by now completely forgotten that the existence of the money still hadn't been proven. Everybody was so excited about giving money to old, crippled, terribly sick Holocaust survivors, that they had taken their eyes off the fact that the money was all hypothetical, and might never be found, and that in any case the issue of oversight had never been properly addressed.

The wretched situation of the Holocaust survivors was raised so often by Bronfman and Singer that the phrase "heartrending" hardly describes the picture they painted. Aging Holocaust survivors living in abject poverty... in horrible and often dirty surroundings in crime-ridden neighborhoods... Bronfman and Singer became positively frantic, daily referring to the fact that if negotiations went on too long, many of the survivors almost surely would die... and indeed, many of these survivors *did* in fact live in wretched conditions, were in poor health, and in fact *could* have used some kind of immediate monetary help to lift them out of their poverty. How could the heartless Swiss bankers not see the absolute necessity of acting on this heart-wrenching humanitarian need?

Here's where the story takes a turn that not even the most depraved, neurotic or cocaine-besotted American writer would dare to inject into a screenplay, short story or novel. The horrifying reality—documented at length by Norman Finkelstein in *The Holocaust Industry*—is that Bronfman, Singer and their World Jewish Restitutions Committee, which ultimately collected billions of dollars from various European governments, never gave all of the money they collected to Holocaust survivors at all, as they had repeatedly stated that they would. Instead they used

104

it to line their own pockets, to pay bogus and exorbitant legal fees, to pay for overhead of various organizations, or to initiate pet projects in Israel and elsewhere, projects that had only the most tangential relationship with flesh-and-blood human beings.

The Dickensian poverty of Holocaust survivors, so frequently invoked by Bronfman during negotiations with Swiss bankers, was the ideological currency of a low-rent, bust-out hustle. The organizers of the appeal had apparently never intended to distribute most of the money to survivors. The claims of the Bronfman/Singer twosome that they would distribute all the money they recovered to needy Holocaust survivors was a lie.

Given that it eventually involved billions of dollars, it was probably the most monumental hustle of human history, and that is exactly what Finkelstein's *The Holocaust Industry: Reflections on the Exploitation of Jewish Suffering* was written to document. The poverty-stricken Holocaust survivors in Europe and Israel ended up getting only a small fraction of the money collected by the organizers of the project; the vast majority received nothing. The dwindling numbers of Holocaust survivors that still cling to life remain as impoverished as they ever were, even in Israel, as we will shortly see. Finkelstein further alleges that this fantastic swindle was part of a larger corruption involving Israel's treatment of the Palestinians, and of the lying and posturing necessary to impose the political line of Israel and its American proxies, to which the ubiquitous President Bill Clinton—perhaps thinking of his wife's future political fortunes—entered at a pivotal moment, happily and shamelessly lending credence to Bronfman's operation. How this all went down we will see later in this chapter.

It would have been different if Bronfman and Singer had been honest, and said from the beginning that they wanted money merely for various pet projects, as well as awarding themselves (and their friends) millions in legal fees, for negotiating the whole shebang. But if they had been that honest, they wouldn't have gotten very much money, and maybe they wouldn't have gotten any money at all. The full extent of the swag depended on their fraudulent claim that they were going to personally distribute the money to individual Holocaust survivors. In fact, they so often invoked heartrending scenes of old and crippled Holocaust survivors reaching out trembling hands to receive money for immediate medical attention, food and shelter that it gradually became the very essence of the controversy they initiated. But those survivors that are still alive today are for the most part just as poverty-stricken as they were before, because most of them—with a few happy exceptions—received not one penny, franc, mark or shekel of the money.

"If [Finkelstein's] indictment is a true one," said the *London Times*, "it should prompt prosecutions, sackings, protest. The book shouts scandal. It is a polemic, communicated at maximum volume." But there would be no prosecutions, sackings, protest—except against Finkelstein himself, for exposing one of the most depraved and despicable swindles in humankind's long history of charlatanism. As always, nobody argued with Finkelstein's facts, only the fact that he revealed them. If some of the European governments had been courageous enough to bring a case against Bronfman and Company, perhaps some abandoned funds could have been recovered, and then actually distributed to Holocaust survivors around the world, beginning with those in Europe. But nothing of the kind happened. What did happen was an international campaign to punish Finkelstein, very often by the same crooks that originally profited from the whole scam.

For his trouble, Finkelstein became the target of a malicious campaign that would ultimately result in making him unemployable in American academia. This probably should not surprise us, since almost anything having to do with the Holocaust—or with Israel—has the ability to make people irrational. On the other hand, American academics keep talking about 'academic freedom' as though it actually existed, whereas it clearly doesn't. In the case of the Holocaust, it is the belief of this writer that it corrupts everything, especially people who use it to raise money or promote their own perceived political interests.

That is because those people that attempt to use the Holocaust in that corrupt manner must, to achieve their goal, refer constantly to its systemic evil; it becomes their secret weapon, with which they can suppress inconvenient facts, repress controversy and frame every issue to suit their own interests. Thus they end up identifying with its dark power, and ultimately internalizing—however unconsciously—its toxic aggression. Because of that, they are likely to act out that aggression against themselves and others without ever knowing why.

9.

The first two sections of Norman Finkelstein's *The Holocaust Industry: Reflections on the Exploitation of Jewish Suffering* set the stage, so to speak, for the remarkable showdown between the Swiss banking industry and Edgar Miles Bronfman, Sr., who postured himself as a spokesperson for the six million who died in the Holocaust. Finkelstein begins *The Holocaust Industry* by describing the ways that the Holocaust is regarded—and used—in American culture. In the first section, "Capitalizing the Holocaust," Finkelstein's contends that there was never much interest among Jews in either the Holocaust or the state of Israel, until after the victorious Israeli victory over the Arabs in 1967. Before that time, Jewish attitudes toward the Holocaust tended to be somewhat understated. After all, West Germany had become our ally against the Soviets; furthermore, concern about the Holocaust was seen as a cause of the Left. For that reason, some Jews—especially in the 1950s—avoided discussing the Holocaust because they believed their concerns might be perceived as a Communist issue.[8]

Furthermore, thinking or talking too much about the Holocaust was often seen as a subtle affront to middle class sensibilities. And Jews, like everybody else, were hesitant to unpack the Holocaust because of what they would find out about human nature. Christians, on the other hand, were afraid of what they would find out about Christianity, since Christians were responsible for it. Many Americans regarded Hitler's Germany as "a period of insanity that should be forgotten as quickly as possible." (The quote is from a character named Dr. Epstein, whose mother is a Holocaust survivor, in Kurt Vonnegut's novel *Mother Night*.)[9]

Norman Finkelstein argues, however, that Jewish leaders in the post-1967 War period saw that the Holocaust could be useful to people engaged in defending Israel. "Given its proven utility, organized American Jewry exploited the Nazi holocaust after the June war." This ideological recasting of history's greatest crime "proved to be the perfect weapon for deflecting criticism of Israel." This ran concurrently with the new concern for the more powerful Israel that emerged after the victory of 1967. "What deserves emphasis here, however, is that for American Jewish elites the Holocaust performed the same function as Israel: another invaluable chip in a high-stakes power game. The avowed concern for Holocaust memory was as contrived as the avowed concern for Israel's fate."[10]

As Finkelstein points out, when President Reagan visited a German cemetery in Bitburg, Germany, which contained some forty-nine graves of SS troops, Jewish leaders were the first to rise in defense of Reagan back in the USA. Finkelstein adds with typical bluntness in a footnote: "Prominent Holocaust-mongers and Israel supporters like ADL national director Abraham Foxman, past president of the A[merican]J[ewish] C[ommittee], and chairman of the Conference of Presidents of Major American Jewish Organizations Kenneth Bialkin, not to mention Henry Kissinger, all rose to Reagan's defense during the Bitburg visit, while the AJC hosted West German Chancellor Helmut Kohl's loyal foreign ministers as the guest of honor at its annual meeting the same week."[11]

This writer well remembers the Bitburg kerfuffle because of the singularly craven role played by Holocaust writer Elie Wiesel. He was asked repeatedly at that time what he thought of Reagan's behavior, but could only reply that he was "perplexed" that President Reagan was visiting a cemetery where SS troops are buried. Wiesel marketed himself as a man on fire over the horrors of the Holocaust, but in this very clear-cut case could not rouse himself to engage in even the mildest criticism of President Ronald Reagan. Wiesel comes across as a typically shallow American celebrity, one who publicly plays at being the *eminence grise* of American human rights activism, but who is constitutionally unable to take the uncompromising, and therefore unpopular, positions that such a role demands. Like many other Americans in public life, Elie Wiesel plays the role of a heroic figure, but is a poor substitute for the real thing.

A real human rights leader would have publicly pleaded for Reagan to visit another German cemetery, a cemetery with graves of Wehrmacht soldiers, perhaps, but without graves of SS troops; and then, if that was unsuccessful, such a leader would have publicly denounced Reagan's choice. But if he'd done so, the ambitious Wiesel would have lost access to the White House, where he was often a guest. Such a public position might also have made it harder to collect the reputed $25,000 he reportedly charges for lectures. Wiesel is best seen as a particularly tacky opportunist, another phony in the American parade of mediocrities that constitute its celebrity culture. But the slippery Wiesel raises an interesting question: to what extent do Americans want opportunists and actors playing the *role* of human rights advocates, rather than figures that might really challenge and upset them?

The second part of Finkelstein's *The Holocaust Industry*,

"Hoaxers, Hucksters and History," continues in the same vein, but deals specifically with the manner in which certain American Jewish leaders have encouraged a superficial obsession with the Holocaust, in order to deflect criticism of Israel while using the Holocaust to raise money and score political points, often posturing themselves as pitiful victims of anti-Semitism when anyone takes exception to their uncritical support of an increasingly right-wing Israeli state. This unhealthy fascination with victim status was probably influenced to some extent by a fascination with victims in popular culture, a phenomenon skewered relentlessly as part of a "culture of complaint" in the book of the same name by art critic Robert Hughes.

But the gratuitous adoption of victim status, central to this same alleged culture of complaint, also offered distinct social advantages to the ambitious and the ideologically combative. Aggressors almost always posture themselves as victims; it is an observable constant in the economy of human aggression. Being able to quickly posture oneself as a victim is also fundamental to the passive-aggressive fighting style.

For Jews in the 1950s and 1960s, however, victim status didn't really fit, since they were doing rather well for themselves. Most American Jews weren't victims, at least not in the same way as African-Americans that lived under segregation in the south. Indeed, Jews had, as a result of their own hard work and respect for education, created a solid niche for themselves in law, medicine and academia, not to mention the garment industry and other trades, and in the entertainment, music and film industries. Jews were at long last beginning to enjoy that sense of power that comes to an immigrant group in America that has become, in the second, third and fourth generations, a powerful cultural and political demographic.

But it came to pass that at almost exactly the same time that Israel became a regional super-power, American Jewish leaders began increasingly to adopt victim status as a tactic in domestic social discourse. "It [anti-Semitism] precluded the possibility that animus toward Jews might be grounded in a real conflict of interests... invoking The Holocaust was therefore a ploy to delegitimize all criticism of Jews: such criticism could only spring from pathological hatred." As Jews gain legitimacy and power in society, in other words, there is a greater likelihood that opposition to the positions of Jewish groups might come from a real conflict of interest, which ought to require the usual democratic process of debate and compromise between them and other groups. But by declaring all adversaries anti-Semites that process could be gotten rid of, through the simple expedient of intimidating and stigmatizing everybody rather than debating them.

The bedrock gambit was, and still is, to use the Nazi Holocaust to deflect criticism of the Israeli state, and its special relationship with the US. But this wasn't just an occasional cultural gambit; according to Norman Finkelstein, it was discernible in the most concrete terms during the intense political debate that accompanied the planning and building of the United States Holocaust Memorial Museum. The Museum became only the most well known of hundreds of concrete reminders of the Nazi Holocaust in every imaginable nook and cranny of American life. "All 50 states sponsor [Holocaust] commemorations, often in state legislative chambers. The Association of Holocaust Organizations lists over 100 Holocaust institutions in the United States. Seven Major Holocaust museums dot the American landscape. The centerpiece of this memorialization is the United State Holocaust Memorial Museum in Washington." All were envisioned in the context of a distinct political role, according to Norman Finkelstein.

"The first question is why we even have a federally mandated and funded Holocaust museum in the nation's capitol. Its presence on the Washington Mall is particularly incongruous in the absence of a museum commemorating crimes in the course of American history. Imagine the wailing accusations of hypocrisy here were Germany to build a national museum in Berlin to commemorate not the Nazi genocide but American slavery or the extermination of the Native Americans." But we know why there are no museums to commemorate the horrors of slavery or the Indian Wars. Americans would not stand for it. It would be seen as "divisive" and a waste of public money. It is much easier to denounce crimes that happened elsewhere.[12]

President Carter's announcement of the building of the Holocaust Museum occurred at the same time that Prime Minister Menachem Begin was visiting Washington, when Carter was being criticized for selling weapons to Saudi Arabia, and the President was also under attack for suggesting that Palestinians have human rights. "Other political issues also emerge in the museum," Finkelstein writes. "It mutes the Christian background to European anti-Semitism so as not to offend a powerful constituency. [How can one understand European anti-Semitism without discussing its presence during a thousand years of European Christianity?] It downplays the discriminatory US immigration quotas before the war, exaggerates the US role in liberating the concentration camps, and silently passes over the massive US recruitment of Nazi war criminals at the war's end. The Museum's overarching message is that 'we' couldn't even conceive, let alone commit, such evil deeds." But of course that is nonsense, and the exact opposite of what the Holocaust teaches us—that normal, ordinary people can be induced to do evil things. If the Nazi Holocaust teaches us anything, it is that we must examine our own capacity for evil, and that of our own country, class and race. The Holocaust Memorial encourages Americans to ignore this fact.

It also went out of its way to pointedly suggest that Israel was the proper destination for the Holocaust survivor, repeatedly showing such refugees making their way to Palestine. (Except that most Holocaust survivors chose to live elsewhere, a great many immigrating to America.) According to Norman

Finkelstein, the Museum subtly suppresses important aspects of Israel's recent history in other ways. "The politicization begins even before one crosses the museum's threshold. It is situated on Raoul Wallenberg Place. Wallenberg, a Swedish diplomat, is honored because he rescued thousands of Jews and ended up in a Soviet prison. Fellow Swede Count Folke Bernadotte is not honored because, although he too rescued thousands of Jews, former Israeli Prime Minister Yitsak Shamir ordered his assassination for being too 'pro-Arab.'" Bernadotte, one of the great men of the 20th century and a great humanitarian, is never mentioned at Holocaust memorials for that reason. History—that is, real history and not propaganda—invariably raises complicated and difficult questions; the Holocaust Museum isn't about that kind of verisimilitude, but about preventing those kinds of questions from arising.

One might think that such a museum, however questionable in other respects, might at least memorialize all the people who died in the Nazi extermination, labor and death camps. But Elie Weisel and other powerful players in the planning of the Museum insisted almost hysterically that the museum be only about Jews. As we know, Roma (Gypsies) were also targeted for genocide, and perhaps two million Poles also perished horribly in the gas chambers; around a half million Roma died. "Multiple motives lurked behind the museum's marginalization of the Gypsy genocide," Finkelstein writes. Right from the beginning, the museum leadership simply didn't believe that a Gypsy life was as valuable as a Jewish one. And Executive Director Rabbi Seymour Siegel opposed Roma representatives from even participating in their discussions, suggesting that they really didn't exist as a people.

A second reason, Finkelstein argues, is that "acknowledging the Gypsy genocide meant the loss of an exclusive Jewish franchise over the Holocaust, with a commensurate loss of Jewish 'moral capital.'" Third: if the Nazis persecuted Gypsies and Jews alike, the dogma that the Holocaust marked the climax of a millennial Gentile hatred of Jews was clearly untenable. Likewise, if Gentile envy spurred the Jewish genocide, did envy also spur the Gypsy genocide?" In other words, when compared to other forms of genocide, the Jewish experience would take its place on a continuum of genocidal human evil in the 20th century, including the Armenian, Roma, Bangladeshi, Cambodian, Bosnian and Rwandan genocides, rather than a completely singular and unique event. This would help us understand more about systemic evil, but the planners of the Museum went to great lengths to prevent this from happening. "In the museum's permanent exhibition, non-Jewish victims of Nazism receive only token recognition."

"Finally," Finkelstein writes, "the Holocaust museum's political agenda has also been shaped by the Israel-Palestine conflict. Before serving as the museum's director, Walter Reich wrote a paean to Joan Peters' fraudulent *From Time Immemorial*, which claimed that Palestine was literally empty before Zionist colonization. Under State Department pressure, Reich was forced to resign after refusing to invite Yasir Arafat, [later] a compliant American ally, to visit the museum. Offered a sub-director's position, Holocaust theologian John Roth was then badgered into resigning because of past criticism of Israel."

"In the wake of Israel's appalling attacks against Lebanon in 1996, climaxing in the massacre of more than a hundred civilians at Qana, *Haaretz* columnist Ari Shavit observed that Israel could act with impunity because 'we have the Anti-Defamation League... and Yad Vashem and the Holocaust Museum.'" As Finkelstein saw it, many in the Israel Lobby experienced the traumatic memory of the Holocaust as a form of political capital, which could be used to justify the various crimes and misdemeanors of the Israeli state; and the Holocaust Museum often served as an institutionalization of that political capital, whatever else it may have been. If the Holocaust is the moral capital of

Israel's traumatic privilege, the ADL, Yad Vashem and the Holocaust Museum are institutional expressions of its destructive entitlement.

The third and last part of *The Holocaust Industry*, 'The Double Shakedown,' is Norman Finkelstein's harrowing (and densely footnoted) account of the greed, dishonesty and criminality that arose in the 1990s as a direct result of this radical corruption in his own community, and in American society in general—a corruption fed, in this case, by unresolved emotions associated with the Holocaust, and the histrionic emotional disorientation, moral degradation and mind-boggling nihilism it has created among individuals within world Jewry, and in Western societies generally. Although it focuses on the depredations of Edgar Bronfman and Israel Singer in the 1990s, Finkelstein's research revealed that this particular story of corruption actually began a long time before, in the 1950s.

10.

The 'Double Shakedown' that Finkelstein documents actually began in 1952, when the West German government concluded some comprehensive agreements—three of them, in fact—for compensation of Jewish victims of the Nazis. These were important, because they were widely seen as tangible evidence of Germany's desire to embark on a new path. One of the three agreements was a settlement with an organization called the Jewish Material Claims against Germany, which is typically referred to by Finkelstein as the "the Claims Conference." This was an umbrella group that included the American Jewish Committee, the American Jewish Congress, B'nai B'rith, a working group called the Joint Distribution Committee, and other Jewish organizations. The Jewish Material Claims against Germany (JMCG), or Claims Conference, probably seemed like a reasonably representative group that would make an effort to disperse money fairly, and it had an organizational leadership already in place that could presumably provide oversight.

But even at that early date, there were hints of trouble to come. For one thing, the Claims Conference made a separate agreement for compensation directly with the new state of Israel. The Jewish state would use the money for settling Jewish refugees in that country—but why should any compensation to a Jewish survivor be dependent on whether they lived in Israel or not? That served the objectives of Zionist *Aliyah* (the immigration of Jews to Israel) but not of reparations. Furthermore, people assumed that the Israeli government would always be fair about the disbursement of funds—but why should anyone believe that about *any* government? In fact, it was simply a convenient method for excluding the majority of Jews who lived outside of Israel, thus making more of the fund available for other uses. Thus the Claims Conference was predicated on the wrong premise right from the beginning. It constituted a financial underwriting, first, of the Israeli state, and secondly, whatever that state chose to do with the money given to it. Most shocking of all, there would be no robust disbursement and accounting protocols, with full transparency and accounting by outside agencies.

As this writer has already pointed out, anybody with real-world experience knows that when ambitious people (and governments) get around large sums of money, the inevitable result—if there are no enforceable protocols guaranteeing transparency and outside accountability—is that sooner or later there will be theft or misuse of the money. Furthermore, those protocols should have been written into the by-laws of the umbrella organization, or otherwise made enforceable by outside parties in a court of law. How could the German government make such an idiotic mistake? Partly, it seems, because in 1952 it was under more pressure to provide tangible evidence of its goodwill than to create foolproof disbursement instruments for the new state of Israel.

In other words, a shaken world was still trying to make an emotional adjustment to the extent and ferocity of Hitler's crimes against humanity. People in the 20th century were being asked to confront evil in its purest form, and there was little to prepare them for it. As a result, a kind of childlike and highly self-serving form of moral accounting had started to take hold in the West. The Nazis were the bad guys, and Jews were their victims. Therefore Jews, being victims of the purest form of evil, would find evil abhorrent and not engage in it in their new Jewish state of Israel. But of course Jews are capable of evil, just as Christians are, not because they are Christians or Jews but because they are human beings.

And regarding specifics, it is precisely recent victims that are most likely to act aggressively and without scruple, rather than less, since they—in order to survive psychologically—have internalized so much of the aggression of their victimizers. (A main exception being those recent victims who take out their internalized aggression on themselves.) These are observable constants in the economy of human aggression, as I've pointed out before, along with the fact that aggressors so often posture themselves—and think of themselves—as pitiful victims. Regarding reparations for the Holocaust, the very powerful emotional influence of human greed eventually comes into play in any situation involving large sums of money, because that is simply the way the human mind and heart operates. The reality is, while there are many honest people who will never steal, there is a very large plurality—and under particular circumstances a majority—of people who will invariably steal or misuse money if there is no very great chance of being punished for it.

Why? Because all people in this world are capable of evil, and greed is very high on the list of evil proclivities; therefore people will steal if they have no internalized moral code precluding such behavior, or if there are no countervailing police or regulatory institutions that can stop them. In fact, since modern societies include so many different kinds of people, and since the temptations of greed are exerted on virtually all human beings, punishment for theft must be institutionalized for society to work at all. Yes, there is a large and heroic group of people who will not act on greed even if they could, and we should learn from them; but once the operation of greed becomes widespread in a particular society or group, such people definitely constitute a minority.

People who do not understand this live in a mental universe created by Walt Disney, whose creations are intended to amuse, challenge and reassure children. It is those people who should study the results of Stanley Milgram's 'Obedience Study,' which revealed conclusively that two-thirds of Milgram's subjects could be manipulated into cold-bloodedly murdering a man in the next room, even as that person screamed for mercy. Yes, we should celebrate and study the one-third who weren't manipulated by Milgram's clever theatrical illusion; but they are important only by virtue of the fact that the majority *were* so manipulated.

All else being equal, most people will be murderers, liars and thieves, if they are exposed to unusual and highly traumatizing situations, and if they do not have to suffer any very great punishment as a result. In fact, once greed is institutionalized in society, it is only a matter of how much money is necessary to corrupt them, and how much temptation and provocation is required to get them to commit the crimes that accompany corruption. People who do not understand this are not yet grown-up enough to understand how systemic evil works.[13]

Nobody in the Claims Conference in the early 1950s talked about reparations without mentioning the fact that the money would go directly to survivors. This was a deeply corrupting element of the entire criminal process, because many of these Conference members must have suspected on some level that most of the money might never reach survivors. Why? Because there was no oversight sufficiently strong to ensure that it would happen; and no government commissions to spell out legally-enforced regulations about how the disbursement would be enforced. But that did not affect the rhetoric of people in the Conference. People privy to these talks, and the news organizations that covered them, invariably spoke of reparations as though there would be individual disbursements of money to deserving Holocaust survivors, on a more or less regular basis. But nobody spoke of how that could be enforced, because there were no provisions for enforcement.

The image was always of some poor Holocaust survivor, perhaps disabled or debilitated mentally and physically, living-hand-to mouth in some out-of-the-way place in Europe or New York, a person probably with no surviving family members, whose life and psyche had been shattered. It was this person that would be sought out, and given a regular pension to help in his or her recovery. This was, in other words, a 1950s preview of the same pitch that would be used in the 1990s.

In the 1950s Claims Conference there was, as in the 1990s, no talk of money being used for Holocaust museums, university chairs in Holocaust studies, or salaries paid to bureaucrats in organizations in New York or Chicago. There was no talk of giving the money to Arabic-speaking and Eastern European Jews to help them immigrate to Israel. There was no talk of using the money for complicated university studies in Israel; and certainly no talk of various attorneys pocketing huge fees worth millions simply because they could get away with it. There was only the image of reparations that would have one purpose and one purpose only—to seek out those Jews that had survived Hitler's Holocaust, and give them economic assistance.

How the survivors would spend the money given to them would be their own business. People active in this 1950s Claims Commission often painted the same piteous picture as the WJRC would in the 1990s, of a poor survivor on the brink of death, waiting in his humble quarters for the world to take pity on him and give him a well-deserved pension to compensate for his suffering. But very few individual Holocaust sufferers received anything from this early Claims Conference.

The Germans were apparently quite suspicious from the beginning of the Claims Conference—they tried repeatedly to get the Conference to sign off on an agreement that would legally require giving money they received to Holocaust survivors. This is the first instance of any institution that had the courage to confront the potential for fraud that exists in such bodies, by insisting on adequate oversight in which the donating government could play a role. The Claims Conference, according to Finkelstein's telling of the story, replied in high dungeon, furious that the Germans would even question their commitment to disbursing money to survivors! Finally, however, they did acquiesce to the West Germans, and signed off on an agreement specifying that the money received from the German governments as reparations would *go only to individuals*—that is, money would go only to individual survivors.

Once they had the first payment of money, however, the 1952 Claims Commission broke their word by doing exactly the opposite of what they'd promised.

Here's Finkelstein's account:

The Claims Conference promptly annulled the agreement. In a flagrant breach of its letter and spirit, the Conference earmarked the monies not for the rehabilitation of Jewish victims but rather for the rehabilitation of Jewish communities. A guiding principle of the Claims Conference was the prohibition of moneys for "direct allocations of individuals." In a classic instance of looking after one's own, however, the Conference provided exemptions for two categories of victims: rabbis and "outstanding Jewish leaders" received individual payments. The constituent organizations of the Claims Conference used the bulk of the monies to finance various pet projects.[14]

The world did nothing, sending a clear message of impunity to Conference members.

So according to Finkelstein, after agreeing that the money would go only to Holocaust survivors, the Claims Conference actually produced its own written protocols *preventing* the disbursement of money to Holocaust survivors. (Unless they were lucky enough to be one of the rabbis and "outstanding Jewish leaders" that were allowed to receive individual payments, as mentioned above.) Predictably, this turned out to include leaders and rabbis in the Claims Conference itself, most of which had never been near a Nazi concentration camp. According to Finkelstein, any money received by individual Jewish victims from the Claims Conference was indirect and incidental. In 2000, German Parliamentarian Martin Hohmann acknowledged that only about fifteen percent of the money given to the Claims Conference actually went to Jewish victims of Nazi persecution.[15]

Lest we think that this kind of dishonesty is unique, it should be pointed out that a similar situation arose after September 11, 2001, in connection with certain representations made by the International Committee of the Red Cross. Immediately after the attack on the Twin Towers of the World Trade Center, the Red Cross set up a so-called 'Liberty Fund' which was represented as disbursing money directly to survivors of the attack, or the families of those injured or killed. By November 6, 2001, CNN reported that the Red Cross had raised more than $564 million for the 'Liberty Fund.'

During a House Energy and Commerce Committee hearing on November 6th it was acknowledged that the Red Cross had disbursed only $154 million of that amount, under circumstances that suggest that even most of the $154 million hadn't gone to families that lost a loved one. Furthermore, the rest of the

'Liberty Fund' would definitely go elsewhere, to projects that had nothing to do with 9/11, as well as to salaries and upkeep associated with the organization's offices and facilities. As a result of public rage at this duplicity, Red Cross President Dr. Bernadine Healy was forced to resign.

But the Red Cross has never admitted that it did anything wrong, nor has it even made good faith efforts to reassure the public that it would behave differently in the future. It is hard not to regard this as symptomatic of the extraordinary dishonesty and disingenuousness all too typical of a great many charities, perhaps a majority of them. People who are given large amounts of money to administer simply begin to believe that anything they do with it will be retroactively redeemed by the money itself, and the power money can buy. What tips us off to the truly malignant nature of the Red Cross incident is that top Red Cross officials didn't think they'd done anything wrong, and still don't, so skewed does the thinking of people become when they have large amounts of money at their disposal.

But the public did not see it that way; and the public was right. The Red Cross was telling potential donors, repeatedly and unmistakably, that money collected by the 'Liberty Fund' was going to go solely to families of victims. (And that would of necessity include a schedule of payments that would probably continue for the lifetime of the person involved, and could be used however the family members chose.) In the public mind, if the Red Cross promises that it is going to give money in the 'Liberty Fund' to bereaved families of a particular catastrophic terrorist attack, it should do so—and I say again, the public is right.

People with power and money often think they are free from the constraints of honesty, but for just that reason must be required to observe those restraints, with prison sentences resulting when they don't. Regarding the Red Cross, the main issue was always trust, and they never saw that—and they still don't. When a humanitarian institution tells the public it is going to disburse collected money directly to survivors, it is legally and morally obligated to do so, and all the complicated excuses for its failure to follow through on its public commitment is the vilest kind of sophistry.

The moral failure of the Red Cross, most blatantly in its unwillingness to re-assess its own behavior, was widely—and accurately—seen as contributing to the distrust that Americans increasingly feel toward big, powerful institutions that publicly claim to do one thing, while actually doing another. When this comes up in the popular media, it is not uncommon to see people laughing uproariously at the idea that any big organization like the Red Cross should actually do what it says it is going to do. This jeering is usually done by people who are themselves personally untrustworthy, and is predictable and disgusting. After all, destroying the very concept of trust is what a great many of those same people are expected to do, because the billionaires that employ them believe implicitly that they have the right to lie to the public, and to break any and all social contracts made in their name.

The Claims Conference that concluded its agreement with the West German government in 1952 did not receive much public scrutiny, partially because reparation for genocide was something new in human experience. No doubt few of the Jewish organizations involved had seen that much money in one place before, and attorneys were needed to formalize agreements that would involve payments to the organizations for a number of years. In such a situation, there are always people, very often attorneys, who will argue with unimaginable fervor that giving away money to individual survivors is not nearly as humane as empowering organizations set up to serve them. That's a lie, of course—giving immediate financial assistance to Holocaust survivors is what the Claims Conference promised to do, and this is what it should have done. But once they got the money, the organizations represented by the Conference coolly decided to break their word. They counted on the world to look the other way, and it did.

When so-called humanitarian organizations lie to people it is a moral disaster for all. I believe the kinds of rationalizations that usually accompany such moral catastrophes must have had an especially corrupting effect on those Jewish leaders involved in the 1952 Claims Conference settlement—they were, after all, committing themselves to a kind of bureaucratic thievery, however self-exculpatory their reasons, instead of helping actual Holocaust survivors. If the Jewish leaders wanted to give the reparations money to Jewish organizations and projects in the Claims Conference, they should have said so. Nobody would have blamed them for holding back a small percentage for their own organizational overhead, but the majority of it should have gone directly to the Holocaust survivors, as they had promised it would. But that generally didn't happen, because of greed and a desire for the power that money brings.

It is hard to imagine why the world allowed the original Claims Conference to do what it did. Memories of the Holocaust—and the horrors of World War Two in general—were still very raw in 1952, and Holocaust survivors themselves were not a rarity in Europe. Even a hardened criminal could not take money intended for a Holocaust survivor and use it to pay for the overhead of organizations with offices in Brooklyn or Chicago (or even Damascus or Warsaw) without becoming corrupted in the process. It was, in fact, one of the first indicators of the extent to which the Holocaust corrupts all who used it to make money or advance their interests.

The dishonesty of this early Claims Conference also accurately prefigured the astonishing series of events that transpired in the 1990s, referred to by Norman Finkelstein as the 'Double Shakedown.' As in the 1952 Claims Conference, it would be the outside organizations and bureaucrats and their lawyers that ended up getting the lion's share of the money. And it, too, had the effect of corrupting everybody connected with it, while further impoverishing actual Holocaust survivors. Edgar Miles Bronfman, Sr., must have had some proprietary knowledge of the 1952 Claims Conference, because according to Norman Finkelstein's research, Edgar's father Samuel was at the center of it. It is perhaps for that reason that Bronfman's operations in the late 1990s remind us so much of the unpleasant denouement of the Claims Conference in 1952.

<h2 style="text-align:center">11.</h2>

As we have seen, by the 1990s rumors had been floating around for decades about money abandoned in Swiss banks by victims of Hitler's terror. Some of these rumors hinged on the idea that the Swiss bankers knew where the phantom accounts were (or could easily lay their hands on them) but refused to do so. The Swiss were supposed to be too lazy or too callous, to thoroughly investigate these lost, dormant or abandoned accounts on their own. Thus the fantasy depended heavily on the impression of incompetence, bad faith or malevolence of Swiss bankers; and this was not a hard sell to many in Europe, who were envious of Swiss prosperity. On the other hand, nobody outside of Switzerland had any idea how to locate these bank accounts, or how much money was in them. (Another aspect of the fantasy was of unlimited wealth, a common ingredient of treasure maps and buried, lost or rumored treasure, the idea being that the money in question exists in unimaginably large amounts.)

In 1995 two things happened. In May of that year, the President of Switzerland formally apologized for his country's refusal to grant Jews refuge into Switzerland during the Nazi period. At about the same time, an Israeli newspaper published another of the perennial journalistic accounts (based on a mistaken source, as it turned out) of Jewish money being deposited in Swiss banks and then abandoned.

The happy coincidence of these two occurrences apparently attracted the attention of some in the World Jewish Congress, and especially Edgar Bronfman, Sr., whose father Samuel had been active in—and thus had a great deal of information about—the corrupt Claims Conference of 1952. (Among other things, Samuel was in a position to know how easy it was to get the world to turn a blind eye to corruption when done in the name of Holocaust survivors.) Edgar Miles Bronfman was also well-connected politically, and had inherited the fortune of the Seagram liquor company. These events likewise attracted the attention of Rabbi Israel Singer, Bronfman's colleague at the World Jewish Congress and Bronfman's partner in high-stakes international negotiating. In time, Bronfman and Singer announced their intent to compel the Swiss bankers to locate the money in the rumored abandoned Jewish accounts, and hand it over to them.

The World Jewish Congress had originally created the Claims Conference of 1952. In 1992—exactly forty-one years later—the same World Jewish Congress created the World Jewish Restitution Organization (WJRO), which was intended to be, and effectively became, a new and improved version of the Claims Conference. In this particular campaign, however, the target would not be a government, but the banks of Switzerland. Bronfman in particular sized up the situation and concluded (in 1995) that now was the time to move on the Swiss banks; Singer, the Secretary-General of the WJC, would be his right-hand man in this enterprise.

Bronfman, a seasoned businessman, a multi-billionaire and an avid Zionist, understood some critical cultural dimensions of the Swiss situation that others either didn't fully grasp, or weren't in a position to exploit. Above all he understood the perennial hatred of Swiss bankers by the rest of Europe, even among those who had secret Swiss bank accounts themselves. And there was an even more powerful factor: Swiss banks could easily be pressured from the US, since thirteen branches of six Swiss banks operated in the US. Furthermore, Bronfman was a crony of President Bill Clinton and other powerful Democrats, and knew that the President's support could make all the difference.

In late 1995, Edgar Bronfman and Rabbi Israel Singer went to sit down for their first negotiating session with a group representing the Swiss banking industry. (Why the bank representatives met with them at all is a mystery—maybe they were simply curious. In any case, they probably had little premonition of the barrage of insults and vilification Bronfman and Singer had in store for them.) Bronfman and Singer met with the bank officials as representatives of the World Jewish Restitution Organization (WJRO), a new incarnation of the Claims Conference that was set up pretty much like the old one, including as before a consortium of Jewish organizations. But Bronfman didn't just represent himself as being there on behalf of certain organizations—he represented himself, as he testified in front of a Senate Committee on Banking, Housing and Urban Affairs, as speaking on behalf of the entire Jewish people. Interestingly but not surprisingly, he also claimed to speak for the six million dead Jews that had perished in the Holocaust, and represented the WJRO as the rightful heir to their assets.[16] (Why he thought his organization, or any organization, could represent dead people, or inherit their personal assets, was a legal point he did not bother to elucidate.)

Now, to represent the dead with any kind of advocacy is tricky enough, but to claim dominion over the assets of the dead is insane—unless, of course, one is a blood relative. If one is not, there exists no legal or normative right of inheritance of another person's assets, and certainly not the assets of millions of people, simply because someone pays a PR flack to say there is. What Bronfman and Singer were about to launch was a major campaign aimed at compelling Swiss bankers to hand over money to them personally.

Once it was in hand, they or others in the WJRO could make

any claim they wanted to. If they wanted to say they held the money in trust for six million dead Jews—as they did, brazenly and repeatedly—nobody could stop them from doing so. In such a case, possession wouldn't merely be nine-tenths of the law; it would also be the entirety of a particular public relations campaign. But everything the WRJO said about its right to receive the funds of the dead was a calculated fiction. The WJRO had no mandate to receive the money of dead people except the mandate it had bestowed on itself.

Secondly, Bronfman, Singer and the WRJO kept saying, just as the original Claims Conference had repeatedly said, that they intended, without any very big exceptions, to give the money they received directly to Holocaust survivors, whether in single cash awards or in payments over a period of time they did not say—but they went out of their way to say, repeatedly and in detail, that their intention was to give the money directly to survivors. To drive this point home, they continued to cite their concern about aging survivors that were in poor health, and who might die without immediate financial and medical help. With these bereft and tragic figures firmly in the world's thoughts, the Swiss were entreated regularly not to stall, not to play games, not to waste any more time, because of the desperate straits in which so many Holocaust survivors found themselves.

The Swiss bankers announced at that first meeting that they could find only 775 "unclaimed dormant" accounts; and that the money therein came, when added up, to $32 million. (To someone unfamiliar with these negotiations, such a discovery might have seemed encouraging, because it suggested that the Swiss had been able to locate some real abandoned accounts, perhaps belonging to real Holocaust victims.) Predictably, however, Bronfman and Singer dismissed the figure of $32 million as insignificant. Bronfman and Singer weren't interested in knowing any more about the dormant accounts included in that $32 million dollars, nor did they suggest setting up independent auditors to investigate the matter, auditors that could question bank employees under oath if necessary.

Once the $32 million was mentioned, Swiss were in effect admitting that there really had been dormant Jewish accounts. Whether they had known about these accounts before, or discovered them in the course of an investigation, is not conclusively known, but there was an assumption—probably an unfair one—that they'd known about the accounts before. In the court of public opinion, that made the Swiss the Bad Guys—why hadn't they said anything about those abandoned accounts before now? This made them seem complicit in a deception, in the eyes of the public. And from the point of view of Bronfman and Singer, nobody had to look any longer for abandoned accounts, now that that the public saw the Swiss bankers as being dishonest. The goal now was simply to drive up the amount the Swiss would be willing to fork over.

The Bronfman-Singer duo's lack of interest in the $32 million worth of abandoned bank accounts was another huge red flag. If Bronfman-Singer were really interested in reclaiming money from abandoned accounts, they would have joined with Swiss accountants in determining who the accounts had belonged to, when they were abandoned, and so forth. But then, of course, according to the law, they would have been compelled to look for living descendants of people who'd left money in numbered accounts, and include them in their calculations. They would, in other words, have cooperated with the Volcker Commission, a committee of knowledgeable and reputable Swiss that was soon to be set up precisely in order to do that. But Bronfman and Singer had never been interested in real accounts. What they were interested in was establishing the *idea* of abandoned accounts, containing huge amounts of as yet unfound treasure that the perfidious Swiss were criminally refusing to turn over to them.

Once the Swiss sent unmistakable signals that they were

looking for some kind of a settlement with Bronfman and Singer, the real purpose of the negotiations was for one side to get the total amount up, and the other side to keep it down. And it had now become clear that the money they were negotiating about had nothing to do with actual dormant bank accounts. Bronfman and Singer now presented the total amount of money the Swiss were supposed to hand over as a species of reparations for the crime of being Swiss, and for not saying anything about the abandoned $32 million accounts until now; also for the fact that the Swiss were relatively affluent and successful and lived in relative peace, and were descendants of a generation of Swiss that had denied refuge to Jews during the Holocaust. The Swiss would pay up, and they would pay up to the World Jewish Restitutions Organization, or Bronfman and Singer would make their lives a living hell. The only issue now was how much the payoff would be.

Meanwhile, Bronfman and Singer of the WJRO played the role of muck-raking crusaders for truth, who simply wanted the two-faced Swiss bankers to stop lying and tell the truth. This version of events was believed by hundreds of millions of people at the time, at least partly because so many eminent and powerful people (such as President Bill Clinton) went on record as also saying it was true. International fury at the Swiss rose. At the same time, the Swiss banking industry and their spokespersons seemed singularly confused and uninformed; part of the reasons they seemed uninformed was because of the secrecy built into such accounts. (The secrecy provisions had first been devised to prevent the Nazis, among others, from seizing Jewish assets.) How they would go about finding out how much money was really there would be a separate issue—and one that never arose, it turned out, because Bronfman and Singer weren't really negotiating about bank accounts, but about extorting a payoff. Their international campaign swung into high gear, and their proxies began to plant stories in daily newspapers around the world.

Hitherto unknown character defects were now discovered in the Swiss. Most of the vitriol was being splashed around by World Jewish Congress executive director Elan Steinberg and Tom Bower, the latter being an investigative writer known for his unauthorized biographies and his work with the BBC current events show, 'Panorama.' Bowers was, by his own report, receiving money from the Simon Wiesenthal Center at this time (in 1996) for "research," also working as a publicist and researcher for both the Wiesenthal Center and Senator Alphonse D'Amato.[17] The full venom of Bower's anti-Swiss rhetoric shortly went on display in his book *Nazi Gold*, published a year later, in 1997; the following is a summary of Bower's attitude, as paraphrased by Norman Finkelstein, concerning the character of the Swiss people:

[The Swiss] boast about their wealth
They profit from blood money
While pretending to be peaceable, they commit unprecedented theft
They have mastered dishonesty as a cultural code
They're instinctively attracted to healthy profits
Self-interest is their supreme guide
Their bankers are greedier and more immoral than most
Concealment and deception are practiced arts among them
Apologies and resignations are not common in their politics
Their greed is unique
Their character combines simplicity and duplicity
Behind the appearance of civility is a layer of obstinacy
They display egotistical incomprehension of anyone else's opinion
They are peculiarly lacking in charm and social skills, have produced no artists or heroes since William Tell, and no statesmen, etc. etc.[18]

Above and beyond specific objections, there is a peculiar aura clinging to this collection of negative stereotypes that is redolent with the unmistakable quality and flavor of a perennial type of anti-Semitism. There is hardly an accusation in the collection of charges listed above that has not been directed at Jews and Jewish culture. It is the most ridiculous kind of racist calumny, pure and simple. There is nothing unique about Swiss greed, duplicity and immorality, just as there's nothing unique about Jewish or Christian greed, duplicity and immorality: these qualities are universal; and being human attributes, they often exist in tandem with nobility, kindness, generosity and integrity. (That is to say, no group or no individual has an option on virtue and wisdom.)

Therefore the anti-Swiss rhetoric, with its strong family resemblance to classical anti-Semitism, comes across not only as a particularly malevolent type of psychological projection—with more than a little self-hatred thrown in—but as a psychology that had been chosen in a very calculated way: it could be used to foster hate of the Swiss as such arguments had once been used to foster hate of Jews. This psychology depended, in fact, on presenting all Swiss as fundamentally evil, but also as a people who enjoyed their own hideous depravity in a particularly leering and diabolical way. If such calibrated use of resentment could be used to foment pogroms, why not use it to shake down Swiss bankers?

Tom Bower's *Nazi Gold: The Full Story of the Fifty-Year Swiss-Nazi Conspiracy to Steal Billions from Europe's Jews and Holocaust Survivors*, which came out in 1997, was an odd mixture of truth, half-truth and what we might politely call fictionalized wishful thinking. (To properly appreciate this, one must remember that it came out of the period in 1996 when he was on the payroll of the Simon Wiesenthal Center.) Bower's history is reasonably accurate concerning earlier attempts to spark investigations into the possibility of dormant bank accounts, but when he gets to Bronfman and Singer's adventures with the Swiss banking industry in the 1990s, the book veers off into a kind of alternative history. One of Bower's most irritating gambits is to constantly and repeatedly write about Nazi loot that was sent to Switzerland for safekeeping—but Nazis sending money and gold to Switzerland has nothing to do with abandoned Swiss bank accounts of Holocaust victims, which is an entirely different issue.

Bower constantly references the anti-Semitism of certain Swiss politicians and industrial leaders, and uses that to smear all Swiss as a people. Conspicuously missing from Bower's book is any mention of Maurice Bavaud, the Swiss theology student who tried to kill Hitler in 1939 and was executed by the Nazis in 1941, or many other Swiss who lost their lives opposing Hitler. And while we're at it, if the Swiss have no artists or writers, what exactly are Hermann Hesse and Paul Klee—talking horses? Interestingly, Bower acknowledges receiving "considerable but un-attributable help from many Swiss bankers and government officials,"[19] so why, one wonders, are such kindnesses un-attributable? Could it be because they contradict Bower's stereotypical view of the unalterably wicked nature of the Swiss?

The present writer is making here the old, old point about the utter falsity of group stereotypes, especially in any discursive investigatory book that invites a judgment; and also about the dishonesty of over-generalizations concerning any group of human beings, whether religious, racial or whatever. There is no "they," because in every group there are good people and bad people, and some effort must be made to separate out the two. Even when people appear to be collectively guilty for something, some are guiltier than others—and common sense, not to mention the rule of law, depends on acknowledging this. Certain Swiss bankers may lie, and others may not; but because some Swiss bankers lie does not mean the man who sells cigarettes on the corner in Zurich or the doctor who treats you in a Swiss hospital have larceny in their DNA.

Banking is not this writer's favorite profession, because bankers are inevitably part of a usurious and unnecessarily exploitive profession that has been known to harm people weaker than themselves; some family members in Kansas and Missouri, for example, lost their farms to the banks during the Great Depression. But that is in the nature of banking, and is not confined to one race, religion, nationality or language group. Indeed, concentrating on a single group of bankers (in this case, the Swiss) is a distraction from what is really needed: an investigation of banking protocols everywhere, especially those that have to do with dormant bank accounts, and the rights of heirs in such cases.

The entire thrust of Bronfman and Singer's PR campaign was calculated to make the Swiss as a group seem like inveterate schemers who had been single-mindedly complicit in a collective con game for the better part of the century, which an idealistic Bronfman and his crusading sidekick Singer were now selflessly devoting their lives to exposing. But as we have already seen, Bronfman and Singer weren't really interested in investigating dormant bank accounts, regardless of what they said when they began their campaign. If anybody was running a con game, it was they.

But their original charges had to be taken seriously, so in April, 1996, before the US Senate hearings on the dormant Swiss bank accounts, representatives of the Swiss banking industry proposed what all parties should have taken up long before—an investigatory group composed of three people from the World Jewish Restitution Organization (WJRO) and three from the Swiss Bankers Association, to be headed by Paul Volcker, former Chairman of the Federal Reserve Bank; the bankers agreed in advance to abide by its findings. (In December the Swiss government would also appoint its own people to the Volcker group, including a well-known Holocaust scholar.)

The reaction from Bronfman and Singer was predictable and

vehement. Before Volcker's investigative group could meet, they began clamoring for an immediate settlement, before the proposed investigative group could actually investigate anything. It is here that Bronfman and Singer tipped their hand completely. One can rationalize their posturing up to now as uninformed enthusiasm, however hateful their racist attacks on the Swiss. But after the Swiss banking industry proposed the Volcker group to investigate allegations of abandoned Jewish accounts, and Singer and Bronfman abruptly and angrily refused their services, one can only conclude that their intentions had nothing to do with their previously announced objectives, but rather with shaking down the Swiss banks and government, to use Norman Finkelstein's pungent phrase. If they really wanted to find out if there were dormant accounts, wouldn't they have waited for the investigations of the Volcker group to establish the facts one way or the other?

Bronfman, Singer and the WJRO had made the claim, which they had broadcast to the world, that there existed abandoned bank accounts that contained money that once belonged to Jewish Holocaust victims. The Volcker group simply proposed to find out whether their claim was true or not, with what sounds like a fair amount of reputable oversight. And once having found out if the phantom bank accounts existed, they proposed to find out how much money was left in them. Hadn't this been what Bronfman and Singer had been haranguing the Swiss to do all along? But an honest investigation was the last thing Bronfman and Singer wanted; instead they immediately sought ways to ignore, undermine and discredit the Volcker group. This tells us more clearly than anything else that they were never interested in finding out whether there was, in fact, money left in bank accounts abandoned by Jewish victims of the Holocaust.

If the Volcker group had been allowed to do a thorough job, they might actually have solved the mystery of the lost Jewish fortunes; they might have been able to actually determine to the extent required by a civil court just how many dormant accounts of Holocaust-era Jews there were, and how much money was in them. That might not have been very much, as Bronfman and Singer were queasily aware, perhaps not much more than the original $32 million the bankers had first mentioned; and Bronfman and Singer were not about to accept such a paltry amount. Bronfman and Singer far preferred to keep the exact amount of money a mystery, so they could float their own inflated figures regarding the amount of the loot in question. They could only make that work by preventing everybody else from doing any real investigation into the matter.

Bronfman and Singer reverted to their previous strategy of emphasizing Swiss duplicity and greed, clearly hoping that negotiations could once again become a discussion about reparations for the ignominy of being Swiss, rather than about real money and real abandoned back accounts. They also fell back on the tried and proven strategy of appealing for sympathy for the poor, poverty-ridden Holocaust survivors who desperately needed assistance in the form of food, shelter, medical help and immediate financial assistance. The Swiss tried to outflank them by offering to set up a "Special Fund for Needy Victims of the Holocaust" until the Volcker Commission finished its investigatory work, in order to immediately start disbursing funds to Holocaust survivors; but disbursing funds to needy survivors was also not what Bronfman and Singer wanted. In response to the 'Special Fund' initiative, Bronfman and Singer choreographed a new round of attacks against the Swiss.

Besides fears of a much smaller settlement, there was another and more sinister reason for Bronfman and Singer's anxiety regarding the Volcker Commission. If Volcker and his people investigated all the dormant Swiss accounts and did indeed find some money, they might have then disbursed the money themselves, or arranged for a government agency to do so. But Bronfman, Singer and the WJRO had no intention of letting that happen. As we have seen, they were actually focused on preventing any disbursement of funds to individual survivors. "In fact," Finkelstein explains, "the Holocaust industry stood only to lose from these findings: if just a few Holocaust-era accounts belonging to Jews were found, the case against the Swiss banks would lose credibility; and even if a large number were found, it would mainly be the legitimate claimants who were compensated, not the Jewish organizations."[20]

The shakedown revolved around three carefully-crafted illusions. **Bronfman and Singer declared with certainty that money belonging to Holocaust victims were in abandoned Swiss bank accounts.** Nobody outside the Swiss banking system had any direct knowledge of money belonging to Holocaust victims in abandoned bank accounts, and even the Swiss weren't sure about it. **Bronfman and Singer postured themselves as investigative reformers who wanted to get at the truth.** But we know that wasn't true, because Bronfman and Singer used their political influence in the US to sabotage the Volcker Commission, which was specifically created to get at the truth.

Bronfman and Singer repeatedly said they were going to disburse any money in abandoned accounts directly to Holocaust survivors. That was falsified by events, since they actually disbursed most of it to the pet projects of various organizations, attorneys and hangers-on that had been supporting their efforts. This is why Norman Finkelstein referred to it as a 'Double Shakedown' — it exploited the banks and governments from whom Bronfman and Singer demanded huge amounts of money, but it also ripped off the Holocaust survivors who were supposed to receive the money.

By this time quite a few people were beginning to understand that something like a colossal hustle was underway, and were speaking out. But the Bronfman-Singer duo had one more gambit up their sleeves, and it was a big one. In a denouement so bold and so big that few seasoned observers saw it coming, salvation for the scheme of the indefatigable Bronfman and Singer was soon to come, not just from a few powerful political friends, but from the most powerful political leader in the world. Incredibly, this politician would cause his allies in the world's most powerful government to line up like obedient Mafiosi to support the 20th-century's biggest shakedown. Bronfman's secret weapon was none other than Bill Clinton, President of the United States, who was poised to dramatically reward one of America's major political donors.

12.

The Clinton administration moved quickly to help Bronfman torpedo the Volcker Commission, which might have actually arrived at a just and honest resolution of the issue. Such a solution was anathema to Bronfman, because it would have defeated his dream of a huge settlement computed on the basis of an unknown amount of money. Furthermore, whatever money was ultimately discovered might have been handed over for honest distribution by some meddlesome entity such as the EU or the United Nations. That could not be allowed to happen. Bronfman was, of course, a major political donor to Democratic candidates in the United States; interested political operatives in the legislative branch moved to serve Bronfman's interests by forcing a settlement before the Volcker Commission could arrive at any conclusions.

To accomplish this, Bronfman, Singer and the World Jewish Restitution Organization received the active support of the entire US government, beginning with individuals at every level in the administration of President Bill Clinton, and involving every aspect of government below that, including high-profile elected US officials. Bronfman, who is nominally liberal on social issues, was an important contributor to Democrats like Clinton, especially in a time when Republicans were starting to receive unlimited billions from the corporate upper class.[21] Bronfman had the deepest pockets around, and Bill Clinton was no doubt already thinking about his wife Hillary's political future.

To help the hapless Swiss better understand their situation, Bronfman, Singer and the WRJO proceeded to activate the most powerful system of political influence the world had ever seen, operating not on the fringes of American life but from its center. Finkelstein explains:

"In December 1995, Bronfman teamed up with [New York] Senator [Alfonse] D'Amato. His poll ratings at a nadir and a senate race not far off, D'Amato savored this occasion to boost his standing in the Jewish community, with its crucial votes and wealthy political donors. Before the Swiss were finally brought to their knees, the WJC, working with the gamut of Holocaust institutions (including the US Holocaust Memorial Museum and the Simon Wiesenthal Center), had mobilized the entire US political establishment. From President Clinton, who buried the hatchet with D'Amato (the Whitewater hearings were still going on) to lend support, through eleven agencies of the federal government as well as the House and Senate, down to state and local governments across the country, bipartisan pressures were brought to bear as one public official after another lined up to denounce the perfidious Swiss."[22]

What Finkelstein refers to as "The Holocaust Industry" now initiated a "two-pronged strategy" to defeat the Swiss investigation.[23] Three class-actions lawsuits were filed by US individuals and Jewish organizations, and were then consolidated in a US District Court judge in Brooklyn, NY. This consolidated class-action suit was significant mainly because one of the lawsuits asked to recover $20 billion in damages. This put the Swiss banking industry on notice regarding the kind of settlement that was being sought. Secondly, the class-action suit was an effective end-run around those people who were working for an honest investigatory committee that might actually find out if there really was any money in abandoned accounts of Holocaust victims, and if so how much.

Paul Volcker, who was supposed to chair the investigative group, pointed out that the lawsuits would impair, perhaps irreparably, the work they were hoping to do. But of course it would—that was the whole point of the class-action suit. That was to tell the Swiss that they were going to have to fork over some big-league bucks, and it now made no difference what the facts were. The Swiss were going to have to pay off the WJRO simply to get it off their back.

The second part of the "two-pronged" strategy was to threaten an economic boycott. Rabbi Singer brought Governor Pataki of New York into the scheme, strategizing with Pataki, D'Amato and Bronfman at his daughter's wedding. Over the next several months several state and city governments tabled resolutions threatening economic boycotts of Switzerland if the Swiss bankers did not give in. Starting with Los Angeles, several cities and states started removing their pension funds from Swiss banks. In December, 1997, Bronfman announced that the settlement would have to be $3 billion or more; D'Amato and New York banking officials were now working to make it impossible for the newly-formed United Bank of Switzerland from operating in the United States. In June, 1998, the Swiss banking industry put out what they hoped was their final offer of $600 million. But they were threatened with new sanctions, so they quickly threw in the towel in August, 1998. In all, they agreed to pay $1.25 billion.

The settlement came before the Volcker group could finish its investigations; and that, of course, was exactly the purpose of forcing a quick settlement. President Clinton hailed the agreement as a triumph of human justice; bipartisan Congressional leaders wrote to the Secretary of State that it was about basic human rights and the rule of law. And in an address to the Swiss Parliament, Secretary of State Madeleine Albright lectured elected Swiss officials about the manner in which alleged bank accounts of Holocaust victims had enriched the Swiss economically. What had supposedly been about dormant bank accounts left by doomed Jewish victims had now become entirely focused on the shocking character defects of the Swiss — which defects were strangely similar to the kind of character defects anti-Semites once attributed to Jews. The Bronfman/ Singer duo's *schtick*-laden performance eventually included not only endless self-congratulation, non-stop exploitation in the form of lies and distortions, and vast amounts of money received; it also afforded the opportunity to endlessly and duplicitously attack the country of Switzerland, one of the most affluent nations in Europe.

But the European shakedown was far from finished. Emboldened by success, Bronfman and Singer proceeded to use the same methodology described above, especially threats to unleash American sanctions and legal actions to shake down other nations, starting with Germany. This time the shakedown included nothing, not even nominally, about bank accounts abandoned by Jewish victims of Hitler. This time the target was German industry — that is, the entire private sector, including factories and productive facilities of all kinds, and their organizations' representatives. The aggrieved group this time was surviving slave laborers used by the Nazis in war production... and the World Jewish Restitution Organization insisted that reparations for their suffering should be paid directly to them, the WJRO. (All to be given to the needy survivors of said slave labor, of course.)

This was complicated by the fact that Germany already had a reparations program for former slave laborers — one that actually included the father of Norman Finkelstein, who received payments from the Germans because of his years in Auschwitz —

and the German reparations program was about as good as such a program could be, in the sense that they actually disbursed real money to real former slave laborers. (The Germans were apparently smart enough not to contract with the Israeli government for compensation of slave laborers, instead disbursing the funds themselves.) Strangely enough, according to Bronfman and Singer, it should be the World Jewish Restitution Organization that received reparation money for former slave laborers; and all this was duly re-enforced by Bronfman and Singer's allies in the US political class, including the President of the US, and other political cronies of Bronfman, who should have known very well by now what was going on.

The Germans, who had seen the Swiss pilloried by the Holocaust Industry, were completely aware of what they would look like once the World Jewish Restitution Organization and its armies of US officials, American political flunkies, propagandists and hired PR flacks unleashed their propaganda campaign against them. They paid the WJRC off, this time the haul being a cool $5.1 billion. Again, most would go to organizations, pet projects, legal fees, and educational programs, and very little would end up with actual Holocaust survivors.

Bronfman and Singer saw no reason to stop their activities at this point, considering how successful they'd been. "The shakedown of Switzerland and Germany has been only a prelude to the grand finale: the shakedown of Eastern Europe," Finkelstein wrote. "With the collapse of the Soviet bloc, alluring prospects opened up in the former heartland of European Jewry. Cloaking itself in the sanctimonious mantle of 'needy Holocaust victims,' the Holocaust industry has sought to extort billions of dollars from these already impoverished countries."

The method used this time, Finkelstein writes, was to call "on former Soviet-bloc countries to hand over all prewar Jewish properties or come up with monetary compensation."[24] Of course, Bronfman and Singer and their World Jewish Restitution

Organization had no right whatsoever to act as legal heirs to millions of dead Jews in Eastern Europe, except the legal rights they awarded themselves. Nor were they interested in actually investigating real examples of pre-war Jewish properties, and hardly bothered to mobilize public opinion in the US. "With the support of key US officials, it can easily break the feeble resistance of already prostrate nations," Finkelstein observes.[25] Again Bronfman and Singer filed a class-action lawsuit (in the same court as they had filed against the Swiss) to force the Polish government to talk turkey. The same pressures would soon be put on Romania and Belarus to pay up.

Again, most of the money would go to Jewish programs and projects, with no independent oversight whatsoever. One of the projects would be "March of the Living." In this Zionist-inspired public theater of trauma, Jewish youth in Israel and from around the world are transported to the death camps in Poland for first-hand instruction in the world's anti-Semitism, after which the Israeli youth are flown back to Israel to fight for the Israeli state. The object of this extraordinary exploitation of traumatic memory is to indoctrinate Israeli young people with stories of the horrors that took place in the death camps, using whatever latent teen angst they can whip up to achieve a carefully stage-choreographed form of group hysteria.

This full immersion in the traumatic memory of the horrors of Auschwitz, communicated in programs presented by Israeli security personnel inside the buildings of Auschwitz, is intended to bond Israeli youth to a lifetime of service to Zionism, which it does—but in emotional terms, it also bonds them to the systematic acting out of the Nazi aggression internalized during the grotesque histrionic drama that "March of the Living" presents inside the walls of Auschwitz. Many of the projects funded by money from the WJRO efforts are 'Holocaust education' of one sort or another, almost all of it in the nature of Israeli indoctrination of the most right-wing sort; many millions of dollars from these awards would end up going into the pockets of the attorneys who eventually attached themselves to the final settlement. Again, although some small amount of the money would end up with needy Holocaust survivors, most of it never would.

The World Jewish Restitution Organization was still continuing its fervent activities in search of further money as Finkelstein finished his book, so information about the efforts in Eastern Europe are inconclusive in Finkelstein's 2000 book. (The Second Edition of 2003 has more damning information about what Finkelstein calls the 'Holocaust Industry,' as well as more information on the WJRO.) At one time Rabbi Singer ecstatically announced that the nation of Austria was holding $10 billion worth of dead Jews' assets, which he believed should be given to Bronfman and himself as representatives of the WJRO. Multiple reports, including a formal investigation by former New York Governor Eliot Spitzer, revealed vast amounts of corruption in the World Jewish Congress.

Rabbi Singer was discovered to have been stealing money from the World Jewish Congress, some of which he placed surreptitiously in an anonymous bank account in Geneva, his period as an accuser of the perfidious Swiss apparently having familiarized him with their accounting and banking practices. He also spent a fair amount of the money for Holocaust survivors on high and affluent living in several venues of the very wealthy; he was eventually fired by his old friend Edgar Bronfman amid multiple charges of embezzlement. There were many other examples of corruption, one recurring motif being of attorneys called in to clear up charges of irregularities, who then billed the WFRO or World Jewish Congress for their services, very often for millions of dollars. Meanwhile, actual Holocaust survivors had started to organize themselves to put pressure on the WJRO to pay them something, or more than the tiny pittance a few had been receiving; but most of them have so far not been unable to match the political, economic and social might of Singer, Bronfman and the World Jewish Restitution Organization. Furthermore, few actual Holocaust survivors had friends with the political clout of Bill Clinton, President of the United States.

Thus did American electoral corruption encourage and normalize the corruption of billionaire charlatans such as Edgar Miles Bronfman, Sr. Equally important was the support of the main Jewish organizations in the US, and the neo-cons that increasingly determine its agenda through their manipulation of traumatic memory and the most irrational kind of religious nationalism. Most Jews, like most Christians, probably knew very little about the machinations of the World Jewish Congress and the World Jewish Reparations Organization. Of the billions the WJRO elicited through a combination of intimidation, corruption, and sheer power plays, the money that actually got through to real Holocaust survivors, I say again, was usually disbursed to a small number of survivors in laughably small amounts. But for Edgar Miles Bronfman, Sr., it was all pay-dirt. He was awarded the Presidential Medal of Freedom, America's highest civilian award, by President Bill Clinton in August, 1999.

Interestingly, the State of Israel has been perhaps the worst offender concerning the disbursement of money to Holocaust survivors living there. It refuses to make any accounting for what it did with all the money it received from the Germans as a result of the first Claims Conference in 1952, and has been particularly notorious for using a variety of complicated excuses to explain their lack of transparency for money received in the 1990s. When it comes to the actual monthly amounts the Israeli government gives to Holocaust survivors, it is so small that most people refuse to believe it when they hear about it. Incredibly, despite all the money the Israeli government has received for disbursement to Holocaust survivors since the 1950s until the present, including the money received as a result of the 1990s shakedown by Bronfman and Singer, it sends only about $20 a month to living Holocaust survivors. This pitiful situation came to a dramatic (and traumatic) reckoning on a bright day in Israel in the early summer of 2007.

13.

On June 8th, 2007, the progressive Israeli newspaper *Haaretz* carried a story that ran under the headline "Survivors' Protest Makes Foreign Journalists Gasp, Security Vanish." What this headline referred to was the ultimate Holocaust nightmare. The reader will recall that early in the 1950s negotiations with the various Claims Committees it was decided that all monies would go to Israel to disburse to individual Holocaust survivors who needed financial assistance. The extent to which Holocaust survivors are demonstrably *not* receiving substantial financial assistance from the various funds that had been collected— including the windfalls collected by Bronfman and Singer in the 1990s—became horribly clear to readers of *Haaretz* on June 8th, 2007.

The story, written by Daniel Ben Simon, was about a demonstration of several thousand Holocaust survivors, which by itself was quite a phenomenon, since so many were quite old. The Holocaust survivors were protesting the Israeli government's measly monthly allowance to them. Again, hard as it may be for many people to believe this, every month Holocaust survivors in Israel *receive the equivalent of $20* from the government of Israel. Although the Israeli state received a handsome settlement from the Germans in the 1950s, and received money afterwards according to the stipulations of the accord, it has apparently never paid out more than a tiny fraction of the money it received to Holocaust survivors. In 2007, they were still giving out only the nearly-unbelievable $20 a month for people, most of whom were in their eighties and nineties; the survivors receiving this insulting sum complained that $20 a month wasn't even enough to starve decently—it was a pittance so small it would hardly buy

146

one's bus fare to the store, much less pay for food.

Part of the anger that drove the 2007 demonstration arose from a casual public statement by a government apparatchik who coolly observed that in two years or so they might be able to increase the stipend, because by that time so many of the survivors would be dead.

But here they were, on June 7th, 2007, shuffling along in the street under the hot Israeli sun by the thousands, leaning on the arms of their grandchildren, hobbling and half-carried by their family members, but nonetheless marching, marching, marching, determined to protest what was being done to them — right up to the very office of the Prime Minister Netanyahu, to protest the indignity of what his Likud government had done.

The foreign journalists present could hardly believe their eyes. What they were seeing staggered the imagination: here were people who had first cheated death to hobble out of the death factories of Europe when they were liberated; and now once again they shuffled by the thousands to face down the incomprehensible disinterest of the Jewish state, survivors in whose name billions of dollars had been received, but to whom so little was given that they now protested their eminent death by starvation in the Jewish homeland.

It hadn't been easy for these double survivors to demonstrate; but they finally decided it was their only recourse, to use shame and guilt where reason and compassion had failed. And they did so by the thousands, may God bless them. That day, the 7th of June, 2007, they marshaled up whatever strength they had left, and marched from a nearby park right up to the Prime Minister's office to express their rage. It was probably the last time in their lives they would be able to press for justice from a callous world, one that had first betrayed them when they were repeatedly denied sanctuary from Hitler's thugs; and now, now that they were again being brushed aside, once again dying not just from the natural ravages of age but again from lack of adequate food, medical care and shelter, here in the bosom of the state supposedly created to provide them with a haven from the world's malignance.

As the foreign journalists watched in horrified amazement, the security personnel assigned to guard the Prime Minister vanished, never to be seen again. (Apparently it was too much for them emotionally.) The silently shuffling legions of aging men and women in their seventies and eighties and nineties, supported by their grandchildren and leaning on canes and crutches as they wordlessly passed like phantoms before the Prime Minister's office, could have been their own grand-parents—in a sense, they *were* their grandparents, and your grandparents, and mine. Can one blame the security policemen for running away in shame?

Here's Ben Simon's full story in Haaretz:

Thousands of protesters marched hundreds of meters from the Wohl Rose Park to the Prime Minister's Office unhindered, while security guards kept a very low profile. The last thing they needed was a violent clash with the Holocaust survivors. Foreign journalists were visibly taken aback by the bizarre spectacle of a Jewish state apparently at war with Jewish Holocaust survivors, who were angrily protesting what they considered a miserable stipend offer from the government.

'I don't think any government in Europe could resist the demands of people who have suffered so much,' one of them said.

Ze'ev Dratva, a Holocaust survivor, was among the marchers. 'How many years do the survivors have left? Barely a year or two,' he shouted. He said he knew survivors who were miserable, and could not afford false teeth or one warm meal a day.

Some survivors were comforted by the sight of the thousands marching for them, including the youths carrying anti-government posters. Yehuda Frenkel, who came from Kiryat Haim, was moved. He could not remember a greater show of solidarity since he immigrated to Israel, after surviving the concentration camps. He had objected to the demonstration at first, if only because of the shame and embarrassment. But in view of the government's callousness, he had concluded there was no other way.

'I want the Germans to know where the money they gave Israel went,' he said angrily.

'I want the Germans to know that Israel took the money we should have received. I want them to answer one question: Where did our money go?'

The demonstration was not only about the meager stipends, it was about the lost honor of people who already had been robbed of their humanity in the Holocaust. As long as their struggle was kept among themselves, they didn't dare to make too much noise. But as soon as their campaign rattled Israeli indifference, they gathered their last bit of strength and went to Jerusalem to show the government that they were nobody's fools.

'I came all the way from Ramat Gan to protest the humiliation of the Holocaust survivors,' said Haya Rosenbaum in a shaking voice. She stretched out her left arm, on which the number 53684 had been etched. She often had considered how much the establishment wished to be rid of those thousands of survivors who were still clinging to life. Otherwise, how could one explain the state's humiliating treatment?

'It doesn't matter how much money we'll get in the end,' said Eva Schoenberger of Petah Tikva. 'It's heartwarming to see [that] so many people have come to support us.'

Bronfman and Singer had gotten multiple settlements less than a decade earlier for billions of dollars. Why had not more of that gotten to these survivors living in Israel? Because the funds had been disbursed to Jewish organizations, some of which were doing good work, some of which used the money to increase the suffering of the Palestinians, far too many of which were fronts for greedy attorneys who took millions for 'legal fees,' and other out-and-out crooks who kept millions for themselves, like Rabbi Israel Singer, who spent his cut of the loot on high living on the Riviera. But little of the money found its way to real Holocaust survivors; and it is those survivors themselves who should have received it, not unscrupulous middle-men and criminal profligates. Why has not the West done a better job of taking care of the survivors, whether living in Israel or elsewhere? That Holocaust survivors could live in such poverty anywhere in the world is a judgment on the world—and the fact that they experience this deplorable privation in a state supposedly dedicated to justice for Jews is especially shocking.

The Israeli state and its proxies in the West too often use the Holocaust for purposes of economic and political manipulation; but for the suffering of real survivors, they have no time. Holocaust survivors—real flesh-and-blood people, as opposed to rhetorical and ideological capital useful for emotional blackmail—are too often used as pawns serving the greed and power-hunger of the super-rich billionaires or government apparatchiki at the top. The Nazi Holocaust was the nightmare tragedy of the first half of the 20th century; the theft of billions from its survivors is the unspoken and unspeakable tragedy of the second.

Although few people will say so, it is both a tragedy of the Jewish leadership class and an indictment of Christianity in the West. The fact that nobody could get it right opened the door to the mountebanks and traffickers of human misery, who make money and create power for themselves out of the suffering of those less powerful than they.

14.

One can best understand the power of Norman Finkelstein's prophetic gift, and the cultural and economic power of those in American that stigmatize him, by looking at the reactions to the publication of *The Holocaust Industry—Reflections on the Exploitation of Jewish Suffering*. "*The Holocaust Industry* evoked considerable reaction internationally after its publication in June 2000," Finkelstein has observed. "It prompted a national debate and reached the top of the bestseller list in many countries reaching from Brazil, Belgium and the Netherlands to Austria, Germany and Switzerland. Every major British publication devoted at least a full page to the book, while France's *Le Monde* devoted two full pages and an editorial. It was the subject of numerous radio and television programs and several feature-length documentaries. The most intense reaction was in Germany. Nearly 200 journalists packed the press conference for the German translation of the book and a capacity crowd of 1,000 (half as many more were turned away for lack of space) attended a raucous public discussion in Berlin. The German edition sold 130,000 copies within weeks and three volumes bearing on the book were published within months. Currently, *The Holocaust Industry* is scheduled for sixteen translations."

The Guardian, a British newspaper, declared it the "most explosive book of the year." The *Times*, a British newspaper, wrote: "These fraudsters need to be unmasked, and Finkelstein believes that he is the man to do it. In 150 short pages he sets out to expose their machinations. If his indictment is a true one, it should prompt prosecutions, sackings, protest. The book shouts scandal." *The New Statesman* wrote: "This is, in short, a lucid, provocative and passionate book. Anyone with an open mind and an interest in the subject should ignore the critical brickbats and read what Finkelstein has to say." And so forth and so on. People everywhere thought it one of the most important books of our time.

But not in America. Here the book—and discussion about it—was systematically suppressed.

"In contrast to the deafening roar elsewhere, the initial response in the United States was a deafening silence," Finkelstein writes. "No mainstream media outlet would touch the book. The US is the corporate headquarters of the Holocaust industry. A study documenting that chocolate caused cancer would presumably elicit a similar response in Switzerland. When the attention abroad proved impossible to ignore, hysterical commentaries in select venues effectively buried the book."

One appeared, predictably, in the *New York Times Book Review*, in a book review by Omer Bartov, an Israeli military historian. Comparing Finkelstein's book to the "Protocols of the Elders of Zion," he used the following words to describe it: "bizarre," "outrageous," "paranoid," "shrill," "strident," "indecent," "juvenile," "self-righteous," "arrogant," "stupid," "smug," "fanatic," but did not disagree with any of Finkelstein's facts—only the fact that he revealed them. Bartov dealt with the issue of Holocaust profiteers with the novel argument that Finkelstein was himself profiting from the Holocaust. A second, *Commentary* senior editor Gabriel Schoenfeld, likewise agreed with Finkelstein's facts, but was careful to denounce him as "extremist," "lunatic," "crackpot" and "bizarre."

Finkelstein replied: "To both savage and appropriate a book's findings is no mean achievement. The performances of Bartov and Schoenfeld recall a piece of wisdom imparted by my late mother: 'It's not an accident that Jews invented the word *chutzpah*.' On an altogether different note, it was my rare good fortune that the undisputed dean of Nazi holocaust scholars, Raul Hilberg, repeatedly lent public support to controversial arguments in *The Holocaust Industry*. Like his scholarship, Hilberg's integrity humbles. Perhaps it's not an accident that Jews also invented the word *mensch*."

15.

The Holocaust Industry is without question Finkelstein's most important book, because of its shocking revelation of the machinations of Edgar Miles Bronfman, Sr., Israel Singer, and the World Jewish Restitutions Organizations (WJRO); and because it first supplied a plausible—and thickly footnoted—theory to explain why Israeli government and its proxies in the US were so obsessed with the Holocaust (to deflect criticisms of Israel, Finkelstein says). There is another reason why the Likud government in Israel is careful to keep the Holocaust in the public eye, this writer would argue: its traumatic memory bonds people to the aggression of the Israeli state. This happens because the Holocaust cannot be tailored to the criminal inclinations of rapacious corporate profiteers or to the power-hungry needs of political operators in the US, without emotionally affecting everybody that comes in contact with that process. Everybody who uses the Holocaust to generate power or money is inevitably corrupted.

There is an unmistakably pathological side to the Holocaust obsession, which the Israel Lobby may not have anticipated when its constituent organizations first began to embrace it as a means to deflect criticism of Israel; but those pathologies invariably kick in whenever the Holocaust is invoked in that manner. One need only consider the noxious depths of self-hatred, inhuman aggression and utter moral degradation to which rich and powerful people were willing to sink, as Finkelstein reveals in *The Holocaust Industry*, as they exploited Holocaust victims and survivors alike in order to make money and increase their own political marketability.

But by so boldly revealing these truths, Finkelstein sealed his fate with the American intellectual, political and academic classes. The time of his greatest importance as an American dissenter and secular prophet began in 1984-85, when he first revealed that Joan Peters' immensely popular *From Time*

Immemorial was a hoax; but it began to wane in approximately 2007, when (after a considerable struggle) he was finally booted out of American academia. After the publication of *The Holocaust Industry*, which came out in a second edition in 2003, Finkelstein produced another undeniably great book, *Beyond Chutzpah: On the Misuse of anti-Semitism and the Abuse of History*, which (despite efforts to suppress it) would be published in 2005, with an expanded edition in 2008. Furthermore, Finkelstein participated in some highly emotional and very public clashes with Alan Dershowitz, a central figure in the Israel Lobby in America. These clashes ended up revealing far more about Dershowitz and the Israel Lobby, than about Finkelstein—specifically, they revealed the profoundly undemocratic nature of the Lobby, and of Dershowitz himself.

All of these things, when taken together with Finkelstein's public speaking and books, probably did more than any other factors to challenge—and ultimately change—what had heretofore been the consensus opinion on Israel/Palestine among most educated people. Some of the same people who drove Finkelstein from his teaching job even began to vaguely denounce the same 'Holocaust profiteers' that Finkelstein had first exposed, while being careful to denounce Finkelstein at the same time.

In October, 2002, a regional director of the Anti-Defamation League tried to sell the idea that Norman Finkelstein was a "Holocaust denier," a laughable (and libelous) assertion considering how many times Finkelstein mentions the fact that his parents were Holocaust survivors. Various functionaries in the ADL continued in this vein for awhile, but finally desisted, probably because a lawsuit for libel was in the offing.

Marc Fisher, a *Washington Post* columnist, tried to pin the label of "Holocaust revisionist" on Finkelstein, but soon had to make a public retraction (which the *Washington Post* was forced to publish). What is particularly unsettling about these episodes is that the individuals involved surely knew that their smears were untrue, but used them anyway. This is one of the main concerns of the present writer: that the Israel Lobby corrupts discourse in US civil society, not just because it presents an inaccurate narrative concerning Israel, but because it ritually launches venomous personal attacks on anybody who disagrees with their uncritical support of the Likudniks, calling them anti-Semites or self-hating Jews, even when they know that to be untrue. Many of those in the Israel Lobby are, in other words, skilled practitioners of gutter politics, engaging regularly in attempts to destroy the reputations of ideological opponents, as well as intensive campaigns to suppress their books and drive them from their jobs.

16.

Finkelstein's downfall was accompanied by a running battle with the indefatigable Harvard law professor Alan M. Dershowitz, whose book *The Case for Israel* came out in 2004. In it Finkelstein might have anticipated the usual garden-variety claims of most Zionists, since Dershowitz—despite his self-promotion as a typical American liberal—is a right-wing Zionist with pronounced neo-conservative and neo-fascist tendencies. (For example, Professor Dershowitz supports the use of torture, probably because Israel does it on a mass basis.) Those regressive political tendencies Finkelstein indeed encountered in Dershowitz's book, but with an unexpected and rather creepy bonus: in certain sections Dershowitz followed very closely the arguments that Joan Peters had used in her discredited book *From Time Immemorial: the Origins of the Arab-Jewish Conflict over Palestine*, which Finkelstein had exposed in the 1980s.

And there was more. Embedded in Dershowitz' book were about twenty phrases and paragraphs which Finkelstein discerned as being lifted almost word-for-word from Joan Peters' discredited book. Furthermore, within these phrases were quotations, some of them replicated with the same errors originally made by Ms. Peters.

Finkelstein knew these phrases very well because, as the reader will remember, it was he who had personally exposed Peters' book as a hoax in the 1980s. Now these same discredited talking points were being recycled by a high-profile author in the Israel Lobby, but (amazingly) without attribution. There was no doubt whatsoever in Finkelstein's mind that whoever had written *The Case for Israel* had borrowed from Peters' book—the only question was whether the author, a high-profile, self-promoting American celebrity, had changed the borrowed material enough to avoid a charge of plagiarism. There was also the fact that Dershowitz was a leading member of the powerful Israel Lobby, which naturally made people wary of contradicting him. It was certainly not to his credit that he borrowed so much material; but if he had changed much of it, and surrounded it with material that was completely original, that would have redeemed to some extent his borrowing, regardless of his book's political message.

The best-case scenario would have been that Dershowitz, having been apprized quietly of his error, would acknowledge publicly that some twenty or so phrases from Peters' book had inadvertently appeared in *The Case for Israel*, perhaps arguing that the way he used them was original, and the rest of the book was his alone. He would then conclude with an apology for the oversight. If he had done this, the controversy would have evaporated. But Dershowitz was too arrogant to consider such an expedient, and it was not in Finkelstein's nature to back down. Neither man was inclined to hide his scholarly lights under anybody's bushel.

Many academics—including those in the "best" Ivy League colleges—are known for letting their students do their research, and 'helping' them write their books and articles. If Dershowtiz had such an arrangement, he would be far from the first academic to do so.[26] But to repeat Joan Peters' discredited arguments, to once again retail her lies and half-truths as though they were some striking modern revelation... what on earth was Dershowitz and his write-by-the-numbers cohorts thinking? To Finkelstein, it was clear that whoever wrote *The Case for Israel* was knowingly and intentionally guilty of plagiarism; and that sincere belief, and his loathing of the recurring recycling of the Peters hoax, ignited the fire in his gut. No matter what else happened, he was going for the righteous kill.

Dershowitz appeared September 23, 2003 on Amy Goodwin's TV news show *Democracy Now!* He later claimed that he showed up on Goodwin's show because he thought he'd be chatting with someone else, which doesn't quite convince; in any case, he was perfectly free to walk out, once he found the notorious Norman Finkelstein lurking about waiting for him. But he didn't, and it was that same notorious, fractious Norman Finkelstein who went on air to challenge him. Again I ask: had Dershowitz no inkling of what was in store for him? Perhaps not; and the fact that he didn't could be construed as circumstantial evidence that perhaps he either didn't remember his book, or hadn't researched, written or edited parts of it. Or perhaps he simply needed more publicity for *The Case for Israel* and didn't care what Finkelstein said, as long as it was sensational. But even Dershowitz couldn't have guessed what was about to transpire.

Amy Goodman introduced the two men. Dershowitz made a longish statement about *The Case for Israel* intended to establish the impression that he is merely an earnest American liberal who supports a two-state solution in Israel/Palestine, whose only interest is peace. He somewhat queasily suggested, apropos of nothing, that Finkelstein refrain from ad hominem attacks against him.

Goodman introduced Finkelstein, who opened with this astonishing statement:

I have no intention whatsoever of getting involved in an ad

hominem debate with Mr. Dershowitz. I'm interested in the facts. I was asked to come in and discuss his new book. I went home, purchased one copy, in fact I purchased two copies. I read the book very carefully. I did what someone serious does with a book. I read the text, I went through the footnotes. I went through it very carefully. There's only one conclusion one can reach having read the book. This is a scholarly judgment, not an ad hominem attack. Mr. Dershowitz has concocted a fraud. In fact Mr. Dershowitz has concocted a fraud which, amazingly, in large parts, he plagiarized from another fraud. I found that pretty shocking, shocking coming from a Harvard professor. I find it shocking coming from any professor.

The debate went downhill from there, although Dershowitz managed to get in more talking points than Finkelstein, including (typically) numerous direct and indirect threats to sue him. But Finkelstein continued to make explosive charges, all of which Dershowitz apparently hadn't seen coming. Sitting next to the Harvard law professor, Finkelstein asserted that Dershowitz was unfamiliar with *The Case for Israel*, the very book that he was supposed to have written and was now promoting, and went on to speculate that Dershowitz, supposedly its author, may not even have read the book. Sitting next to Finkelstein during this highly personal and very public denunciation, Dershowitz appeared to be gnashing his teeth.

Dershowitz was highly regarded by the eastern academic establishment, was on intimate terms with major players in the Israel Lobby, and was himself an unusually vigorous self-promoter. Despite this—or perhaps because of it—Finkelstein felt compelled to expose him. One suspects the object was not just a definitive exposé of Dershowitz the individual, but also by way of sending a message to other powerful operatives of the Israel Lobby, whose books Finkelstein felt were rarely given close scrutiny by critics, because everybody was terrified of 'the Lobby.' Didn't Finkelstein anticipate retaliation? Almost surely he did, because no one could have made such an accusation against Alan M. Dershowitz during a live television broadcast without expecting retaliation—and he was prepared to defend himself. Finkelstein's downfall, however, was to trust in the integrity of academia in American and to take seriously its frequent protestations of academic freedoms.

It was clearly because of Dershowitz' position as a stalwart of the Israel Lobby that Finkelstein wrote his next book, *Beyond Chutzpah: The Misuse of Anti-Semitism and the Abuse of History*, in which he analyzed Dershowitz' claims about Israel while attempting to demonstrate plagiarism in *The Case for Israel*. In this book he expanded on his previous thesis that whenever the suffering of the Palestinians seemed to catch the public's attention, Israel's proxies around the world would bring up the Holocaust as a way of deflecting attention from the injustices suffered by the Palestinians.

In *Beyond Chutzpah* Finkelstein proceeded to systematically challenge Dershowitz' thesis that the Israeli Defense Forces almost never made mistakes or engaged in atrocities, taking certain events referred to by Dershowitz and comparing them to much different accounts by Human Rights Watch, Amnesty International and the Israeli human rights organization B'Tselem. Also he dealt at great length with Dershowitz' alleged plagiarism of Joan Peters' notorious *From Time Immemorial*, which to Finkelstein's mind was compelling evidence that he hadn't written his most recent book and perhaps hadn't even read it. Dershowitz' ultimate intent in using Joan Peters' arguments and quotes was to disseminate disinformation about the Israeli state, according to Finkelstein, so to him it was further deceit in the service of a bad cause. *The Case for Israel* was, according to Finkelstein, "a collection of fraud, falsification, plagiarism and nonsense."

When Alan Dershowitz found out that Finkelstein would soon be coming out with a new book (*Beyond Chutzpah: On the Misuse of Anti-Semitism and the Abuse of History*) he immediately kicked off a campaign to have it suppressed, using his status as a well-known law professor and spokesperson for the Israel Lobby. Finkelstein originally had an arrangement with New Press, a non-commercial publisher in New York that published activist and progressive works. But long before the book went to press, in early summer of 2011, Dershowitz launched his campaign of intimidation. According to Gary Younge of the *Guardian* in Britain, Dershowitz got hold of the home addresses of the New Press Board of Directors and started sending them letters, indirectly threatening to sue New Press for libel.

Colin Robinson, the publisher of New Press, says in the *Guardian* article that he received three letters himself from Alan Dershowitz. ("The atmosphere for publishing critical stuff on Israel here [in the US] is very intimidating," he is also quoted as saying.) The author of this same article, Gary Younge, helpfully points out to his British readers that "the scope for discussing these things [Israel/Palestine]" in the US is "relatively narrow compared to the rest of the western world." Indeed.

But was not the New Press a "progressive" publishing organization? Perhaps, but it is also true that so-called progressive presses, theaters and artistic organizations in the US are often more susceptible to pressure from the Israel Lobby than any other, especially in New York. Although it is considered bad form to talk about it, Zionist billionaires and pro-Israel organizations are major donors to the Democratic party, as we've already seen, and of certain progressive and artistic organizations; thus super-rich Zionists are likely to give to such organizations not because they are themselves liberals or inordinately interested in the arts, but do so in part to maintain the leverage necessary to keep serious discussion of Israel/Palestine off the table. Until very recently, the entire American Israeli Public Action Committee

(AIPAC) operation has existed to keep the Democratic Party in line, through the simple expedient of giving money to its elected politicians to run their campaigns. Now that AIPAC has shifted to the right it gives money to both parties—indeed, it now gives so much money, according to some reports, that an actual majority of elected persons in the legislative branch, both Republican and Democrat, are on their payroll.

Partly for that reason, and partly simply to avoid rancorous discussion, there has long been in American liberalism an unspoken rule not to discuss Israel/Palestine, because of the fear of splitting the Rooseveltian liberal-labor-minorities coalition that is at the heart of progressive domestic politics in the US. In fact, this agreed-upon silence among American liberals has greatly contributed to the failure of US efforts to achieve a resolution of the Israel/Palestine conflict, since the only Middle East diplomats the Israel Lobby will tolerate are right-wing Zionists and neo-cons—that is, advocates for the Israeli right-wing party Likud and the fanatics of the religious parties—and by so doing, it has brought the Middle East (and the world) each year closer to religious war.

When it began to seem likely that the New Press was likely to cave to Dershowitz' relentless threats, Finkelstein took his book to the University of California Press, and got a book contract there. At UC Press the editors were determined to stand up to Dershowitz's intimidation—for one thing, they had probably concluded that Finkelstein's main points were essentially correct, and that therefore Dershowitz would not dare sue; and that even if he did, it would be great publicity for the book. Furthermore they respected Finkelstein's gifts as a scholar and writer, and actually believed in academic freedom. When he realized he couldn't get anywhere with the editors of UC Press, Dershowitz wrote to the Governor of California, Governor Schwarzenegger, asking *him* to block publication of the book.

The Governor promptly had his legal affairs secretary write

back to say that he would not get involved, rightly citing academic freedom as his reason. (Why Dershowitz thought Schwarzenegger could help him is anybody's guess—perhaps he had a couple of political IOUs he thought he could cash in.) Jon Weiner, who is both a writer for *The Nation* and a history professor at UC Berkeley, has written that the frantic Dershowitz engaged a well-known law firm in the Bay Area to write threatening letters to the university regents, to the university provost, and a grand total of seventeen directors of the UC Berkeley press, not to mention nineteen members of the press's faculty editorial committee. Luckily, they all held firm, if for no other reason than Dershowitz' annoyingly transparent attempts to intimidate people had succeeded in infuriating them.

For Finkelstein, it was a good time for the publication of *Beyond Chutzpah*, because it was about to become a little easier to discuss Israel/Palestine. Jimmy Carter's book *Palestine: Peace Not Apartheid* would be coming out in 2006, and Walt and Mearsheimer's essay about the Israel Lobby would come out in the London Review of Books that same year. (*The Israel Lobby and US Foreign Policy* would come out in book form in 2007.) But it still wasn't easy to rationally discuss Israel/Palestine without being attacked as an anti-Semite or self-hating Jew—Walt and Mearsheimer's original 2005 essay on the Israel Lobby had to appear first in Britain, because no publication in the US would dare publish it.

Thus *Beyond Chutzpah*, if taken together with the rest of Finkelstein's controversial work, can be seen as constituting the first public attempts in the early 21st century to open the American mind to what was really happening in Israel/Palestine—and to make Americans aware of the disproportionate influence of the right-wing Zionists, neo-cons and religious nationalists in American life and politics. This became especially important after 9/11, when the rightward-shifting Israel Lobby began to support and disseminate Islamophobia—

that is, religious bigotry against Muslims. American thought and culture owes a great deal to Noam Chomsky and Norman Finkelstein in that area, because those two prophetic Jewish voices insisted that we see certain truths about our country we would rather ignore. And there were many other courageous people involved in the publication of *Beyond Chutzpah*, heroes who are mainly nameless, such as the editors and publishers at the University of California Press who would not back down in the face of threats by Alan M. Dershowitz.

Finkelstein's objective had always been to expose the Israel Lobby in its entirety, to expose the mixture of propaganda, money, political influence and intimidation it uses to suppress free speech and in general operate as a Thought Police. He believes they are corrupting Jewish consciousness and values, and furthermore believes they are bad for Israel, the Palestinians, and America. Finkelstein saw *The Case for Israel* as a representative example of Israel Lobby propaganda, and Dershowitz as an arrogant, dictatorial figure who likes to push people around, and who prefers to kill debate rather than engage in it. In order to demonstrate how Dershowitz operates—to smoke him out, in other words—Finkelstein chose to publicly taunt him in order to make him attack, using himself as bait.

This may seem extreme, but it is consistent with Finkelstein's underlying preoccupation as a prophetic intellectual defending basic—and essential—Jewish values against those Jews whom he believes are betraying those same values. In addition to setting the record straight regarding Israel, he focuses on fighting those in the Israel Lobby that use the traumatic memory of the Holocaust to deflect legitimate criticism of Israel—what I have referred to as *traumatic privilege*—since he is convinced that human rights for Palestinians, and historical truth regarding the Holocaust, are both part of the same battle. In fighting that battle, Norman Finkelstein continued, and continues today, his mother's struggle with her Holocaust memories by taking his socially-beneficial activities to a new level, the level of critical debate in American public life.

In so doing, he believes he is defending the best Jewish and American values, as well as standing tall for peace in Israel/Palestine. Furthermore, he sees degradation of Jewish values—as well as rhetorical and physical attacks on the Palestinians—as typically emanating from those that use the Holocaust to make money, manipulate power, or oppress Palestinians. Finkelstein wanted to draw the Israel Lobby into a fight that would cause it to reveal its essentially anti-democratic nature, and he was about to succeed beyond his wildest dreams. But even Finkelstein could not have guessed the personal price he would be forced to pay.

17.

Besides writing modern history, Finkelstein has one other love, teaching; and those who have been in his classes say that he is rigorously, even fanatically, solicitous to all points of view, despite his reputation as the country's leading and most disputatious cultural radical. Working as a contract instructor at Rutgers, New York University, Brooklyn College and Hunter College, Finkelstein left the latter in 2001, after they cut back on his teaching hours and salary; but since the publication of *The Holocaust Industry* he had increasingly engaged in various speaking and lecture commitments. But as Finkelstein has often pointed out, teaching was in his blood; and it was a singular victory when he succeeded in getting hired as an Associate Professor at DePaul University in Chicago. DePaul was the country's largest Catholic college, serving around 25,000 students, and had a reputation as being a home for the social-justice teachings of Catholicism, especially those teachings associated with the ministry of the 17th-century Roman Catholic saint St. Vincent de Paul. De Paul served the poor and the suffering, and was known for his compassion and generosity; his followers formed a Roman Catholic order commonly referred to as Vincentians.

Finkelstein settled in at DePaul, and with his fame as a scholar seemed in line for tenure. Yes, he was controversial, but so are most first-rate thinkers, including those at DePaul. And he was an excellent teacher, something that is not always obvious to those who see him only as a public intellectual involved in various political and academic controversies. The faculty at DePaul viewed him primarily as an excellent teacher who had written some highly controversial books, not all of which were of any particular interest to the average student or faculty at DePaul. But Finkelstein made a powerful impression on his students, partly because he was a dynamic thinker and speaker, and partly because he had an impressive ability to keep his opinions out of the classroom, something far less controversial instructors have trouble with. There was no reason to suspect that his tenure would be anything but automatic.

But it was anything but automatic, once Alan Dershowitz and the rest of the Israel Lobby intruded themselves into the scene. How Dershowitz did so was a lesson in institutional aggression, not to mention the cowardice of academia—he simply started sending threatening letters to all the main players at DePaul University: faculty, administration, or anybody whose address he could get hold of, telling them they shouldn't give Finkelstein tenure, and instructing them in the reasons why they shouldn't. The extent to which he threatened legal action is not known, but as during his attempt to suppress Finkelstein's book he had often indirectly threatened lawsuits. The recipients of the letters were clearly not prepared for this, probably because no academic from another university had ever tried to intervene in tenure deliberations before. It was undoubtedly against the unspoken rules of how such things are done, but it is hard to believe that such high-level intrusion by outside forces are not also against the written rules.

It is instructive that nobody involved in this dispute set clear limits for Dershowitz from the very beginning, bringing him up on charges in the appropriate academic organizations, and in general making it clear to him that there would be unpleasant legal and administrative consequences if he kept trying to interfere in DePaul University's affairs. Dershowitz is a bully, and like most bullies is also a coward; and if confronted directly for his unacceptable conduct, he would probably have backed down. But nobody at DePaul ever did confront Dershowitz, because they lacked the courage to do so. Dershowitz was a powerful member of the Israel Lobby, and because of that all the things that should have happened, didn't. Other organizations involved with the Israel Lobby also weighed in on what had now become a national controversy, but it was Dershowitz who would be on point during this assault, the better to act out his own revenge and personal animosity.

The controversy became public early in 2007, when the DePaul University Political Science department voted to give Finkelstein tenure, 9 to 3, and the College of Liberal Arts and Science Personnel Committee approved Finkelstein's tenure by a margin of 5 to 0. The Dean of the College, Chuck Suchar, tipped his hand early in the game as an opponent of tenure, encouraging the three Political Science professors who had voted against Finkelstein's application to write a report stating their objections. Suchar's objections became public when a memorandum he had written was leaked, first appearing on the blog of Professor Peter N. Kirstein, who was at the time of the Finkelstein affair active in an Academic Freedom and Tenure committee of the American Association of University Professors.

Suchar's objection to Finkelstein was similar to the main objection his critics have always made: Finkelstein's tone was disturbing. To this Suchar added that Finkelstein seemed to aim at destroying the reputation of those he attacked. This occurred at a time when Alan Dershowitz was himself trying to destroy

Finkelstein's reputation at DePaul, as part of a dispute in which he had no business interfering—but Suchar not only refused to set limits for Dershowitz, he completely but predictably ignored the asymmetry in power between Finkelstein and those established political and cultural figures whose bono fides he was interrogating. This is from Suchar's leaked memorandum:

> The departmental minority report cites Dr. Finkelstein's personal and reputation demeaning attacks on Alan Dershowitz, Benny Morris, and the holocaust authors Eli Wiesel and Jerzy Kosinski. My own examination of Prof. Finkelstein's works corrobarates (sic) the minority report's claims and conclusions in this regard. My reading of Dr. Finkelstein's work, especially *The Holocaust Industry*, where in one chapter alone Goldhagen, Morris, Wiesel, Kosinski and many others are collectively attacked as "hoaxers and hucksters," typifies his apparent penchant of reducing an argument and oppositional views to the inevitable personal and reputation damaging attack, demeaning those with whom he disagrees.[27]

Any harm that had accrued to the reputation of Alan Dershowitz probably came from his own poor judgment, his political extremism, and his bullying tactics. Similar demurrals could be made concerning Israeli historian Benny Morris and author Eli Wiesel; and although Jerzy Kosinsky committed suicide on May 3, 1991, his supposed Holocaust-era memoir had already been proven to be fraudulent. As for Goldhagen, he personally demeaned Finkelstein by dismissing him as a "Hamas supporter."

When Finkelstein calls powerful and corrupt people "hoaxers and hucksters," that is nothing compared to calling sincere critics of Israel's government anti-Semites, self-hating Jews, or crypto-Nazis, as Dershowitz and others in the Israel Lobby regularly do, a practice that is especially despicable because Dershowitz and his friends know those charges to be, in the vast majority of cases, completely untrue. But were the people Finkelstein wrote about "hoaxers and hucksters," or were they not? If they weren't, Finkelstein was guilty of libel; but nobody ever sued Finkelstein for libel.

Indeed they were everything Finkelstein said they were, and he could prove they were, as seems clear from the evidence presented; and for that reason, such dissenting public intellectuals such as Finkelstein are especially precious to the American republic, the better to warn the public of the charlatans and hucksters in American life. Dershowitz, on the other hand, was simply engaged in advancing the power of the Israeli state—and the Likud party—in American institutions and culture, as a means of advancing his own interests and enhancing his own corrupt power.

But what are we to make of the charge that Finkelstein's muckraking tone was a violation of Vincentian values?

Let us look for a moment at the life and world of Saint Vincent de Paul. He was a rich man in 17th-century France who took up the cause of the poor and the oppressed, who lived with the poor and regularly argued their case to the wealthy. But are the Palestinians, the group whose human rights Finkelstein embraces, not also oppressed? Finkelstein does not have Saint Vincent's humility, but he is clearly more restrained in his expression than Alan M. Dershowitz, who—when discussing Palestinians and Palestinian culture—is little more than a gutter racist. But Finkelstein does, in a very direct and unmediated way, demonstrate a passionate, unmistakable Vincentian generosity and concern for the poor and the powerless. Do his enemies, who use the Holocaust to get power and to scam people for money, who support apartheid in the Occupied Palestinian Territories, ever think once of the poor and powerless? No, they do not, because most of them are power-hungry operators out for themselves.

Where Suchar went wrong—where institutional Christianity almost always gets it wrong—was to support the powerful against the powerless, by groveling before an undemocratic, well-financed lobby that sought to destroy a prophetic voice and render him unemployable; in so doing, Suchar became complicit with the ultimate crime against Vincentian values. Suchar, in other words, supported Goliath against David—as Christianity has done on a regular basis since the fourth century, when it became the imperial training academy for Constantine's ecclesiastical toadies.

Suchar has nothing but contempt, as institutional Christianity usually does, for the spiritual, cultural and moral argument for social justice. Although religious institutions sometimes do good things, when the chips are down they care more about their own power than the values they profess. Ultimately, Finkelstein cares more about justice than power—or, to put it another way, Finkelstein sees justice as a form of psychological and spiritual power that is superior in quality to tribal religion and money. Suchar drove a knife into the heart of Vincentian consciousness by siding with the rich over the poor, all too typical of the betrayals of humanity witnessed every day within institutional Christianity.

In his concern for academic propriety, Suchar passes over the fact that the weak have never been able, short of violent revolution, to get the strong to stop their exploitive or murderous behavior, except by exposing their activities—and that is a process in which it is far easier for people to blame the messenger than make a sober assessment of the message. Shaming the oppressor and exposing the demagogue are the only way the weak and the oppressed can ever hope to get a hearing, short of terrorism and violent revolution—that is the great value of the muckraker, and the prophetic voice generally. That is also the great value of a free press, and of freedom of speech in the marketplace of ideas. If the American truth-teller cannot find refuge in academia, where will he find it? And if truth does not outweigh in importance the ruffled feathers of an outraged propriety, what is truth?

On June 11, 2007, Finkelstein was denied tenure as the result of a 4-3 vote by DePaul University's Board on Promotion and Tenure, affirmed by the Rev. Dennis Holtschneider, the University's President. The utter hypocrisy of Holtschneider and Suchar hit its dreadful nadir in their claim that their decision was based entirely on the case's merits. But that is belied by the facts. As a part of Holtschneider and Suchar's abject surrender to the Israel Lobby, they also made a deal to deny tenure to international studies assistant professor Mehrene Larudee, in spite of the fact that she had received unanimous support from her department, the Dean and the Personnel Committee.

Professor Larudee had strongly supported Norman Finkelstein—but there was much, much more to it than that. Mehrene Larudee was a member of 'A Jewish Voice for Peace,' which—because it strives for peace in Israel/Palestine, and supports human rights for Palestinians—is the arch-enemy of the Israel Lobby. Furthermore, her brother had been involved with the International Solidarity Movement, which is a network of progressive Christians—many from the historic peace churches, such as Quakers, Church of the Brethren and Mennonites—who use non-violence to try to protect Palestinians from racist settlers on the West Bank. Clearly, 'the Lobby' saw a chance to clean house at DePaul University. Denying tenure to Dr. Larudee, as well as Finkelstein, sent a strong message to American academia that anyone who bucked the Israel Lobby could expect immediate retaliation.

And it wasn't just tenure—Dr. Larudee had just been approved as the chair of the International Studies Department of DePaul University. As a result of pressure from the Israel Lobby, that appointment was made void. Everyone at the University knew what was happening, and few had doubts as to how it had come about. The University Board on Faculty Promotion and Tenure—the same Board that denied tenure to Finkelstein—also denied tenure to Dr. Larudee, with the clear intent of making it impossible for her to serve as chair of the International Studies Department. The fact that Father Holtschneider, president of the University, accepted both decisions, thereby canceling her appointment to be chair of the International Studies Department, suggests the extent of the pressure from 'the Lobby,' and his cowardice in not standing up to it, and the even greater heights of hypocrisy in denying his own cupidity in the matter.

If the main problem was Finkelstein's temperament, why did the college block tenure for Mehrene Larudee? Clearly the Israel Lobby had demanded that she be gotten rid of too, and Suchar's protestations to the contrary were clearly more of his lies. "I played by the rules, and it plainly wasn't enough to overcome the political opposition in my speaking out on the Israel/Palestine conflict," Professor Finkelstein said grimly in an interview. "This decision is not going to deter me from making statements that, so far as I can tell from the judgment of experts in the field, are sound and factually based."

There was more, of course—Finkelstein was supposed to teach some classes the next year, but when he filed a lawsuit the administration canceled his classes. There were a couple of awkward incidents in the hallways, including one caught on film, in which it appeared that Finkelstein and one of his detractors were on the brink of fisticuffs. The powers-that-be decided to settle, paid Finkelstein off with an undisclosed amount of hush-money, and participated in a joint press conference with the embattled scholar in which the administration representatives said nice things about him. (They praised him as "as a prolific scholar and outstanding teacher," among other things.)[28] It was time for Finkelstein to pack up his car and get out of Dodge.

From his power base at Harvard, the ever-tasteless Dershowitz scolded DePaul for saying nice things about Finkelstein after the settlement, characteristically maintaining that by exerting a minimal level of civility to Finkelstein the university had "traded truth for peace."[29] Dershowitz' lack of 'Vincentian' values—or even the most fundamental common decency—provoked no comment from DePaul administrators. After all, Dershowitz had a powerful political lobby behind him, and Finkelstein was just another smart-aleck public intellectual who needed to be hustled out of town before he made any more trouble. When it came to a test between the world's powers and principalities, on the one hand, and the academic freedom the DePaul administration likes to talk about, the compliant clerics that ran DePaul University knew exactly on which side their daily bread was buttered.

18.

Why did the administrators of DePaul behave as they did? That is, why did they behave in such an extreme and despicable way? The administration of DePaul Administration behaved as they did because academic freedom in America is a sham. Education in America is marketed on a fee-for-service basis, bonding young people to twenty or more years of serfdom as they pay off their loans to corrupt financial institutions that are busily compounding interest on the original loan. The idea that these institutions of higher learning would actually stand up for academic freedom, if they weren't paid to do so, is ridiculous. After all, they're businesses, aren't they? There is only academic freedom for the mundane; there is no academic freedom when it counts.

Noam Chomsky was right. Academia is a gang of frauds. If they really believe in academic freedom, as they want us to think, why did not one university in America step up and offer Finkelstein a job, since he was so clearly denied tenure for political reasons at DePaul University? Wouldn't people who believe in academic freedom want to protect that same academic freedom? Finkelstein himself has said in an interview that he has already asked some 40 universities for a job, but none will touch him. The fact is Finkelstein is blacklisted. When some university offers Finkelstein a job, then one can again believe in academic freedom. Until then, let's see it for what it is—a lie designed to help institutions of 'higher learning' make more money.

And while we're at it, where was the moral influence of religion in this painful conflict? We have already seen the corruption of certain leaders of the Jewish establishment, and the political corruption of the US political class. The behavior of the top administration at DePaul is likewise sadly typical of the ongoing corruption of Christianity. Institutional Christianity is, and has been for many centuries, on the wrong side of almost every conceivable social and political issue. If only because it taught hatred of Jews for a thousand years, culminating in the Nazi Holocaust, institutional Christianity must be seen, in the early 21st century, as a failed religion.

That does not mean that individual Jews and Christians should forgo interrogating and investigating their own religious traditions in the process of fashioning their personal moral psychologies. It is better to seek spiritual truth within one's own traditions, rather than embracing—and thereby unconsciously trivializing—a religious tradition one does not really under-stand. But for the time being, one must agree with the late Lenny Bruce, who once remarked that it's a good thing that people are "leaving the church and going back to God." That is to say, we are probably at the place in history where the search for God, and for the kind of moral psychologies that can guide daily behavior, must be values that are framed, defined and acted out mainly by concerned secular people and religious dissenters. By itself, institutional religion just can't be trusted.

19.

Finkelstein is not just a public intellectual, however: there is something too explosive about the subjects he writes about for that category to completely contain him. He acts out a role that is Grecian in its cosmopolitanism, Abrahamic in its prophetic intensity. It is a role all Christians, Jews and Muslims instinctively—if subliminally—recognize. He is the archetypical prophet who warns the people in his tribe to stop dancing around the Golden Calf, and tells of their impending doom if they do not. He is Cassandra, who foresees the downfall of her nation; he is the Abrahamic prophets Isaiah, Daniel, and Jeremiah, as well as the heroic figure of Joseph, who astounds the Pharaoh by telling him what his dreams are *really* about. He is a figure Americans recognize, although they do not want to. He is the Puritan preacher, hurling bolts of rhetorical fury in modern Jeremiads; he is Daniel in the lion's den; he is tormented and selfish and at times uncouth, but is also unexpectedly Christ-like, refusing to abandon his message despite scourging by critics.

He is the Quaker John Woolman denouncing slavery, and he is Thoreau; he is James Baldwin and Noam Chomsky. He warns us like prophets have always done, prophets whom we have always ignored in daily life, but whose warnings ensconce themselves in our brains. When their warnings are ignored, terrible things follow. Historian G. M. Trevelyan put it best: "Close your ears to John Woolman one century and you will get John Brown the next, with Grant to follow." We usually *do* close our ears to Woolman, sadly, and Grant usually *does* follow, with Sherman in close pursuit.

When he writes about Israel/Palestine, Finkelstein is the prophet of a crisis that will ultimately tear apart American Judaism, tear apart American liberalism, and tear apart American culture. Zionism operates in the West by propaganda, money, political influence and intimidation. Because it is tribal, irrational and propelled by powerfully self-destructive impulses, it will devour and divide every aspect of life. While it was once driven by a kind of desperate idealism, the religious nationalism at its center has gradually become—at least if you are a Palestinian in the Occupied Territories—a form of religious fascism. It is bad for America, for the West, for Israelis and for Palestinians. Arising out of the nihilism of the Holocaust, it continues to operate out of that same nihilism, creating new chaos and new victims.

Finkelstein saw the suffering that traumatic memory of the Holocaust inflicted on his mother, which is why he internalized so many of her demons. But he also inherited from his mother the ability to overcome those demons, and act out the truth of social justice as he perceives and embodies it. He does not completely understand the psychological process of internalization—who does?—or understand its power to unconsciously drive behavior, but sees clearly enough the connection between the Holocaust and the way oppression of the Palestinians has always been rationalized. Most important of all, he sees the way to escape from the pathology of Holocaust-inspired violence. He sees how the lying necessary to cover up oppression of the Palestinians, and to cover up the corrupt exploitation of the Holocaust, continues to distort and corrupt Jewish life. He sees that the systemic evil of apartheid in Israel's occupied territories is what must be opposed.

Most of all, he feels in his bones the public immorality of those who use the Holocaust to make money and gain political power and influence. All these things are distractions from what we should be learning from the Holocaust—that there is a Nazi in all of us, Jews and Palestinians and Americans alike, and an anti-Nazi as well; and that our capacity for evil is waiting to come out, with the right emotional circumstances and the right ideological justification. The creation of a Holocaust industry is the desperate attempt to make a Faustian bargain with evil; but by so doing, such people not only make an adjustment to systemic evil, but also internalize it in its most powerful form, and are therefore bonded to its sadism. Their lives become a continuation of the Holocaust by other means.

Ultimately, few of the inconvenient truths Finkelstein has uncovered in his books have been challenged, and that tells us something very important. What makes people hate Finkelstein is not his personal or literary style; it is that he was, for a very important period in American history, engaged in systematically exposing lies that were so painful for people to confront that it was everything they could do not to become hysterical. He took it upon himself to probe the traumatic memory of the Holocaust and of Israel/Palestine, and few could stand what he discovered. Let those who say they hate Finkelstein separate out his facts from his style, I say, the better to assimilate the terrible story he reveals; but they do not. Ultimately, it is really the truth of the revelator that they hate, not his style.

But now, we must face the question raised by Finkelstein himself. Why did people like Edgar Bronfman, Sr., and Bill Clinton, President of the United States, behave as they did? To begin with, greed, pure and simple, and the calculations of ambitious people who need the deep pockets of rich donors. This writer votes for Democrats, and would vote for a Democrat over just about any Republican one might name, given the extent to which the Republican party promotes racism, religious bigotry, loathing of women and hatred of science. But I also believe in seeing the world as it is, and not as I want it to be. Clinton and other Democrats enthusiastically sought money from the large donors such as the late Edgar Miles Bronfman, Sr., because that is the nature of the oligarchy America is becoming. For his part, Bronfman probably behaved so brazenly at least in part to impress others like Bill and Hillary Clinton, so that he could reap the benefits of their political influence whenever he needed to. In return, the billionaires like Bronfman were expected to lend a hand to the Clintons' projects (such as their charity Global

Initiative) and give money to the electoral campaigns of their friends.

I think this tells us far more about the way power works in America than we want to believe. It is run by billionaires who wish to buy out our electoral politics, and will spend endless millions of dollars to elect the candidates they want. The ultimate goal is to destroy electoral democracy as it has existed in the past, and replace it with government that operates as a casino. That is greed, but it is greed of such a malevolent and addictive nature as the world has not seen since the Roman Empire. Money is no longer the mother's milk of politics; it is the heroin of imperial American power.

There was a manic quality to the depredations of Bronfman and Singer, something insane, something malignant—something that is not, in other words, explainable solely by greed. There was something about the way they denounced the affluent Europeans—invoking constantly the death and destruction of the Nazi Holocaust—that caused them literally to run amuck. They seemed to find it especially exciting to refer constantly to the suffering of the survivors they were supposedly helping, whilst knowing very well on some level that those same survivors would see little of the money they would ultimately obtain.

But they also seemed to feel, for just that reason, that by operating in such a dishonest way they were wreaking a perverse revenge on the Europeans, by forcing them to become complicit on a gutter level to behavior and political posturing that all concerned knew to be despicable. Bronfman was simply taking the opportunity, perhaps, to humiliate a bunch of European Christians who looked to him very much like the Christians that had once humiliated his ancestors; but such gambits always end up hurting those that use them, because they show that the victims learned nothing and have become just as cruel and deranged as the bigots that once persecuted them. And

Bronfman not only harmed the Swiss whom he stigmatized, he harmed himself and the organizations with which he was associated.

The question remains: Why did Bronfman and Singer do what they did? Singer we may safely dismiss as a bold if contemptible minor-league criminal. But what about the late Edgar Miles Bronfman, Senior?[30] He was one of the world's richest men, one experienced in the ways of the world, and quite familiar with the various machinations that flourish in the twilight worlds of philanthropy, politics and political influence. The fact that he conferred with powerful political operators at the wedding of a friend's daughter suggests the casual but highly-focused way he moved through various worlds of power. (Shades of Coppola's *The Godfather*!) Why, then, did Bronfman, an extremely wealthy man, do things that harmed Holocaust survivors, whose stories of destitution he used to raise money and whom he was supposed to be helping? Why, in fact, did he do things that were bound to harm Israel—and Jews everywhere—when the full truth came out?

I don't think that greed is nearly enough to explain what happened. There was a gratuitous quality to the lies told by Bronfman that greed cannot fully explain, almost as though he wished to be caught and punished. I think it far more likely that this was another example of the way traumatic memory of the Holocaust operates. Those who use it to exploit other people do so at their own risk: the trauma associated with the Holocaust has an uncanny tendency to destroy, twist and harm everybody who tries to use it, making them dangerous to themselves and to others. And the Holocaust itself, far from being merely a memory, has the power—for reasons nobody fully understands—to corrupt everybody and everything.

This does not require personal exposure to the Holocaust. Simply to know about it is enough, because to know about what was done by the Nazis is to understand, in a visceral way, the unalterable evidence of human evil. Yes, most of us have the capacity for evil, but the Holocaust was something completely extraordinary, an explosive outbreak of a kind of systemic evil that only the word 'demonic' can accurately describe. Furthermore, the moral collapse of Germany warns us of the extent to which good people can be pulled into acting evil out, if it is part of a powerful ideological system with its roots in aggressive emotional orientations. Those who were deeply traumatized by such evil almost invariably internalize some of its aggression, to be acted out later, either against oneself or against others. And where does the aggression come from? It is embedded in the traumatic memory itself, to be acted out by those who have internalized it.

The Nazi Holocaust is our shared traumatic memory, and it is still very much alive, because we still do not understand how and why its memory is so deeply affecting us. Not only did the Holocaust overturn the cultural balance of power in Europe, by destroying Europe's most highly motivated and progressive ethno-religious group; it also overturned the world's geo-political balance of power, leading directly to the creation of the state of Israel and the displacement of the Palestinians. But such was the insane quality of the aggression involved in the Nazi horror that it continued to operate a dangerous moral blowback on anyone—such as Bronfman—who had the chutzpah to posture himself as an appropriate spokesman for the six million.

Using the Holocaust to make money or amass power is extremely dangerous, because its traumatic memory has a radioactive half-life far longer than most people imagine, and it can hurt people in ways they would never suspect. Rabbi Israel Singer, Bronfman's confederate, seems to have fallen victim to it, acting out in various acts of false witness the noxious inhumanity of the Nazis, which he appears to have thoroughly internalized. Bronfman did not learn from this hard lesson, but instead continued to use the traumatic memory of the Holocaust to raise money in Eastern Europe. For not making sure that money went to actual Holocaust survivors, as they promised it would, Bronfman and Singer sinned against their own people, and they sinned against the world. This is an objective reality that is true whether or not they had the gift of introspection, or the ability to feel shame.

Could the rot of this monstrous corruption have begun earlier, in the systematic deceit adopted by many Jewish leaders in the US regarding the ethnic cleansing of the Palestinians? American Jews were not complicit in the dispossession of Palestinians—it would be too much to say that believing lies is by itself complicity, given humanity's incredible propensity for self-deception. But it was hard to be an observant Jew without to some extent being influenced by those lies and prevarications that were ladled out to American Jews by Jewish leaders, and also by the Christian denominations, and by the US political class. We know this because Christians believed exactly the same lies as Jews did. The corruption begins when someone hears a rational-ization of some terrible state violence, whether Israeli or American, a rationalization that doesn't sound quite right, and makes a conscious decision not to probe too deeply into things that one instinctively feels to be wrong.

The corrupting effect among American Jews of worshipping a state that engages in systemic evil (as any state will do if given unlimited impunity) simply compounds the traumatic memory of the Holocaust, introducing profound distortions into American Judaism. The deceit about 'the Nakba,' an Arabic word for the ethnic cleansing of Palestinians, also introduced a viral distortion into American Judaism that could eventually stunt and lacerate it at its heart, and demand a thorough reformation by the pure in heart. The rise of neo-conservatism—which is really little more than an argument for Israeli/American imperialism—further corrupted Judaism in the US, especially because neo-cons became adept at activating the trauma bond at the heart of religious nationalism, cynically triggering at will the latent paranoia that Jews carry deep inside them because of a thousand years of persecution by Christians.

The criminal greed of the Holocaust Industry added to the corruption that had already begun with America's drift into oligarchy; but to many American Jews (and Christians) it seemed but one more unfathomable event that began with the Holocaust. The rich and powerful organizations of the American Jewish establishment—the ADL, the Simon Wiesenthal Center and the American Jewish Congress in particular—now identify with their own corruption. This was the inevitable result of the impunity the US political class granted not only Israel, but the Israel Lobby in America. And why did the political class give the Israel Lobby in the US this impunity? Not because of any moral or political principle, or to protect any discernible US interests, but because America's politicians in Congress want to receive the money of the American Israel Public Affairs Committee (AIPAC) to conduct their electoral campaigns.

Therefore one might think that thoughtful Jews would be thankful for Finkelstein's exposure of the fraud and greed so typical of the Holocaust Industry's activities in Europe. But breaking a trauma bond is not that easy for those who do not have Finkelstein's hard and tragic vision. As Freud learned long ago, the attempt to neutralize the influence of past trauma will be resisted as though it were death itself. Driven by the hostile mechanisms of the victim-aggressor, and the arrogance of those whose crimes and misdemeanors are given impunity, the Jewish cultural and political elites have been corrupted, a corruption aided by the pre-existing corruption of the Christian elites. Perhaps many people within the organized Jewish community assume that perhaps such corruption is the inevitable result— and price—of gaining power. But that kind of self-exculpation is exactly the ideology of bondage to organized aggression.

Given what has happened to them in the past, Jews must have

power to protect themselves. The problem is that bad leaders have chosen the wrong kind of power; and those same leaders all too often use the Holocaust to make money and get power for themselves. The price of that kind of corruption is too high, and the form of the corruption too pathological, and in addition too dangerous for the world. Neo-Zionism and the destructive hysteria of its attendant religious nationalism are the ultimate False Messiah. Thus ordinary Jews must begin to talk about what has happened to them, and look for a better way. Interestingly, Finkelstein has found such a way, a way to break the trauma bond and beat the Holocaust. And it's a way out not just for him but for Jews, Palestinians, the Americans, and everybody else.

20.

So how does one break the trauma bond, and beat the Holocaust?

The reader will remember that there are two steps (a 'recovery dualism') this book suggests for recovery from traumatic memory, and the aggression contained in it. **First, one must talk about what happened**. In most cases, this will mean talking in a clinical setting, where a trained counselor, psychiatrist or psychologist can help the individual process his or her emotions. But it can also mean talking or writing about the traumatic memory in ways that are considered taboo by the aggrieved group, or by the rest of society. Maryla Husyt Finkelstein raised this process to the next level by making connections between the aggression embedded in her traumatic memory, and the unacceptable imperial aggression she saw in the world around her. Norman Finkelstein adopted this same method, instinctively using whatever intergenerational trauma he had internalized as a yardstick for the systemic evil he saw around him, and interrogated it—as his mother had—in the present moment. But it all began with speaking about the unspeakable. That lesson Norman Finkelstein learned well from his mother.

Secondly, one should engage in a socially-beneficial

activity—and if possible, that activity should in some way oppose the social dynamics that set in motion the original trauma. Finkelstein sees the oppression of the Palestinians, and the torture, murder and collective punishment that circumscribes their lives, as very similar to the horrors experienced by Jews in Europe. But it is a bit more than that. It is the theory of this book that the brutality that Israelis use in dealing with Palestinians is a *direct result* of their experiences in Europe. The Zionists thought they had left behind a thousand years of anti-Semitism, but instead they had internalized that same anti-Semitism, and then brought it with them to the Middle East to act out against the Palestinians, their fellow Semites from whom they took the land for their new country.

Finkelstein has found a way out not just for him, but for all Jews; and—I would argue—for all people. He has found a way to break the trauma bond created by the Holocaust, which bonds people to the aggressive emotional orientation at the heart of traumatic memory. The Palestinians are the most prominent current victims of something that began with Christian anti-Semitism sixteen centuries ago, acted out in a chain of anti-Semitic events against Jews that culminated in the Holocaust, which in turn caused its traumatized survivors to create the state of Israel. Israeli apartheid—and the torture, murder and collective punishment of the Palestinians—is an expression of the aggression of the Holocaust internalized by its Jewish victims; it is a further expression of the same patriarchy, militarism, racism and aggression that originally caused the Holocaust. Furthermore, it was the *traumatic privilege* of their internalized aggression that caused them to believe they had the right to ethnically cleanse the Palestinians in the first place.

Israel has fought ten bloody wars, all conflicts made inevitable by the ethnic cleansing of the Palestinians. To deconstruct the traumatic memory of the Holocaust in the present moment, one has also to deconstruct the added trauma of aggression against and by the Palestinians, because these various traumas have become conflated and intermingled, and they to some extent potentiate each other. Because of this conflation, Jews will not be free of the trauma created by the Holocaust until they can see the Palestinians as human beings like themselves, people who were also victims of circumstances, people whose only crime in the Neo-Zionist scheme of things is that they have the wrong religion and the wrong ethnicity, and who (like most Jews) do not consciously wish to be either victims or executioners. Jews will be free of the trauma of the Holocaust only when they stop traumatizing Palestinians, and work with them to overcome their shared traumatic memory.

This means making big political changes in Israel. It means giving up the illegitimate power of the longest and most brutal military occupation in modern history. It means re-writing the Israeli legal codes to make Jews and Palestinians equal under the law, including the Palestinians' right to own property. It means understanding that the Israeli state is a government of both Jews and Palestinians, and not a 'Jewish State.' It means permitting Reform Judaism in Israel, instead of the regressive state-sponsored national-religious Judaism, with its exhortations to achieve salvation by killing Palestinians. It means making changes that the political class in Israel will oppose to its last breath. But all one's exhortations to brotherhood and sisterhood mean exactly nothing if such changes do not occur. Change may start with having the right feelings, but ultimately means having the right laws, and the right political strategies to get those laws.

Finkelstein's life and work is a good example of the 'recovery dualism' required to break free of shared traumatic memory. Individuals in an aggrieved group struggling with a shared traumatic memory seek to deconstruct the fears and anxieties they feel personally, but sense that there are larger social contradictions that exacerbate their personal struggle. The smart and courageous people in the aggrieved group then work to confront the social injustice that first generated the traumatizing events. The rape victim seeks personal relief through counseling, but makes progress more quickly if she works with other women to oppose patriarchy in society. The combat veteran can deconstruct the after-effects of war more quickly by advocating for proper treatment for all vets, and for a world without unnecessary wars. And so forth.

Victims may begin as individuals caught in a trauma bond, but gradually become aware that they must ameliorate and eventually abolish the social injustice that keeps the trauma alive. This is especially important in Israel, where traumatic memory of the Holocaust is deliberately exacerbated by the right-wing and religious parties that are in government, and whose aggressive ideas and rhetoric predominate in the political class. It is not something that Israeli Jews will do quickly on a mass basis, because people do not give up their bondage to past aggression easily, nor do people give up supremacy over other people without a struggle.

To some extent they must be forced to do so; and that begins with defeating their proxies in America—but Finkelstein made straight a path in the American wilderness for people to see not only the necessity of it, but the advantage of doing so. Jews do not need to love Palestinians, for love is overrated as a social motivator; what is both possible and necessary is to respect them as human beings with the same human rights as everybody else. This difficult process is necessary for Jews to jettison the traumatic memory they carry around inside themselves, because if they do not deconstruct the aggression that is at the heart of that traumatic memory, they will continue to act it out against the Palestinians, and against themselves.

For a thousand years Jews suffered the aggression of European Christians, and in making an adjustment to such an unremitting hatred, Jews have internalized many of the unresolved contradictions—much of the hate and aggression—of the Christians that oppressed them. Now they have redirected that same hatred and aggression against Palestinians. They do this, always, in the name of Israel's security. But Israeli Jews will never have security until the Palestinians have security.

And, Finkelstein says clearly, we must also confront corruption in America. Let's not forget the egregious way the Clinton administration used the collective power of the entire US government to help Bronfman and Singer get the billions they sought. Finkelstein, to his great credit, showed how this corruption at the center of American power also leads directly to Israel's torture, murder and collective punishment of Palestinians, and the reason why Americans support these crimes with the taxpayers' money. No man would dare to reveal such a thing, and incur such loathing and insults, if he did not love Jewish culture and American democracy much more than most.

Renegotiation of the power relationship with Palestinians is the key to deconstructing Jewish traumatic memory. The Palestinian, so feared and hated as the enemy in Israel, paradoxically holds the key to the Jewish future—not to be loved or hated, embraced or shunned, but simply to be a person (and to be recognized as a person) with the same legal rights as a Jew. That is the gut lesson of Finkelstein's work and life, acted out at such cost to his career. In addition Israeli Jews, as well as their proxies in the US, must reject the 'traumatic privilege' that arises from past victimization, which demagogues like Benyamin Netanyahu use to generate torture, murder and collective punishment of the Palestinian people. If Jews do not reject traumatic privilege, they will become hopelessly bonded to the past, and so enmeshed in fresh violence that the trauma bond to aggression will be virtually impossible to deconstruct. Traumatic privilege, if not challenged, will become—and has already in part become— destructive entitlement, which always results in self-destruction as well as sadism toward the perceived enemies of the state.

For showing the way, despite torrents of public calumny that would have driven a weaker person insane, Finkelstein has won a measure of immortality, not just as a prophetic intellectual and hard-working servant of humanity, not just as a fighter for truth who struggled against seemingly impossible odds, but as one who has become, despite his best efforts to adopt an outlaw stance, one of the great culture heroes of the modern American panorama.

When individual Jews renegotiate their relationship to Palestinians, it becomes the definitive argument against the aggression and narcissism of religious nationalism. But the greatest power of this process is that by negotiating with the Palestinians, and acknowledging their right to self-determination, it can release Jewry from the traumatic memory of Hitler's nightmare, and begin to dissolve the trauma bond created by the Holocaust. The Jews of the world will then have begun the painful process necessary to deconstruct forever the aggression they internalized during the moral collapse of Europe. When Jews look in the mirror and see a Palestinian who has the same human rights as a Jew, Judaism will finally have won the war the anti-Semites unleashed against it so long ago in Europe.

Chapter Three

The Eric Lomax Story: Breaking the Trauma Bond of Torturer and Victim

1.

Eric Lomax was a young British soldier who was taken prisoner after the fall of Singapore in February, 1942, at which time he became a POW of the Japanese Imperial Army. He was brutally tortured for a week by the agents of the Kempeitai, Imperial Japan's equivalent of the Nazi Gestapo, and was forced to stand by helplessly while two of his friends were beaten to death. The traumatic memories of these experiences—as well as certain things that happened during the torture that Lomax couldn't bring himself to remember—made Lomax's life a living hell, as the memories over time became more disabling than the torture itself. In time it interfered with everything in his life, including his marriage to a vivacious and intelligent woman whom he loved dearly.

He was never able to talk to anybody about being tortured; and because of that, the traumatic memories had gradually taken over his consciousness. He realized that decisive action was necessary to save his marriage, not to mention his sanity. It was for this reason that Eric Lomax found it necessary, some fifty years after he was brutally tortured, to talk to the man that had tortured him.

How could such a thing be imagined, much less carried out? Two seemingly unrelated factors conspired to bring it about. Through what seemed like pure chance, Eric Lomax discovered the name of his torturer; and he also—again, seemingly by chance—found out where this man was living in Japan. The second factor was the acute insight of his wife, Patti, into Eric's agonizing dilemma, and her steadfast conviction that they must

188

do everything possible to find a solution, and do it together. What was at stake was not only Eric's mental health, but their marriage.

For his part, Eric Lomax wanted desperately to overcome the traumatic memories that kept him awake at night and threatened to destroy everything good in his life; but how was he to do that? If he went to Japan, took the law into his own hands, and retaliated against the man who tortured him, he would spend the rest of his life in prison. Yet the memories of his ordeal would not go away. Once he found out where his former torturer could be found in Japan, Lomax felt a growing compulsion to act.

2.

As a young Scottish boy living in the 1930s, Eric Lomax was fascinated—in fact he was obsessed—with trains and railroads. Lomax says that the modern word 'trainspotter' was not one he had ever heard in those days, or ever used; yet he wrote that "steam engines occupied most of my free hours between 1933 and the moment when I volunteered for the army in 1939. I read histories of engineering, of companies that were long gone even then, haunting the second-hand bookstores around George IV Bridge in Edinburgh and finding beautiful old books on railways that I could buy for a penny each."

Even his holidays at school were spent traveling around Britain in pursuit of the unalloyed thrill of observing the largest and most powerful steam engines ever constructed, and seeing them tear ahead at full speed. "I didn't just sit and dream about trains, but traveled to look and see, waiting on cold embankments and cuttings in the hope of catching a glimpse of some rare and famous locomotive. I thought nothing of riding fifteen or twenty miles on my bike to watch an engine hammer past on a rural line, and turning around to ride back to my parents' house as happy as though I had seen a girlfriend."

It is therefore beyond irony that this young train enthusiast would end up, along with untold thousands of other British POWs, being sent by the Imperial Japanese as slave laborers to build the notorious Burma-Siam railway, still known to many as the Railway of Death. Tens of thousands of POWs and Asian laborers perished there of starvation and exhaustion under horrific conditions.

Soon after war was declared in 1939 Lomax volunteered for the Royal Corps of Signals, which recruited directly from the Post Office Telephones where Eric worked. (In that manner he avoided the drilling and weapons training known in the US as 'basic training.') Eric soon applied for a commission, and was sternly reminded that the life expectancy of a second lieutenant in the Great War had been two weeks. Perhaps there was an element of reverse psychology in this warning, for in the event he persisted, was given officer's training, and eventually mobilized in Scarborough in North Yorkshire on the North Sea coast, en route to posting in India.

Nobody was supposed to know when they left, but family and friends appeared from nowhere before dawn on the day of departure to see the boys off. It was an uncanny and unexpectedly emotional scene, as parents whispered gaily in the pre-dawn gloom, striving valiantly to appear cheerful and encouraging, as both they and the sons they were seeing off faced an increasingly dark future. Eric caught a glimpse of his mother trying desperately to smile; although he could not know it then, it was the last time he would ever see her.

Once in India, Eric settled into a "passable imitation of the Indian Army Officer's life in Rawalpindi," as he put it in his book *The Railway Man: A POW's Searing Account of War, Brutality and Forgiveness*.[1] Rawalpindi was the largest permanent garrison of the British Army, and had been since 1851; Lomax kept himself busy lecturing on telecommunications to audiences of mixed officers and enlisted men. Ultimately he was transferred to Singapore, where one of his commanding officers mentioned that

British troops might be required to fight the armies of Imperial Japan. But their combined British forces would quickly defeat them, the officer added cheerfully, by the convenient expedient of fighting only at night—luckily for the British, this officer said, the Japanese soldiers all suffered from incurable night blindness!

Lomax ended up at Fort Canning, General Percival's office in Singapore City, where they soon discovered that the highly disciplined and combat-hardened Japanese soldiers were formidable enemies. After three weeks of heavy fighting, Singapore fell; the mainly disarmed British troops were ordered to walk to Changi, where the first stories of Japanese atrocities toward prisoners began to circulate. Six of Lomax's brother officers were shot dead on the beach when most of the men refused to sign 'no-escape' clauses; as a result of this and other atrocities, the men eventually signed them. Not long afterwards Lomax was taken with a detachment of others to Ban Pong, Thailand, which was to be the central location for Imperial Japan's efforts to build a vast new rail system that was intended to become the Burma-Siam railroad. Eric Lomax was assigned with several others to a separate workshop for repairing the track-laying equipment.

Eric ended up in one of the repair shops. Food was barely sufficient in the workshop at Ban Pang; but he quickly became aware that working conditions further up the line were not merely appalling but literally murderous, since there was progressively less food available the further one traveled toward the actual track-laying. "The track-laying gangs were thus unknowingly working themselves to death," he wrote in *The Railway Man*. "This is brutally heavy work: exhausted and ill-fed city boys and dragooned Asian laborers did not have a chance. Rest periods were rare, and any slackening was met with abuse or violence." (About 90,000 Asian laborers and 16,000 POWs would eventually die working on the railway.)

The horror of the Burma railway would be immortalized by Pierre Boulle in his book *The Bridge on the River Kwai*, a fictionalized and greatly sanitized version which was eventually made into an extremely popular film. In reality, the bridge—and the entire Burma-Siam rail project—was a meaningless waste of life, much of the railroad turning out to be so badly constructed that it wasn't even appropriate for commercial traffic, and in any case it was never connected to rail lines in Burma. The Burma-Siam railway was, as Eric Lomax wrote, "not only the last cruel enterprise of the railway age, but the worst civil engineering disaster in history."

The hunger for information among British POWs was enormous, given that the men were being held virtually incommunicado in a part of the world completely unlike anything they'd experienced before. Therefore it was natural that some began to laboriously construct small and extremely primitive radios that could receive All-India Radio located in New Delhi. Driven by a collective desire to know about the progress of the war, many prisoners worked together to build the receivers. (Someone had been prescient enough to smuggle in parts sufficient for the creation of a headphone—other prisoners had brought with them parts that might aid in constructing a radio. Prisoners even traded stolen Japanese tools with a local trader for needed valves.) Lomax compared it to "reinventing wireless telegraphy," as they scoured the slim pickings in their tropical prison camp for the needed materials. Sergeant-Major Lance Thew had owned a radio shop back in Sunderland in north-east England, so it was quite natural that he became the main radio-maker. A 'quarter-wave' aerial was hidden in the rafters of his hut, since a full-length antenna was out of the question.

Lomax writes of their eventual success: "We arranged a security system in the main hut. POWs apparently engaged in reading or doing their woodwork were stationed in strategic places, on the lookout for guards, while Thew worked in his bed-space with assistance from the others. We finished one night, and Thew crawled under his blankets and tuned in his primitive detector. He had a pencil in his hand, I remember, and he emerged smiling from ear to ear with some scribbled notes. It had worked beautifully. He had heard the crisply modulated English voice of the announcer cutting through the static." From then on, Thew would take on the task of listening for news of the war each night, assembling his tiny radio before each listening session and dissembling it afterwards, as all the while POWs kept up a careful watch for Japanese guards.

Eric Lomax was one of the people involved in this collective project. Once the receiver was operating, Thew would crawl under his blankets and listen for news of the war, and then report to others what he'd heard. It was a way of creating a connection to the world they'd left behind them when they were sent to this distant outpost of Japan in Thailand; most importantly, it gave them information about the progress of the war they'd never have had access to otherwise.

Early in February, 1943, the British POWs at Ban Pong learned that they were to be moved to Kanchanaburi—or 'Kanburi', as the English-speaking prisoners called it—as the entire railway-building project moved north. As before, the prisoners' job at Kanchanaburi was the mechanical upkeep of equipment necessary for building the new railroad, especially lorries needed for transporting track-laying equipment. Here Eric Lomax came in contact with the prisoners to whom he would become closest. Major Jim Slater was now the camp's highest-ranking British POW; Alexander Morton Mackay, another Scot, became a trusted friend. Two others were Jack Hawley, a scholarly man from Ireland, and Lieutenant Stanley Armitage, "a man who enjoyed the clubs and the ease of pre-war Singapore, where he had worked for the British American Tobacco Company."

It was an unlikely collection of men in this isolated corner of Asia, but thanks to their radio they were acutely aware of the progress of the war, and all were concerned with achieving some level of ongoing sabotage against the enemy. They were, after all, engaged in building a major railway for the Imperial Japanese Army. So while their immediate goal was sabotage, they were equally concerned that it should be the kind of sabotage that would not be immediately noticeable, but nonetheless effective over the long run.

"In the workshops, we found subtle ways of keeping overworked lorries in apparently good mechanical condition, but with an unfortunate tendency to break down a week after they left our hands," Lomax wrote in *The Railway Man*. "I was learning the arts of subterfuge and quiet resistance, and I was becoming a competent thief." Lomax was assigned the job of camp timekeeper, and he contrived new ways of making the regular ten-hour working day consist of less than ten hours. "More than anything else, we wanted to delay [the Japanese], to hinder their efforts, to do shoddy work in such a way that the origin of the nuisance could not be traced back to one man or group. Even people who were working on tasks like stone-breaking—which was considered a 'light' job—would work unbelievably slowly, giving the absolute minimum of co-operation."

Interestingly, Lomax wrote that every prisoner became a slacker and a saboteur, adding that "of course some of us are doing it to this day, having spent so much time creating quiet havoc in our early manhood." But the most ferocious havoc would be the kind visited upon the prisoners by their Japanese captors, as we will see.

The hope of escape never quite disappeared among the POWs at Kanburi. But there was no easy way out of the north of Thailand, where they were being held; and certainly not the remotest hope of organizing an escape without a good map. Eric therefore set himself the ambitious but dangerous task of creating a first-rate map of that part of Asia. "I took a large sheet of plain paper, over two-feet square, from the chief engineer's desk. In the storehouse I noticed a small atlas that included much of South

East Asia and Siam; I 'borrowed' it and slowly copied the relevant pages with a pencil, working on a scale of about 50 miles to the inch. It was too small for practical purposes really, but it gave me such hope as I filled in details gleaned from POW lorry drivers who had been some distance up the railway, and memorized topographic facts from Japanese plans and documents left lying around the stores."

Once again a secret radio was carefully constructed, Lance Thew now aided by Fred Smith, who had smuggled radio parts with him from Changi. "It was still the same ritual every night: the tense guard around the hut, Thew huddled under his blanket, the earnest discussion of the news afterwards." News from the BBC received on their primitive receiver was supplemented by bush telegraph, which not only informed POWs in the repair shops at Kanburi but also carried news to those suffering and dying further up the track. "The news was passed along by trusted men, through hundreds of different mouths, around the workshop compound and up the miles of railway track to the real death camps." One man was regularly briefed on the latest news and tasked with making sure it got up the line to the north. "Who knows how the news was distorted as it went along, how truth became legend and vice versa; but having these scraps of information was a wonderful boost to our morale and to our sense of connection with the world we had lost. The radio meant more to prisoners than anyone can imagine: it literally gave meaning and normality to our lives; now we felt we knew what we were living for."

While at Kanburi, Lomax witnessed over a period of months the advance guard of 'F' and 'H' forces, exhausted and demoralized British forces that had been selected to go directly to the track-laying areas up north. "'F' and 'H' Forces had the highest casualty rates of all the POW drafts on the railway. They were to give the work a final boost, to complete the line earlier than planned—a kind of expendable shock force." Eric and the other prisoners tried to get food and water to them, but their fate was already sealed; and indeed as Lomax wrote later, one in three of them would perish, and a great many of the rest would be incapacitated for the rest of their lives by lingering injuries or debilitating tropical illness. The brutality of the conditions seemed consciously intended simply to kill or injure those laboring on the railway. Eric Lomax and his comrades already knew that Admiral Yamamoto, the strategist of the attack on Pearl Harbor, had been shot down in the Solomon Islands. Was it partly retaliation for that, they wondered among themselves, that was spurring the cruelty of the Japanese?

Mountbatten, who eventually became the Supreme Allied Commander in Asia, believed that Japanese soldiers were so brutal to their POWs because of the Japanese warrior code: because the British had chosen to surrender rather than die fighting, they were therefore deemed unworthy of respect. But that seemingly reasonable theory doesn't explain the sadism of Japanese soldiers during the Rape of Nanking (or Nanjing, as it is now called), since their brutality was mainly acted out against civilians; arguably, much of the brutality throughout the areas that the Imperial Japanese Army controlled was motivated by an imperial intent to condition soldiers to act with utter sadism in their behavior toward all identified as 'enemies,' POWs, civilians and combat soldiers alike. The ruling classes of Japan at that time were under the influence of a violent kind of ultra-nationalism, and deliberately inculcated fanaticism and extreme cruelty in their soldiers (and in fact in the Japanese population at large) in much the same way that the Nazis consciously sought to inculcate cruelty and fanaticism in the German people.

It is notable that both Japanese and German cultures stressed the importance of not questioning authority; both countries had a warrior class that was deeply admired and perceived as being above the ordinary rules of civil society; and the Japanese were led by a Sun-God Emperor who was supposedly divine, or the descendant of divine beings. As part of a conscious plan by Japan's leadership class, these factors were used to create a generation of Japanese soldiers who were to a large extent morally depraved, men who did not hesitate to kill civilians on command or torture their prisoners of war; or—as in the case of Nanjing—to engage in mass rape and sexualized torture of civilians for sport. The gradual breakdown of discipline that normally accompanies military setbacks could not help but make this ingrained aggression worse.

Memories of a youth spent studying—and watching—the great railroad trains of Britain and Europe came gloriously alive for Eric Lomax for a moment, as the Japanese brought up a new locomotive to test the track that their slave laborers were laying. Amazingly, Eric saw that this locomotive was a "beautifully preserved, turn of the century machine built by Krauss of Munich, its origin described on a magnificent black plate. I remember the joy of its sudden appearance on that dusty and degraded siding under the palm trees." A moment later, he felt intense guilt for the pleasure that the sight of this classic locomotive gave him, because he was in a place of so much suffering—but the suffering Eric Lomax would soon personally endure would exceed even that experienced by men working further up on the Railway of Death. His Japanese warders had discovered the camp radio, and partly because of his background in the Royal Corps of Signals he quickly became one of the main suspects.

3.

After roll call on August 29th, 1943, the Japanese guards forced the entire camp to stand at attention while they spent the morning going through the huts. The atmosphere was tense: clearly the Japanese guards were looking for something specific. Sure enough, the Japanese found Lance Thew's radio—and they also found three other small radios as well, carefully constructed imitations of Thew's original creation. When the prisoners were dismissed, they silently went back to work, unable to imagine what would come next. Understandably, few slept well that night, as the entire camp waited for the other shoe to fall. Next morning Lance Thew and another soldier were summoned by the Japanese Camp Commander, who punished them in various ways before sending them for interrogation at Kanburi.

"It is impossible to describe the emotional state of POWs at a time like this," Lomax writes, "as retribution gathered momentum. Work and feeding went on as if nothing had happened, but there was everywhere a desperate haunting fear, superimposed on the normal perpetual uncertainty which filled the mind of every prisoner." Soon word came from Kanburi that Thew had been beaten mercilessly. Eric's friend Fred Smith soon followed, and was made to stand at attention for four days. There were also stories of several POWs being shot out of hand, supposedly for trying to escape.

Throughout this time Eric Lomax had a secret: the intricate map of the area that he'd been working on sporadically still hadn't been found: "It was now rolled up in a hollow bamboo tube in the back wall of our latrine behind the hut. It represented, I supposed, a slim chance—a remote glimmer of hope. It was the only carefully drawn general map of the area in the hands of any prisoner, as far as I knew, and I kept it in case we needed to run for it, in case we needed to set out on that thousand-mile walk to the Burma Road. And it was a beautifully drawn map."

This map was to be Lomax's undoing. Seven officers, including Eric Lomax, were caught in the dragnet, and removed from the camp for further questioning on September 21. In an act of desperate hope (and spectacularly bad judgment) he decided to take his beautiful map along with him. As Lomax remembered it later, he was convinced that they might soon face a firing squad, and reasoned that if they ran for it they'd have little chance of the long trek to freedom without a map. That much is true, but what are the chances, really, of successfully making a break for it when being taken to the killing field?

The image of the last-minute jailbreak is the recurrent fantasy of men facing the hangman's noose or the firing squad; it was only much later that Lomax regained his perspective sufficiently to realize that the chances of interrogation and a thorough search were much more likely than instant death, if for no other reason than that his captors wanted more information for their reports. He slipped his precious map into his canvas kitbag, concealed in a leather case with some Signal Corps instruments; it was almost guaranteed to be found in the inevitable search of personal belongings, as indeed it was. The only redeeming aspect of this dizzying sequence of events was Lomax's memory of the camp inmates standing to salute the seven departing officers as they were taken away.

First they were taken to a main military camp at Kanburi, where they were searched and made to stand at attention for long periods. Then the beatings started, beginning with Major Smith and Eric's friend Morton Mackay. "To have to witness the torture of others and to see the preparations for the attack on one's own body is a punishment in itself, especially when there is no escape. This experience is the beginning of a form of insanity." Then came Lomax's turn, an entire team of soldiers using pickaxe-shafts. "I felt myself plunging downwards into an abyss with tremendous flashes of solid light which burned and agonized. I could identify the periodic stamping of boots on the back of my head, crunching my face into the gravel; the crack of bones snapping; my teeth breaking; and my own involuntary attempts to respond to deep vicious kicks and to regain an upright position, only to be thrown to the ground once more."

"I do know that I thought I was dying. I have never forgotten, from that moment onwards, crying out 'Jesus,' crying out for help, the utter despair of helplessness. I rolled into a deep ditch of foul stagnant water which, in the second or two before consciousness was finally extinguished, flowed over me with the freshness of a pure and sweet spring."

Somehow he did not drown in the water-filled ditch, probably because his captors pulled him out for more torture. "I awoke and found myself standing on my feet. I do not recall crawling out of that ditch but the sun was already up. I was an erect mass of pain, of bloody contusions and damaged bones, the sun playing harshly on inflamed nerves. Smith and Slater were lying on the ground beside me, blackened, covered in blood and barely conscious." Lomax joined his associates on the ground shortly, unable to stand. Around noon the camp interpreter sent for a bucket of tea to revive them. Apart from one attempt by the camp commandment to force them to stand—which they were unable to do in any case—they were left to lie in the dirt all day and all night.

The next morning something odd happened, a detail that stuck in Lomax's memory. A young Japanese interpreter approached the brutally-beaten Eric Lomax and said in pompous but half-respectful way, "You are very brave men—yes, indeed, you are very brave men."

Eric Lomax was taken to the camp's makeshift hospital, where he was treated by a doctor who was a Dutch POW. "For my part, both my forearms were broken and several of my ribs were cracked. One hip was clearly damaged. There did not seem to be any skin on my back. What astonished even the doctor was that there was not a single patch of white skin visible between my shoulders and my knees, down both sides of my chest, hips and legs. Most of the skin was in place, but it had turned a uniform blue-black, swollen and puffy, like velvet in texture. I was in such pain I could not begin to locate its source. The four others were in as bad a condition; everyone had broken ribs; but by some chance I was the only one with fractured limbs." Eric's broken bones were set, the bone-setting being done entirely without anesthetic since there was none available for prisoners. Lomax remembered that the pain from the beating was so great that he hardly noticed the additional pain from the bone-setting.

In time they heard four more British officers from their camp—Hawley, Armitage, Gilchrist and a fourth officer Lomax didn't know—being brought and forced to stand at attention all day in the sun. That night, at exactly 10 PM, the beatings with pickax handles began, ultimately lasting all night. The next morning, their POW doctor discovered that he could do nothing to help Hawley and Armitage. In an act that was typical of Imperial Japan's loathing for its perceived enemies, as well as its own moral and spiritual degradation, the Imperial Japanese soldiers did not take the time to bury the two dead British POWs. Instead they simply took away their bloodied bodies and flung them down a deep latrine.

Lomax and the other officers were in such debilitating pain it was almost impossible to process what was happening. Lomax and his brother officers were experiencing physical and emotional trauma, drifting in and out of consciousness. During moments of lucid thought, Lomax could concentrate on little more than fear of what might come next. One morning some Japanese officials arrived with some personal items belonging to Lomax and his brother officers. When Lomax went through his kit, he discovered that all his belongings were there, with one disturbing exception: his carefully-drawn map was gone.

4.

The Japanese no doubt assumed that every officer in the prison camp had guilty knowledge of the proscribed radios, and to a great extent the beatings were by way of punishing them for their assumed complicity. To be sure, torture in war is often administered to gather intelligence, but even more often to get prisoners to sign confessions to specific acts of which their captors already believe them to be guilty. But any close study of torture will reveal that obtaining actionable intelligence is usually second to simply administering pain. The reality is that much modern torture, like much of the torture administered in the Spanish Inquisition, is simply a form of state terrorism focused mainly on deterrence. The object is to create a paralyzing fear of the consequences that would arise from future disobedience, and by that means to generate a state of absolute mental and emotional submission. (During the Spanish Inquisition the required submission was to the Church, today to the armed state.) It also sends the message that aggression is the highest and most authentic form of power; this is something that the people that authorize torture already believe, and which they attempt to impose on others in a variety of ways, including aggression in the form of agonizing pain.

Why did the Japanese interpreter go out of his way to compliment Lomax on his bravery? Most likely as a way of softening up his resistance to torture. In effect, he was saying, "You have demonstrated what a brave man you are; and as a fellow soldier I appreciate bravery. Therefore, why don't we take the next step and help each other?" Perhaps to some extent the interpreter really felt like encouraging his victim—in fact, everything that we will learn about him later suggests that he may indeed have felt pity for him. Nonetheless, in most instances, this kind of momentary friendliness, when accompanied by the suggestion of underlying mutual interests, is usually used by the torturer to subtly suggest compliance as an honorable way to end the agony of the torture. Lomax was himself aware that the alternation of aggression and kindness was a way of creating a feeling of emotional ambiguity, "of keeping a prisoner off-balance," as he put it later in his own account.

The interspersing of aggression with kindness is to the interrogatories of power, whether legitimate or illegitimate, what the King's Pawn Opening is to chess—its use is omnipresent because it works so well, and its results are predictable. It plays on the utter dissimilarity of the two most powerful of all human emotional orientations, aggression and kindness. The Argentine editor and writer Jacobo Timerman, who was tortured by the Argentine military, writes of how his interrogation proceeded: "A brief pause. And then words of hope. A brief pause. And then insults. A brief pause. And then questions."[2] The mental and emotional disorientation produced by the alternation of kindness, when followed by terrifying and threatening insults, and then mind-numbing pain, can be overwhelming.

The fluctuation between seeming kindness and physical aggression reaches heights of pathology—not to mention the most brutal criminal behavior imaginable—in 'battered woman syndrome.' Almost all writers on this subject mention the manner in which intermittent kindness and cruelty is used by the battering spouse, and the enormous emotional disorientation this creates in the victim. (A kind of disorientation, by the way, that greatly strengthens the trauma bond created by the abuser's violence.) The apparent kindness of the abuser, and the fact that he can go for long periods without abusing, causes the victim to identify with the good times, rather than the bad ones. But abusers almost always go back to systematic violence if they think they can get away with it, no matter how long they have refrained before.

Finally, one must mention the manner in which hostages in hostage situations often identify with all manner of small kindness by their captors—a psychological reality that can lead to an intense identification with the hostage-taker. Torturers are also likely to use the rapid alternation of extreme cruelty and contempt with seemingly kind comments, and even kind gestures, such as pausing in the torture to offer the victim a cigarette. Even if they do not identify with the torturer, victims *will* internalize the aggression they have endured, and whatever they can remember of the torturer can quite easily come to represent all that was most excruciating in the experience— indeed, how could torture victims survive psychologically *without* internalizing some of the aggression they experienced in such a situation? The greater danger, as with all victims of aggression, is that having internalized such toxic aggression they will act it out later, often against themselves but sometimes also against the people they love.

5.

Before dawn on October 7, 1943, officers of the Kempeitai, Imperial Japan's equivalent to the Nazi Gestapo (referred to as 'Kempei' in British POW slang) appeared at the hospital hut to pick up the four prisoners. Eric Lomax had both broken arms in stiff splints, so his belongings were rounded up by his friend Morton Mackay. They were driven out of the camp to a street that ran parallel to the Mae Klong River, where they were hustled into what turned out to be the local Kempei headquarters. They were put into small cells, each about five feet long, not quite three feet wide and less than five feet high. Each prisoner was allowed one blanket each, something to drink from and whatever they happened to be wearing. Lomax was just able to lie down diagonally in the cell, but large red ants crawled over him which he was unable to brush away, because his arms were immobilized.

Lomax thought later that the interrogation started after a full day and night. He was taken to a dimly-lit room where he was questioned by a Japanese Army NCO, assisted by the same youthful but frail-looking interpreter who had spoken to him before. The interpreter, who had the rank of private, spoke in what Lomax recalled as "a heavily-accented, uncertain but quite fluent English." The NCO informed his prisoner at the outset that he would be executed, but suggested that if he immediately confessed to everything it would go easier for him. The NCO "spoke, or rather shouted in a series of short barks, and the small man began his task of translation. Their styles of delivery were, and remained almost to the end, very different: the NCO relishing his own aggression, assuming my guilt and utter worthlessness in the contemptuous way he put his questions, the younger man speaking like a mechanical conversational voice doing its duty, with almost no inflection or interest."

Since Lomax was the only Royal Signals officer in the nearby POW camps, he was not surprised that they were suspicious of him, and was certain from the beginning that he would ultimately be executed. Clearly they suspected him not only of leading "anti-Japanese" activities in the camps, but of somehow being in touch with allied forces coordinating resistance activity in the area. "They hammered away at this endlessly, and I could see that for them I was a piece in some crazed jigsaw puzzle that linked Singapore, Malaya, Thailand and elsewhere—wherever they were having trouble or there was resistance to their occupation. I knew that to give even the appearance of having such contacts would be absolutely fatal; and of course we had none."

Lomax was forced to give a detailed account of his family history, the absurdity of which did not escape him. "Here I was, trying to explain the migrations of my Lancastrian and Scottish ancestors to a couple of uncomprehending Japanese men in a Siamese village." They even forced him to discuss his passion for trains and railways as a young man. Then they moved on to Lomax's thoughts about the course of the war in which they were all involved. Who would win the war? Why? Where will the allied landings be? There were many other questions of that nature.

Lomax found himself identifying with the interpreter, and hoping that this younger man might be as frightened of the NCO who shouted questions as he was. At times he found himself believing—or hoping against hope—that there was an undercurrent of shared values between them. "There was something earnest and studious about the young interpreter, something in the way he seemed to relish—or was I imagining this?—our exchanges about British life and culture. I found it hard to tell because I loathed his endless sing-song questions, his dreadful persistence and smug virtuous complicity with what they were putting me through; I was beginning to feel that he and I had been in this room for months."

"But I asked him anyway to tell me something about the Japanese educational system during some exchanges about my own education, to which they had returned, as though the clue to the crumbling of their imperial ambitions could be found in the teaching of the Royal High School. He volunteered some account of his own schooling, and we had an interesting little chat about language teaching. At that moment, and there were others, he became a hated intimate, a sort of lifeline—simply because we could share a language and a moment of curiosity about each other."

The NCO interrogator would ask questions related to English-language bulletins put out by the Japanese, suddenly inter-spersing them with nonsense questions such as, "Do you enjoy eating rice?" Lomax could tell that they were cross-referencing many of his answers with information they had already gotten from interrogations of other prisoners, especially Lance Thew, the POW who had constructed the first radio in the prison camp. This brought about a slip in which they revealed that both Fred Smith and Lance Thew were still alive, and being held in the same building. Lomax gradually began to get an idea of how much information they already had, and what that information was. "Where I knew they knew something, I gave them straight-forward corroboration, but of course this in turn allowed them to produce a list of apparent discrepancies between my version and previous version of events, and so it started all over again."

This followed the usual course of such interrogations—but of course both prisoner and interrogator were aware that the Kempeitai was not getting what it wanted: irrevocable proof of a conspiracy of resistance, directed from outside but extending throughout the prisoner-of-war camps. The truth—that the building of radios was more the natural result of curiosity about the course of the war than resistance directed from outside—was something the Kempeitai did not seriously consider.

Specifically, the Kempeitai was obsessed with the notion that the POWs had in some manner constructed a transmitter, despite the fact that it could not have been made from a receiver. "I was floundering in the gap between their knowledge and mine, and was suddenly the victim of my whole upbringing and culture; for my interrogators were from a relatively backward society. It is hard to imagine this now, after half a century of astonishing technological development in Japan, but in 1943 the Japanese army was a technically primitive organization, reflecting in this the partly feudal state of its homeland. The two men sitting across the table from me simply did not know enough to judge what I was telling them, which was that the technical problems of making a transmitter were too great, and that no group of prisoners with the pathetic materials available to them could work a miracle."

At a certain point the burly NCO shouting questions seemed to grow suspicious of the slight interpreter: "The interpreter was simply meant to be a channel of communication, and when it got blocked or distorted the NCO would shout at him too. Although I felt that the interpreter was in some way a human being like me, I hated them both; hated the interpreter more, because it was his voice that grated on and that would give me no rest." But in due time the Kempeitai higher-ups brought in a new NCO to shout questions at the prisoner. "So far they had not laid a finger on me, but the endless disorienting abuse relayed by the impassive young man, the barrage of ludicrous questions, and the deprivation of sleep were bad enough. I sat hour after hour balancing my broken arms on my thighs, longing for rest. It all became a featureless blur, eighteen hours a day from what seemed like early in the morning till well after dark. Once or twice they woke me at night and brought me to the [interrogation] room. The endless wearisome repetition wore on and on. There was so little inflection in the interpreter's voice, [that] it filled my dreams with its flat repetitive questions."

When he could think at all, Eric's thoughts and fears focused on his interpreter, who inevitably became a malevolent representative of all that was tyrannical and brutal about Imperial Japan. This became even more toxic because he sensed a certain kindness and humanity in his interpreter, but one that was totally absorbed in the service of systemic evil. "I thought that I must be the first English person he had spoken to, after his training. His first interlocutor in another language a person he is helping to break down: would this make him feel proud? I hated him more and more. He was the one asking the questions, driving me on. I was sick of the sight of him, I would have killed him for his endless insistence, his boring mechanical curiosity about things I thought he would never understand." Eric Lomax was nearing a breaking point. He began to have religious dreams and visions, hearing voices from the Bible, William Blake and nursery rhymes.

"I remembered all that POW talk about the moment when you are absolutely doomed and you take one of them with you. It was easier said than done with two broken arms, but it came to me all the time now and I wanted to do it. It was the interpreter I would have tried to kill."

Lomax was caught in the worst dilemma a person in that situation could experience, which was to know how much to lie, and what kind of lies to tell. "I could not spin them a yarn, of course, or go into complete fantasy because I feared their violence when they found me out. I did not know for sure what they knew, only what they wanted to know; my task was to give them sufficient information to satisfy them without incriminating any other person. You have a fraction of a second in which to think up answers and I felt so close to disaster all the time, through one careless word."

"They wanted to know who our contacts were, how the information went up the railway, who we were buying parts from, so I would say that it was a man who wore a shirt without insignia so we could not tell what unit he was in; that it wasn't me who passed on the information, it was another soldier in another hut whose name I didn't know; that we left a note outside our hut and never saw who picked it up." This heightened desire not to incriminate anyone else and its concomitant shading of reality affected everything else in prison—Eric deliberately avoided communication with the British prisoner in the cell next to him, for example, since "the less we told each other the better we knew it would be."

The NCO who was questioning him was becoming increasingly aggressive. Lomax sensed that the interrogations were building to a climax. One day he was brought to the interrogation group to find that his carefully drawn map of the area lay on the table. Neither the NCO nor his young interpreter said anything. Instead they simply stood at the window with their backs to him. Lomax knew that today would be different than previous days.

"Then they turned and from both of them came a storm of fake anger. They had obviously known about it all along, but were now trying to shock me. This is a very good map… why did you make it? From where did you steal the paper, where did you get your information? There must be other maps from which you got your information… Where are they? Were you planning to escape on your own? With others? Who are they? And then they kept returning to one thing: who we were planning to meet up with, whether there were villagers who had promised to help us, whether we received instructions by wireless, whether any villagers had radios. Were you in contact with the Chinese? And so on."

It was on this day that the most severe torture began. It is not so much from the things done to generate pain that the harm is done, as Lomax describes it—it was the sense of utter helplessness, the belief that one is dying, and the nightmarish blurred memories that occur years or decades later. The worst thing about torture, in other words, is not the actions or the pain in themselves, but their affect on the personalities of victim and torturer. So one should describe what was done as objectively as possible, as Lomax himself did in his book *The Railway Man*, and simply go on to the rest of the story.

Lomax was suddenly grabbed by the NCO and dragged out of the interrogation room, with the interpreter walking quickly in close proximity, to translate the verbal abuse of the torturer. Quite simply, Lomax was taken into a room with a bathtub, and his head was shoved repeatedly under the water. (With both arms broken and still in splint, he was completely unable to defend himself.) This crude form of water torture, not unlike the water torture used by US troops during the American intervention during the Philippine-American War and later in the CIA black sites after 9/11, gives the victim the sensation of drowning—and in the case of torture in which one's head is shoved below water, the victim really *is* drowning: that is, he holds his breath as long as possible, until his lungs start to fill with water. But the sheer agony and panic comes from the process of asphyxiation.

There is a great deal of misinformation about the use of water torture. Americans are told that the water torture used during the administration of President George Bush generated pain because of "simulated drowning," as though it were a kind of trick or practical joke that deluded the victim into thinking he is drowning. This is not true. Water-boarding by CIA contract employees consisted of pouring water on a square cloth over the nose and mouth, which effectively blocks out the air. The immediate cause of pain in this kind of torture is *asphyxiation*— that is, the systematic cutting off of air when one is trying desperately to breath in oxygen. There is perhaps no other agony as horrifying as the deliberate asphyxiation—the cutting off of air— of a torture victim by a torturer. Eric Lomax had no clear memory of this experience, but was told about it later by British POWs who happened to witness some of it.

Lomax was then dragged out into the courtyard of the prison and tied to a bench on his back. He was then beaten relentlessly on all parts of his body, including his broken arms. All the time the little interpreter was whispering orders from the NCO, insisting that he tell them what they wanted to hear, the information about mass resistance in the prison camps that they were sure he possessed. The interpreter hovered at his shoulder. "Lomax, you will tell us. Then it will stop." The little interpreter even put his hand on his shoulder, or at least Lomax remembered it that way.

Now the NCO brought a hose and directed it at his face. "He directed the full flow of the now gushing pipe on to my nostrils and mouth at a distance of only a few inches. Water poured down my windpipe and throat and filled my lungs and stomach. The torrent was unimaginably choking. This is the sensation of drowning, on dry land, on a hot dry afternoon. Your humanity bursts from within you as you gag and choke. I tried very hard to will unconsciousness, but no relief came. He was too skilful to risk losing me altogether. When I was choking uncontrollably, the NCO took the hose away."

"The flat, urgent voice of the interpreter resumed above my head, speaking into my ear; the other man hit me with the branch on the shoulders and stomach a few more times. I had nothing to say; I was beyond invention. So they turned on the tap again, and again there was the nausea of rising water from inside my bodily cavity, a flood welling up from within and choking me." Lomax lost track of time. "They alternated beatings and half-drowning for I know not how long. No one was ever able to tell me how long all this lasted, and I have no idea whether it finished that day, or there was more the following day. I eventually found myself back in my cage. I must have been dragged there."

Two unexpected things happened during that sequence of

horrors. After it was over, Lomax remembers the Kempeitai NCO appearing at his cage to hand him a cup of warm milk. "This was an incredible delight," Lomax wrote, "but even at the time I knew it was not an act of kindness: it was a way of maintaining ambiguity, of keeping a prisoner off-balance." That was the first unusual event.

The second was a little different, because it was not something he could remember; but it did indeed happen to him, because it was witnessed by others. It seems, according to others in the Kempeitai compound, that at some point he had come so undone during the long days of torture that he had cried out for his mother. (This is not unusual in war—virtually all writers on the subject of war and combat report wounded and dying soldiers crying out for their mothers.) But Lomax was never able to remember doing that; and because he could not remember, he came to feel that he had lost something primal in his personality, lost some vital part of himself, whatever it is that gives people intentionality or control over their emotions, and over their memories.

Although his memory contained the sheer aggression of being tortured, and large parts of the pain, aggression and desperation, it wouldn't allow him to remember exactly how it had all happened in the later stages, and what he had said during the worst parts of it. He would never remember calling out for his mother, but would be informed about it much, much later, by POWs who were there at the Kempeitai station at the time he was being tortured. Although Eric Lomax was never sure how long the torture lasted, this phase of the torture seemed to have lasted about a week, every day long hours of torture by drowning, interspersed with repeated interrogation.

It was not long before all the British prisoners were told to get their gear together, because they were about to be moved from the compound at Kanchanaburi. One of Lomax's friends helped him into the waiting truck. The young interpreter who had been present during Eric's most agonizing hours of torture moved closer to him. "Keep your chin up," Eric heard him say.

"He stood there in the yard," Lomax wrote many years later, "a tiny figure standing among the larger regular soldiers. The truck pulled away."

But the overwhelming feelings of hate and fury would not be left behind so easily.

6.

First the prisoners were taken to Bangkok, where they were subjected to a rudimentary court-martial. Lance Thew and Fred Smith received 10 years each, and Eric Lomax and three of his comrades five years each. The prisoners were overjoyed—they had assumed that a firing squad awaited them, and with these sentences it was now established that they would apparently survive, barring some further disaster. From Bangkok there were transported 1200 miles to the Outram Road Gaol in Singapore, which had been the main civil prison in Singapore until the late 1930s. His cellmate was Fred Smith, "an uneducated working-class man, a 'rough diamond' in the language of the day, but in the situation we found ourselves in rank and class counted for nothing." Eric and Fred looked out for one another, and spoke in whispers on work detail and in their cell. The worst thing about this prison was the random violence of the Japanese guards, the lack of food and liquid, and the fact that some prisoners seemed to disappear without notice.

Because of the very small portions of food, most of the prisoners had been reduced to walking skeletons; furthermore, the men were ravaged by horrific skin diseases. Eric practiced driving up his pulse rate in order to be taken to the 'sick cells' for prisoners that were seriously ill. He became so successful at elevating his pulse rate that he was taken to the POW camp at Changi. When he woke up there he thought he had gone to heaven: "I was surrounded by the concerned and grinning faces of ragged British and Australian prisoners. My stretcher was the centre of caring bustle and activity and after a few minutes I was carried into the ground floor of a two-storey block which my bearers called HB. I was in the safest possible hands, in the care of sympathetic and supportive British and Australian servicemen. Then I began to cry, an uncontrollable cascade; tears of relief and joy."

There wasn't much food except rice (camp doctor Bon Rogers tried to get milk and the occasional egg to Lomax), but there were actual showers, toilets that really worked, and real beds with mattresses, sheets and pillows. Eric was reunited with comrades from Kanburi and rapidly got to know other prisoners there. He was painfully aware, however, that he was simply on medical leave from Outram Road and could be returned there at any time. According to what Lomax was hearing (somebody at Changi had access to a radio, although Lomax was careful not to ask about it) the Axis powers were clearly losing the war. Now fears of an unknown future took a new form: what would the Japanese do when they realized they were losing? In the chaos that would inevitably accompany such a defeat, might not the Japanese high command — or individual commanders in the field — be tempted to retaliate by punishing or systematically killing off British POWs?

The end was closer than Lomax or any of the others POWs could imagine. Word among the prisoners was that the Nazi armies in Europe were almost defeated, and Rangoon had been taken from the Japanese. On the other hand, POWs were oppressively aware that there were also rumors of trenches being dug nearby by their captors, as though in preparation for mass murders. In August the camp doctor, Bon Rogers, gathered the prisoners around him in the infirmary to impart some unbelievable news. "He said that a new type of bomb had been used over Japan, that it had destroyed the city of Hiroshima, that it was a weapon of terrible power developed in secret by the

Allies, and that there was talk of surrender, but none of us believed it." Yet soon there were reports of a second bomb, and another Japanese city leveled.

Six days later Japan capitulated, and four days after that all surviving British POWs were brought from Outram Road to Changi. A radio loudspeaker appeared on the outside wall of the Changi prison camp, with excited British voices on All India Radio, proclaiming victory. The prisoners danced; the Japanese guards were in shock. Soon some British officers were parachuted in and the Japanese handed over their arms.

When Eric Lomax had regained a modicum of his physical strength, he found himself a serving officer in the British army once again; but the normality he sought was of necessity something of a pose: something inside him had been broken, wounded and changed forever. Of course, he told himself that once he was back in Britain and demobilized, his war would be over. "My 'unpleasantness', as I often called it, for we survivors almost competed with each other in laconic understatement, seemed to have ended with the surrender of Japan. I was more worried about my physical injuries: my arms, my exhaustion, the skin diseases which I could not eradicate; I still had ringworm when I left Changi. I didn't understand yet that there are experiences you can't walk away from, and that there is no statute of limitations on the effects of torture."

Lomax's choice of word ("unpleasantness") to describe his traumatizing experiences was absolutely typical of a particular generation of British men, particularly in the military; but it also had the effect of personally minimizing, in his own mind, the experiences he had endured. But those experiences were not through with him yet, because there was something about being tortured that took up permanent residence in his personality, and would cause him endless anguish long afterwards—until at long last, fifty years later, he did something about it.

7.

What made the Imperial Japanese Army so cruel in World War II? We must remember that there is little connection whatsoever between the generation of Japanese soldiers that fought in World War Two, and the Japanese people of today. In talking about the soldiers of Imperial Japan, we are talking about a generation that had been systematically conditioned to behave with utter ruthlessness toward perceived enemies of Japan. And even during the worst of the killing, there were individual Japanese who deplored the war and its excesses. But those same excesses were quite widespread, affecting ultimately the great majority of the men in the Imperial Japanese Army, as well as a big plurality of the total population of Japan; and we can say with some exactitude that the historical, cultural and emotional pressures that brought about the outbreak of systemic evil in the Imperial Japanese Army had been building for some time.

Behind the Japanese attack on the Chinese in Manchuria, as well as the attack on Pearl Harbor, were various forms of religious and cultural fanaticism, especially a uniquely aggressive form of religious nationalism; and behind religious nationalism, we know, is always the same objective: to inflict maximum pain and death on the identified enemy, followed by a belief in martyrdom as a transcendent and desirable state. In the end, it would be the civilian population of Japan that suffered most from this insanity, most notably in Hiroshima and Nagasaki. The disasters that lay ahead for Japan could easily have been foreseen, with the single exception of the two atom bombs, if the political and cultural leaders of Japan had been thinking clearly. How could they possibly imagine that America would not fight back after being attacked at Pearl Harbor?

In Japan patriarchy and nationalism reached insane heights of intensity that could not be sustained, but which contributed directly to an ongoing idealization of the warrior—samurai— ethos; this slavish apotheosis of the warrior in turn had everything to do with a certain paranoia about the outside world, as well as a rampant but unproductive patriarchy. Underlying this paranoia was a gnawing and unacknowledged sense of inferiority, since the West had achieved certain social and economic goals that Japan seemed incapable of realizing. While the Japanese coveted the benefits of industrialization, they seemed to have little idea of the economic and emotional investment necessary to achieve them. Furthermore, throughout the 19th and early 20th centuries a great deal of the free-floating aggression in Japanese society was reinforced by an emphasis on coercion, harshness and violence in child-raising, and in extreme patriarchy expressed in the worship of war and in the domination of women by men.

But it was the influence of nationalism that was strongest. Consider, for example, that until the end of World War II most Japanese actually believed Emperor Hirohito was divine—it was not until General McArthur forced Hirohito to admit over the radio that he was not divine, but rather an ordinary human being, that the Japanese learned the truth. (Britain was likewise determined to eradicate Japanese imperialism for all time, a determination that caused British Rear Admiral Lord Louis Mountbatten to force General Itagaki—who commanded Japanese forces in Southeast Asia—to ceremonially hand over his eleventh-century sword to Mountbatten personally.) It is hard for us, living in the early part of the twenty-first century, to imagine what it must have felt like to live under an Emperor whom one believes to be a god—but let us not be too smug in the West: the attitude that the Emperor was beyond human good and evil, and therefore did not have to be accountable for his behavior, is simply an Asian version of the way many Germans felt about Hitler. The Japanese simply subscribed to a religious kind of nationalism, whereas German Nazis practiced a secular version of the same kind of fanaticism.

The Shinto religion, like any other religion, is what its practitioners make of it, which means that it has served various purposes during various epochs. On one level, it is simply a vast body of mystery wisdom indigenous to Japan—mythology, folk beliefs, mystical traditions, poetry and the like—that came together in the eighth to twelfth centuries. Today it is mostly associated with certain public monuments that express traditional Japanese values. Literally it means "way of the Gods," implying a search for harmony among animistic spirits (rather like Taoism's *I Ching*); and that in turn means that while it is important, it is not exclusive, in the sense that it is very common for Japanese families to celebrate a Shinto rite at the birth of a child and observe a Buddhist rite at that same family member's death.

Interestingly, the Wikipedia section on Shinto seems to say rather confusingly that whereas 80 to 90 percent of Japanese believe in Shinto, only a paltry four million or so *really* believe in it. In other words, Shinto is a faith that one observes rather than believes, very often while actually believing and practicing another religion entirely. In its favor, then, one must say that this characteristic makes it potentially one of the least exclusive religions on the face of the earth, but also one of the most arbitrary.

From the 17th century onwards Japanese scholars were increasingly convinced that Shinto could become a centralizing force that could hold the Japanese nation together, despite the centrifugal forces of modernist reforms, by using the supposed divinity of the Emperor as a rallying point. This strategy was employed with great intensity from the time of the Meiji in 1868 until the collapse of Imperial Japan in 1945. The government established a bureaucracy called the Shinto Worship Bureau; and in 1871 all Shinto shrines were taken over by the state.

The post-war Japanese religious historian Shigeyoshi Murakami has thoroughly demonstrated the late 19th and early 20th century penetration of this form of religious nationalism—

which he accurately refers to as State Shintoism—in all areas of Japanese public life, with its powerful and unrelenting emphasis on veneration of the Emperor and imperial values. But there were two great moral anomalies in this campaign. To being with, it tended to justify as a nationalist duty (and therefore a virtue) the extreme brutality involved in imperialism, which after all is simply the domination of one people by another. Secondly, the belief in a divine Emperor is strikingly incompatible with science and modernism generally—one inevitably undermines the other.

This extreme nationalism and patriarchy, reverence for the Samurai warrior as a culture hero, combined with an uncanny emphasis on cruelty as potentially beautiful or a source of spiritual authenticity (not to mention the inevitable concomitant of a modern police state), flowed into Japanese society from many directions, and began to achieve critical mass in the decades before the Japanese invasion of Manchuria in 1931. One cultural conduit (although certainly not the only one) was Zen Buddhism, which was used in a particularly dangerous and self-serving way by nationalist writers and religious scholars. As a number of scholars have pointed out, D.T. Suzuki, one of the Beat Generation's favorite exponents of Zen Buddhism in America and a darling of bohemian writers and poets in California, was a fanatical Japanese nationalist who vehemently supported the criminal enterprise that was the Japanese Imperial Army, right up to 1945—something he was at pains to cover up later, and something his American accolades were at pains not to know about.

One of the most hilarious of post-war American phenomena, if one is possessed of a sufficiently dark sense of humor, was the idolatry of Suzuki and his writings by successive legions of California bohemians, a phenomenon this writer personally witnessed living in the San Francisco Bay Area. In reality, Suzuki was a particularly malignant but ultimately unrepentant religious nationalist, one of the worst of the 20th century, as were virtually all of the other leading Zen Buddhists in Japan before and during World War II. There is a convenient subjectivity about Zen Buddhism that makes it particularly amenable to misuse by religious nationalists, not to mention every other kind of charlatan. A very famous quote from Harada Daiun Sogaku, a leading Zen teacher of the Soto school during the Second World War, went as follows: "[If ordered to] march: tramp, tramp, or shoot: bang, bang. This is the manifestation of the Highest Wisdom." In other words, be sure to murder or torture when ordered to do so, because therein lies the Highest Wisdom. With mystical thought like that, you don't need stupidity.

Suzuki was a shrewd marketer of his corrupt religious product in America. As David McMahon pointed out in *The Making of Buddhist Modernism*, Suzuki carefully takes Zen out of its "social, ritual and ethical contexts and reframes it in terms of a language of metaphysics derived from German Romantic idealism, English Romanticism and American Transcendentalism"—as well as Anglo-American Theosophy and a fair amount of New Age hokum, I might add. Thus it ends up with a solipsistic stew of profound-sounding cultural reference points that can mean anything, and therefore justify anything. Suzuki correctly saw this as the kind of thing that would strike Americans as profound and wise, and indeed there was indeed a robust market for his writings among the intellectuals and pseudo-intellectual bohemians of the 1950s and 1960s. For the best account of Suzuki's unremitting support for Japanese militarism see *Zen at War* by Brian Daizen Victoria, published in 1997, followed by Victoria's *Zen War Stories*, a further exploration of the role of Zen Buddhism (and institutional Buddhism generally) as a central supporter of Japanese militarism, patriarchy, nationalism and cruelty generally.

The entire society in Japan was rife with such pressure-generating contradictions, the strongest of which was the insistence on believing in the divinity of the Emperor, by all accounts a weak and not very bright individual. As Japan grew increasingly bereft of creative initiatives to deal with its own internal contradictions, it fell back on an insistence on its own uniqueness, the classic gambit of neurotic nations and individuals, which led to one of the most toxic forms of nationalism in the world outside of pan-German nationalism. Such nationalism seems to have been based mainly on mass narcissism, and driven by a deep sense of national inferiority, to be overcome in the same way as the individual narcissist overcomes his own lack of self-esteem — by creating a super persona that is always right, a persona so unique and wonderful that he does not have to play by the rules, or observe even the most common kinds of decency.

In the mass narcissism of Japanese nationalism, the omnipresent failings of a nation that could not address its own contradictions was resolved by the shared fantasy of a morally, aesthetically and physically superior society, one that did not have to follow international law, listen to anybody or consult anything outside its own pathological imaginings. Thus did the fantasy of moral superiority, driven by the profound anger and frustration arising from Japan's inability to resolve its own entrenched social problems, lead to the expression of a completely malevolent aggression.

In the end everybody suffered. To perpetrators who operate out of a profound aggression, and the deceit and self-deception inherent to systemic evil, it matters little whether the victims are one's own people or the supposedly "inferior" races they seek to punish. The armies of Imperial Japan and Nazi Germany killed millions of civilians under the most horrible circumstances imaginable; and in the end it was precisely the civilians in both the German and the Japanese homelands that experienced — in Hiroshima and Dresden and many other terrible venues — the full measure of the suffering unleashed by their corrupt and pathological leaders.

8.

It is a proud and enduring testament to the discipline of the British armed forces that there were few acts of revenge by British soldiers against surrendering Imperial Japanese soldiers and bureaucrats in the Far East. That does not mean, however, that British officers were not painfully aware that atrocities had been perpetuated against British and other POWs. As soon as Eric Lomax and the other prisoners held at Outram Road and Changi were able to do so, he began—with the full cooperation of his immediate military superiors—to create a comprehensive and complete record of prisoners who had been in the military section of Outram Road and at Kanburi. The intent of this was much more than simple record-keeping.

"I also drew up detailed complaints about our treatment at Kachanaburi, taking statements from the survivors. Major Slater, as the senior officer among us—ranks suddenly mattered again—signed the statement. The Kanburi Radio Affair, we called it in our statement after we agreed [to] a final version; the designation began to seem a kind of euphemism. We were becoming history, and we could tell how close we were to being forgotten already."

But *they* had not forgotten, and they would not let the atrocities they witnessed be forgotten: "This meticulous, orderly registration of witnesses and participants and descriptions of the criminals was a wonderful displacement of anger and revenge. It still astonishes me that there were not more spontaneous outbursts of summary justice on the guards, but our normality reasserted itself very quickly, and that did not include lynchings."

The "meticulous, orderly" recording of wrongdoing—so similar to what happens in the civilian legal process when long-standing crimes are finally adjudicated—helps greatly in putting such atrocities into perspective, partly by giving them a historical context. By abjuring violent revenge in favor of legal retribution, the victim of atrocity sends a strong message to himself and the world that *his values are better than his torturers' values*, and that by rights their evil behavior should not be given the power to control one's feelings. The deliberate exercise of objectivity in describing an atrocity may also diminish psychological trauma, and therefore to deconstruct the aggression internalized during the torture itself. The careful recording of atrocities on a mass basis also helps the historian understand the spectrum on which such atrocities occur; in this case, what was involved was documentation of the moral degradation of nearly an entire generation of Japanese soldiers in the Far East.

All these things to some extent tend—not completely, of course, but to some extent—to objectify the horrible crimes that were committed, making them less threatening and more manageable to victims in the short run, by describing them as part of a social pathology that can be studied, just as a doctor or a medical researcher can study a physiological pathology. All of these things by themselves cannot completely deconstruct the after-effects of torture, but taken together they can potentially make it easier to handle.

Eric Lomax was at first most concerned about the physical effects of his ordeal: weakness and overall debilitation, and skin diseases such as ringworm, which continued to plague him. "I didn't understand yet that there are experiences you can't walk away from," he wrote in his book, "and that there is no statute of limitations on the effects of torture." Lomax was given a number of tasks, including the reorganization of Indian troops around Changi that enabled him to use hard work to repress the negative emotions that periodically overcame him. Then he was sent to India, and thence to Britain. (Interestingly, in India he was told to do nothing but rest, and the "sudden requirement to do nothing was more than my system could bear," causing a kind of breakdown that required him to be hospitalized for three days.) On ship finally, bound for Southampton in England, he was filled with anticipation of being once again in his parents' house, and especially of seeing his mother again. Eric was sure he would be able to talk to his mother about what happened to him, especially the torture.

But that would never happen. On his arrival at Southampton in October, 1945, he was informed in a letter from his father that his mother had died, and that he had remarried. The shock was compounded by the fact that his father had married a woman that Eric had always considered insincere and acquisitive. "All the calmly-constructed images of home which I had been nurturing on the voyage back simply vanished. I was so shocked that I could not tell grief and anger apart, sorrow for my mother almost eclipsed by my response to what seemed like a betrayal by my father. It was a quick and brutal indication that I was not returning to anything I would find familiar." Many other soldiers had a similar disillusionment—six years of wartime was simply too much time for things not to change significantly. The loss of his mother Eric found particularly hard, for there "were things I could probably have told her that proved hard to share with others."

At first he went to his fiancée's family, and only afterwards to his father's house at Joppa, an Eastern suburb of Edinburgh. It was not a successful meeting. "Over my natural formality was laid the instinctive caution and blankness of the prisoner used to hiding his feelings. I hardly knew it then, but I had begun the process of shutting down my emotions, pulling back into cold anger at the first sign of confrontation rather than expressing myself." He could not rid himself of the sense that his father's new wife "cannot have been indifferent to his good pension and comfortable house when she took him on." But in what is clearly a judgment on his own feelings as well as his father's, he adds: "Within two days I was in a world that seemed cynical and petty compared to the companionship and the seriousness that comes from facing death which I had found in the camps and Outram Road."

It is when the combat veteran returns from war that civilian life often appears to be grotesquely petty, when he inevitably finds himself comparing the triviality of many civilian experiences to the extreme emotions and high mortal stakes of combat, not to mention life in a prison compound. The returning veteran slowly realizes that he may never again have such powerful experiences as those he had in war. There are many vets, of course, that embrace the trivia of civilian life as a welcome relief to the murderous tempo of war; but some are overwhelmed with contempt toward the hum-drum pace of regular life, and find themselves shaking their heads with disbelief over the manner in which civilians invest emotional capital in what often seem to be completely inconsequential ideas and activities.

Three weeks after returning Eric Lomax married his fiancée, who had waited for him through six years of war. Clearly it was an attempt to create a refuge from the confusion and pain he was feeling, made up partly from shock at the loss of his mother, but clearly enhanced by emotional trauma related to being tortured. "She [his fiancée] was the nearest safe haven I could find from my father's betrayal and the pain that I could not get rid of or understand. I was already living in a world of my own; the privacy of the torture victim is more impregnable than any island fortress. I could not have begun to understand that in 1945, for I did not have the words to describe what I was going through."

"Nor did anyone I knew; and certainly not the army. The entire extent of my attention from the British Army after the war consisted of a brief medical examination at an army centre in Edinburgh in November 1945. I could walk across the room, was warm to the touch and had no incurable diseases, so they turned me loose. 'Get on with your life,' the doctor seemed to say, as though it was the easiest thing in the world. The wounds were not on the surface, nor detectable by stethoscopes. My rush to marriage was a symptom of their presence."

Writing from the vantage-point of retrospection (his book *The Railway Man* was published in 1995), Lomax wrote that he had discovered that one must be proactive to overcome trauma; but in 1945 he had no clue how to deal with his growing emotional alienation: "Here was Eric Lomax playing the part of the newly-wed, pretending he was what he had been in 1941, before he left for the East, when his innocence and much of his emotional life had not been ripped out of him... I had grown up appallingly in the years I had been away. I was much harder, less able to enjoy other people's pleasures easily and certainly less able to sympathize with their smaller misfortunes. Yet I stepped back confusedly into the tide and it carried me away, as it did so many other young men in that winter of 1945." His new bride suffered as well. "I was broken down; her own romantic ideas were rubbed up against the reality of this nervous, pale and debilitated young man. She was as much a victim of the war as me."

Being able to talk about emotionally traumatizing events is absolutely necessary for the victim to recover from them. The absence of his mother was of extreme importance in Eric's case, because he felt he could talk to her. In fact he made a valiant effort to talk to his young wife about his experiences, but that effort foundered badly. "One of the first unbridgeable distances between us was created simply by our inability to talk. I have spent most of my life unable to talk about my experiences in South-East Asia, but I am pretty sure that in those early years of intimacy with my wife I wanted to try to tell her, to explain to her what it had been like. It was hard for her to be interested. I was expected to behave as though my formative years had not happened. My fumbling attempts to begin a description of the effects of what my comrades and I had experienced in Kanburi, or to talk about the Japanese who had done these things to us, were brushed aside. She naturally felt that she had had a hard time of it too: for civilians there had been the difficulty of getting eggs, the air raid warnings, the waiting in lines."

"She simply did not know, and I am sure that tens of thousands of returning soldiers walked bewildered into the same incomprehension. It was as though we were now speaking a different language to our own people. The hurt I felt silenced me as effectively as a gag. It was hard to talk, but my wife made it easy not to." But it was not just that his young wife didn't know about what happened, it was that she didn't *want* to know, a tendency that Lomax noticed everywhere. All these things reinforced the negative effects of the trauma he had experienced when he was being tortured.

One day Lomax noticed a small paragraph in the *Daily Telegraph* to the effect that the two officers in charge at Kanburi (Captain Kiomai Mitsuo and Sergeant-Major Iijima Nobuo) had been hung at Changi for two of their many war crimes, the murders of two British POWs, Lieutenant Armitage and Captain Hawley. Somehow Lomax found little relief in their punishment, partly, this writer suspects, because it all happened so far away, and the victims played no major part in it; when terrible crimes are committed, it is frequently good for the recovery of the victim if he can be part of the legal proceedings. The victim knows that the crime has been adjudicated properly, and that the revenge exacted is in accordance with the rule of law, but he still has the satisfaction of seeing perpetrators punished.

At the same time, participation in adjudicating atrocities gives the victim an opportunity to talk about their horrific experiences, and the deep anguish—not to mention the disorientation—that the emotionally traumatized person quite naturally feels. In fact, allowing victims in criminal trials to confront the perpetrator in order to give a statement expressing their anger, frustration and sorrow, as we do in America, is one of the few great modern innovations of Anglo-American law, an extremely important reform arising out of the American Victim Rights' Movement.

What perhaps bothered Lomax the most was the fact that the

trial and execution of two of his tormenters was relegated to the bottom of the newspaper's back page. "Other people had suffered more than we had—the horrors of the European camps and the scale of the massacre of the Jews were beginning to sink into the minds of an unbelieving population—but that did not entirely explain the relegation of our experience to the bottom of the page. The British public was not very interested in the Far Eastern war crimes trials, in general, and official policy was to downplay them for the sake of reconstructing Japan as an ally of the West."

This alludes in part to an observation that has been made often by writers on the Second World War, which is that while enormous amounts of historical study have been directed toward the horrors of Nazism in Europe, people almost invariably show less inclination to deconstruct or acknowledge the systemic evil practiced by Imperial Japan. On the surface, this appears to suggest that the West unconsciously experiences the Second World War in Europe as more important than the same conflict in Asia. But this historical syllogism, so often repeated that it has become a stereotype, was at first not quite true in America. As Norman Finkelstein has pointed out, Americans during the 1950s also avoided discussing the Nazi Holocaust—so much so that the greatest historian of the Holocaust, Raul Hilberg, was forced originally to self-publish *Destruction of the European Jews*, his classic work on the Holocaust. Why? Partly because middle-class Americans seem to think it in questionable taste to acknowledge the existence of evil of that magnitude; but also because West Germany was being reconstituted as America's new ally in the Cold War. It seems something similar happened in Britain in regard to war crimes of the Imperial Japanese Army in World War II.

Eric Lomax began to regularly experience horrible dreams, usually about being imprisoned in solitary confinement, waiting for something that he dreaded but could not name. "In the cold light of day my anger was more often turned to the Japanese who had beaten, interrogated or tortured me. I wanted to do violence to them, thinking quite specifically of how I would like to revenge myself on the goon squad from Kanburi and the hateful little interrogator from the Kempeitai with his dreadful English pronunciation, his mechanical questions and his way of being in the room yet seeming to be detached from it. I wished to drown him, cage him and beat him, to see how he liked it. I still thought of his voice, his slurred elocution: 'Lomax, you will be killed shortly'; 'Lomax, you will tell us'; you remember phrases from encounters that have hurt you, and my meetings with him were cast in a harsh light."

So there was a substantial probability his careful accounts of the murders committed by Mitsuo and Nobuo, written up in the Far East just after the liberation of the Outram Road prison, had resulted in the two war criminals being punished. "I regretted that there were not more of them going to the gallows; I felt that thousands of them were guilty. There was unfinished business between me and the Japanese people as a whole, and a few of them in particular." Here he refers to the Japanese who tortured him—but he could find no military records of them.

It was as though they had disappeared into the fog of war that had swallowed up so many people. "No trace of my interrogator or his brutal superior the Kempei NCO, who had irritated me so personally, was ever reported. I had never even made a statement about them, though I remembered them more than the killers of Hawley and Armitage, who to me were simply a faceless bunch of club-swinging thugs; I remembered the faces of the Kempei men almost every day." One of the horrors of torture is that the torturer may take up permanent residence in the former victim's traumatic memory, which puts him in a perfect position to continue the torture indefinitely—something that Eric Lomax experienced on an almost daily basis. And Eric's now-entrenched inability to talk about his experience as a victim of torture, with his wife or anybody else, was making things worse.

Obviously he needed to talk to *someone* about what had happened to him, but a variety of barriers got in the way. "Not being able to share memories was, as I've said, a common affliction among those who returned from the war, and I could not talk about what had happened to me with a soul. The single and partial exception was anyone who had been through similar experiences; but in the crush of everyday life, there were few encounters with ex-POWs. I became close to one former POW, however, and we could talk to each other, guardedly and euphemistically. I saw in him some of the same traits I had developed, his capacity for enthusiasm and joy replaced by surface coldness and docility. When I applied for an appointment in the Colonial Administrative Service, he did too. I felt he was drifting, as I was in a different way, and I had become briefly part of the tide that was pulling him along. He was following me passively instead of determining his own fate."

Eric Lomax began to realize early on, not more than four years after he married, that his marriage had been a mistake. "After our first daughter was born in December 1946, my wife's own mother did not see us or the child for about six years; there was an absolute break. Her family cultivated feuds; she had relatives in the Scottish borders, for example, and few of them would communicate with her." The reason for the feuds seemed stunningly petty. "Certain of her relatives would not speak to her because when we sent out the traditional little boxes of wedding cake to our friends and relatives at the end of 1945, they went out in two or three batches, and this meant that some people got theirs before others. And the ones who were in the second and third deliveries were infuriated because it implied that the recipients of the first wave of little sugary wedges were considered more important than them. These were people who were not even aware of their own entrapment."

"This intolerance over things so surpassingly trivial was very hard for me to take. I had felt less morbid vindictiveness towards the Japanese guards in Changi than these seemingly normal Scottish middle-class people were displaying to their own blood relatives."

This was exactly the wrong emotional environment for someone in Lomax's situation. "Of course it takes more than one person to create what Milton called 'disconsolate household captivity,' and my withdrawals into cold and blank anger in the face of hostility, pulling my shell around me and locking it tight, cannot have made things easier. Confrontation threatened my whole being, triggering flashes of memory that I could not articulate to anyone, and most tragically of all, not even to my wife."

She made it clear that she didn't want to hear about his experiences, which constituted an important part of his entrapment, nor did the horrendous bickering at their church help. "The feeling of claustrophobia was worsened by the [Charlotte] Chapel, where fierce feuds, outbreaks of ostentatious remoteness and snorting resentment would break out over seating priorities." The Chapel was the Charlotte Baptist Chapel in Edinburgh, where Lomax and his wife had been married, and continued to attend. Its bleak church politics reflected the inevitable social influence of centuries of harsh Calvinism, but were similar in tone to his in-laws' interminable feuds.

Instead of humor, sympathy and a taste for frank discussion about human emotions, the people with whom Lomax came in contact seemed to suffer almost invariably from the miasmal cultural sensibility defined by the word "dour," as one uses the word in the Scottish and northern dialects. The idea was to suffer life's iniquities as silently (and as sullenly) as humanly possible, and to cultivate feuds instead of friendships, which was exactly the opposite of what Lomax needed. Compassion seemed especially in short supply, both at his church and among his wife's family.

"One woman who had been going to Chapel for thirty years complained loudly one day when my wife and I inadvertently sat in which she regarded as her personal pew. I could not help noticing that most of the veterans had done very little in the war; their complaints about how awful fire-watching duties had been did not, under the circumstances, engage my full sympathy."

It is not surprising, then, that he welcomed an assignment from the Colonial Service in London for the Gold Coast—going to Africa was a chance to get away from the Chapel, and from his wife's joyless and problematical family. His wife accompanied him, however, and their mutual estrangement was deepened by the loss of their son Eric, who died a day after his birth in Takoradi. Meanwhile, Lomax well understood that he was one of the last colonial administrators of a fading Empire, and did his best to do a credible job. He took early retirement in 1955, and devoted himself to teaching, specializing in personnel management and better industrial relations.

But despite his relative success, due in large part to his hard work and a pronounced native intelligence, the violence of the past continued to rule his waking and sleeping life. "I had to behave all the time as if the past had not occurred. I did not think that I was any different from anyone else, despite my terrible nightmares, which I refused to acknowledge as a problem. I wanted to believe that it had all been buried, yet Outram Road kept coming back, night after night. Silence, disease, hunger, fear, above all the intensity of the uncertainty and fear. It was almost always that terrifying scenario of being inside the gaol again after the war, and since there was no reason for my imprisonment, this time there could be no reasons for getting out."

With great economy this perfectly suggests the Kafkaesque sense of entrapment generated by a recurring dream—if there is no reason to be trapped there will certainly be no reason to get out. In other words, since the dreamer does not know what brings the recurring dream on, he has no idea how to stop it from coming back. "My wife did her best to reassure me, but the distance between us was hard to bridge. I would cry out at night, wake up sweating as though I had run up a hill with a heavy load and shake with relief when I found myself in the damp heat of Sekondi or the cold Edinburgh night."

"Curiously, I recognized the symptoms in others, especially in one man in the Gold Coast who had been in Germany as a POW, and was now nervous, defensive, in bad health. But nobody ever spoke about it and I never brought it up. The only way in which 'my war' came up would be around the subject of the Japanese, when I could and would say that I hated them with absolute totality."

Somehow the filters that most people use to keep bad things at bay until the conscious mind can put them in perspective had been permanently removed. "I found it difficult to tolerate grey areas in my life, to accept ambiguity or uncertainty of any kind, and I could not easily forgive the mistakes of others, what is euphemistically called not suffering fools gladly. Trifles bothered me, or perhaps it is truer to say I could not be bothered with them, and I would find ways of procrastinating over the small irritations with which life bombards us. For example, while my professional work was extremely organized and I brought real energy and dedication to it—I could organize my thoughts and speak without notes with military precision—I found bills, circulars and, especially, demands for personal information more or less unbearable. They were contingencies, distractions, irruptions of uncertainty into a life that craved regularity. It was better to concentrate on one thing at a time."

"I was often inward-looking, a victim of a strange passivity that made me absorb experiences like blotting-paper but which made it difficult for me to give; it made me appear slow, yet I was anything but lazy. I felt sometimes like a guest in my own house. When confrontation came, I would resist with immense stubborn energy, [as though I were] revenging myself on the Kempeitai and the guards in every encounter. Although I could not have admitted it, I was still fighting the war in all those years of peace."

Many victims of war-related emotional trauma—including torture—could say exactly the same thing, especially the feeling of being a guest in one's own life. The experience of being completely subjected to the sadism of a torturer is so destabilizing that it practically demands that the victim transform his or her life to take into account an awareness of systemic evil in the world, and to devise a strategy to oppose it. But Lomax continued in the frozen half-life of the emotionally traumatized, oppressively aware of the past violence and its hold over him but being completely at sea about what one could do about it to neutralize its hold over the imagination.

His only defense was hard work. "Work and the strong pull of the currents that run through everyday life—no matter how threatening they can seem to someone whose memories are bad—give the illusion of sweeping us away from the past. Like many men who went through Japanese prisons, I found I could allow my professional life to crowd out my desire to settle those old accounts." This continued for several decades, until his final separation from his wife in 1981 and his retirement in 1982.

But now, without work to function as a defense for suppressing traumatic memory, Eric Lomax found himself wanting to know more about what had happened to him, and if possible to get the names of those who had tortured him. "After my retirement in 1982, I could put off no longer the need to know, the desire became more intense than ever. I wanted to find out what had really happened; why the Japanese had made the search of our hut on that particular day, and if somebody had tipped them off. I wished to establish the exact sequence of events."

"I also wanted to find out more about the Japanese responsible for the beatings and murders, apart from those already brought to justice, and above all more about the Kempeitai personnel who had tortured me at Kanburi. I knew nothing about their units, their names or their fate after the war. The prospects of finding the right men, of finding them alive, even of making a start were so remote; but as the events receded the obsession grew. It was like trying to reconstruct a coherent story from evidence reduced to tattered rags, faded documents, bones and rusty rails. And memories, which are even less durable."

"Perhaps I was trying to recover something of what I had been before being sent to war and put to work on an insane railway." One of the overriding obsessions of those who have suffered emotional trauma in the past is a desire to mentally reconstitute the exact sequence of events that traumatized them, as if to find out the moment-to-moment passage of occurrences would somehow free the victim of its effects; and the desperate hope that in finding out exactly what happened, one could miraculously recover the innocence the events had taken away. But these quests are usually doomed to failure, because it is not the events that changed everything—after all, the events are over, they're in the past—but the experience of the victim in response to those events; and that, in turn, all too often includes not knowing how one should go about deconstructing the aggression embedded in the traumatic memory. Even if the victim finds out exactly what happened to him so long ago, it will change nothing if he is not able to neutralize the internalized aggression he carries around inside him.

Suppose, for a moment, that the torture victim could find out all about his ordeal, and even the names of those responsible for torturing him, and their current addresses. What would he do with these facts? "The more I thought about it, and thought about it, the more I wished to do damage to the Kempei men if I could ever find them. Physical revenge seemed the only adequate recompense for the anger I carried. I thought often about the young interpreter at Kanburi.... the interpreter was the link; he was centre-stage in my memories; he was my private obsession. His slurred and struggling English; his endless questions; his repetitiveness; the way he gave voice to the big torturing NCO: he represented all of them; he stood for all the worst horrors."

To the victim, murder often seems the only response to being tortured, because murder is the physical equivalent of the radical emotional harm done by torture. It is not the logical, conscious mind that demands violence as recompense—it is the aggression internalized by the torture victim that demands repayment in kind. But the consequence of murdering one's torturer would be life in prison. And there is no guarantee that killing one's torturer would stop the agony of the traumatic memory—the reality is that it could make the psychological pain that much worse.

9.

Victims of emotional trauma often have a pronounced fear of conflict and of expressing anger, feeling that if anger were to be expressed directly something terrible might happen. Ironically, the resulting conflict-avoidant behavior often creates such tension that a fair amount of frustration and anger is created anyway, which arguably becomes far more unpleasant than if the original anger had been appropriately expressed and its causes discussed. There are certainly exceptions to this, but some people struggling with traumatic memory feel that they have lost or been denied an appropriate way to express anger. As a result, conflicts can become off-limits for discussion, making the victim's psychic pain significantly worse.

As we have seen, Eric Lomax became obsessed with finding out the exact sequence of events when he was tortured, especially during one period he could not remember. This desire to find out the truth is understandable, and may have historical importance, so it should not be discouraged if the victim does not let it get out of hand. But the victim's real challenge is not finding out the precise sequence of past events, but in deconstructing the aggression he has most likely internalized as a result. His problem is not what happened *then*, but the power of the traumatic memory *now*, and the aggressive emotional orientations that he internalized during the original trauma and that now accompany his memories of it.

Victims of psychological trauma sometimes believe that if they can discover the exact sequence of events concerning the atrocities they have endured, they'll be able to recover the personal innocence—and the emotional resilience—they seem to have lost. But no historical verisimilitude can bring back lost innocence, because the traumatized person has been made aware of evil, and cannot escape from that knowledge. Until society accepts the existence of evil as a *psychological* reality that people experience in powerful *subjective* ways, society at large may not be able to fully understand that aspect of recovery. In the meantime, victims struggle to regain their emotional equilibrium. It is important, then, for them to remember that they may not be able to neutralize all evil in the world, but they *can* neutralize the effects of the specific evil they personally experienced, by finding a way to get rid of the compacted aggression they internalized long ago in order to survive.

The manner in which the deconstruction of aggression is accomplished may be different for each person, but the purpose of this chapter is to tell the story of Eric Lomax's struggle to find such a way out of his personal nightmare, and his ultimate success in so doing. *First*, Eric Lomax was about to find, after many decades, people to whom he could talk about the horrors he had experienced. That alone would be a kind of miracle. *Secondly*, he would conceive and participate in an extremely radical but socially-beneficial experience that was so risky that almost everyone advised him not to do it. Yet he became convinced it was the only way.

Eric Lomax knew he had to do something. There were his

nightmares and night sweats, a brooding debilitation in mental concentration, and a tendency to fly off the handle at the mistakes of others. Perhaps worst of all, there was an omnipresent feeling of being alienated from his own life ("I felt like a guest in my own house"), a sense that the world had become "uncanny," as Freud once famously put it. Perhaps the most stressful circumstance for Eric Lomax was the isolation of having to suffer from past violence alone. This happened partly because a comprehensive understanding of post-traumatic stress only began to cohere in the last decades of the century; partly because Eric's wife was unwilling to discuss his problems with him; but also because of British—and to some extent Scottish—cultural traits that discouraged open sharing of emotions by men, with the British component holding up the man with the 'stiff upper lip' as the highest male ideal. Finally, Eric Lomax himself didn't understand the importance of talking about the torture he'd experienced, and over the decades had become incapable of speaking about it.

With nobody to talk to about the after-effects of torture, Eric Lomax and people like him were effectively alone in the world with little more than their ghosts and their despair at ever getting better. But something radical was about to change in Lomax's life. He was about to meet the one person who could be the appropriate catalyst for change that he needed, and she arrived just in time.

10.

Maybe we should not be surprised that Eric Lomax met his future and second wife Patti on a train, since trains and railways had become such a controlling metaphor for Eric's life. She was English, much younger than he, and lately living in Canada. Eric was by now separated from his first wife for the last time, and attracted to the vivacious but poised younger woman. Long an owner of an antiquarian bookstore in Montreal, she had once worked in the north of England, and greatly appreciated Lomax's historical knowledge of the towns they were passing through. Lomax experienced a kind of instant rapport between them that caused him to engage in a long and animated conversation with her; and apparently she did as well, since she accepted his invitation for lunch the next day in Glasgow.

Lomax summarizes their situation in *The Railway Man*: "It emerged quickly that we were both living rootless and not altogether happy lives; her marriage was as reduced as mine." Even after she had returned to Canada, Lomax refused to let her go ("there were many letters and long-distance calls after her return"). Lomax understood that he was hopelessly in love; and the upshot was that Patti came to live with him in Edinburgh. Eric now found himself part of an extended family consisting of her children, a family as open and friendly as his previous in-laws had been harsh and judgmental.

All this couldn't have been more emotionally stimulating—and unsettling—since he was getting closer to knowing more about the people who tortured him, particularly the young Japanese private who functioned as the interpreter during the torture. Eric had placed a notice in a newsletter for former prisoners of war, soliciting information about the events occurring in Kanburi in 1943. He specifically asked for information about the interpreter at Kanburi; but although he received twenty letters in reply, none had information relating to his torture.

Then Lomax made contact with a former regular army Chaplain from Oxford, a man named Babbs, who had participated in an official War Graves Commission that traveled the entire length of the Burma-Siam railroad looking for mass graves or cemeteries of British soldiers that perished there (they located 144 cemeteries in the jungle near the railway, and remains of over 10,000 bodies buried there). Babbs mentioned that there had been a Japanese interpreter with them who might have information that Lomax needed. He offered to make inquiries; Lomax was relieved that Babbs offered to do so, since direct contact with a former Japanese soldier would have been unthinkable to him.

As a result of his quest to illuminate the events at Kanburi in 1943, at one point Eric Lomax found himself at the Public Record Office in Kew in 1985, going through old records relating to war crimes, some of which he had written himself. The official file relating to his torture (and to the deaths of Captain Hawley and Lieutenant Armitage, the two officers that had been beaten to death), was File WO235/822. Lomax wrote in *The Railway Man* that he remembers going into a kind of trance as he read the files. "Perhaps the most remarkable element in this experience was the curious sensation that I was reading something in which I was not personally involved. I was seeking these exact truths on behalf of some person I barely knew."

In the short term, the search for "exact truths" about traumatizing events often heightens the victim's personal feelings of alienation. As I have suggested before, the reason for this may be that the real problem resides not in what happened *then*, but in the victim's emotional orientations *now*. Because of Eric's inability to talk about what had happened to him, the toxicity of the traumatic memory—driven by the aggression he had internalized—had developed a power of its own; and over time actually became just as bad (or worse) than the original events themselves. As we know, an untended and infected wound is worse than a fresh one, and all other things being equal, an abscess in an impacted tooth might be generally worse than one in a normal tooth.

Meanwhile Eric and Patti had married, and although they found great happiness, the marriage also suffered from the pressures of Eric's buried memories. He had rather haltingly begun to tell her of his experiences in the Far East, and she had become quite aware that she was "living with someone with unusual problems," as Lomax puts it in *The Railway Man*. Meanwhile Eric was making progress in finding out more about the circumstances of his torture as Babbs, the former army Chaplain with whom he had been corresponding, wrote with information about the building of a Buddhist temple near the now-famous Bridge on the River Kwai, dedicated to the slave laborers that died building the Burma-Siam railway. The man behind the building of the temple had also, according to reports, held a meeting of 'reconciliation' nearby.

Lomax found the reference to the 'reconciliation' meeting or service intensely distasteful: the 'reconciliation' sounded to him "like a fraudulent publicity stunt," not least because of the proximity of the River Kwai Bridge. (For most former Far East POWs that would be a sore point, since the David Lean film of that name had, in their opinion, given a ridiculously rosy picture of POW life under Imperial Japan.)

Of his life with Patti, Lomax wrote in *The Railway Man*: "It was becoming more and more difficult for the person I loved most to bear with me. The ex-prisoner, even after several decades of 'forgetting', can puzzle and frighten others. It is impossible for others to help you come to terms with the past, if for you the past is a pile of wounded memories and angry humiliations, and the future is just a nursery of revenge. At times my good qualities, which I am self-aware enough to know that I have, could almost be crowded out by sudden triggering of frightened anger. A confrontational edge to a voice could bring all my shutters down. All of this made it difficult to imagine a way of healing my wounds."

"Patti had to suffer the sudden icy rages, the withdrawals of affection and contact, of a man who could not stand being teased even lovingly. My hurt response was never deliberate; it was a way of disappearing into myself, of adopting the impassive hurt features of the victim; I shut down as a way to protect myself. Patti was bewildered by it. I recall not speaking to her once for almost a week because of some imagined insensitivity. Another time, I woke from an afternoon nap after some wonderful days in which we had been getting on so well, and possessed by the spirit of loving fun I crept downstairs naked, intending to surprise my wife as she prepared dinner in the kitchen. When I appeared like a ghost at the door behind her she turned and, matching my high spirits, threw a wet dish-cloth at me to cover my indecent condition. This harmless gesture pitched me into a frightened remoteness, ruining a delightful piece of hilarious intimacy."

As so often happens, it was the wife who not only identified the problem, but demanded that they do something about it. "Patti suspected that I had been seriously damaged by my wartime experiences, and that they were at the bottom of our difficulties, and decided that something had to be done about it; neither of us could bear the thought of our relationship breaking down." There was nothing left for husband and wife to do but to join together to co-strategize Eric's recovery.

It had never occurred to Eric that he should speak to a psychotherapist of some kind, and it seems to have been well outside the norm for the average ex-POW. "Not talking becomes a fixed habit, a way of shielding ourselves from those years, and this is doubly true for the victim of torture, who most certainly does not talk." But Patti was not to be discouraged; she contacted Dr. Peter Watson, a senior Medical Officer of the Department of Health, who had written about psychological problems of former POWs. He arranged for Eric to be seen at the RAF Hospital at Ely, in Cambridgeshire, first to rule out lingering tropical disease, and then a psychiatric evaluation.

Lomax found his traumatic memory so impacted that he was unable to speak about what had happened to him in the Far East. "I solved the problem by writing the story of my misadventures in the form of a Memorandum, which ran to over fifty typewritten pages. I presented this to an astonished Squadron-Leader Bloor, the consultant psychiatrist at Ely. I could not possibly have told him any of it by word of mouth, but the

Memorandum gave us a basis for discussion. For the first time in my life, I felt that a barrier was being pushed aside." Dr. Bloor called Patti to reassure her that her husband was indeed suffering from "a straightforward case of psychic damage arising from wartime trauma," which he compared to a kind of prolonged battle-stress.

The next stop for Eric Lomax was the Medical Foundation for the Care of Victims of Torture, which had set up shop in a disused hospital in London. In 1987 he was seen there by Mrs. Helen Bamber, the Foundation's director. "She was utterly unhurried, and this is what impressed me more than anything. She seemed to have infinite time, endless patience and sympathy; but above all she gave me time. It was astonishing simply to know that the pressure of everyday life would not drown out what I had to say. I remembered the half-hour medical examination in 1942, when I was still raw and sore, and there was no interest or time. Half a century later I was still livid with suppressed anxiety and now at last here was someone with the time. Not only that, there was the easing of mind that came with knowing I was not uniquely crippled or mad."

Lomax described his first meeting with Helen Bamber as similar to "walking through a door into an unexplored world, a world of caring and special understanding."

"Helen Bamber is a remarkable woman," Lomax wrote. "A small person, whose stillness and calm presence belie an extraordinary energy for her seventy years, she has spent most of her life working with the victims of cruelty. The Medical Foundation of which she is a founder is probably the only organization in the world whose staff and consultants are expert in the problems of the tortured. Helen entered Bergen-Belsen with the Allies at the age of nineteen in 1945, and stayed for two and a half years. It is an illusion to think that the inmates of the Nazi camps were 'liberated' and went home; most of them had nowhere to go, and it was people like Helen who looked after their tuberculosis, their memories of cannibalism, murder and the grotesque selection procedures that sent some to work and some to the gas chamber. She learned as a girl in Belsen the importance of allowing people to tell what had been done to them, the power of listening to their testimony and of giving people the recognition that their experience deserves."

For several years Mrs. Bamber had been working with Amnesty International. Sadly, the demand for her services for victims of torture increased so rapidly that she set up her new organization. "We've learned so little in my lifetime that torture is now a global epidemic: Helen's small group has seen 8000 cases in its ten years of work."

"Our first meeting was an exploratory one, but after an attempt to interest my local health service in taking me on—when I was told by a young psychiatrist that ancient history did not fall within her brief—I received an invitation from Helen Bamber to become the first ex-serviceman from the Second World War to be accepted as a patient of the Foundation. This changed my life, at nearly seventy years of age."

Throughout 1988 and 1989 Eric and Patti went once a month to the Foundation in London, where Eric continued to receive treatment for his inner wounds. "The doctor assigned to me, Stuart Turner, was a man of infinite tact, and he persuaded me in his 'guided conversations' to reveal more and more, gradually bringing to the surface every fragment of my experiences from early 1942 onwards. He seemed to have wide and painful knowledge of the world's tortures and of their effects on victims. I had never before met a doctor who was so perceptive and so willing and so quick to understand."

"I was aware of myself for the first time as a person for whom the idea of torture might hold some answers—why I was such a strange combination of stubbornness, passivity and silent hostility; why I was unable to express open anger, and why I found authority so difficult; and why I was sometimes unable even to feel."

"Stuart once told me that I was the only patient he had ever met whose face was so inscrutable that he could not tell what I was thinking. I had never heard my mask-like expression described so objectively; it must have slipped on whenever I wanted to hide from his questions for a moment."

As he continued to find out more about the way torture had affected his personality, he continued to seek information about what had actually happened in 1943. There was a kind of cognitive dissonance between the two quests, Lomax wrote, "and yet in the course of these two years, my search changed its character only very slowly. The need to identify the Japanese responsible for these particular cruelties was reasonable enough, but the idea of revenge was still very much alive in me." Yet there was something in the healing process Eric was experiencing that seemed to be leading him in a different direction.

As he continued to gather accurate information about the activities of Imperial Japan in 1943, he encountered specific information that unexpectedly brought him closer to identifying the interpreter who had helped in torturing him. This was just as confusing and morally disorienting as the desire for historical verisimilitude had been, and even more challenging to his emotional recovery. The twin quests—to know the facts, on the one hand, and to escape the agony of traumatic memory, on the other—were about to overrun each other, or perhaps collide, putting his hoped-for recovery in danger.

Eric Lomax's impending crisis was so important that I must allow him to tell his own story at this point: "One of the men I had found in my belated search for information was Jim Bradley, who had lived in the bed next to mine at Changi in 1944. He published an account of his experiences as a member of the Wilkinson escape party in 1943 and his subsequent mistreatment, and after reading a review of his book I found a copy in which I read a warm tribute to 'the late Eric Lomax.' It was a pleasure to write and surprise Jim with my insistence on living. We met and renewed our friendship."

"In October 1989 I went to stay overnight with him and his wife Lindy at his home in Midhurst, a village in Sussex on the edge of the South Downs. We had a pleasant evening, talking about the good old days, and over breakfast the following morning Lindy gave me a photocopy of an article from the Japan Times of 15th August, 1989. This is an English-language paper published in Tokyo and not a publication I was ever likely to buy. Lindy had been sent it by a member of the War Graves Commission in Japan, who knew of her extensive collection of cuttings about the war in the Far East, and she thought that this article might be of interest to me because it mentioned Kanchanburi."

"The article was about Mr. Takashi Nagase, the interpreter who had helped the Allied armies find their dead along the railway after the way, and Padre Babb's eager correspondent. As I read it, I experienced a strange, icy joy of the weirdest kind. A photograph accompanied the piece. It was of a slightly elderly man, dressed in a dark collarless shirt and leaning back in a chair against a wall full of books, his arms spread out to the side making him look resigned and vulnerable. Behind his right shoulder was a large photograph of the River Kwai Bridge with its distinctive spans in the shape of minor arcs. The face was unsmiling, thin and familiar with pain, the face of an ailing seventy-one-year-old man; but the text with its short paragraphs and neutral prose revealed a younger face behind it."

"The article described how Nagase had devoted much of his life to 'making up for the Japanese Army's treatment of prisoners-of-war'; how he had been ordered to join the Allied group trying to locate the graves along the railway, and how, although he had seen trains loaded with POWs leaving Singapore for Thailand in 1943, he was unaware of what occurred on the upper reaches of the railway until he went with the Allied party and saw the corpses in grave after grave in the primitive trackside cemeteries. On the trip, Nagase was quoted as saying, he decided to dedicate the rest of his life to the memory of those who died constructing the railroad."

"This was the man I remembered from Padre Babb's account, and about whom I had been so scathing. But there was more. The article described his ill health, his recurrent heart disease, and how every time he suffered a cardiac attack he had flashbacks of Japanese military police in Kanchanburi torturing a POW who was accused of possessing a map of the railway. One of their methods was to pour large amounts of water down his throat. 'As a former member of the Japanese Army, I thought the agony was what I have to pay for our treatment of POWs,' Nagase said."

"I did not say anything in the Bradleys' kitchen that morning; I probably showed no reaction at all, the impassive mask gripping my face with a vengeance. I stared at the article and read and reread it all the way from the nearby station to London on the train and by the time it pulled into Waterloo Station I knew that this was the man I wanted. His face was recognizably the face of the interrogator, his sunken cheekbones and eyes and mouth an older edition of that serious young man's features. He was speaking about me, and guardedly admitting that he had been there during my torture. I felt triumphant that I had found him, and that I knew his identity while he was unaware of my continued existence."

"I had been haunted by what he described for half a century, but so, it now seemed, had one of my tormentors—the only one with a face and a voice, the only one I had ever been able to endow with a personality across the years. He too had nightmares, flashbacks, terrible feelings of loss. The article talked about Nagase atoning for guilt, about visiting Kanchanaburi many times since 1963, when the Japanese government deregulated foreign travel, laying wreaths at the Allied cemetery, and setting up a charitable foundation for the survivors of the Asian laborers who died in such vast numbers. In my moment of vengeful glory, triumph was already complicated by other feelings. This strange man was obviously drawn on in his work by memories of my own cries and distress and fear."

"I had apparently found one of the men I was looking for and I had the near certainty, shadowed by only a tiny cloud of doubt, that I knew who he was and where he was. I was in such a strong position: I could if I wished reach out and touch him, to do him real harm. The years of feeling powerless whenever I thought of him and his colleagues were erased. Even now, given the information about what he had done since the war, and my own changing feelings about revenge, the old feelings came to the surface and I wanted to damage him for his part in ruining my life."

"When I got back to Berwick much later that day, Patti said it was the first time I'd looked truly delighted for years. On my next visit to the Medical Foundation, liberally handing out photocopies of the Japan Times article, I was interested to be told that for the first time in the staff's experience I could be described as 'animated.' Facial inscrutability was impossible now."

"I still did not know what to do about Nagase. I made enquiries about him, writing to the British Ambassador in Tokyo and to experts on Japan's dreadful record of coming to terms with its past. Nagase's activities were well known, it seemed, to people concerned with the threat of a renewed Japanese militarism, but what I could not tell was whether his expressions of remorse were genuine or not. I needed to see that for myself. The thought was entering my head, distantly at first, that perhaps I should try to meet this man, to make up my mind with that face in front of me again. Many people could not accept the reality of our injuries after the war because they had not been there, because they could not make the leap of imagination out of their comfortable lives, but I wanted to see Nagase's sorrow so that I could live better with my own."

"This half-thought desire took a long time before it could be expressed. One or two people suggested that perhaps it was time for me to forgive and forget. I don't normally argue openly about anything, but I began to argue just a little about this. The majority of people who hand out advice about forgiveness have not gone through the sort of experience I had; I was not inclined to forgive, not yet, and probably never."

And yet—the concept, the idea, of some forgiveness, no matter how conditional, had been planted: an idea that would have been impossible before.

"Throughout the next two years I could not decide what to do with my information, which seemed the product of incredible and precious coincidence. Meanwhile, for the first time, and solely to benefit the Medical Foundation, I allowed myself to be interviewed by journalists. Hitherto, the prospect of anything resembling interrogation filled me with horror, but I managed to get through an interview with a woman from the *Sunday Times* and even, late in 1990, a television programme about the Medical Foundation, which was broadcast in January 1991."

"I spent that year at my periodic meetings with Dr. Turner discussing the effect of the discovery of Nagase on me and considering what I should do. I still thought often about striking him down, but Stuart helped me to see beyond murder. He thought that I should not try to meet my former interrogator at all, arguing that to do so would be to enter uncharted territory. Despite the range of their awful experience, not one of the Medical Foundation staff could find any precedent for a meeting such as I proposed. Helen Bamber could not recall a voluntary encounter between a person closely complicit with torture and his victim in the history of post-war Europe; while Stuart Turner more than once reminded me that there were many records of US veterans of the Vietnam War suffering traumatic flashbacks when confronted with strong reminders of their wartime experiences."

Later there would be commissions of reconciliation in places such as South Africa, in which the confrontation of the state perpetrator by the victim would at certain points become the norm. But even then (and still more now) it was never certain whether the object was reconciliation, forgiveness or redemption—or perhaps just the search for a way for the victim and perpetrator to live together without killing each other, or going mad. In retrospect, it seems that what the early reconciliation commissions of the late 1990s and early 2000s aimed at doing was to create a basis by which failed states and societies could once again function. But Eric Lomax found himself a pioneer considering things never before contemplated by psychologists and psychiatrists. He was a stranger in a strange land, a pioneer, as it were, of a new approach to aggression and systemic evil that everybody seemed to be making up as they went along.

"Still consumed by the desire to make Nagase suffer fully the consequences of his actions, I decided that I would like to surprise him, reveling in my superior knowledge and his ignorance of me. Aid for this vengeful plan came from an unexpected quarter. The director of the brief television film about the work of the Foundation and my own predicament, Mike Finlason, became so fascinated by the story which he saw unfolding that he decided to try to make a full-length documentary about Nagase and me. My intention was that a meeting should be arranged but that Nagase should be told only that I was a former Far East POW, and not be told that I had identified him as a member of the Kempei. At first Finlason acceded to my plan, but he became understandably and increasingly reluctant to stage a surprise assault on Nagase of the kind I wanted."

"The ways of television were completely new to me, but I soon learned that there is many a slip between the full cup of excited plans for a film and the actual lip of the audience. Mike Finlason was then an independent director and this was his personal enthusiasm. Funding for the film proved elusive, and the early summer of 1991 passed without any of my plans nearing fulfillment—a delay that has almost certainly infinitely benefited at least two people's lives. Stuart Turner was warmly concerned about my intentions, and suggested that I should try to meet some Japanese people socially to prepare myself for the encounter which I was determined to arrange. Given that I had not spoken to a single Japanese person since 1945, this was no easy matter, but I agreed to try. Various schemes were canvassed: visiting a Japanese travel or airline office, for example, so that I could flee without difficulty if I found it necessary to do so."

"No embarrassing meetings with startled Japanese ticket clerks had taken place when one day, in early July 1991, I answered the phone at home, which I very rarely do; Patti has screened calls for a long time past, at my request, and she was out when the phone rang. The caller was a historian of my acquaintance, who asked whether I would be willing to meet a Japanese professor of history, a woman from Tokyo called Nakahara Michiko, who was researching the exploitation of POWs and Asian laborers by the Imperial Japanese Army on the Burma-Siam Railway. I said yes. My wife returned to find that I had arranged a meeting with a Japanese person at our own house. She was more than a little astonished."

"For a few days before the meeting in late July I was frightened of my own response, but when the time came it was a revelation. It was a beautiful summer day, our best clear and light northern weather. Patti went to meet her at Berwick Station, and a little later I heard our garden gate clatter open. I saw my wife walk up the garden path besides a petite, smiling woman wearing elegant trousers and a black silk jacket, her hair a striking deep blue-black. We shook hands. Professor Nakahara spoke superb English, and within a few minutes I could tell that it was going to be all right. She is a considerate and learned

251

woman, and after lunch we sat outside in the garden exchanging information and looking through papers, books and relics."

"Her husband, she told us, had been wounded at Hiroshima. She wanted to rescue the laborers from obscurity; dozens of books have been written about the POWs, but almost nothing about the *romusha*, as they were known to the Japanese. There were a quarter of a million of them: Malays, Indonesians, Chinese, Burmese, Tamils, a disorganized and starved multilingual army with no internal leadership or organization, unlike us. Michiko was interested in my memories of work in the railroad camps; I was fascinated by her as my first new link with Japan. She told me that she had once met Nagase."

"The man who had crept under my skin and stayed there in 1943 seemed different through the eyes of others, and aspects of Japan began to interest me. Here, for example, was a historian unafraid of the truth, delving into her country's most shameful actions, and I liked her. Soon after her return to Japan, she wrote to us to say that she had received an invitation to the Akasaka Palace to give the new Emperor Akihito a lecture on modern South-East Asian history, prior to his tour of the area. She accepted with the condition that she be allowed to speak freely."

"In the month of Nakahara Michiko's visit I was given a copy of a small book by Nagase which he had published in Japan. All I knew was that it was called *Crosses and Tigers*, since my Japanese studies had not progressed much since my efforts with Bill Williamson in 1943, but I learned that an English edition had been published in Thailand in 1990. I ordered a copy and eventually a small package arrived. The book was a tiny paperback, with a picture of the railway bridge over the Kwai on its light green cover; it had less that seventy pages of text, roughly printed with bad type, but I sat down to read it as though it were a rare manuscript."

"The book opens with a brief introductory account of Nagase's conscription in Tokyo, in December 1941, when I was waiting for his Emperor's army at Kuantan. He was classified B3, presumably an indication of low physical fitness, and the photograph he reproduces, taken on 20th December, 1941 shows a very slender young man with a face I remembered too well—an intense , fine, timid and mournful face, dressed in Japanese Army uniform and forage cap, clutching a sword that looks too big for him. He describes how he was sent to Saigon to serve with the oddly-named 'Literal Intelligence Bureau' of the General Staff Office, and how he was then sent to Java to interpret for an intelligence officer collecting information at the end of the Indonesian campaign."

"By early January 1943, he was working in 'transport operations' at Singapore, snooping on POWs who were being sent up to the railway, and presumably searching their baggage for precious fragments of the kind that Fred Smith had taken with him on his way to Ban Pong. In March 1943, when we were already in Kanburi, he was assigned to Bangkok, to the headquarters of the Railway Construction Staff, and in September he received an order to serve with what he calls the 'military police platoon' at Kanburi. He acknowledges the terrible cost of the railway, and that a prisoner or laborer must have died for every sleeper laid; and that today it runs for less than a third of its original length."

"The rest of the little book has three main sections: his memories of Kanburi; his reconstructed diary of his three-week expedition with the war graves group, including Padre Babb, in September-October 1945; and some brief remarks about his post-war experiences in Thailand."

"The first section, and especially the first five pages of it, held me spellbound. Nagase arrives at Ban Pong in dark and cloudy weather. The scene as he recalls it is hellish, the sky overcast and grey, flocks of large black vultures perched on roofs and in the branches of tall teak trees. He thinks at first that vultures are native to this place, but then realizes that they are attracted to the smell of carrion around the prison camp."

"The next day he goes to Kanburi. ('Again there were ghastly flocks of vultures when I walked across the field of tall weeds. The birds moved their heads back and forth every time they made a forward step.') Nagase meets a funeral procession of prisoners, carrying a body on a stretcher covered with a faded Union Jack, followed by a Japanese soldier with a gun and behind him four or five vultures nodding their heads to and fro. He sees the rough bamboo fence of the camp and is told by the sergeant accompanying him to pretend to be an inspector of the camp, since he is unknown and the prisoners may unwittingly give him information. He is shocked at the sight of the camp, and sees shabby roofless huts, sick prisoners shivering in soaking blankets, malaria victims rolling feverishly on their bedding or on the floor."

"The rain starts falling as a British officer comes up to him, pleading for improvements in their conditions, telling him that they have had no roof on their hut for over a week with malaria patients exposed to the rain. The 'weak dimmed eyes' of the malaria patients affect Nagase badly. He remembers seeing the same mournful gaze when prisoners were being packed thirty at a time into box cars in the scorching sun at Singapore railway station. There a blue-eyed British officer had persistently asked him where they were headed, over and over again, repeating the question, but Nagase was unable to answer. 'Why do blue eyes look so sad?' he asks."

"He is assigned at Kanburi to the squad responsible for *Tokko*, intelligence and counter intelligence. He accompanies the head of the squad or a tall sergeant with a 'bluish, clear shaven face', at all times. Sometimes he is asked to impersonate a Thai and to talk with the prisoners in order to learn their thoughts and movements. I had not known that he also spoke Thai, or perhaps he was mimicking a Thai villager who knew a little English."

"Some time before the opening of the railway in October they suspect that a radio is in operation among the prisoners, and that we are listening to Allied broadcasts. They discover the set when they inspect the prisoners' belongings without warning. When all the 'suspects' are brought to his intelligence squad, he writes they have already been beaten badly. He thinks that one prisoner has been beaten to death."

Lomax knows that he is about to read about his own torture. "Suddenly it's as though [Nagase] steps out from behind a screen and I am looking at a scene familiar to me distanced as though in a dream." Nagase writes:

> Let me talk about a prisoner for whom I worked as an interpreter. It was found that he had a rough sketch of the Thai-Burma railway with the names of all the stations when the inspection of their belongings took place. He claimed that he was a railway fanatic and intended to take it home as a souvenir. His explanation was not convincing because the railway was a secret matter in those days.

Nagase says that they had to approve the charge of spying against this prisoner in order to commit him for court martial. He is interrogated but the POW stubbornly denies the charge, knowing that he will be condemned to death if he admits to being a spy.

> The fierce questioning continued from morning till night for over a week, which exhausted me as well. The military policeman sometimes shouted at me because he got too excited to differentiate between the prisoner and me. The suspect looked weak and good natured, but he repeated his stubborn denials... the MP beat him with a stick. I could not bear the sight, so I advised him to confess to avoid further mental and physical pain. He just smiled at me. Finally, the policeman applied the usual torture. First they took him to the bathtub... Then his broken right arm was placed on his front and his left arm behind his back, tied with a cord.

They laid him on his back with a towel loosely covering his mouth and nose. They poured water over his face. The soaking cloth blocked his nose and mouth. He struggled to breathe and opened his mouth to inhale air. They poured water into his mouth. I saw his stomach swelling up. Watching the prisoner in great torture, I almost lost my presence of mind. I was desperate to control my shaking body. I feared that he would be killed in my presence. I took him by the broken wrist and felt the pulse. I still remember clearly that I was relieved to feel an unexpected normal pulse.

With the prisoner screaming and crying, 'Mother! Mother!' I muttered to myself, 'Mother, do you know what is happening to your son now?' I still cannot stop shuddering every time I recall that horrible scene.

Eric Lomax now knew how long the torture had gone on—it had lasted an entire week, as he had previously suspected. Nagase's account confirmed the one part of this horrible experience that he'd never quite been able to remember, the thing that had taken his innocence and smashed his personality in a fundamental way. At the height of his suffering, when he was unconscious but not yet dead, he had cried out to his mother. The terrible irony was that by that time his beloved mother, the most important person in his life, was already dead—the mother who would never hear what happened to him, and would never again comfort her son.

11.

The rest of Nagase's book is mainly about his immediate post-war period. He was assigned by the British to accompany Padre Babb and other officers as they searched for abandoned graves by the Burma-Siam railway. At the end of the line in Burma, there is one tense and potentially violent confrontation with rogue Japanese troops whose commanding officer at first refused to salute the British captain leading the search party.

Nagase describes how his feelings matured, how he came to

understand the systemic evil at the heart of the Japanese military system, which for him was symbolized by the Imperial Rescript, an oath of loyalty that all recruits had to memorize. Over time he came to an appreciation of the Western respect for individual human rights. But always he was motivated by a desire to redeem his part in the crushing mistreatment of Allied POWs, as well as the so-called *Romusha*, the tens of thousands of Asians whose slave labor was used to build the Burma-Siam railroad. (Their situation was so bad that Nagase found entire villages of displaced Asians along the railroad, of slave laborers who for one reason or another felt unable to go home.) But clearly Nagase experienced the torturing of the tall British officer, torture that lasted a week, as the height of the cruelty in which he himself participated, and was in fact the most shocking incident practiced by his own government and its military establishment that he had personally been a part of.

Nagase and his wife then spent the immediate post-war years advocating for the *Romusha*, working to keep up the cemeteries of the POWs, and speaking out for peace and against militarism. He opened a temple dedicated to international peace in the vicinity of the River Kwai bridge. Perhaps most significantly, he mentions an experience he had while visiting the war cemetery at Kanburi with his wife:

> *My wife and I moved forward to the white cross and offered a wreath at its base. The moment I joined my hands in prayer... I felt my body emitting yellow beams of light in every direction and turning transparent. At that moment I thought, 'This is it. You have been pardoned.' I believed this feeling plainly.*

A few days after her husband read the slim book, Patti read it through herself. She immediately sensed the next step that needed to be taken. "The passages which I've quoted on Nagase's trip to the War Cemetery at Kanburi filled her with anger, much more than I had felt. She wanted to know how Nagase felt pardoned. How could his sense of guilt simply 'vanish' if no one, and me in particular, had pardoned him?"

"Patti's sense of indignation was such that she wanted to write to Nagase immediately and asked my permission to do so." Eric gave her permission, as she had asked, and she drafted a letter and sent it in late October 1991. Interestingly—and providentially, given the adventure her husband was about to embark upon—she also sent a photograph of Eric.

Patti writes in her letter that since Eric "had lived all these years with the after-effects of the cruel experience he suffered," she hoped "contact between you could be a healing experience for both of you." But the letter also contains a blunt and provocative question. "How can you feel 'forgiven' Mr. Nagase, if this particular former Far Eastern prisoner-of-war has not yet forgiven you? My husband does understand the cultural pressure you were under during the war but whether he can totally forgive your own involvement remains to be seen and it is not for me, who was not there, to judge..."

It was, to say the very least, a provocative challenge.

12.

A powerful example of Patti Lomax's intuitive understanding of her husband's situation was her decision to send a picture of Eric to Takashi Nagase. Of course, on one level it was simply a courtesy to Nagase, to help him compare his memory of the young Eric to the older man he had become. But it also neutralized any lingering fantasy that Eric might have had about surprising Nagase to harm him, because his face would now be known. In that sense, it was, however unconsciously, a benign but unequivocal 'spoiler' that sent a strong message to both men that physical revenge was off the table.

In the letter sent to Nagase by Patricia Lomax, some extremely important points are articulated, some of which may have been

conscious, and some unconscious. To begin with, she appropriately points out that for most non-Japanese in the West, or at
least most non-Buddhists, forgiveness is interactive; it must
happen *between people*, rather than spontaneously arising from
the cosmos as Nagase had perhaps experienced it. Secondly, her
interest is very clearly not in whether Nagase feels forgiven, but
to help her husband Eric decide if *he* can forgive his torturer. She
does not object specifically to Nagase's desire to experience
forgiveness, but simply points out that his mystical experience,
in which he saw his body emitting yellow light and experienced
a powerful sense of being forgiven, took Eric out of the equation
in a manner that was not acceptable to her personally. While she
clearly understood Nagase's situation, *her* interests lay in helping
Eric reach a point where he could recover; and she had reached
the conclusion that for her husband, forgiveness of his former
torturer would be necessary.

This book is the third of a trilogy presenting a theory
concerning the economy of human aggression: its pivotal and
most important observation is that victims tend to internalize the
violence of the aggressor, and to act it out against others or
against themselves. What is the relationship between the
aggression that the victim internalizes, and the traumatic
memory itself? One can think of the internalized aggression as
being *the same as* the traumatic memory, since the feelings
associated with it cause an aggressive reaction when triggered in
the present moment. But one can also conceive of the aggression
one internalizes as being in some way *separable from* the
traumatic memory. The goal, then, is to deconstruct the
aggression while leaving sequential memory more or less intact.

We know that Eric Lomax internalized an enormous amount
of aggression because of his frequent fantasies and dreams of
killing his torturers, and because of the way the memories of
torture continued to torment him with sleep disturbance,
emotional alienation, and much else. In Eric's case, the goal was

to deconstruct the aggression he had unfortunately internalized, while leaving sequential memory relatively intact: the memory would still exist, but the violence at its heart would be deconstructed. The reader will remember that this book suggests a two-step 'recovery dualism': *first*, one must talk about what happened, in a clinical setting if possible; *second*, one must act out some socially-beneficial behavior that in some way relates to the social forces that originally drove the traumatizing events. Having already discussed his experiences with the clinicians that were helping him, Eric Lomax had taken the first step; it was the second step that he now contemplated acting out.

Does deconstructing a traumatic memory necessitate forgiving a perpetrator? In some cases it plays a role, but in other cases it doesn't. In general, the more the victim is concerned about the issue of forgiveness, the more important it could be to his recovery. In this situation, the victim's forgiveness of the perpetrator increasingly seemed important, and even necessary, because for Eric Lomax the threatening face and persona of Takashi Nagase had come to symbolize the entire episode of being tortured. If Eric could forgive Nagase for torturing him, the traumatic memory of it would no longer have the same power over him as before. But it would be difficult, and there were no guarantees that Eric was capable of forgiveness. Furthermore, everybody involved in this volatile situation was operating in unknown waters. As much as she might understand the dilemma of Takashi Nagase, Patti correctly stipulated that whether her husband forgave him or not was entirely up to Eric, since he was the victim. In so doing, she gives her husband maximum power to act as he chose, while recognizing Nagase's centrality to the process.

By now it was clear that there were circumstances in this situation that made forgiveness at least possible, beginning with an understanding of the cultural pressures Nagase experienced as a very young man. Nagase had been in a military-police organization and was under orders at the time he participated in torturing Eric: that fact did not remove the trauma, nor did it relieve Nagase of his complicity, but it did make understanding of his participation easier. Above all, there was Nagase's intense remorse for his youthful complicity in the systemic evil of which he had been a part. Nagase sought redemption for the evil he had acted out; Eric Lomax sought relief from the traumatic memory arising from that same evil—therefore they shared a common interest. Like many people (and certainly many men), Eric Lomax had assumed that relief might come from killing or punishing his torturer.

But there is a kind of emotional uncertainty principle that begins to apply whenever one becomes familiar with the person one dreams of killing. Unless one is a sociopath, it becomes increasingly hard to imagine killing someone one knows, if that person has human qualities not unlike one's own; indeed, recognizing the humanity of someone one longs to kill might even begin, at some point, to add to one's trauma, since the fantasy of revenge would no longer give the same psychic release as before.

Imagine, then, the dilemma that Lomax was now in—he must do something about Nagase to rid himself of the traumatic memory; but he had started to understand *why* Nagase had participated in Imperial Japan's brutality (not least because of his extreme youth) and was now also aware of Nagase's profound remorse for what had happened. His traumatic memory of Nagase's aggressive persona had long haunted and badgered him, but this new knowledge of the man behind the persona was already taking Eric well beyond the place where he could seriously consider killing him.

Both men sought freedom from the emotional after-effects of involvement in systemic evil, one as victim and one as perpetrator. In a sense it seems grotesque to say that they had a common interest, since they were at opposite ends of a system that destroyed millions of lives; yet clearly they did, since forty years later both were bound together by the emotional after-effects of the same evil system. Could the two men help each other? It might be more accurate to say that they were now cooperating with each other to help themselves—to work together to arrive at a solution. And Nagase's remorse, a remorse that is not often present among perpetrators, created an extraordinary opportunity.

Over the years the traumatic memory had itself become a problem, independent of the events that caused it. Because Eric had not been able to talk about what happened to him, his memory had become impacted, and in time began to play a disproportionate and highly disorienting role in his personality. His memories grew stronger and more threatening, partly because he had no comprehension of what was going on in his personality, and partly because he had come to believe that he would *never* be able to discuss what he'd endured, even as his symptoms got worse. (Remember that when he got around to seeking help at the RAF Hospital, Eric was so terrified of talking about his experiences that he submitted a 50-page memorandum instead.)

His inability to discuss his memories led to a growing belief that the memories had the upper hand over his volition, and indeed, over his entire personality. His ultimate belief that the memories themselves prevented him from discussing them—that they were literally unspeakable—gave them a negative charismatic power over his personality. Only his love for his wife made him realize that recovery was necessary if he was to save his marriage.

What is it that causes traumatic memory of past aggression to take over a person's personality, and to become something just as bad, or sometimes worse, than the events that generated it? All too often it begins with the inability or unwillingness to discuss the memories. This can result in an inability to leave behind the disturbing emotions, while perhaps being unable to remember exactly the events themselves, or to understand why they have become so important. Secondly, it is the aggression encoded in the memories themselves, which can end up creating a paradoxical identification with a past aggression the conscious mind doesn't quite remember. But this is enhanced by an even more maddening emotional conundrum: the *inexplicable* nature of the violence experienced.

The logical conscious mind involved with executive decision-making cannot understand aggression, and aggressive emotional orientations cannot understand logic. They are too often mutually exclusive worlds which are never on speaking terms, much less in opposition to each other. When aggression of an extreme nature has been deeply internalized into the unconscious mind, the logical mind becomes uncomfortably aware that a powerful negative energy is now driving—or at least profoundly influencing—the personality.

But it has no idea what this energy is, or where it is coming from. All the conscious mind knows is that something happened that changed everything, and that its power cannot be easily explained or comprehended. To the conscious mind, it is nothing less than the *unknowable nature of past evil* that seems to reverberate in the aggression at the heart of traumatic memory. The victim knows that the traumatic memory is the most powerful psychological force in his personality, but it is also the least understood. Therefore its functions seem both unknowable and uncontrollable, and therefore incapable of being integrated into the personality.

13.

The ball was now in Nagase's court. Patti had written to him with Eric's blessing, baring her deepest thoughts about the matter that concerned all of them.

Nagase Takashi's reply was not long in coming; and it came, as Patti's had, in the form of a short letter. Patti saw an express airmail letter from Japan lying on the floor just inside the front door, and although it was evidently for her, she brought it upstairs to her husband unopened.

Eric sat on the edge of his bed in his pyjamas and read the letter:

Dear Mrs. Patricia M. Lomax

I am now quite at a loss after reading your unexpected letter. And I am thinking that it is very natural indeed for me to expect such this letter. The words you wrote to me 'If this particular former Far Eastern Prisoner of War has not yet forgiven you has beaten me down wholly, reminding me of my dirty old days. I think having received such a letter from you is my destiny. Please give me some time to think it over and over again.

But please tell your husband that if I am a bit useful for him to answer any questions that he has had in his mind, I am willing to answer them.

Anyhow, I am beginning to think that I should see him again. Looking at the picture, he looks healthy and tender gentleman, though I am not able to see the inside of his mind. Please tell him to live long until I can see him.

Most sincerely yours

Takashi Nagase

p.s. Please let me know your Telephone number.

p.s. Excuse that my mind has confused after reading your letter and I could only write what you read here. I will try to find out the way I can meet him if he agrees to see me.

And thank you very much for your taking care of him until today for a long time.

The dagger of your letter thrusted me into my heart to the bottom.

The last line suggests the extent to which Nagase had been traumatized, not just by his role in the war but by the long-term traumatic memory that he suffered from afterwards; by his own account, maturity had gradually brought with it a growing awareness of the systemic evil of which he had been a part, which helped him integrate his experiences; but because of their extreme brutality they had created a personal crisis, which Nagase had dealt with through his work for reconciliation between former enemies, and honoring those who died on the Railway of Death. For her part, Patti found it "an extraordinarily beautiful letter." Certainly she was in agreement with it—she had evidently come to the conclusion that an actual face-to-face meeting with Nagase was necessary to completely unravel Eric's longstanding and complicated emotions as a victim of torture.

Eric's counselor at the Medical Foundation for the Care of the Victims of Torture was opposed to the meeting with Takashi Nagase because he feared it could trigger a psychotic flashback of the kind often experienced by torture victims. But Eric had made up his mind to go ahead. This willingness to move ahead despite the risks was significant, because it reflects the extent to which Eric Lomax was no longer a victim but a survivor, and was about to become something even more important: he was determined to become a protagonist in his own perilous life story, to seize hold of this opportunity to face down his demons. Some things in his life might remain unknowable, but Eric Lomax was now beginning to assume control over his attitudes toward both the knowable and the unknowable.

Because neither Eric nor Patti were wealthy, it took about a year for them to get together enough to pay for a trip to the Far East, and to make all the arrangements that become necessary in such a situation. No doubt that was a blessing in disguise, since it gave both Eric and Patti time to prepare emotionally. No one can adequately predict what one will feel in such a meeting as the one they contemplated; but one can think through a number of scenarios, and imagine what one's reaction might be. One can even rehearse in one's mind what one might say—such an expedient might serve to diminish fear by making it seem more familiar, and less frightening. But Eric's real advantage lay in his relationship with his wife Patti, and the fact that he could discuss his situation with her on a moment by moment, day by day basis.

In her, Eric now had an advocate and friend who perhaps possessed more insight into his personality, at least in certain areas, than he did himself. He was beginning to have a firm and very practical idea about what he wanted from the meeting with Nagase. What Eric wanted was relief from the traumatic memory that had robbed him of the integrity of his personality. And he wanted to deconstruct the profound aggression in his traumatic memory so that his marriage—a marriage to which he and Patti were both deeply committed—could succeed.

Eric had almost sought financial aid from the Sasakawa Foundation, which facilitated cooperation between Japan and Britain, but certain interested parties wished to make a documentary film of Eric and Nagase's relationship. Soon, however, the would-be documentarians became embroiled in the perennial struggle of all filmmakers, the quest for funding. "In the end," Eric wrote, "believing that Nagase and I could not wait much longer and that the world of film would wear us down, I went to the Sasakawa Foundation and they agreed to help to finance our trip."

"They also felt that the proposed documentary would have some effect in promoting their aims of reconciliation and under-standing, and agreed to loan money for that too. I agreed, as long as the Medical Foundation could own the film when the costs were recovered. With these organizational contingencies at last out of the way, I was ready to face my old enemy eagerly and in good heart."

14.

Bangkok was noisy and hot, but someone had arranged for an air-conditioned Rolls-Royce to drive Eric and Patti the three hours to their hotel. A couple of days later they set out on their rail journey to Kanburi, through Nong Pladuk and then Ban Pong, where the track divided in two; the line diverging to the right would lead to the Burma Siam-Railway where so many people had died. There was no trace of the POW camp at Ban Pong, however; instead Eric, still a railroad fanatic, spotted an old Garratt engine, a "giant handsome workhorse with two sets of eight-coupled wheels; why it had been placed here I couldn't imagine, but it had the aura of a great piece of human effort and it awakened all the old passion in me." Then, a little past Kanburi, the platform at the River Kwai Bridge. That evening Eric and Patti dined at a restaurant owned by Tida Loha, a friend of Nagase who had given him land for his temple of peace. Ian Kerr, an employee of the Medical Foundation, was on standby in case the meeting with Nagase took a bad turn.

The next morning Eric and Patti crossed the river on the bridge, up to a broad veranda overlooking the bridge. There was a museum nearby devoted to the history of the bridge, but Eric and Patti could think of nothing but the impending meeting. And in fact at that point Eric thought he saw Nagase walk out on the bridge: "It was important for me to have this last momentary advantage over him; it prepared me, even now that I no longer wanted to hurt him. I walked about a hundred yards to an open square, a kind of courtyard overlooking the river, where we had arranged to meet."

In situations such as this, one's environment can become so emotionally charged that it feels like a vision or fantasy. In addition to a huge smiling figure of Buddha, Eric "realized that there was another benign presence throwing a shadow on to the wide expanse of terrace: a carefully preserved locomotive, a veteran of the Royal Siamese Railway, built in Glasgow, I noticed, in the year of my birth. This exquisite relic could have come from a brightly-lit dream, with me sitting on an empty square, a silent steam engine close at hand, waiting for something to happen." It was as though Eric's lifelong fascination with trains had suddenly physically manifested itself in real time, offering mute witness not just to the personal enthusiasms of his youth but to the tragic reality of the Railway of Death. The inexplicable but crowning touch was that this magnificent locomotive had been built in the year of his birth.

But then suddenly the world of dreams gave way to something else, something real.

"He came on to the terrace, walking past the engine. I had forgotten how small he was, a tiny man in an elegant straw hat, loose kimono-like jacket and trousers. From a distance he resembled an oriental carving, some benign wizened demon come to life. He carried a shapeless blue cotton shoulder bag. As he came closer I could see that he wore around his throat beads of dark red stone on a thick string. I remembered him saying to me again and again 'Lomax, you will tell us,' other phrases he had recited in the voice I hated so much..."

"He began a formal bow, his face working and agitated, the small figure barely reaching my shoulder. I stepped forward, took his hand and said, 'Ohayo gazaimasu, Nagase san, ogenki desu ka?' 'Good morning, Mr. Nagase, how are you?'"

"He looked up at me; he was trembling, in tears, saying over and over 'I am very, very sorry...' I somehow took command, led him out of the terrible heat to a bench in the shade; I was comforting him, for he was really overcome. At that moment my capacity for reserve and self-control helped me to help him, murmuring reassurances as we sat down. It was as though I was protecting him from the force of the emotions shaking his frail-seeming body. I think I said something like 'That's very kind of you to say so' to his repeated expression of sorrow."

"He said to me, 'Fifty years is a long time, but for me it is a time of suffering. I never forgot you, I remember your face, especially your eyes.' He looked deep into my eyes when he said this. His own face still looked like the one I remembered, rather fine-featured, with dark and slightly hidden eyes; his wide mouth was still noticeable beneath cheeks that had sunken inwards."

"I told him that I could remember his very last words to me. He asked what they were and laughed when I said 'Keep your chin up.'"

"He asked if he could touch my hand. My former interrogator held my arm, which was so much larger than his, stroking it quite unself-consciously. I didn't find it embarrassing. He gripped my wrist with both of his hands and told me that when I was being tortured—he used the word—he measured my pulse. I remembered he had written this in his memoir. Yet now that we were face to face, his grief seemed far more acute than mine. 'I was a member of Imperial Japanese Army; we treated your countrymen very, very badly.'"

"'We both survived,' I said encouragingly, really believing it now."

"A little later, I'm sure he said: 'For what purpose were you born in this world? I think I can die safely now.'"

Interestingly, both Eric and Nagase wanted to visit the Kempeitai house in Kanburi, where Eric had been tortured, but the house was gone. "The yard where the 'monkey houses' were kept is now occupied by a family dwelling," Eric Lomax wrote in *The Railway Man*. "Places where such things have been done can be wiped out so easily. Torture, after all, is inconspicuous; all it needs is water, a piece of wood and a loud voice. It takes place in squalid rooms, dirty back yards and basements, and there is nothing left to preserve when it is over." Nothing left, that is, except the emotional affects on both torturer and victim.

15.

One of the most interesting and unexpected emotional outcomes of this meeting was the growing realization by Eric Lomax that Nagase's suffering had been, if experienced in a different way than his, at the very least just as acute and as longstanding. As a result, he began to understand Nagase's need to be forgiven, especially in terms of his Buddhist faith. "I still needed to consider the matter of forgiveness, since it so concerned him. Assuming that our meeting, in itself, constituted forgiveness, or that the passage of time had made it irrelevant, seemed too easy; once somebody raises forgiveness to such a pitch of importance you become judicial. I felt I had to respond to Nagase's sense of the binding or loosening force of my decision."

This understanding of Takashi Nagase's need to be forgiven made it easier for Eric to be objective about his own need to forgive, in order to recover from his traumatic memory. But it also relieved him of the egocentric predicament in which he had formerly been trapped—Eric Lomax no longer thought of his experience of torture as exclusively or even primarily a private matter, but as a phenomenon of history in a particular time and place, which he had experienced as a victim. He was beginning to understand that the enemy was not the Japanese—at least not anymore—but torture itself.

Lomax wrote in *The Railway Man*: "A kind Thai woman who we met that week tried to explain the importance of forgiveness in Buddhism to me; I understood that whatever you do, you get back in this life and if what you have done is tainted with evil and you have not made atonement for it, evil is returned to you in the next life with interest. Nagase dreaded hell, and it seemed that our first meeting had made parts of both our lives hellish already. Even if I could not grasp the theology fully, I could no longer see the point of punishing Nagase by a refusal to reach out and forgive him."

"What mattered was our relations in the here and now, his obvious regret for what he had done and our mutual need to give our encounter some meaning beyond that of the emptiness of cruelty. It was surely worth salvaging as much as we could from the damage to both our lives. The question was now one of choosing the right moment to say the words to him with the formality that the situation seemed to demand."

In the meantime, they continued to get to know each other.

Not surprisingly, their conversation sometimes took on the black humor of the survivor. Among other places, they visited the Peace Memorial Museum in Hiroshima. "Nagase asked me when I had heard about the nuclear attack on Hiroshima."

"'On 8th August,' I told him."

"He was astonished: this was at least two days before he and his unit were told about it. He wanted to know how we could possibly have known, locked up as we were in Changi and deprived of contact with the outside world. Ah, I told him, but of course we had a radio. And for some reason, that set us off, even in a place of such awful seriousness... There we were, two old gentlemen laughing our heads off in this sanctum of peace."

At the same time, Eric was gradually becoming aware of subtle distinctions regarding Nagase's approach to war, torture and redemption. "Nagase and I had talked about historical truth and he was concerned—almost to the point of obsession—with ensuring that the Japanese should be aware of what their army did in the name of the Emperor before 1945. He believes that there must be a break with all vestiges of the cult of obedience to authority; he is a militant spiritual humanist. He often talked about how there was so little in the way of good history to put into Japanese schoolchildren's hands; so little encouragement to face up to the past and come to terms with it. Nagase's crusading spirit, which is courageous and laudable, can become a little wearing, as when he wished to publicize our outings; but the more he talked the more I could understand his zeal. His obsession had become atonement and reconciliation, which need publicity—whereas mine had been with private remembering and revenge."

Lomax was surprised that he felt no anger toward Nagase during all the time he was with him, "no backwash of that surge of murderous intent I had felt on finding out that one of [his torturers] was still alive." He was beginning to feel, now, that it was time he found some formal way to forgive Nagase. While

Eric and the others in their party visited Kyoto, Nagase was laid up with his chronic cardiac problem; this, in turn, caused Eric to feel that he should express his forgiveness soon, lest the old gentleman die without closure. Therefore he asked to meet with Nagase alone in his hotel room the next day in Tokyo. With some trepidation, Patti left with Yoshiko, Nagase's wife. As Yoshiko left, she softly murmured the word *heart*, a reference to her fear that the impending conversation might be sufficiently strenuous for Nagase as to trigger a heart attack.

"After they had gone I went next door. There in that quiet room, with the faint noise of trains and the city streets rising up to us, I gave Mr. Nagase the forgiveness he desired." Lomax used an improvised ceremony of his own devising: he had written out a short letter expressing his forgiveness, elaborating on it in several paragraphs. "I read my short letter out to him, stopping and checking that he understood each paragraph. I felt he deserved this careful formality. In the letter I said that the war had been over for almost fifty years; that I had suffered much; and that I knew that although he too had suffered throughout this time, he had been most courageous and brave in arguing against militarism and working for reconciliation."

"I told him that while I could not forget what happened in Kanburi in 1943, I assured him of my total forgiveness."

Nagase was overcome with emotion again. After their private ceremony of forgiveness, they spent some time in Nagase's room, two victims of the most destructive war in human history, "talking quietly and without haste."

16.

When Eric Lomax realized that he no longer felt anger toward Nagase, he understood that his recovery was real. The young Takashi Nagase, who had been complicit in his torture in 1943, *no longer existed*. A certain memory of Nagase had ensconced itself in Eric Lomax's unconscious mind fifty years before, and from that vantage point had become a kind of torturer-in-residence, which along with the internalized aggression of the torture itself, had continued to negatively influence everything in Eric's personality and experience. But outside of Eric Lomax's traumatic memories, the real world had moved on; and when Eric became aware that his anger toward Nagase had dissipated, he understood that he, too, had moved on. Patti's intuition had been proven correct: it really *had* been necessary for Lomax to meet Nagase face-to-face to understand that he need no longer fear and hate him. When Eric Lomax finally confronted the demonic enemy who had so long haunted the darkest recesses of his emotions, he encountered only an ancient, harmless revenant—another old man like himself!

Takashi Nagase was profoundly remorseful for what he'd done, and long before meeting with Eric had taken many concrete actions to atone for his actions. Eric Lomax and Takashi Nagase were now free to create a rational relationship that included redemption for both men. And that is what they proceeded to do, concluding with Eric Lomax's brilliant, intuitive idea of a formal letter outlining his reasons for forgiving Nagase.

Its formal nature was in keeping with a certain Japanese preference for the ceremonial that Eric had become aware of, and which he wished to accommodate—interestingly, however, it was also consistent with Eric's very British predilection for formality (*"I read my short letter out to him, stopping and checking that he understood each paragraph."*) It was, in effect, an epistolary contract of forgiveness, binding on two willing parties who had met precisely for this purpose. This writer finds the manner in which Lomax carried out his decision to forgive Nagase especially admirable. This was no impulsive, self-congratulatory New Age interaction, aimed at manipulating short-term relief or spurious notoriety.

Eric specifically made it clear that he could not forget what had happened in 1943, while at the same time forgiving Nagase for his role in it. This is the essential, archetypical contract for forgiveness of systemic evil in our time: that we dare not forget systemic evil because we are determined to oppose it; yet we are able to forgive those persons complicit in it whom we feel are deserving of forgiveness, partly to reward the former aggressor who renounces past evil behavior, and partly to help the victim deconstruct his traumatic memory.

Above all, the victim must always reserve the right to recover from traumatic memory, even if the perpetrator is unknown or beyond redemption. We can see, then, that this was an extremely serious social contract, one that Lomax had carefully considered for a very long time, perhaps even before he had become aware of the necessity to write it down; and because of that—because he cared so much about it—he was careful to reduce it to a written form, so he could get every word right. It was not a game for him: the success of his marriage hung on his recovery. And the fact that he went to such pains to get it right must have made it more meaningful to Nagase as well.

As he and Patti started their journey back to Britain, Eric could hardly contain his amazement at everything that had happened. "As the plane tilted us over the bay of Osaka, I held my wife's hand. I felt that I had accomplished more than I could ever have dreamed of. Meeting Nagase has turned him from a hated enemy, with whom friendship would have been unthinkable, into a blood-brother. If I'd never been able to put a name to the face of one of the men who had harmed me, and never discovered that behind that face there was also a damaged life, the nightmares would always have come from a past without meaning. And I had proved for myself that remembering is not enough, if it simply hardens hate."

For Eric Lomax, returning to the Far East was not so much a return to the scene of the emotional trauma he had suffered, as it was the realization that the historical past had vanished. What he really wanted to do was to make a new future with Patti, and to do that it had been necessary to meet with—and ultimately forgive—Takashi Nagase, who had similarly been seeking to remake his life as an author and activist opposing Japanese nationalism and militarism. This remaking of lives, it should be added at this point, this redemption between two people, occurred not by some primal magic nor as part of a thrilling fantasy, but through halting, painful steps that the two principals laboriously undertook, sometimes separately and sometimes together. And it is also the story of two resolute wives, who were willing to accompany their psychologically wounded husbands to the gates of hell, if that would help them achieve mental health, and cause their marriages to flourish.

Another way to look at Eric Lomax's journey is to see it as a rejection of the tyranny of the past, which for him was not only a good thing, but a necessary thing, for many reasons. To begin with, a memory may be significantly different from what actually happened, and furthermore, memories continue to change over time. When past events tyrannize the present moment, what may matter most is not so much what really happened, but the way the victim's traumatic memory is evolving to keep the traumatic events alive in the victim's unconscious and conscious mind. It is natural for victims to believe that recovery can be found through revisiting the past, but that part works only if the victim does so in order to invest in the future. The story of Eric Lomax is an extreme but inspiring example of a person making a different kind of life for himself and his wife, but doing so in a way that acknowledged the past while deconstructing the past's aggression.

The moment of recovery for Eric began, as noted above, when he realized that Takashi Nagase was no longer threatening to him: which is to say, he finally comprehended that the man he had hated for so long actually existed only inside his own mind and memory, and his own personality. Since the youthful Nagase no longer had any objective reality in the world, Eric had no need to be afraid of him. But simply saying that had not been enough—he needed to *experience* it, by seeing Nagase as the old man he had become. Again, that's why the meeting with Nagase was so important, as Patti Lomax had intuitively understood. Eric's decision to write a letter forgiving Nagase, and reading it slowly to him, had further solemnized and made more concrete his decision to move on, to affirm life and reject the brutality of the past.

The Eric Lomax story is an inspiring narrative of a recovery that worked in a specific instance, although it is not intended to be an invariable prescription for everybody. Still, it embodies certain recurring elements in recovery from traumatic memory: *first,* it illustrates the extreme importance of talking appropriately about traumatizing events as soon as possible after they occur, before they become an unspeakable secret. *Secondly,* Eric Lomax's project of meeting with the man who once tortured him was a superb example of socially-beneficial behavior (public reconciliation with a former enemy) that was also fundamental to Eric's psychological recovery. As a result both men were able to deconstruct much of the aggression they had internalized fifty years before.

Eric Lomax bore his heavy burden for fifty years before choosing the road of recovery to save his marriage—and by so doing, he saved himself. At the same time, he joined Takashi Nagase in heroically confronting the war crimes committed by the Imperial Japanese Army. With the crucial help of their supportive wives, Eric and Takashi broke out of the lethal cycle of aggression and systemic evil that binds and lacerates humankind. Both men acted out in exemplary fashion the 'recovery dualism' recommended in this book. *First:* They spoke about what had happened to them, Nagase first in his books and articles, and Eric to the clinicians who treated him, and then by writing his own book. *Second:* They acted, despite their fear and at some risk to themselves, as part of a socially-beneficial project that enabled them to become better people, while creating a better world. In these accomplishments, and in their unforgettable story, are encoded the entirety of the 'recovery dualism' advocated in this book.

Chapter Four

"The Things They Carried": Art, Artifice and the Deconstruction of War Trauma

The surprising thing, next to their progressive corpulence, is the amount of paper that is scattered about the dead. Their ultimate position, before there is any question of burial, depends on the location of the pockets in the uniform. In the Austrian army these pockets were in the back of the breeches and the dead, after a short time, all consequently lay on their faces, the two hip pockets pulled out and, scattered around them in the grass, all those papers their pockets had contained.

A Natural History of the Dead

Ernest Hemingway

1.

During the time when the Vietnam War was being escalated, this writer worked at Rincon Annex of the San Francisco Post Office, a huge postal facility near the waterfront. For a year or two I worked in FPO and APO parcel post, in what was called the 'Nixie' section. ('Nixie' is a word used by postal workers for damaged items that must be repaired before they can be sent on.) It was the sworn duty of this writer to rewrap packages that had for some reason come apart in the military mails, packages that contained the personal items belonging to American military personnel deployed in Vietnam. Most of the packages were from soldiers sending things home; others were being sent to military personnel in Vietnam from the USA; and a few contained items from soldiers that had been killed or were missing in action. Instead of coming home themselves, it was now their personal belongings that were coming home.

Almost all the packages, whether headed for Vietnam or

coming from that country, contained drugs of some kind, if you looked hard enough. Given the intense antiwar attitude then prevalent in San Francisco, it was our unofficial policy—that is, the postal clerks in the Nixie section, who were mainly younger people—to ignore drugs ('contraband'), especially cannabis, and certain other illicit items. Our refusal to enforce postal regulations in this matter was because we did not want to add to the problems of people who were already under a great deal of stress. One might call this a small act of solidarity. (There was also a sense that there was something problematical about any war that so regularly involved the use of drugs.)

Although I have repressed a great many memories relating to that time period, I can still remember the incredible depression I felt after handling the belongings of soldiers killed in action, or in some cases items that had been sent by friends to soldiers who were later reported as killed in action. (In my memory these packages were marked 'deceased,' although this may be wrong. They may have been marked 'K.I.A.', for killed in action.) Handling belongings of the dead, or even belongings *intended* for the dead, was terrible. There is no way to prepare for the tactile shock of handling and seeing such artifacts; but it is not hard to understand the reason for their power. Soldiers take certain items off to war, and then into combat, to remind them that there is a better place than war, and as proofs that they might at some point resume a normal life in spite of the death they are experiencing. These little artifacts, these *chachkas*, remind anyone who sees or touches them that they were once carried by living people, persons who wanted very much to stay alive. Very much like ourselves.

So the artifacts of the dead intrude on life—but so do the frivolous paraphernalia of life intrude on lethal scenes of death after battle. A young Ernest Hemingway writes, in the quotation at this chapter's beginning, about the magical intrusion of personal papers of the living into a battleground filled with dead soldiers. Letters, photos, poems and an insane variety of lucky charms are carried faithfully into battle, more as symbols of life in the midst of death than any sustained belief that they can guarantee a good outcome. If there are two worlds, the quick and the dead, the soldier's personal memorabilia are the connection between the two. They are carried as *emblems* of life outside of war: tokens, signs, symbols and representations of a different and better world—irreducible proof, as it were, that such a better world exists, and that the soldier might someday resume full citizenship in it.

My Oxford English Dictionary gives one felicitous definition of the word *emblem* as the "picture of an object (or the object itself) serving as a symbolical representation of an abstract quality, an action, state of things, class of persons, etc.," but the word can also mean "that which is inserted into some other substance," such as inlaid metal in a wood cabinet. The small personal items carried by soldiers are *emblematic*, in the very midst of organized murder and destruction, of the better and saner world of civilian life, a life that the soldier once knew intimately and which was now going on "back in the world." The emblems, the remembrances, and the personal items of the soldier vividly suggest what might await him in civilian life, if only he could manage to survive.

The greatest (and most dangerous) temptation of every soldier is to *become* war, to internalize completely its logic of death, despite the fact that on the surface that seems like a good strategy for minimizing psychological pain. (Once you identify completely with war, it can no longer overwhelm you, because you belong totally to it and in it.) But once one *becomes* war, how does one get back to the civilian world in which one previously resided, in which murderous aggression is no longer rewarded but punished? If the warrior loses all sense or remembrances of the civilian world, there will come a time when he is tempted to validate his temporary identity by becoming a war casualty—that is, by becoming a certifiable statistic of the certifiably dead.

Thus the personal items, the emblems of life carried by the soldier, are terribly important, because they help him remember where he came from; and that, in turn, can help him understand that the war zone in which he operates is temporary, necessarily pathological, and necessarily bereft of meaning, except to kill or be killed. Thus a lucky charm from one's children, a letter from a friend, or some quotation or poem on a card, may be uniquely capable of helping the soldier avoid the death-wish that periodically comes upon even the most aggressive and patriotic warrior.

The magical quality inherent in such personal items is carried to extreme and sometimes hilarious lengths in Tim O'Brien's *The Things They Carried*, perhaps the best novel to come out of the Vietnam War. O'Brien's powerful work consists of interconnected stories in which the same characters appear and reappear, almost all of whom are American combat soldiers in Vietnam in a platoon (Alpha Company) commanded by First Lieutenant Jimmy Cross. The first story, *The Things They Carried* is mainly about some letters carried by Lieutenant Cross, the letters wrapped in plastic and concealed at the bottom of his rucksack. Lieutenant Cross's letters are from an attractive young woman named Martha, who is studying English at Mount Sebastian College in New Jersey; Cross also carries two rather unremarkable photographs of her in his wallet.

The letters are not love letters, nor are the photographs the kind a woman would ever share with a lover, because Cross's relationship with Martha had not progressed to the point of sexual intimacy—or any other kind of intimacy, actually; nonetheless, Cross is doggedly hopeful that the relationship might become a romantic one at some point in the future. Over a period of time Lieutenant Cross has fallen deeply in love with Martha—or at least, with the photographs of her that he carries.

"In the late afternoon, after a day's march, he would dig his foxhole, wash his hands under a canteen, unwrap the letters, hold them with the tips of his fingers, and spend the last hour of light pretending. He would imagine romantic trips into the White Mountains in New Hampshire. He would sometimes taste the envelope flaps, knowing her tongue had been there. More than anything, he wanted Martha to love him as he loved her, but the letters were mostly chatty, elusive on the matter of love."

While Martha's letters are well-written and informative, there is not the slightest indication that she cares about Cross romantically, or is ever likely to do so. It appears that Cross receives no other letters of similar import, at least not from women. One must ask oneself why a young woman such as Martha would expend such effort writing letters to someone with whom she is clearly not emotionally involved. One must also ask how Lieutenant Cross, who seems a thoughtful and unusually introspective person, could fall in love with Martha—a woman he really doesn't know very well—and believe that Martha might someday love him.

"She often quoted lines of poetry; she never mentioned the war, except to say, Jimmy, take care of yourself. The letters weighed 10 ounces. They were signed Love, Martha, but Lieutenant Cross understood that Love was only a way of signing and did not mean what he sometimes pretended it meant. At dusk, he would carefully return the letters to his rucksack. Slowly, a bit distracted, he would get up and move among his men, checking the perimeter, then at full dark he would return to his hole and watch the night and wonder if Martha was a virgin."

Cross clearly values these artifacts from Martha so highly because they have the power to generate intensely romantic and sexual feelings, not to mention hope for a romantic future with the object of his infatuation. But it seems equally likely that Martha composes the letters she sends to Lieutenant Cross as exercises in creative writing of the epistolary variety—after all, she's an English major—rather than out of any regard for him. (We are told that she writes beautifully "about her professors and roommates and midterm exams, about her respect for Chaucer and her great affection for Virginia Woolf.") She may not be interested in men. She may even feel sorry for Lieutenant Jimmy Cross. He is, after all, fighting in an unpopular and perhaps losing war, and she may hope that her well-written letters can provide diversion in an otherwise stressful situation. Interestingly, we aren't told whether Cross responds to her missives with letters of his own, and how often he does so. Yet it is clear that Cross regards Martha's letters and photographs as the most important things he carries in his knapsack, besides the implements of war.

What the soldiers carried "varied by mission," O'Brien says. "On ambush, or other night missions, they carried peculiar little odds and ends. Kiowa always took along his New Testament and a pair of moccasins for silence. Dave Jensen carried night-sight vitamins high in carotene. Lee Struck carried his slingshot; ammo, he claimed, would never be a problem. Rat Kiley carried brandy and M&M's candy. Until he was shot, Ted Lavender carried the starlight scope, which weighed 6.3 pounds with its aluminum carrying case. Henry Dobbins carried his girlfriend's pantyhose wrapper around his neck as a comforter. They all carried ghosts. When dark came, they would move out single file across the meadows and paddies to their ambush coordinates, where they would quietly set up the Claymores and lie down and spend the night waiting."

The mentioning of M&M candy is oddly evocative, although in *The Things They Carried* O'Brien does not tell us why. M&Ms had long been popular with soldiers, long before Vietnam, because of its hard sugar coating, which prevents it from melting when carried in a rucksack. ("Melts in your mouth, not in your hand.") But it was also part of a benign scam in which unspecified numbers of Vietnam medics were complicit. Evacuation of wounded was generally rapid, according to most reports, but for those who were dying of mortal wounds, something else was needed. When someone is dying, and there is no chaplain available, something else is always needed. The M&Ms were used as a placebo given to wounded men who were probably not going to make it. They were told that it was a painkiller, when in fact it wasn't. It was a lie, but one told for benign reasons.

One must imagine that the sugary-sweet M&Ms were often a comfort both to the dying soldier and the medic that treated him; and apparently it often worked, more or less: when a half-conscious, dying soldier was told that the M&M was a painkiller, the placebo effect would sometimes kick in. Even when it didn't, it would allow both the medic and the wounded soldier to pretend that his pain wasn't so bad and would quickly pass, and that the wounded man wasn't in such bad shape after all. It gave medic and soldier an encouraging illusion they could both engage in, and a ritual in which they could jointly participate. At the same time, most soldiers in Vietnam must have known about the M&M scam, so it is hard to understand how the placebo effect could have ever worked.

Perhaps dying soldiers knew very well on some level that the M&Ms really weren't painkillers, but willingly bought into the illusion on the spur of the moment, in the desperate expectation that the placebo effect would kick in. In *The Things They Carried*, Tim O'Brien never tells the reader the full story of M&Ms—that is, he never fully explains their tricky psychological function in the dreamlike world of American combat soldiers in Vietnam— but not letting the reader in on the secret is consistent with his idea that in combat what is important is not a particular reality, but the feelings you have later about it. Seen from that perspective, the M&Ms end up as a half-articulated, mysterious symbol of something in the American character that causes us to seek out and regard as necessary certain psychological illusions. (One thinks of the murderous American doctrine of 'manifest destiny,' which nineteenth-century Americans were supposed to accept because it was framed as being completely self-evident.)

Like the M&Ms, the letters and photos of Martha that Jimmy Cross carried were also placebos, the effect of which was likewise to kill pain; but like the M&Ms carried by the eccentric medic Rat Kiley, they exist only as part of an illusion, albeit one that Cross must believe in for it to work even temporarily. Cross's intermittent belief that Martha will someday love him enables him to imagine being alive after he leaves Vietnam—a perfect example of magical thinking in war. But for the magic to work Jimmy must believe that he loves Martha in the present moment; and to believe that he loves her as much as he wants her to love him. It is an entirely self-generated and self-fulfilling lie, one that exists only in his imagination; but his fear, and the intense sexual longing that he uses as a defense against his ever-present consciousness of it, keeps it going. Martha's letters and photos are for him the connecting link between the world of death in which he is immersed, and "back in the world"—that is, the world of life elsewhere, outside of Vietnam.

But it is death itself that breaks this connection, not of Martha but of one of Jimmy's men. The crisis began with Lieutenant Jimmy Cross's receipt in the mail of a good-luck charm from Martha. It was an oval-shaped pebble, which strikes Cross as resembling a miniature egg. "In the accompanying letter, Martha wrote that she had found the pebble on the Jersey shoreline, precisely where the land touched water at high tide, where things came together but also separated. It was this separate-but-together quality, she wrote, that had inspired her to pick up the pebble and to carry it in her breast pocket for several days, where it seemed weightless, and then to send it through the mail, by air, as a token of her truest feelings for him. Lieutenant Cross found this romantic. But he wondered what her truest feelings were, exactly, and what she meant by separate-but-together." (To this writer, Martha's together-but-separate idea, while aesthetically attractive, sounds suspiciously like the precursor to a 'Dear John' letter, the lethally poetic kind an English major might be tempted to write.)

But Cross is entranced. "He loved her so much. On the march, through the hot days of early April, he carried the pebble in his mouth, turning it with his tongue, tasting sea salt moisture. His mind wandered. He had difficulty keeping his attention on the war. On occasion he would holler at his men to spread out the column, to keep their eyes open, but then he would slip away into daydreams, just pretending, walking barefoot along the Jersey shore, with Martha, carrying nothing."

But the war intervenes. Later, on that same patrol, Cross sends one of his soldiers into a Viet Cong tunnel preparatory to blowing it up. At the same time, one of Cross's soldiers, Ted Lavender, is coming back from urinating in the jungle, and is shot in the head, dying instantly. For reasons unknown, Cross does not order his men to return fire, nor does he order them to fan out and flank the sniper. Instead everybody spends a great deal of time simply internalizing, thinking and talking about the precipitous manner in which Ted Lavender fell after taking the head wound. Then they retaliate by burning down the nearest village.

"After the chopper took Lavender away, Lieutenant Jimmy Cross led his men into the village of Than Khe. They burned everything. They shot chickens and dogs, they trashed the village well, they called in artillery and watched the wreckage, then they marched for several hours through the hot afternoon, and then at dusk, while Kiowa explained how Lavender died, Lieutenant Cross found himself trembling."

Lieutenant Jimmy Cross is now in full crisis. He has concluded that his obsession with Martha had distracted him to such an extent that he hadn't taken sufficient precautions, and had therefore put his men at risk. He assumes responsibility for the death of Ted Lavender, although his death is clearly not Cross's fault. But blame, responsibility and guilt are to a great extent intangibles—yes, even responsibility—and Cross feels responsible for Lavender's death. Lavender was under his command, and Cross was daydreaming about Martha at exactly the moment that Lavender took the bullet that ended his life.

"He felt shame. He hated himself. He had loved Martha more than his men, and as a consequence Lavender was now dead, and this was something he would have to carry like a stone in his stomach for the rest of the war." Cross digs his foxhole, and sits in it for a long while, alone. "In part, he was grieving for Ted Lavender, but mostly it was for Martha, and for himself, because she belonged to another world, which was not quite real, and because she was a junior at Mount Sebastian College in New Jersey, a poet and a virgin and uninvolved, and because he realized she did not love him and never would."

"On the morning after Ted Lavender died, First Lieutenant Jimmy Cross crouched at the bottom of his foxhole and burned Martha's letters. Then he burned the two photographs. There was a steady rain falling, which made it difficult, but he used heat tabs and sterno to build a small fire, screening it with his body, holding the photographs over the tight blue flame with the tips of his fingers." Even as he burns her letters, Cross thinks about what Martha looked like playing volleyball in her white gym shorts and yellow T-shirt. He thinks he sees her moving in the rain. He decides to dispose of the good-luck pebble.

Cross has decided that from now on, he will no longer lose himself in reveries about Martha, but will concentrate wholly on being a better commanding officer. "He would now determine to perform his duties firmly and without negligence. It wouldn't help Lavender, he knew that, but from this point on he would comport himself as an officer. He would dispose of his good-luck pebble. Swallow it, maybe, or use Lee Strunk's slingshot, or just drop it along the trail. On the march he would impose strict field discipline. He would be careful to send out flank security, to prevent straggling or bunching up, to keep his troops moving at the proper pace and at the proper intervals. He would insist on clean weapons. He would confiscate the remainder of Lavender's dope. Later in the day, perhaps, he would call the men together and speak to them plainly. He would accept the blame for what had happened to Ted Lavender. He would be a man about it. He would look them in the eyes, keeping his chin level, and he would issue the new SOPs in a calm, impersonal tone of voice, a lieutenant's voice, leaving no room for argument or discussion."

"Among the men there would be grumbling, of course, and maybe worse, because their days would seem longer and their loads heavier, but Lieutenant Jimmy Cross reminded himself that his obligation was not to be loved but to lead. He would dispense with love; it was not now a factor. And if anyone quarreled or complained, he would simply tighten his lips and arrange his shoulders in the correct command posture. He might give a little nod. Or he might not."[1]

The emblems of love that Jimmy Cross carries are no longer powerful enough to stave off the reality of imminent death. From now on he will put his trust solely in his willingness to realize his own vision of himself as the complete soldier; and he will live totally in the present moment, not in fantasies about Martha: his sense of responsibility for his men will be his single connection to life after the Vietnam War. The decision to live in the present moment is usually a good one; yet one cannot help but marvel at the power of Martha's photos, letters and her talismanic pebble from the Jersey shore, and the role they assumed up to that moment in Cross's mind, memory and emotions. Evidence for this can be seen clearly in the night and morning after Ted Lavender is killed. It is Lavender's death that causes Lieutenant Jimmy Cross to get rid of Martha's photos and letters, but his tears of grief aren't for the dead soldier, but for Martha, the fantasy lover who is now lost to him forever.

What has this to do with recovery from emotional trauma? Cross's decision to connect on a deeper level with his men is a first step toward connecting with a real future, rather than an imaginary one. The problem with fantasy lovers, as with dreams of instant wealth through a winning lottery ticket, is that they take the dreamer nowhere. You can make your imaginary lover do anything, except those unpredictable things that only a real, flesh-and-blood lover would be likely to do. Fantasies of love are essentially self-serving, because they do not help the dreamer connect with life-giving things in the real world, they do not help him learn the social skills necessary to win a real lover, nor do they help him talk out his problems with a real, flesh-and-blood person. A fantasy lover such as Martha is essentially an experiment in magical thinking, an attempt to bring about a reality simply by believing that it will happen. It is the kind of thing that happens when people are under great stress, such as combat soldiers, prisoners of war, torture victims and people in solitary confinement.

But such fantasies can be treacherous, because the real people on whom the fantasies of love are based usually do not turn out to be the people they seem to be in one's fantasy world. Furthermore, dreaming of something that is probably impossible is not how to build a better future, or a better world. One recovers from the tyranny of past human violence by connecting with real people in the present moment (hopefully those who understand where you're coming from) and not to imaginary friends and lovers. One must find some way, some *modus vivendi*, some way of getting along with others, to work toward the person one wants to be, and toward the world one would like someday to see; and the only way to do that is to interact with real people.

Hell is other people, as Sartre famously said, and sometimes it is; such horrors as the Vietnam War would not happen if people didn't have a hellish side. But the abiding mystery of humanity is that other people—real people, not imaginary ones—can also be, and often are, the conduit or means of recovery from traumatic memory of human violence. It is real people to whom one must talk, however, not to idealized figures in a fantasy, to make changes in oneself and in the world.

Jimmy Cross is in a terrible war. As he himself observes early in *The Things They Carried*, he got into the war because he lacked the courage to resist it. But once he finds himself in it, he has a responsibility to the men under his command. As obscene, violent and occasionally crazy as the soldiers in Alpha Company may be, Lieutenant Jimmy Cross is better off connecting with them, and identifying with their survival, than strolling on an imagined Jersey shore with an imaginary lover. Jimmy's expectations of Martha were bogus; the men with whom he is serving are real. Talking to other people about your feelings, people who understand what you are going through even if they don't agree with you, is where the path out of the emotional thicket of war begins, the path to "the world," the path to the world outside of war and the trauma induced by human violence. The irony is that to get out of war, Jimmy Cross must identify with other men who are, like him, in the thick of that violence.

2.

No, I am not a child. I am grown up and already strong in the face of hardships, but somehow, at this moment, I yearn deeply for Mom's caring hand. Even the hand of a dear one or that of an acquaintance would be enough. Come to me, squeeze my hand, know my loneliness, and give me the love, the strength, to travel all the hard sections of the road ahead.

Last Entry of Dr. Dang Thuy Tram
Last Night I Dreamed of Peace, translated by Andrew X. Pham

On June 22, 1970, soldiers from "D" Company of the 4th Battalion, Americal Division, were on patrol in Central Vietnam. (The 23rd Infantry Division—more commonly known as the Americal— was the same Division in which Tim O'Brien, author of *The Things They Carried*, had served two years before.) It was morning; and on this particular day the American infantrymen were surprised to hear distant music and voices. Later on that same day, soldiers of the 2nd Platoon saw four people moving toward them on a jungle trail, and opened fire. They killed two of the four, one of them a woman, while the other two escaped, apparently without returning fire. The woman they killed was Dr. Dang Thuy Tram, a young North Vietnamese doctor who had been serving under various Viet Cong commands. The things she carried were as follows: a radio, a rice ledger, bottle of Novocain, a medical notebook with drawings of the wounds she had treated, bandages, a photograph of a Captain serving in the North Vietnamese Army, and poems written to him.

She also carried a small diary, which became the property of the US Army.

Fred Whitehurst, a young American officer in an intelligence unit at Duc Pho, an American base in southern Quang Ngai Province, eventually came upon the diary. He had been ordered to go through captured North Vietnamese documents and burn those that had no military value, throwing them into a fire in a 55-gallon drum. He picked up Thuy's diary and was looking into it, when—according to Frances Fitzgerald, who wrote the 'Introduction' to the English translation of *Last Night I Dreamed of Peace*—Whitehurst's translator, who was standing nearby, saw the diary in Fred's hand and made a strange but highly evocative comment that would change Whitehurst's life.

"Don't burn this one," the translator said. "It has fire in it already."

The document Fred Whitehurst was examining consisted of several small pages sewn together, with a cardboard cover, hardly bigger than a pack of cigarettes. At that moment Fred Whitehurst made a decision that would influence the rest of his life, and touch many others' lives as well, both American and Vietnamese. Instead of burning the small diary, he saved it for his own personal use (along with another diary by Thuy that likewise fell into American hands). Whitehurst was curious, and asked his translator, Sergeant Nguyen Trung Hieu, to read to him from the diary at night. It isn't known exactly what made Whitehurst so curious to hear the passionate voice encoded in the entries of this extraordinary diary; but the young patriot quickly began to realize that reading, hearing and internalizing Thuy's words was affecting him emotionally. To better understand how this worked, one must remember that Fred Whitehurst was incurring a fair amount of risk by keeping the dairies, rather than burning them. Not only did he disobey a direct order in the short term, Whitehurst took the diary home to America with him after three tours of duty in Vietnam, again disobeying military regulations regarding captured enemy property—in this case, property he had been ordered to destroy.

Why did Fred Whitehurst take such risks? Whitehurst has been quite forthcoming about what had happened to him. In the diary he encountered a complex but honorable person who— despite the fact that she belonged to the educated elite of America's sworn enemy—possessed many admirable qualities, including a capacity for selfless dedication that is rare in all times and places. But while she was supremely confident in the historic cause for which she labored, she was, at the same time, capable of questioning her own motives, and often expressed despair at what was happening around her. She was also a person who—if somewhat naïve politically—exhibited an almost unbelievable resolve in carrying out her militarily important but essentially humanitarian mission. In addition, the young woman who wrote the diaries seemed to encapsulate in her writing style—and exemplified in her life—a certain perennial quality of spiritual beauty in the midst of great suffering, something one usually encounters in religious mystics.

In the diaries of Dr. Dang Thuy Tram, Fred Whitehurst saw a young North Vietnamese woman whose patriotism very nearly mirrored his own. As always happens when one sees oneself (and one's own highest values) reflected in the life and values of someone designated as 'the enemy,' it was a profound emotional shock. Thuy's diaries touched Fred Whitehurst's personality on a deep level, gradually becoming the agent of a profound and unexpected emotional transformation.

"Person to person, I fell in love with her," was the way he put it.

3.

Dr. Dang Thuy Tram's father was a surgeon at Saint Paul Hospital in central Hanoi, a large medical complex formerly administered by the Catholic Diocese of Hanoi under the French. Her mother lectured at the Hanoi School of Pharmacology; among other things, she was an expert on the uses of medicinal plants. Francis Fitzgerald tells more about her family in her 'Introduction' to *Last Night I Dreamed of Peace*: "Her parents weren't rich—no one was in North Vietnam at the time—but they were cultured people who filled their small house on Giang Vo Street in Hanoi with books and flowers. Her father played Western classical music to relax after surgery and taught Thuy to play the violin and the guitar."

The oldest of five children, Thuy went to the Chu Van An high school. "Founded by the French in 1906 as the Lycee du Protectorate, the school with its campus on the West Lake had trained generations of prominent Vietnamese intellectuals, artists, and politicians. For four years Thuy, dressed in a white *ao dai*, studied in the handsome French colonial buildings with their spacious classrooms, the breeze coming through the transoms over the high louvered doorways. Her concentration was science, but she loved literature—Vietnamese poetry and the French and Russian novels sent from the Soviet Union. According to classmates, she was beautiful, intelligent, and warm-hearted, and all the boys were a little in love with her. She went on to Hanoi University Medical School and, following in her father's footsteps, trained as a surgeon. On graduating, she was accepted for advance study in optical surgery, but chose instead to serve in the war zone of the South."

Why would a young professional woman of twenty-four volunteer for such dangerous duty? In North Vietnam—and in many places in South Vietnam—people saw themselves as part of a long and heroic national struggle for independence, first from China, later Cambodia, then the French imperialists and finally the Americans. That, as many of them saw it, was their destiny, to participate in an ongoing armed resistance that had been going on for centuries. Quant Ngai, the province to which Thuy was headed, had been a center for guerilla activity since 1930, when the first revolts against the French had occurred; it had become a center for resistance to Japanese occupation, then again against the French and finally the Americans.

The Viet Minh (precursor to the Viet Cong) had been so powerful in Quang Ngai that the French never had full control of the province. People in the province had enthusiastically welcomed the declaration of independence by Ho Chi Minh, and in many ways considered themselves part of North Vietnam, despite being cut off from it by the creation of South Vietnam. For the idealistic young, the final defeat of the European and American imperialists was usually seen as the ultimate good, a final success that all Vietnamese should sacrifice to achieve, and which they could celebrate together as the culmination—and final acting out—of the deepest meaning of their history.

Americans never understood the extent to which many Vietnamese experienced communism as an extension of Vietnamese nationalism. For example, here is Thuy's definition of Ho Chi Minh's revolution: "The revolution has forged a noble people and bound them into a unit firmer and more solid than anything in this life. Could anything make one prouder than to be part of this revolutionary family?" So—is this a description of Marxist-Leninist comradeship, or of the Vietnamese people involved in a national liberation struggle *as a people?* Surely it is the latter.

Rachel Boeve, writing for the Institute for Global Engagement, argued that the success of Communism in Vietnam also "depended on the deeply spiritual nature of the Vietnamese people. Tram's diaries reveal the quasi-religious nature of her devotion to the people." The way the diaries were framed may seem like political fanaticism to outsiders, but they were based squarely on values that were deeply embedded in Vietnamese culture, revolving around the idea of self-sacrifice in the struggle against outside invaders. These values were shared by people at all levels of Vietnamese society, from peasants to professionals to militant political cadres.

Of course, the tactics of the North Vietnam Army and the Viet Cong included the sustained use of terrorism—by the Viet Cong especially—but to the average Viet Cong cadre this would simply have been seen as an inevitable part of the struggle to liberate their people from the humiliating occupation of American imperialists. Thuy, along with all elements associated with the National Liberation Front and the Viet Cong in Quang Ngai, were deeply and agonizingly aware of the Americans' saturation bombing, a campaign that was ultimately responsible for somewhere between two and three million dead throughout Vietnam as a whole. They would have considered this a form of state terrorism, next to which their occasional deployment of terrorism was hardly remarkable. While Thuy's diary included much self-doubt, any doubts about the necessity of Vietnamese liberation from Americans and Europeans would not have occurred to her, nor would it to millions of other young patriots in both North Vietnam, and those parts of South Vietnam under the influence of the Viet Cong and North Vietnamese Army.

American scholars—many of them supported economically by the Pentagon or State Department—reached consensus early in the Vietnam War, generally arriving at the conclusion that the main social dynamics of rural Vietnam had long tended to revolve around clandestine military organizations; but that did the Americans little good in developing a coherent counter-insurgency doctrine. They were typically too fixated on *militarily* defeating "the threat of Communism" to understand the deeply emotional—and in fact quasi-religious—nature of Vietnamese nationalism and patriotism. Instead of boldly presenting a vision of a better society, the Americans sought to defeat their enemy with money, power and saturation bombing, things that generated fear and corruption but no sense of national purpose. Thus the Americans and their proxies could offer no historical task to the Vietnamese people as compelling as the national liberation struggle initiated by Ho Chi Minh.

Again, the NVA and VC victory occurred not so much because the North Vietnamese Army and Viet Cong leaders were Communists, but because military resistance to invaders was the major preoccupation of Vietnamese literature, legends and history generally; and because the national liberation struggle against the French and Americans was seen as operating in a parallel way to similar national liberation struggle of Africans, Latin Americans and Asians around the world. The American involvement in what was actually a domestic civil war was perceived even by non-Communists in the Third World as a form of imperialism or neo-colonialism.

It was this kind of bone-deep patriotic idealism described above that animated Dang Thuy Tram as she joined the teams sent from North Vietnam to provinces in the South. "On December 23, 1966," writes Francis Fitzgerald, "she boarded a truck in Hanoi with a group of civilians—journalists, photographers, and doctors—and drove 250 miles south to a staging area in Quang Binh Provice. From there, she and her companions set off on foot with heavy packs on their backs and walked for three months down what the Americans called the Ho Chi Minh Trail though the mountains of the Trung Son range. Their destination was Quang Ngai, the fifth province below the demilitarized zone that divided the North from the South, and they reached it in late March or early April." As mentioned above, this province had been a center of revolutionary activity for as long as anybody could remember. "In Quang Ngai, the influence of the Saigon government never reached beyond a few of the larger towns. By the time the first regular American troops arrived there in 1965, a whole generation of young people in the rural areas had grown up, as Thuy had, in the revolution."

Thuy's clinic was in Doc Pho District, in a mountainous area "with trails that ran through it like tunnels," located near a river. As it was quite cold in the autumn and winter, Thuy was obligated to cut firewood, dig shelters and transport rick sacks, in addition to her medical duties. "Sometimes army units would bring dozens of patients with serious wounds, and she would have to work through the night, making diagnoses and perform operations without electricity. The soldiers would stay for a while, then move on, leaving the clinic with only the dead and dying. Then Thuy would have time for reflection." Thuy had begun a diary soon after leaving Hanoi, but it was lost. The dairy that was later recovered she began after a year at Quang Ngai, and according to Frances Fitzgerold, "at a time when she was desperately unhappy."

Fitzgerald writes of the reason for her unhappiness: "Thuy had gone to the South out of patriotism but also because of the man she calls M., whom she had loved since the age of sixteen. M., whose real name was Khuong The Hung but who used the pen name Do Moc, came from another intellectual Hanoi family, and his parents were close friends of Thuy's. Handsome and intelligent, he wrote poetry and composed music. A match between them would have been entirely suitable, and he courted her in her college and medical school days. But he was six years older than she was, and in 1962 he left and worked for a while with a troupe of singers and actors, then joined the guerrillas in central Vietnam."

"He wrote her letters, and on her graduation five years later, Thuy, 'following the calls of country and love,' set out for Quang Ngai, hoping to see him from time to time. By then M. had become the captain and chief political officer of an NLF sapper group, and had earned a reputation for heroism.[2] Because of the loss of Thuy's first diary, it is unclear what happened between the two of them, but by April 1968, Thuy understood that he didn't love her in the pure, bright way that she loved him. Was it that he had dedicated himself entirely to the struggle and assumed he would die in it? Or was it that he had affairs with other women? She had her pride, but to her he represented all her hopes and dreams of happiness, and she couldn't bear to give them up—certainly not amid all the hardships and dangers she was experiencing. 'Oh, why was I born a dreamy girl demanding so much of life?' she asks herself plaintively."

Thuy witnessed the incredible destructive power of the US military as it attacked the civilian population of the province, and the attacks of both NVA and main force Vietcong soldiers. "The roads were mined and booby-trapped; the American patrols were ambushed, and their bases were often mortared or attacked by sappers. Unable to find the guerillas amid the population that supported them, the American forces used their overwhelming firepower against the villages. As a matter of policy, the Marines bombed and shelled the hamlets from which they took fire and the hamlets they believed were contributing food or labor to the enemy. 'The US Marines will not hesitate to destroy immediately any village or hamlet harboring the Viet Cong,' one leaflet dropped on the villages read." It would have been difficult for a village *not* to harbor Viet Cong, since most of the province had long been under their control.

Quoting the journalism of Jonathan Schell, author of *The Village of Ben Suc*, Fitzgerald writes that Marine and Army units "had destroyed 70 percent of the hamlets on the coastal plain, caused countless civilian casualties, and driven some 40 percent of the 650,000 people in the province into towns and refugee camps along Route One. By then, the US command had come to see the 'generation of refugees' not just as an unavoidable consequence of military operations but as a means of depriving the guerillas of the population they needed for support." In other words, the US military had come to believe that in those areas where a majority of the people supported the Viet Cong, the Americans had to destroy most villages and hamlets, killing people as they did so, in order to terrorize them and turn them into refugees.

"Some of the hamlets along Route One remained standing, but much of the district had become a free fire zone where people lived in caves or in tunnels that also served as bunkers for the guerrillas." (A free fire zone is one in which anything that moves is considered a legitimate target.) "Many of the hamlets had been burned or bulldozed to deny the guerrillas shelter; the fields were pocked marked with craters, and the nearby forests defoliated." At that time tens of thousands of civilians were dying horribly from napalm dropped on their villages, not to mention rockets, mortars and harassing fire from gunships used on civilian centers that were thought to "harbor" Viet Cong.

The Americal Division at Duc Pho was a patchwork of different units. "The Americal eventually became known as the worst division in the American army," Francis Fitzgerald remarks briskly. "Its three unrelated brigades never fully cohered, and other units were often transferred in or out of it. The 11th Light Infantry Brigade, based in Doc Pho, was a particularly troubled unit. It went into action without combat training, with few veteran officers or NCOs and a great many raw recruits." It was on March 16, 1968, that a platoon from this brigade killed some 504 civilians in what was later called the My Lai massacre, in the northern part of Quang Ngai, the province where Dang Thuy Tram was stationed, and where she wrote her diary; she and local VC cadre most likely heard about the slaughter through their own sources. In any case, the Americal Division suffered enormous problems with morale, but they were not different in kind from the problems endured by American troops in other parts of South Vietnam. It is important to go into this a bit since the reasons for it resulted in so much American disillusionment with the war, and ultimately made Vietnam so traumatic for many Americans.

American soldiers had been told, as Americans in general were, that our troops were going to Vietnam to help the people there fight off an invading Communist force. And then, depending on the area where they were deployed, those same soldiers were often ordered not to help the indigenous people of that area, but to kill, displace and brutalize them in a variety of ways, because that is the nature of counter-insurgency. That came as a big shock to many American soldiers, who came to feel that they'd been lied to. The fact that so many rural Vietnamese actively followed a movement led by Communists was astonishing to US soldiers; the fact that soldiers in the American military were being used in a civil war (and that most Vietnamese were motivated more by nationalism and patriotism than by Marxist theory) were things they learned about only after they arrived. To anybody with common sense, it began to appear — especially after the Tet Offensive — that the Viet Cong and the National Liberation Front were ultimately likely to prevail. The desertion rate among the Army of the Republic of Viet Nam (ARVN) was very high, and there were a variety of other indicators that might lead a reasonable person to conclude that the South Vietnamese troops were likely to ultimately be defeated by the North Vietnamese-led insurgents.

To top it all off, over time many American soldiers became aware that in the 1950s a multi-national conference had been held in Paris to resolve the problems of what was then called Indochina. In April 1954, the conference decided that there should be elections in the South of Vietnam in July of 1956. After first appearing to agree with the idea of a vote, the US rejected the elections, believing that the South Vietnamese would vote for the "wrong" candidates. (That is, the Americans thought that Ho Chi Minh would win.) In this way America sought to undermine a democratic solution to the Indochina conflict.

The point, as the reader is probably already guessing, is that the American war in Vietnam never needed to happen. If the American government and their proxies in South Vietnam had let the election go forward, the Vietnamese could have decided who they wanted to run their country, and the death and destruction of war could have been avoided. Even those US soldiers who didn't know about the suppressed election in 1956 had begun to feel that there was something morally wrong with the war, as the many antiwar newsletters and newspapers written, published, circulated and read by soldiers at that time demonstrate.

There was also a surge of Black Nationalism sweeping through the African-American troops, a nationalism that identified with near-insurrections by Blacks in American ghettoes, which many Black soldiers identified with the national liberation struggles being waged around the world. In 1968 both Dr. Martin Luther King and Bobbie Kennedy were assassinated in the US; increasingly it seemed that only violence could change the course of American history. As a result, there was a powerful and violent movement within the US military aimed at the officers, a deeply political antiwar movement in the very bowels of the war itself. Colin Powell, who was a major in the 11th Infantry for a few months in 1968, has written revealingly about this.

According to him, it was necessary to move his cot around to a different place every night. Why did he do this? Not just because of the likelihood of Viet Cong attack, but also because he was afraid of possible attacks from his own men. Attacking unpopular officers with fragmentation grenades—'fragging,' it was called—was increasingly practiced by enlisted soldiers. Drug use by soldiers was rampant everywhere in the country, and its use did nothing to improve anyone's judgment or morale. Perhaps worse was the effects of an intangible that few historians wish to deal with, which is the feeling by American soldiers that their government had knowingly, consistently and cynically lied to them about what kind of war it was. By 1970, morale was so bad among enlisted US troops in Vietnam that the Army and even the Marines were close to collapse.

On the other side of the war in Quang Ngai, the idealistic young doctor Dang Truy Tram was experiencing the inevitable effects of mass bombing and constant US patrols, and the fear and anger they generated. In early April 1969, Thuy was driven from a compound where she had set up a small clinic. From that time on, she and her helpers in the clinic were constantly on the move, constantly looking for a safe place for the clinic. (She had sought to train some local people in the basics of nursing, and had apparently succeeded.) Frances Fitzgerald vividly describes the harrowing experiences of that desperate year. "She watched jets on bombing runs, gunships firing streams of bullets and tracers, helicopter assaults, and sweeps by the American forces. She notes how the defoliant Agent Orange debilitated herself and her fellow cadre, and how a white phosphorus shell roasted a man's body. She saw hamlets that had just been bulldozed and the survivors wandering around through the devastation, unwilling to leave their homes. On a night emergency mission, she walked across the national highway and through hills so bright with lights and flares she felt herself on a stage. Another night she walked through an area she calls Khe Sanh, the rice bowl of Duc Pho District, which the Americans guarded with artillery, constant patrols, and an electronic surveillance system. She slept in underground shelters, spent a night up to her chest in water, and was almost killed many times."

In June, 1970, a temporary clinic was bombed, and five people killed, and she was once more driven to search for a safe place. Eventually all the wounded were evacuated, and the clinic resupplied. Why Dr. Dang Truy Tram was out on a trail on June 22, 1970, we don't know, and probably never will. Her life was ended by a single bullet through the forehead. Her body was discovered by a highlander of the local H're people, a tribal mountain people, and she was buried by them.

In a gesture that suggests the extreme reverence of the Vietnamese for those who were heroes in the national struggle, a man who had been one of her patients and a good friend returned after the war to the Doc Pho District of Quang Ngai province and made inquiries about Truy, but discovered that she was dead. He located her grave and notified her family. (Sadly, Thuy's father in Hanoi, upon hearing of her death, had a paralytic stroke and died soon afterwards.) Her body was taken to North Vietnam, and ultimately re-buried in Tu Liem Martyrs Cemetery, where it became a destination for many who came, and still come, to pay their respects.

4.

The diaries of Dang Truy Tram changed the life of Fred Whitehurst. Like Thuy, he was—and is—a patriot. But the full measure of his service to America is painfully suggestive of the paradoxical times that we live in, and our own changing attitudes about what that service should be, and what patriotism really is. Back home in America, he earned a doctorate in chemistry at Duke University, and ultimately a JD at Georgetown University; eventually he was hired by the Federal Bureau of Investigation as a forensic scientist, and from 1986 to 1998 was a supervisory special agent in the Federal Bureau of Investigation Laboratory.

During that period Whitehurst discovered extremely serious cases of scientific malpractice, and reported them to the higher-ups in the FBI. When they engaged in a cover-up, Whitehurst became one of the most important whistle-blowers in American history. It couldn't have been a role that Whitehurst relished— he'd already done three full tours in Vietnam, and had broken strict army regulations in 1972 by taking the Tram dairies home with him. But it is a testament to his unbending moral code that although the FBI, the Department of Justice, and even people in the Clinton administration conspired to retaliate against him during this period, he continued his campaign to reform laboratory protocols.

In the end he prevailed; after twelve years of exhaustive, debilitating struggle his documentation of wrongdoing compelled the FBI to initiate some forty reforms in their forensic laboratories, and to go through a rigorous accreditation process. These extremely important reforms may have resulted in freedom for many unfairly convicted defendants, and without question it impacted, in one way or another, almost all of the procedures that would soon be used in investigating terrorist atrocities. (Whitehurst's specialty was in the science of explosives and explosive residue.)

Fred Whitehurst's whistle-blowing campaign to reform the FBI's laboratory practices was not a quick or easy one. As a result of the FBI hierarchy's implacable campaign against him, Whitehurst was obligated to hire a law firm that was well known for its aggressive defense of whistle-blowers. Despite all the obstacles he encountered, he was able to give extremely valuable testimony regarding abuses in FBI laboratory protocols, not only because he knew what the main scientific issues were, but because he also understood their implications for investigatory practices and ultimate adjudication. Perhaps most important of all, he had not only the integrity but the raw courage to carry out his campaign for reform despite attempts by some of America's most powerful people to discredit him. Fred Whitehurst could not be frightened off by threats or intimidation—and it's lucky for America that he couldn't. For one thing, he was perhaps the one man in America who was ideally situated to document FBI malpractice, who not only understood the legal implications of that malpractice but who comprehended in detail the changes that had to be made.

These are clues to Whitehurst's nature, and there are other clues as well. We know, for example, that at the age of seventeen he had rescued someone from a freezing lake, and was awarded the Army-Navy Corps Medal of Heroism. He received four Bronze Stars and other military honors while in Vietnam, but didn't talk often about them. Finally, he was offered a Purple Heart but refused it, perhaps because he thought the wound too inconsequential. He received the highest commendations from virtually all his commanding officers.

What do these things tell us about Fred Whitehurst? That he is a patriot goes without saying, but his love of country is motivated not by governmental power and force of arms, but the ability of its people to do the right thing, regardless of obstacles. He was capable of seeing the good in someone defined as 'the enemy,' and was driven to speak out against corruption and malpractice in the governmental agency that employed him. Above all, he is a person who feels honor bound to correct—or try to correct—whatever he knows to be wrong. His deepest values seem closest to the ideal of universal human rights, rights which go beyond particular governments or government policies, although the US government can and should observe them.

Whitehurst's personal evolution continued, this writer believes, because once he read the diaries of Dung Thuy Tram they began to help him, on an emotional if not a cognitive level, to personally come to terms with the Vietnam War, and the devastation he witnessed there. (And perhaps accept the defeat of a cause that Whitehurst had seen as virtuous.) His original motivation in keeping the dairies was a determination to return them to the family members of Dang Thuy Tram, if he could locate them—a determination that by itself demonstrates a great sensitivity to the suffering of people on 'the other side' of the chasm that was war. As time went on, it seems likely that he—and perhaps also his brother, also a Vietnam veteran—began to see the possibility of post-war reconciliation between Vietnam and the US, and the manner in which the diaries might serve this purpose.

Furthermore, he saw that the diaries were the record of a life lived in service to ideals that America must arguably try to understand, even if it does not entirely share them, so that our country can be sufficiently informed to function well in a diverse world with strong but divided loyalties. The diaries unquestioningly have a power to bring people together; and to help them learn—by sharing in the intense and shining compassion of a very young doctor caught up in a very long war—from one of the most brutal conflicts in history, and in so doing to make the future different. Above all, there is something about the diaries of Dang Thuy Tram that have the power to make the reader question the use of war to resolve human differences.

All the time that Fred Whitehurst had the diaries in America, he apparently never stopped thinking about delivering the diaries back to the family of Dang Thuy Tram; but there was a big problem: as an FBI whistle-blower engaged in a intense internal struggle with the FBI hierarchy, he could hardly approach people in the Vietnamese embassy, particularly since his powerful enemies in the FBI (and the Department of Justice) would surely have used that against him. Eventually, however, he found a way. He shared them with his brother Rob, who was married to a Vietnamese woman and spoke Vietnamese. Both Fred and Rob became obsessed with publishing the diaries, hoping that would help them locate Thuy's family.

In March 2005, the two brothers met an Air Force veteran who planned to travel to Hanoi, and he agreed to help the Whitehurst brothers locate the Tram family. This veteran in turn consulted with Do Xuan Anh in the Hanoi office of the Society of Friends, or Quakers, who are greatly respected in Vietnam for their antiwar beliefs and their humanitarian work. Working together they were able to locate Dang Thuy Tram's surviving family members, including her mother Doan Ngoc Tram; as a result of this information, Fred Whitehurst subsequently exchanged emails with her youngest sister, Kim Tram, who although an engineer is also a translator of English-language children's books into Vietnamese.

In April 2005, the diaries were hand-delivered in Hanoi to Thuy's mother, Doan Ngoc Tram, apparently by an American who represented the Whitehurst brothers.

At some point Fred Whitehurst and his brother must have been invited to Vietnam, because Frances Fitzgerald writes: "Rob and Fred were adopted into Thuy's family as 'sons' and 'brothers,' and in August they went to Hanoi to meet the family. To their amazement, they had become celebrities. Dozens of people, among them journalists, came to greet them at the airport; later, they were interviewed on television and welcomed by Vietnamese officials, among them the Prime Minister, Phan Van Kat."

This "adoption" of American servicemen into the extended family of Vietnamese, including those families who lost family members during the war, is not unusual, as we will see later in this chapter. Such acts of reconciliation are encouraged by the Vietnamese government because it seeks reconciliation with the US itself—it is in that government's economic and political interest to do so; but it is also of great benefit psychologically to the Vietnamese people, because it gives them an opportunity to reach out to their former adversaries in the 'American war,' as they call it. The healing effects of this process for Americans are also very powerful.

For American veterans to be unquestioningly accepted into

the families of people who lost family members in the war also has an incredible emotional resonance for both Vietnamese and Americans. This reconciliatory process says, in effect: "We're all in this together, because both Americans and Vietnamese suffered. That suffering in some way makes us brothers and sisters." American veterans that visit Vietnam often have the opportunity to talk with men who served on the other side, and for certain Americans it may have been the first time they had talked at length about their service.

There is no more powerful agent for healing and reconciliation. For Fred Whitehurst, that process began in 1972, when he refused a direct order to burn the diaries of Dang Truy Tram. The diaries now belong to all of humanity, and have been translated into many languages, including English. The name given to the English-language translation was *Last Night I Dreamed of Peace: The Diary of Dang Thuy Tram.*

5.

In her 'Introduction,' scholar Francis Fitzgerald wrote of the diary's publication in Hanoi:

"Thuy's diaries were published in Hanoi on July 18, 2005. To the surprise of the book publisher, they caused an immediate sensation. By the time the Whitehurst brothers arrived, twenty thousand copies were in print, the diaries had been excerpted in a newspaper, and a television film about Dang Thuy Tram was in preparation. A year and a half later, they had sold 430,000 copies—this in a country where few books sell more than 5,000 copies. The diaries struck a particular chord among young readers. Two-thirds of all Vietnamese were born after 1975, and for them the war was ancient history, and a history that was taught in a dry, stylized fashion. Other war diaries had been published, but, like the textbooks, they spoke mainly of invincible heroism and great military victories."

"Thuy's diaries broke the mold. Here was a brave, idealistic young woman, but one with vulnerabilities and self-doubts: a romantic in spite of all her discipline. Her descriptions of the pathos of the soldiers, as well as of their heroism, reminded readers that those who had died for their cause were people much like themselves. Furthermore, the government, which had previously censored novels about the horrors of war, seemed to understand that the diaries brought the war to life for the young in a way that the old rhetoric of invincibility did not."

"On a second trip to Vietnam in the spring of 2006, Rob Whitehurst, Fred's brother, found that hundreds of people had visited Thuy's grave in a cemetery [Tu Liem Martyrs Cemetery] on the outskirts of Hanoi. In Duc Pho [the former Republic of Vietnam], ground had been broken for the Dang Thuy Tram hospital, and a memorial marked the place where she had died in the mountains. She had become a folk hero." Rob also traveled to Duc Pho in Quang Ngai Province, in the former South Vietnam, where he met some of the people Thuy had treated during the war.

The publication of the diaries was a turning point for the Vietnamese people. Instead of portraying the war through grandiose Stalinist slogans, the government appeared to understand that it was now time to consider the human cost of the war—and to grieve. The diaries of Dang Truy Tram are all about self-sacrifice in the name of a transcendent national struggle, but makes the point repeatedly that such self-sacrifice does not happen without suffering; the publication of Dang Thuy Tram's dairies gave the Vietnamese people permission, as it were, to identify with the suffering that triumph had brought, and perhaps to allow themselves to feel a pain they many had previously suppressed. The diaries allowed them to do that because they were written by a national hero, one who was writing under conditions of enormous stress, surrounded by death and violence, who was yet a person who—far from suppressing her fears, guilt, anger and disappointments—embraced them as part of her sacred path to the heart of national service.

The translator, Andrew X. Pham, drew heavily on the experiences of his own father, Thong Van Pham, who was born in Tong Xuyen and grew up in Hanoi, not far from where the Tram family lived. He understood the nuances of life during a certain era in Hanoi, and the motivations of educated families in that time and place. Pham was also aided in the translation by Thuy's sister, Kim Tram. Andrew X. Pham writes: "Dr. Thuy Tram wrote her diaries under extreme duress. She penned these entries in battle trenches, bomb shelters, and triages, and in wards filled with dying patients. Through destruction, hunger, extreme fatigue, loneliness, and psychological trauma, this remarkable young woman still had the presence to reach for the literary and the sublime."

"Her writing leaped nimbly from prose to poetry, from meditation to self-examination, from confession to reflection. In some places she talked to herself. In others she held conversation with absent friends. She switched viewpoints frequently, from the first to the second to the third person, with ease and without warning. The reader will find it helpful to keep in mind that she wrote in the flowery literary style of her era; she was innocent in the ways of the heart, an inexperienced romantic; and she died without knowing anything more intimate than kisses. Such were the traditional values of her generation."

"Regardless of how the diaries are read or perceived, there are three undeniable truths about the author. First, her heart was noble. Second, her life was guided by ideals. Third, her sacrifice was as tragic as it was heroic." Regarding her idealism, I would specify a particular characteristic of her ideals, one that has already been mentioned. That was a bone-deep faith in Vietnamese patriotism that was essentially religious, animated by self-sacrifice and driven by an unshakable conviction that this transcendent spiritual force would defeat the West's technological sophistication and military power. This quasi-religious force was, in fact, the secular or civil religion of three generations of Vietnamese who followed Ho Chi Minh's leadership, based in turn on a shared traumatic memory of a thousand years of resistance to foreign domination.

I believe that someday the Vietnamese will find their way to some form of democracy, because the longing for multi-party representational government is nearly universal. That will be another struggle in which the profoundly spiritual nature of Vietnamese patriotism will doubtless play a role. But the Vietnamese must do it themselves, in their own time and in their own way. It is almost unbearably tragic to consider that the Vietnamese could, in 1955-56, have voted for their own leaders, if the Americans had permitted that. But the weak South Vietnamese government, supported by the US, refused to hold the elections.

In intelligence work one develops an odd intimacy with the enemies one studies; and since an intelligence officer often has more information about circumstances in play than the subjects under surveillance, he may think he knows more about the motives of the people he studies than they do themselves. But reading Thuy's diary was a completely different species of experience. The emotional impact of Thuy's diary seems to have been part of Fred Whitehurst's disengagement from the war, and from the internalized aggression that invariably accompanies organized human conflict. How did that disengagement gain traction? Was saving the diaries despite military orders to destroy them part of the process? Or was it the emotional effects of Dang Thuy Tram's idealism?

It certainly helped Whitehurst understand, from the point of view of an 'enemy,' what the people of Quang Ngai Province had been experiencing under continual bombardment, free-fire zones, and the relentless destruction of up to 70 percent of the villages in the province. But there was more. There is something about Thuy's emotional vulnerability that disarms the reader.

What the diaries ignite, finally, is a deep and incandescent awareness of the irrevocable evil of killing people who are just as patriotic, just as dedicated, and just as good as oneself.

Fred Whitehurst's spiritual journey began in war, and ended with becoming a 'brother' to the people he once fought. The extent of his journey, and his own maturation, is suggested in an extraordinarily honest statement made by him: "You know, I joined the army to go kill Communists. I wasn't against the war at all, and I think [I was] very effective as a soldier. I didn't damn my army or damn my nation. But I've always known since in Vietnam when I did it, when you put a bullet into a human being you cannot take back that thing called life. You cannot get it back, and Dang Thuy Tram describes so deeply what that thing is... and a bullet went right through her forehead, and in that instant, she was gone. Can we think of another way to do this?"[3]

6.

Chu Lai was an air field and a US Marine and Army Base from 1965 and 1971 in Vietnam, but its name was not Vietnamese; rather it was a Chinese abbreviation for the name of the American military commander, Marine General Victor Krulak. (Interestingly, the Hanoi government has kept the name, now calling it Chu Lai International Airport.) It was located in Quang Nam Province at Dung Quat Bay, its task being to complement the larger air fields at Da Nang and Cam Ranh Bay, and also to resupply Swift Boats in the bay. It supported major operations in nearby Quang Ngai Province, directly southeast of Quang Nam. (Quang Ngai Province was, the reader will remember, the place where Tim O'Brien of *The Things They Carried* was stationed, the province where Dang Thuy Tham wrote her diary, and the area in which the ill-fated Americal Division operated.) Like Quang Ngai, the province of Quang Nam was a Viet Cong stronghold and a major deployment area for the North Vietnam Army (NVA); Quang Nam was the site of several critical battles, culminating with the disastrous retreat from Hue and Da Nang in 1975 that turned into a rout, ending the war in defeat for America and the South Vietnamese government, and victory for the North Vietnamese and Viet Cong.

Rich Luttrell knew precious little about the history of the province on the day when he found himself on a trail near Chu Lai. He was a poor kid from the projects in Illinois, barely eighteen years old, just old enough to sign up; but by 1967 he had been assigned to an outfit in the 101st Airborne Division, an historic army division (the "Screaming Eagles") that had previously specialized in air assault operations. (By the time Rich joined up, of course, its operational transport had become helicopters.) From 1967 to 1971, the 101st was assigned to operations in I Corp, consisting of the five northernmost provinces in South Vietnam; which—because they were so close to North Vietnam—often resulted in intense fighting with well-trained and battle-hardened regular troops of the North Vietnam Army. Rich Luttrell was nervous about his ability to stand up under enemy fire. He would indeed be profoundly challenged, but in a way—and to an extent—he would never have imagined.

He was airlifted directly into the jungle by helicopter, and spent the next few days carrying a heavy rucksack through steaming and nearly impenetrable jungle. Then came the day when he was on a path with his unit, and off to one side he saw something moving. It was a NVA soldier, squatting down, an AK 47 in his hands.

In a television report decades later, he spoke of what happened next. "I had to react," he said. "I had to do something—it was my decision." He and the enemy soldier looked at each other square in the face. "It seemed like we stared at each other a long time." Then slowly, as though dreaming, he pulled the trigger. "And I just started firing, full automatic."

The enemy soldier went down.

As Rich Luttrell told the story to Keith Morrison of 'Dateline

NBC,' there was a "pretty heavy firefight," so there must have been other NVA soldiers involved. "And I wasn't smart enough to hit the ground—and somebody tackled me, and took me to the ground."

It was kill or be killed, and Rich Luttrell survived the action by killing an enemy soldier who, had he fired first, might very well have killed him. Killing an enemy soldier did not surprise or demoralize Rich; it was exactly what he had come to Vietnam to do, and he would kill again before his tour was over. As it turned out, it was something else that made this day a traumatizing and difficult one, something uncanny and completely unpredictable.

As he contemplated the NVA soldier he had just killed, he noticed something sticking out of the soldier's pocket. It was a photograph. Forty years later, in an interview with Keith Morrison of NBC News, he tells about seeing it: "I'd seen this picture sticking out, partially out. It looked like the face of a little girl with some long hair or something. And I pulled it out and it was real tiny. And it was a picture of a soldier and a little girl. I can remember holding the photo and actually squatting and getting close to the soldier and actually looking in his face and looking at the photo, and looking in his face." Sure enough, the man in the tiny photo was the same man whom he'd just killed in the firefight.

Let's cut directly to his NBC interview with Keith Morrison:

KEITH MORRISON: (Voiceover) *Here was the man he had just killed. But who was that little girl? His daughter? They seemed so serious. So sad, somehow. Like the picture had been taken just before they said goodbye. Before her father went off the war.* (To Rich) And that hit you?

RICH LUTTRELL: It hit me really hard.

KEITH MORRISON: (Voiceover) *Not for long, mind you. Rich stuffed the tiny picture in his wallet. And within minutes they moved out again. Not for a moment, by the way, should you believe that Rich was a reluctant soldier. When it came time again to use his weapon he did not hesitate. He developed an uncommon expertise at the dangerous and gruesome business of clearing underground tunnels of enemy personnel. He became skilled at hand-to-hand combat, at surviving.*

RICH LUTTRELL: I can remember being on a hill one night, and mortar rounds just pounding in the dark, and hearing guys screaming and getting blown out of holes. And pulling my rucksack over my head and thinking, 'God, don't let one hit me.'

KEITH MORRISON: (Voiceover) *He had just 20 days left, when the bullet ripped into his back. The wound that sent him home.*

RICH LUTTRELL: I can remember, when I got on the helicopter, all of a sudden this tremendous guilt hit me, like, 'Where are you going? What are you doing? What are you leaving these guys for?'

KEITH MORRISON: *Rich came home to a case full of medals and married his childhood sweetheart, Carole. And as the 60s gave way to the 70s, the 80s, he tried to put Vietnam behind him.*

CAROLE: He really didn't talk about Vietnam for years. It just was something he kept very personal and very hidden.

KEITH MORRISON: (Voiceover) *But all the while, there in his wallet, was that picture. The little girl who would not let him go. Of course he didn't know yet—how could he?—what that little image had in store for him.*

RICH LUTTRELL: I really formed a bond, especially with the little girl, in the picture.

KEITH MORRISON: (Voiceover) *It was so odd, so strange. All the horrors Rich had seen in battle... and it was this little face that kept coming back to haunt him.*

RICH LUTTRELL: Here's a young daughter doesn't have a father thanks to me.

KEITH MORRISON: (Voiceover) *Year after year, he kept it in his wallet... As the torment he felt failed to go away... as it settled on his life like a darkening cloud.*

CAROLE: The only thing I could ever say was, why don't you just get rid of it? You know? Let it go. And get it out of your life and you can forget it and go on.

Twenty years after Rich first told Carole about the picture, an opportunity presented itself. They were on a vacation in Washington DC, where the Vietnam Veterans' Memorial is located. It suddenly occurred to Rich that here was an opportunity to finally get rid of the small photo he had been carrying so long. He would write a letter to the man whom he had killed, and leave it at 'the Wall,' along with the picture. When Rich told Carole of his decision, her face lit up. So he sat down in that hotel room and composed a note to the man he had killed so many years before.

RICH LUTTRELL: I sat down on the bed with just the scratch pad that was in the hotel room, I started thinking, I thought, if there was any way possible that you could talk to that soldier, what would you say, you know? And in like, just a couple of minutes, I scribbled out a little note.

KEITH MORRISON: Not that he regretted being in that war... not that he regretted serving his country. No, he didn't. It was instead that unending guilt, that uncontrollable sorrow, of having taken away a young father's life.

Here's the note Rich Luttrell wrote:

Dear Sir, for 22 years, I've carried your picture in my wallet. I was only 18 years old that day we faced one other on the trail at Chu Lai, Vietnam. Why you didn't take my life I'll never know. You stared at me for so long, armed with your AK-47, and yet you did not fire.

Forgive me for taking your life, I was reacting just the way I was trained, to kill V.C... So many times over the years, I've stared at your picture and your daughter, I suspect. Each time my hearts and guts would burn with the pain of guilt. I have two daughters myself now... I perceive you as a brave soldier defending his homeland.

Above all else, I can now respect the importance that life held for

*you. I suppose that is why I am able to be here today… It is time for
me to continue the life process and release my pain and guilt.*

Forgive me, Sir.

The next day Rich put the photo, along with the letter, at the foot
of the monument, under the names of the 58,000 Americans who
were killed in Vietnam.

RICH LUTTRELL: And at that moment, if was like I had just
finished a firefight and dropped my rucksack and got to rest. The
load I was carrying was gone. It was gone.

Why did Rich Luttrell leave the photo and the short letter
asking for forgiveness at the Vietnam Veterans' Memorial?
Because that part of the Memorial that contains the names of
people killed—the Vietnam Veterans' Memorial Wall, or simply
'the Wall'—became, from the very beginning, a place where
people could bring small artifacts and mementoes associated
with an event or a person, and leave them there as a sign of
respect, or as an act of remembrance and mourning.

This apparently began spontaneously, after which the
National Park Service, realizing the deeply emotional nature of
the practice, adapted to it by respectfully collecting, cataloging
and storing the artifacts. Supposedly the practice of leaving
items began during the actual construction, when it is said that a
Vietnam Veteran threw the Purple Heart his brother received
posthumously into the concrete of the memorial's foundation.
Since that time many thousands of items are left at 'the Wall'
every year.

Artifacts left at the Vietnam Veterans' Memorial are collected
by National Park Service employees and taken to an NPS
Museum and Resource Center, which catalogues and stores all
items except flowers and unaltered flags. (The flags are redis-
tributed.) National Park Service employees at the site tend to be
Vietnam Veterans; and perhaps not surprisingly, they are trained

to counsel people that are overcome by emotion while at the site, especially vets struggling with issues relating to the war. The Memorial is one of the most emotionally fraught sites in America, all the more impressive because it is located in the nation's capital, an acknowledgement of war's devastation at the center of national power.

KEITH MORRISON: (Voiceover) *Every day, hundreds of people say goodbye to bits and pieces of the war and leave them here along these granite walls and every single thing—sacred and profane—is collected and boxed up by park rangers. Including Rich's photo. Which just happened to land at the top of one of these boxes, which just happened to land face up... which just happened to be seen by another Vietnam Veteran who knew right away that this was something different.*

DUERY FELTON: I thought 'what is this?' So I leaned down and picked it up.

KEITH MORRISON: (Voiceover) *Duery Felton is curator of the Vietnam Veterans' Memorial collection. He has seen just about everything here. But a picture of an enemy soldier?*

DUERY FELTON: I really did a double take.

KEITH MORRISON: Don't often see something like that at the Wall?

DUERY FELTON: Well, I haven't seen it in about thirty odd years, that green uniform.

KEITH MORRISON: (Voiceover) *And he read Rich's letter of apology.*

DUERY FELTON: I read that letter and it was about taking a life. It's very difficult to do that. That decision has to be made in a matter of seconds. And you have to live with that decision for the rest of your life. So it was somewhat comforting, if that's the proper term, to know that someone else has been through that, and they set it down on paper.

MORRISON: (Voiceover) *And before long the little photo and all the emotion it conjured up, infected this veteran, too. A tiny determined spirit floating from one old soldier to the next, reminding them both of the price they paid for pulling the trigger.*

DUERY: That haunted me for years and years as to who the little girl was.

MORRISON: What is it about that image that was so powerful that you'd hang onto it? That he'd hang onto it? That you couldn't let it go in a way?

DUERY: I think it resonated someplace in my psyche. You have to understand I was in a combat unit. This is about taking someone's life.

Back in Rochester, Illinois, Rich Luttrell had no idea that someone in Washington DC was agonizing over the same tiny picture he had once found so painful to look upon. But at the NPS Museum and Resource Center, it seemed to Duery Felton that his fascination with the photo increased over time rather than decreased. Who was that little girl, and what had her life been like without a father? When the time came to put together a book about the things people left at the Vietnam Veterans' Memorial Wall, Duery Felton put Rich's letter—along with the photo of the NVA soldier and the little girl—right in the middle of the book. And since Rich now worked for Veterans' Affairs, he received his own personal copy of the book, entitled *Offerings at the Wall: Artifacts from the Vietnam Veterans' Memorial Collection.*

And when he opened it and turned to page 53, there it was— the note he had written to the soldier he'd killed, and the photo of the soldier with his daughter. To Rich it felt like the little girl was in some sense haunting him. It was almost as she had something to tell him, something important that she wanted him to know. "It was almost like, little girl, what do you want from me? You know, what do you want from me?"

He contacted Duery Felton at the NPS Museum and Resource Center, and Felton flew across country to return it personally to him. It was about this time that Rich had an improbable but deeply compelling idea. What if he could return the photo to Vietnam, return it to the little girl who was in it, wherever she was now, using the opportunity to say how bad he felt about killing her father? If he found the little girl, found the family of the slain soldier, would that not give him some redemption, or at least some closure?

It was a long shot, of course. Carole, his wife, knew how improbable it was—but she did not discourage him. She could see that he was struggling to find peace, and she was willing to stick it out with him until he found it.

Rich met with a journalist from the St-Louis Post-Dispatch and told him his story, and it ended up on the front page of the Sunday edition. Rich sent the article, along with a letter, to the Vietnam Embassy in Washington DC; a newspaper editor in Vietnam got hold of it, and published the photo with an appeal to anyone who knew the people in it. This newspaper was used as wrapping paper by a man in Hanoi who sent something to his mother. In a village north of Hanoi a woman saw the picture, and recognized it. She took it to a neighboring village, convinced that a woman there was the little girl in the picture.

"This is your father," she said.

At some point the government in Hanoi apparently became involved, and it was not long before Rich received a letter from Vietnam. It was from a woman named Lan, who said the man in the picture was her father. Rich wrote back, explaining his motivation for seeking her. It was not regret that animated him, he said, because he was proud to serve his country. It was guilt, for having taken away a child's father.

By this time Rich had begun to think about going back to Vietnam, to return the little photograph to the daughter of the man he had killed. But could he go through with it? In his interview with Keith Morrison on NBC Dateline, he revealed his deepest fears: "How do you tell a little girl, "Hey, I killed your father in Vietnam?... There's a risk there, there really is. There's really a risk. I don't know how they're going to react."

Rich told Keith Morrison that he'd almost rather go back into combat than face that little girl. The irony, of course, was that the little girl in the photo was now a woman in her 40s; and he was far from the teenager from the projects who signed up to serve his county. In his wildest dreams, he never would have thought he'd end up going back to Vietnam. But now he was going there. "The whole thing's bigger than I am," he told Keith Morrison. "It's hard for me to understand it myself sometimes."

Of course, his wife Carole would be with him, she would be by his side, just as she had been by his side every step of his journey up to this point. They would face the unknown together.

7.

At the airport in Hanoi Rich and Carole are met by officials of the Vietnamese government, who are happy to facilitate Rich's mission. Shortly they are in a van heading to Lan's village. The weather seems foreboding, dark clouds threatening rain. Rich is nervous. Even though Carole is with him, these last minutes are difficult. What will Lan say, what will her reaction to him be?

They get to the village and the small group heads toward Lan's place of residence. They turn a corner and head toward the small group waiting for them. Rich thinks he sees her. *"I've already seen her,"* he murmurs, *"I know who she is."* He walks up to her and they stand looking at each other, Carole a step or two behind.

Rich stops before the woman who stands at the center of the group. He speaks in Vietnamese, a brief memorized statement.

"Today," he says, "I return the photograph of you and your father, which I have kept for 33 years. Please forgive me."

Lan seems to dissolve in tears, shaking with grief for a father she never knew. She pitches forward slightly, clinging to Rich; as she weeps, she buries her head in his chest. There is a long moment during which Rich also tears up. The feeling is not tension, but sheer, total grief for all the people hurt by the war.

"Tell her this is the photo I took from her father's wallet on the day

I shot and killed him and that I'm returning it. He died a brave man, a courageous warrior."

The government officials are somber, and very respectful; they bow their heads in silent witness to the grief engulfing them. Then Lan's brother tells the group that they believe that their father's spirit lives on in Rich. They don't expect people to consider this as anything more than a private superstition; it is simply something they have come to believe. Today, they say, is the day their father's spirit has returned to them.

The group goes into Lan's modest dwelling. Food has been prepared, and the guests sit down around the table—Rich and Carole first—as family members bustle about. They share the prepared food together, talking in both English and Vietnamese. It seems more like a homecoming than a strangers' meeting—and perhaps it is, as Lan and her brother believe, that a long-missing and perhaps half-forgotten father has finally come home.

Some of Rich's pain was still there, but being here in Lan's home gives the pain a context, makes it less uncanny, less lacerating. There's no question now that Lan forgives Rich for killing her father in a firefight. By inviting Rich into her home, by making him part of her family, by perceiving in him the spirit of her father, the woman Lan—with the blessing of her government—has found a path to helping all of them (including herself) come to terms with the loss of a family member in a war that had once divided them.

Above all, Lan and her family understand Rich's pain, because it's the same pain they've been feeling—it belongs to both of them, because it comes from the same war, the same path near Chu Lai, the same moment of armed confrontation, the same bullet. There are few things that can make people closer than that, if you are brave enough to make the connection and to live with it. Having been taken into Lan's family, Rich shares a meal with them, as they prepare to live—to the extent that they can— in a world free of war and its haunting trauma, fears and self-recriminations.

8.

The stories of Fred Whitehurst and Rich Luttrell, as well as much of Tim O'Brien's fiction, provide examples of warriors who strive—and not without risk—to fashion something redemptive and good out of the traumatic memories of a brutal war. In each of these stories some personal article or articles plays, because of the fraught nature of this war, a seemingly momentous role in bridging death and life. American artist and designer Maya Lin managed to create something quite similar, but in a different and completely unexpected way. The miracle of her work is that although the design of her memorial is unapologetically in the realm of high art, it also serves a profound vernacular purpose: it invites Americans to bring simple, powerful, personal artifacts to the dead, to celebrate loving memories by the living.

Maya Lin is the designer of the Vietnam Veterans' Memorial in Washington, D.C., better known as 'the Wall.' Here is the first paragraph of Lin's winning entry, submitted in 1981, to the open competition for a design of the Vietnam Veterans' Memorial:

Walking through this park-like area, the memorial appears as a rift in the earth—a long, polished black stone wall, emerging from and receding into the earth. Approaching the memorial, the ground slopes gently downward, and the low walls emerging on either side, growing out of the earth, extend and converge at a point below and ahead. Walking into the grassy site contained by the walls of this memorial, we can barely make out the carved names upon the memorial's walls. These names, seemingly infinite in number, convey the sense of overwhelming numbers, while unifying these individuals into a whole....

At the time Maya Lin wrote these words, she was a 21-year-old undergraduate student at Yale. When she won the competition to design the Vietnam Veterans' Memorial, it revolutionized the world's way of honoring the war dead. In the past, war monuments have tended to be grandiose, emblematic of the battles themselves, not the people who died in them. The Memorial is the exact opposite of patriarchy, and the patriarchal ethos encoded in most war monuments. Standing at 'the Wall,' the living are forced to see their own reflection on the surface of polished, cut-stone masonry—thus they see themselves, even as they see the names of the dead. This is a monument not to battles, but of the people who died in them, and their momentary unity with the countrymen and countrywomen who mourn them. Everything in the monument is created to focus thought and emotion on the war dead, what they were and what they could have been; and the faces of those who cared—and still care—about them.

Maya Lin seems to have been born to design the Memorial. Her collateral ancestor, Lin Juemin, was part of an armed struggle to end imperial rule and institute the democratic ideas of Sun Yat Sen in China. Before being killed in battle he wrote a "Letter to My Wife," a precise inversion of a 'Dear John' letter, a memorandum of love and appreciation by a soldier to his wife before dying in war; it is now considered a modern literary classic in China. Maya Lin is the niece of the first female architect of China (Lin Huiyin), her brother is a poet, and her father a ceramist; her vision is of quiet containment of adversarial energies, of peace rather than chaos at the meeting of opposing forces. The stunning austerity of the Memorial design creates a peaceful space between the two great opposing forces of life and death, war and peace, aggression and love.

In this border place between the two great competing adversaries, the living are respectfully and without comment invited to grieve in whatever way they choose. The genius of this idea—which like many great artistic ideas is predicated on extreme simplicity—made Maya Lin perhaps the most famous architectural designer and artist in the world. It also made her a 'public artist,' in the same way that a political thinker is a 'public intellectual,' because of the way her landscape art makes a statement about honoring the dead. Her public statements are like her designs: assertive and without adornment; but without exception they contain a depth that is best explored over a period of time.

A realization that the 'the Wall' was more than a monument set in when people began, unbidden and without any formal permission, to bring small artifacts to the Memorial, in order to place them at or near the wall. Art is about coming to terms emotionally with death; artifacts are about the tactile experience of life in the present moment. The design of 'the Wall' incorporates both emotional orientations, and goes beyond them. The Vietnam Veterans' Memorial encourages memories of the dead, making them dynamic rather than inanimate. Once the habit of bringing small artifacts to the wall got traction, people began on a mass basis to grieve there while bringing objects, tokens, memorabilia, little bits of their own and other peoples' lives; and often things that in some way once belonged to the dead, but which the grieving person wants to share with the dead, in a shared communion with the past.

Without anybody planning for it to happen this way, 'the Wall' became a place to invite survivors (including Vietnam veterans, but also other kinds of survivors) to bring traumatic memory—survivor guilt and resentment and every kind of aggression, not to mention gnawing memories of loss—and to do that in the company of one's fellow countrymen and countrywomen, both the living and the dead. There is no judgment at 'the Wall.' There is grief and acceptance of grief. And the miracle of it is that the bringing of artifacts was not planned by anyone, but was simply brought into being by the American people themselves. Yet there is something about this Memorial as a work of art that seems to invite the bringing of artifacts.

When people began to leave things at 'the Wall,' the custodians of the Park Service were unsure what to do with all those little artifacts. It soon became clear that these were pieces of people's lives, given importance not by their physical meaning but by intense, intangible and often overwhelming feelings of people who brought them there. When a woman wants to say goodbye to a lover, an airman who 'augured in' (was shot down), she brings her goodbye letter to 'the Wall'; when a man wants to say goodbye to the dog who accompanied him on patrol, he brings his letter to 'the Wall'; when a winner of the Medal of Honor wants to give it back to the government because of his opposition to government policy in Central America, he leaves the medal at 'the Wall.' (A lot of medals ended up there, it seems, and they were probably left there for a variety of reasons. Again, there's no judgment at 'the Wall.') So the custodians of the Memorial gather them up every day, then carefully and respectfully store and document them at the National Park Service Museum and Resource Center.

People leave the things they carry at 'the Wall' because they experience the Vietnam Veterans' Memorial as something completely different than a monument. Right from the beginning, the people who came there experienced it as a *shrine*, and a shrine (unlike a monument) has life-giving properties. By leaving the small articles of life to the dead—the *emblems* of life—such a shrine animates our memory of them. Nobody completely understands how this works, but it seems to be a particularly American (and rather pragmatic) form of civil spirituality. If we remember the dead, and refuse to forget them, they live in our memory— and so do their best values, if we make up our minds to act on them. That seems to be the essence of it. So every day people carry their small artifacts to 'the Wall,' from the most sacred to the cheerfully obscene, and leave them there. Maya Lin's vision is only half of Vietnam Veterans' Memorial; the other half is what people use it for, and make of it.

Of course, there were objections to Maya Lin and her design. Some didn't understand the simplicity of it at first, and began to appreciate its radical minimalism only later, after the general idea had a chance to sink in. Some were upset that the design competition was won by an Asian-American woman. (To his everlasting discredit, third-party candidate Ross Perot referred to her as an "egg roll," when it became public knowledge that the designer of the Vietnam Memorial was Chinese-American. There were other public comments, many of them much more offensive.) And to be sure, there are many influences in the design, not least of all an Asian concept of balance between competing or opposing forces; to be fair, such a conception probably would never have occurred to most white American males, since its classical simplicity is the exact opposite of patriarchy. (You get the feeling that many people would have been more comfortable with conventional statuary representing war as heroic.) But our American leavening of different cultural influences is arguably one of the best things about us; and—I would argue—it is our racial and religious diversity that gives our art and literature its resilience and its unpredictable spiritual depth. It was perhaps because of this that Maya Lin's design seemed to come out of left field, championing a completely new concept that would be widely copied, first in America and then throughout the world.

The only objection that really rang true in the Vietnam Memorial debate was the lack of the human form. So an addition (designed by Frederick Hart) was made to the Memorial—three young soldiers, one African-American, one Latino and one white; and after some spirited advocacy by Maya Lin, they were placed at a short distance from 'the Wall.' They are portrayed as staring, looking into the distance, as though looking for lost comrades; but one soon realizes that what they are looking at is 'the Wall,' where they at last find their lost comrades among the dead, in the wall itself. This seemingly vulgar compromise, which threatened to destroy Maya Lin's vision, ended up being a disturbing but haunting completion to a brilliant idea—but not for the reasons its advocates thought. The three forever-young soldiers stand looking for a deliverance they can only receive by comprehending the full loss of the American dead. The Vietnam Veterans' Memorial is the most visited memorial site in America.

Lin has spoken about her first thoughts regarding the proposed site of the Vietnam Memorial. "It wasn't going to be something that was going to say, 'It's all right, it's all over,' because it's not." Note the ease with which Lin handles the essential tragedy of all who have lost people to death: you want to be with them, but all you really have is memory; yet the simplicity of her memory art has encouraged thousands of pilgrims to leave artifacts with which to communicate, however, briefly, with those that have gone on. To explain the emotions she sought to arouse with her design, she said this: "I thought about what death is, what a loss is. A sharp pain that lessens with time, but can never quite heal over. A scar. The idea occurred to me there on the site. Take a knife and cut open the earth, and with time the grass would heal it. As if you cut open the rock and polished it."

Maya Lin's definition of death is also a good definition of psychological trauma. It's a wound that never quite heals, but it can be managed. The power of Maya Lin's design is that it suggests the spiritual and emotional beauty, the maturity and quiet strength, with which a great many people manage exactly those kinds of wounds.

9.

When soldiers participate in violence, and are in an essentially violent environment for long periods, their personalities change. How could they be in something as violent as war and *not* change? Sadly, victims, witnesses and perpetrators of violence in war tend to *internalize* aggression, both the violence that they act out and the violence they endure. This happens because of a need to adapt oneself to the attacker's style and techniques, especially in a counter-insurgency; but in order to survive the violent chaos of war, soldiers also often end up internalizing a great deal of the chaotic aggression they hoped to leave behind.

As a result, combat veterans may have aggressive emotional orientations that continue long after they have left the battlefield. Furthermore, the traumatized vet is at risk to act out that aggression, either against others or against oneself. Or vets may seek street drugs to repress their pain, and to control the aggressive emotional orientations they have internalized. To avoid this, and all the additional trouble that comes to people that have participated in violence, the traumatized individual must find a way to *deconstruct* the violent emotional orientations created by war.

In a way, the phrase 'internalizing aggression' is somewhat misleading, because it sounds like a physiological process, as though the victim were injecting or consuming blood-borne pathogens. But it isn't a physiological process, at least not primarily so. When a military platoon on patrol is ambushed, or subjected to repeated ambushes, firefights and mortar attacks, the individual soldier's personality is subjected to a kind of radical realignment process in which sensory functions are greatly heightened, cognition is often replaced by intuition, and a dreamlike feeling temporarily prevails. This apparent shutting down of cognition allows the unconscious part of the personality to focus on survival, and allows one's military training to kick in.

In this writer's previous book *Trauma Bond: an Inquiry into the Nature of Evil*, the process is described this way. "It's a sharp, violent and emotional response to aggression, in which the victim's emotions violently reorient themselves and take on an aggressive emotional orientation that the victim didn't have before. The unconscious mind isn't just *accommodating* the aggression it is experiencing—it is unconsciously *imitating* and *conforming* to the aggression being visited against it, in a desperate bid to survive it. The longer the aggression goes on, and the longer the victim is in a threatening or violent environment, the more these changes are likely to occur, and to affect the victim's personality later."

"The bad part is the price the victim will pay later, perhaps struggling with powerful feelings of irrational anger arising from the aggression internalized during combat. This aggressive orientation is likely to grow stronger if the conscious mind cannot retrospectively make sense of the violence endured—and it usually can't, if the victim cannot create some kind of moral context for the aggression experienced."

The best short-term way to establish that context is to start talking about the traumatizing experience as soon as possible after it happens. When you talk about what happened to you—and above all, the way it made you feel—you are creating a context for it in the morality play that is your life. Above all, by talking about what happened one creates a narrative that can be seen as separate from the personality, that to some extent *externalizes* a great deal of what one previously *internalized* during the events themselves. By talking about what happened, one gets it out of one's personality, and no longer has to carry the traumatic memory entirely, at least not in an unconscious part of the personality where it can influence one's behavior.

People that have internalized a fair amount of aggression are likely to unconsciously adopt a worldview based on the idea that aggression is the most authentic and transcendent experience human beings can have, and winning through violence and coercion the highest good. They may fight this orientation, they may believe it to be wrong, but it operates not out of reason but out of their emotions; and until they find ways to deconstruct the aggressive orientations *emotionally*, instead of trying to resolve them cognitively, they will continue to influence their thoughts and behavior. It could cause them to act out violently against others, but it could also cause one to suffer greatly from sleep disturbance, depression, anxiety, and hyper-vigilance typical of an aggressive emotional orientation.

This book is about ways people can help each other *deconstruct* these aggressive emotional orientations. It is, in other words, a book about managing and reducing the tyranny of past violence in one's life, so one can live without fear and aggression in the present moment. Let us say it again: traumatic memory is a wound that doesn't heal, but it can be managed, and for many combat veterans that's a big challenge, as we will see. This book suggests a two-step 'recovery dualism' for people struggling with traumatic memory, but first—before we reiterate that—let's look at some therapies currently being used to help combat veterans. Everybody seems to agree that talking about what one has experienced is the best first step, and probably the sooner one does it the better.

10.

Here's what a friend of this author tells young recruits at the police academy: "If you're a police patrolman in a radio car and having a rough night, talk about it with your partner, the way it makes you feel, the way it affects you physically, and the frustration you may feel. There's satisfaction in being a cop, but incredible tension, especially if you're in a high crime area every night on patrol. If something violent goes down, talk about it right away with your partner. (Don't put it off, because the longer you put it off the more you'll want to let it slide.) Talk about it before you go to sleep, and if you can't talk to the partner you work with, talk to your wife or significant other. But whatever you do, talk about it before you go to sleep, before it gets into your dreams, and 'goes viral' in the unconscious part of your personality."

Why does talking about traumatic events make it less destructive to you emotionally? Nobody really knows completely. As pointed out before, talking about a bad experience somehow helps you *externalize* the aggression you previously *internalized*, by making it part of a narrative that is to some extent separate—or at least separable—from your personality. Yet paradoxically it also helps you integrate the painful experience into your memory and personality in a way that makes sense to you, and therefore makes it easier for you to manage it more effectively. Talking about human violence you have endured or witnessed robs it of its "uncanny" nature, and helps you put it into perspective. That's the basis for the whole idea of the "talking cure," as good old Doctor Freud put it. Talking about violent, traumatizing experiences to another person who understands your situation seems to rob it of a great deal of its negative power, and makes it easier to live with. As I said, nobody really knows for sure why that is so, but it works.

As indicated above, the sooner you talk about violence you've witnessed or participated in, the less likely it is to come back and haunt you later on. But what if you were in a war a long time ago, and you didn't get a chance to talk about how you were feeling about it then? Does that mean you should sit down today and talk to a therapist or counselor about something bad that happened to you thirty or forty years ago? Yes, if it's still adversely affecting your life, if that experience still bothers you in some way. The miraculous thing about the 'talking cure' is that talking about a traumatizing or dicey experience you had a long time ago can actually help you in the present—and the statute of limitations on traumatic memory never expires completely. Of course, it's better if you can talk about a traumatizing experience right away rather than thirty years after it happens, but it will probably still help you to talk about it, no matter how much time has passed, especially if you've been fearful of talking about it before.

Talking about war is different than talking about any other kind of event, however, which is probably why the expression *war story* has come to be synonymous with any kind of intense narrative that involves both physical and psychological wounds. (The expression *war story* is very popular with recovering alcoholics and addicts, who use it to describe the half-remembered saga of what they did and said when they were active drinkers and addicts. It is, in other words, a story of past destruction, incompletely but vividly remembered from a sober vantage point in the present.) And it's the same when you talk about being in a war. Talking about a war in which you were involved has nothing to do with historical truth—writing and talking about a war you were involved in is really about emotions and memory.

When O'Brien writes about particular episodes in *The Things They Carried*, he writes his narrative as though it were in bits and pieces, a little part remembered in a certain way, and another part remembered in another way. What O'Brien is really doing is recreating with a particular literary style the way *psychological trauma affects the way people remember*. You don't remember all the things that happened, and you'll probably have more of a series of impressions of what happened than a narrative memory with a beginning, middle and end. Your imagination may have added details that didn't really happen, yet you may have forgotten many things that really *did* happen. You will have a kind of pastiche memory, of certain things at some times, and certain things at other times. Some things you remember are true, and other things aren't. The memories you get in the end may not fit together as a logical whole; but there may well be little jagged pieces of it that are problematic, that stick in the memory in a painful and intrusive way that you can't stop thinking about.

The reason I emphasize this is because of the way some people focus on figuring out the exact sequence of events that traumatized them. (Rape victims tend to spend an enormous amount of time trying to figure out what they did wrong, but it is rape that is wrong, and not what the victim did.) They believe that if they could remember exactly what happened, they can arrive at the answers that will liberate them from the burden they are carrying, and make them feel better. Figuring out the exact sequence of traumatizing events is a little like taking apart a broken watch. You may figure out exactly how the inner workings of the watch fit together, but that's usually not enough to restore their proper functioning—you need a different kind of skill for that. In a similar way, the literal, historical truth may not be where recovery from traumatic memory lies. The way of recovery is to understand the way the past *is interfering with the present*, and that usually has less to do with what actually happened as it is with the way events are lodged in one's memory, and the aggressive emotional orientations that one has internalized along with the memories themselves.

On the other hand, some people spend so much time repressing memories of traumatizing events that they must confront them before they can move on. The Veterans' Administration is now widely using what is called Prolonged Exposure Therapy with Vets with the PTSD diagnosis, and results are reported as good. The idea is to get the veterans to repeat the details of the traumatizing events over and over, in order to desensitize them to the disturbing memories that are causing them problems. There may be many dynamics in operation in this particular treatment modality, since there is so much about memory that is not completely understood.

For example, celebrities who give many public interviews say that if you tell your story over and over, it begins to sound unreal, even though the story itself is factually true. If you tell your story enough times, the story of your life starts to sound totally contrived, as though it were about someone else. For some, Prolonged Exposure may engage that same quirky psychological tendency for therapeutic purposes, giving the veteran who is being treated the distance and perspective that is required, paradoxically, for him to integrate the disturbing experiences into his personality. Anthropologist Michael Jackson has suggested that story-telling is one way of unfreezing the present from the tyranny of past trauma. Telling your story "externalizes" some of the aggression previously encoded into the violent memories. Above all, it makes the memory less threatening because now it belongs to the world, and not just to you. This is also one of the great advantages of talking with a group of combat vets in a clinical setting.

Prolonged Exposure often includes "assigning" the vet to do certain things—like driving in traffic—that have previously operated as emotional triggers causing anxiety. If you have an irrational fear, such as a fear that you may encounter an Improvised Explosive Device (IED) while driving on the familiar streets of your city, you may be "assigned" by your therapist to drive there every day. Your fears of getting hit by an Iraqi-style IED will gradually fade as you keep driving day after day without encountering one—even if the irrational fear doesn't go away completely, the patient becomes aware that it isn't logical or rational, so it doesn't have that much power anymore. Of course, being able to talk to a trained therapist on a regular basis, while acting out these "assignments," is itself therapeutic.

Can science find a way to disengage the pain of traumatic memory from the memory itself? "I want to disentangle painful emotion from the memory it is associated with," said Daniela Schiller, a researcher in psychological trauma who was quoted in a recent *New Yorker* article. "Then somebody could recall a terrible trauma, like those my father [who was in a Nazi labor camp] obviously endured, without the terror that makes it so disabling. You would still have the memory, but not the overwhelming fear attached to it."[4] This was important to Schiller because her father went most of his life without being able to discuss his Holocaust experiences.

But it may not be possible to disengage pain from memory without deconstructing the aggression that caused it. Holocaust memories aren't just *about* evil, they *are* evil, because they are a living experience of specific crimes committed against victims by specific Nazis acting out a radical form of systemic evil. These memories consist of evil in its rawest form. One can't pretend that the Nazis didn't exist, or that their behavior wasn't evil, or that people didn't suffer—and continue to suffer—from that same evil. But one *can* deconstruct whatever aggression one has internalized, by talking about what happened, and then—secondly— by living out a moral alternative to the sadism and aggression that animated everything the Nazis did.

Science can do many things, but it cannot remove the awareness of evil from those who have experienced it, nor can it be automatically expunged from the collective memory of the world—the very attempt to do so is suggestive of modern psychology's inability to grasp the moral issues at play in much psychological trauma, and typical also of a certain refusal to believe that human evil exists. But the bottom line is this: if victims of systemic evil *can* talk about what happened, to begin with, and secondly, if they *can act out values* that defy the evil they saw and endured, they can over time deconstruct the brutality they internalized. That is the essence of the 'recovery dualism' advocated in this book.

Another therapy often used by the Veterans' Administration these days is Cognitive Processing Therapy (CPT), an offshoot of Cognitive Behavior Therapy. As in Prolonged Exposure, the veteran with the diagnosis of PTSD is asked either to write or give a detailed account of a traumatizing event during his active service. The therapist then asks the individual to specify how specific details of the remembered behavior may be affecting him in the present moment. People who use this therapy believe that individuals have difficulty integrating traumatic memory because the unconscious part of the personality arrives at a skewed interpretation of reality subsequent to the traumatizing event. As a result of a buddy getting killed near him, an individual may come to feel that anybody he cares about will be hurt; that if he gets angry, the person that he's angry at will die; or that it is impossible to trust anyone. A skilled cognitive therapist, by asking the right questions and using ordinary everyday logic, can gradually reveal those points where the veteran has unknowingly arrived at certain beliefs in ways that were deeply irrational as well as self-destructive.

From all accounts Cognitive Processing Therapy has been quite helpful in treating combat veterans, because while it doesn't shy away from past traumatizing events, it continually asks the patient to relate them to the present. In the world of CPT, the problem is not what happened *back then*, but the way it is intruding on your life *right now*. I understand the necessity for some people to go back and confront the events that actually traumatized them, as in the Prolonged Exposure approach; but I have some concerns about therapies that cause patients to focus too much on the past, because it can subtly reinforce the feeling that organized aggression is humankind's most authentic emotional state, and therefore the underlying dynamic of human life. (The objective, it seems to me, should be to find an alternative to that emotional orientation.)

In a recent Sixty Minutes segment on PTSD in veterans, men in a sixteen-man group, many of whom experienced Prolonged Exposure Therapy, were asked, as they discussed combat experiences, how many of them would "go back there." All sixteen people in the group raised their hand. That desire to go back to the place in time and space where one was traumatized is a profound instinct among trauma victims, but it probably isn't the best way to manage traumatic memory.

For many men, combat was the only time they were allowed to be emotionally intimate with other men. For a great many men, that's a very, very powerful experience, one that causes them to remember combat as the most deeply-felt experience of their lives. It can also cause them to develop a worldview in which combat is a heroic and transcendent activity, but one that incidentally—for some reason they can't quite figure out—gives them bad dreams and disabling anxiety that interferes profoundly with daily life. They're not quite ready to live in the present moment because their emotional orientations are still about living in that heroic, powerful part of the past. That's too bad, because the real reason they want to go back is to recover something they lost. A better way is to start building a better life in the present, rather than returning to the past. To this writer CPT seems safer than Prolonged Exposure, because although it deals with the patient's narrative of past events, it constantly relates the past to present symptoms.

How do you keep from getting stuck in the past? In my book *Trauma Bond: an Inquiry into the Nature of Evil*, I mentioned a well-known residential program for Vietnam Veterans that lasted two weeks. Vets from all walks of life came together to talk to each other; and, since it was a residential program, they all lived as in-patients in the facility where the meetings were held. The first meeting was all about 'the Nam,' and they talked about every-thing that happened during the time they were in the Republic of Vietnam: the drugs, the lost buddies, the punji sticks, the firefights, and so-called "re-entry" problems afterwards. As one might expect, there were a couple of emotional meltdowns, but that was all part of the experience. They didn't leave anything out, including the after-effects, the bad dreams, the anxiety and depression, but it was all focused on stuff that happened in Vietnam. That was the first week.

Then came the second week. *The second week they weren't allowed to talk about anything having to do with Vietnam.* The second week they were allowed to talk only about the future, about what they wanted to be in the future, what they wanted their future itself to be like. The kind of jobs they wanted to work into, the way they wanted to improve their relationships with spouses and girlfriends, the kind of spiritual and emotional growth they'd like to experience. Most of all, the kind of person they wanted to become. It was a brilliant way, this writer believes, to take people back to Vietnam for a week, let them confront the traumatic memories, and then—after they'd made that one-week trip back to 'the Nam'—to turn them around and bring them back home, back to the world, and force them to talk and think about the kind of life they wanted in the future, and the kind of person they wanted to become.

It was, in other words, a simple but effective way to get people talking about everything that happened *back then*, and then bringing them the hell back to *right now*. By being designed that way, the program did a couple of very important things: first, it got people talking about their traumatizing experiences in Vietnam with people who understood what they were talking about; secondly, it made sure that nobody could get stuck in the past, because during that whole second week it made them talk about the future. It seems to this writer that Prolonged Exposure *could* be an important addition to the available therapies, and Cognitive Processing Therapy is even more likely to play a pivotal role. But as a precaution I would build into every program a requirement that at some point the vet start talking about the kind of person he or she wants to be in the future. Some people gradually come to identify with their traumatic memories so much that they have no reason to get better.

11.

Again: talking about traumatic memory is the first step of recovery. But for many, it may not be enough. There is relief in talking about painful experiences, there is insight, and there is very often the partial reintegration of the personality—but it still may not be enough. Why? It may not be enough because the people that design the various talk therapies we've examined very often aren't taking into consideration the moral dimension of armed combat. They may not even believe in the existence of evil, or of systemic evil in organized societies; yet in war there is invariably a profound moral quandary, and all soldiers involved in war are aware of it, even if the politicians and military organizations and social institutions and psychotherapists that send them off to war pretend that it doesn't exist.

The moral problem is this: *War is about killing people. And killing people is wrong.* Is there not a Commandment, 'Thou Shalt Not Kill?' And do not almost all people, both believers and secularists, have a gut feeling—despite the enormous human capacity for aggression—that killing people is wrong, especially if there is some way to avoid doing so? To compound the problem, we are increasingly aware that most casualties in modern war are innocent civilians.

Yet there are times in the fortunes of our nation when we feel it necessary to engage in war. The difficulty in reconciling those two things is so harrowing that many young people in the military don't even try to do so, instead focusing on becoming good soldiers, airmen and sailors. But the moral quandary will catch up with them sooner or later; and if they suffer psychological trauma, this terrible unanswered question is likely to interfere with their recovery, however deeply into the unconscious part of their personality they may push it.

People involved in modern wars must be prepared to kill strangers, or those same strangers will kill them. Of course, simply being in an environment where one suffers a constant fear of imminent death is enough to give many people long-term after-effects, and survivor guilt is also devastating. (Why did my friend die, and not me?) But the really disorienting thing, the thing that traumatizes soldiers the most deeply, is the fact that people, strangers to each other, are killing each other. The fact that young people can be traumatized by killing, or seeing people get killed in terrible ways, is paradoxically a sign of their moral soundness—only a sociopath could find killing people an easy task.

In fact, war is so terrible that it should be fought only when the outcome would be much worse if the war *wasn't* fought. If our country is physically attacked, for example, do we not have to respond aggressively? Yes, because in that instance killing in war, even though it's wrong, is the lesser evil when compared to the destruction of the nation, which would result in the enslavement of our people. So fighting back against a physical aggressor is one example of war that is justified, because the outcome if we didn't take up arms would be so much worse.[5]

Veterans of the Second World War went into World War II knowing that the US had been attacked at Pearl Harbor, and feeling also that if Imperial Japan and Hitler weren't stopped, the most brutal kinds of enslavement of the American people would follow. Everything they heard about the death camps in Europe and the brutality of the Japanese POW camps in Asia reinforced that belief. Many soldiers of that era believed that stopping Hitler and Imperial Japan was a moral imperative—and indeed, it became the great task of an entire generation, with many of the left/progressive Popular Front organizations devoting themselves to little else. This sense of being an important part of a great historical movement provided a *moral context* for the war, and created the sense that not opposing fascism would have been far worse, regardless of loss of life that was surely to occur in World War II. Imperial Japan and Hitler are two examples of a greater evil that had to be defeated, because to let those evil systems dominate the US—not to mention the world—would have been even more evil than going to war against them, despite the massive, horrendous nature of the killing necessary to defeat them. Can you imagine what the world would have been like if Hitler and Imperial Japan had won?

Here's another concrete example. This writer's great-grand-father, a man named James Quinn, was a Quaker who lived in Kansas. When the Civil War came along, he realized how terrible it was going to be, because civil wars are the most savage wars imaginable, with brothers often ending up killing brothers. He realized that killing people was wrong—I mean he *really* realized it, because 'Thou Shalt Not Kill' was absolutely and totally fundamental to the Society of Friends, or Quakers. The Quakers had been resisting war for several centuries, and I'm sure that James prayed about it a fair amount. But in the end, he decided slavery was an even greater and more malignant sin than killing, because he'd seen it up close in Missouri.

If slavery extended into Kansas, the western states would be lost, and it would be one big Slave Power—brutal, corrupt and totally undemocratic. So he joined the Union army, and put on the blue uniform. Because he was a good horseman and had a certain humorous authority in the way he interacted with others, he was eventually given the rank of Captain in the US Cavalry. It couldn't have been easy. But he believed absolutely and totally in every cell of his body that slavery *had* to be ended, or the country would be finished, kaput, done with. That *moral context* made it possible—necessary, actually—for him to be a soldier; and made it possible for him to excel at it, even while believing that war was a sin.

Here's a third example. Osama Bin Laden, whom the US had supported during the Afghan war against the Soviet Union, ultimately launched a surprise attack against America that killed 3,000 of our people. The war in Afghanistan was therefore necessary, because the Taliban sponsored Osama bin Laden, who attacked our people on 9/11; it was necessary to deny him sanctuary in Afghanistan, and ultimately to kill him. So the moral algorithm goes something like this: war is killing people, and killing people is wrong, but sometimes societies find it necessary. Why? Because a worse evil would occur, and ultimately would become a greater wrong, if one doesn't take up arms in the short term; in those situations societies fight and kill for a reason that is more important, and longer-lasting, than the killing itself. Yet the young people that do the killing suffer terrible after-effects that often last a lifetime.

Unfortunately, we live in a world where leaders sometimes declare wars that are *not* necessary, which therefore *can't* be justified. Sadly, the Vietnam War *wasn't* necessary, because the US could have followed the Paris Accords of 1954 and allowed elections in South Vietnam, but was too blinded by imperial pride to do so. The Iraq invasion wasn't necessary either, because Iraq never attacked the US—that war happened because of the imperial pride of George W. Bush, and the crazy neo-conservatives that advised him. When people begin to find out that they have been fed half-truths and lies, and that the terrible wars they rushed into couldn't really be justified, those wars became impossible to rationalize; when that happens, it creates a widening dissatisfaction in the society, and ultimately affects military personnel in a profound way. In 1970, distrust of the government and the top military commanders was so great in Vietnam that the various branches of the military faced an almost complete collapse of morale.

Since many politicians lie, it is very important for the future of America that young people, and their parents, learn how to distinguish between necessary wars (when we are attacked) and unnecessary wars (based on made-up stories about Weapons of Mass Destruction, for example). I believe young people should refuse to serve in wars that cannot be justified. But the war fever stirred up by politicians can become so strong, and most young people are so intellectually and emotionally immature at the age when they are likely to enter the military, that they may not be able to distinguish between a necessary or unnecessary war. When they find out later that the reasons given for getting into the war were mainly lies or distortions, the moral algorithm breaks down. That, and a sense of being betrayed by the government or by powerful politicians, can make recovery from war trauma more difficult.

But here's the good news.

Believe it or not, a veteran can create the all-important *moral context* for his service *after the actual service is over.* Once our precious young people in uniform are back home, and trying to recovery from any after-effects they may be experiencing, the politics of the war are no longer important. What the veteran then needs to concentrate on is getting better, and getting treatment for any delayed stress—or Post-Traumatic Stress Disorder (PTSD)—they may be experiencing. The veteran is no longer called on to make a decision about being in the war, because he's already been there; but he *can* make a decision about how to handle traumatic memories of it.

And the way to do that is, first, by talking about it, and gaining insight into how it has affected one's personality. But it is also through social interactions—however minimal—in some *socially-beneficial activity.* This kind of personal moral engagement with something going on in the world, identifying with the need to make the world better (even as one makes oneself better) is at the heart of the 'recovery dualism' that this book advocates. Clearly it's applicable to veterans, as we can see from the dramatic examples recounted in this book.

Fred Whitehurst defied direct orders to save the diary of Dang Thuy Tram. Rich Luttrell traveled to Vietnam to give a small photograph of a man he'd killed to that man's daughter—and he ended up going back twice after that. Eric Lomax traveled all the way to the Far East to meet with a man who had tortured him. And Tim O'Brien has written some awesome books about the emotional effects of his service. Those are examples of people who are making positive decisions about how to handle their memories—and their *socially-beneficial behavior,* while associated with their memories of war, helped them determine how best to integrate the entire experience of war into their personalities. At the same time, their socially-beneficial actions also made the world a better place.

Yes, these were extraordinary actions of extraordinary

people—but the point is, they went out of their way to create a *moral context* for their experience in a particular war, by taking some action regarding that war that was positive, life-giving and creative. All of them took some risks in so doing, but they were determined to do something good with their military experience, something that went beyond the fighting itself. That's how they created a moral context for something that was over a long time ago—and so can any veteran of any war. How they do it is up to them, but I'll make some suggestions later on in this chapter.

The one population that has led the way toward this 'dual recovery' approach has been victims of rape and sexual assault, a primarily civilian population. Many rape victims start their recovery by getting the counseling they need, but then go on to greatly benefit themselves, and all of us, by becoming vigorous critics of patriarchy and rape culture. Combine those two things—counseling by peers and advocacy against patriarchy— and you have the ideal dual recovery strategy. Rape victims do need to start their recovery with counseling, and that is appropriate and desirable, but their recovery can happen more quickly if they work with other women and men to oppose those social forces, such as patriarchy, that can lead to rape. (*Patriarchy* includes the belief that men have the right to be violent and coercive with women, which is a big part of rape culture.) Rape victims have a certain authority when they speak out against patriarchy, because having survived the terrible experience of a sexual assault they have special credibility regarding the malignant effects of patriarchal culture.

Rape victims have had all personal power violently taken from them by the rapist, and need to get that power back; vigorous advocacy against patriarchy, and the prevalence of rape culture on college campuses and in the military, allows these former victims to empower themselves. Veterans who seek treatment could also work for a better world in a somewhat similar way, even as they work to get better. Both combat veterans and rape victims may begin their recovery as individuals caught in a trauma bond, and begin with talk therapy; but both should also become aware, over time, that they can also work with peers to confront, reduce and seek to abolish the social injustice that once generated the trauma, and to some extent keeps the traumatic memory alive.

So while receiving personal counseling is the proper place for rape victims to start their recovery, it seems to work best if they cooperate with other women and men to work *for* a world without rape, and work *against* those misogynist beliefs and emotional orientations that create the cultural/psychological climate in which a rape culture flourishes. By raising consciousness around such issues as date-rape and rape culture on college campuses and in the military, former rape victims have empowered themselves by directly challenging toxic, pathological attitudes that support that same 'culture of rape.' It's not an alternative to counseling for victims of sexual assault, and certainly not an alternative to prosecuting and adjudicating offenders, but it gives the victim a way of being empowered—it gives them a feeling that they count, that they're making a difference, and the hope that if they speak out against patriarchy maybe women in the future won't suffer the same sexual assaults they have endured.

Socially-beneficial activities tend to support the emotional growth that should occur in recovery, taking the individual out of her private concerns and helping her hook up with the world outside her rehabilitative program. Above all, a dual recovery strategy *empowers* the victims of trauma, taking them out of victim status by showing them that they can make a difference.

It's about going into oneself and discovering the best parts of one's personality, while at the same time journeying out into the larger world to connect with those engaged in making the world better. If you're serious about making *yourself* better while you make the *world* better, pretty soon you'll start making connections between the two. You'll discover the good things in yourself, and by standing up for something good in the world, you end up working with other good people who are similarly inclined.

12.

So what kind of 'socially-beneficial' activities should veterans embrace?

The concept of reconciliation of soldiers with former enemies is a recurring theme in this chapter, and there's no denying its power for healing. Reconciliation occurs, in its best and most liberating incarnations, between a former soldier and the country where the veteran was once deployed—by participating in some charitable activity, the veteran enjoys the privilege of helping the country heal at the same time he or she heals. Several agencies have sponsored such activities, among them the Quakers (Society of Friends), several Non-Government Organizations (NGOs), and a variety of nonprofits.

The services they offer to civilians in former war zones are quite extensive. In Vietnam these services are aided by the fact that the government there supports reconciliation with the US; Iraq and Afghanistan are unfortunately still war zones, so veterans of those conflicts should limit their involvement to donating through established organizations that have a presence in those countries. The beneficial effects of helping civilians, especially children, can still be enjoyed at a distance.

But there is another way ex-servicemen can participate in a socially-beneficial activity, and this way is really a game-changer. They can join a nationwide mass movement for better services for veterans, *all* veterans, but especially our returning Afghanistan and Iraq veterans. God knows, such a movement is needed, and the individual can get involved on any level that he or she chooses. The Veterans' Administration may acknowledge that the lengthy wait times for veterans are an emergency only when there is such a massive groundswell of compassion and concern for our vets that they can no longer ignore the crisis. Returning vets can play a positive and important role in advocating for better services. 'Iraq and Afghanistan Veterans of America' is doing a terrific job of coordinating this important movement, and there are many more organizations that are also taking up the cause.

This is a 'socially-beneficial' service of supreme importance. Veterans returning from wars often suffer from delayed stress, yet the long wait time and denial of services can gravely compound these problems. By advocating for better service for veterans, the vet sends himself an all-important message that he is important, that he counts in the scheme of things, and that he has certain rights. That by itself will help the veteran deal with personal stress, but it does so by trying to change something in the world that is *causing* stress. Veterans should try to find a niche that is comfortable for them, while trying to interact regularly with other vets with whom they can talk about how they're feeling. When they're taking this dualistic approach to recovery, they are sending the world—and themselves—a message that the world can become a better and more humane place, at the same time that they're stabilizing themselves emotionally. It's a powerful and compelling process.

Another reason for the dual approach is this: traumatic memories are *endogenous*, but activated by triggers that are *exdogenous*. That is, traumatic memories are a stressful condition that exists *inside* the personality of the victim, but the stress gets triggered by things *outside* of the victim's personality; and usually—unfortunately—outside of the victim's control. Participating in socially-beneficial activities can begin to heal the connection between the interior life of the victim and the world outside, empowering social contracts and restoring trust. The events that traumatize in war were beyond the control of individual soldiers, and so, perhaps, were the depression and anxiety they may have felt when they came home. But by learning to advocate for themselves the returning veterans acknowledge the dual nature of the world, and signal their willingness to play a role. The veteran advocating for better services helps himself and also helps others in his situation — that's a powerful connection. The recovering veteran senses that he is helping other veterans in the future avoid some of the stress he is feeling, and that is a source of deep satisfaction.

The situation at many Veterans' Administration hospitals is in crisis. Even though the treatment in the Veterans' Administration is excellent once you are in the system, returning vets are suffering because of the extremely long wait times, and some vets with PTSD may be committing suicide because they can't be seen. Too many politicians are responding by using it as an opportunity for scoring political points! Things won't change until enough people put pressure on the system to open up the intake process and shorten the wait times. I'm not advocating anything violent or extreme, please understand that — *but the time is ripe for a mass, non-violent movement for veterans' rights*. If you're a veteran, or even if you're *not* a veteran, do something today for all returning veterans! Start by writing a letter to your local newspaper about the necessity of change within the Veterans' Administration. Be polite, but be forceful.

Don't be surprised if writing a letter makes you feel better — a vigorous, thoughtful exercise of free speech can do wonders for one's morale! If there's something that drives you crazy about the way vets are being treated in the US, write about it, write a letter to the editor of your local paper about the VA backlog, or whatever it is about veterans' treatment in US society that is important to you. If you're a veteran and are already in the system, and receiving good treatment, write a letter telling how much you appreciate it. If you're still on a wait list, write a letter about how that feels. If you don't think you can write a letter, get another veteran to help you. You'll be surprised at how good you feel when that letter is printed in the newspaper! You're sending yourself, and the world, a message that you count, that your welfare is important!

This is basic, simple stuff, but it's important. Veterans need to have the feeling that they can make a difference where their own treatment is concerned, that where treatment is concerned they don't have to be victims. The purpose here is two-fold—first, to actually improve the treatment of military vets; two, to encourage vets to realize that they're not helpless, that there's a problem, yes, but that they can be part of the solution. And believe me, better treatment for military vets is a cause whose time has come! This may be partly a political issue, but it should be approached as a humanitarian one, and it's one that Americans of all political persuasions understand and support; our precious vets need to realize how important they are to the American people. Furthermore, vets can have a powerful national voice when they stand up for each other!

The need for immediate treatment for Afghanistan and Iraqi veterans is critical. Because of the enemy's use of Improvised Explosive Devices (IEDs), severe head trauma is widespread among vets, including many with the Post-Traumatic Stress Disorder (PTSD) diagnosis. The exact relativity between the two may never be known completely, but it seems likely that the two conditions overlap, and can potentiate each other—and in fact, it may be very difficult to tell where one ends and the other starts. The military often demotes in rank those who have difficulty following orders, but forgetfulness of an order, or the way it should be executed, may be a symptom of these two conditions (PTSD, severe head trauma, or both) rather than intentional disrespect for the command structure. The need for diagnosis and long-term treatment for these vets is absolutely central to the future of the Veterans' Administration, and to the future of America! Their treatment should be given the highest priority. You can help, whoever you are, by adding your voice to those who are demanding shorter wait times and quicker intake into VA treatment programs, even opening up the intake process to practitioners in private practice if necessary.

Furthermore, the Veterans' Administration needs to fast-track new med protocols for returning vets from Afghanistan and Iraq. In Iraq particularly, soldiers doing their third or fourth tours of duty were often given psych meds to help them get through it. That was an inappropriate use of psychoactive medications, but it happened, because the meds were the only tools the doctors had to combat stress. As a consequence, VA doctors back in the US are sometimes reluctant to prescribe certain meds, saying that they have been 'over-prescribed.' In other words, our soldiers serving in Iraq got too many meds when they didn't need them, and now that they need them, they can't get them. It's a perfect Catch-22. The doctors at the Veterans' Administration need to confront this conundrum directly, and work out an acceptable compromise, so that they will have appropriate protocols to help their patients. The sooner they get to work on this problem, the sooner it will be resolved.

Again: practitioners working with vets should consider 'socially beneficial' activities as a useful adjunct to conventional treatment. Individuals struggling with traumatic memories as a result of human violence need to deconstruct the fears and anxieties they feel personally, but they almost invariably end up sensing that there are larger social contradictions, forces that are connected to the circumstances that originally caused them to be traumatized. The smart and courageous ones then find (sometimes almost by accident) that along with treatment for their own problems, it helps them to work for a less traumatizing world, and that this has a way of empowering them *personally* — that is, it not only makes the world a better place, but also helps them recover more quickly.

Some rape victims end up working for agencies that counsel recent victims of rape, working to guide victims through the psychological and legal steps necessary to simultaneously apprehend criminals and care for the psyches of victims—and making sure that rape counseling is available at the hospital, making sure the rape kit is used correctly, helping victims navigate the police interview; and above all, talking about the rape with a counselor as soon as possible. Throughout this process peer counseling is given a high priority. This book strongly supports the concept of peer counseling for returning vets with PTSD or other problems, including those on a wait list.

Each vet should get a "navigator"—that is, another veteran, someone who has already made it through some of the administrative hurdles—who can familiarize veterans on the wait list with the Byzantine complexities of the Veterans' Administration, and advocate for them as they enter the system. The idea of 'navigators' was embraced in various states to spur enrollment in the Affordable Care Act, with great success. Shouldn't we consider such peer empowerment in the treatment of returning veterans?

13.

Reducing war trauma isn't just a matter of treating it after it already happens. If war trauma and its attendant risks for violence, addictions and traumatic memory constitutes a public health problem, as this writer believes it does, our concern for victims of war trauma should extend to prevention as well. That means opposing wars that aren't really necessary, while supporting those that are. Remember, war is far too important to leave to the generals and the politicians, because they usually aren't the ones who get killed or grievously wounded.

Therefore one great task before our American young people and their parents is to understand what would constitute an unnecessary war, and a necessary one. The reader will already have seen that the Vietnam War was unnecessary, because an agreement had been reached in Paris in the 1950s to allow the

Vietnamese people to choose their own leaders in internationally-supervised elections. But the US and its client state in Saigon refused to allow the elections, because the US thought they could simply defeat the North Vietnamese and the VC militarily. Some two to three million Vietnamese were killed in the resulting war, most of them civilians, and the Americans lost the war. A lot of our young people saw the killing of civilians up close, and when they began to realize they'd been misled, it created an enormous problem in public confidence and morale.

In more modern times, the Taliban in Afghanistan gave sanctuary to the terrorist group Al Qaeda, which eventually carried out an attack that killed 3,000 of our people in New York and Washington DC. Clearly, we had no choice but to deny Al Qaeda sanctuary; so we were right to go into Afghanistan, to fight the Taliban, and ultimately to kill Osama bin Laden. On the other hand, in 2003 President George Bush invaded the country of Iraq, which had never attacked the US. The world could see what a terrible mistake this was going to be, and how badly it hurt America's reputation, even if Bush couldn't. In this unnecessary war, the US got rid of one group of brutal, corrupt crooks in Iraq and replaced them with another group of brutal, corrupt crooks. But the real tragedy is that as many as two hundred thousand Iraqis, mainly civilians, died in the conflict. And those Iraqis, along with our military women and men, died or were maimed for no really good reason, though our troops performed admirably.

Of course, to people under the influence of patriarchy, war may *always* seem good and necessary, because it is part of patriarchic culture. In *The Things They Carried*, Tim O'Brien writes in "On the Rainy River" about making a decision to go to Vietnam, rather than going to Canada. The person in this story, who we are encouraged to believe is a lot like Tim O'Brien, had already decided that the war in Vietnam was unnecessary—and he had gotten some idea of how destructive it was going to be, both to

Americans and to the Vietnamese. He believed that the right thing for him to do, the moral thing for him to do, would be to go to Canada as a war resister, and not go to Vietnam. But he couldn't. Some powerful force was preventing him from doing what he thought was right, and was pulling him toward being a soldier in Vietnam. What it all boiled down to was that he was afraid of disappointing all the people he'd known in his life, starting with his parents—he was afraid they'd all think he was a coward and a traitor.

O'Brien has his narrator put it this way: "I survived, but it's not a happy ending. I was a coward. I went to war." O'Brien's narrator is perhaps the first in American literature to say that one is a coward for not resisting a war one believes to be wrong. I think O'Brien is right. Of course, one would be just as cowardly for *not* fighting in a war that you believe really *is* necessary. So what I am advocating is not pacifism. I am advocating fighting in necessary wars, and resisting wars that aren't.

And what was that powerful force that kept O'Brien's narrator from resisting a war he knew to be wrong? It was, and is, the idea that aggression is the most transcendent force in human affairs, and that men killing and dominating other people through force of arms is the highest test of manhood. This is called *patriarchy*, and it has many other sides to it besides war, including a belief that men have the right to enslave and dominate women; but at the heart of patriarchy is a belief that armed conflict is fundamentally good because it established excellence in leadership. Instead war produces a great many broken bodies and souls, and it also produces people who are bonded to aggression, some of whom are eager to impose their patriarchal values on everybody else.

Physical bravery is admirable when wars are necessary, but killing is never good in itself, and making war simply to make war is never a good idea. The ideals of patriarchy must be set aside so that new instincts for morality, cooperation, and justice can arise. There is no quick or easy way to do this, but people can make this happen (and it's already starting to happen) only as we—*all* of us—keep working to deconstruct whatever aggression we have internalized, and to recognize internalized aggression in others. In certain ways, women may lead the way in this, because of their verbal skills and their willingness to advocate against patriarchy, which as a cultural force is often associated with internalized aggression.

In any case, there is a profound moral dilemma at the heart of war, a conviction that killing is wrong, accompanied by a concurrent belief that in certain situations wars must nonetheless be fought to stop an even greater wrong. This moral dilemma is faced squarely in this book because it inevitably contributes to the psychological trauma of people caught up in war's violence—we know that it does because veterans so often speak of feelings of guilt at having to take another life. (Remember Rich Luttrell's story?)

But just as these dynamics are involved in *causing* trauma in war, they can also be used in *recovery* from war trauma. Once back in civilian life, the objective of the veteran is to reduce and manage any negative psychological after-effects of war. And as I have pointed out earlier in this chapter, veterans can create a moral context for whatever traumatic memory they may have— and they can do that by working for a better world in socially-beneficial activities that are life-giving and creative and compassionate. It sounds paradoxical, but it works. It can not only help the veteran integrate and move past his or her experiences, it can turn the veteran's military service into a lifelong resource—for the veteran, and also for the world.

This book's suggested path to recovery from traumatic memory is a 'recovery dualism,' because it consists of two powerful but complementary elements. One begins managing one's traumatic memory by discussing the traumatizing events in the past, hopefully with a counselor or psychotherapist, achieving as much insight as possible into the way it influences present behavior. The second part occurs when one engages in some socially-beneficial activity, activity that in some way relates to the cause of one's past trauma.

The socially-beneficial activity need not be something dramatic, but simply something in which the individual has some emotional investment, the goal being to make oneself better at the same time that one makes the world better. This second part of the 'recovery dualism'—helping others even as one is being helped by professionals—operates to address the conflicted feelings that arise from the moral dilemma of war, and helps restore the connection between the soldier returning to civilian life and the rest of the world. But it restores that connection in a way that gives the veteran the moral initiative, the moral high ground, and the power that goes with them.

14.

Sometimes reconciliation between former enemies happens in ways one could never imagine, much less predict. Most of us know about the My Lai massacre, in which a platoon of men from the Americal Division under Lieutenant William Calley killed several hundred civilians on March 16, 1968, near the hamlet known as My Lai, part of the four villages of the Son My network. Less known is the fact that it was an Americal helicopter crew, composed of Hugh Thompson, Jr., Lawrence Colburn and Glenn Andreotta, who heroically intervened to stop the My Lai massacre. The reader will remember that the Americals have figured prominently in the stories told in this chapter, and not always in a good light; therefore it is especially important to acknowledge the extreme bravery of Thompson, Colburn and Andreotta, who saved many innocent lives. And there's an aspect of their stories that turns out to be unexpectedly important regarding the theme of reconciliation between former enemies.

Thompson immediately reported the massacre to his superiors; but there was, as one might imagine, a cover-up by army brass. Colin Powell, who was serving with the Americal Division, was assigned to investigate the rumors of a massacre (and Thompson's detailed report about it), but his investigation—like other "official" investigations—conveniently came to nothing. Tragically, Glenn Andreotta, one of the soldiers that helped stop the slaughter by men under Lieutenant Calley, was killed in action three weeks after the My Lai massacre. Hugh Thompson, Jr., was awarded the Distinguished Flying Cross, and Colburn and Andreotta received the Bronze Cross, with Andreotta receiving his posthumously.

Thompson, who watched with horrified incredulity as an elaborate cover-up was set in motion by the top military brass, disgustedly threw his DFC medal away, since it was accompanied by an account of the incident that was completely fabricated. The truth eventually came out, however, thanks to the letter-writing of Ron Ridenhour—a helicopter gunner serving with the 11th Infantry Brigade, Americal Division—and the cutting-edge investigative journalism of Seymour Hersh. Thompson's extreme courage in stopping a rogue operation by American troops is regularly cited as an example of courage in ethics manuals of various military organizations. Thompson may actually have stopped further slaughter as well—similar 'operations' were planned in other villages, but were called off because of his fearless advocacy, in which he referred to Lieutenant Calley's actions as 'murder.'

Although Thompson was criticized by some conservative American politicians for stopping the slaughter—and afterwards telling the truth about what really happened—the people and government of Vietnam did not forget the heroism of Colburn and Thompson, the two Americans who stepped up in the midst of mass murder and managed to save many lives. Thompson and Colburn returned to Vietnam in 1998, exactly thirty years later, where they were greeted by government representatives and people representing the villagers in the hamlet of My Lai. In addition to speaking personally with many of the villagers he saved, he also appeared in a ceremony to dedicate a local grade-school for the area's children. (Apparently one of three built by a group of Quakers from Madison, Wisconsin.) Several former American and Vietnamese soldiers were at this ceremony.

Thompson talked to and interacted with many people whose lives he had saved thirty years before. One of the people there, Phan Thi Nhanh, had been only fourteen years old when the massacre happened. In a statement that could stand as a thoughtful analysis of how traumatic memory can be managed, she said: "We don't say we forget. We just try not to think of the past, but in our hearts we keep a place to think about that." That seems especially appropriate considering the role of family and ancestors in Vietnamese culture.

On 2008, there was another anniversary of the massacre—the fortieth—and there was another ceremony, and another get-together of former American and Vietnamese soldiers. Larry Colburn returned, but Hugh Thompson, Jr., was not there—he had passed away on January 6, 2006. At the ceremony Colburn happened to run into Bo Da, a My Lai survivor who had lost his mother, his brother and his sister in the massacre. He was delighted to see that Bo Da had a new wife and a 14-month-old daughter. It meant a lot to Colburn. "Today I see Bo Da with a wife and baby," he said wonderingly. "He's transformed himself from being a broken, lonely man. Now he's complete. He's a perfect example of the human spirit, of the will to survive." That's one of the most intriguing things about reconciliation with former 'enemies'—you look at them, and you see them living their lives, and you think, 'If they can recover, so can I.'

15.

While reconciliation with the Vietnamese people is not the policy of the US government,[6] there is no lack of American organizations working with Vietnamese organizations in projects that are mutually beneficial to both Americans and Vietnamese—and in many cases, beneficial especially to US Vietnam Veterans. The *US-Vietnam Dialog Group on Agent Orange/Dioxin*, a group sparked by the Aspen Institute in the US, is blessed with a strong array of both Americans and Vietnamese, including both scientists and public figures. Many readers will know that 'Agent Orange,' or dioxin, was sprayed on foliage throughout South Vietnam during the period of 1965-1970, with disastrous results on plants, animals and people. (Dang Thuy Tram writes in her diary that in Quang Ngai Province all the birds were killed, so that between bombardments an uncanny silence prevailed.)

Today the Vietnamese government gives monthly stipends to about 200,000 people affected by dioxin, although there are probably many more sufferers than that. The Vietnamese government has established "peace villages," each of which takes care of some 50 to 100 patients; and outside Hanoi there is a "Friendship Village" which is actively supported by Vietnam Veterans from several countries, including many from the US, a fair number of whom also suffer from illnesses having to do with Agent Orange.

The *US-Vietnam Dialogue Group on Agent Orange/Dioxin* (founded in 2007) includes prominent private citizens, scientists and policy-makers on both the Vietnamese and US sides, working on issues that the governments of the two countries haven't yet been able to agree on. The role of the *US-Vietnam Dialogue Group* has been to call attention to the need for five key actions to be undertaken in a humanitarian spirit, according to Wikipedia: "To establish treatment and education centers for Vietnamese with disabilities; cooperate with the US and Vietnamese governments to contain and clean up dioxin, beginning at three priority airport 'hot spots'; set up a modern dioxin testing laboratory in Vietnam; foster programs for training of trainers in restoration and management of damaged landscapes; and educate the US public on the issues."

Leading the Vietnamese side at the time this book was written was Ambassador Ngo Quang Xuan, vice chair of the Vietnamese National Assembly's Foreign Affairs Committee; and leading the US side was Walter Isaacson, president and CEO of the Aspen Institute. The convener of the group was Susan Berresford, former President of the Ford Foundation. The group is promoting a ten-year plan for getting rid of Agent Orange in Vietnam. Of course anything learned from these initiatives in Vietnam will help our own Vietnam Vets here in American who also may be suffering from illnesses related to 'Agent Orange.' The *US-Vietnam Dialogue Group* is a very practical group that can do good work in the present, and is aimed at healing the wounds of war in a way that can help both Vietnamese and Americans.

16.

Joseph Campbell, an author widely known for his work in comparative mythology and comparative religion, wrote a very famous book called *The Hero with a Thousand Faces*. In this book he argued that some of the most famous myths cherished by humanity follow a fundamentally similar pattern, or sequence of events. A hero (usually a male, but sometimes a female) goes to a distant country, a place of danger and magic. He passes certain tests, and performs certain feats of valor; and as a result receives certain powers and gifts, which he takes back to his home country and bestows on his countrymen and countrywomen. This is actually a foundational mono-myth, one that occurs in a great many cultures—with many variations—and a story that has fascinated humankind for millennia.

It seems to this writer that the dilemma of the traumatized combat veteran resembles this basic myth-narrative, but with one huge difference. The traumatized soldier goes to a far country, a place of danger and magic, a Place of Wonders, but never quite makes it back home. Somewhere in that far country he sustains a terrible wound; and he is doomed for a time to wander in the borderlands—the badlands, one might say—until he is whole again. What is this part of him that was wounded? Innocence, perhaps; a sense of himself as a good person; or a moral code that once worked, but was overwhelmed by violent events.

The warrior with traumatic memories, or one who has received the Post-Traumatic Stress Disorder (PTSD) diagnosis, is stuck in the borderlands between a distant war and the homeland to which he is trying to return. To such combat veterans I would say this: it's not the end of the world. It gets better. Furthermore, many writers, artists and poets are stuck in that same borderland, sometimes for life. And it's not the terrible thing you might imagine—being a non-violent outlaw in the wild places gives you a certain freedom to be who you really are, rather than what society wants you to be.

The point is, you can take as long as you need to learn how to get your thoughts and feelings back in some semblance of order, to integrate into your personality what you've learned, and reorient yourself so you can live with a reasonable amount of integrity. To become that new and better person you are meant to be—*that's* what recovery from traumatic memory is all about. And you can take as long as you need to get there.

In fact, the mono-myth that Joseph Campbell articulates is fundamentally patriarchal, this writer would say, because it does not acknowledge that warriors get hurt, that they don't automatically slay all the dragons, and don't always emerge triumphant from the field of battle with special powers. The challenges of the warrior whose wounds are unseen are much more complex and interesting, and the challenges he or she faces much more relevant to society, than simply slaying dragons and winning fair maidens in a distant land.

The person in recovery is basically an anti-hero, but he is also an iconic figure in a society seeking to re-define itself, because he does not seek to dominate or impress, but rather to create a new way of life. To accomplish that, the traumatized warrior needs emotional and moral courage, which is far more important to our modern world than physical courage. It is the gentle warriors who accept the challenges of becoming new and better people, and not necessarily the decorated war heroes, who are the unacknowledged exemplars of our time.

To the combat veteran struggling with traumatic memories I say again that the first step is to tell someone—preferably a professional in a clinical setting—about the things that happened to you, and how those things make you feel today. But I would also encourage you to engage in some socially-beneficial activity that could help make the world a little less dangerous, a little less violent, a little better. I don't know exactly what that thing would be for you, but it would in some way probably be related to your status as a veteran. As I've already suggested, you might consider becoming part of the movement for veterans' rights, a movement whose time has come. You might also consider helping those Non-Governmental Organizations or charitable groups that work for peace, or that work to help civilian reconstruction in formerly contested lands. You might want to consider getting a degree in international relations, or getting trained as a counselor who could help other veterans. There are many things you can do. But in my experience, people who first *talk* about what they experienced, and then *act* in some socially-beneficial manner to make the world better—well, they're the ones most likely to recover well.

To reinvent, to re-discover, or to live without some wounded part of oneself is, in fact, the great spiritual challenge we all face, because of the great changes that are taking place around us: we must learn to live in a world that is changing so fast that one barely recognizes it from season to season. Because people in transition need new myths, I encourage victims of war trauma, those still suffering from the after-effects of traumatic memories, to write the stories of their lives. When I was a counselor, I used to ask them to use no more than three pages—not the whole story, but a page or two, a story in outline form. *At the top of the first page write about who you were when you were young; the middle part is what happened to you; then on the last page, what you want to become.* If you're still in the borderland, that's fine—just write about the person you'd like to become once you're all the way home.

Such a story is both art and an artifact. Artifacts help us want to stay alive, because they fix our mind's eye on the present; art, on the other hand, helps us to come to terms with death, including those deaths that we may have caused, the death of friends, and ultimately our own death. Remember what Tim O'Brien is telling us in *The Things They Carried*: that the real story is always about our emotions, about those parts of our memory that were changed or branded in some way with powerful experiences. Write about the way your memory organizes the emotionally important things that happened to you; the way memory influences the present; and the way you can manage the whole shebang.

Again: write about where you've been, where you are now, and what you want to become. That story becomes the myth of your life, which is just as important as any other life on this planet. It reflects where you are now in your pilgrim way, so hang onto it and take it out in ten years or so—it will be a valuable artifact, because it'll be an accurate indicator of where you are right now; but it'll also be art, because it's about what you are becoming, and what you ultimately want to be in the great scheme of things.

Above all, remember that you are simultaneously the narrator and protagonist of your own life story: no one can ever take that away from you, because it belongs to you alone. And if by chance, when you sit down to write the story of your life, you find that you're still in the borderland between past and future, please remember that you can take as long as you need to get back home. The truth is we're all on pretty much the same journey.

Chapter Five

Gerry Adams and Others: Deep Trauma and Redemption in the Irish Quagmire

1.

James Carroll, perhaps America's best Catholic writer, had this to say about Padriag O'Malley's *The Uncivil Wars: Ireland Today*: "Padraig O'Malley is the first author in years to treat the mad subject of Ireland as if it can be understood." To be sure, Ireland was forever a 'mad subject,' but the money phrase here is the delightful qualifier *as if it can be understood*. Understanding of anything Irish is not an easy or automatic thing, even for—or especially for—the Irish themselves. Ireland is simultaneously a beckoning reverie for pilgrims, a nattering memory of exiles, an Unholy Land beset by religious fanaticism, an artistic obsession that too often becomes an aesthetic of death, a high concept for personal theater, and a martyr nation whose irreconcilable conflicts generate violent emotions ranging from the gleefully nihilistic to the densely sadistic. Interwoven through these things is a traumatic memory of tragedy and oppression going back 800 years, a fair amount of which came from the Irish themselves, but most of which came from a certain English distrust and hostility, bordering on racism, toward the Irish people.

States of Ireland, by Conor Cruise O'Brien, managed best to suggest—despite the fact that Cruise O'Brien fell victim to his own extremism—the epic manner in which Ireland is at the center of several wildly differing (and often opposing) world-views, or states of mind, depending on which tribal aspect of Irish-ness one is a part of, or wishes to invoke. Cruise O'Brien's great victory was in describing the profoundly different emotional orientations of Catholics and Protestants in Ireland and Northern Ireland. His great defeat was in hating violence so much that he ended up opposing peace, a peculiarly Irish accomplishment.

Such emotional orientations usually emanate from powerful group loyalties, which in both Ireland and Northern Ireland tend to mean group grievances. In 1916 there was a failed Irish uprising against Britain; in the immediate aftermath of that attempted revolution, the astonishing stupidity of the British in executing its ringleaders swung the support of the Irish people behind the revolutionaries. (The leaders of the uprising had declared a Republic, so those who supported it were called Republicans.) After the First World War there commenced a brutal national liberation struggle against the British, fought by the Irish Republican Army, until in 1921-22 a peace treaty was negotiated. Sadly, however, in 1922 this peace treaty ('the Treaty') divided the Republicans into pro- and anti-Treaty factions, leading to the Irish Civil War. This division prefigured and to some extent paralleled another strong and ongoing divide in Irish life, between parliamentary (nonviolent) nationalism and 'physical force' (violent) nationalism. The Civil War ended in 1923, and within a relatively short time, as these things go, the Republic of Ireland was achieved through political, diplomatic and entirely nonviolent means, a process that picked up momentum in 1937 and was completed in 1949.

But the war was not over, as we now know. Six counties in the North had been divided by 'the Treaty' into a separate country called Northern Ireland, because its Protestant majority hated and distrusted the Catholic hierarchy, which it tended to regard as evil incarnate. Within Northern Ireland in the last half of the 20th century resided about a million and a half people, about a third of whom were Catholics identifying with the Republic of Ireland, and two-thirds Protestants violently opposed to any kind of merger with that same Republic. The two-thirds Protestant majority increasingly defined themselves by their burning antipathy to the politics and goals of Irish

Republicanism, and to Irish Catholics generally. Thus the antipathy between the two groups in Northern Ireland: the Catholics believing that Northern Ireland was destined to become part of Ireland proper (partly in order to protect the rights of Catholics) whereas most Protestants violently resisted any connection to a country in which policy would be decided by Irish Catholics, whose dominance they feared.

Those Catholics that once sought to merge the six counties of Northern Ireland into the Republic of Ireland were the Republicans; the Protestants that violently opposed that expedient were called loyalists, or unionists. These two groups, Republicans (overwhelmingly Catholic) and Unionists (overwhelmingly Protestant) sought to represent the interests of the two religious communities in Northern Ireland; and both were parties to the armed conflict in Northern Ireland that lasted from about 1968 until 1998—approximately 30 years—a time that people in both communities called 'the Troubles.'

Since long before 'the Troubles,' however, there had been built into the social order in Northern Ireland certain extreme structural advantages for Protestants, in the form of institutionalized discrimination against Catholics—including the gerrymandering of voting districts—aimed at keeping in check the already impoverished Catholic community. But although the Catholics of Northern Ireland were objectively far more discriminated against than Protestants, those same Protestants felt deeply threatened by the preponderance of Catholics on the island as a whole; furthermore, in Northern Ireland itself, 'the Prods' came to detest and fear the Catholic minority they oppressed, a familiar mania of those who practice or benefit from oppression. Both factors contributed to the gnawing fear that drove traditional Unionist thinking. Both religious communities in Northern Ireland were beset by the paranoia, aggression and resentments typical of aggrieved minorities: the Catholics saw themselves—correctly—as a persecuted minority within Northern Ireland; the Protestants felt themselves potentially a persecuted minority in the island as a whole.

This chapter deals to a great extent with one person's experience in Northern Ireland, that of Gerry Adams, who—although he still declines to acknowledge it directly—was in the leadership of the Irish Republican Army in Northern Ireland during much of 'the Troubles,' as the urban guerilla war in Northern Ireland is called. These upheavals, lasting roughly thirty years, began in the late 1960s with violent Protestant pogroms staged against Catholic neighborhoods, and ended, for most combatants, with the Good Friday Agreement of 1998. Adams probably joined Sinn Fein (a political party closely affiliated with the IRA) as early as 1964, at the age of 16; but was also part of, and was deeply radicalized by, the failure of the Northern Ireland Civil Rights Association to nonviolently address discrimination against Catholics.

Their nonviolent marches and demonstrations were met with police brutality, Protestant intimidation and—in 1972—with the killing of 14 unarmed demonstrators. The Irish Republican Army had already split over tactics, the Provisional IRA taking the position that the time for armed struggle had arrived, with Adams siding with the Provisional side. 'The Troubles' commenced, consisting of a period of intense and almost unbearable urban civil war until the IRA and most other parties, including most Protestant paramilitaries, formally accepted the Good Friday (Peace) Agreement of 1998. Reversing decades of IRA thinking, Gerry Adams became the main proponent, within the Provisional IRA, for the adoption of a constitutional (that is, electoral) strategy, in which the Provisional Sinn Fein would support candidates for office whilst conducting armed guerilla operations. He later advocated for the even more radical idea that he and his colleagues could achieve their goals politically, through their historic political party Sinn Fein (pronounced 'Sheen Fain'). His advocacy won out, Sinn Fein was successful electorally, and ultimately the IRA decommissioned their weapons.

The problem of Northern Ireland—not just during 'the Troubles' but also afterwards—is the problem of shared traumatic memories so powerful, so continuous and so dense that everything else pales in comparison to it; in such a situation, the political becomes so personal that it dominates everybody's waking and dreaming lives. It affected everybody in Northern Ireland during 'the Troubles,' and spilled over regularly into the Republic to the south; such a process also inevitably results in the wholesale internalization of aggression, and a burning identification with aggression as a way of life, since violence was the most striking aspect of the environment shared by the warring parties. I refer here not just to the daily violence of urban warfare, but to the grinding brutality of institutional religious discrimination and bigotry by the Protestant establishment against the Catholic minority. Add to that the fact that the IRA retaliated with the most horrific kind of terrorism, a prime example being the nearly simultaneous setting off of twenty-six bombs in Belfast on 21 July, 1972. (Eleven people, nine of them innocent civilians, lost their life in that operation.) Not to be even momentarily dissuaded, the IRA reportedly set off upwards of 1,300 bombs that year alone.

The problem of Gerry Adams is the problem of a ruthless, perhaps fanatical, terrorist leader in a civil war, who unexpectedly—after advocating and committing many violent acts—finds himself the advocate for certain policies capable of bringing peace to a tortured country. The moral problems are obvious. To what extent should anyone work with someone like Gerry Adams in a peace process, or in political life? (That is, to what extent should a terrorist escape punishment—or at the very least, public condemnation—for the crimes they have personally committed?) Under the law, a homicide is always a homicide, because for that crime there's no statute of limitations. When and why, therefore, does a particular society, struggling to extract itself from the vicious cycle of violence in a civil war, decide to suspend all rules of law and morality and seek the help of the terrorist himself instead of imprisoning and executing him? The answer seems to be, "When he is able and willing, for whatever reason, to help bring an end to the terrorism, through the expedient of a peace settlement." To assimilate that idea completely, we must examine the particulars of the conflict, strive to balance social pragmatism against the moral sense, and above all—because this problem is essentially a moral one—closely examine and interrogate the connection of forgiveness and redemption to traumatic memory, and the internalized violence that is the inevitable product of civil war.

And there's yet another problem, one with both moral and psychological implications. If, as this book insists, psychological trauma as a result of human violence tends to bond people psychologically to aggression as a way of life—and tends to contribute to a worldview that sees aggression as the arbiter of history—what qualities enable certain people to break free of it? What gives them the strength to opt out of the addictive cycle of violence and trauma to which they are bonded, to break free of the shared traumatic memory that defines their world, and deconstruct the internalized aggression that drives their crimes and misdemeanors? This question took on an almost unbelievable urgency at the very moment that peace seemed likely to descend on the tortured country of Northern Ireland, as Gerry Adams—the most feared commander of the IRA—was forced to confront the existence of the most profound kind of evil in his own family, as he discovered incontrovertible evidence of profound sexual abuse against children committed by his own father and brother.

2.

Northern Ireland is a small and rather congested little country of a million and a half people, one that was ideologically at war long before the latest round of 'the Troubles' began. That undeclared war was mainly expressed through anti-Catholic prejudice, reinforced by Northern Ireland's segregated schools (Catholics in their schools, Protestants in theirs). Since it was in the past accompanied by institutionalized discrimination aimed at keeping Catholics poor and powerless, this anti-Catholic prejudice was an objective social reality as well as a set of entrenched attitudes. Beginning in the late seventeenth century, at some point over the last three centuries it became as much a psychopathology of oppression as a strategy for religious containment.

Here is Anthony Storr, in his 'Foreword' to Morris Fraser's *Children of Conflict*, a study of affected children in Northern Ireland: "[Morris Fraser] gives convincing evidence that the Catholic ghettoes of Derry and Belfast have formed in exactly the same ways as the black ghettoes of Harlem and Watts. In other words, the conflict is not about equals professing differing ideologies, but is the revolt of minorities that have become scapegoats for an insecure, and therefore intolerant, majority."

"The pejorative phrases that, in America, white Anglo-Saxon Protestants apply to blacks are word-for-word the same as Ulster Protestants apply to Catholics. They "breed like rats"; their estates are "rabbit warrens"; they are "subhuman," "lazy," and so on. 'Daddy says we're poor because the government takes his money to give to the Catholics and all their children and priests to keep them in luxury because they don't work...' This, from an Ulster boy of eight."

"The Catholics are the untouchables of Ulster, and like their counterparts in India and Japan, are scapegoats—hated, despised, and yet, at the same time, feared. Dr. Fraser reviews the economic and other factors, now familiar to students of poverty, that lead to the revolt of the ghetto. These are the same in Ulster as elsewhere: rising prosperity in the surrounding areas combined with frustration in the ghetto when a hoped-for sharing in the prosperity is disappointed." At the same time, Storr remarks, such revolt is not necessarily a sign of nihilism, but strong circumstantial evidence of hope for a better way.

"Dr. Fraser, through his studies of individual children and of ghettoes everywhere, has amply established that in America, as in the southern states of America, emotional prejudice is so deeply rooted that political solutions alone will not abolish it." One of his main recommendations is to the integration of schools in Northern Ireland, which may be hard to achieve since many Catholic parents prefer Catholic education. But there is an overriding advantage to it: "It is more difficult to imagine Catholics as rats if, as a Protestant child, you have habitually learned and played with them."[1]

Dr. Fraser and his colleague Dr. Anthony Storr are, in the quotes above, describing the emotional ravages of poverty, prejudice and the exigencies of ghetto life. One can imagine, then, how these pressures were exacerbated when, in 1969 and 1970, mainly in those same ghettos, an unrelenting urban war broke out. "Between 1971 and 1982, there were over 28,500 shooting incidents in Northern Ireland, over 7200 bomb explosions and another 3100-plus bombs neutralized, over 9600 armed robberies, and over 17,000 civilian injuries—an injury or death in one out of every twenty households. Which means that in the tight-knit community that is Northern Ireland there is hardly a family that does not personally know at least one other family that has sustained at least an injury as a result of the violence of the last decade."

The result was not only psychological trauma but also societal depression: "Belfast, ugly and sore to the eyes, the will to go on gone, signs of departure everywhere. In ten years it has lost one quarter of its population. Buildings are boarded up. There is little construction, and no skyline. Business is desultory, pace lacking, energy absent, burned-out housing estates a vivid reminder of the sectarian tensions that mark the quiet expression of passion in private places. The tall, silent cranes of the Harland and Wolff shipyards look down on a modern wasteland, on what is perhaps the first-real-life laboratory of urban guerrilla warfare."[2] These lines were written in the early 1980s, fifteen years or more before the 1998 Good Friday Agreement would bring peace, and some measure of economic rejuvenation to Northern Ireland.

How did the people of Northern Ireland get to that point?

In urban guerilla war, people become accustomed to body searches and requests to see identification by soldiers, not to mention the ever-present helicopters, shots fired on a daily basis, and the sound of bombs going off. During a bombing campaign everybody listens, consciously or unconsciously, for the next explosion; some people are arrested or shot dead because their cars backfire at the wrong time. But the worst thing about it is that children are inevitably drawn into the fighting, since the war is fought in the ghettos where they live. War has its terrors, says one commentator on 'the Troubles,' but "stress takes on new and horrifying meanings in a war where there are no civilians — where children and their parents are themselves the combatants, drawn into conflict by powerful forces with vested interests in a deeply divided community."[3]

"Children now [the early 1970s] at school have never known streets free of armored cars, bullets, petrol bombs, stone throwing, broken glass, and the perpetual threat of death. Children of eight and upwards participate in violence — hurling missiles, making bombs, setting traps of wire for armored cars. Most appalling of all, because the soldiers are reluctant to fire on them, children are often used as front-line combatants, hurling bombs in situations into which adults dare not venture, acting as a protective screen behind which their fathers, armed with rifles, can take aim and shelter."[4]

In Northern Ireland urban warfare, children and teenagers

found themselves involved as rarely before in the annals of guerrilla warfare. The result could be compared only to Black children threatened with death by segregationists during the US Civil Rights struggles of the 1960s, according to Dr. Morris Fraser, who compared a child in a Catholic ghetto to "a Negro youngster fleeing before a segregationist mob," his Catholic equivalent in Northern Ireland portrayed as a "dirty-faced urchin, his back to a barricade, facing steel Saracens[5] with his last weapons—half a brick, or a rag stuffed into a milk-bottle dripping with cheap petrol."

"Children's tears speak plainly in any language. Or do they?"[6]

3.

Gerry Adams' maternal great-grandfather was a Fenian[7] terrorist who (during the 1870s and 1880s) conducted a violent campaign of bombing in England on behalf of independence for Ireland. Gerry Adams' paternal grandfather was a member of the Irish Republican Brotherhood during the Irish Civil War, as were two of his uncles, Dominic and Patrick Adams, who were interned by governments in Dublin and Belfast. Another of his uncles was election agent for Eamon de Valera in 1918 in Belfast. Gerry Sr., Gerry Adams' father, joined the IRA at the age of 16, as his son would later do; Gerry Sr. was often on the run, interned, or imprisoned. (He drew eight years for an ambush on a RUC patrol.) Gerry Adams' mother, Annie Hannaway, was a member of *Cumann na mBan*, the woman's branch of the IRA. During 'the Troubles,' in 1974, one of Gerry Adams' cousins, Kieran Murphy, was kidnapped and murdered by the Ulster Volunteer Force.

Gerry Adams was one of eleven children, many of whom were involved with IRA or Sinn Fein activities during 'the Troubles.' To grow up Catholic in Northern Ireland, even before 'the Troubles,' meant being exposed to a continuum of highly emotional stories, songs, legends and secrets regarding past crimes and glories of various Republican campaigns. All of it was extremely violent. (One of Gerry Adams' brothers developed a pronounced stutter after a raid by British troops; all of them sustained wounds of one kind or another, mainly psychological ones. No doubt this added to a discernible tendency to alcoholism among Republican families.) Furthermore, children in this situation didn't always know exactly what position older family members held in the confusing and often-changing welter of Republican politics, and these affiliations might remain secret for generations. (For example, Gerry Adams told Tim Pat Coogan, a scholar whose academic specialty is the IRA, that he hadn't known that one of his uncles, Dominic Adams, had been IRA Chief of Staff during the 1940s, until he read it in the UK edition of Coogan's book.)

This happened because of the extraordinary secrecy surrounding IRA activities. You could know exactly how a family member felt about particular political positions—and in fact such a family member might expound on them for hours—without others in the family being aware of his exact place in the hierarchy of armed struggle. But very often the ones who were least talkative were most active in armed conflict and terrorism. In any case, if anyone was asked directly if they were an IRA volunteer, he would deny it. Gerry Adams has always denied that he is an IRA volunteer when asked directly, but it is well known that he was a top commander. Lying about IRA membership is simply part of the self-imposed discipline of membership, the way a spy or spymaster would automatically lie about his spy-craft, and strive to maintain "plausible deniability," a highly suggestive phrase often used by US intelligence organizations.

This combination of secrecy and violence generates a 'knowing, but not knowing' mentality, in which one has a vague idea of the true activities of a family member, but no certainty. There is also a poetic Celtic otherworldliness adhering to Irish religion, and it is at least conceivable that within Catholicism it could have been enhanced by the confidentiality—or secrecy, if you will—of the confessional. Gerry Adams and his siblings adjusted well to this twilight world, perhaps too well—the 'knowing, but not knowing' habit would play a central role in the personal trauma that Adams would be forced to face after peace came. It led to various kinds of play-acting, in which true motives are hidden and relationships become a kind of shadow dancing.

To adjust to this, children growing up in such families were likely to adopt an 'as if' sensibility toward the claims of everybody around them, in which the young person had to create his or her own standard for authenticity. (The child would have little doubt, however, that violence played a big role in the lives of adults around him, without knowing exactly why or how.) In such a situation, it is easy to see how violence can come to seem the standard for personal authenticity to a young person, who would be likely to internalize the rationalizations for political aggression as well as the aggression itself. If you were willing to give you own life, as well as take others, surely you meant business. Ideology made it easier: you internalized violence all the more easily because you needed it to drive the British out and defeat 'the Prods.' Aggression was just part of the deal. You were born into it and you inherited its powerful traumatic memories.

Violence was not questioned, at least partly because it defined all of life that young people like Gerry Adams experienced; and as violence defined everything, so did the traumatic memory it left in its wake. A fair amount of the trauma experienced by young Catholics in Northern Ireland probably came from various forms of multigenerational trauma already present in the family system, but would then be reinforced by personal experiences on the street. Or to put it another way, one heard about this kind of violence repeatedly, and when one began to smell the tear gas or lose friends to the bullets, one said, "Ah yes—this is it, this is what it's all about." In addition, smart young people growing up in a Catholic ghetto quickly realized that their oppression gave them a paradoxical power, because although the Protestants despised them, they were also terrified of them. The outcome of this was the non-stop psychological trauma that bonded individuals in both communities to aggression as the arbiter of social life in Northern Ireland. To young people who became volunteers for the IRA, the violence it promulgated was already all around them in the ghettos where they lived, except that now they were acting it out, and becoming a victim-aggressor rather than merely a victim.

Gerry Adams was born in 1948, on lower Falls Road in Belfast, the historic center of Catholic Republicanism in Belfast. At the age of 16, Adams joined Sinn Fein and Fianna Eireann, a youth group aligned with Sinn Fein and the IRA. In that same year, 1964, something happened that greatly radicalized the young nationalist. He volunteered to work for a nationalist candidate whose office was on Divis Street in West Belfast. An Irish Tricolor, the flag associated with Irish Republicanism, was situated squarely in the window. Technically a violation of Northern Ireland's Flags and Emblems Act, the Royal Ulster Constabulary—a police force with Protestant sympathies—ignored it, since it was in an out-of-the-way area. But a young, right-wing, anti-Catholic minister named Ian Paisley became aware of it and began to agitate against it among other anti-Catholic Protestants, insisting that no flag but the Union Jack should ever be displayed in Northern Ireland. Fifty police broke the door down at the office, and removed the flag. The flag soon reappeared, and the police reappeared in force. Significant rioting broke out, reminding some people of a similar riot in the area in 1935 in which 20 people had perished.

The 1964 Divis Street riots had a great effect on Gerry Adams, who concluded that the government of Northern Ireland derived its power only partly from its electoral franchise, but even more from the systematic use of force on behalf of a particular ideology. (This would have resonated well with Sinn Fein thinking, which held that only "physical force" was capable of winning their main goal, the integration of Ulster[8] into the Republic of Ireland.) Adams also saw that the British—in a classic example of colonial divide and conquer—had in the past counted on fanatics like Ian Paisley to keep the Catholic and Protestant communities divided and at each others' throats.

1966 was fast approaching, which would be the fiftieth anniversary of the seizing of the General Post Office in the proclamation of the Irish Republic in Dublin. Both governments, of the Republic of Ireland and of Northern Ireland alike, were apprehensive, although neither could have said what they were apprehensive of. In general, they were most afraid of some kind of operation by remnants of the IRA, and there were no dearth of reports and rumors, including some grossly inaccurate intelligence reports regarding IRA intentions. What really bothered the leaders in both countries, in other words, was the possibility of people 'picking up the gun,' and of civil or rhetorical excesses that could lead to such an eventuality. (Harold Wilson, Prime Minister of Britain, actually sent a battalion of troops to Northern Ireland, ostensibly for training the Royal Ulster Constabulary, or RUC.) He needn't have bothered. The IRA had ceased its 'Border Campaign' in 1962, and dumped whatever remained of its ancient weapons. The smarter people in Dublin were more afraid of Paisley, the anti-Catholic fanatic, than of the IRA, since he was capable of initiating anti-Catholic riots that could, over a period of time, be used as a rationalization for armed intervention from the Republic of Ireland on behalf of the Catholic ghettos.

The Catholics in Northern Ireland were, however, given permission in 1966 to march in celebration of this important aspect of Irish history, probably because it would have been even more provocative to deny them that right. A few banners were flown, a few barricades thrown up (to commemorate the barricades in Dublin, perhaps?), and people marched—despite some failed attempts at provocation by Ian Paisley—down one of the main roads of Belfast, in unabashed celebration of the Easter rising fifty years before. It was all very quiet but dignified, but it had an effect on people seemingly out of proportion to the event itself. Peter Taylor, another of a handful of scholars who study the IRA, tells the story of a young man named Martin Meehan, from the Ardoyn area of Belfast, who was deeply impressed by this Commemorative parade on April 17, 1966. His father had been active in the IRA in the 1940s, but he'd never had the opportunity to discuss it with him, because his father wouldn't allow it—the subject was taboo in their home.

But something in this Commemorative parade of proud Catholics, some of whom were probably not nationalists, and many more who were in no sense Republicans, but who nonetheless had joined together to celebrate the memory of a tragic insurrection both nationalist *and* Republican, moved him in such a very deep place that he found it impossible to deny its effect on him. After that, he said, his single ambition was to join the IRA, which he eventually did.[9]

The aspect that affected Catholics in Northern Ireland the most, however, was the appalling conditions under which they lived. Much has been written about this, but the extent of the conscious, institutionalized discrimination against Catholics in Northern Ireland is still shocking. Everywhere in Northern Ireland the voting districts were gerrymandered in such a way that there could never be a Catholic majority in any municipal council, even in areas—and some towns—in which Catholics were a majority. (The phrase 'power-sharing, which was soon to be employed by those seeking some solutions to the problems of Northern Ireland, was clearly a reference to the negative presence of 'the gerry,' as gerrymandering was popularly known.)

Likewise discrimination in employment was profound and unmistakable—at the Belfast shipbuilders, Harland and Wolff, out of a workforce of 10,000, only 400 were Catholics. (And this tiny contingent had the least skilled and mostly menial jobs.) "Most of the province's employers were Protestants who tended to look after their own. Catholics often only had to mention their name or address to guarantee rejection."[10] An oppressed minority, indeed. And the worst part was the unremitting hatred from Protestants that went along with it, which after being internalized by Catholics could become a very toxic form of self-hatred.

Enhancing the problem was the fear and horror felt by Ulster Protestants toward *any* discussion of unification with the Republic of Ireland. Under a Republic of Ireland government, elected by a huge majority of Catholics, they would be likely to experience a great many polices as objectionable, from the inability to purchase decent birth control pills to an anti-British foreign policy. Most of all, however, they would, in Northern Ireland, lose the considerable privilege and power they had traditionally enjoyed at the expense of their Catholic minority. There can be no doubt, however, that these political objections of Protestants to Catholics in Northern Ireland were routinely exaggerated, and gradually took on an apocalyptic tone more typical of pathology than politics. It is for this reason that Protestants found even the slightest reform threatening. Give the Catholics an inch, and they were bound to take a mile; after all, hadn't the Protestants done the same, in their relations with Catholics? The argumentation of Northern Ireland Protestants had, therefore, over time developed more of the characteristics of a psychological obsession than a real political discussion.

Ian Paisley had, along with a few other fanatical Protestant ideologues over the centuries, developed an aggressive theology in which Catholicism was not only the greatest evil in the world, but *the* manifest demonstration of *all* evil. He believed in his bones that Catholicism was—not metaphorically but literally—a modern political vehicle of Satan, which made whoever was

Pope a modern anti-Christ. Once he got into the inter-European parliament, the excitable Paisley went out of his way to insult the Pope personally, since Paisley believed that the Pope was using the UE as an opportunity to consolidate his power over Europe (by reconstituting the Holy Roman Empire, according to some Ulster Protestants). To Paisley, Catholics in Northern Ireland were but the frontal assault forces of a vast and abominable Popish plot (historical pun intended) aiming at taking over the British Isles, then Europe, and then the world.

The problem with this kind of lunatic worldview is that by conceiving of any very large group of human beings as *intrinsically* evil, one tends to bring the phenomenon of psychological projection into play. Whatever is wrong in one's own personality, or in one's own church, is immediately projected onto the Evil Ones, and becomes one more revolting characteristic of the group you are denouncing. One of the reasons Christianity stagnated in the Middle Ages, this writer believes, was its anti-Semitism, its obsession with the supposedly inherited guilt of the Jews. When one can only see the evil in others, it makes emotional and social growth very difficult, because one is deprived of the ability to be self-critical. At the same time, a supposedly evil minority can quickly become a scapegoat for all the suppressed guilt and aggression of the majority group, which is exactly the direction in which anti-Semitism took Europe. In Northern Ireland, the anti-Catholicism of the majority group led to a certain profound mediocrity in the culture and religion of Ulster Protestantism. This inherent mediocrity would show up repeatedly and flagrantly in the Democratic Unionist Party, Ian Paisley's party.

There is little doubt, then, that the Catholics of Northern Ireland were an oppressed minority. And the Protestants of Northern Ireland would fight to the death to keep from being part of the Republic of Ireland, and felt that oppressing Catholics was the only way to prevent that. The question is, then, what does one do to change the situation, starting with religious discrimination against Catholics? Luckily, there were people with the good sense to try to achieve reform without violence. In the late 1960s a new group appeared called the Northern Ireland Civil Rights Association, so-called in conscious imitation of the Civil Rights Movement in the US, whose non-violent tactics it imitated. Early organizers included Bernadette Devlin and John Hume, the latter of whom was eventually to play a pivotal role in the 1990s peace process. The NICRA attracted many moderate IRA members who would later found the Workers' Party, which rejected armed struggle. Also involved were the more militant IRA and Sinn Fein members who would later be major combatants in the approaching civil war.

A great deal has been made of the fact that IRA people were involved in the early days of the Northern Ireland Civil Rights Association (NICRA), but it should be pointed out that many of those IRA members were at that time against armed struggle, and were in favor of an electoral approach. They were, in other words, willing to give non-violence a try as a tactic; their participation in the NICRA was part of a political evolution. The lesson here seems to be that while terrorists do not become angels overnight, nor do practitioners of non-violence become terrorists overnight, since both are capable of some moral and political evolution; those that reject terrorism do so for reasons— including moral and legal ones—that make sense to them. (Finding out what those reasons are is important to creating a program to convert terrorists into ex-terrorists, usually involving the opportunity for terrorists to disseminate their political program through non-violent means, ranging from demonstrations to electoral involvement.) The NICRA was organized by people from widely differing political backgrounds, some of whom had previously advocated violence and many who hadn't, but they all wished to give peaceful protest a chance in this particular instance.

Critics claimed that NICRA wished to bring down the

Northern Ireland government—but in fact Protestant over-reaction was far more likely to do that, not anything the demonstrators did or said. And such critics always left out the important fact that for most Catholics, the government had no legitimacy to begin with, because the Catholic vote was systematically suppressed by Protestant gerrymandering. In any case, even those NICRA marchers who wished to see the government fall also wished, in their capacity as civil rights marchers, to accomplish that goal *using nonviolent tactics*, and to do so outside the familiar institutions of the state. That was something new in Irish politics. Its failure brought on urban guerilla war.

The NICRA was formed along the fault lines of two great Irish controversies. First, its organizers were willing to address oppression against Catholics *separate from the traditional Republican demand* to unite Northern Ireland with the Republic of Ireland. They were interested not in Republican orthodoxy, but in protesting religious discrimination. Secondly, they were willing to adopt Gandhi's tactics of nonviolent protest and civil disobedience. In addition to rights for Catholics, they also advocated civil and human rights for Irish Travelers,[11] a significant minority in Ireland and Britain, as well as nuclear disarmament. Ultimately the NICRA were mainly concerned with religious discrimination in housing and employment, and the gerrymandering of electoral districts. Although it eventually ended in tragedy, NICRA was proof that many were willing to try nonviolent methods—and it was not lost on close observers that it received significant support around the world for precisely that reason.

The first march of the NICRA was April 27, 1968, of about 2,500 people in Dungannon. They were met by 400 members of the Royal Ulster Constabulary, which refused to let them proceed. The next march was in Derry (Londonderry), and began in the Protestant section of that town. Only 400 people were there to kick off the march, but there were important observers that the

RUC probably knew nothing about; these included the Republican Labor MP Gerry Fitt, who had brought with him three labor MPs from the British parliament. As they had before, the Royal Ulster Constabulary prevented the march from going forward, instead attacking the marchers. At some point Catholic youths from a nearby ghetto got involved and were driven back, after some rock-throwing at police. In terms of public impact, by far the most important thing that happened was that the clueless RUC beat up Fitt and his British friends, putting the lot of them in the hospital; film of this event clearly showed highly armed police mercilessly beating unarmed protesters. Some historians believe that this was a big turning point; international opinion swung decisively behind the NICRA marchers—and Catholic activists generally—because of the merciless beating of the Labor MPs.

Toward the end of 1968, the NICRA announced a temporary cessation of marching due to some small governmental reforms having been made. Attempts to hold further marches were made, but these attempts to air grievances seemed regularly to lead to violent clashes between Catholics and the RUC. Later in 1969 wide-scale rioting broke out in which many people were killed, and in which the RUC and Protestant supporters initiated the mass practice of entering Catholics' houses and attacking Catholics simply because they were Catholics, in what were essentially pogroms.[12] In response to continued widespread rioting in April and July, Catholics began to organize for a defense of their neighborhoods—which included gathering weapons—and to set up vigilante patrols. The NICRA activists tried to take pressure off Catholic neighborhoods that were so attacked by holding marches in adjacent towns or neighborhoods, hoping to draw police of RUC away from residential areas.

Gerry Adams was involved in the Northern Ireland Civil Rights Association at every point, and despite his membership in the IRA respected NICRA's strategy of nonviolence. But he was acutely aware that the Dublin leadership of the IRA failed to understand the depth of sectarian loyalties on the part of the Protestants. The Dublin IRA leadership thought class interests would trump culture; but then, as now, it's the other way around: culture tends to trump class interests. (Indeed, after three centuries of exquisite conditioning, one might say that Protestant class interests *were* its sectarian interests.) The same problem occurs in a slightly different form in the US—fifty years after the Civil Rights and Voting Rights Act, Fox News and the modern Republican Party still appeals to racial resentment against Blacks and Latinos, as well as religious bigotry against Muslims; and in most cases these powerful forms of prejudice are stronger that class interests, especially among white people in the middle-west, southern and border states.

What does this mean? It means that prejudice is likely to be, in the short term, stronger than enlightened self-interest. The failure of idealistic social reformers to realize and understand this occurs to a large extent because of a modern inability to understand the problem of aggression, and to recognize the existence of evil, especially systemic evil. Racial and religious prejudice is evil: people under its influence derive pleasure from the suffering of their perceived enemies: it is essentially a negative emotional orientation that affects all thought and behavior: and it is not—as many liberals believe—merely a failure to understand the other person's point of view. Gerry Adams saw, and understood, that all the chatter of the Dublin IRA about making common cause with working-class Protestants was, at least for his generation, a pathetic exercise in folly.

Another influence on Gerry Adams was the general tone of rebellion that young people in Northern Ireland felt. Richard English stresses this point, quoting Adams:

People [in Northern Ireland] did not live their lives in

isolation from the changes going on in the world outside. They identified to a greater or lesser extent with the music, the politics, the whole undefined movement of ideas and changes of style. Bob Dylan, the Beatles and the Rolling Stones, long hair and beads, the 'alternative society,' music and fashion were all markers put down by a new generation against complacencies of the previous one, and one of the most important to come across was that one *could* change the world.[13]

Before 1969, the people of Northern Ireland had been caught in a kind of mental time warp, when any public discussion of institutional injustice was seen as tantamount to advocating the violent overthrow of the government. But the young generation of Catholics was desperate to find some way to fight the injustices that surrounded them and held them down. The irony that many authors have emphasized is this: even the staging of nonviolent marches stimulated the violent sectarian frenzies of the Protestant establishment. To the Protestant establishment, even the *thought* of changing power relationships provoked histrionics, provoking also the conviction that such thoughts should everywhere be met with violence. To the Protestant establishment, the Civil Rights marchers were criminals for even *talking* about their grievances, and therefore deserved whatever they got, because they should have stayed home, kept quiet, and allowed things to go on as before.

One might say that the NICRA sought an over-reaction from the government, just as Dr. Martin Luther King sought to bring to the surface the underlying institutional violence of American segregationists. Some say that approach is to deliberately court disaster. But were not NICRA's civil rights demonstrations a necessary stage in addressing the full dimensions of Protestant tyranny, so that the world could see it and the nation deal with it? It is hard to imagine any other way such entrenched brutality could be challenged, without some risk of retaliatory violence; but the courageous activists of NICRA vowed to continue to demonstrate, even though they could never have imagined how great a price they would pay for their efforts to find a nonviolent solution.

And was not the Protestant over-reaction, this determination to burn and wreak havoc and ultimately to kill Catholics who were marching peacefully, clear evidence of a profound spiritual and mental derangement that plagued the Ulster establishment and the Protestant mobs? Religious apartheid and discrimination cannot be tolerated in a modern industrialized democracy, and exposing it became the job of an entire generation of Catholics in Northern Ireland. This is in no way a defense of the later violence of the IRA, but it *is* a defense of the Northern Ireland Civil Rights Association that must be made, and often isn't. However radical their politics may have been as individuals, the NICRA marchers were good people who were bravely addressing one of the most outrageous examples of social injustice in modern Europe, and they were trying to do it nonviolently, just as Martin Luther King did when he confronted segregation in the American south.

Then, in August 1969, came the 'Battle of the Bogside,' which occurred in the Catholic neighborhood in Derry known as 'the Bogside.' Wikipedia refers cryptically to this traumatizing orgy of violence as a "very large communal riot," but in reality it was a three-day series of pitched battles between Catholics and the RUC and Protestant mobs. This, in turn, provoked resistance in almost all the Catholic nationalist neighborhoods in Northern Ireland. There was provocation on both sides, to be sure; but in almost all of these instances it was the RUC or Protestant mobs that entered Catholic neighborhoods and drove people—or attempted to drive people—from their homes. These incursions by Protestant mobs, which the RUC either participated in or made no effort to stop, had the classic characteristics of a pogrom. Many people were killed, a great many Catholic homes

386

were burned, and as many as several thousand Catholics expelled from their homes. On August 13, Jack Lynch, Taoiseach [Prime Minister] of the Republic of Ireland, announced on the radio that he "could not stand by," and rather provocatively sent a detachment of medical personnel to the border of Northern Ireland, supposedly to treat wounded victims of police violence.

On August 14, the next day, James Chichester-Clark, Prime Minister of Northern Ireland, asked British Prime Minister Harold Wilson to send British troops. The 1st Battalion, Prince of Wales' Own Regiment of Yorkshire, soon arrived from the HMS Sea Eagle, where they had been waiting for some time. It is one of the great anomalies of this strange conflict that the Catholics of the Bogside at first welcomed the British troops, actually serving them tea, since their presence impeded the murderous assaults of the RUC. But the descent into madness was already well underway, and it would not be long before the British troops would themselves become targets for IRA sharpshooters.

During the worst of the Bogside fighting in early August, 1969, the IRA was caught completely off guard. They had started to gather weapons, mostly ancient firearms left over from past IRA campaigns, many long buried in secret armories, but were otherwise unprepared: the armed defense of Catholic neighborhoods had not previously been a policy of the IRA, because this was the first time in modern times that large incursions—or pogroms—had occurred, with Protestants entering the Catholic neighborhoods on a mass basis. Still, a few IRA veterans gathered whatever weapons they could, and tried to defend some key Bogside areas. Peter Taylor repeats an account by young Brendan Hughes, later to be an important leader of the IRA, of his experiences as a boy caught up in the Bogside fighting:

> My old school was being attacked by loyalist crowds with gasoline bombs. One of the IRA men who were there at the

time had a Thompson submachine-gun and asked if anybody knew the layout of the school. I did and I went with this fella. Gasoline bombs were coming in all over. There was a man on the roof of the school and people were shouting at him to fire into the crowd and he was shouting back that he was under orders to fire over their heads. That's exactly what he did. He fired a Thompson submachine-gun over the heads of the crowd and it stopped the school from being burnt down. That was my first contact with the IRA.[14]

After the fighting died down the IRA got little credit, however— signs saying "IRA, I Ran Away" appeared on some of the walls. A hard core of IRA fighters, mostly from Belfast, decided that as senior Republicans in Northern Ireland they had to take a central role in defending Catholic communities or they would become irrelevant. On 24 August, just a few days after the worst of the rioting, some leading Belfast IRA men met and determined to break free of the Dublin-based IRA leadership. On September 22, three armed men, including Gerry Adams, burst in on the Belfast IRA leadership and accused the leaders of not adequately protecting the Catholic neighborhoods.

An IRA convention was held in December, 1969, and after much argumentation the rebels split off into a new organization, called the Provisional IRA. Nine out of the thirteen units in Belfast sided with the Provos, as they were called, consisting of well over a hundred hardcore fighters and 500 trusted supporters. Over the next two years the Provisional IRA would inherit or create the vast majority of fighting Republican units, and weapons, in Northern Ireland. (For purposes of clarity, all references to the Provisional IRA henceforth will simply be to the IRA.)

Somewhere—perhaps during violent Protestant attacks on the early civil rights marches, perhaps during the riots of August 1969—Northern Ireland had crossed a line. 'The Troubles' were on.

4.

For some Catholics in Northern Ireland, it still wasn't too late to undertake the staggering task of trying to reform the country nonviolently, through agitation, strikes, demonstrations, informational prayer vigils and other tactics. And the Northern Ireland Civil Rights Association (NICRA) was very much still in the game, and still committed to demonstrating nonviolently— that would be its main tactic, to publicly articulate demands and grievances that had been virtually taboo before. Their goal was to end discrimination in housing and employment, and reform the corrupt electoral system. By way of demonstrating its tactical acumen, it did not address the smoldering question of eventually reuniting Northern Ireland with the southern Republic. Its main goal was to put an end to discrimination against Catholics and achieve a just peace based on the rule of law.

And although there were IRA members in the Northern Ireland Civil Rights Association, most of NICRA's activists were "people with far less radical views—people for whom the thrust of the campaign was the entirely reasonable demand for fair treatment within a state which had not hitherto provided it." Rather than the IRA hijacking the nonviolent movement, as unionist politician Brian Faulkner thought, "it was the IRA that had helped to initiate a civil rights campaign which grew to encompass many people who did not share the IRA's philosophy."[15] This was not a defeat, but a sign that it was not only the Republican groups that sought justice—and Northern Ireland would need precisely such people, those who sought peace through constitutional activism, if reform were to be achieved. But the ultimate failure of the Northern Ireland Civil Rights Association would come at the hands of the Protestant establishment and British troops, and it would open the door to those Catholics that advocated urban warfare. The peaceful marchers would become the victims of a horrible atrocity that changed everything, and convinced a great many people that nonviolent protest was no longer possible.

One reason this happened is that the Protestant establishment, entrenched deep within the Ulster Unionist Party—the main Protestant party—saw little difference between a Catholic with a picket sign and a Catholic with a gun. They were all part of the same subversive assemblage to the UUP, and therefore both were intolerable. To many of the unionist/loyalist[16] persuasion, the Catholic with a placard was perhaps even more dangerous than a Catholic with a gun, because it was harder to justify killing or interning the nonviolent protester. For these reasons, Protestants in the Ulster Unionist Party saw no advantage in keeping the conflict nonviolent. Like the segregationists of the American south, to a great many people in the UUP *any* questioning of the prevailing system, however unjust that system might be, was unacceptable, and therefore deserving of violent punishment.

There was sporadic rioting at various times in 1970, at least partly because the opportunities for nonviolent expression of grievances was drying up. For one thing, it was becoming increasingly dangerous to appear in a public demonstration challenging the status quo. Then, in July 1970, a government ban on 'parades and public processions' (that is, all demonstrations) was announced, and was intended to last until January 1971. In August 1970 the Social Democratic and Labour Party was formed, with John Hume and Gerry Fitt as leaders; it would draw most of the Catholic vote until Sinn Fein began to compete with it electorally. Despite some small reforms, in October serious rioting broke out in Belfast's Ardoyne area, lasting three days. The IRA was buying and distributing weapons, and there had already been serious incidents—the IRA had begun operations in earnest. In 1971 an estimated 30 British soldiers were killed.

Throughout the first months of 1971, several small reforms in the area of housing were made, which raised hope that an end to discrimination in housing might be in sight. On 9 August, 1971, however, the government, under the Special Powers Act of 1922, moved to intern 342 individuals. These were people that the British and Northern Ireland authorities considered dangerous, but the internment proceeded without trial. Gerry Adams was among those caught up in the sweep, and was held by the British on the *HMS Maidstone*. (In June he was released to take part in secret talks in Britain. The talks produced nothing, but it is highly significant that Adams' IRA comrades insisted that he be released to be part of the negotiations.)

Instead of a body blow to the IRA, the August 1971 internment resulted in support for the interned and anger at the government and British troops who carried it out. Very bad rioting immediately broke out throughout Northern Ireland, the worst violence since August of the previous year. An estimated twenty-one people were killed in three days of rioting, and as many as 7,000 people, mostly Catholic, were driven from their homes. The fledgling SDLP withdrew all its representatives from public bodies and announced a campaign of civil disobedience. The real question, however, was how the Northern Ireland Civil Rights Association would react. Certainly there could be no greater offense against civil rights than people being interned without due process. Furthermore, it had become known that *only Catholics had been interned*, and no Protestants, despite violence from recently-organized Protestant paramilitaries; and this caused support for the IRA to rise precipitously in the Catholic community, higher than at any time since the Anglo-Irish War of 1916-1921.

The NICRA, after much discussion, decided to march nonviolently against internment, despite the danger involved. How could they not meet the challenge, when people were being interned without trial, at the same time that the window for nonviolent expression of grievances was closing? A small anti-internment march was held on January 2, 1972. On the 18th all parades and marches (that is, demonstrations) were banned until the end of the year. The NICRA promptly replied with another and larger anti-internment demonstration; this was met with severe beatings, as the demonstrators tried to reach the internment camp but were stopped by troops.

What to do? NICRA knew the risks, but the entire burden of seeking justice nonviolently had now fallen on them. They organized a mass march against internment without trial, while according to the Irish News [28 January 1972] "placing a special emphasis on the necessity for a peaceful incident-free day" on January 30. Countless books, films and articles have been written about the tragic events of that day, so this writer will not give a blow-by-blow description of the tragedy, but rather concentrate on its political fallout. Suffice it to say that on January 30, 1972, a day that would later be called "Bloody Sunday," 26 unarmed Irish demonstrators were shot down, with 13 dying immediately and one dying later. It was one of the worst political massacres of modern European history. On 15 June, 2010, almost forty years later, Prime Minister David Cameron declared that the killing by British troops was "unjustified and unjustifiable," and made a formal apology on behalf of the British government.

Cameron's apology came thirty-eight years too late for the people of Northern Ireland. On 30 January, 1972 the fate of the Northern Ireland Civil Rights Association was sealed. The time of peaceful marches had now ended, because nobody could ever be sure again that they would not be shot down in the street for demonstrating, no matter how peacefully they did it. The British had driven Catholics from the street, and into the arms of the IRA. The time of the gunman had arrived.

5.

In his comprehensive study of the IRA, Tim Pat Coogan states that the entire IRA in Northern Ireland had exactly ten guns in their possession during August, 1969. A frantic search for weapons began, both by the IRA and Defense Committees that had begun to form in the neighborhoods. At first there were only very old weapons from former IRA campaigns. After the split in the IRA, the Provisional IRA took over all the arms depots, but found that they contained mainly leftover weapons from the Second World War, including Thompson machine guns and Bren light machine guns. During the period of 1969-1972, an arms purchasing operation was set up, run on the American side by George Harrison, an IRA man who had lived in New York since 1938. He bought guns from a Corsican arms dealer, mainly Armalite assault rifles. The weapons were then smuggled on the regular runs of the Queen Elizabeth II to Southampton, England, thence to Northern Ireland, where they were collected by an IRA cell in Belfast. The Armalite weapons could be folded, making it easy for IRA seamen to pack them in their lockers. The AR-18 was the IRA's weapon of choice, since in addition to its folding stock, it was small, light, and fired high velocity rounds in rapid fire.

There was an enormous fetishization of the Armalite AR-18 among the IRA volunteers; there was the feeling among those same volunteers, especially the younger ones, that if they had the right weapons the IRA was sure to win. ("Winning" by that time meant driving Britain out of Northern Ireland so that it could be integrated into the Republic, after which the conditions of Catholics would surely be automatically improved.) Some of the young IRA recruits had an almost sexualized affection for the Armalite, which they were sure was their ticket to victory. Peter Taylor, in *Behind the Mask: The IRA and Sinn Fein*, quotes Brendan Hughes, who had become second in command in the Lower Falls area of Belfast:

I remember sitting in a house and this guy who was in the Merchant Navy came back from America with this booklet on the Armalite. It really praised this weapon. It could be folded up, dumped in rivers, buried, almost anything. Everyone was talking about it—this "Super Weapon." The brochure said if a person was shot in the arm, it would break every bone in his body. It was light and it was powerful. Everybody went wild about it because up until then there were only M1 carbines, .303s and old Second World War weapons.

Everyone was saying, 'this weapon is going to change the whole war.' The Armalites came in and that I think helped change the whole situation because then the IRA had a weapon that was effective, easily dumped, easy to handle and easy to train on. If it did half the things that it was supposed to have done, the war was going to be over in a couple of years. At that time most people didn't think long term. They thought of next year or next month or six months' time. But that was it. No one was thinking of ten years, or five years or even three years.

He tells about receiving the smuggled arms in Belfast:

I remember a car driving up. The boot was opened and there were ten to fifteen Armalites in it. The magic Armalites were there. Fifteen of them. I remember the people who were there being amazed at their fire power. It was a big jump from a couple of M1 carbines. I know people felt, 'This is it. We're really moving up a stage here with these things.'[17]

Perhaps not surprisingly, the Armalite rifle shows up in several songs from those violent times. It first makes an oblique appearance, for example, in the Gang of Four's 1978 album *Damaged Goods*. But another reference is in the folksong "My Little Armalite," in which the IRA volunteer articulates his affection for his weapon. Some words are below:

I was stopped by a soldier he said "you are a swine"
He hit me with his rifle and he kicked me in the groin
I bowed and I scraped, sure my manners were polite
Ah, but all the time I was thinking of me little Armalite!

A brave RUC man came walking up our street
With 600 British soldiers gathered round his feet,
Come out ya cowardly Fenians come on out and fight
But he cried 'I'm only joking' when he heard my Armalite!

Chorus:
And it's up along the Bogside, that's where I long to be
Lying in the dark with the Provo company
A comrade on my left and another one on me right
And a clip of ammunition for me little Armalite[18]

Note the heavily sexualized content. The British soldier emasculates the Catholic boy by kicking him in the groin, but later the lad gets his power back with his Armalite, even causing the Protestant RUC man to give up without a fight. In the chorus the singer imagines an idyllic situation—fraught both with sexuality and great tenderness—in which he lays in the dark with an IRA lad on either side and "a clip of ammunition for me little Armalite." (Two versions of this song on the internet actually open with the distinctive hollow tapping sound of an Armalite being fired in short bursts. As in so many Irish songs about their wars, the tune to "My Little Armalite" is incongruously upbeat and cheerful.)

The 'magic Armalite' quickly assumed a transcendent importance to the younger volunteers. Terence "Cleeky" Clarke, who became involved in the IRA as a young man, was somewhat typical of younger volunteers who simply wanted to fight the enemy in the streets, but knew little of the issues involved: "I remember on one occasion a certain person telling Sean MacStiofain [IRA Chief of Staff] that he was a gunman not a politician. MacStiofain hit the roof. He was going to have his scalp. But that was indicative of how we all felt then. We were gunmen and [Clark] was saying, 'We just want to shoot. We don't want to talk or find out.' It's a sad reflection on us at the time."[19]

Much of this excitement on the part of the IRA volunteers regarding the Amalite is painfully consistent with the phenomenon of young males with an entrenched patriarchal worldview, but who are themselves without any power. Above all there was the frustration of being Catholic in that time and place, and the hatred of Catholics that many of them had no doubt internalized, not to mention lack of work and skills, and an abiding grievance against a social system in which the cards are stacked against them... those are all ingredients that can, in times of social upheaval, lead to an apocalyptic love of combat and violence. Yet these same young males were eventually to learn that the power one felt while firing an Armalite also meant a slow and extremely agonizing death to the ones hit by its 5.56 rounds. And in Belfast and Derry, the fighting was too close not to know—to see and feel—the impact of the high-velocity bullets on the people you were killing.

In 1971, the IRA killed 42 British soldiers. In 1972, it was 64, mostly the work of snipers. Brendan Hughes describes how daily operations were planned, with a strong emphasis on sniper attacks, both planned and opportunistic:

There would probably have been a group of twelve to fourteen Volunteers in a particular area, plus back-up. Some would meet in a house that particular morning. [Operations were planned and staged at different houses to avoid electronic surveillance.] There'd be an Operations Officer there whose job it was to pick particular operations for bombings or for shootings or for ambushes or for robbing a bank if money was needed at that time. It was called 'jumping the counter.'

It would be normal enough for five or six operations to go ahead in one day. Plus, they would put a 'float' out. There's two men in a car with one man driving and one man in the back with a particular weapon. They'd be 'floating' around the area just waiting until targets came along. Men would be picked to do the particular operation. Someone would be sent to steal or highjack a car, someone else would hold the driver while someone else carried out the operation, whether it was a bombing in the town or a 'float.' The circumstances at the time would dictate what operations took place.[20]

As Northern Ireland descended into madness, the killing became nightmarish. Here is an account from a British soldier of the death of one of his mates on March 4, 1973:

It was the very last patrol of their tour and they were suddenly called to an incident. When this happens, the Commander usually yells, "Follow me!" and they make off at a helluva rate of knots. Unfortunately this soldier was left behind. He didn't think nothing of it. It was getting dark and he thought, 'Well, it's best to stop here. They'll come back and fetch me on the way back.' Of course, they didn't. The women in the area very quickly realized the young lad was on his own. They surrounded him. I can't understand what went through the lad's mind, probably pure terror, but they held him there and ripped his face with their nails. There was no skin left on it. And they held him there for the local gunman to shoot with the soldier's own weapon. The actual terror that this lad must have gone through while he was being held down by these women must have been terrific.[21]

Brendan Hughes, who was a commander with the IRA, remembers this incident well:

There was a gun battle that took place that day and this young soldier was left behind. He was killed and I remember feeling very, very sorry for him and I don't think it should have happened. He was killed by local IRA people and I am told by people who were there at the time, that he was only a kid and the young fellow was crying for his mother. It certainly had an effect on me when it happened. I always felt sorry for him and I regret it very much. It bothers me when I think about that young soldier sometimes.[22]

These are traumatic memories that don't go away. One must ask how it was that IRA volunteers stood up to the constant stress. Studies done by the US army during World War Two indicate that infantry soldiers became unable to function after about two hundred days at the front. Subsequent armies have made sure, when possible, that this limit is not exceeded. So how did IRA volunteers continue to function, under those conditions? According to statements made by Gerry Adams in a recorded speech, it was sometimes necessary to order volunteers to go to a neutral place—somewhere in the south, most likely, during 'the Troubles'—simply to rest and recuperate emotionally. Furthermore IRA volunteers typically spent a great deal of time in internment or in prison; this created something of a break in urban warfare, although there was a tight IRA hierarchy in prisons and internment camps, and IRA volunteers were expected to do as they were told. Most important, however, was what IRA volunteers thought to be the sacred nature of their combat.

Interestingly, once they came out of prison, IRA volunteers were not necessarily expected to resume their IRA activities. If they wanted to—and many did—they could; but if they were not inclined to do so, they didn't have to. That makes the IRA quite different from most disciplined criminal, paramilitary or under-ground terrorist organizations, from which it is quite difficult, if not impossible, to resign. If someone in a criminal gang or a terrorist group begins to drift away, their trauma bond will neces-sarily loosen, and they might be inclined to reconsider their loyalty to the organization, and reveal secrets to strangers. For that reason, then, once one enters one of those groups, they will be expected to stay with it for a lifetime. If their loyalties are seen to waver, their superiors in the group may assign them some egregiously violent task to renew the bond. But that level of discipline apparently did not exist in the IRA in Northern Ireland.

At the beginning of 'the Troubles' the IRA had a policy of not engaging in sectarianism in its urban warfare—that is, they would not execute Protestants just because they were Protestants, whereas the Protestant paramilitaries often killed Catholics just because they were Catholics. The IRA would kill British soldiers and members of the RUC because they saw them as part of an apparatus of oppression; or they would kill a Protestant who was part of a mob in the act of attacking Catholic homes. For this reason, they denied being sectarian in the same way that the Protestant paramilitaries were. On the other hand, the IRA began at some point to use explosives and car bombs. How could you be sure you were killing only British soldiers or RUC with a bomb?

Obviously, you couldn't, and many innocent people, both Catholic and Protestant, died horribly in these bombing attacks. The use of explosives in the 1970s crossed the line from supposed urban warfare into pure terrorism. On 20 March of 1972, the IRA set off its first car bomb, which succeeded in killing four innocent civilians along with four RUC officers and a soldier of the UVF, the Ulster Volunteer Force, a violent Protestant paramilitary. There would be many more bombs, from both the IRA and the UVF, the majority of which killed innocent people as well as military targets.

Trauma bonding was definitely operating in the Irish Republican Army in the 1970s and 1980s, but as mentioned before the psychological trauma of individual events would have merged with the traumatic memory—and the intergenerational trauma—that most of them had inherited. The psychological trauma came from two sources: first, simply the reality of being Catholics in Northern Ireland, and the oppression that involved; secondly, being the heirs, once they had joined the IRA, of what they regarded as the only true political authority in Ireland, an authority that had always been betrayed. According to the ideology in which their leaders believed, and which they gradually internalized, the Free State had betrayed the Republic in 1922-23, as had the main government parties: since the IRA had always defended the Republic against those who would betray it, the IRA Army Council was the supreme political authority in all of Ireland. The individual became bonded first to aggression and to terrorism as a way of life, and then to a worldview and an ideology that attempted to rationalize that lifestyle.

And the IRA volunteers sealed that authority with their willingness to shed blood, their own and others. Were they not willing to kill, and if necessary to be killed, were they not willing to operate in total secrecy, to defend the apostolic authority of the 1916 Republic? The psychic energy that kept IRA volunteers going was the trauma bond of daily killing, the shared traumatic memory of growing up in a society where they were hated, and a shared traumatic memory of a betrayed Republic whose authority existed only in their minds. In this shared traumata the gun was the supreme and only arbiter of social life, and one's personal authenticity was proven by a willingness to kill and be killed. The shared traumatic memory didn't just accompany the ideology, it *was* the ideology.

6.

In March 1972 Gerry Adams was interned for the first time without trial. By now he had become well known as a top IRA commander. But as mentioned before, Adams was abruptly released from internment in June, so that he could participate in peace negotiations in Britain. The peace talks came to nothing, but it was a high-powered delegation of top Irish Republicans including Martin McGuinness, Sean MacStiofain (IRA Chief of Staff), Daithi O'Conneill, Seamus Twomen and Ivor Bell. The older IRA and Sinn Fein stalwarts insisted that the young Adams accompany them in their delegation—his talents as a speaker and writer had become known, as well as his physical courage. But there was probably another reason why the old-timers trusted the young volunteer: the fact that his family had been Republicans, and IRA members at that, for several generations. In any case, the stakes were high on both sides. In March 1972, the same month that they interned Gerry Adams, the British government dissolved Northern Ireland's government and established direct rule.

With the breakdown of peace talks, Adams returned to Belfast, and immediately took up where he had left off. On May 13 and 14, after the bombing of a Catholic pub, gun battles broke out throughout Belfast, with seven people killed. On July 13 and 14, there were again gun battles all over Belfast, and again many casualties. On 21 July, the IRA detonated 22 bombs at different locations around Belfast, with the usual disproportionately high civilian body count—six civilians, two British army troops and one UVD volunteer killed. On Operation Motorman, on July 31, some 12,000 British troops, supported by tanks, opened up the 'no go' areas created by the IRA. The Republicans went deeper underground and continued their operations. Gerry Adams was probably involved with these events—although not necessarily all of them—on a daily basis.

Adams was again interned July 1973, and sent to the Long Kesh internment camp. While there he participated with IRA comrades in a mass escape attempt, for which he was convicted of a crime and sentenced to a prison term. While in prison he wrote a series of influential articles using the pseudonym 'Brownie,' in which he criticized some of the decisions of top IRA leaders, and was especially vehement in opposing assassinations of leaders of other Republican groups. There was also, in these articles, the beginning of his questioning of the policy of non-participation in electoral politics and the introduction of the idea of political involvement in tandem with the IRA's traditional paramilitary initiatives. He was released in 1976, rearrested for IRA membership in 1978, and released again for lack of evidence.

It probably wasn't hard for Gerry Adams, who was a part of the peace talks, to figure out why peace didn't happen. The British knew that Adams, IRA and Sinn Fein were only one small, very fanatical and very violent part of Catholic nationalism in Northern Ireland, and at that time represented only themselves. Furthermore, since it was their violent paramilitary activities that made them different, it was easy to see them as a criminal or military problem, and not a political one. The problem, as Gerry Adams saw it, was not to give up their Republican heritage, but to find a way to position Sinn Fein and the IRA as the representative of the majority of Catholics in Northern Ireland. And the best way to accomplish that would be to create some common front with other Catholic groups. The time was not yet ripe for it, but that would eventually lead to working with the Social Democratic and Labour Party, which in the late 1970s represented by far the majority of Catholics.

Gerry Adams had married Collette McCardle in 1971, and both he and his wife had to adjust to the unique pressures of the family of an IRA commander, the main issue being that Adams was either in prison, interment or on the run most of the time. And it was a rare day when Adams wasn't personally in some kind of dangerous or violent situation. He had made the mistake, when negotiating with the British in 1972, of saying that under certain conditions, "all bets are off." The next time Adams heard those words were while lying on the floor in the Springfield Road Barracks being kicked by a Special Branch interrogator who was gleefully declaiming, "All bets are off, now, Gerry!" (Adams later claimed permanent kidney damage from that incident.) In fact, both the British and the RUC were developing new methods of interrogation that would easily fit the United Nations' definition of torture.

The RUC would take away special category status for crimes committed by the IRA after March 1, 1976. The idea was to treat IRA members as simple criminals, in order to damage their morale and weaken group resolve. Both the British and the RUC had already made good use of informers, many of them recruited after violent interrogation. We still don't know the exact contribution of Gerry Adams to the reorganization of the IRA, but he and other leaders completely overhauled the IRA structure. To defend against informers, the IRA now operated through Active Service Units, or ASUs; each ASU was a small cell of members on full-time duty status—three, four, five or perhaps six—who were completely separate from the rest of the organization. No ASU knew who was in the other ASUs, or even where they operated. Brigades and Battalions were kept, but the cell leaders would interact only with the Brigade Operations Officer. This prevented leaks through infiltration and torture. Under the Prevention of Terrorism Act (POTA) suspects could be held and interrogated for a week.

Top IRA commanders had embraced the idea of a "long war," but were now considering the possibility of a political component to it—a component that could lead to a mass movement. At about this time Brigadier James Glover of the British army's intelligence staff did an analysis of the IRA, which was stolen by parties unknown, and somehow found its way into the Sinn Fein newspaper, the *Republican News*, where everybody in Northern Ireland had a chance to read it. Glover was sure that Gerry Adams was behind most of the reorganization of the IRA, as well as inventing and promoting new strategies:

For some time we'd always thought that, sooner or later, a charismatic figure would emerge from within the ranks of the

IRA who would succeed in transforming it from being the old-fashioned organization that it was into something very modern. It became evident that Adams was starting to fulfill this role, both when he was in the Maze [internment camp] and probably even more so when he was outside. One of the things I've never really quite been able to understand is how, while he was locked up in the Maze, his influence spread outside into the North and obviously trickled down to the South as well.[23]

Glover also predicted in his purloined intelligence report that the IRA would start targeting high profile individuals in government and elsewhere. And indeed, on 27 August, 1979, the IRA killed a member of the royal family, Louis Mountbatten, first Earl of Burma, by blowing up his boat in the harbor of Mullaghmore, County Sligo; also killed at that time were Lord Mountbatten's grandson and two other innocent people. This tragic incident infuriated the British establishment, since the last Viceroy of India was greatly beloved, and not just by the royal family—he was also a great favorite of the British people. This shocking incident also led indirectly to one of the most notorious public expressions of anti-Irish prejudice in modern history.

This contretemps occurred on the occasion of Princess Margaret's visit to Chicago, where she attended a dinner party given in her honor by the Mayor, Jane Byrne. Ms. Byrne remarked that she had attended Mountbatten's funeral in London, which elicited the following from Princess Margaret:

Princess Margaret: The Irish. They're pigs.

Pause.

Princess Margaret: Oh dear. You're Irish.

Mayor Byrne was indeed Irish-American, and she spent the rest of the dinner party, according to eye-witnesses, in a state of intractable, silent rage.

Afterward Byrne—perhaps fearful of an international

incident—attempted a little damage control by suggesting that the words of Princess Margaret referred only to the IRA, and not to the Irish as a whole. But it did not seem that way to the people who attended the dinner party, nor to most Irish readers, who received this juicy gossip in their newspapers. Therein lay a significant problem of the British Establishment, in which we may include Margaret Thatcher: many of the angry, dismissive or negative things she and others said in response to 'the Troubles' came across to the Irish themselves not as denunciations of the IRA—denunciations with which most Irish might have agreed, at that point—but of the Irish as a group. And very often the British government did not go out of their way to make any such distinction.

Meanwhile there were, by 1979, some 300 "blanket men" in the Maze—men who refused to wear the prison uniform. The protest wasn't working, some felt, so there was much discussion about how it could be broadened. Beatings by prison guards were common, they said, especially when they went to shower. Therefore they stopped showering. For reasons this writer does not completely understand, the blanket men began to smear their excrement on the walls. (Some say it was because the guards deliberately spilled their chamber pots in the cells.) By January 1980 a consensus was growing among prisoners for a hunger strike. At first top IRA commanders were against it, but eventually relented. This, like so many tactics used during the civil war, would have repercussions that no one could have predicted. Before it would be over, ten men would die on hunger strike, and public opinion in the Catholic community would be deeply affected.

The main hunger strike began March 1, 1981, led by Bobby Sands, a committed young man who fully understood that people were going to die in this battle of wills. Margaret Thatcher, now British Prime Minister, was only too happy to let them die; the IRA was "playing its last card," she crowed. Then there suddenly occurred one of those rare anomalies of history that changes everything, and in this case transformed not only the hunger strike but the entire Republican movement, and the future of Ireland. There would soon be a by-election for MP in Fermanagh-South Tyrone, in Northern Ireland, and at the last moment Bobby Sands was entered as the Sinn Fein candidate. Miraculously, on April 19, 1981, Bobby Sands won the election. Out of a massive turnout of almost 87 percent, Bobby Sands beat his opponent by almost 1,500 votes. On May 5, 1981, he died of starvation secondary to his hunger strike.

He was given a funeral with full military honors by the IRA. The amazing thing was that one hundred thousand people followed his coffin to its final resting place; there were media from dozens of countries. There was also an outpouring of statements from foreign leaders and movements in support of Sands and his comrades. The sight of one hundred thousand Catholics in Northern Ireland, marching in the streets, was a sight that Gerry Adams and the other leaders found astonishing. Here was what they had so laboriously been looking for—a way to create a mass movement! Mairead Corrigan Maguire, a co-founder of the Peace People[24] and the recipient of the Nobel Prize for her peace-making efforts—and no friend of the IRA—was quoted in Padriag O'Malley's *The Uncivil Wars: Ireland Today*:

I watched Bobby Sands' funeral. The coffin stopped at the bottom of our garden in Andersontown. I saw at the funeral of Bobby Sands people who had been at my sister's funeral, who walked at the children's funeral, who marched in the peace rallies, walking by the coffin of Bobby Sands because people are emotionally tied into the prisons. It's not that they support violence or the Provisional IRA. But they are all men from our community. We know how they have come to be there. And above all we don't want them suffering within the prisons.

When Bobby Sands died, many of us felt, it's back to square

one. In fact, further back and further divided than even square one was. If you tried to call a peace rally now in Andersontown—and I'm from Anderstontown, so I know it— you wouldn't get anyone to come. There is far more bitterness and a feeling of anti-Britishness in many communities. People who never even used the term *Brits out* started to use the term.[25]

Had Bobby Sands' election to Westminster, while dying in prison, been the transcendent event that changed everything? If that were true, it was merely common sense for Sinn Fein to run more candidates. This all began in a completely anomalous situation regarding IRA hunger strikers, but with the stunning turnout at Bobby Sands' funeral—and the fact that he had won an important election—everything changed; and the thought naturally arose that electoral activity could no longer be automatically ruled out.

7.

It was because of this that at the Sinn Fein *Ard Fheis* [convention], IRA volunteer Danny Morrison stood before the assembled Republicans to ask, however rhetorically, a question no one thought they would ever hear: "Who here really believes we can win the war through the ballot box? But will anyone here object if, with a paper ballot in one hand and an Armalite in the other, we take power in Ireland?"

"No!" the crowd roared, signaling their approval.

This became known as the "Armalite and ballot box" strategy. The astonishing nature of this abrupt change must be assessed in view of the fact that Irish Republicans had traditionally refused to cooperate in elections, regarding them as illegitimate. (Some participated, but refused to sit in the bodies to which they had been elected.) In 1981, it was assumed that those who ran for office would refuse to sit in the British House of Parliament or any power-sharing arrangement in Northern Ireland either, for that matter—but that, too, would soon change. Underlying all of this was the shock of seeing the mass turnout for the funeral of Bobby Sands—a hundred thousand Irish Catholics in the street, the largest march in Irish history!—and the outpouring of sympathy for the hunger strikers from people in struggle around the world. This was something that Gerry Adams and the other leaders couldn't afford to ignore, and they didn't.

But Prime Minister Margaret Thatcher did; her misapprehension of the Bobby Sands phenomena—and probably her unwillingness to find an accommodation to the IRA prisoners' demand that they wear their own clothes—were more examples of British misunderstanding of the Irish. Allowing Bobby Sands and the other hunger strikers to perish was an incredible windfall for the IRA. Hundreds sought to join the "ra," as the IRA was called in the Catholic ghettoes; Sinn Fein was treated as though it had a serious chance of standing for, and winning elections. This happened because, just as it had in 1916, the British government supplied the key to success for the Republican with their rigidity, behind which probably lay a certain dislike of the Irish as a people.

As in 1916, the IRA had limited popular support, even among most Catholic nationalists—until the British were seen to be killing them. Of course, Margaret Thatcher didn't personally kill Bobby Sands, but she was quite happy to stand by while he died, making nasty remarks about his criminality at every point. Margaret Thatcher's sneering repudiation of all things Republican—which because of their peculiarly disdainful tone were increasingly experienced by Irish Catholics as a repudiation of all things Irish—was the magic ingredient which brought instant renown and appreciation for the hunger strikers and their IRA comrades.

The war ground on through the 1980s, with the main change being Sinn Fein's willingness to contest elections. The armed dimension of such a struggle, waged mainly by urban guerilla forces, depended heavily on terrorism. In a milieu of extreme daily violence, the amount of aggression internalized by combatants and their victims was enormous. Some psychological trauma can come from being attacked, some from witnessing armed attacks—and perhaps most of all from staging and carrying out those attacks oneself, particularly when one witnesses the agony and death of an enemy at close range. Even worse is the knowledge that with bombs one has killed innocent civilians. In this situation, the stress was compounded by the fact that nobody could see a way out of the cycle of violence. Worst of all was simply being there, witnessing the descent of two religious communities into madness, and hearing the stories, the gunshots, the explosions, the ambushes—all the appurtenances of war in poor neighborhoods, where people were simply trying to live.

In 1982, the IRA assassinated Lenny Murphy, leader of the 'Shankill Butchers.' This gang had been indicative of a new and frightening level of sectarian violence. He and his gang would drive through Catholic ghettos looking for Catholics, and would kidnap, torture and kill them, usually by slashing their throats. He and his gang were responsible for twenty-three known deaths, although there may have been many more. Interestingly, Murphy's gang was ultimately so out of control that he also began to kill Protestants, either former members of his gang whom he didn't like, suspected informers, or simply people who irritated him for some reason. Some investigators believe that the IRA hit squad that ultimately took his life was, in effect, given permission by Unionist paramilitaries to kill Murphy, particularly since the hit went down in a Protestant neighborhood.

An Anglo-Irish Agreement was signed in 1985, which Margaret Thatcher hoped would win some support from Catholics. This Agreement gave some consultative powers to the Republic of Ireland in the government of Northern Ireland. It sent the Protestant unionists into a frenzy of paranoia—all unionist representatives in Westminster resigned their seats—and the Republicans also refused to support it because they felt it gave legitimacy to the ongoing division of Ireland. Again, this represented yet one more failing of PM Thatcher to understand how people in Northern Ireland were experiencing events on the ground. She was aware that a traditional demand of Irish Republicans had been for the unification of Ireland, and thought that the consultative privileges of the Dublin government in Northern Ireland might suggest a move in that direction—or suggest it just enough for the Catholics to feel it was a concession.

What she didn't realize was the ferocity of the daily violence in Northern Ireland. While the old demand for reunification was still there, it had been largely replaced in importance by the demand for Britain to leave Northern Ireland, and to create a timetable for its departure. The Republicans and a great many Catholic nationalists had convinced themselves that this would give them victory, and probably also the end of hostilities, because the loyalists would realize that the jig was up. Of course, Britain was not willing to contemplate such a move, and it is hard to see that Britain could have created any kind of a timetable for withdrawal, so enmeshed had it become in the fighting. Furthermore Britain knew that if it left anytime soon, the result would likely be an even more ferocious civil war. The irony here—one of many—is that eventually, after Gerry Adams and the Sinn Fein leadership had decided on peace, they would need the hated 'Brits' to enforce many of the provisions of the peace process.

At the November, 1986, Sinn Fein party congress in Dublin, the majority voted to end the policy of abstentionism—that is, refusing to take seats they had won in the Irish Parliament, or in any future power-sharing arrangement in Northern Ireland. This was a huge step for the party, but after the infusion of support and money as a result of the Bobby Sands election and funeral, such a move had most likely become inevitable. In 1988 Gerry Adams met with John Hume of the Social Democratic and Labour Party of Northern Ireland. John Hume had the idea that they should pool their resources to achieve something truly revolutionary—initiating a peace process. The people were getting tired of war, both men knew, and needed something to look forward to besides more killing; Adams wouldn't have admitted it as openly as Hume, but he was in a position to know that it was true.

Could the two Catholic nationalist parties posture themselves as the leaders of a search for peace? The SDLP was the party that got the most votes from Catholics in Northern Ireland, but saw that the IRA and Sinn Fein had to see some benefit in peace, enough to contemplate it, or there would be no peace. Gerry Adams quickly saw that by cooperating with SDLP, he and Sinn Fein would achieve greater credibility, and would finally be seen as working more for the majority of Catholics, rather than the narrow historical agenda associated with the IRA worldview. Adams was now the President of Sinn Fein, and had, it seems likely, turned over operational paramilitary matters to other IRA leaders. This meant that the majority of people within the IRA-Sinn Fein spectrum were coming to believe that Adams could serve the movement better as a negotiator and politician than a gunman and a commander; and John Hume and the SDLP were soon to be of that persuasion too. As the new head of Sinn Fein, Adams was now free to work the political possibilities inherent in the situation, and he was free to come and go as he pleased, as long as he didn't again pick up the gun.

Why would Gerry Adams want peace? To begin with, he was the first to understand the prestige—local and international—that would befall anyone who succeeded in stopping the hostilities. And the paradoxical reality was that one of the most violent secret armies in the world was in the best position to bring peace about, through negotiations leading to a ceasefire. If Sinn Fein could bring peace, it would—precisely because of the violence of its guns—bestow a prestige that the gun had never done. If it could at the same time change the laws that had previously barred full social participation for Catholics, it would be winning the war and the peace at the same time! Furthermore, Adams now saw something that John Hume had perhaps not yet seen: that in time Sinn Fein could, if it was serious about peace, successfully contest elections in districts that the SDLP had traditionally won.

Simply by voting for Sinn Fein, Catholics could demonstrate how fed up they were with the Protestant establishment, and signal conclusively that they would never go back to the old ways of discrimination against Catholics—and they could make that point at very little personal risk, by secret ballot. Adams well understood that the war would have to go on until enough people had decided they were willing to take some risk in stopping it. But the truth was that he, and many others, had become wearied by the extraordinarily bloodthirsty toll that guerilla urban war had taken on parties in the conflict.

Of special concern was that the British Special Air Services had undertaken 'shoot to kill' operations, apparently approved by Margaret Thatcher. Roughly the same as the order to take no prisoners in a land war, it meant that even if during an operation an IRA volunteer attempted to give up, the SAS would still shoot and kill that person, even if they were unarmed. (It should be pointed out, of course, that the IRA had often done exactly the same thing—but most people would hold a democratic government to a higher standard.) These were basically assassinations, and the SAS was to some extent operating as a death squad. This was brought home to Adams by the deaths of three IRA volunteers on assignment in Gibraltar. Planning to detonate a bomb at a British army ceremony, all three—including one woman—were shot dead by SAS operatives, despite the fact that they were unarmed. This shooting, called Operation Flavius by the SAS, was reportedly given the green light by Margaret Thatcher herself.

At the funeral of the IRA volunteers, at which Gerry Adams and Michael McGuire were present, a loyalist named Michael Stone mounted a pistol and grenade attack on the mourners, killing three people and wounding sixty. This surrealistic attack was filmed in real time by TV crews that were present, causing disgust and shock around the world. Two days later, two under-cover British corporals somehow got caught up in yet another IRA funeral procession (for one of Stone's three victims), and the mourners—fearing another attack by loyalists—pulled the men from the car, stripped them and shot them dead. Ironically, the priest who gave the two young British corporals last rites was a major contact between the IRA and the British government, and was himself a Republican. But he, like many others, had come to feel that finding a path to peace was more important than fighting.

But how could peace come about? There seemed no end in sight, and no way out. The fateful truth was, as the top leaders in both Sinn Fein and the IRA were beginning to see—even if they did not verbalize it—that there was no way they could win with the gun, the gelignite bomb, or the paper ballot. (Or even with the potent combination of all three.) The British weren't leaving; the Protestants despised the Catholics, and would never be a part of a united Ireland in the foreseeable future; and nobody was winning. Militarily and politically, they were at stalemate. What to do? Adams was increasingly contemplating peace as a major goal: that at least might in the end be doable, and even if it wasn't, it would make Sinn Fein and the IRA—and the Catholic leaders generally—look good, if they took the lead in demanding peace talks. It would also create a situation in which Britain would have to force the Protestant establishment to improve conditions for Catholics as part of any proposed peace agreement in Northern Ireland.

If Sinn Fein could be a major contributor to a peace process, they could take credit, first, for having defended Catholic neighborhoods with arms in hand during the bad years of 'the Troubles'; and secondly, helping to bring the peace that everybody thought was impossible. Since the funeral of Bobby Sands, the far-sighted Gerry Adams had also seen something else: if Sinn Fein played its cards well, if it could deliver peace to Northern Ireland, it might find itself in a position to politically challenge the two older parties in the Republic of Ireland, Fianna Fail and Fine Gael; and in Northern Ireland, Sinn Fein candidates would stand a very good chance of victory in elections for any power-sharing government. Adams might appeal to the anti-establishment Catholic young as an iconic Republican warrior who stood up to the British, while to others he might be seen as the softly-spoken negotiator who brought peace to a tortured country when nobody else could pull it off. In reality, both would be true.

But why would the majority of Catholics turn to Gerry Adams and Sinn Fein to lead them, rather than John Hume and the SDLP? Part of it was simply the way the ongoing trauma of violence had bonded people to the most prominent leader of the gunmen. Certainly John Hume was in many ways the better man than Gerry Adams, a man who had seen the need for peace earlier than anyone, and who was willing to step aside and give leadership to Adams to achieve that peace. Such men and women are rare in this world, and are therefore a nation's most precious resource. But despite Hume's clear moral ascendancy, Gerry Adams had the authority of the gunman, by virtue of having been the top commander in the thick of the war. If you want to get people to put down the gun, you must get the chief gunman to demand a ceasefire—that was the unspoken thinking of the time. Catholics were coming to see Gerry Adams as the only public representative of the gunmen who would have the authority to get them to dump arms, and give up armed struggle for political struggle.

8.

The person mainly involved in bringing together John Hume of the SDLP and Gerry Adams of Sinn Fein was Father Alec Reid, a Redemptorist priest whose parish was the Clonard Monastery in Belfast, where he served for 40 years, through the worst times of 'the Troubles.' The Redemptorist Monastery at Clonard stood at the intersection of Shankill Road, a working-class Protestant enclave, and his strongly nationalist Catholic parish. Father Reid had sought to operate as a go-between and negotiator between the IRA and the British establishment, a position that was respected on both sides. It was Father Reid who gave last rites to the two battered British corporals shot dead by Catholic mourners, as mentioned above.

A photo was taken of him as he did so, which became iconic in its accurate representation of the futility and horror of the mayhem into which Northern Ireland had fallen. What most people didn't know was that in his pocket Father Reid was carrying a letter from John Hume to Gerry Adams. Father Reid had become convinced that a way to peace had to be found—not least, one suspects, from the violent things he heard about in the confessional, and also by the many last rites that he had to administer.

His strategy at first was to encourage a 'pan-nationalist' grouping of the SDLP and Sinn Fein, which is why he first brought John Hume and Gerry Adams together. But that was the least of his involvement. In his obituary in *The Guardian* (he died on 22 November, 2013) it was noted as follows: "He was especially energetic for many years in trying to obtain information about a dozen people abducted by the IRA and buried without trace. This confidential and delicate work in the shadows was never acknowledged in any way, save privately, by the beneficiaries." In addition to his contact with the British government, he also functioned as a contact person with the Dublin government from 1987 until the 1998 signing of the Good Friday Agreement in Northern Ireland. He had numerous private meetings with Republic of Ireland government officials, including Charles Haughey, the Taoiseach (Prime Minister) of the Republic of Ireland, as well as with leaders of the Fianna Fail party. In all of these meetings, he tried to represent the ideas and interests of the wider nationalist community, which in practice means that he represented the thinking of John Hume as well as Gerry Adams, while being careful to emphasize the difference between the two.

Father Reid first became well-acquainted with Gerry Adams as a result of ministering to the IRA prisoners in the Maze Prison. By the late 1980s and early 1990s, according to his Guardian obit, he had become a trusted go-between. "By then Reid was at the epicenter of an undeclared cross-community peace movement, involving fellow visionary clergy from non-Catholic denominations and other community figures. Reid's initial objective was to bind together republicans and nationalists into a single body to advance their cause. That achieved, he believed constructive inter-government and all-party negotiations could begin. Having slowly converted Adams to his view, Reid became the contact for private exchanges between Adams and John Hume, the SDLP leader and figurehead for peaceful nationalism, at first written, and later face to face." Both Father Reid and John Hume were raising the same point to Gerry Adams—if your Republican principles are any good, they can win politically, if you've got the stomach to argue them publicly. And Adams was gradually being won over to this point of view.

On 29 April of 1991, the Protestant militias announced a two-month truce. There was no response from the IRA, which continued operations. On August 31 of 1994, the IRA announced a complete cessation of hostilities, a truce that would last for two years. On 13 October, probably in response to the IRA announcement, the combined Protestant paramilitaries also announced a ceasefire. A broadcasting ban on Sinn Fein was lifted in the UK and the Republic of Ireland, allowing Gerry Adams to articulate the evolving Sinn Fein position. And in 1995, a Sinn Fein delegation actually met with the Northern Ireland Office, something that had been unthinkable before. A Joint Framework document was agreed to by the Irish and British governments. And in the US, Gerry Adams was treated to a reception by Bill Clinton, President of the United States.

But peace, which seemed ever closer, momentarily slipped away. There was an unwillingness of the unionist parties to meet with representatives of Sinn Fein, or even to allow Sinn Fein into the peace negotiations, until their weapons were "decommissioned," which lead to the freezing out of Sinn Fein from the all-party negotiations—which in turn lead to a resumption of hostilities of the part of the IRA, which (after a telephone warning) blew up the London docklands. Negotiations slogged on in Stormont, the Northern Ireland government, but without Sinn Fein. Sinn Fein responded by blowing up the city center of Manchester, England, the largest bomb exploded in Europe since the Second World War. A realization was setting in that the IRA would have to be included, despite the extreme repugnance of that idea to most Protestant loyalists, represented by the two main unionist parties.

To break the logjam, American negotiator George J. Mitchell devised a simple but clever solution to the "decommissioning" problem—all parties would decommission their weapons piecemeal *as they negotiated a peace agreement*. Meanwhile, momentum for peace was building. In November, 1995, US President Bill Clinton appeared at a humongous rally at Belfast City Hall, in Northern Ireland, proclaiming—in a phrase that might have come from Yeats—that terrorists and secret armies were "yesterday's men." There was another huge peace rally in Belfast in February, 1996; and in May, 1996, Gerry Adams announced that Sinn Fein would sign the Mitchell Principles, if all the other parties and paramilitary groups would do so. (The Mitchell Principles asked the parties to give up violence, and was especially concerned with stopping revenge killings.) The fact that Sinn Fein agreed first to these principles, and challenged the other parties and paramilitaries to the same, seemed to give credibility to Sinn Fein's commitment to the peace process.

In 1997, Sinn Fein made significant gains in Northern Ireland elections; Gerry Adams was one of two MPs elected to Parliament in Britain (but declined to take his seat). On 18 July, 1997, John Hume and Gerry Adams appealed to the IRA to declare a ceasefire. The next day the IRA announced that a ceasefire was going into effect—and this one would hold. In August 26, 1997, in Belfast, the Irish and British government set up an Independent International Commission on Decommissioning. On August 29, the Secretary of State for Northern Ireland, Marjorie Mowland, announced that her government accepted the ceasefire by the IRA as genuine, at the same time inviting Sinn Fein into the multiparty talks at Stormont. Substantive negotiations began, as all parties signed off on the Mitchell Principles, which was basically an agreement to stop the violence. On January, 1998, the talks moved to London, and—clearly as a good faith gesture— Prime Minister Tony Blair agreed to open a new investigation of the "Bloody Sunday" massacre in Derry in 1972.

Then, in a classic negotiating gambit, on the 25th of March negotiator George Mitchell announced a two-week deadline for all parties: this was to let them all know that the time of statements and photo ops was over, and the time for an agreement was nigh. On Good Friday, April 10th, 1998, a peace agreement was signed; it is generally referred to as the Good Friday Agreement, or GFA. Campaigning for approval by the people in both the Republic and in Northern Ireland was intense, with enormous international pressure for approval. President Clinton again came to Northern Ireland, and a few days before the referendum on the GFA—in a cultural event whose importance has not been properly recognized—the Irish band U2 played a concert for peace in Belfast, during which it invited onstage both David Trimble (a Protestant unionist) and John Hume (main Catholic parliamentarian of the SDLP).

The fact that both were willing to appear on the same stage together, at a rock concert, was typical of the fervor with which everybody in the political class had thrown themselves behind approval of Good Friday. It would either be peace, they realized, or perhaps a war that might last for much of the 21st century. The people agreed that it was time for peace. In the actual 1998 referenda, 94.39 percent of the people in the Republic of Ireland voted for the Good Friday Agreement; in Northern Ireland, 71.1 voted for the GFA. It was a tremendous victory for peace and common sense.

One outcome of the referenda was that the Republic of Ireland changed its Constitution, so that it no longer claimed sovereignty over the six countries of Northern Ireland. The Northern Ireland version of the referendum emphasized the role of 'consent,' specifying that the Republic of Ireland and Northern Ireland would be united only if a majority of the people in both countries wanted it. In subsequent speeches, Gerry Adams stated that Sinn Fein now found both the Republic of Ireland and the power-sharing arrangements of Northern Ireland to be constitu- tional and proper: this, too, was a huge change, since before Sinn Fein had considered both governments bogus for a variety of reasons.

Among other things, Adams' statement signaled the willingness of Sinn Fein to compete robustly in conventional politics without raising constitutional issues going back to 1916. The ceasefire held, and on July 28, 2005, the IRA announced that it had "formerly ordered an end to the armed campaign." It added unambiguously: "All volunteers have been instructed to assist the development of purely political and democratic programs through exclusively peaceful means. Volunteers must not engage in any other activities whatsoever."

There would be sporadic violence afterwards, of course; there would be tiny splinter groups that would continue the lonely, violent life of the bomb and the gun. Perhaps there always will be such groups, in Ireland and Northern Ireland, as it will be the job of law enforcement to track them down. Physically, these splinter groups could still do great damage, but they could not compromise the Good Friday Agreement, because the public overwhelmingly supported it; and that same public had decisively turned against the gunmen as representatives of Irish integrity.

There would be charges and counter-charges between Protestants and Catholics and their representatives in Northern Ireland, and there would be much posturing for the TV cameras. But it would be done in the context of running for political office, and not as a political adjunct to an armed struggle. Sinn Fein was becoming a professional, modern political party; it was attracting new members; and it had already successfully contested political districts that the SDLP had formally won. But there was an odd but welcome dichotomy involved: Sinn Fein was becoming popular to the extent that the IRA was losing its luster. There had been too much killing, and a traumatized people desperately longed to be quit of it. The public supported Gerry Adams and Sinn Fein because it talked of a future of peace, and was only too happy to leave the war stories and songs of conflict behind.

In the same year that the IRA abjured violence once and for all—2005—many of its volunteers seemed to be struggling to find peace in their personal lives. Alcoholism had long been endemic amongst IRA volunteers and among the loyalist paramilitaries as well. In Belfast a man—an IRA volunteer—was killed by two other IRA men in an unusually savage pub brawl. This had the effect of greatly diminishing support in Belfast for the now at-liberty IRA men, at least partly because of the extreme brutality

420

of the killing they had once engaged in. The IRA had difficulty coming clean about the fact that its men had been involved in the Belfast brawl, which further damaged its standing in the public mind.

From a secret band of brother-warriors arraigned against the British empire, it had come down to this: alcoholic, undisciplined and traumatized men involved in squalid quarrels in pubs over reported insults to somebody's girlfriend. Once feared and respected if not universally supported warriors, these pathetic and out-of-control individuals now seemed more like social parasites with psychological problems. It was truly now beginning to seem, as President Bill Clinton had said, that the gunmen of Northern Ireland were indeed on their way to becoming "yesterday's men."

9.

Was civil war in Northern Ireland inevitable? We can never really know, nor can we really say how a continued campaign of nonviolent resistance would have worked if "Bloody Sunday" had not happened. The reality is that by the time of "Bloody Sunday," in January of 1972, a majority of the Catholic people of Northern Ireland could no longer live under Protestant oppression; and after "Bloody Sunday," those most involved in fighting for Catholic rights simply didn't believe that further nonviolent resistance could be justified. In such a situation, a vocal and active minority will choose armed struggle; and so they did.

But why did so many young men make the *personal* decision to pick up the gun? To a very large extent because their history told them to do it, and that history consisted of one long, shared traumatic memory. That is what they had done before over the centuries, when the Protestant ascendancy shot them in the street and burned down their homes: they picked up the gun and the bomb, and learned the arsonist's trade. Terrorism it was, indeed; but Irish terrorism did not arise out of a vacuum, but rather in response to a particularly claustrophobic kind of oppression. In Ireland, oppression was the terrorism of the rich Protestant ascendancy, and over many centuries terrorism became the oppression the poor visited on the rich. (Thus the pronounced British fear of the 'wild Fenian' with his torch and bomb.)

Terror it was, but it was also mixed up in the Irish mind with self-destruction through alcoholism, which is not surprising. This self-destruction came not just because of the Protestant ascendancy's objective social exploitation of the Irish peasant class, but also because of Protestant (and British) prejudice against anything Irish, and the Irish people's internalization of that anti-Catholic and anti-Irish prejudice, whence it became an undercurrent of self-hatred expressed in violence against oneself, and against others.

How were Irish males to rid themselves of such a burden? Often with a kind of peculiarly Irish form of redemptive violence: self-destruction with the drink, and social destruction with the revolver and the AR-18. The gun was such a part of the Irish experience that even the centrist parties in the Republic of Ireland never tired to referring to it. "Thus, many see the Dublin government's professed repugnance at the tactics of the IRA as at best self-serving and at worst hypocritical," writes Padriag O'Malley. "For it was those very tactics—the clandestine bomb, assassination on the street, murder from a ditch, destruction of property, and random terror—that shaped the struggle between the IRA and the British in the years 1918 through 1921, and that led to the independence of the Twenty-six Counties and the foundation of the Irish Free State."[26]

To a great extent the history of the Irish, to the Irish themselves, is made up of traumatic memory that is oddly amenable to dramatic treatment in the writing, speaking and singing of it. To be Irish is most likely to mean that one is a prisoner of history, or several histories, all of which are suffused with suffering and psychological trauma, and several of which are at war with each other. Because of the searing nature of the legends and memories of violence, the songs and stories and preoccupations with tragedy and oppression in generations past, the particular version of Irish history one embraces inevitably creates a profoundly conflicted identity. Such an identity suggests not only a certain kind of political affiliation, but— however unconsciously—some strategy for political and personal redemption, since so much of Irish history was associated with aggression, resentment, oppression and its accompanying pathologies.

Unfortunately, in Northern Ireland—as so often before in Irish history—personal redemption from real or imagined injustices came in the form of ever more social violence, the more ferocious examples of which in Northern Ireland in 1968 to 1998 were "Bloody Sunday," the use of torture and internment without trial, endless killing by IRA volunteers using the Armalite assault rifle and car bombs, the 'Five AM Knock' of the death squad at one's doorstep, not to mention the kneecapping and murdering of heretical Catholics and dissident Protestants. 'The Troubles' were themselves nothing but mass trauma bonding in a very small country over a period of thirty years, a people born into the thick of traumatic memory who endured the daily experience of ever more traumatizing events, experiences that bonded them many times over to aggression as a way of life. It should be no surprise that so many young people picked up the iconic tools of death that long haunted the collective Irish imagination and the public mind, the gun and the bomb being the greatest of those.

The long wars the Irish always lost over a period of 800 years, the forced exile of its Catholic leaders, the lost Catholic aristocrats of the Wild Geese, the horrible Great Famine, and finally the shock of dying and killing for a Republic in 1919-1921 that turned out to be counterfeit, because it was a Free State and not quite a Republic after all. And through it all a lyrical but unhealthy apotheosis of Irish suffering, and a deeply embedded, and deeply felt, sense of inferiority as a leaderless peasant people, especially when compared to other peoples, all of it based on the internalized hatred that had originated with the Protestant ascendancy throughout the land. Irishwomen and Irishmen internalized that tribal prejudice; and in the end the internalized hatred became a burning self-hatred, only partly ameliorated by a gift for poetry and song. The Irish responded to this dilemma with Irish nationalism. And what is nationalism but a form of mass narcissism, a desperate attempt to overcome a negative self-image?

The narcissist deals with his low self-esteem by creating a conception of the Self as a kind of privileged persona who isn't required to follow the rules, but who is always right, and who transcends ordinary human categories. That is how individuals with narcissistic personality disorder often tend to deal with low self-esteem. The Irish nationalist deals with his low self-esteem by creating in his mind a *national* persona that doesn't have to follow the rules, that is never wrong, and that transcends ordinary human categories—he creates in his mind a national persona that is, in fact, very much like God, in the sense that it transcends both the world and historical time. Therefore this national persona is always right, and cannot be contradicted. This means that it is deeply felt, and also becomes the touchstone for right and wrong. If something serves Irish nationalism it is right; if it contradicts Irish nationalism—especially the Republican variety—it is wrong.

But that is a dream of power, and if there is one thing the young Catholic men in Northern Ireland didn't have very much of, it was power. They didn't have personal power, and they didn't have institutional power. For many of them nationalism was the ticket out of that cul-de-sac. For those attracted to the Republican version of Irish nationalism it was a dream of power, especially as acted out in the bold daring of the IRA; but it was also about the nobility of dying, which in turn is driven by a uniquely Irish form of death-worship.

Conor Cruise O'Brien, in a debate with a leader of the Official IRA in 1971, dealt with this directly: "For that movement true, legitimate authority is derived only from the generations of the dead who died for Ireland, and is properly wielded in the present by the organization of men and women [that are] prepared to repeat the blood sacrifice. To some people, and certainly to a significant minority in this country, that idea—of the authority of the dead and those who volunteer to die—will seem more noble than democracy. I would even agree. It is more noble. Being noble is what it is all about."

"To belong to a military elite is noble—in the strictest, earliest meaning of the word—and the authority of a military elite is the real present-day meaning of this movement. The dead can only validate: real power is wielded by the living military elite. They decide who is to die and when, and they possess the prestige which the power to decide that confers."[27] I would only add to this that such a military elite manipulates the words of the dead, in an attempt to impose dead meanings on living situations. But Cruise O'Brien is right about the origins of the nobility that he deconstructs: it is the warrior's authority of being willing to kill and to die. It is the perfect dream of power—perhaps the *only* dream of power—available until recently to young Catholic men and women in Northern Ireland.

This inverted dream of death-power is inadvertently supported by a key idea of Christianity, the idea of Christ's blood sacrifice to save the world from sin, which also sends a message that there is something redemptive about violence. Why does Jesus' capacity to confer salvation come from being tortured to death in public, rather than through his teachings and his example? Because the idea of blood atonement has always been promoted as the central idea of organized Christianity, perhaps—this writer would argue—to distract from the revolutionary nature of Jesus' teaching. During the time of the long and very public death of Bobby Sands, it seems apparent that profoundly Catholic emotional orientations regarding death and redemption were being evoked in a very direct way. That is why 100,000 ordinary Catholics in Belfast—most of whom were not supporters of the IRA—took to the streets to bury him.

A paragraph or two ago I wrote that this dream of being able to kill and die deeply appealed to many young Catholic men in Northern Ireland. But it wasn't just a dream of nobility available to all, nor was all of it an unconscious acting out of the Christian theme of redemption through suffering. The young men who became IRA volunteers were also affected by a third and very profound cultural tradition, that of rampant patriarchy. I won't say that Irish Catholicism is any more patriarchal than any other religion, but it is there in all three of the main Abrahamic religions, and there are strong strains of it in Irish culture generally. In addition, patriarchy is a dream of power that is very attractive to young males who are completely powerless.

Patriarchy is all about a small group of strong fighting men ruling all other men and women, and it idealizes and apotheosizes conflict as the highest good in life. It is also about controlling the sexual and domesticating power of women. That is exactly what the IRA was all about—the power of a few men who abjured ordinary family life, in order to assume power over who lives and who dies, that life-and-death power arising from their skill as clandestine guerilla soldiers—and, I might add, their willingness to die along with their victims. This is not fascism, because IRA ideology aimed at religious equality rather than religious discrimination; but there is a strong family resemblance between the violent means employed by fascism and those of the IRA. And there is also, I might add, a strong connection between fascism and Republican violence in the way young males are likely to find those violent means attractive, and the way those

426

means can cause them to become bonded to aggression as a way of life.

Patriarchy is above all a dream of power, the power to control women (and to a peasant people afraid of sex, that is a heady temptation indeed); but also to be part of power to be exercised by a small male group over everybody else, both men *and* women—and this power is always defined and acted out in the arts of war. I say again, when men without power adopt the dream of total power inherent to patriarchy, they are likely to become very dangerous to themselves and to others. And in Ireland, because of the dense traumatic memory associated with its history, this small, brave, noble elite is also seen by some as the only legitimate source of power and therefore can do anything in the name of the nation.

There are other cultural factors that feed into the attraction to a clandestine army. One is a certain obsessive quality in Irish life; it is this obsessive quality that drove some people to believe that the IRA Army Council, at most representing a few thousand supporters, is—or should be—the only legitimate executive power in an entire island of six million people, without ever asking the opinion of the aforementioned millions. They could feel this way because the IRA did not represent the living, as Conor Cruise O'Brien accurately pointed out, but rather the sacrifices of the mighty dead, the heroes of modern Ireland: Connelly, Pearse, and all the others killed by the British in 1916.

It is this same obsessive tendency, however, which caused Conor Cruise O'Brien—whose loathing of the IRA gradually became an unhealthy obsession—to oppose the peace process in Northern Ireland, because Sinn Fein had been involved in negotiating it! People who have been overtaken by an obsession often have a tendency to adopt large, intricately reasoned but rather schematic perceptions that—despite being highly detailed—are nonetheless quite mad and therefore useless overall. Obsessions reflect the fixations and pathologies of the individual, not a correct perception of the shifting political realities of the real world; obsessive thinking gets in the way of one's ability to assimilate new evidence, and adapt to changing situations. It almost always involves an element of grandiosity as well, frequently backed up by narcissistic traits. This appears to have been the fate not only of many IRA volunteers, but also of Conor Cruise O'Brien, who hated political violence all of his days but never ceased for a moment to oppose the Northern Ireland peace process.

All these complex and sometimes terrifying cultural elements tend to support political violence in Ireland and Northern Ireland, but it was traumatic memory that bound these disparate elements together. Since Irish history is a history of oppression and defeat, Irish history *is* traumatic memory, whether in books, songs, poetry or the stories of elders. Irish history begins to make sense if you view it in that context, as do many of the main preoccupations of the Irish. Trauma and traumatic memory change the brain, and therefore affects everything else in the personality, including the things we believe, the way we define our identities, our ability to feel empathy and sympathy, and our ability to trust and form relationships. If you want to know how the people of Northern Ireland tend to view their own history, imagine how victims of trauma view their *personal* histories. Even those in Northern Ireland who were least damaged by the 30-year civil war tend to think of themselves in the context of the country's shared trauma.

Human aggression deeply affects one's ability to trust other human beings, and interferes with one's ability to create and affirm social contracts. It also interferes with one's judgment regarding *whom* to trust, since even in the US—a hypercompetitive and often corrupt society—a great many people are not worthy of trust. The ultimate effect of psychological trauma resulting from human violence—war, sexual abuse, crime—is to make it harder to have relationships with other people, because the person beset by traumatic memory often doesn't know how trust works, even if he is lucky enough to find someone trustworthy. The unwillingness of many Irish men to marry until middle age is undoubtedly based to some extent on this inability to form relationships and make social contracts, although it is doubtless enhanced as well by the dread of sexuality typical of peasant cultures.

Unfortunately, ideologies and theologies that arise from traumatic memory are not simply another point of view. They are that, but they are also—and more importantly—psychological problems that require attention and healing. Unfortunately, when traumatic memory is widespread, the people themselves must often struggle to find some method for treating and healing themselves, both individually and as a community. This usually happens when enough individuals start facing aspects of their own behavior that they wish to change. Through positive attempts to change behavior (in law, custom or through some aspect of the cultural apparatus), people can in that way follow the threads that lead back to the traumas they have assimilated.

In Northern Ireland, because of the intense divisions dating back to the late 17th century, and the modern influence of fanatics such as Ian Paisley, ideologies rising whole from traumatic memory are assimilated as the gospel truth. And they are *felt*, rather than believed—that is, they are emotional orientations as much as—and often more than—belief-systems. Beliefs arising from psychological trauma aren't merely another point of view. They are efforts to act out the traumatic memory in the present moment, and they are usually acted out in violent, coercive and exploitive behavior. This is nothing more or less than an addiction—people cannot stop acting out their traumatic memories because they do not comprehend the inner and outward circumstances that cause them to behave as they do, and have in some sense become unable to see beyond the circumstances of the world in which they are trapped.

The behaviors begin in traumatic memory, as the result of internalizing aggression from specific traumatizing events; but once the violent or coercive behavior gets underway it develops a momentum of its own. Traumatic memory is, because of the aggression inherent to it, the emotional equivalent to a self-fulfilling prophecy: the traumatizing events keep repeating themselves, and the violent actors become victims of their own violent personalities.

In Northern Ireland, traumatic memory became multigenerational trauma, transmitted from parents to children in families, promulgated by the Protestant parties in order to preserve their privilege, and likewise promulgated in a more secretive way by IRA and Sinn Fein adherents to protect *their* privilege, which was to kill when and whom they chose. It is consistently true that very poor people who inherit a certain traumatic memory at birth, and who are themselves victims of traumatizing events, have their own lethal form of 'traumatic privilege.' And 'traumatic privilege,' if not stopped early, is likely to be institutionalized as 'destructive entitlement,' which might be described as an institutionalized right to harm or kill whom one chooses.

So how did this play out during 'the Troubles' in Northern Ireland? Catholics had long been traumatized by Protestant hate, by living in a ghetto, and finally by the guerilla war that surrounded them—and to survive emotionally, they internalized a great deal of the aggression that they witnessed. Aggression, once internalized, creates pressure to be acted out, especially in young males who have a hard time sublimating strong desires and feelings. And yes, many of the young men so affected in the period 1968 through 1998 in Northern Ireland experienced a certain 'traumatic privilege' in a powerful form. They had been hurt, and they felt they had the right to hurt others, even the innocent, *and their history told them how to do that*. It told them you could pick up the gun; and once these same young men got their hands on the 'magic Armalites,' their fate disappeared into the fog of war.

The problem is that as one's profound exposure to violence is internalized, it becomes a kind of addiction, and it also becomes connected to everything else the gunman feels or knows in his bones. It's not just that one always has to commit another murder, drive another bombing run, to blot out the pain from the last killing or bombing (although that too is true). The problem is the 'traumatic privilege' that the young gunman is acting out becomes the only source of power in his universe—it alone has the power to redeem him from the exigencies of the criminal and ghetto games into which he has fallen. 'Traumatic privilege' is his Higher Power, roughly commensurate to the Holy Spirit in the Catholic Trilogy. It is seen by a corrupt world as a criminal power, but the young man knows it to be a noble and morally ascendant power. How many people have the right to decide who lives and who dies? The young gunman does. He may experience that as a form of salvation giving meaning to a violent life, suffusing him with a sweet albeit troubled personal integrity.

And it is not only a response to the circumstances that enslave him, but arises also from his sense that his 'traumatic privilege' is something that normal, average people don't have, and is a form of power that only he—and people like him—can enjoy. It is his ticket to understanding and transcending his unjust and traumatizing world. The addictive nature of this privilege is something he tries to ignore, when he can—and his history tells him to persevere, to keep fighting, even though the Irish always lose. At a critical point the personal trauma merges with the shared traumatic memory of Irish history, and here is what it tells him: *The Irish always lose because they are better than everybody else.* (Certainly better than the money-grubbing, power-worshipping British, who conquered three quarters of the world only to lose their souls.) It is these things, and the 'destructive entitlement' that was institutionalization of murder-by-the-gun, that constituted the trauma bond of the IRA and Sinn Fein in Northern Ireland during the thirty years of 'the Troubles.' But none of this arose out of a vacuum. It was all there in Irish history, waiting to be unpacked and re-activated.

The gunman and his fatal attraction was never put on display better than by Sean O'Casey in *The Shadow of a Gunman*, first performed by the Abbey Theatre in Dublin in 1923. It is a play not so much about an actual gunman—although there is a couple of working-class IRA volunteers who are characters in the play—as about the enormous and dangerous prestige of the gunman in Ireland, who overnight became a figure of legend during the Irish War of Independence in 1919 through 1921. The play tells the story of the mistaken identity of a young man who is thought to be an IRA volunteer, but who actually has no relationship whatsoever to the ongoing street-fighting outside on the streets of Dublin. This young man fraudulently allows an attractive young woman in his rooming house to believe that he is a hardened gunman in order to impress her, when he is anything but.

The duplicity of the young man suggests a certain deceit in the way that Irish society lionized the IRA volunteer, as well as the dangers of identifying with a tradition that has, although it may have at times seemed justified, inevitably corrupted Irish society. After all, had not those same gunmen engaged in an extremely bloody civil war, in 1922-23, when Sean O'Casey's play was first produced, as part of which the Free State supporters actually executed by firing squad scores of their own former IRA comrades? *The Shadow of a Gunman* evokes these tragedies in a delightfully colloquial and consummately ironic (and Irish) way, while at the same time exposing the hypocrisy and brutality of British rule. And it does so in a way that just about everybody could understand. Rarely has a prophet or poet eviscerated his own tribe's totems and bloody fetishes with such a sure hand, while eviscerating his tribe's enemies at the same time; and rarely have they done those things so thoroughly, and yet so gently, in a way that all the world, friend and enemy alike, could see the sorrow and the terrible beauty of it.

Given all that, then, and given the intense negative charisma of the gunman's place in the Irish half-conscious scheme of things, how, then, did the IRA leaders in Northern Ireland during 'the Troubles' break the trauma bond, abandon 'traumatic privilege,' and choose peace? We may never have all the answers to this question, but we know that the people of Northern Ireland were tired of war, tired of the bombs and the killings, the leaders no less than everyone else. And the leaders themselves had to face certain undeniable and terrifying evidence of the systemic evil with which they'd been complicit, not just in the larger society but also in their own families.

10.

Gerry Adams' personal encounter with systemic evil after the Good Friday Agreement came not from the Protestant Establishment, nor even from his past behavior as an IRA commander, but from shocking revelations of incest and sexual abuse of children in his own family. The ninth circle of Dante's *Inferno* is where the sin of treachery is punished, wherein the souls of spiritual traitors are frozen in ice for the crime of betraying humankind's most precious relationships. There is no greater treachery to the modern mind, no greater betrayal, than adults who sexually exploit children; so it is natural, then, that the crime of incest and predatory sexual abuse of children set in motion shock waves of horror and disgust, both in the families personally affected and in society at large. The family, in this case, was perhaps the most famous Republican family in the Republic of Ireland and Northern Ireland, a family under constant scrutiny by friends and enemies alike: the family of Gerry Adams. A country accustomed to odd and unprecedented horrors now had one more horrific mystery to ponder.

As often happens in such cases, the sexual abuse had been secret for some time, at least from the public. The accused were Gerry Adams' father, Gerry Senior, and Gerry's brother, Liam. In a TV interview in 2009 with Aine Adams, daughter of Liam, the painful allegations began to come out. In this program on UTV, Northern Ireland's independent commercial TV station, Aine stated that she had been raped and abused sexually by her father, Liam, for about six years, from 1977 until 1983. Interestingly, she revealed that she had made a report about it to the police in 1987—the Royal Ulster Constabulary, at that time—when she was thirteen years old, but according to the BBC "she did not pursue it" until 2007, when her father Liam was arrested in Dublin.

Shortly after the UTV interview, in December 2009, Gerry Adams dropped a further bombshell. In a statement reported around the world, Gerry Adams revealed that his father—not his brother Liam, but his *father*, the IRA stalwart Gerry Adams, Senior—had sexually abused family members over an extended period of time. The first part of Gerry Adams' carefully-worded statement reads as follows:

In the late 1990s we discovered that our father had been sexually, physically and emotionally abusing members of our family. This abuse happened over many years. This discovery and the abuse that preceded it have had a devastating effect on our family. We are still struggling to come to terms with what happened. We live with the consequences every single day. We have been dealing with this with the support of a number of professionals who have the expertise to deal with these matters. We thank them for their help.

Abuse of any kind is horrendous but sexual abuse, particularly of a child, is indescribably wounding and heartbreaking. Our family have debated for some time whether we should publicize our father's abusive behavior. We do so now in the hope that, in time, this will assist the victims and survivors to come to terms with what happened and help them to move on from these dreadful events.

And there was more: "All citizens need to be educated and children need to be listened to, empowered and protected," the statement says. "Victims of abuse in our family are still, years later, recovering from the trauma inflicted on us." Gerry Adams observes that his family is now united, and that they have determined that "there is a way out of this awfulness." All in all, the experience of sexual abuse in one's own family comes across in this statement as something as overwhelming and difficult to extricate oneself from as any civil war. The statement closes with a cautionary note regarding sexual abuse of children in society: "Anyone affected by these issues should contact the Samaritans or any appropriate agency."

It's a good statement, balanced and compassionate. It's easy to believe that the family is indeed immersed in treatment by counselors, psychiatrists or other professionals, because Gerry Adams uses many of the ideas and even much of the nomenclature of social work and psychological recovery, as well as the language often used by clinicians that specialize in family systems. And his conclusions about what is important in this situation seem like the right ones. But the revelations raised new issues. What did Gerry Adams know, and when did he know it?

The timeline for these events is still a matter of controversy, but it can be set out in outline form as follows: Aine Adams, Gerry Adams' niece, alleged that she was raped and sexually abused by her father over a six-year period from 1977 to 1983. In 1987, she made a police report to the RUC, but didn't follow it up. Sometime in the 1990s—the exact sequence here is foggy—family members compared notes, and the family—including Gerry Adams, Junior—became aware that Gerry Adams, Senior, had engaged in sexual abuse of children in the family, and that the abuse had continued for some time. Then in 2000 came the second bombshell: in Dundalk, County Louth, while Liam Adams and his brother Gerry Adams walked in the rain, Liam Adams confessed to a single incident in which he raped his daughter Aine. (Sexual predators may try to conflate many behaviors into a single incident in order to minimize their guilt, and thus their punishment.) By several accounts Gerry Adams then took his niece Aine and her mother to confront his brother Liam. After this encounter Gerry Adams became convinced of his brother's guilt.

In 2007, after Sinn Fein had voted to accept the newly-reorganized police of Northern Ireland, the Police Service of Northern Ireland (PSNI), Gerry Adams told them about his brother's criminal abuse of his daughter. In 2009 he contacted the PSNI again to tell them that Liam had personally confessed to his crime to him in 2000—that would be important for the police to know, since Gerry Adams could testify under oath to hearing the confession. Liam Adams was extradited to Northern Ireland from Dublin in 2011. In October, 2013, Gerry Adams' brother Liam was found guilty of rape and gross indecency and eight other offenses against his daughter, Aine, and on October 27 was sentenced to prison. Since Gerry Adams, Senior, died in 2003, his alleged crimes can never be adjudicated.

If Aine went so far as to make a police report of her father's abuse in 1987, it seems at first hard to believe that Gerry Adams didn't know about his brother's guilt until 2000—hard to believe, that is, until one considers the extreme secrecy in which sex crimes against children are committed, and the cloak of secrecy that often remains after the crime becomes known in the family. (A deliberate secrecy, in fact, that was not unlike the extreme secrecy in which IRA volunteers learned to operate, and the way in which this psychic habit could be used to conceal crimes against children.) Abuse such as this can go on in a family for decades without the other family members knowing about it—

and that would be especially easy in a family in which secrecy is placed at such a premium.

Some critics ask why Gerry Adams didn't report the criminal offenses of his brother Liam as soon as he found out about them in 2000—why, they ask, did he wait until 2007? The answer is that Republicans—and most Catholics—did not trust the police in Northern Ireland when it was still the Royal Ulster Constabulary, because of its anti-Catholic and anti-Republican past, and because of its perceived collusion with the Protestant paramilitaries; and for that reason, the official policy of Sinn Fein was not to cooperate with it. The police were reorganized into the Police Services of Northern Ireland (PSNI) in 2001; and in 2007 Sinn Fein voted to treat it as a legitimate police, and cooperate with it. Critics reply that in cases of sexual abuse, one cannot pick and choose regarding the behavior of the police agencies responsible for receiving such reports, nor can one put the protocols of one's political organization above the law.

Sinn Fein may not have voted to treat the PSNI as the legitimate police until 2007, say the critics, but according to some that was a case of putting ideology and party discipline above the needs of the sexual abuse victim, whose healing is partially dependent on receiving justice. No doubt the critics have a case here, although it is not a conclusive one. (There may have been other considerations that kept Gerry Adams from reporting the abuse until 2007, such as the need of some family members to receive counseling and psychotherapy before the case became a matter of public knowledge.)

One particularly outspoken critic of Adams has been Eilis O'Hanlon, a journalist in the Republic of Ireland, who has publicly denounced Gerry Adams at length for his failure to report the sexual abuse sooner; indeed, she has an annoying tendency to imply that he was somehow collusive in the abuse itself. She has also written at length against Sinn Fein, arguing (correctly, this writer believes) that it and the IRA are bastions of

Irish patriarchy—but so is the *Irish Independent* and the *Sunday Independent*, for which Eilis O'Hanlon writes, since they have a long history of smearing public figures they dislike, willingly paying out huge damages in libel awards as a kind of legal tribute for the corrupt privilege of printing lies. Ms. O'Hanlon is one of those who believes that Gerry Adams may someday run for Prime Minister in the Republic of Ireland; and although she says she is not trying to use the abuse timeline to "get" Gerry Adams, it is clear that she would like to.

And... like so much in Irish life, there is more to Eilis O'Hanlon's campaign than at first meets the eye. Eilis O'Hanlon's late mother was a lifelong Republican in Belfast, being the sister of long-time IRA commander Joe Cahill; and Eilis is herself the estranged sister of the late Siobhan O'Hanlon, onetime IRA volunteer and longtime aide to Gerry Adams. Her hatred of Sinn Fein, then, is a visceral and obsessive thing, linked to her estrangement from her mother and sister; and like Conor Cruise O'Brien's hatred of Sinn Fein, it is not as helpful as one might imagine, since in both cases critical thought and rational analysis end where prejudice and obsession begin. She is typical, to a large extent, of the way in which much of the discussion about sexual abuse in the family of Gerry Adams—a discussion that Irish society should have, nonetheless—ended up centering almost entirely on the character of Gerry Adams and the politics of O'Hanlon herself, rather than abuse of children.

Gerry Adams first became aware of his own father's abuse of family members in the 1990s, according to what he has said publicly; and if that awareness had come before Good Friday in 1998, and he had told the RUC at that time, there is an excellent chance they would have tried to use the allegations of sexual abuse to turn family members into informers, probably by arresting them one at a time on the charge of failing to report the commission of a crime. I can see why Adams would have wished to avoid that. And after 2001, when the reorganization of the police in the Police Services of Northern Ireland was more or less complete, Sinn Fein had still not decided as a group to trust it. (Remember that it was not until 2007, when Sinn Fein had decided to accept the authority of the PSNI, that Adams reported the abuse of his brother.) Of course, Adams could have reported the abuse, first of his father and then of his brother, to a social service agency which could have maintained a certain level of confidentiality; but considering the extreme bitterness of 'the Troubles,' and the extent to which those troubles subsumed everything else, there is little doubt that it would have leaked out. And then, of course, it is always the case that there were family members who may not have been psychologically ready in 2001 for the world to know about what had happened.

In the end, I find that I cannot judge Gerry Adams' decision, informed by the input of family members, to report to the police the criminal offenses of his brother when he did (in 2007); or the timing of their decision to make public the abuse of his father by releasing a joint family statement about it (2009). Yes, he may have put his Sinn Fein loyalties—and perhaps, without realizing it, his own political career—before the emotional needs of his niece. But that is all too typical of the mistakes people make in struggling to handle these kinds of problems. And like the psychic wounds sustained from thirty years of war, the Adams families will not heal faster by beating themselves up over past mistakes. Learning from their mistakes, and vowing to act differently in the future, is all we can expect of them, and of ourselves.

The reality seems to be that Gerry Adams and his family were all subjected to an unwanted tutorial on the problem that no family wants to have, the problem of sexual, physical and emotional abuse, and how exactly one handles it, especially if one is in public life. This is a part of the larger issue of violence against women and children; but the disgusting injustice of sexual offenses against children is especially difficult to deal with. *Why didn't the family know? Why wasn't more done to protect the innocent ones?* In any family affected by this issue, the questions will keep coming for a very long time. And in roughly the same timeframe that the Adams family was learning how to deal with the revelations of sexual abuse, making mistakes along the way, so was the rest of Northern Ireland. In that part of the world that includes the industrialized democracies, as well as many places in the developing world, we are just starting to come to terms with sexual and physical abuse against women and children, and the family systems and patriarchal values that cause it.

One thing is sure: oppression, war and institutionalized aggression tend to exacerbate violence and abuse against women and children. In times of violent social upheavals, the ones who end up being victimized by aggression the most, in the form of rape and other forms of physical and emotional abuse, are women and children. Sexual abuse against children in families is hard to quantify, naturally, because it is typically kept secret by both predators and victims, and by their families. But when adults are born feeling powerless, or when they are reduced to the powerlessness in an oppressive society that practices extensive discrimination against their religious, racial or tribal group, abusive people within the aggrieved group will take out their aggressions on those that are closest and most defenseless; and some people, almost always men, will end up beating and abusing family members and using them as sexual objects.

The recovery of Gerry Adams' family, like the recovery of Northern Ireland as a nation, is something that will take a long time. It's one more example, sadly, of the way aggression and psychological trauma change everything, starting at the top and working down the social ladder to ultimately harm the weakest and most vulnerable at the bottom, which in a patriarchal society are the women and children.

11.

The blind man's wife needs no paint, it is said; her husband's hands already know the deeper truth about her beauty. If anything good came out of 'the Troubles,' it was that the people of Northern Ireland now appreciate peace in a way most people never will. In Belfast and Derry, they lived for thirty years with the most hideous kind of religious war, as people shot and bombed each other in the dense and impoverished neighborhoods in which they lived; and in that seemingly endless war of treacherous ambushes and monster bombs that could irrevocably maim and take lives in the twinkling of an eye, people lost brothers, spouses, children, parents to faceless assassins. That kind of war is felt in the gut and bones, and the peace that arises afterwards is likewise felt in the gut and bones. The Good Friday Agreement was the great redemption of Northern Ireland: and although it felt like a gift from God (and in some ways may have been), the miraculous reality is that it was made by the people of Northern Ireland themselves.

If there is an Irish tendency toward blind and obsessive fanaticism, there is also an Irish gift for political negotiation. And the special truth that this book examines is the astonishing reality that the larger part of this negotiation came from men addicted to clandestine killing, not to mention worship of the dead. It was born of a traumatic history, this addiction, and acted out in an even more traumatic present. So how, on the Catholic side, did Gerry Adams and the IRA volunteers do it? How did they break free of the unrelenting trauma that bonded them to killing, death and fear? And how should we feel toward the gunman when he puts down the gun: does he redeem his former crimes in the eyes of society by rejecting political violence, or is he still guilty of his crimes?

First, we should acknowledge the centrality of the IRA/Sinn Fein in achieving peace in Northern Ireland. That is important to understand. The parties could have negotiated forever, but if the

IRA did not choose peace, there wouldn't have been any. Just as there would have been no war if the IRA had not chosen armed struggle in 1969, only the IRA could stop the war that arose out of that decision. *The peace process could not have happened without the IRA.* Therefore it was absolutely necessary to include the IRA/Sinn Fein in peace negotiations, because—as experienced negotiators are fond of pointing out—we do not make peace with our friends, but with our enemies.

And to get the IRA into the negotiations, it was necessary for the Protestant establishment to accept that they must remove institutional oppression of Catholics. One of the great ironies of Northern Ireland is that the Protestants, who thought of themselves as British, had for centuries benefitted from a most un-British religious apartheid. This they would have at last to give up—and the entire panoply of British institutions stood ready to explain to them, while listening patiently to their rampant fears and obsessions, the obligations of government in an industrialized democracy in the 21st century. The British played a critical role in helping the Protestants of Northern Ireland deconstruct the oppressive laws, customs and private arrangements that had constituted religious apartheid.

But again: how did the IRA break loose of the trauma bond that operated at the center of the maelstrom that was urban guerilla war? If you accept the fact that political violence in Northern Ireland had an addictive dimension to it, leading both Protestants and Catholics downward into a heart of darkness with each new escalation in violence, how did they recover from it? Part of the answer lies outside social psychology, in the personal human psychologies of the two peoples of Northern Ireland. It's already been pointed out that much political struggle in Ireland contains an unconscious strategy for redemption.

Instead events began to happen, even as 'the Trouble' raged, that made people acutely aware that redemption would come, at least for them, from hard choices that were simultaneously personal and political. There was the young girl who was blinded by a horrific bomb at Omagh (Claire Bowes, nee Gallagher) whose grace and spiritual beauty touched everybody around her. (George Mitchell, the American peace negotiator, was so touched by Claire Bowes that he named his daughter after her.) There was the Protestant man whose daughter was killed in an IRA explosion who subsequently begged the Protestant paramilitaries not to retaliate for her death. There were a multitude of such events, many unknown and most never to be known, in which individuals began to realize that they could not go on with their old retaliatory business as usual, and that their society had to change *fundamentally* in order to redeem itself. And something told them that the change, although it must be institutional, had to begin with them as individuals, in the very midst of their own troubled lives.

With each act of terrorism, the IRA volunteer's thrill of exhilaration at a successful operation is closely followed by fear, depression and guilt. Those negative emotions can only be successfully repressed by engaging in another operation, which in turn enhances the internalized aggression, and reinforces the gunman's violent lifestyle. But after each act of violence the negative emotions of fear (what if I die tomorrow?) repressed guilt (it could have been me) and hatred (the Brits/Prods make us do this because they oppress us) are also enhanced. These negative emotions can only be successfully repressed by participating in yet another violent operation, which leads to even more negative emotions. The addictive nature of that kind of violence is experienced on a personal as well as a society-wide level. It is the very essence of trauma bonding in civil war.

And then there were the claustrophobic pressures under which the IRA operated, which were probably almost intolerable, despite the momentary excitement of successful operations. (Thus the very high rate of alcoholism.) Above all was the fear of being killed at any moment. In an interview with Tim Pat

Coogan, editor of the Irish Press and probably Ireland's greatest living journalist, Gerry Adams casually mentioned that a few weeks before the interview with Coogan, his wife and child had been subjected to a grenade attack at their home, luckily escaping injury; the casual way Adams mentioned it left Coogan with the impression that such attacks were simply a part of his life, and that he accepted them as such. Adams was shot at innumerable times; in March 1984 a squad of Ulster Freedom Fighters almost took him out for good, putting three bullets into him, from which he recovered.

The descent into political violence can be accompanied by alcoholism or other substance abuse or, as in the case of two of the men in Gerry Adams' family, by predatory sexual abuse. This latter trauma has many levels, beginning with the abuse itself, and creating more shock waves as knowledge of it percolates through the family and the tribe, and then becomes public knowledge; then, if the family has some special fame or notoriety, the affected family must confront it along with the effect it is having on the public at large. It is an extraordinary thing to realize that at the very time that Gerry Adams was fighting other men in a guerilla war, the cancer of incest was eating away at the core of his extended family, with its horrible toll on the mental health and self-esteem of the children involved. How could he know? He was too busy with other things. And there are indications that Adams himself understands his culpability in that regard. In familial as well as political aggression, there is always 'collateral damage'—a horrible phrase that simply means that violence is experienced in different ways, but most traumatically by the weakest, the women and children, who are ironically most innocent.

Alcoholism is part of the Irish story, and one senses that Gerry Adams had his struggles with it. What we know for sure is that he started his working life as a barman in a pub, and at some point along the way became a teetotaler. One of his big complaints after entering the Irish Dail Eireann in the Republic of Ireland was to remonstrate against the parliament's habit of leaving the Dail's pub open until four AM on the nights of important votes. When did Gerry Adams stop drinking, and why? How did he do it? We don't know and probably never will, but there is enough anecdotal evidence among former IRA volunteers to know that alcohol and alcoholism is a huge untold story in the IRA and Sinn Fein leadership. (One thinks of the 2005 drunken brawl in which two IRA volunteers killed another, and tried to cover it up.) And the progressive nature of alcoholism— progressive in the sense that it always gets worse—often seems to run parallel to the progression of political violence.

There comes a point in the course of an addiction—let us say alcoholism, because of its cultural relevance to the Irish—in which the addict reaches a point where he simply can't go on. He will either go mad, kill himself (often with an overdose), or act out some gratuitous physical violence that will put him in prison for life. Or he will try to recover from his addiction. What awaits him if he tries to live without his comfort drug he does not know; all he knows is that he cannot go on as he has before. This is commonly known as "hitting bottom" in recovery circles. To get better—that is, to recover—he will probably have to receive help from others. This often includes help from other alcoholics or addicts who have similarly chosen to live without the substance that was once at the center of their lives.

Once the alcoholic has crossed the line into alcoholic drinking, or the addict traverses into addictive rather than recreational use, the only safe recovery for many people is to never use the drink or the drug again. If alcoholism and addictions are, as this writer believes, something very close to a personality disorder, the decision to put down the drink or the drug is an unbelievably wrenching one. The most painful part will be living a daily life in which the person in recovery can no longer use a sedative for emotional pain. He is entering a completely different kind of world, the world of sobriety, with its own byways and hypocrisies, its own conventions and privileges. It will feel different, and its values are different. All the traumatic memories the alcoholic or addict had repressed and anesthetized must now be faced and dealt with in real time; it is now time for looking in the mirror, and the long conversations with bottled-up demons. All these things start to happen when the alcoholic "hits bottom."

That is the reason why the IRA/Sinn Fein was able to make such a dramatic turn in its fortunes: they were addicted to political violence, and then, after the addiction threatened to destroy them, they—to their own endless surprise—hit bottom. Imagine: here is an organization that long demanded (throughout most of the whole 20th century, in fact) that Northern Ireland had to break off its connections to Britain, so that Northern Ireland could become part of the Republic of Ireland. That was demonstrably impossible, but countless IRA volunteers died making exactly that demand. And now, the IRA/Sinn Fein acknowledges that it cannot be done at the present time. (For one thing, everybody needs the Brits to make sure that the conventions of the Good Friday Agreement are followed.)

Of course, Gerry Adams believes that his organization can use politics to make the case for the eventual reunification of Ireland, and hopes that over time the Protestants of Northern Ireland can be convinced to give up their ancient cultural and political identification with Britain. But by adopting peaceful means to make their case, IRA/Sinn Fein acknowledge, without saying as much, that unification may never happen. There are no guarantees, one way or the other.[28] That is cultural and emotional growth of a kind the world rarely sees.

And all this happened, this writer believes, because the IRA/Sinn Fein hit bottom in their addiction to violence, arising from their 30-year war of attrition in Northern Ireland against the Protestants and the British. To be sure, the position of Catholics in Northern Ireland was greatly improved, to a great extent because of the insistence of the British government that the Protestants reform their society, as well as pressure emanating from Catholic parties to the conflict. But the other demands, the demands that could never be met in the real world, had to be given up. The horror of the war could not be sustained. The gunmen could recover from their addiction to violence and coercion, go mad, or die—and if the war had gone on, Northern Ireland would surely have died, slowly and agonizingly. So the gunman had to give up his gun.

Of course, there were distinct benefits awaiting Sinn Fein as a political party. Sinn Fein has become the third largest party in Ireland as a whole, and the second-largest party in the power-sharing Northern Ireland Executive, with four ministerial posts. Adams and his Sinn Fein comrades apparently decided that his notoriety had become a distraction in Northern Ireland, and that he would be better employed in the Republic to the south. In the election of 2011, Gerry Adams left Northern Ireland to effort-lessly win a seat from Louth in the parliament of the Republic of Ireland. Sinn Fein is the fourth-largest party in the Oireachtas, the parliament of that Republic, but with excellent prospects for the future—health and education seem to be its main issues. Click on the website of Sinn Fein, and you'll see four very nice-looking young people standing around Gerry Adams, two women and two young men, and a great deal of thoughtful infor-mation about various political positions they are promoting, positions that could be described as progressive in the social-democratic sense, but not necessarily radical.

In short, in the words of the Wikipedia entry regarding Gerry Adams, under his leadership Sinn Fein has gone from being a revolutionary movement to becoming "a professionally organized political party in both Northern Ireland and in the Republic of Ireland." Indeed. Gerry Adams' personal political prospects are rocky in the short term, because other politicians are afraid of him; there will be a long period in the Republic during which no other party will dare make a coalition with Sinn Fein. But if Sinn Fein continues to pursue thoughtful policies, feelers will gradually manifest themselves.

Her majesty's government made its contribution to the 1998 peace settlement (after a discreet interval) in a uniquely understated British way, by raising to the peerage anybody likely to undermine the Good Friday Agreement. By so gentrifying the rough cobs in the equation, so to speak, the occasional contrarian opinion or lunatic behavior might be made to seem eccentric rather than sinister, and then politely ignored. In June 2006 David Trimble was created Baron Trimble of Lisnagarvey in the County of Antrim, and was made a lifetime peer. Lord Trimble (whose full title is the deliciously lugubrious *The Right Honorable The Lord Trimble of Lisnagarvey)* promptly bailed from the rowdily sectarian United Unionist Party to join the much calmer, predictably patrician Conservative Party, and has furnished the world with a website outlining his adventures in the House of Lords. These consist mainly of making speeches and writing short articles of a surpassing, but not unpleasant, mediocrity.

The scabrous Ian Paisley was created a life peer as Baron Bannside, of North Antrim in the County of Antrim, in June 2010. In a speech to the House of Lords later that year he interrupted the afternoon slumbers of the assembled peerage by mysteriously revealing that there were certain Secretaries of State that he would have liked to "punch," but that "we neither punched them nor disagreed with them in a muscular fashion, and today we are here in the quiet of this House." Nor was John Hume bereft of honors—both he and David Trimble shared a Nobel Prize for their labors on behalf of peace.

I have seen film footage of Gerry Adams speaking in the Republic of Ireland, in the Dail Eireann, for more transparency in the government management of charities in Ireland. He is softspoken, thoughtful, courteous and sometimes politely ironic. He throws in a sentence of two in Irish from time to time, an implicit rebuke to many of the mainstream politicians in the Republic who have perhaps let their Irish language skills lapse a bit. He presents as very much like most of the other politicians in the chamber, although better-looking and somewhat better organized; his gentle demeanor seems to say, *this is business as usual*. Yet people are quiet when he speaks, and there are probably few people who can forget the tumultuous events of which he was lately a part. Some fault him for betraying the revolutionary nature of Sinn Fein to improve his personal political opportunities, and perhaps there is some truth in that. But most people will tolerate and even celebrate personal ambition, if it will lead from killing to peace without killing. And they are right to do so.

So how does one regard Gerry Adams, the former terrorist and IRA commander who became a statesman? Did he redeem himself for rejecting violence and adopting the arts of peace? He has indeed sought and achieved redemption, although not quite in the way most people might imagine. Peace with justice was the great prize; and the cost of it—and it was a cost that had to be paid—was an amnesty for both Protestant and Catholic paramilitaries, which meant leaving unpunished untold thousands of crimes committed by those that murdered in the name of the armed Protestant and Catholic groups, of which the IRA was one. The people of Northern Ireland had no choice but to accept that as a price that needed paying; and if possible forgive their enemies—and themselves—simply because that was the best way to move on. That is not acquiescence but acceptance, and is the hard compromise that must sometimes be hammered out when people go from war to peace. Some can do it, and some can't; but the truth is that there was no other way to make peace in Northern Ireland.

As for Gerry Adams, there is little doubt that he was the most energetic and articulate advocate for a peace agreement within Sinn Fein and the Irish Republican Army, and played a major role in negotiating the Good Friday Agreement. Yet even many who agree with this advocacy, and are profoundly grateful for it, will long continue to have their nightmares and their shadow encounters with the demons of traumatic memory, because for them there is no forgetting the past. Nor will those blinded and maimed by terrorist bombs long be able to forget their wounds. But it is the people *of the future* that will benefit from the transformation of Sinn Fein from a party of guerilla war into a "professionally organized political party," and the peace that followed logically from that transformation. Some people will be uneasy with this, and they are welcome to their unease: there's plenty of it to go around in Ireland. But the hard home truth is that achieving peace in Northern Ireland was more important than the settling of scores, whether on the street or in a court of law.

Gerry Adams fought his way out of the deep trauma of the Irish quagmire, and brought countless others along with him. He did this, *first*, by talking openly about the unacceptable condition of Catholics in Northern Ireland, and then about the necessity of achieving IRA/Sinn Fein goals politically. In seeking peace, he challenged the traumatic memory of centuries and disestablished the 'traumatic privilege' of the gunman. He also spoke out publicly about the sexual abuse that had occurred in his family. *Second*, he acted in a socially-beneficial manner to lead the campaign for the Good Friday Agreement, first within Sinn Fein and the IRA, and then in Northern Ireland as a whole. Countless generations of the future, especially the precious children and young people, will be spared the horrors of sectarian guerilla warfare because of the Good Friday Agreement. It is because of what Gerry Adams did *for them* that he, and others that accepted political compromise in order to negotiate a lasting peace, have achieved redemption.

Chapter Six

'Stealing' the Holocaust: Deconstructing Traumatic Memory, Resisting Systemic Evil

Clearly I must introduce my Holocaust to you so that you can understand the splendor of which I was robbed. I must also share with you the story of its theft, for otherwise you won't know how a Holocaust is stolen, will you?
Noam Chayut, *The Girl Who Stole My Holocaust—A Memoir*

The Girl Who Stole My Holocaust—a Memoir is an astonishing coming-of-age reminiscence by Israeli author Noam Chayut, a bitterly introspective *Bildungsroman* of war and oppression that has many of the literary characteristics of *The Things They Carried*, the Tim O'Brien Vietnam memoir referenced in this book's chapter on war trauma. Like *The Things They Carried*, it employs many of the literary conventions associated with 'metafiction,' a type of writing that seems realistic on the surface but nonetheless contains both real and imaginary elements, travels forwards and backwards in time, and self-consciously (and often ironically) attracts attention to itself as a literary exercise rather than a sequential narrative.

It tells a story, but it is usually a story about emotions rather than chronological events. It is a style particularly appropriate to writing about war, because in jumping from events in the past to emotions in the present, and creating stories about powerful emotional orientations rather than clearly defined events, it simulates the effects of psychological trauma in war.

Chayut's memoir has many of the markings of an archetypical experience: A young man grows up in Israel, living through and emotionally absorbing the full range of experiences typically encountered by people growing up there. Embedded deep in

Israeli culture (and what we might call the collective Israeli unconscious) is the shared traumatic memory of the Holocaust, which keeps showing up in public ceremonies, personal relationships and certain entrenched public attitudes; furthermore, it is constantly referenced by right-wing political leaders. According to the right-wing political parties, the Holocaust—since it is history's greatest crime—invariably justifies Israel's aggression against perceived enemies of the state.

Furthermore, many of these right-wing leaders in Israel insist that identification with the horror of the Holocaust is essential to Jewish identity. Israeli children in the 11th or 12th grades are regularly transported to Poland to visit the death camps Auschwitz and Majdanek, and on those trips are subjected to indoctrination by right-wing teachers, counselors and state security personnel, who tell them that the entire world hates Jews, that their only hope is Israel, and that they must support the Jewish state unhesitatingly. Otherwise, the children are told, another Holocaust may happen. It is in that atmosphere of dread, traumatic memory and internalized aggression that our narrator-author is raised.

Noam Chayut unquestioningly internalizes the aggressive emotional orientations associated with this kind of indoctrination, although he increasingly sees there is something simplistic and self-serving about it; in any case, he internalizes enough of what he experiences to become a successful officer in the Israeli Defense Force (IDF). But as an IDF officer he witnesses the systematic violations of Palestinians' human rights inherent to Israel's military occupation. One day he sees a young Palestinian girl looking at him in terror, then turning to run away—that is, she is running away from the military unit in which he is an officer. Suddenly he realizes that the Holocaust, which happened in the *past*, can no longer justify brutal oppression in the *present*.

This ignites a tumultuous emotional upheaval in Chayut's

personality, which takes him several months—years, actually—to completely process, to understand, and to come to terms with. Eventually he quits the military and joins 'Breaking the Silence,' a group of Israeli veterans who speak publicly about the violations of human rights committed by the Israeli Defense Force in the Occupied Palestinian Territories (OPT).

This is an important—and probably representative—story for several reasons. Chayut's memoir is, first of all, a narrative about the dangerous and often cynical way that right-wing politicians in Israel and elsewhere manipulate traumatic memory. Specifically, it is a case study of the way that traumatic memory of the Holocaust is used to keep a harsh right-wing government in power, and to disseminate openly racist ideas throughout the Israeli political class. The right-wing parties in Israel constantly refer to the Holocaust as the pivotal event of history, and encourage Israelis to identify with it, while insisting that their own political and military behavior as merely a response to it: torture, extrajudicial executions, imprisonment without trial, and collective punishment. Chayut's memoir, in other words, is a detailed and honest look at Israel's use of 'traumatic privilege,' the personal cost of that strategy for individual soldiers, and Noam Chayut's decision to break free of it and seek a better way.

Clearly the Holocaust is quite useful in keeping in power those in the Israeli political class who use the shared traumatic memory of the *past* to bond people to state violence in the *present*. They not only believe that past injustice justifies brutality in the present, they feel it on a very deep level, as most right-wing religious nationalists tend to do; and they are therefore quite passionate, and quite successful, in eliciting those same emotional orientations in others who share a common traumatic memory. That is the power of the trauma bond on a mass basis in Israel.

The Girl Who Stole My Holocaust also tells the story of one person, the author Noam Chayut, who sees through the volatile dark matter of Israeli *hasbara*[1] and embarks on educating the world about the things he saw and witnessed as part of the considerable brutality of Israel's occupation of Palestinian territories, an occupation that has now morphed into an ill-concealed colonial strategy of slow ethnic cleansing. Therefore this book, while it is important for the rest of the world to read, is of even greater value to the Israelis themselves, because it is a personal story of one Israeli's pilgrimage to emotional freedom and social justice. Such an incredible journey was not only facilitated, but actually made possible by, the author's courageous reverse-engineering of the political uses of traumatic memory by the current Israeli government.

2.

Noam's first consciousness of the Holocaust came from his youthful participation in a Holocaust Memorial ceremony at his Israeli *moshav* [farm village] when he was in the fourth grade; and the memory, as he describes it, is both hilarious and disturbing, since it coincides with his first awareness of sexuality, which arrives in the form of his first erection. At the end of the Holocaust Memorial Day ceremony, he writes, he asked a pretty girl in his group to be his girlfriend. He remembers crying during the ceremony, too, but in his memory that emotion is somehow mixed up with his feelings for the pretty girl whose cheeks were "chubby, red and wet with enticing tears."

Holocaust Memorial Day was when "everyone gets serious, wears a deep and concentrated look and cries together, mourning the 'splendor of youth and glory of courage.' *Do not forget, do not forgive*," intones the speaker during an opening prayer; yet even as they grieve the victims of the Holocaust, the young people in this Israeli farming village are also focused on their own gamut of juvenile pranks, games and secret obsessions common to children of all times and places. Perhaps because of that—and because of the way memory works—it might be easy for a child's memory to be filled with an oppressive sense of the Nazi Holocaust as something horrifying in the past, but also something eternally threatening in the present moment; a danger that can only be kept at arm's length through constant exertions and never-ending acts of courage. As Chayut tells it, a deep—and sometimes desperate—sense of shared traumatic memory is the powerful, elemental, and charismatic force that seemed to hold the farming community of Noam Chayut's youth together.

"I acutely remember the unbearable feeling I experienced during one of those [Holocaust] ceremonies. For years afterwards it would flood back, filling me to bursting whenever I watched Holocaust Memorial Day films, black and white with horrible camera work. They showed naked, emaciated human beings piled on top of each other or stuffed into train cars, or standing in endless lines waiting to be incinerated, shot dead or just plain humiliated." The boy's queries about the inexplicable nature of human evil were answered by adults who simply said that "the perpetrators were Nazis, were *absolute evil*, and such evil did not *make sense* the way normal people's actions did—and if there was no sense, naturally everything was possible."

Of course, the Nazi Holocaust happened not as a random cosmic accident, but as the result of human evil. Yet that evil occurred in association with specific historical, cultural and psychological forces that can be studied and analyzed. But if you're a victim of the Holocaust, or you're underground or on the run because of it, the situation is no longer answerable to logic: it has moved beyond reason into an omnipresent sense of total horror and desperation. And because of the traumatic memory of that desperation that arose at the very height of the Nazi Holocaust, and the multigenerational trauma that keeps such feelings alive, a great many people will inevitably experience those feelings in the same way in 1959 or 1989 or 2009: as something beyond normal comprehension, and indeed almost paranormal, and therefore beyond reason.

455

But of course *everybody* is capable of evil, given the right historical circumstances, including Jews—but that kind of introspection was probably not a sensibility that most Jewish parents in Israel wished to convey as Noam Chayut was growing up, because it could raise questions about Jewish behavior in the Promised Land. The evil *they* wanted to convey was the evil first of the Nazis, and then of the Arabs, because the Arabs were still experienced as an existential threat to the new country. A great many people—especially those associated with Likud and the religious parties—discovered that it was all too easy to continue to see themselves as victims long *after* the Holocaust: victim status is uncannily seductive, partly because the victim is always right, and therefore never has to do anything or make any changes.

That's a perfect way to avoid dealing with the awesome moral responsibilities involved with running a country, especially one engaged in a brutal military occupation. Furthermore, many Israelis were—and still are—unable to contemplate the malignant effects of Jewish nationalism on state power, because Jews have never had the collective experience of wielding political and military power before. It was a new experience, and Israelis had no idea how many ways it could go wrong. Thus the Likudniks consciously encourage the backward-looking fascination with victim status, which has combined with an aggressive religious nationalism to drive Israel rapidly to the right politically; and in the US these elements, among Jews and right-wing evangelical Christians, would someday contribute to the neo-conservative call for religious war.

To Noam Chayut, the feelings evoked by Holocaust Memorial Day were the same as those aroused on the Memorial Day for Fallen Soldiers—the day to remember Israel's war dead; and to the extent that both days were ruled by thoughts of the dead, both had become conflated in his mind, emotions and memory. The idea generally invoked on these days of remembrance was that the world was perpetually intent on harming the Jews; the only difference was that in the Fallen Soldiers ceremonies the focus is on the perfidious Arab rather than the malevolent Nazi. What child in Chayut's *moshav* didn't know the story of the siege of Jerusalem, and the betrayal of those who sought to bring food to besieged Jews?

The story goes something like this: A man from Noam's *moshav*, along with some forty-four others, sets off to smuggle food to besieged Jews in Jerusalem. On the way they meet an 'Arab'[2] shepherd, and beg him not to tell his 'Arab' friends where they're headed. Of course, the shepherd boy betrays them, and the forty-four perish. The point is simple: never trust the 'Arabs.' (This can be also interpreted as suggesting, without being terribly explicit about it, that under certain circumstances prisoners of war can be killed, as both Israelis and Egyptians did in the October War of 1973.) The more generalized point is painfully transparent: the evil of the Nazis has been replaced by the evil of the 'Arabs,' but is the very same in both cases: it has no rational basis! It didn't *make sense* in any way that normal people could acknowledge; therefore negotiation with it was out of the question. It could only be resisted, and those Arabs that acted on it had to be obliterated, imprisoned or collectively punished by the state.

An unconscious but often hilarious rebellion against the emotional blackmail inherent in Zionist nation-building soon makes its appearance in *The Girl Who Stole my Holocaust*. Naom takes up the trumpet in fifth grade, as a result of a grandiose plan to play at ceremonies celebrating the dead, or perhaps at recruiting get-togethers where the IDF marching song is featured. "I distinctly remember the first memorial ceremony where I played the trumpet. It was a total fiasco. IDF Memorial Day is a serious event where not even a snicker is tolerated. So no tomatoes were hurled at me on such a solemn occasion, but still some people bothered to comment: 'Something went wrong there when you played.'"

Naom's unconscious rebellion begins to resemble sabotage, or at the very least self-sabotage. He is supposed to play the trumpet when the flag is lowered on IDF Memorial Day, and then raise it again on the next day, which was Independence Day—but Chayut manages to "forget" to raise the flag. "And so our flag always remained at half mast, and still every year we would lower it anew, as if to verify that we still do get very sad. For me this was rather convenient, as the bugle call for lowering the flag was much easier to play than the call for raising it."

'Playing war' is the amusement of choice among the boys in the *moshav*, and many of the girls as well, a game rigidly reinforced by the summer camps most children attended. At one of the youth camps that Naom attends he has a special role in night maneuvers. "I walked at the end of the line with my friend Ran, who was much cooler and better-looking than I. When the call 'grenade!' rang out, we lay down last, facing each other. After waiting on the ground for a long time, we had to make sure none of the kids had fallen asleep—from battle fatigue, or from staying up late to pull pranks, like painting the faces of the girls while they slept or stealing flags from nearby encampments. Ran and I knew we were putting ourselves at risk, but we also knew it was for the good of the whole force. Just like Nathan Elbaz did."

The troubling story of Nathan Elbaz was apparently a big favorite with camp counselors. Nathan Elbaz, it turned out, was a soldier whose job had been to take care of grenades, the detonators of which were supposed to be neutralized. One day one of Nathan's grenades, for reasons unknown, emitted a tell-tale *click* that meant that Nathan had exactly four seconds to figure out a response. Many soldiers were sitting out in a nearby ditch, where he might otherwise have thrown the grenade, and there were too many soldiers around the tent. He decided to sacrifice his own life to save the lives of his comrades. He fell on the grenade, heroically protecting everyone in his vicinity from the lethal effects of its blast, and at the same time killing himself.

"On one Memorial Day, our counselor asked us if we would do what Nathan Elbaz the hero did: after all, he could have thrown the grenade far away and then his mates would only have been wounded, and he wouldn't have been hurt at all. But no, not Nathan Elbaz. He didn't risk his friends' lives. He jumped on the grenade."

"At this time there were still battle and sacrifice stories mixed up in my mind with tales of vampires threatening to suck my blood. But Nathan Elbaz really did jump over the grenade. His story was real. Unlike the vampire stories, there was no surprise ending that saved everyone from danger. Instead, at the end of Nathan's story was the question: Would you do as he did? Would you die for our sake? And you?"

There was little question in Noam's mind that he wants to soak up the glory of being a war hero. "I wanted stories to be told about me, about my courage, my resourcefulness and cleverness. I dreamt of being a battle hero." But Chayut makes no attempt to answer the counselor's portentous existential question (*would you fall on a grenade?*), and seems at about this point to have become conscious of his conflicted feelings about the macho posturing going on around him. After all, performing heroically in battle and then living to enjoy the resulting acclaim was one thing; ending one's own life to benefit one's friends seemed a less attractive prospect.

It is at this point in the story of Noam's rather rocky progress toward manhood that the real indoctrination goes into high gear. "Like everybody else," he writes, "I traveled to Poland with our school delegation. We Jewish Israeli high school students got to visit the death-camp of Auschwitz and other Holocaust commemoration sites as a part of our national grooming, a year before we graduated and enlisted in the military. On the same bus as our group was a delegation from the Israel Air Force technical school, so we had boys in uniform. Throughout the trip, the Air Force flag was flown along with the Israeli flag, all the more impressive and official looking for it."

Chayut's own account of his experience at Auschwitz suggests the conflicted emotions generated by such an experience. "In Poland I was proud and happy. The piles of shoes and ash at Auschwitz and Majdanek, and the stories of the witness who accompanied us (who had been one of Dr. Mengele's 'children'), the descriptions of starvation in the woods—all these are not exactly a recipe for happiness, of course, but still I was happy." The overwhelming sense of Chayut's often fragmentary memory of this time is that the Holocaust became central to his own identity, to his experience of being Jewish; but it is clear that he did not completely understand what that meant, or why the people who organized this trip thought it was so important to connect the Holocaust to one's Jewish identity. Nor does Chayut report any conscious attempt to teach values that could keep Israeli Jews from slipping into the same emotional orientations as the Europeans that had participated in the Holocaust.

Noam sang *kaddish*, the traditional Jewish prayer for the dead, for his dead relatives, during which he found himself weeping along with the other children there. "I burst into very real tears and wept for a very long time, a loud, visceral, unstoppable weeping. It was the first time I ever read this list that we were asked to bring along and my mother prepared for me before we left. It was photocopied from the town register of Sokolka. What a horrible list: names and names and more names, truly depressing." Afterwards he concludes that there was something questionable about grieving for so many people he'd never known, and tellingly refers to his dead grandfather as an 'imaginary' figure. How, he seems to be asking, can you really grieve for people you've never met?

"I had not worked on a roots project in the seventh grade, not even copied my sisters' projects, as did many other third sons of deep-rooted families. I was lazy, just as I was too lazy to photocopy that list myself or at least give it a glace before our departure, and that's why I didn't know how large my family had been. And perhaps, too, because my grandfather passed away long before I was born and my grandmother did not even live long enough to celebrate my father's Bar Mitzvah, and so I had no one to relate that huge murdered family to." But seeing the list of dead ancestors, or at least those who had the name from which the Hebrew transliteration Chayut had supposedly been derived—seeing them, moreover, in the very bowels of Auschwitz, in a place where they might have died a horrible death—opens the floodgates; and he finds himself overwhelmed by tears and emotion that he does not quite understand.

The Auschwitz experience at first empowers him, even as Noam senses its dark side. "Now, in Poland, as a high school adolescent, I began to sense belonging, self-love, power and pride, and the desire to contribute, to live and be strong, so strong that no one would ever try to hurt me." His trumpet-playing was also now seen in a different light. "As I played I took revenge on all those who hated us. If any Nazi villain, I thought, is hiding in Argentina or Brazil, if some miserable train worker of that war is now sitting in his living room in Germany or Poland, he is surely going crazy at the thought that in spite of all the extermination efforts, our State has come into being."

"This was sweet revenge. I drew power from my Holocaust and this power pushed me on, to want to enlist and serve in a select recon unit, possibly in the Nahal[3], for my dad served there and that would strengthen my roots. (And also because there are fewer bullies in the Nahal and my time there would be more fun.)" He is aware of the connection—constantly stressed by the counselors and security people associated with this program—between going to Auschwitz in one's junior or senior years, and then embracing the opportunity to serve in the Israeli Defense Force. "This is the force that later pushed me to go to officers' training at the end of my training as a combatant."

But by this time some competing emotions are beginning to haunt him. To put it simply, he was surrounded by a military culture that was also a culture of duplicity; this was—and is— certainly not unique to Israel, but was nonetheless at odds with the purity of the youthful nationalism with which Chayut had been indoctrinated at such length; and even more at odds with the shining public-relations image of life in Israel that the government wanted to project. "I had been instructed that 'credibility and truth are foremost in the army,' but I never realized they didn't really mean it. Even years later, when I would join 'Breaking the Silence'[4] and would tell anyone, any journalist who listened, how houses were blasted and what it was like to use a human shield and how it felt to command a dozen soldiers and 2,500 Palestinians on a normal 'workday' at Qalandiya Checkpoint[5]—even then I would still think that credibility and truth come first."

"It would take a long time for me to gradually realize that for many people, truth is worth nothing. When I realized this I was deeply disappointed in human nature, just as I felt when as a child, I discovered what rape was and was ashamed of being male, and just as I felt when I discovered how many guys cheated on pilot training exams. There were only a few nerds who watched their ass and they didn't really mind what the others did. When the squadron commander arrived to deliver a speech about credibility and warned us not to cheat, I wondered whether he had once been one of the few nerds and not like all the rest. Suddenly, I didn't believe him. I got sick to my stomach and cried that night, cried like a kid on the shoulder of my buddy, the other nerd in the course."

"I cried because I missed my girlfriend, and because of the lies. Everyone lied. Even I lied. I had lied to her two years earlier. I had gone as a 'young ambassador' to represent our country in Argentina and Chile. I told them what a cool place Israel was and that they shouldn't listen to the news about us because everyone lied and we in Israel only wanted peace, and that boys and children were the same everywhere, maybe except for those in countries where they are brainwashed and it was not their fault." While in Chile, Noam also cheats on his girlfriend with another girl.

Once in the military, he talks to a brother pilot-in-training about his emotional fatigue regarding the nonstop duplicity they seem to be a part of; and that same brother officer uses the information obtained during this little heart-to-heart chat to seduce Noam's girlfriend just twenty-four hours after Noam breaks up with her. The young Noam Chayut experiences duplicity—both national and personal—as a kind of spiritual weight that one must carry, a weight that always gets heavier rather than lighter, freighted with the Israeli façade of victim status and Noam's somewhat queasy identification with—or rather, his inability to *really* identify with—the six million dead Jews of Europe. The constant emphasis on the Holocaust, military service and unquestioning obedience to the state do little to make his burden lighter, or his questions easier. From a very early age it feels to him like there is something subtly out of kilter in the entire process of growing up in Israel; but he lacks the perspective, not to mention the life experience, to figure out what it is, and what to do about it.

3.

The Holocaust program Noam Chayut writes about is called 'March of the Living,' which is an Israeli program that arranges for the yearly transportation of tens of thousands of Israeli youth to the ruins of the World War Two death camps (Auschwitz and Majdanek) in Poland. The state carefully prepares them for their trip with ideological discussions led by right-wing teachers, counselors and Israeli state security personnel, who accompany them on their pilgrimage to the sites of the Holocaust death camps. Its objective is not to teach history, but rather what can only be called a form of state indoctrination.

In fact, the entire program is a classic example—if a particularly disturbing one—of the way in which traumatic memory can be intentionally imposed upon young people by the state. And the young people themselves have little choice in the matter, since many of their adult mentors in school, youth associations, and in the summer camps they attend, are constantly telling them they should participate in this program. It is also conceived by the Israelis as a way to prepare them for military service.

The upshot is that millions of Jewish children are taught that identifying with those who died in the Holocaust (not those who *opposed* the Holocaust but those who *perished* in it) is central to being a Jew. But to make the Holocaust pivotal to Jewish identity, in such a way that one's personality and social identity are built around it, is a sadly mistaken and extremely dangerous strategy. It gives entirely too much power to the Holocaust itself—you cannot base *identity* on the Holocaust without also internalizing its *aggression*, because you cannot take in one without the other. The immediate effect, consciously intended by the founders of the 'March of the Living' program, is to make good soldiers and to bond young people to the state, since these same founders have convinced themselves that the state of Israel in its current right-wing incarnation is all that stands between them and the destruction of the Jewish people.

But what the young people in 'March of the Living' are really bonded to, through a variety of spookily effective candlelit rituals inside the death camps themselves, is the aggression of the Holocaust itself. Traumatic memory of the Holocaust is used to bond the children to each other, as well as to the Israeli state, preparing them emotionally for the ecstasy of service in the Israeli Defense Force—during which many of the young people will presumably be able to act out the aggression they have internalized against the Palestinians.

One highly interested observer of all this governmental indoctrination was a bright young Israeli man named Yoav Shamir, who decided to make a film about these yearly pilgrimages—or at least the most important aspects of them—called *Defamation*, a film that eventually ended up winning a large number of awards. *Defamation* opens with the filmmaker haunted by a question he cannot answer, a question about his country and about himself. Why, he asks, are the Israelis so obsessed with the Holocaust sixty years after it happened—and with anti-Semitism generally? Why not more emphasis on positive goals for the future? Here they are, a brand-new country, and all the media and government can talk about are the tragedies of the past.

"In the Israeli media I kept hearing three words, 'Nazi,' 'Hitler' and 'Holocaust.' That struck me as strange, living in a country that was supposed to provide a safe place for Jews. And hearing about anti-Semitism all the time made me curious, because I'd never experienced it." So—exactly what *was* this thing, anti-Semitism? Is it one form of bigotry among many others, or is it the dark matter that drives all human consciousness, as many Israelis seem to think? Seeking answers, Shamir goes to a conservative newspaper to interview a renowned Israeli journalist (a Holocaust survivor), who tells him that *everybody* is anti-Semitic, at least outside Israel.[6]

The renowned journalist's assistant shows him information on a computer to demonstrate how widespread anti-Semitism is, remarking rather innocently—but tellingly—that anti-Semitism is newsworthy because "it sells more newspapers." When Shamir asks him where he gets his information about anti-Semitism, the assistant says it comes from the famous Anti-Defamation League in New York, supposedly the largest and most well-funded Jewish organization in the world, headed by the famous Abraham Foxman. So Shamir decides to visit Mr. Foxman, the Director of the ADL, hoping to find out more about this mysterious subject. (Thus the film's subtitle, *Anti-Semitism: the Movie*.)

That's the setup for the film, which proceeds to explore those two explosive but nonetheless intimately connected issues: the career and allegations of the ADL's Abraham Foxman, and the state indoctrination of Israeli teenagers through the 'March of the Living.' The connection, he quickly discovers, lies in the way Foxman—and Israel's Likud government—exaggerate the presence and influence of anti-Semitism in order to raise money and enhance political power. The editing of the film follows an emotional rather than a narrative logic, as Shamir takes the viewer through his personal hegira; he turns out of be a kind of post-modern pilgrim with genius-level satiric instincts, and a deadpan manner of asking questions and making observations that could be described as *The Good Soldier Schweik* meets *Catch-22*, with a pinch of Lenny Bruce maybe.

Such is the complexity of his film, however (not to mention the systematic absurdity of the world he explores) that Shamir is perfectly happy to let much of his material satirize itself. Those who have read *The Good Soldier Schweik* (the inspired antiwar satire from World War One by Jaroslav Hasek) will remember that it is precisely Schweik's frantic desire to do every task extremely well that reveals the underlying insanity of the tasks themselves.

Before he leaves Israel for New York, Shamir tries to explain his quest to his grandmother, whose remarks are riotously funny and constitute easily the most anti-Semitic dialogue in the film, if they were not uttered by somebody's beloved grandmother. So why does Shamir keep this footage in his documentary? Well, she's ninety-some years old, and... she's his grandmother. Besides, it sets the stage for *Defamation* in a truly uncanny but effective way, by demonstrating that wildly negative generalizations about Jews, or any other group, can come from damned near anywhere, including one's own family members.

So the film follows Shamir to New York, where he tells Abraham Foxman of his plan to make a film documentary about the ADL's struggle against anti-Semitism; Foxman's media instincts appear to go on red alert with the possibility of starring in an Israeli documentary. Foxman announced to two underlings that there has recently been a threatening "wave of anti-Semitic and racist manifestations," and that New York seems to be at the epicenter of this tsunami of hate. Shamir is delegated—that is, handed off—to several people down the food chain of organizational responsibility (every journalist, or anybody who has ever made a film documentary, will recognize this process) ending finally with a woman who appears to be a clerk. As a middle-level ADL executive rustles about a bit nervously in the background, the woman studies data on the computer. All she can uncover are three or four minor incidents. But where's the "wave of anti-Semitic and racist manifestations?" Apparently it doesn't exist.

Finally, however, Shamir engages with what seems like a real anti-Semitic incident. A group of black youths throw rocks at a bus transporting Jewish students, breaking two windows. A real attack! But even here, there seems to be some historical background that makes the incident appear less like an anti-Semitic attack than a social problem. In the area where the incident occurred there is a long history of tension between Hassidic Jews living in Brooklyn—mainly the Chabad-Lubavitch Hassidim—and their African-American and West Indian neighbors. During August of 1991 in Crown Heights, the long-simmering tensions between the Hassidic Jews and their neighbors boiled over, and a three-day riot ensued. Given the history of tensions between Hassidim and their neighbors in Brooklyn, the charges that the rock-throwing is anti-Semitism seem at least questionable.

Shamir interviews some of the Black citizens in the area; one or two refer rather vaguely to the "Protocols of the Elders of Zion," which reminds us again that trace elements of anti-Semitic stereotypes are still alive and well, and are likely to turn up where least expected. Next Shamir talks to Rabbi Shea Hecht, himself a Chabad rabbi, who is completely disillusioned by the ADL, suggesting that Abraham Foxman is little more than a charlatan invested in keeping talk of anti-Semitism alive in order to reinforce his own power. "Look," this rabbi says, "if a group of black kids throw rocks at some Jewish kids, or steal a Jewish women's purse, that's not anti-Semitism. You may want to put the criminals away for a longer period for attacking a soft target, okay, but it's not anti-Semitism." Others make similar comments, suggesting that the problems of the Hassidim in Brooklyn are mainly about the high crime rate, not religious bigotry, and are best addressed with better law enforcement, good community relations and continued inter-community dialogue.

Abraham Foxman's talk of a "wave" of anti-Semitism in New York is clearly untrue. The Anti-Defamation League presents itself as the world's foremost authority on anti-Semitism—and boasts a annual budget of 70 million dollars, much of it from rich donors—but can't produce enough anti-Semitism to create a decent segment, much less a whole film. So Shamir turns his gaze back to Israel. The implied question here is: *if Abraham Foxman doesn't know what anti-Semitism is, how can the Israeli government hope to teach us about it?* But the Israeli state, like a great many other governments, doesn't really care about educating its youth. What it really wants to do is to *indoctrinate* its youth, especially since they are going into the army in a year or two.

We see that indoctrination in progress in the next scene, in which an Israeli teacher shows film footage of Nazi death camps in a school classroom. The students to whom the footage is being shown are preparing to go on 'March of the Living,' the government-sponsored journey to reconstructed Nazi death camps in Poland. (These death camps are today a destination for well over a million people annually.) As the children watch footage of Nazis loading Jews into cattle cars and pushing Jewish bodies into the flames at Majdanek, Shamir remarks a bit laconically that the teacher showing the film footage is "responsible for their mental preparation." Throughout the preparation, and during the trip itself, state security professionals, right-wing counselors and teachers, and others that specialize in students' "mental preparation" will be ever-present, and full of ideas about how the world hates Jews.

At one point the teacher says, "Everybody must describe your motivation for going on this trip [to Auschwitz]." One teenage boy says that he is a "third-generation Holocaust survivor," but when he looks at the face of his grandmother he can see that she's feeling something, but he can't feel it himself. He believes that she is feeling, "Never forget—never forgive." He wants to have that same feeling himself, he says. Other young people similarly hint at the likely presence of multigenerational trauma. You have the feeling that the students are aware that they are supposed to feel and say certain things, but don't yet know what they are, and are waiting for the adults to show them.

The teacher in charge of their "mental preparation" makes her pitch about the reason they are going to visit the reconstructed death camps. This is what she says, word for word, translated from Hebrew:

> Try to understand the connection between then and now. Anti-Semitism has not ended. Israel was formed as a result of the Holocaust, but anti-Semitism still exists. If you read the newspapers, there are anti-Semitic incidents in Europe and in other countries. You as Jews, as [the] next generation, who are about to join the Army, you will also have to face this aspect of our life. Secret Service people will go with you, so you will not be in contact with the local people. You will meet people who do not like us. [Raising her voice] You will see that they do not like us, even today they do not like us!

Afterwards, some of the teenagers sit around to discuss their reactions to the footage of Nazi atrocities, and what the teacher has said. "That's what makes us special," a boy named Yaiv says, "that no one can stand [Jews], but we're proud of it." A girl named Adi remarks: "We are raised in this spirit, that we know we are hated, and if a kid knows from the start that he is hated, about what happened to his ancestors in the Holocaust, it evokes anger toward the other side: pain, anger, even hate." A girl named Nofar says: "Everybody knows that Jews are hated. We were raised that way, with hatred and anti-Semitism. I can't remember a single moment, when there was no anti-Semitism." The kids sound like they're trying hard, but still don't quite know what the adults are getting at—there's even a slight undercurrent of resentment at having to deal with ideas that don't quite make sense. The pretence that they've spent their entire lives surrounded by anti-Semitism is particularly ludicrous, considering that they have been raised in Israel, surrounded by Jews.

The children are duly transported to Yad Vashem, the secular cathedral in Jerusalem built by the Israelis to memorialize the death of the six million. As the children are herded through the museum, they are shown diorama statuettes or figurines of people being killed in a Nazi death camp. Little is told about the lives of the victims, since the entire emphasis in on the machinery of death. "There's where they burned them in the ovens... the bodies were on top... the fuel was underneath... that's the place where they put the Zyclon B in the gas chamber... there's where they pulled out the teeth with gold..."

All of which seems like the regular fetishization of the tools of death one sees in certain Holocaust museums. But is morbidity the whole story at Yad Vashem? Is not the obsession with the aggression of the Holocaust offset to some extent by the pictures of the 600 Jews that perished in the Holocaust in the famous Hall of Names, arranged in a cone-shaped spiral on the ceiling? Yes, perhaps, to some extent—but the dead in those photographs wanted to live; and at Yad Vashem they are useful to the state only as victims, not as people who once lived, people with stories. Therefore we cannot identify with what they did that is good, or even learn from the mistakes they made, because their lives are not what make Yad Vashem important. What is important about Yad Vashem is soon revealed: after the horrors of the Holocaust are fully assimilated by the young people, a magical door in the rear swings open to reveal to the young people—wait for it—the shining sunlit beauty of Israel's New Jerusalem!

The message is clear: the only hope for the living, indeed the only hope for the dead, lies in the power of the Israeli state—its military victories and its ability to transform Jewish suffering into operational power, not to mention its 200 nuclear weapons that make it the regional superpower. Yad Vashem, to which the diplomats and world leaders are invariably required to visit first upon arriving in Israel, is—besides being a temple for the remembrance of the dead—an unmistakable message to the international community, that the enormity of the Holocaust might put the Jewish state beyond the requirements of international law, not to mention ordinary morality. It is different from other Holocaust museums, such as the facility at the Simon Wiesenthal Center in Los Angeles, not merely because it has a political function, but that its political function is so explicit.

But the very-much-alive Israeli teenagers who are shown through Yad Vashem are now looking forward to their adventure in Poland. The next scene in *Defamation* shows the children yelling and enjoying themselves as an El Al plane takes off en route to Poland, and picks up their pilgrimage after they arrive there. The handlers are taking the kids to a particular street in Krakow. (Auschwitz is about a hundred kilometers away from Krakow.) "The Germans were throwing Jews from the windows," one of the handlers explains helpfully, "and a young girl named Danka hid under the stairs." A girl hides under the stairs, and her friends take pictures of her. "Now I know what

Danka felt," she says.

The government handlers have been telling the kids not to talk to local people in Poland, because all Poles hate Jews, and are likely to grab them and harm them in some unspecified but horrible fashion. In *The Holocaust in American Life*, Peter Novick describes 'March of the Living' in this fashion: "American teenagers join Jewish youths from around the world in a meticulously orchestrated 'Holocaust to Redemption' pageant in which the Zionist message is driven home. At Auschwitz, an American rabbi, Shlomo Riskin, tells them: 'The world is divided into two parts: those who actively participated with the Nazis and those who passively collaborated with them.' At Majdanek, another rabbi informs the kids that the camp could become operational again within a few hours. Armed Israeli security guards who accompany the tour do everything possible to convince the youngsters that they're in constant danger in Poland."

"'Run straight to the buses,' they are told. 'Don't stop for anything.'"[7]

In other words, Polish anti-Semites might attack them at any moment, and Auschwitz *might be put back into operation in a few hours*, for the sole purpose of asphyxiating the Israeli children that are there taking the tour. This is an 'as if' quality to this, a kind of lurid role-playing or agitprop-theater in which the children are expected to participate; and since teenagers tend to love high drama, they're all too willing to go along with this spine-chilling make-believe. (After all, the adults keep saying it's important to being a good Israeli citizen—and their country has transported them all the way to Auschwitz—so why disappoint their mentors by not playing along?) The objective is clearly to get the young people to internalize emotionally the conception of a world in which everybody hates Jews. 'March of the Living' is the introduction to what will soon become the hard-sell version of that same idea.

The idea is that *all* Poles in the early 21st century live in an ever-present frenzy of hatred toward *all* Jews. But far from existing in a rabid state of ever-present Jew-hatred, today's Poles have developed an entire kitsch industry based on a weird form of philo-Semitism — weird, but not lethal. Figurines of idealized *shtetl* Jews can be bought everywhere, and there are actually cafes based entirely on Jewish themes, featuring performers dressed like 19th-century Jews and doing Jewish dances. The point here is that while anti-Semitism has been rife in Poland for centuries, the idea that in the early 21st century the average Pole would think of nothing else but harming Jews, and secondly, would want to impulsively grab them off the street (and do what? Drink their blood?) is beyond silliness, even for a state indoctrination program as blatant as this one. It's also a complete trivialization of historical anti-Semitism in Poland, and an insult to every Polish Jew that ever suffered from it.

In Yoav Shamir's *Defamation*, the teenagers disembark from their bus, and there is an incident. A group of old men sitting in the sun attempt to communicate with the girls. The girls talk back, but one of the girls seems to remember that something else is expected of her. She breaks free of the conversation.

"Oh! They're saying bad things about us. They're saying we're bitches." She runs to join her friends. (One of the old men says, *What a bunch of funny girls. What were they chatting about?*)

Later Shamir seeks out a conversation with this same girl, who informs him that the security men are there "to protect us from anti-Semitism and stuff, so that no one comes and hurts us."

"Do you think that could happen?"

"Yes, in the morning we saw some old men on a bench. They heard that we were from Israel, and they made faces. They called us monkeys and donkeys. We almost got into a fight."

Shamir had observed the interaction, and says, "They didn't say anything of the kind."

"They did."

"Did not."

The girl doesn't seem entirely sure that she actually heard these words, but she also seems somewhat resentful that she is being questioned for following the script that the adults have given her. In the evening, the kids are raising hell in the hotel, attracting the attention of the manager. "Why aren't you going out?" Shamir asks the kids.

"There are Neo-Nazis here in Poland. They are a threat. We're in danger. They could knock on our doors, and throw things through the windows."

A boy says: "At dinner they told us that. They briefed us that we're not in a friendly country. We are in a relatively hostile county. There are demonstrations out there. They could throw stones at us. Two weeks ago some Neo-Nazis came in and started banging on the doors."

"Who said that?" Shamir asks.

"The Secret Service guy. He's crazy. We were all eating and suddenly he says that he has something to tell us. Then he started talking about neo-Nazis. We were all shocked. We couldn't eat anymore."

A girl says: "That's all for our safety. We're not allowed out, so we should go to our rooms right after we eat."

"Why?"

"Because [the Poles] are anti-Semitic."

Boy: "They don't like us."

Girl: "At the airport the soldiers walk like Nazis, rigidly."

Boy: "The one that stamped our passports looked like an SS officer."

One can only lament the missed opportunities here. What an opportunity to call in a couple of trained historians at this point, who could give some informed presentations to the kids on the history of anti-Semitism in Poland, perhaps accompanied by some inspiring stories of Jewish resistance, and stories of non-Jews who hid Jews from the Nazis. But the Israeli government isn't interested in creating a nuanced presentation of history, nor does it want more informed and morally imaginative young people; it wants good soldiers. Furthermore, any nuanced and honest presentation of recent history would quickly dispel the idea that modern Poles are chronically addicted to hanging out on street-corners waiting to pounce on Jewish kids.

Furthermore, there could be another reason why the Israeli state probably doesn't want a nuanced historical presentation of anti-Semitism—it might remind some students of anti-Palestinian racism, and some kids might connect the dots. In any case, the object of these government-sponsored trips is not education, but indoctrination—and that is something that happens not through balanced presentation of the facts but through intense emotional manipulation (and the strategic use of traumatic memory) to bond people to the state, to each other, and to the aggression they will need to oppress millions of Palestinians.

The next day Shamir interviews a security man. You have to wonder if he's the guy the kids were talking about, who inter-rupted their dinner to tell them they were all in danger from neo-fascists. But all we really know is that he's one of the government handlers. Suddenly, without warning, he goes off-script—he speaks from the heart about his job, and about the kids. This is what he says, translated from Hebrew:

We live with the feeling that death is always with us. Whether that feeling is good or not, I don't know. It is always hanging over us, and here in Auschwitz you see how it becomes an industry, an industry of death. The Germans started it all, and we are perpetu-ating it. I thought a lot about it, whether this 'March of the Living' is good or bad, this death industry... We perpetuate death, and that's why we will never become a normal people: because we emphasize death and what happened. We have to remember, no doubt, but we live too much in it, and it's preventing us from being a normal people. It leads to...

Without warning another security man comes up and stops the interview.

It's hard to say exactly what triggered the first security man's sudden honesty, but it sounds as though he might have been pondering the underlying agenda of 'March of the Living' for quite some time. You also get the feeling that maybe this is going to be his last trip to Poland with students—state security personnel are not supposed to be so introspective, and so morally acute. But he sums up the whole project with chilling accuracy: *"The Germans started it all, and we are perpetuating it."*

The group heads to Auschwitz, and the kids are singing and dancing in the bus that is transporting them. The driver tells them on the bus's amplification system that he expects serious attention from them—and the kids fall silent for the moment. The trip's security men proceed to show footage of starving Jews in a concentration camp on a TV screen located *in the bus.* The kids are not yet a captive audience—indeed some are resisting a bit, eating chips from a bag as they watch footage of starving prisoners. (One reviewer called this brief scene "definitely worthy of Seinfeld.") But by now the kids are starting to get hooked—the Holocaust is heavy stuff, generating the kind of high-octane hysteria and morbidity that is likely to attract adolescents, who because of the biological changes in their bodies tend quite naturally to be specialists in various kinds of drama, angst and hysteria; and the adults are giving them a green light to emote a little.

Jewish author Hajo G. Meyer believes that when the Holocaust is "collectively remembered in ritual settings," such discussion may "serve the same role as the previous traumatic experiences." As we have seen, talking about one's traumatic experience is almost always therapeutic, but *ritualized* and *repeated* remembrances of trauma may actually serve to empower the trauma rather than its victims. "Collective remembrance thus acts as fresh trauma," writes Meyer. "Since the number of previous traumatic experiences that the Jewish people have suffered throughout history is so large, and as observing Jews have to remember many of them so often, the amplification of trauma is very great indeed."[8] Meyer assumes that de-escalating traumatic memory is always desirable, but it is precisely the *amplification* of traumatic memory that the Israeli state wants. Indeed, that is evidently the purpose of 'March of the Living.'

Once Shamir and his crew are inside of Auschwitz with the young people, the indoctrination begins in earnest. It is hard to see if it is day or night, but one assumes it is night, because the faces are bathed in candlelight. The children are encouraged to talk about how they feel. One young woman says she knows that she should feel horror, but doesn't feel anything yet—this is encouraged by one of the teachers for its honesty. The children are now encouraged to read the names of those who died in Auschwitz or other death camps, a process for which they have already been prepared. They read the names, and as they do some begin to tear up, and some begin to cry. The young people take each others' hands and embrace each other as well. One of their handlers stops to remind them that even today, Jews are hated everywhere—even today, the death camp of Auschwitz could become operational again in only a few hours. The world has always hated Jews, and they always will. The Holocaust proves it.

And inside Auschwitz, by candlelight, reading the names of dead relatives, the kids are really starting to get into it. The tears start to flow; the mood of desperation and open-ended trauma is starting to take over. Carefully orchestrated by the state security people, some of the young people begin to emotionally testify to their own feelings of horror, anxiety and dread concerning the Holocaust. Some continue to read the names of the dead. The state handlers remind the kids again and again that their enemies still want to kill Jews. Kids cling to each other and sob. The objective of the process is clearly to share as deeply as humanly possible the traumatic memory of sadistic acts that occurred within these walls, internalizing in the process the aggression at its heart. In such a manner can the children be bonded to each other for life, and to the Israeli state.

The kids will also share a willingness to sacrifice for the state, and to unquestioningly obey it—after all, is not the state of Israel the only thing that stands between them and another Holocaust? One of the last scenes in *Defamation* is of the Israeli youngsters having a group picture taken at the very gates of Auschwitz, under the words made famous by the Nazis, and now appropriated for its own purposes by the Israeli political class: *Arbeit Macht Frei*.

4.

Noam Chayut's experiences as an Israeli teenager consisted not only of being indoctrinated, but in indoctrinating others. He is sent to a variety of venues, including Chile and Argentina, to plead for support of the new Jewish state. Their lectures—which were apparently made mainly but not exclusively to potential donors and supporters in the Jewish communities of those countries—consisted almost entirely of tear-jerking appeals to religious nationalism, martyrdom in the cause of the Israeli state, and references to Jewish suffering in the Holocaust.

"At every lecture we gave, Deborah and I raised the topic of the Holocaust and its inevitable lesson: that our country, the State of Israel, must exist and be strong. The idea of talking about the Holocaust was mine, but Deborah played the principal role in this show. At times she made the audience weep as she told about her survivor grandmother who could not possibly throw away food, not even a single crumb, and forced the whole family to eat everything on their plates, down to the last morsel."

"Slowly, the telling of the Holocaust became our mission's

main topic. I recall how one evening, in the province of Misiones, Argentina, I touched the heart of the mother of our host family. We spoke about the Holocaust and the refugees who arrived on a rickety boat from blood-drenched Europe and immediately went forth to fight the Arabs. I described in detail the myth of the Jew who migrated to Palestine on his own, without any family relations, disembarked in Jaffa port, was handed a gun and ran east to fight for Jerusalem and fell there on one of its rocky hills, and now he is buried nameless, and has no one to mourn him or honor his memory."

The pressures that accompany that kind of narrative are obvious, not least because heroic war narratives never sound quite real—we instinctively know that the people they honor are invariably more (and invariably less) than a narrative that is mainly about war and not about them. Furthermore, Noam is always to some extent aware of the fact that such narratives were intended to raise money. "And so my brain—washed with a single dogmatic truth—combined with my youthful innocence and my skill at moving hearts made tears flow in faraway Argentina. I kept those tears in my memory along with the tears I gathered while reading aloud what I had written about the imaginary grandfather in Poland. The next tears I proceeded to reap were tears of the love for homeland and flag, tears proud and uplifted, tears of rich Jews and very rich American Jewish mothers and grandmothers, tears falling on checks and contracts for investment in bonds, which we collected every evening."

The animal energies of youth help him suppress his doubts about these activities, and his intense desire to serve his country prevails; he joins the IDF and goes on active duty, after a time becoming an officer. Many of his duties have to do simply with going into troublesome Palestinian villages to "make a show of presence" in various ways. "This meant rumbling through them, raising a racket, hurling teargas canisters into markets and balconies, blasting stun grenades, amusedly yelling swearwords over the commander's Jeep loudspeaker, firing live ammunition at house walls, piles of dirt and trash or vineyard terraces. I knew such villages like the palm of my hand."

There are certain streets where he and his men go where stones are thrown at them. "Once, I entered that street, and it was a mistake that someone had to pay for; someone always had to pay for those first, one-time mistakes. For example, a kid paid for running slowly while trying to escape chaos. He was caught and shackled in front of his mother or older sister, who screamed and wept, and he was thrown into the Jeep, driven an hour's walk away, then lightly pushed out of the Jeep. I don't remember whether we freed his hands or let the other price-payers do it. Anyway, we figured, this kid learned his lesson."

"And it was not only kids who were there to pay for the humiliation we felt after making such mistakes. Shopkeepers, too, paid when we fired teargas into their shops because we thought the curses or stones had originated there. Or their name was very similar to one of the names on our wanted list. Or their shop was on Shaheed Street, and Shaheed,[9] we all thought, means terrorist, so it makes sense that on 'terrorist' street we'll find the guilty parties who must pay for humiliating us."

"This was all done in order to 'make them pay the price for disturbing the peace'—these were the exact words used in written orders when the authorities wanted to define the need for scapegoats." Sometimes it meant simply parking in a military vehicle in front of a Palestinian restaurant, so no Palestinians would enter to buy a meal. There was also "the girl whose family home we had broken into late at night to remove her mother and aunt. And there were plenty of children, hundreds of them, screaming and crying as we rummaged through their rooms and their things. And there was the child from Jenin whose wall we blasted with an explosive charge that blew a hole just a few centimeters from his head. Miraculously, he was uninjured, but I'm sure his hearing and his mind were badly impaired."

"And there were the elderly women who had difficulty walking and we still made them march from one side of the checkpoint to the other and stand in the crowded line and wait like everyone else. And there were the proud men who suddenly broke down and wept, and the children who watched their father, the head of their family, second only to God—looking through the tears and seeing him being shackled and blindfolded and removed from his home, thrown into the Jeep. There were thousands, most of them chosen at random only because on our map their home was marked with an X."

"Later, when we were sent on 'massive arrest missions,' as these were officially called, we no longer marked maps with Xs but simply arrested everyone—all the boys and men between fifteen and fifty-five years of age. They were detained, shackled and blindfolded. Sometimes they would be stripped, sometimes taken out of bed in pajamas and into the street. We would pass from house to house, boring holes in the walls and entering through them. We would take out the man of the house and his older children—in front of the whole family, petrified with fear— and concentrate them in groups outside. Nowadays, whenever I see a blind person in some city walking along or waiting to cross at a pedestrian crossing, I recognize that special gait and stance, leaning forward slightly, of our detainees who would wait, blind-folded, for the truck to drive them to the interrogation facilities."

"On one of our missions, I was the one who collected hundreds of detainees from the refugee camp Nur al-Shams in Bethlehem and moved them to an improvised holding pen between 'curlies'[10] in the fields of the Israeli village Nitzanei Oz. I was riding in a small military lorry, and behind us was a Safari, a large, heavy, armored personnel carrier. Both vehicles were filled with detainees, the first batch of whom were beaten up as they were unloaded into a pen by the military policemen. In response, I got off the truck and went berserk, jumping at one of the soldiers who raised a hand to my shackled detainees. I gripped him by the collar and shook him with great force. I yelled that if anyone here dared to hit someone again, I'd personally break his bones and send him to jail."

"I spent minutes looking for the commander of the soldiers to make him watch them, but I couldn't find him and was running out of time. I couldn't wait any longer without damaging my vanity as the best urban navigator in my battalion. I was already being rushed on radio by company commanders who wished to rid themselves of more and more 'packages'—that's what the locals are called when they are shackled and waiting to be transported into custody. I threatened the military policemen once more, perhaps added some curse, and left my detainees there."

"I led the convoy back to pick up the second round, and felt that I was definitely a humane officer, one who even protected terrorists. An officer of the most moral army in the world... the most moral army in the world... The most moral... *Lucky for them I am here... Lucky that people like me... Fortunately it is I who do this job and not somebody else, good that I...*"

Clearly the Palestinians didn't clearly understand how compassionate and decent Noam was. Once, when a girl needed to get to the university on the other side of a checkpoint, the checkpoint was closed. "Why wasn't she allowed to cross? Because that day the checkpoint was sealed shut. When would it open? I don't know. Either it would or it wouldn't." It wasn't Noam's fault—he didn't close the checkpoint. It was just closed.

"And that student, what guts she had to stand up to me, without looking away, without lowering her gaze, without pleading, without asking me to make an exception just for her. She told me instead, in a restrained, controlled tone, as one human being to another, how much I make her and her friends suffer when I block them on their way to their final exams. That must have been no less important to her than her pride. How beautiful she was, I thought."

But her beauty did not deter him. Noam knew these things

had to be done. Had not the enemies of the Jews been trying to destroy them forever, culminating finally in the Holocaust? And were not these Palestinians simply the latest version of that eternal evil? Would they not conduct their own Holocaust, had they the chance?

And so it went.

Until the day the girl stole his Holocaust.

5.

On that day he was escorting a senior army officer, one who went out of his way to insult Noam's deputy battalion commander. Noam Chayut understood instinctively that the humiliation of his deputy commander would be passed on down the line, "down to the child who was too slow to run away and [who] would pay for the humiliation suffered by the legendary deputy battalion commander, as the general scolded him in front of his subordinates." (But how and why would such a child, however much endangered and ultimately humiliated, steal his Holocaust?)

On this particular day the mission of the security officials and senior army officers was to post notices of land confiscation on ancient olive trees. Palestinians could appeal in special courts, supposedly, but in these struggles over land and houses the Palestinians rarely won; the entire system was skewed against them. Noam explains in memorable detail how the law works in the Occupied Palestinian Territories: "On such occasions, 'locals,' as they were called, often materialized out of the fields or houses, wishing to present documents to the administration people or the 'officer in charge,' which in their jargon meant the supreme authority in the region." Sometimes "they waved and showed all kinds of maps, documents, writs of ownership dating from the Ottoman Empire. The papers were colorful and decorated with official Turkish stamps, which in their opinion were ample proof of their claim to the land." But what the land would be used for was not up to Palestinians, if it had been purchased by some Israeli or American Jew who wanted it for reasons of his own. In that case, they had no rights whatsoever. "After all, I just need to ensure the well-being of the fellow who is here to survey this plot of land and pass the map on to whoever ordered it, made and paid for it and will build whatever he will on it."

But on this day the object was not to survey the land, but to post notices of its immanent confiscation. Noam sees the folly in posting notices. "I don't recall the exact worlds, of course, but I do remember that even then it seemed ridiculous to post such notices on the trunks of centuries-old olive trees that did not speak Hebrew, and anyway they had been planted there long before laws and regulations and edicts had been issued in Hebrew in this country, at least this time around, and if an olive tree were found that was old enough to understand, its owner certainly wouldn't, and even if he did, he would not be allowed to cross the checkpoint in order to appeal to the proper legal authority."

But it was in a nearby village, a village no doubt within the area soon to be confiscated, that something caught his eye. "Back at the village outskirts, I remember very well a group of children playing, and you among them, my little thief. When I saw you, with your face totally engrossed in the game, I gave you a 'charming smile.'" Noam Chayut had once been a counselor for young people, and had become quite skilled at a particular smile, a kind of cheesy but practiced smile that radiated both authority and sensitivity. "But I knew myself for quite a few years by then, and I knew exactly what kind of mask I had on for every one of those seconds. After all, these were the very seconds during which you stole my Holocaust."

"You did not smile back at me as had been the custom ever since I acquired that smile as a youth-movement counselor. No, you froze on the spot, grew very pale and looked terrified. You neither screamed nor ran off. You only stood there, facing me with a horrified face and your black eyes staring. Normally, I don't remember the eye color of my interlocutors and acquaintances. This is an important detail in a person's description, but when I have no intention of describing them, I don't commit their eye color to memory. But I do have a precise recollection of your eyes and their color, and I will forever."

"The rest of the children ran off immediately, some crying, others generating the same hubbub that had resonated throughout their playing before we cut if off with our arrival. Only you waited there, staring at me for another shuddering moment. Then you shook yourself out of your frozen stance, turned silently—a scrawny girl in light-colored clothes—and ran off, not looking back. You ran and disappeared among the olive trees, appeared again, and then disappeared into the village alleys, forever."

"And I don't know why, of all people, it was you who stole my Holocaust."

At that moment, everything changed, although Noam would not realize how much things had changed until months afterward. "I understood only much later what that scrawny girl in light-colored clothes had taken from me: she took away my belief that there is absolute evil in the world. She took from me the belief that I was avenging my people's destruction by absolute evil, that I was fighting absolute evil. For that girl, I embodied absolute evil. Even if I was not as cruel as the absolute—Nazi—evil in the shadow of which I had grown up, I didn't have to achieve its perfection and force in order to fulfill my role in her life. No. I was merely who I was, playing the role of absolute evil in the play of her life. As soon as I realized the fact that in her eyes I myself was absolute evil, the absolute evil that had governed me until then began to disintegrate."

What Noam Chayut is writing about is 'traumatic privilege.' Up to that moment he had possessed the right to do anything he wanted to the Palestinians, in order to serve the Israeli state. He had that right because it was built into the traumatic memory that he had internalized as he was raised. The Jews had suffered in the Holocaust, and it gave them the right to transfer that pain to the Palestinians. As an Israeli he was expected to continue that cycle of violence, because of the aggression built into that memory, the aggression everyone internalized along with the Holocaust that was constantly being talked about and memorialized by the state. Emotions do not go away by themselves, so when you internalize that much aggression you must somehow express it.

But now, inexplicably, that precious 'traumatic privilege' was gone. The little girl that had stared at him so long with mingled terror and hatred had stolen his Holocaust.

"And ever since," Chayut writes, "I have been without my Holocaust. Ever since, everything in my life has taken on new meaning: the sense of belonging is blurred, pride has gone missing, belief has weakened, regret has grown strong, forgiveness has been born."[11]

6.

Some people *inherit* traumatic memory, by growing up in particular familial, national or religious systems. Because they are so often exposed to stories of violence and aggression, children who grow up in such cultures, countries and families tend to feel endangered even when danger is not objectively present. As we saw in the chapter on Norman Finkelstein, many children of Holocaust survivors identify with aspects of their parents' past trauma (and internalize so much of its aggression, and suffer so much of its anxiety and hyper-vigilance) that they are said to suffer from *intergenerational, multigenerational, trans- generational* or *historic* trauma.

The Likud government of Israel tells its citizens that the Holocaust could happen again, that the whole world hates the Jews; and by so doing, it manages to keep the traumatic memory of the Holocaust operating in the present. It does this because it is the ticket to power for the Likud party, as well as for Likud's proxies in the US. Indeed, people exposed to this kind of toxic propaganda may *feel like the Holocaust is still going on*. This provides the emotional basis and ideological framework that can be used to justify systemic abuse of Palestinians, the sadistic elements of which are highly addictive, and which ultimately heightens rather than reduces anxiety. This internalized aggression can be neutralized if people become aware of the way the government is manipulating them—especially if they are simultaneously aware of their own capacity for evil. Since Jews were victims of Christian anti-Semitism in Europe for over a thousand years, Israeli Jews might be expected to have a hard time acknowledging their own capacity for persecuting others.

Aggressors are *always* aggrieved, they *always* feel like victims—that is one of the observable constants in the economy of human aggression. Trauma bonding is a process in which the victim seeks to overcome his trauma by identifying with the attacker's aggression, in the process internalizing that aggression, and acting it out against new victims, or against himself. As this dynamic plays out, the victim is likely to become a victim-aggressor, an archetypical personality type in modern Israel. Such a personality needs victim status to justify his crimes and misdemeanors, but also needs to act out his internalized aggression by punishing real or imagined enemies among the Palestinians.

For Noam Chayut, this entire toxic system is compromised when he realizes that the Holocaust, which happened sixty years before, can no longer justify violence in the present. This insight is triggered when he sees a terrified child running from him, which forces him to understand the effects of Israeli apartheid on its victims; and over a long and difficult period of time, he begins to understand the changes going on in his personality. As his victim status is compromised, and his identification with the

Holocaust begins to weaken, his internalized aggression begins to dissipate, and his need to act aggressively likewise begins to dissipate.

7.

At the end of his service in the Israel Defense Forces, Noam Chayut is sent to America to sell Israel Bonds, and in so doing speaks to audiences of the heroism of the Israeli soldiers—that is to say, he addresses his American audiences as he imagines a heroic Israeli soldier would, always remembering that his specific task is raising money from affluent Americans. But things have now changed; he's no longer so sure of Israel, or of himself, and as a result memories of that time have an increasingly dreamlike nature. "Over time I have suppressed the story of that trip to such an extent that at moments I can hardly believe the words I write. Luckily, my parents have kept picture albums and newspaper clippings, proving that this was no figment of my imagination—that I was in fact sent to Miami on behalf of the IDF and Israel Bonds to tell tales of courage."

This suppression of memory suggests a struggle to break free of traumatic memory. "The time that followed can be described either as a sobering elevation or as deterioration, as humanist insight or treason. One thing is obvious, though: my own picture begins to warp because memory delivers dark things it had previously suppressed. My life was a simple oil painting in which a small child is seen near a house and flowers against a neat, clear background, until someone added layers of pain that blur the clean lines. Lines blur and other lines come into focus, new victims enter my picture. Gradually I begin to see another truth, which no longer contains my Holocaust."

What he doesn't talk about to the rich Americans to whom he sells his Israel bonds are the things that are done to Palestinians to maintain the Israeli occupation, because he knows the Americans do not want to hear about that. Indeed, his job is precisely to present an Israel of such surpassing heroism and beauty that it is incapable of evil, incapable of doing anything that is not inspirational and wonderful. It is thrilling beyond the power of words to describe, a dream come true to many of the people to whom he spoke, Jews anxious to bequeath their funds to something that will outlive them: the excitement of nation-building combined with military empowerment, the first time Jews have ever had such power. There is also an unmistakable religious dimension to it: for many of these people, the worship of God—or at the very least, the search for God—has been replaced by an awed worship of the new Israeli state.

Noam Chayut has a chance to practice his Israel-Bonds pitch before he ever leaves Israel, and delivers it to his commanding officers. He says exactly what they want to hear—that the Palestinians are ungrateful enemies of the state, on the one hand hiding terrorists and on the other making propaganda out of any accidental damage that occurs. "I didn't tell them that our APCs [Armored Personnel Carriers] and tanks and bulldozers entered Ramallah—a handsome, modern city, even impressive—and crushed and destroyed private and public property while grinding to dust any part of the town's infrastructure which they happened to run across. Sidewalks and roads and bus stops, traffic dividers and road signs, public parks and drainage ditches, telephone poles, playgrounds and decorative tress, hedges and stone walls—everything was pulverized and smashed to smithereens like sandcastles on the beach. Nor did I tell them how our heavy equipment crushed cars at roadsides, sometimes with barely disguised pleasure, sometimes by mistake, sometimes with regret that there was no other option."

It wasn't just the physical damage. "I didn't tell them that the regional brigade commander opened live fire—in violation of his own official orders, incidentally—at a demonstration that was taking place 300 meters from us up the Muq'qtq'a road. The shooting stunned us and surprised even our legendary battalion commander. I didn't tell them how the demonstrators who ran away later came back with Molotov cocktails and burning wooden wheels and threw stones, and how a line of Border Patrolmen dispersed this demonstration with more live fire, teargas and beatings. The clothes of the detainees in the Border Patrol Jeeps were drenched with blood, because all of them, when trying to run off, 'fell with their faces on the asphalt.' That's the explanation on the medical report because under our enlightened occupation, every detainee sees a doctor to whom you have to account for the wounds. *Can't just go ahead and beat them up, order must prevail!"*

"Nor did I tell them that, sometimes, in order to have a safe night's rest, we would choose some chance [Palestinian] house and enter, locking up the whole family in one small room and settling down in the rest of the house. And that we preferred comfortable, heated homes, with the excuse that the house of our choice was the safest. Nor did I describe to them what such a residence looked like after twenty men, filthy with dust and mud, lived in it and did in it as they very well pleased." That was not what his military superiors wanted to hear.

It was the same for the rich Americans of Miami. "In Miami I repeated the same things time and again to a different audience each day: we shall pursue the terrorists wherever and whenever we shall see fit. It is our right and duty to fight terror and destroy the infrastructure of Palestinian terrorism. (I loved that expression—'the terror infrastructure'—and used it a lot when I answered questions at the end of my talk.) I mentioned the Israeli army's operation to free the hijacked French plane in Entebbe, Uganda: 'Remember that the Palestinian Liberation Organization terrorists, whose successors we are fighting now, freed the French passengers and sent the Jews to the left, just as the Jews had been selected by the Nazis and sent to their death in Auschwitz all those years ago. Our IDF said loud and clear: Never again! Never again will Jews be selected and sent off to die! We didn't just say it, the IDF sent forth the best recon unit to rescue them. Ladies and gentlemen, my dear hostess, rest assured that back then, as on this very day, we shall not let anyone hurt us just because we are Jews!"

And at the end of every speech, 'Hatikvah' was played. Behind me was a large Israeli flag and while we played and sang the national anthem, I wore my beret over my prim dress uniform and saluted the flag. This was the highlight of the evening; the audience was moved every time."

But for Noam Chayut, the transcendent vision of Jews fighting terrorism had long since begun to fade. Because it wasn't about hunting terrorists at all—it was about occupying territory where millions of people lived. It was about destroying just enough property, killing just enough people, beating up just enough demonstrators, to terrify and oppress the people who lived there. The so-called military 'assignments' were increasingly make-work, nonsensical excuses for being occupiers of Palestinians territory. Of course, he didn't point this out to his army superiors, nor did he mention it to the people who came to hear him in Miami.

"I didn't tell them that the number of our superfluous assignments grew and grew and even then, had I opened my eyes, I could have understood that the main point of my being there was being there per se." It wasn't about fighting wars with neighboring Arab states; it wasn't about killing or capturing terrorists; it was about being an occupier of Palestinians' areas while those same areas were being subjected to slow ethnic cleansing.

And he became intimately aware of the real meaning of the impressive but deliberately impersonal military terms used by the IDF:

Exposure: Razing—uprooting trees and flattening buildings;

Targeted prevention: Extrajudicial execution;

Show of presence: Humiliation, intimidation, vandalism;

Neighbor procedure: Using a random unarmed bystander as a

human shield in order to enter a Palestinian house;

Passer-by Procedure: Same thing, after 'neighbor procedure' was ruled illegal by Israel's High Court of Justice;

Searches: Entering homes and damaging their contents;

Deterrent fire: Opening fire indiscriminately in all directions;

Making them pay the price: Revenge, letting off steam and collective punishment;

Mapping: Invading the last vestige of privacy in the refugee camps: entering every home, drawing the layout of the rooms, listing the names of the inhabitants, scanning their mobile phones, checking out family relations...

"I did tell the truth in my speeches," Chayut writes. "I just didn't tell all of it. I didn't lie, didn't distort. I didn't even exaggerate. But I didn't tell the true story." Above all, he did not tell them about the girl who stole his Holocaust. He was still struggling to come to terms with the big changes that this charismatic moment, when he saw the young girl looking at him with such fear, had unleashed in his personality. One change he understood quite well, however—it was getting harder, much harder to rationalize what he did as an Israeli soldier.

8.

There's nothing that victims hate worse than being told they've internalized much of the aggression that they've endured. Men abused by their fathers, for example, don't like to be told that they've internalized a great deal of their own fathers' aggression, and are at risk for acting it out against others. Israeli Jews, for their part, don't like those cartoons regularly created by cartoonists around the world, in which IDF troops are portrayed as wearing uniforms that are slipping or being torn off, to reveal a German Wehrmacht or SS uniform underneath. Yet there is a historical basis for that artistic perception. With the rise of fascism in Europe, some Jews not only internalized fascist aggression, but became active fascists. And those same Jews rose to power in the new state of Israel.

Most Jews, of course, responded to fascism by supporting liberal and center-left policies and parties. All saw the anti-Semitic tendencies within fascism, which were a central part of the German Nazi party. Nonetheless, certain Jewish intellectuals begin to advocate fascism in both style and in ideology—that is, they presented fascism as a political style Jews should follow and emulate. Most outspoken of these was Ze'ev Zabotinsky, the founder of Revisionist Zionism, who was the main ideologist of the Betar youth groups and militias, first in Europe and then in Palestine.

The young people in the Betar groups wore fascist-style uniforms and used fascist salutes; the Betar groups also regularly engaged in military-style marching and sang songs that praised racial purity and extolled violence in the Zionist cause. (For a while the Betar groups wore black uniforms in imitation of the Italian fascists, although various groups later used both black and brown uniforms.) The Betar movement became quite numerous in the 1930s, especially in Poland. Although Betar tended to attract alienated young Jews inclined to violence, it also established militias wherever it could, first in Europe and then in Palestine. Not heard of it? One shouldn't be surprised. It's not a part of the story most Zionist historians are anxious to reveal, although Betar's ideas eventually came to dominate in Israel.

Zabotinsky, the chief ideologist of the group, encouraged typical fascist ideas, idealizing armed force as a purifying spiritual force and the only way to achieve Jewish aims in Palestine. In Poland, Zabotinsky's estimated 40,000 followers, led by Menachem Begin, were given military training by the Polish government, as Betar placed great emphasis on military drilling of various kinds; the group was greatly influenced by Polish nationalism, and absorbed many of its nationalist ideas at that time, along with the ideas and orientations of Italian fascism.

The Betar alumni soon commenced immigration to Palestine, where they set about organizing paramilitary and terrorist organizations. Not surprisingly, in Palestine the followers of Zabotinsky advocated massive retaliation against innocent Arab civilians in response to every Arab attack. (This eventually won acceptance as 'collective punishment,' a tactic ultimately used by all subsequent Israeli governments against Palestinians, despite being condemned by the United Nations.) They were also extensively involved in terrorism against Palestinians, and against rival Jewish groups.

Betar members were pivotal in organizing Irgun, a terrorist organization led by Menachem Begin, two of whose main operations were blowing up the King David Hotel, killing 91 innocent civilians, and the Deir Yassin massacre, in which Begin's men killed well over two hundred unarmed Palestinian men, women and children, according to a representative of the Red Cross that visited the site of the massacre. (As Begin would proudly proclaim later in the Israeli Knesset, the largely successful goal of his terrorism was to terrify Palestinians in the area into fleeing Palestine, so their property could be taken over by Jews.) In December 1948, Menachem Begin came to the US to raise money for his group. His arrival was met by a remarkable letter that appeared in the *New York Times*, signed by Albert Einstein, Hannah Arendt, and other Jewish notables. Einstein and Arendt denounced Begin's group as clearly and unmistakably fascist, and dangerous to both Israel and America. "This is the unmistakable stamp of a Fascist party for whom terrorism (against Jews, Arabs and British alike) and misrepresentation are the means, and a 'Leader State' is the goal."

Begin immediate went back to Israel, his plans to raise money defeated by the *Times* letter; but he continued to agitate for his violent, ultra-nationalist vision there. With his followers he founded the Herut party, which later became the center for the Likud party in the 1970s. The Likud party—the heir of Begin and

Zabotinky's openly Fascist movement—would ultimately become the most powerful in Israel, especially after the election of Benjamin Netanyahu; subsequent to the collapse of final status negotiations with the Palestinians in 2000 (and the loss of a negotiated settlement on which most Israeli liberals and the Labor party had pinned their hopes), Likud's dangerous ideas would be embraced by almost the entire Israeli political class. And those ideas, as we have seen, began with fascism and still retain most of their fascist qualities, especially for Palestinians in the Occupied Palestinian Territories.

And under Netanyahu, the Likud party has, if anything, become more authoritarian, more nationalist, more demagogic— and, if you are a Palestinian in occupied territory, more openly fascist. There's no sign that Netanyahu wishes to move toward the political center; on the contrary, he is clearly striving to take Likud even further to the right, to fend off challenges by right-wing challengers and extremist religious parties on the right. His bombastic, racist declarations about Palestinians, as well as his openly demagogic use of the Holocaust to manipulate Jewish emotions, seem to come from nothing more or less than a particular kind of fascist temperament adapted to the exigencies of the Middle East. But it should also be seen as incontrovertible evidence of the extent to which Netanyahu and his right-wing party have internalized the fascist worldview, and the extent to which that worldview is increasingly internalized by the Israeli political class.

9.

The second part of *The Girl Who Stole My Holocaust* is about a man who is leaving behind exactly those right-wing cultural and political tendencies that first formed his worldview, without really understanding how fast he was going, and how far it would take him. Noam Chayut explains: "This part of the story of the theft of my Holocaust took place in between the theft itself and the realization that something was no longer a part of me. I suppose this time lapse was necessary. It could have taken years, perhaps a lifetime, and then my story would have been one of those old men's tales told upon their deathbed. In my case, for reasons unknown to me, the revelation came sooner."

At one point, while driving with his mother, Chayut asks her not to read historical markers about the siege of Jerusalem, because "those damn signs are what made me go to the army and commit crimes in the Occupied Territories." Afterwards he is surprised at his words, because he is not yet conscious of feeling that he has committed crimes. At another point he falls in with a dangerous bunch of Bedouin drug smugglers, realizing about halfway through one particularly tumultuous night that he probably won't survive to see the morning, and beats a hasty exit to save his skin. At another point he falls in with a 73-year-old Bedouin goatherd who is a gifted storyteller, who tells him how he experienced events in 1948:

"Then he told me how one day soldiers came and ordered everyone to leave. The soldiers fired in the air and announced that whoever did not leave would be killed. He described their flight on carts, on foot, with their livestock and all the belongings they could carry." His father stopped at this hill, he said, the hill where he herded his goats, because from this hill the families could see their homes and land—the homes and land they'd just left behind. The first night they slept in the open, and during that first night the family watched as the soldiers moved into their old home.

But the few Bedouin families apparently built new dwellings higher up on the hill, and became refugees "just a few kilometers from their home." Cursing Arafat and the Israeli soldiers as part of the same plague, this story-teller—like his father before him—had been loyal to King Hussein; but he felt betrayed by him for abandoning him to the Palestinian Authority. But he vowed to stay on within eyesight of his old home: "Here he would die, he said, and gazed at his father's land."

Chayut takes to hiking through the countryside, investigating old villages and half-forgotten ruins. This hearty outdoor activity brings him closer, little by little, to a certain home truth about Israel: that its towns, cities and roads had been built entirely on the ruins of another country, with its networks of villages, farms and orchards, and its many forgotten stories. Now when he reads the historical markers celebrating the heroism and industry of Jewish settlers along the roads and trails where he hikes, he begins to see a new reality.

"I began to re-read them, and the girl who stole my Holocaust forced me to fill in the images with new faces, truths and facts. I faced the plaque describing the valorous battles around Kibbutz Tzova, one among hundreds of such plaques through the country perpetuating the memory of dead Jewish underground fighters. The tin plaque itself now contained stories that my eyes could read, like those stories I never told my interviewers before going to Miami: victories now contained the vanquished, the enemy was now also embodied in the plaques—it's fighters, women, children, homes, herds and lifestyle."

In Israel, this sympathy with the Palestinians and the identification with their humanity could be experienced as a kind of political subversion. But Noam can't stop the process—he is too curious, to begin with, and there are now too many memories, which raise too many questions. He remembers a beautiful spring named 'En Yizre'el located about thirty minutes' walk from his parents' house. It was one of his favorite hiking destinations when a child, and he loved to bathe in it. Among the eucalyptus trees surrounding the pool was a memorial for a soldier named Tzvi Karmeli, who fell during the battle of Zar'in, the name of a Palestinian village in the neighborhood before the largest Kibbutz, Kuibbutz Yizre'el was founded.

"But what was that battle over Zar'in? I never asked this question, neither as a child nor as a teenager. I knew that Zar'in was the village situated there before Kubbutz Yizre'el was founded. But where did that village disappear to? Where did all the people and animals go? What happened to the fields and fruit groves? I never asked, and was never told."

"Today, without my Holocaust, I sometimes try to imagine what happened in Zar'in when Golani infantry battalion 13 entered the village and cleansed its houses of their inhabitants, 'because they put up a heavy resistance,' as the ceremony texts put it. I've heard that Tzvi Karmeli was killed by a mine that he and his mates went out to lay at the spring. A mine at a spring? The spring of a neighboring village? Impossible. I can't believe that.

"After all, they burned out fields, they were thieves and murderers, and we defended ourselves and tended the land that we had purchased with money earned by the toil and sweat of our brows. We fought disease, mosquitoes and malaria. We built by day and guarded by night. In the books I read, the *Palmah* commandos carried out their secret missions while carefully avoiding unnecessary harm to civilians. An explosive charge at a village spring? Impossible. Simply impossible."

"I don't know if things could have been done differently, and the truth is I don't know what really went on. This is actually the worst fact of all: we know the story about Ahab, who murdered and inherited, we are familiar with Gideon's path down Gilboa Mountain to Harod spring and Sisra's escape route after his army sank in the valley's mud. We are learned, so we even know the geological epochs in which the Gilboa emerged and its strata formed, we know that some of them are water-penetrable and others are not, and thus Artesian springs were formed, like 'En Yizre'el and Harod spring nearby."

"We learn all of this in school, and we saw all of it on our youth movement outings. But we don't have an inkling of what happened here yesterday, right here, in our own 'En Yizre'el, the beautiful spring that over the years has also turned into a barbecue site where piles of trash abound after weekends and public holidays. The rushes and reeds that used to grow down to the water are no more. The eucalyptus clump has thinned out and the old pump house in the center of the pool has been cleaned and emptied of is equipment."

"The basalt memorial still stands there, commemorating Tzvi Karmeli, but for me it is a reminding of something more, even if only blurred: the memory of the men, women and children who lived in their villages, got up in the morning, tended their trees, herded their livestock, pumped water from the spring, built stone houses, prayed to God to grant them a good harvest, loved, hated, married, bore children, were unfaithful, happy, annoyed, cheated, stole, died, buried, cried. Lived. Villagers, owners of property, who became homeless overnight, left their houses and trudged south on the road at the foot of Gilboa Mountain, towards the city of Jenin. I met their children and grandchildren face-to-face in the refugee camps, on behalf of Saul. Not the king. The chief of staff."

One can have such thoughts and sympathies in Israel; but to articulate them, and act on them, could be dangerous—or at the very least, it could make life difficult. When Noam Chayut was a youngster at one of the many summer camps of his youth, he remembered sitting in a circle with the other children around a large sheet of paper on the floor of the meeting house. Their counselor proceeded to draw a big triangle, and next to each of the three points wrote these words: "Jewish," "Zionist," and "Israeli."

Each child was supposed to mark the spot inside the triangle and write their name nearest to the identity they felt most closely allied to.

But what if you wanted to affiliate yourself to some completely different identity, such as "justice-lover" or "entertainer" or "healer" or "truth-seeker," or any one of a thousand other identities of your own stubborn creation?

You couldn't. It wasn't on the triangle, and therefore wasn't permitted.

10.

My Holocaust was stolen from me in that village, but I understood nothing yet. Changes taking place in me were of the internal kind and I was unaware of them until my encounter with 'Breaking the Silence,' as the organizations would eventually be known.
—Noam Chayut

"'Breaking the Silence' is an Israeli non-governmental organization (NGO), located in a western part of Jerusalem, established by Israeli Defense Forces (IDF) soldiers and veterans who collect and provide testimonies about their service in the West Bank, Gaza Strip and East Jerusalem since the 'Second Intifada,' giving serving and discharged Israeli IDF personnel and reservists a platform to confidentially describe their experience in the Israeli-occupied territories." Thus does Wikipedia describe the controversial Israeli organization, 'Breaking the Silence.'

It summarizes the group's goal as follows: "The organization's stated mission is to 'break the silence' of IDF soldiers who return to civilian life in Israel and 'discover the gap between the reality they encountered in the [occupied] territories, and the silence which they encounter at home.' Since 2004, 'Breaking the Silence' has run a testimonies collection project called 'Soldiers Speak Out.' They have collected several hundred testimonies from 'those who have, during their service in the IDF, the Border Guard, and the Security Services, played a role in the occupied territories.' By publishing soldiers' accounts, 'Breaking the Silence' hopes to 'force society to address the reality it created' and face the truth about 'abuses toward Palestinians, looting, and destruction of property' that is familiar to soldiers."

J.J. Goldberg, an editor in the US for the *Jewish Daily Forward*, once characterized 'Breaking the Silence' as a "left-wing soldiers' protest organization," but Goldberg's characterization is inaccurate; in its demographic and ideological composition it has always been more than that, and in terms of its impact it has become something to be reckoned with. Yehuda Shaul, perhaps the most important original organizer of 'Breaking the Silence,' turned out, when Noam met him, to be an orthodox Jew with a thick beard and a black skullcap, about as far from being a secular leftie as one could imagine. Yehuda Shaul proved to be one of those rare individuals with the capacity to be both a good political organizer and a good friend. "Eventually, I would have the privilege of getting to know him very well—his capacity to listen, his willingness to make decisions only after consulting his partners in the organization and reaching unanimity, for which endless discussion and mutual persuasion were often needed. It became a privilege to know him and to work with him."

In 2004, toward the end of the 'Second Intifada,'[12] Noam Chayut, Yehuda Shaul and Avichai Sharon, all Israeli ex-servicemen and founders of 'Breaking the Silence,' publicly exhibited a photographic exhibit with texts submitted by IDF personnel who had served in Hebron. The exhibition was attended by thousands of Israelis, and overnight 'Breaking the Silence' became a center for organizing veterans and IDF personnel. In Israel, where people go out of their way not to publicly discuss violence toward Palestinians by security or military personnel, it signaled the beginning of a new kind of truth-telling. With a minimum of emphasis on torture and extra-judicial execution by security forces, the exhibition focused instead on the kind of petty harassment, destruction of property, beatings and arbitrary house demolitions that ordinary soldiers were expected to carry out.

These beatings and destruction of property—often accom-panied by indiscriminate shooting into houses—were often retal-iation for Palestinians who had filed complaints against soldiers, or non-violently demonstrated against right-wing settlers stealing their land or destroying their crops. Or shooting in houses was simply a form of 'collective punishment' to relieve the tensions felt by Israeli troops.

Chayut began to run into soldiers and ex-soldiers serving in Hebron who had been—and were being—changed emotionally by participation in the occupation; this produced "a few testimonies of another kind: deeper, not merely dry descriptions of unpleasant sights, but stories dealing with feelings and emotions, admitting personal responsibility, engaging in self-reflection. These were testimonies of combatants who even during their service realized that they were responsible, that their actions enabled the existence of that whole surreal apparatus that totally paralyzed life in the center of a big city while serving a few hundred [Jewish] settlers."

Noam begins to realize that he, too, was partly responsible; indeed, one suspects that this feeling began at the point that he, Yehuda Shaul and Avichai Sharon dreamed up their explosive truth-telling project in the first place. It had simply taken Noam a very long time to realize what personal responsibility felt like to him. He was beginning to realize that as he argued for his society to change, he was also changing his own personality— and vice versa.

To a great extent, Noam writes, he found himself following the example of his friend Yehuda Shaul: "When Yehuda Shaul looked in the mirror after his discharge, he did not see the smiling orthodox-religious boy who loved to hike throughout the country and help the needy. He saw a monster terrifying the streets of Hebron. He was horrified at his own image. Why him of all people?"

"Maybe because he did not grow up with my Holocaust. For him, enlisting in the army was a breach of social custom among the religious circles of his youth. Perhaps this was his reason for discovering the monster on the day of his discharge, the moment he turned in his army gear."

"Yehuda Shaul is not a normal person. Instead of going to a shrink or wiping his mind clear with drugs in India, or suppressing and denying and waiting for the day it would all burst out, he roared: 'If I look in the mirror and see a monster, then every member of the society that sent me must see this monster, too. I will show it.'"

"And so he did."

'Breaking the Silence' was the first time 'the most moral army in the world' acknowledged both its dreams and its nightmare, through the testimonies of serving and former members; and it happened where all of Israel could see it. That included what I regard as the most revealing outcome of an atrocity in a recital of atrocities. It seems the IDF wanted to kill some uniformed official in Gaza in retaliation for something Hamas had done. So they decided to assassinate a Palestinian policeman directing traffic in Gaza. But the shell missed, and instead hit a car with a family in it. The gunner in that tank, according to rumor, climbed out of his tank and carved swastikas all over his body, screaming, "I'm a Nazi!"

11.

"Few Israelis," Chayut writes, "know anything about their own army's rules of engagement. Fewer still oppose them. But whoever learns about them and dares to put two and two together will reach an inevitable conclusion: procedures have executors, and for every person killed, there is a killer. That killer might very well be the youth movement counselor you admired, or your neighbor's delicate son, or the intimidated boy from your grade-school class. Perhaps even your own boyfriend—imagine that!"

So whose fault was it that the family in the car mentioned above was killed? Was it just a big mistake? Was it the fault of the shell itself? Or was it the order from above to conduct an extrajudicial execution of a policeman?

When the Likud government—and its US proxies—use the Holocaust to justify Israeli's draconian policies toward the Palestinians, what does that do to Judaism? *How many dead Palestinians does it take to redeem six million dead Jews?* The strategy of redemptive violence doesn't work; one murder never redeems another murder, but simply creates more murder; and this bondage to aggression as a way of life can, and will, degrade the nature of a people, and ultimately whatever is left of their religion.

12.

There was one more step Noam Chayut needed to take, one more thing he needed, to complete the process that began with the girl that stole his Holocaust. Like so many other things in the 'Breaking the Silence' collaboration, it was his friend Yehuda Shaul, the fearless filmmaker, who knew where he needed to go. Working with some British students who were filming at the Qalandiya Checkpoint, Yehuda suggest that Noam meet him there so that he could be interviewed. Noam was apprehensive about this, because he had once commanded troops at this checkpoint.

"I was afraid of Palestinians and, even more, of my own feelings. For I actually had unpleasant bodily sensations whenever I traveled to the Occupied Territories as a civilian at the time: a strange malaise of sorts, slight nausea and even an unfamiliar sense of self-revulsion that made me want to wash up urgently. But even the cold, refreshing shower at home would not help. It did not relieve me of this irrational sense of filth."

Noam goes to meet the British students filming at the Qalandiya checkpoint. "When I arrived for my interview with the British students, I was surprised by the number of stalls. When my own company was assigned to the checkpoint and I was its commander for eight hours out of every twenty-four, we didn't let the venders get so close. One of the company's recon Jeeps was tasked with chasing them off. We wrote cardboard signs in Arabic instructing the venders to get the hell out. They immediately removed the signs. We often hurled teargas and stun grenades at them. Whenever a taxi driver insisted on waiting too close to the checkpoint—hoping he would be the lucky one to get passengers—we would hurl a teargas grenade into the cab through the window, just to make certain that this driver would not earn anything in the next few hours and would learn his lesson and never come so close again."

"In the interview I told [the British students] how I felt as a check point commander, how fatigue aggregated with fear to become apathy as the days rolled by, how human compassion and judgment are gradually lost. I described the mental process that a soldier at the checkpoint undergoes, how at first he tries to be nice, to smile, to explain, keep calm. How, eventually, he turns into an automaton, and how at the end of this process he no longer sees the Palestinians as human beings."

"During my army service I thought I believed all humans were equal, that everyone had the right to live in dignity and freedom. I believed that this situation I was in was temporary and imposed upon us in order to cope with terrorism. Now, in my memory—film-like—replays the events that transpired when I was in charge at Qalandiya Checkpoint, I know this was all a lie, a denial mechanism and a distortion of reality, a mechanism that enabled me to function without contradicting my own set of values, which in turn were being warped."

"Now I know that had I seen the crowds in front of me as human beings just like me, I would see how they were harassed even before carrying out my assignments: in the endless waiting forced upon them, standing in the baking sun behind high fences, in horribly crowded conditions, in an unbearable cacophony of shouts, quarrels, crying babies, pleading women and elderly people, screaming venders and the stench concocted by massive crowding and heat."[13]

He tells the students about how he and his soldiers sometimes engaged in "drying out" a recalcitrant Palestinian by making him stand, hands shackled behind his back in tight plastic cuffs, feet also shackled on occasion, and blindfolded. Why? Because he has been rude, yelled, cursed, bypassed the line, or any number of small infractions. There that Palestinian must stand, until perhaps the commander decides to give him a drink of water, or loosen his handcuffs.

He also tells them about an incident that he didn't see coming until it was already underway. "The line, as usual, was long and crowded. I was standing by the checking posts, making sure everything was operating smoothly. I looked at the line and noticed a young blond woman in western summer clothes standing dressed in between sweating me and the high fence. I approached her and signaled to her to get out of the line and bypass it. I would check her passport and let her proceed, I thought." But the blonde woman did something unexpected. "She made some room between herself and the others around her, waved her finger at me and yelled in foreign-accented English: 'What's the difference between me and the rest of the people here?'"

I didn't say anything but she repeated the same words again and again, and got more and more flushed. 'Tell me what the difference is! Why shouldn't they come around with me?' I smiled and answered her quietly, calmly and politely, that if she wanted to stand in line, suit herself. '*Tfadhali*, you may wait.'"

These are the stories Noam Chayut is telling the British students making their film about the injustices done to the Palestinians. So far all has gone as planned. But now something completely unexpected happens. Noam's friend Yehuda Shaul had an idea neither Noam nor any of the students could have predicted. There they were, waiting as the endless line of Palestinians files past, not saying very much—simply watching.

"Then Yehuda did something I did not understand, and at

first even tried to resist. He forced me deep into that crowed waiting line and said something like: 'I did this myself in Hebron. It's good for you, stand in line!' I tried to turn around and get out, but he gently gripped my shoulders and pushed me back inside. I stopped resisting."

"It was already noon. I felt as though I was watching a complex thriller from the middle and not understanding the plot, but it was shaking my every nerve ending, touching every bit of my skin. At times the film would go mute. I saw a vender selling sunglasses call out to me but did not hear what he said. Suddenly the sound was back and I realized he had called out to me a few times. I refused him with a nod, not uttering a word, so as not to identify myself and break the silence I was in."

"With that same mute nod I refused the child who offered me coffee in a small plastic cup. I shuffled further along the queue. Through the wire fence I saw soldiers get out of a staff Jeep at the same spot where two years earlier I had gotten out of such a Jeep. It was a changing of the guard at the checkpoint. I looked at the soldiers from the new shift approach their pals at the observation and checking posts and exchange words with them."

He watches as the Israeli soldiers go through the routine of changing the guard, remembering the hassles it usually involved. "Suddenly, I was terribly startled. Looking at the Palestinians crowded around me, I felt they could hear my thoughts and figure out that I was in fact a soldier like the ones across the fence. I was also afraid of the soldiers. What if that idiot over there had not unleaded the machine-gun point at us, or if I moved a few steps to the right and back and thus lost my place in line to some boys who crowded ahead of me. But now at least I was out of the soldiers' sight."

"Then my turn came. I wasn't ready for this. I hadn't thought at all about what I would say. I was standing in front of that concrete cube, facing a female soldier, her helmet a bit loose, her lips dry and sub-burnt, and she was yelling. 'Where's your ID?'

and I was silent. Confused. Not understanding where I actually was. I looked right and left at the concrete posts at my sides. Behind every one of them were soldiers. Palestinians were exiting the waiting line one by one, holding out their IDs. Again she yelled: 'Your ID already!!' I stared at her, petrified. A vein stood out in her flushed neck. 'Give me your passport!' she screamed in English. Quiet, then another scream: 'Your passport!'"

I came to my senses and took out my wallet, and out of it, my blue (Israeli) ID. "You're Israeli!" she barked at me. "Idiot, what are you doing here?!" She took my ID and went off to get someone.

I was alone facing the empty concrete block. I looked sideways and back and saw dozens of eyes staring at me. My ears were still ringing with her shout: "You're Israeli, what are you doing..." And suddenly I was scared of those stares, afraid of the crowd around me.

Someone behind me yelled in Hebrew: "Why are you messing with them and holding us all up!?"

I looked around for an armed soldier to protect me from them. But the female soldier was already gone and the two soldiers at the side posts did not even lift their eyes from the IDs they were checking. I felt like one of the soldiers at the checkpoint, threatened on every side, but unlike them—naked, exposed, no helmet, no bullet-proof vest, no gun. More moments of fear passed until an older gray-haired soldier came along, in his bullet-proof vest and helmet, his rifle hanging from his neck. My ID was in his hand and he approached me and asked in a calm voice. "You're from Afula. What are you doing here?"

"Before I found a good answer, he asked, 'Do you know where you are?' I nodded. 'You are not allowed in there. This area is closed to Israelis.'"

"'Closed to Israelis' he tells me, as if I don't know, I thought. Slowly I felt my sense of orientation return. I knew the man facing me was at least forty-five years old and past his reserves-duty days. I knew he was volunteering at the checkpoint to relieve some of the burden the young soldiers were bearing, and to 'solve moral issues' as we called it. Indeed, officially he was a soldier like all others and subordinate to the checkpoint commander, but in fact his role was to help the young soldiers out, using his personal experience and judgment—'humanitarians,' such people are called these days."

"I too had had humanitarians at the checkpoint. I saw them try, on their first shifts, to be gracious to Palestinians and keep up the appearance of an enlightened occupier, fair and composed. But I also saw them, after their third or fourth shift, begin to lose patience just like all the rest of us. Then exhaustion kicked in, too, and they found themselves tyrannizing people for no reason, grumbling, not listening, even throwing teargas and stun grenades and firing in the air like everyone else."

"The man standing in front of me showed me soon enough that he was already in that phase, for before I even answered him, began yelling at me: "I'll summon the police. Who do you think you are coming here, feeling the big hero, eh?" and immediately began to body-search me roughly. He also summoned another soldier, although I did not resist him at all."

"I decided I didn't want to complicate matters further and be handed over to the Israeli police. I did what was called for in order to get out of there quickly and quietly. I signaled to him to approach and whispered in his ear: "Listen, I was commander of this checkpoint for a long time." I showed him my reserve-officer card, and said: "Listen, pal, I don't know what I did. I went a bit crazy out here and have come back to see what was going on. Let's keep it quiet so that these guys here'—I pointed discreetly at the Palestinians—'won't slaughter me.'"

"He relented immediately and gave me back my ID, saying: 'Go wherever you want.'"

I began to make my way back among the people in line. My fear of the Palestinians crowded around me returned in full force. I feared every boy and man I passed. Then I saw Yehuda coming with the camera crew and I calmed down."

"'Don't film here!' the soldiers yelled at the British students who were filming me again as I passed by the line. A moment later the humanitarian showed up again and ran towards us shouting angrily that he was calling the police. He must have felt deceived. The cameraman lowered his camera."

"But one of the Palestinians cried out: 'Go on, film us! So people can see how we're caged in here, like cattle. Film these shits, go on!'"

More soldiers approached. We hurried away from the spot, but then I heard my name loudly called out from the checkpoint. The first question in my mind was: how come a soldier was calling me by my first name and not my last name, as I was called in the army? A fellow got out of the Jeep and came up to shake my hand through the fence: 'What are you doing out there? Come through here. It's much easier.'"

"The soldier was from my own village, five years younger than me. When he was in the seventh grade I was his youth movement counselor. He also used to come over to play computer games with my kid brother. My brother put off his own checkpoint hell by one year to do civilian volunteer duty in the *moshav* movement. The soldier suddenly noticed the film crew: 'Are you with them?' he asked, grimacing."

"'Yes,' I answered, and wanted to terminate this meeting. Again I noticed surprised and suspicious looks around me: a moment ago they were looking at a brave journalist, and now they are looking at a friend of a soldier. Once again, I didn't know who to fear most."

"Being at the checkpoint, on its other side, was the most profound psychological transformation I had ever undergone. I recommend it whole-heartedly to any checkpoints soldier whose mind has been scathed."

13.

The turning point for Noam Chayut is giving up societal privileges associated with an imagined victim status—in other words, he stops using 'traumatic privilege' as an excuse for doing things he knows to be wrong. As we've seen, it is very common in Israel that those who are bonded to aggression by a shared traumatic memory use it to justify the Israeli state's violence. When that kind of 'traumatic privilege' begins to seem false to them, however, when it no longer makes emotional sense, such people begin to understand that past trauma—no matter how horrendous—does not give them the right to oppress and traumatize new victims in the present, nor does it give the Israeli state that right.

The people who arrive at this conclusion include both those who have inherited 'traumatic memory' through intergenerational trauma, and those who have been psychologically traumatized in the recent past by violence against or by Palestinians, or a combination of both. (In Israel the shared traumatic memory of the Holocaust is often conflated with the trauma and guilt derived from violence against Palestinians.) But when the combined burden becomes too heavy, when 'traumatic privilege' no longer rings true, the psychological bond to aggression begins to break down. When that happens, the institutionalized forms of 'destructive entitlement' embedded in the Israeli state begin to weaken.

The individual under the influence of traumatic memory is likely to believe—and to *feel*—that violence is the proper response to social problems. He is, in other words, bonded by shared trauma to aggression as the fundamental dynamic of life. He is also likely to feel that his internalization of aggression, and the pain associated with the psychological trauma that caused it, gives his country—and him personally—the right to support violent solutions to social problems, and violent institutions to carry them out. The refusal of 'traumatic privilege' occurs when the individual understands *on an emotional level* that past violence is not an excuse for present violence, and likewise relinquishes the idea that the government of his country has such a right.

In The Girl Who Stole My Holocaust there are two points in this narrative at which the writer Noam Chayut gives up—or loses—the 'traumatic privilege' he has inherited. He loses the 'traumatic privilege' associated with the Holocaust, first, when he sees a young Palestinian girl looking at him with terror in her eyes and on her face, and running away in fear. The indoctrination of a lifetime is broken; his right to oppress Palestinians disappears, Chayut writes, because the Palestinian girl had 'stolen' his Holocaust. (That is, it no longer makes sense *emotionally* to hate and oppress Palestinians because of a shared traumatic memory of the Holocaust.) This starts out as a cognitive transformation, but over a period of months becomes a wracking emotional one, a transformation of Noam Chayut's entire personality.

Secondly, there is the equally transformative event when Noam is shoved, by his friend Yehuda Shaol, into the crowded line of Palestinians waiting at Qalandiya Checkpoint. Going through the checkpoint, he is forced to see the checkpoint as Palestinians see and experience it. It is a powerful and transformative event, absolutely one of the most important of his life. After this experience, all 'traumatic privilege' goes out the window permanently.

The Israeli organization 'Breaking the Silence' is all about speaking the unspeakable, talking about those subjects in Israel that have previously been taboo, subjects that nobody is supposed to discuss. It means, in other words, talking directly about the dangerous undercurrent of unspoken violence, fear, guilt and anger that accompanies the societal aggression involved in oppressing Palestinians. As we have already seen, the Israeli state instinctively understands the pivotal importance of shared traumatic memory in supporting apartheid and its attendant cruelties in the Occupied Palestinian Territories. A public discussion of what soldiers must do as part of Israel's occupation army is profoundly helpful psychologically to the soldiers and ex-soldiers, but it is also increasingly necessary— although excruciatingly painful—for Israeli society to know what is done in its name. And for that reason it is perceived as profoundly dangerous by the Likud government.

A similar taboo regarding the open discussion of Israeli violence against Palestinians operates also in the US, and is enforced by the Israel Lobby. To publicly discuss in America the everyday brutality that is practiced by Israel's occupation army, not to mention the use of extrajudicial execution and torture by Shin Bet and other security forces, is to invite immediate—and often hysterical—attacks that one is an anti-Semite, a self-hating Jew, a crypto-Nazi, or whatever. But such gratuitous personal attacks don't work as well now as they did once. Increasing numbers of people, including a great many Jews, see such attacks for what they are: evidence of an underlying pathology. They're likewise more willing to stand up to the Israel Lobby leadership and the right-wing billionaire donors that support them.

The Girl Who Stole my Holocaust tells the story of Noam Chayut's struggle to break free of an inherited, shared psychological trauma, and the internalized aggression that proceeds from such trauma. One is the traumatic memory of the Holocaust that is present at all levels of Israeli society, and which results in certain entrenched attitudes in that society; this traumatic memory is purposely kept alive, and systematically and consciously evoked by the Likud and other right-wing parties, to maintain political power for Netanyahu and his cohorts. To talk openly about this arouses intense anger and retaliation on the part of those who keep this toxic secret, in both America and Israel. That is the power of the trauma bond in Israel today; but the young in America are increasingly willing to speak about the unspeakable, because they know that to do so is the only way things will change.

In many ways, modern Israel resembles the American South before the triumph of the Civil Rights and Voting Rights Acts in 1964 and 1965. There, too, people were unable to discuss the unspeakable: they were unable to speak about the crimes used to keep Blacks in subjugation, and from which whites benefitted, but the toxic emotional effects from which neither whites nor Blacks were capable of escaping. People had the same suppressed guilt as one encounters among Israelis, causing them to despise the people they oppressed. And white southerners had the same impulse to drown all doubts in the emotional anesthesia of violence, which has likewise become the answer to everything for a great many Israelis.

The profound emotional transformation that Noam Chayut experienced in this amazing memoir could only happen because he began to realize, at some point, that nothing would change until Israeli society changed. He realized that simply feeling uncomfortable about the brutality against Palestinians wasn't enough; what was needed was to tell the truth about what the IDF was doing in the occupied territories, in the process moving Israel/Palestine toward some political resolution that could stop or greatly diminish its violence. The resolution would be difficult, because it had to provide security for both Jews and Palestinians—but simply by working to change his society, Noam Chayut greatly enhanced his own transformation emotionally. In his case, it all happened rather quickly, partly because of his energy and his self-confidence, and partly because of his friend Yehuda Shaul, who at times understood Noam's emotional needs before Noam did himself. This reminds us of the importance of emotional support in the recovery process, as we have seen in previous chapters.

In their relationships to other world leaders, Prime Minister Netanyahu and the Likud party do their best to posture themselves as victims rather than occupiers. This is standard practice for aggressors; as this writer has already observed, the claiming of victim status by aggressors is an observable constant in the economy of human aggression. *All aggressors are aggrieved*—this seems to be the rule. This is at least partly because the aggressor often *feels* like a victim, even as he devastates other peoples' lives. As mentioned before, the victim-aggressor is a recurring personality type in Israel, since the right-wing Likud government constantly postures itself as a victim, even as it administers ruthless policies in the territories it militarily occupies.

The similarity of this stance to the sociopath is striking, since the sociopath *always* considers himself a victim, even as he rapes, murders, lies and steals. The difference between the sociopath and the Israeli victim-aggressor is that the former has a personality disorder, whereas the latter has a situational disorder, driven by the internalized aggression of a shared traumatic memory, which he acts out as a form of state-supported systemic evil. Therefore the latter is potentially capable of eventually understanding his dilemma, *if* there are compelling reasons for him to do so. But the systematic uses of aggression and coercion are quite addictive, which means that many people caught up in them won't be able to change until they are forced to do so. That means their form of systemic evil must be challenged by the world, by American Jews, and by America itself, which supports their predations financially by giving Israel more money than any other country.

Noam Chayut's main contribution to Israeli society is clearly in his work with 'Breaking the Silence,' a project that has provided a way for him to engage in the 'recovery dualism' that this book recommends for people with traumatic memory. In fact, 'Breaking the Silence' is the recovery dualism writ large. *First*, in 'Breaking the Silence' Noam Chayut not only publicly speaks about his own traumatizing experiences in the occupied territories, but also about the generalized psychological burden of systematically oppressing other people, as he publicly interrogates the relativity between trauma, violence and systemic evil against Palestinians, exactly the subjects that the Likud government in Israel doesn't want people to discuss.

Secondly, Noam Chayut isn't merely discussing traumatizing events with a small circle of friends, but with the larger society that sent him to serve in the Occupied Palestinian Territories. This makes 'Breaking the Silence' a socially-beneficial project on a magnitude of influence rarely available to the individual in modern societies. Noam's self-deprecating humor, openness to emotional change, his clarity regarding personal deficits and assets, and his moral and physical courage, make him a formidable humanitarian. *The Girl Who Stole My Holocaust* tells the truth about the treatment of the Palestinians by the Israelis, and the toxic effect it is having on everybody in Israel/Palestine; but whether the Israelis are able to benefit from that truth—at least as much as Chayut does in articulating it—remains to be seen.

Chapter Seven

Writing about Atrocity: The Brilliant Life and Tragic Death of Iris Chang

Humanity is outraged in me and with me. We must not dissimulate or try to forget this indignation which is one of the most passionate forms of love.
George Sand

1.

This book is about people struggling to break free of the bonds of traumatic memory. But not all people are successful in doing so: to pretend otherwise would be to lie about the power of our subject matter, and in so doing to trivialize it. Managing an oppressed group's traumatic memory can often be an extremely difficult task, especially when that shared trauma isn't recognized, or minimized and denied by the majority culture. It is in the context of shared trauma that secondary or vicarious trauma can very often enter the mind and memory, and can be especially destructive to the person who is emotionally vulnerable in other ways. Why is this important? Because the tragedies of those who succumb to psychological trauma, including those that suffer from secondary and intergenerational trauma, can often teach us just as much as the narratives of those who manage it successfully.

The life, work and tragic death of Iris Chang, author of *The Rape of Nanking: the Forgotten Holocaust of World War II*, have become part of the legendry of modern American thought and scholarship. At the height of her fame as an internationally renowned author and speaker—at the age of 36—this brilliant and seemingly indomitable young woman was struck down by mental illness; three months after her breakdown, she took her own life. In addition to a previously undiagnosed mental illness, she also suffered from intense forms of secondary trauma as a result of writing about unthinkable war atrocities. There were repeated episodes in which Chang showed clear signs of being psychologically and even physically overwhelmed by interviews, photographs and written accounts of World War II Japanese atrocities that she was writing about.

This became acute during 2003 and early 2004 when Iris Chang was conducting interviews for her proposed fourth book, which was to be on the Bataan Death March. Not only did she conduct intensive interviews with American GI survivors of the Death March, but also personally typed up transcripts of the interviews, doing both these things at a time when she found it almost impossible to sleep. The horror of the interviews (and her increasingly profound sleep disturbance) clearly potentiated each other, contributing directly to her breakdown in August 2004 and her suicide three months later.

Iris Chang was the most successful—and from both a literary and historical point of view, the most important—modern writer on atrocities committed by the Japanese Imperial Army in Nanking in 1937-38, during what is usually called the Rape of Nanking. She was also this country's outstanding nonfiction writer on the Chinese-American experience. Chang's main historical importance is that by sheer will and imagination she courageously brought to light and vividly described a major historical event the West knew little about, and for a variety of reasons seemed determined to suppress or ignore. In so doing, Chang became a major culture hero in China and the Chinese Diaspora, where people bought her book on Nanking by the hundreds of thousands. But few knew the personal price she was paying. The life and death of Iris Change are harrowing examples of the toxic danger of internalizing too much of the aggression inherent in accounts of events in which mass murder and mass rape—as well as public dismemberment, torture and mutilation—are part of a shared traumatic memory.

2.

Chang Tien-chun, Iris Chang's grandfather, was a poet and journalist who lived in Nanking in the 1930s. He worked for the Koumintang, Chang Kai-Shek's political movement, educating government officials in the ideology of the Nationalist party; except for the hot summer months each year, Nanking was a pleasant place in which to live. But war clouds had been inexorably building since the early and middle 1930s, especially since Imperial Japan had invaded and occupied Manchuria in 1931. Even so, nobody, not even in their wildest nightmares, could have imagined what would eventually happen to Nanking in 1937-38.

Sun Yat-sen declared the Republic of China in 1911, and in 1928, under the Nationalists, Nanking once again became the capital of China. (It had been the capital of China from the third to the sixth centuries.) Nanking was a center of culture and the arts, of language study, of Chinese literature and Buddhist scripture; the democratic influence of Sun Yat-sen lingered after his death in 1925, and despite unending political upheavals within the Nationalist Party, usually involving Sun's successor Chang Kai-Shek, the city developed a rather cosmopolitan atmosphere in which both foreigners and an educated and growing middle class mingled freely.

As an educated Chinese writer and democrat, Chang Tien-Chun no doubt understood the threat posed to the rest of Asia by the growing ferocity of Japanese nationalism, and Japan's insistence on war (and political power as defined by the warrior's code) as the pivot upon which Asia's future should devolve. But he probably hoped, as many people who lived in Nanking at that time surely did, that the time of reckoning could somehow be deferred, or that if war came Chiang Kai-shek would be able to defend Shanghai and Nanking. Only later would Chiang's tragic shortcomings as a general become part of the historical record.

Chang Tien-Chun realized by autumn of 1937 that his family was not safe in Nanking, so he sent his wife and their small child to her village at Tai Hu Lake, between Nanking and Shanghai. He visited her once, in November; but upon returning to Nanking, he was surprised to discover his entire governmental department engaged in packing up to evacuate the city. They were supposed to regroup at the city of Wuhu, on the Yangtze River, so Tien-Chun immediately sent word to his family to meet him there. As so often happens in such crises, middle-class professionals and educated people in Nanking had begun to flee, because they—like Chang Tien-Chun—had the resources to do so; first to evacuate were those involved with government departments that could sponsor large-scale movements of people, most of whom brought their family members. The ones who were left in Nanking were the poorer classes and newly-arrived peasants from the countryside, who had hoped to find safety behind Nanking's ancient walls. In all, about half the people of Nanking were able to leave, leaving the other half—the poorest and least defensible half—to await their fate in the city.

Meanwhile, Chang Kai-Shek threw his best troops into the defense of Shanghai. Their determination to defend the city came as a considerable shock to the Japanese, who had convinced themselves that the Chinese were a subhuman race, and therefore incapable of mounting an effective defense. It was as though all the propaganda they had been hearing for many years, as well as their training as soldiers—in which concepts of racial and cultural superiority played a critical role—were being refuted on the battlefield. The result was a deep and sustained anger. Furthermore, as the Japanese finally took Shanghai, there was a concomitant organizational breakdown in the Chinese forces, and something close to a complete breakdown in morale.

Unfortunately, Chang Kai-Shek's best troops had been lost in Shanghai, and the troops that remained tended to be new and undisciplined; in retrospect, the decision to retreat to Nanking was a disastrous strategic mistake: Nanking was surrounded on two sides by the Yangtze River, and the three Japanese army groups advancing on Nanking effectively cut off escape. Chang Kai-Shek and his governing bureaucracy were able to organize a small and effective retreat across the Yangtze, but he inexplicably left hundreds of thousands of his demoralized Chinese troops behind, trapped and abandoned to their fate, without any kind of instructions or command structure to help them fight back, break out, or otherwise defend themselves. Tang, the ineffectual, opportunistic commander he left behind, was caught up in a retreat that became a mad rout, with untold numbers of his troops drowning in the Yangtze.

The Imperial Japanese Army began committing mass atrocities against both Chinese civilians and soldiers even as they marched from Shanghai to Nanking, burning cities, raping women, and killing people at will. According to one Japanese journalist with the Japanese troops, "The reason that the [10th Army] is advancing to Nanking quite rapidly is due to the tacit consent among the officers and men that they could loot and rape as they wished."[1] It was on the march to Nanking from Shanghai that Toshiaki Mukai and Tsuyoshi Noda, two Japanese officers, conducted their notorious and widely-reported 'killing contest' to see who could first kill 100 Chinese using swords. (Both men were executed for war crimes after the Second World War.)

Meanwhile, Chang Tien-Chun waited anxiously in Wuhu for the arrival of his wife and family members. For four long, agonizing days he waited on the docks for them, but they were nowhere to be seen. Would he have to leave without them, assuming they were not coming, or stay in Wuhu to face the advancing Japanese? In despair he cried out his wife's name to the heavens: *"Yi-Pei!"* To his utter astonishment, a distant voice from far out in the Yangtze River answered him. It was not an echo from heaven, but rather his wife herself, in one of the very last sampans to reach the docks of Wuhu. That tiny boat contained his wife, his daughter, and several of Chang Tien-Chun's relatives. They proceeded to relative safety, as Chang Kai-Shek eventually set up his new government in Chungking.

This incident entered the family's lore as one of many miracles of their survival. It was in this way that the miraculous story of escape from Nanking came down to Iris Chang, the American-born granddaughter of Chang Tien-Chun. Also passed down to Iris—perhaps enhanced by her parents' knowledge that for reasons of class they had been able to escape something that many with more limited resources could not—would be the parents' horror regarding the incomprehensible nightmare that had been unleashed upon the people remaining in Nanking: the *Nanjing Datusha*, or Great Nanking Massacre.

3.

Iris Shun-Ru Chang was born on March 28, 1968, in Princeton, New Jersey, to immigrant Chinese parents. Her mother, Ying-Ying Chang, was a biochemist and microbiologist, and her father Dr. Shau-Jin Chang, a physicist. The couple had met and married while studying at Harvard. When Iris was two, they moved to the Champaign-Urbana area in Chicago, and Ying-Ying and Shau-Jin worked for the next three decades teaching and conducting research at the University of Illinois. Iris attended the lab school at the University, and attended the school with other children of the university faculty.

Iris Chang's parents were enlightened, kind people who consulted Benjamin Spock's *Baby and Child Care* but also taught their children to be proud of their Chinese culture and heritage. Iris and her brother, Michael, were raised bilingual in English and Mandarin; they were also taught by their father to raise silkworms, as many children in China still do. (This experience may have been in the back of Iris' mind when she chose the title for her first book, *Thread of the Silkworm*.) In the third grade, she participated in a class project in which the children were asked to choose an American hero about whom they would write reports. Iris chose Clara Barton, the nineteenth-century nurse who founded the American Red Cross, because of Barton's courage, she said, but also because "she cares."

Iris was an extremely fast reader, and at one point was reading so many books that her parents wondered if she was reading *too* many of them. In grade school she also started winning literary contests, which caused some of her friends' parents to whisper that her mother was writing her poems for her. ("Alas!" Ying-Ying responded, "I wish I *could* have written them!") Iris participated in a regional authors' conference for young writers; at this conference, a best-selling author gave a speech and signed books. "Iris's eyes were sparkling throughout the conference," her mother wrote later. "From that moment on, I think the fact that being an author was glamorous was planted in Iris's mind."

It was a comfortable life, but—in a way that reminds one of families that struggle with traumatic memory associated with the Holocaust—it included an awareness of a sometimes unspoken but powerful evil in the family's collective consciousness. Iris Chang dealt with this directly in the 'Introduction' to her book on the Nanking massacre.

"I first learned about the Rape of Nanking when I was a little girl. The stories came from my parents, who had survived years of war and revolution before finding a serene home as professors in a Midwestern American college town. They had grown up in China in the midst of World War II and after the war fled with their families, first to Taiwan and finally to the United States to sturdy Harvard and pursue academic careers in science. For three decades they lived peacefully in the academic community of Champaign-Urbana, Illinois, conducting research in physics and microbiology."

"But they never forgot the horrors of the Sino-Japanese War, nor did they want me to forget. They particularly did not want me to forget the Rape of Nanking. Neither of my parents witnessed it, but as young children they had heard the stories, and these were passed down to me. The Japanese, I learned, sliced babies not just in half but in thirds and fourths, they said; the Yangtze River ran red with blood for days. Their voices quivering with outrage, my parents characterized the Great Nanking Massacre, or *Nanjing Datusha*, as the single most diabolical incident committed by the Japanese in a war that killed more than 10 million Chinese people."

"Throughout my childhood *Nanjing Datusha* remained buried in the back of my mind as a metaphor for unspeakable evil." But if it represented the acting out of complete and total evil in her parents' world, Iris wanted to know more about it. To her shock and surprise, she could find no information about it—there was a complete blackout on the subject in books about the Second World War. "While still in grade school I searched the local public libraries to see what I could learn about the massacre, but nothing turned up. That struck me as odd. If the Rape of Nanking was truly so gory, one of the worst episodes of human barbarism in world history, as my parents insisted, then why hadn't someone written a book about it?" The West understood the moral importance of Hiroshima and Dachau, but about Nanking it was clueless.

That remained the reality right up to the time Iris Change published *The Rape of Nanking: The Forgotten Holocaust of World War II*. As Chang herself points out, nothing about Nanking appears in *The American Heritage Picture History of World War II*, for years the best-selling single-volume history of the war; nor was it mentioned even once in Winston Churchill's *Memoirs of the Second World War*.[2] The impact of the stories told about the *Nanjing Datusha* by Chang's parents, combined with the curious fact that western historians seemed intent on excising it from the written and photographic record, made a deep impression on Iris Chang. If something of such enormous evil had occurred, why did historians refuse to mention it? Was there a kind of hidden protocol that certain facts had to be covered up, and banished from the historical record?

Over the next two decades Iris Chang finished her education, got married, moved to California and launched her career as a successful author. She graduated from the journalism department at the University of Illinois, during which she worked as a stringer for the New York Times, writing six front-page stories over a period of a year — an incredible coup, it seems to this writer, for a student still in college. There were two brief jobs with the Associated Press and with the Chicago Tribune; afterwards she studied at the Writing Seminars at John Hopkins University. And she also married Bretton Lee Douglas, a name so delightfully and unabashedly WASP that it almost seems contrived. But it was very real, and so was their love, real enough to sustain long separations before and during marriage.

According to her friend Paula Kamen, the marriage came about as a result of typical Iris Chang chutzpah: "One day in college, she decided she wanted a boyfriend. Someone suggested that frat parties were a good place to meet guys. So she went to one, and there she met her red-haired husband-to-be, a star engineering candidate from a small farming town. He was delighted with — instead of taken aback by — her drive and candor." As were a great many others: there was something so open about her drive and ambition that people found it engaging, at least in college. And her sense of humor and her physical beauty likewise impressed many.

Paula Kamen mentions another Chang characteristic: a pronounced tendency toward perfectionism. "As the features editor of our college paper, I had edited her articles — or actually *never* edited them — because they always came in perfect. The facts, grammar, punctuation, gerunds, everything." But at some point in the early 1990s, when the two young women got together, Paula noticed some worrisome signs: "During that meeting, or perhaps another one, I was immediately sorry to see that the grueling hours at her new job at the Associated Press were wearing her down. In college, she was a steamroller of energy. But now she was frail and told me her hair was coming out. I saw then for the first time just how hard she worked, how she put a piece of herself into every story she covered."[3]

Writers as a group tend to be obsessive, but the fact that Iris Chang presented as frail, and reported that her hair was falling out, was a red flag. This same phenomenon would repeat itself several times: intense work, going without sleep for many days at a time, sometimes also going without food, would lead to tears and anxiety, often followed by a report that her hair was falling out. Both cause and symptom of these harrowing episodes, it appears in retrospect, was the more or less constant sleep deprivation to which she regularly subjected herself. Her extreme intensity, her obsessive perfectionism, the contemptuous rejection of her own body's need for sleep, and the tendency to put work projects above her own psychic and physical needs—all would play a role in her eventual breakdown. On some level, of course, she greatly enjoyed the ability to stay up all night and work twice as hard as everybody else—she saw such intensity as an asset that would help her achieve her goals. But going without sleep had already become a habit, one that would have dangerous consequences for her mental and physical health.

There was an interesting sidelight to the friendship of Paula Kamen and Iris Chang. Jews, a demographic to which Paula nominally belonged, had long been perceived as producing academic stars in higher education. But Iris Chang was an Asian-American who had, during their time together at college, won many of the scholarships and internships that Paula had competed for. Although it was important for many other reasons, their friendship was also emblematic of the way in which Asian-

Americans were now coming to challenge the reputation that Jews had formally held as academic over-achievers.

Paula had, at one time, been intensely jealous of Iris Chang's success, but quickly got over it; and in so doing, she revealed the one quality that Iris needed but didn't have, which was a capacity for introspection concerning her own gifts and limitations—that, and a more balanced attitude toward what is possible for the human mind and body. Paula Kamen would go ahead to write *Finding Iris Chang: Friendship, Ambition, and the Loss of an Extraordinary Mind*, a deeply insightful book about Iris' life and self-inflicted death that at present constitutes, along with the book by Iris' mother Ying-Ying Chang, the best things written about Iris Chang.

It was after moving to California (after her stint in the John Hopkins writing program) that Iris picked up her life as an important American author. Her first book, *Thread of the Silkworm*, told the cautionary tale of Chinese scientist Tsien Hsue-Shen, who was driven from the US by McCarthyism and ended up contributing in major ways to China's ballistic missile program; his forced exile from the US prefigured a similar McCarthyist campaign against Chinese scientist Wen Ho Lee in 1999-2000. Such events contributed to Iris Chang's later belief that Chinese-Americans could never completely assimilate to American culture, because they would never—on some level—be considered "real" Americans.

But Iris Chang had never forgotten the stories her parents told her of the Rape of Nanking, about the Japanese soldiers "cutting up babies into thirds and fourths," and the Yangzte River running red with blood. After *Silkworm*, Chang made contact with a network of young Chinese Asian-American writers and filmmakers involved in film projects documenting the Nanking massacre. Iris Chang felt—correctly, I believe—that a great many first- and second-generation Chinese-Americans experienced a need to document the Rape of Nanking because of a sense of loss and grief after the Tiananmen Square massacre of 1989: "The pro-democracy movement left behind vast, intricate webs of Internet relationships; out of this network a grassroots movement emerged to promote the truth about Nanking."

The trauma that Tiananmen evoked was very real. This writer was living in student housing at the University of Massachusetts in Amherst in 1989, at a time when UMass hosted a great many students from mainland China. Almost all of them sympathized with the students at Tiananmen, and the vast majority had signed respectful but strongly-worded petitions to the Chinese government supporting the students. When the massacre began, a wave of despair and depression washed over the Chinese students in student housing; not only were they watching in real time as their contemporaries in Tiananmen Square were being slaughtered, but over the next 24 hours came the horrifying realization that many of them might never be going home again, because of their very public petitions on behalf of the Tiananmen students. Those same students had now been declared enemies of the state by Chinese government. It was among such networks of radicalized Chinese students that, according to Chang, the trauma of Tiananmen generated a movement to vigorously make public—to force the world to see and acknowledge—the suppressed trauma of Nanking.

These Chinese-Canadian and Chinese-American networks were, in effect, operating out of a double traumatic memory: first of Tiananmen, and then of the even more horrible (and histori-cally suppressed) memory of what really happened in Nanking. Whether Tiananmen or Nanking, to be deeply touched by a massacre that the world doesn't much know or care about, and furthermore doesn't want to remember—that is doubly trauma-tizing.

As Iris' interest in Nanking grew, she found out about an organization called the Global Alliance for Preserving the History of World War II in Asia, which was intent on telling the story of

Nanking to the world, and in so doing commemorating its dead. Ignatius Y. Ding, who would later mentor Iris, was very active in this group. Iris found out about a conference they were holding in Cupertino, California, in the Silicon Valley, and decided to go. Perhaps because they were having such difficulty getting the world to believe what had happened in Nanking, this group made the decision to display huge poster-size photographs of atrocities committed by Japanese soldiers during the seven weeks of the Rape of Nanking occurring in 1937-38.

The day that Iris went to the exhibition—December 13, 1994— was a day that changed her life forever. When Iris Chang arrived at the community center in Cupertino, she discovered that the photographs were not just pictures of the dead. These were huge, poster-sized photographs of unthinkable atrocities taken *as they were being committed by Japanese soldiers*. The graphic nature of these photographs—the acute horror they revealed and documented—was beyond anything she could have expected or anticipated, because it exceeded anything most people could imagine.

What Iris Chang saw at the Cupertino conference were photographs of dead and mutilated women with foreign objects protruding from their vaginas, mass executions, people being used as bayonet practice, piles of dead babies, beheading contests by Japanese soldiers, rivers full of bodies, naked women tied to furniture to be repeatedly raped, and Japanese soldiers engaging in the sadistic sport of burying prisoners alive, not to mention dousing people with gasoline and setting then on fire. The soldiers were also engaging in many other acts of sadism difficult for the normal mind to imagine.

Iris Chang was above all a sensitive person; so it is not surprising that suddenly being exposed to these photographs was a traumatizing experience, as she herself reported; according to her mother and all who knew her well, she became determined at that moment to tell the world about Nanking. It is a strange but haunting detail that this date, December 13, the day that Iris visited the Cupertino exhibition, was the same date in 1937 on which Nanking fell to the Imperial Japanese Army.

In "The Photos that Changed Her Life," a chapter in her book about Iris, Iris' mother Ying-Ying Chang wrote that her daughter's decision to write about Nanking "came all of a sudden, in December 1994. As Iris told us, and as described in [her] book, she made up her mind to write about this most atrocious chapter of history when she was attending a conference in Cupertino, California on December 13, 1994."[4] From that moment on, Iris Shun-Ru Chang was committed to writing the definitive English-language book on the Nanking massacre.

After writing *The Rape of Nanking*, Iris was asked by a Japanese reporter about her decision to write the book. Iris replied that when a child, her parents had told her about the Nanking massacre, and it had made a powerful impression on her. But when she tried to research it, she found that no books had been written about it. "The event remained a question mark in my mind for years," Iris said, "until I saw an exhibit of photographs on the subject in 1994. The horror of those photographs inspired me to write the book."[5]

Iris Chang was well aware that her attendance at the Cupertino conference on December 13, 1994, had changed her life. In *The Rape of Nanking*, Iris Chang describes the effects of the large photographs on her: "In the conference hall the organizers had prepared poster-sized photographs of the Rape of Nanking—some of the most gruesome photographs I had ever seen in my life. Though I had heard so much about the Nanking massacre as a child, nothing prepared me for these pictures—stark black-and-white images of decapitated heads, bellies ripped open, and nude women forced by their rapists into various pornographic poses, their faces contorted into unforgettable expressions of agony and shame."

"In a single blinding moment I recognized the fragility of not just life but the human experience itself. We all learn about death while young. We know that any one of us could be struck by the proverbial truck or bus and be deprived of life in an instant. And unless we have certain religious beliefs, we see such a death as a senseless and unfair deprivation of life. But we also know of the respect for life and the dying process that most humans share. It you are struck by a bus, someone may steal your purse or wallet while you lie injured, but many more will come to your aid, trying to save your precious life. One person will call 911, and another will race down the street to alert a police officer on his or her beat. Someone else will take off his coat, fold it, and place it under your head, so that if these are indeed your last moments of life, you will die in the small but real comfort of knowing that someone cared about you."

"The pictures up on that wall in Cupertino illustrated that not just one person but hundreds of thousands could have their lives extinguished, die at the whim of others, and the next day their deaths would be meaningless. But even more telling was that those who had brought about these deaths (the most terror-filled, even if inevitable, tragedy of the human experience) could also degrade the victims and force them to expire in maximum pain and humiliation. I was suddenly in a panic that this terrifying disrespect for death and dying, this reversion in human social evolution, would be reduced to a footnote of history, treated like a harmless glitch in a computer program that might or might not again cause a problem, unless someone forced the world to remember it."

I do not blame the organizers of the Cupertino conference for posting the poster-size atrocity photographs. They were furious at the world for not recognizing what had happened at Nanking, and rightly so; they were at the point where they had to take strong action to get the world's attention. Furthermore, while it is almost certain that Iris Chang was traumatized by the photographs, she did the one thing that such a person should do, which is to talk about the traumatizing event. And she *did* talk about it, in what were finally thousands of different public appearances, explaining why the world had to come to terms with what had happened. But she did not often talk about what it did to *her*, and the exceedingly personal way she went about internalizing the suffering of the victims of Nanking.

At the Cupertino event she stands next to a photograph taken of a woman during the Rape of Nanking.[6] This woman is weeping helplessly into her crippled hand: two of her fingers appear to be smashed. Iris Chang stands next to this photo, leaning against the wall, with her face pressed close to the suffering woman's face. The message is clear: *she will share this unknown woman's suffering and horror*. It was a stunning and strikingly explicit indication of what Iris Chang sought to do. But one must ask, is it advisable to stand in such unrelenting proximity to suffering, without drawing boundaries for one's own protection? Is it right to share the despair of victims one is writing about? If one does, how long can such identification with another person's despair continue without negative consequences to the project, and to the writer?

Iris Chang's vivid memories of her parents' stories about Nanking had long functioned as a kind of illustrative subtext for her necessarily limited understanding of evil. But here was that same evil *as it actually happened*, documented in scores of unforgiving, terrifyingly real photographs—large, *poster-sized* photographs. She was not prepared, as she said later in interviews, to see that kind of radical evil. Nobody is, in reality, but because of her extreme sensitivity, Iris Chang was particularly vulnerable.

Imagine, then, how writing about the sadistic frenzy that was Nanking must have affected Iris Chang. Her self-description of being "suddenly in a panic" during that single blinding moment in which she understood life's fragility, is a tip-off to the depth of her response to the photographic exhibit in Cupertino; it was a moment that changed everything. This was the evil that her grandparents had fled, the evil that had caused her mother's voice to tremble when she talked about it, the evil that had launched the family on its long flight that would end in America; here it was. Yet there was nothing in the history books about it— one of the most evil episodes in human history, and it had seemingly been eradicated from history! In January of 1995, encouraged by Chinese-American activists in the Bay Area, she flew back east to undertake research on the Nanking massacre at the Library of Congress in Washington DC and at the Yale Divinity School Library, where some key documents were housed.

In retrospect, there were two pivotal turning points in the life of Iris Chang. One was the Cupertino conference of December 13, 1994, when she first saw the photographs of the Nanking atrocities of the Imperial Japanese Army. The second date was ten years later, on August 12th, 2004, when she became psychotic in a hotel room in Louisville, Kentucky, whence she had gone to interview survivors of the Bataan Death March. There was a tragic connection between the two dates, although no one could have predicted or comprehended it at the time. After seeing the photographs of Japanese atrocities in Cupertino, Iris would devote the next few years of her life to researching and writing her classic *The Rape of Nanking: The Forgotten Holocaust of World War II*, which would sell half a million copies in English, be translated into at least 15 languages, and become not only the definitive book about the Nanking massacre but one of the great works of narrative nonfiction of our time.

4.

There are several factors that make the Rape of Nanking unique in the history of human evil, as well as the attempts of journalists to record it and historians to understand it. One factor is the pervasive sadism—which should rightly be called radical evil—

of the atrocities committed by the Japanese soldiers. Another is the fact that it went on so long: seven weeks, most historians say. Third is the seemingly incomprehensible fact that the atrocities were so *public*. Most armed groups intent on committing atrocities try to conceal their crimes; but the Japanese troops tortured, raped and murdered in broad daylight, as photographers took photos and traumatized witnesses watched in speechless horror.

Here is a brief summation of the events,[7] in roughly the same order as Iris Chang wrote about them in *The Rape of Nanking: The Forgotten Holocaust of World War II*, and whenever possible quoting directly from her book:

The atrocities began with an order from the top commander, Prince Asaka, to kill all the Chinese POWs. There is some controversy about who gave the kill order, but what is important is that once it began, nobody at any point of the command structure tried to stop it. (Previously the Imperial Japanese Army had asked for permission from the Emperor to deal with prisoners-of-war as they wished, the implication clearly being that they sought the right to kill POWs.) On the morning of December 13, 1937, as the Japanese broke through the gates of Nanking, the Japanese 66th Battalion received a direct order to kill all Chinese soldiers taken prisoner. *"All prisoners of war are to be executed. Method of execution: divide the prisoners into groups of a dozen. Shoot to kill separately."* Inside Nanking, marauding groups of Japanese soldiers simply killed Chinese soldiers whenever they encountered them. Larger groups of Chinese POWs that surrendered as a group were to be taken to various killing fields adjacent to — or in the vicinity of — Nanking. *"From the discussion it is decided that the prisoners are to be divided evenly among each company (1st, 2nd and 4th company) and to be brought out from their imprisonment in groups of 50 to be executed."*

But groups of 50 were not large enough. Prisoners were gradually separated into somewhat larger groups. "Because of their limited manpower," Iris Chang writes in *The Rape of*

Nanking, "the Japanese relied heavily on deception. The strategy for mass butchery involved several steps: promising the Chinese fair treatment in return for an end to resistance, coaxing them into surrendering themselves to their Japanese conquerors, dividing them into groups of one to two hundred men, and then luring them to different areas near Nanking to be killed. Nakajima hoped that faced with the impossibility of further resistance, most of the captives would lose heart and comply with whatever directions the Japanese gave them."

Probably the most massive slaughter of POWs happened in the vicinity of Mufu Mountain. It lay due north of Nanking, between the city and the Yangtze River. According to Chang's sources, some 57,000 civilians and POWs were executed in this region. One such organized mass execution was an incident in which some 14,777 soldiers fell into the hands of the Japanese near the 'artillery forts' of Wulong Mountain and Mufu Mountain.

"According to Kurihara Riichi, a former Japanese army corporal who kept diaries and notes of the event, the Japanese disarmed thousands of prisoners, stripped them of everything but their clothes and blankets, and escorted them to a row of straw-roofed temporary buildings. When the Japanese military received orders on December 17 to kill the prisoners, they proceeded with extra caution. That morning the Japanese announced that they were going to transport the Chinese prisoners to Baguazhou, a small island in the middle of the Yangtze River. They explained to the captives that they needed to take special precautions for the move and bound the captives' hands behind their backs—a task that took all morning and most of the afternoon."

"Sometime between 4:00 and 6:00 PM, the Japanese divided the prisoners into four columns and marched them to the west, skirting the hills and stopping at the riverbank. 'After three or four hours' waiting and not knowing what was going on, the prisoners could not see any preparations for crossing the river,' the corporal wrote. 'It was then growing dark. They did not know... that Japanese soldiers already encircled them in a crescent formation along the river and they were in the sights of many machine guns.'

"By the time the executions began, it was too late for the Chinese to escape. 'Suddenly all kinds of guns fired at once,' Kurihara Riichi wrote. 'The sounds of these firearms mingled with desperate yelling and screams.' For an hour the Chinese struggled and thrashed about desperately, until there were few sounds still coming from the group. From evening until dawn the Japanese bayoneted the bodies, one by one."

It was a horrible death, but the death of the Chinese solders was at least a relatively quick one. The fate of the civilians was considerably more brutal. "The torture that the Japanese inflicted upon the native population at Nanking," wrote Iris Chang, "almost surpasses the limit of human comprehension."

In *The Rape of Nanking* she documents the following forms of torture, rape and mass murder:

Live burials: "The Japanese directed [live] burial operations with the precision and efficiency of an assembly line. Soldiers would force one group of Chinese captives to dig a grave, a second group to bury the first, and then a third group to bury the second and so on. Some victims were partially buried to their chests or necks so that they would endure further agony, such as being hacked to pieces by swords or run over by horses and tanks."

Mutilations: "The Japanese not only disemboweled, decapitated, and dismembered victims but performed more excruciating varieties of torture. Throughout the city they nailed prisoners to wooden boards and ran over them with tanks, crucified them to trees and electrical posts, carved long strips of flesh from them, and used them for bayonet practice. At least one hundred men reportedly had their eyes gouged out and their noses and ears hacked off before being set on fire. Another group of two hundred Chinese soldiers and civilians were stripped naked, tied to columns doors of a school, and then stabbed by *zhuizi*—special needles with handles on them—in hundreds of points along their bodies, including their mouths, throats, and eyes."

Death by fire: "The Japanese subjected large crowds of victims to mass incineration. In Hsiakwan a Japanese soldier bound Chinese captives together, ten at a time, and pushed them into a pit, where they were sprayed with gasoline and ignited. On Taiping Road, the Japanese ordered a large number of shop clerks to extinguish a fire, then bound them together with rope and threw them into the blaze. Japanese soldiers even devised games with fire. One method of entertainment was to drive mobs of Chinese to the top stories or roofs of buildings, tear down the stairs, and set the bottom floors on fire. Many such victims committed suicide by jumping out of windows or off rooftops."

Mass Rape: Somewhere between twenty and eighty thousand women were raped, a great many (probably the majority) tortured and killed during or after the rapes. Dismemberment and mutilation of women often occurred after or during the rapes. Those women who were raped and lived afterwards often committed suicide. Many women who carried resulting pregnancies to full term ended up killing the babies after they were delivered.

"Another form of amusement involved dousing victims with fuel, shooting them, and watching them explode into flame. In one infamous incident, Japanese soldiers forced hundreds of men, women, and children into a square, soaked them with gasoline, and then fired on them with machine guns."

Chang adds that the Japanese deliberately froze thousands of victims by forcing them to break the ice on a pond and plunge into the water; another particularly diabolical method of torture was to "bury victims to their waist and watch them get ripped apart by German shepherds." She adds, however, that these incidents are "only a fraction of the methods that the Japanese used to torment their victims. The Japanese saturated victims in acid, impaled babies with bayonets, hung people by their tongues. One Japanese reporter who later investigated the Rape of Nanking learned that at least one Japanese soldier tore the heart and liver out of a Chinese victim to eat them."

And throughout the seven weeks, on a daily basis, the Japanese soldiers were engaged in mass executions. Many times these daily killings took the form of mass beheadings. But Chang doesn't just document available statistics—she tells stories about survivors, including one about Tang Shunsan, an elderly survivor that she personally interviewed in China. This man, who was a twenty-five-year-old Chinese shoemaker's apprentice at the time of the Nanking massacre, originally found a place to hide during the massacre. Because he was curious about what Japanese soldiers looked like—he had never seen a person from Japan, but had heard these resembled Chinese—he boldly but unwisely left his hiding place, and was quickly taken into custody by Japanese troops. Soon Tang found himself near a freshly dug, rectangular pit already filled with fifty or sixty Chinese corpses.

"Then, to Tang's horror, a competition began among the soldiers—a competition to determine who could kill the fastest. As one soldier stood sentinel with a machine gun, ready to mow down anyone who tried to bolt, the eight other soldiers split up into pairs to form four separate teams. In each team, one soldier beheaded prisoners with a sword while the other picked up heads and tossed them aside in a pile. The prisoners stood frozen in silence and terror as their countrymen dropped, one by one. 'Kill and count! Kill and count!' Tang said, remembering the speed of the slaughter. The Japanese were laughing; one even took photographs. 'There was no sign of remorse at all.'

"A deep sorrow filled Tang. 'There was no place to run. I was prepared to die.' It saddened him to think that his family and loved ones would never find out what happened to him."[1]

The killing contest lasted for about an hour. When the man standing in front of Tang was beheaded, Tang fell backwards with the dead man's body into the pit. Now the Japanese soldiers had grown tired of beheading, and were simply slashing throats. Tang lay very quietly under the bodies on top of him. "Later that afternoon, at about 5:00 PM, Tang's fellow shoemaker apprentices Big Monk and Small Monk came to the pit, hoping to retrieve his corpse. Through a crack in the brick wall of their house, they had seen the Japanese herd Tang and the others away and assumed that he was now dead with all the others." But when they spotted him moving around, alive under the dead bodies, they quickly pulled him out and hustled him back to his hiding place. He lived to tell the harrowing story of his near-death experience to the youthful Chinese-American author Iris Chang as she interviewed survivors fifty years later.

How many people died in the Rape of Nanking? What was the final death toll, in other words? Estimates vary, but it is possible to arrive at a consensus range of estimates. Officials at the Memorial Hall of the Victims of the Nanking Massacre by Japanese Invaders claim 300,000 deaths. The International Military Tribunal of the Far East (IMTFE) cautiously estimated "more than 260,000" fatalities. Another estimate, using Chinese burial records—when added to a lengthy confession of a Japanese major awaiting trial for war crimes—arrive at 377,400 deaths; other authors (James Yin and Shi Young) are comfortable with the figure of 355,000 deaths. Even the Japanese themselves estimated that the dead were at least 300,000, arriving at this figure shortly after the massacre was over.

Burial records, while greatly beloved by historians because they are so concrete, are not particularly persuasive when arriving at total fatalities for the Rape of Nanking, since many bodies were unceremoniously dumped in the Yangtze River, burned, dumped in ditches or mass graves near the killing fields, or surreptitiously buried by family members in order not to attract attention. This writer suspects the true body count was closer to the higher end of most estimates. In any case, somewhere between 300,000 to 400,000 estimated deaths resulting from the Rape of Nanking, while leaving much unknown, is probably as close to the truth as modern scholarship can come.

5.

For many reasons, some of which are obvious, *The Rape of Nanking: the Forgotten Holocaust of World War II* was not an easy book to write; the emotional toll on Iris Chang ended up being greater than anything she may have imagined. Iris' mother, Ying-Ying Chang, writes in her own book about Iris that during the time her daughter was researching and writing her most famous book, she complained of extreme emotional and physical debilitation while reading untold numbers of documents describing atrocities.

"The Japanese soldiers carried out the rapes, tortures, and executions of innocent women and men with unspeakable cruelty. [Iris] read hundreds of such cases. She felt numb after awhile. She told me she sometimes had to get up and away from the documents to take a deep breath. She felt suffocated and in pain. One day in March 1996, she read a document that described a nine-year-old weeping girl being dragged screaming into bedrooms to be raped by Japanese soldiers. She felt a cold rage sweep through her. She could hardly contain her anger."

"One night in April, she called and told me that she could not fall asleep lately. She had nightmares and had lost weight. Her hair fell out in clumps in the shower. I was alarmed and very worried when I heard that. As her mother, Iris' health was my prime concern. I asked her whether she really wanted to continue to write this book. She said, "Yes, Mom. What I'm suffering right now is nothing compared to those victims who perished in the massacre." She added, "As a writer, I want to rescue those victims from oblivion, to give a voice to the voiceless." This was typical of episodes in her life during which she reported feeling oppressed by her writing or research, experiencing great anxiety, some depression, an escalating inability to sleep, and the alarming discovery that her hair was falling out—yet she could not step back from the material long enough to take a break.

Iris' friend Paula Kamen writes knowingly about Chang's vulnerability in her book *Finding Iris Chang: Friendship, Ambition and the Loss of an Extraordinary Mind*: "She was genuinely shocked at the atrocities she had exposed, and reacted with a pure, honest rage—like someone seeing evil for the very first time. She couldn't understand the possibility of knowing about such things and *not* writing about them. Part of the power of her interviewing was that she had no filters to block out anything that was being said to her; I suspect she didn't even know that people came with filters."

Two months later Iris and her mother met in New York. "Iris told me all her worries and concerns," Ying-Ying wrote. "She had apparently lost some weight. Writing *The Rape of Nanking* definitely had taken a physical toll on her. She said she had lost a lot of hair, and she could not sleep well at night. Beside the fact that the story of the Rape of Nanking depressed her, Iris was also unhappy about a number of other things." Iris complained that she was not sure she would get a sufficient advance on the book, yet felt under tremendous pressure. "I told her I was amazed that she would drive herself so hard. Why should she torture herself?"[8]

Why *did* she inflict such torture on herself? Because she felt compelled to do so. She knew that no books had been written about the Rape of Nanking, and that in the West this extremely important historical event was practically unknown. And she understood the anger—and the shame—of people in China and the Chinese Diaspora, regarding the fact that the suffering of

Nanking's victims was still being covered up and ignored. Above all she felt the shame of her parents that the West knew nothing about this pivotal event in the history of Asia.

Iris Chang knew that she was ideally situated to remedy this situation. She had been raised to speak both Mandarin and English, and since her grandparents came from Nanking, most likely various colloquialisms of the Nanking dialect would be familiar to her. She would be able, then, to personally interview Chinese historians, as well as surviving victims; and she did, traveling to Nanking and conducting interviews with many living victims of the Nanking massacre.

Furthermore, it was Iris Chang's belief, once she comprehended the full horror of the massacre, that its suppression by historians was essentially a second rape—the first rape being of Nanking, and the second rape being the suppression of all historical memory of the victims' suffering. "[*The Rape of Nanking*] describes two related but discrete atrocities," she wrote in her 'Introduction.' "One is the Rape of Nanking itself, the story of how the Japanese wiped out hundreds of thousands of innocent civilians in its enemy's capital. Another is the cover-up, the story of how the Japanese, emboldened by the silence of the Chinese and Americans, tried to erase the entire massacre from public consciousness, thereby depriving its victims of their proper place in history." Even Asian-Americans, she wrote, often didn't know what Nanking was. "By writing this book, I forced myself to delve into not only history but historiography—to examine the forces of history and the process by which history is made."[9]

In short, Iris Chang felt, because of her language and writing skills, that it was her duty to step up and set the record straight, not only for herself but for all Chinese—if the world cared little for the dead of Nanking, she thought, it would after she became their voice. It was only after she was well into the research that she realized how debilitating telling their story was going to be.

Perhaps the most remarkable of Iris' historical sources—and

she had a profound ability to ferret out hitherto unknown sources—was the discovery and publication of the diaries of John Rabe, a German national (and member of the Nazi party) who lived in Nanking, and who became the chairman of the International Committee for the Nanking Safety Zone, an area of refugee camps clustered around the American Embassy. The International Committee worked to save the lives of as many as 250,000 people who lived in the Zone, led by Rabe, who often risked his own life by personally confronting Japanese officers and soldiers in the act of committing atrocities. Rabe also kept highly-detailed dairies of the Imperial Japanese Army's descent into depravity.

"Before his death, [Rabe] left behind a written legacy of his work in China: more than two thousand pages of documents on the Rape of Nanking that he had meticulously typed, numbered, bound, and even illustrated; these documents included his and other foreigners' eyewitness reports, newspaper articles, radio broadcasts, telegrams and photographs of the atrocities." Iris excitedly began long and intense negotiations with Rabe's grand-daughter Ursula Reinhardt, who after some hesitation agreed to their publication. Iris also discovered the previously "lost" diaries of another German Nazi who was on the International Committee, Christian Kroeger, who was tied up and beaten by the Japanese for trying to save a wounded Chinese man.

Chang also brought to light—and used as a primary source— the diaries of Minnie Vautrin, the acting head of Ginling College in the Safety Zone of Nanking, who repeatedly risked her life challenging the marauding Japanese soldiers intent on rounding up men to be killed, and women for mass rapes and military brothels. ("How ashamed the women of Japan would be if they knew these tales of horror," Vautrin wrote in her diary.) Minnie Vautrin, whom Iris Chang refers to as "The Living Goddess of Nanking," was an idealistic single woman from Illinois, in America, who had dedicated her life to missionary work for the

United Christian Missionary Association. Unable to recover from the psychic wounds of the Rape of Nanking, Vautrin had a breakdown in May, 1940. Clearly suffering from what we would today call PTSD, Minnie Vautrin blamed herself for not being able to stop the mass slaughter of Nanking, and especially the mass rape of thousands of Nanking's women, whom she had tried tirelessly to protect. She attempted to jump overboard several times on the boat home to America; and on May 14, 1941, back home in Indianapolis, she sealed the doors and windows of her apartment with tape, and committed suicide by turning on the gas.

Ying-Ying Chang described the emotional effect of Minnie Vautrin's diary on her daughter, not just as an important primary source but as a tragic human documentation of one woman's pain. (Reading this diary would have been particularly difficult for Iris Chang since she understood from the beginning that it would end with Minnie's suicide.) Iris called her mother while reading Vautrin's account of the Rape of Nanking at the Yale Divinity School library: "After she read Minnie Vautrin's diary, [Iris] was so moved that she broke down and cried and right there she called us and told us Minnie's story." Ying-Ying fills in some of the important facts about Minnie's valiant struggle to protect the people of Nanking, adding: "Minnie's diary and her suicide had affected Iris greatly, perhaps because Minnie was a woman with such courage, or perhaps because Minnie had also graduated from the U of I [University of Illinois] as Iris had. In any case, Iris described Minnie's story whenever the Nanking Massacre and Safety Zone were mentioned in the years to come."

The historical value of Minnie Vautrin's diaries was never in doubt, but one wonders about Iris's response to them: when one breaks down in tears while reading words written by a primary source, is that a red flag? It would probably depend on the person. It is a fact that little of value is accomplished in historical science, the arts, or anything else, without some passion that drives one to seek a higher form of truth, despite the suffering that quest may cause. But for someone of Iris' sensitivity—and considering her intense and almost primal loathing of human evil—are not tears something of a warning of problems to come? Such questions are personal, and can only be answered by the people directly involved; but in this particular case one has to wonder if Iris Chang identified too much with this distressed if heroic voice from a violent past. Needless to say, Iris continued to work at all hours of the night and day, all too often without eating or sleeping, often going for days at a time in this manner.

Monica Eng, who did a piece about Iris after her death for the *Chicago Tribune Magazine*, wrote: "It was during these late-night writing sessions, as she poured over diaries, interviews and photos depicting unspeakable acts of rape, murder and torture, that her work began to take its toll. She told people that clumps of her hair fell out, she lost weight, suffered nightmares, often became sick and frequently broke down and weeping at her computer." Her mother told Eng that the book "definitely affected her mentally." During a 1997 interview with *John Hopkins Magazine* Iris Chang herself said: "I was weak the whole time I was writing the book. I was very unhappy." Yet it was this book that brought her the greatest fame, and that astounded the world partly because of its graphic descriptions of radical evil.

Iris Chang was almost surely affected by what is called 'secondary trauma'—also referred to as 'vicarious trauma'—a condition that often affects people that are privy to various forms of human evil. Frank Ochberg, MD, an expert on psychological trauma, speaks of it as being trauma that can result from being close to, trying to help, identifying with and caring about people subjected to violent and horrendous events. (In the same way that Iris Chang identified with the victims of the Rape of Nanking, let us say, and later with the victims and survivors of the Bataan Death March.) People likely to suffer from it include clergy, psychotherapists working with trauma survivors, frontline social service workers, health care and humanitarian workers, investigative journalists, authors and first responders. Symptoms include social withdrawal, emotional lability, aggression, great sensitivity to violence, intrusive images and thoughts, and—unfortunately for Iris Chang—enhanced sleep disturbance. It is also known to cause problems with trust, self-esteem, intimacy and control. There is little doubt that Iris Chang's already pronounced difficulty with sleep disturbance was exacerbated by secondary trauma and that the two worked in tandem to make sleep even more difficult.

"Too long," Paula Kamen wrote in *Finding Iris Chang*, "the ethic in journalism has been the short-sighted macho one of swallowing feelings, maybe compartmentalizing them, and facing trauma all alone, perhaps by medicating sorrows in drinks after work. Or reporters just leave themselves to feel the impact years later with a worsening of health. Journalism schools lack a basic curriculum to teach about trauma, along with a vocabulary for expressing it, the impact on victims, and its possible fallout to those who report about it. This is especially negligent considering that so much journalism involves trauma, from day one; typical first-year beat reporters pay their dues, as I did, covering crime and major accidents."[10]

Nanking [now Nanjing] professor and historian Sun Zhaiwei put it even more succinctly: history, he told the *London Times*, sometimes involves "torture of the mind." He is further quoted as remarking: "Nuclear scientists wear protective clothing and have their health checked by doctors. Perhaps we historians of the extreme need similar measures. Yet for now we have to take care of ourselves. Maybe that was Iris' problem—she cared for the dead but failed to take care of herself."[11] Yet at the height of her career Iris' dynamic, deeply-felt writing, speaking and interviewing style, combined with a seemingly inexhaustible high energy, seemed to carry her through, despite her frequent physical and emotional debilitation.

When Iris had done interviews of Nanking survivors in China, she discovered that almost all of them lived in conditions of extreme poverty. One of the reasons Iris wrote the book was to advocate compensation to survivors from Japan; but it gradually became clear that reparations would never happen. Japanese nationalists and ultranationalists responded in fury to her book, insisting that the Nanking massacre never occurred, and that she had faked historical evidence. The ultranationalists were particularly dangerous—although small in number, they have disproportionate influence in Japan because of their willingness to use violence against historians who write truthful accounts of Japanese war atrocities, and politicians who talk about those atrocities. Even in the US, there were people who accused Iris Chang of "Japan-bashing," much as human-rights advocates for the Palestinians are sometimes called "anti-Semitic" by far-right supporters of the current Likud government of Israel. Many of the Japanese Studies departments in US academia are financially supported by Japan or by corporations that seek trade with Japan; furthermore, the US State Department is well known for trying to discourage historians from writing about Japanese atrocities during the Second World War for the same reasons, because they seek advantageous trade arrangements with Japan.

Finally, for a variety of reasons (one of which was the failure of the US to insist on it in the early 1950s) the political class in Japan has never found a completely thoroughgoing way to come to terms with the past; centrist politicians try to control the ultranationalists by giving them concessions, but that simply makes them stronger and more violent. When speaking about the ultranationalists, many Japanese politicians repeatedly sound the same theme: criticism of Japanese actions during the Second World War make the far right in Japan more powerful; therefore historians everywhere need to censor themselves and stop writing about past Japanese atrocities, and stop using the mass media to discuss them. (And stop making demands on the current Japanese governments for compensation for survivors of atrocities!)

They couldn't be more wrong, both about the responsibilities of the historians, and about their own domestic political responsibilities in Japan. Furthermore they are completely wrong about the way democracy actually works, and the way people ought to handle the burden of traumatic memory. What is needed is *more* thoughtful analysis of past systemic and radical evil, whether it is slavery and racism in the US, militarism and nationalism in Japan, or the moral collapse that occurred under Hitler in Germany.

This final challenge—writing about radical evil—gradually became Iris Chang's vocation. But modernism and post-modernism offer few convincing philosophical or theological explanations for the existence of radical evil; so the reader who confronts atrocity after atrocity in *The Rape of Nanking* soon begins to ask, *why?* Why did they do it, why does such rampant evil exist? Chang did not supply a conclusive answer to the perennial *why*, but she did rather clearly show *how* such radical evil could be elicited.

Officers of the Imperial Japanese Army systematically ordered large groups of their men to participate in traumatizing events— such as "contests" to see who could cut off the most heads of Chinese civilians—and once they had participated, once they had been made to experience their own personal complicity in the atrocities, the men could much more easily be ordered to commit more atrocities in the future. In other words, the officers of the Imperial Japanese Army used crude but effective forms of trauma bonding.

6.

As they moved toward Nanking, large groups of Japanese soldiers were ordered to witness atrocities committed by their officers in ritualized settings, so that they would internalize the aggression of these atrocities—and shortly afterwards were ordered to commit exactly the same kind of atrocities, again in groups. It was an unimaginably intense form of mental and emotional conditioning, in which ordinary Japanese soldiers were systematically traumatized by extreme violence, the purpose being to bond them to the kind of aggression they were expected to act out. This culminated in the mass sadism and sexualized violence that occurred in Nanking, a form of aggressive behavior that can only be called radical evil. But this use of trauma bonding by the officer corps of the Imperial Japanese Army was consciously or unconsciously extrapolated, at least to some extent, from certain cultural values that had been disseminated over several decades prior to the Japanese invasion of China.

In Japan's militarized educational system, students were taught that the individual counted for little, while the imperial state was everything. Shinto had gradually become nationalized to the point that it, as well, had become little more than worship of the state. The values of *Bushido*, the way of the warrior, had been institutionalized at all levels of society. Most dangerously of all, a master-race mentality had been encouraged and ultimately instilled throughout Japan. The Japanese were supposedly superior to all, including the West: but running underneath all this state-sponsored posturing there was a distinct undercurrent of acute insecurity, inferiority and lack of national self-esteem.

Obsequious conformity to domestic authority, on the one hand, and prejudice and arrogance toward foreigners, on the other, is an extremely dangerous compound, which ended up being directed at the United States as well as the other peoples of Asia. Ultimately this combined envy and hatred led to a kind of apocalyptic anti-American thinking typified by this statement in a book by Okawa Shumei, a nationalist activist, and quoted by Iris Chang in *The Rape of Nanking*:

Before a new world appears, there must be a deadly fight between the powers of the West and the East. This theory is realized in the American challenge to Japan. The strongest country in Asia is Japan and the strongest country that represents Europe is America…. These two countries are destined to fight. Only God knows when it will be.[12]

Ultimately, this undercurrent of insecurity almost surely goes back to the great humiliation Japan experienced at the hand of US Navy and Commodore Matthew Perry, who sailed to Japan in 1853-54 with a fleet of steam vessels with the express purpose of forcing Japan to open its markets to American and international trade. This still rankled in the collective consciousness of the Japanese in the 20th century, but the intricacies of Japanese culture, having been hijacked by successive waves of nationalism, could no longer rationally manage or even analyze such challenges. Nor were the Japanese governing elites capable of the introspection necessary to understand that the perceived threats from America, and from the West, originated to a great extent in their own fears and resentments, and in the aggressive emotional orientations instilled by their worship of the warrior ethos.

Instead there was a steady drumbeat of militarism, accompanied by the insistence on the idea that all problems in Japan—and in the world—could be resolved through the ruthless violence of the professional warrior. Japan could not produce anywhere near enough food for its people to eat, and it had long ago lost the bargaining skills necessary to negotiate a resolution of this problem with its neighbors. The result was a steadily building frustration that the ruling elites of Japan could no longer analyze, contain or manage. Given the predominance of the warrior ethos, the building momentum within the Japanese elites could only lead toward one outcome: war, in order to get even with the United States for Admiral Perry's humiliation of Japan, and to conquer and exploit the rest of Asia to solve Japan's economic problems.

In July, 1937, Imperial Japan invaded Shanghai; the fighting was extremely fierce. Although it was an undeclared war, Japan's goal was clearly to conquer and dominate China. And there was soon a dangerous new factor added to the already lethal equation. The Imperial Japanese army had recently petitioned Emperor Hirohito for the right to get rid of all constraints of international law regarding the treatment of prisoners of war; and had Hirohito refused this request, history might have been much different. But he didn't. On August 5, 1937, Emperor Hirohito agreed to this murderous request by the Imperial Japanese Army.

What Hirohito's decision meant, as a matter of practical application, was that the Imperial Japanese Army could now kill, torture or otherwise mistreat prisoners of war in any way it chose. And since captured prisoners of war were now explicitly denied legal protection, it might logically follow—at least in the minds of top commanders—that civilians should be similarly killed or tortured. To be sure, the proposal to suspend international law originated with the army; but in a society whose people had been taught that their Emperor was divine, Hirohito's agreement to reject international law was a clear provocation: it implied that his soldiers could best serve their Emperor by treating prisoners of war in the most brutal way imaginable. It was perhaps inevitable that the officer corps would quickly interpret Hirohito's attitude of murderous cruelty toward prisoners of war as also applying to all civilians.

That's the historical back story that set the stage for the Rape of Nanking. But the specific question remains, *how* and *why* did it happen that ordinary soldiers and officers behaved with such sadistic frenzy? The best answer for *how* such violence was elicited comes in two parts, both of which involved trauma bonding. The first occurred as part of the built-in, ongoing brutality of the Japanese military toward its own soldiers. Chang is quite specific about that: "Before the invasion of Nanking, the Japanese military had subjected its own soldiers to endless humiliation. Japanese soldiers were forced to wash the underwear of officers or stand meekly while superiors slapped them until they streamed with blood." This was accompanied by perverse sadomasochistic rationalizations: "Using Orwellian language, the routine striking of Japanese soldiers, or *bentatsu*, was termed an "act of love" by the officers, and the violent discipline of the Japanese navy through *tekken seisai*, or "the iron fist," was often called *ai-no-muchi*, or "whip of love."

"It has often been suggested that those with the least power are often the most sadistic if given the power of life and death over people even lower on the pecking order, and the rage engendered by this rigid pecking order was suddenly given an outlet when Japanese soldiers went abroad. In foreign lands or colonized territories, the Japanese soldiers—representatives of the emperor—enjoyed tremendous power among the subjects. In China even the lowliest Japanese private was considered superior to the most powerful and distinguished native, and it is easy to see how years of suppressed anger, hatred, and fear of authority could have erupted in uncontrollable violence at Nanking. The Japanese soldier had endured in silence whatever his superiors had chosen to deal out to him, and now the Chinese had to take whatever he chose to deal out to them."[13] The Japanese military was, in other words, a training school for extreme brutality. The soldiers internalized the violence they endured from their officers, and acted it out against Chinese civilians.

A second and more specific method for eliciting rage and cruelty has already been alluded to above. It was used by the officer corps of the Imperial Japanese Army to prepare soldiers *specifically to murder civilians*. This method—what we might call the pedagogy of mass murder—was employed as the Imperial Japanese Army moved closer to Nanking. "The Japanese soldier was not simply hardened for battle in China; he was hardened for the task of murdering Chinese combatants and noncombatants alike. Indeed, various games and exercises were set up by the Japanese military to numb its men to the human instinct against killing people who are not attacking."

"For example, on their way to the capital, Japanese soldiers were made to participate in killing competitions, which were avidly covered by the Japanese media like sporting events. The most notorious one appeared in the December 7 issue of the *Japan Advertiser* under the headline 'Sub-Lieutenants in Race to Fell 100 Chinese Running Close Contest.'" Photographs make it clear that the victims of the 'friendly contest' were mainly civilians. The casual, offhand manner in which the newspaper reported this event seemed calculated to make the reader feel complicit in the atrocity, since the soldiers committing them were presented not as despicable but heroic. "Such atrocities were not unique to the Nanking area," Chang wrote. "Rather, they were typical of the desensitization exercises practiced by the Japanese across China during the entire war."

The goal of such 'exercises' was clearly to cause trauma. "For new soldiers, horror was a natural impulse. One wartime memoir describes how a group of green Japanese recruits failed to conceal their shock when they witnessed seasoned soldiers torture a group of civilians to death. Their commander expected this reaction and wrote in his diary: 'All new recruits are like this, but soon they will be doing the same things themselves.'"

"But new officers also required desensitization. A veteran officer named Tominaga Shozo recalled vividly his own transformation from innocent youth to killing machine. Tominaga had been a fresh second lieutenant from a military academy when assigned to the 232nd Regiment of the 39th Division from Hiroshima. When he was introduced to the men under his command, Tominaga was stunned. 'They all had evil eyes,' he remembered, 'They weren't human eyes, but the eyes of leopards or tigers.'"

"On the front Tominaga and other new candidate officers underwent intensive training to stiffen their endurance for war. In the program an instructor had pointed to a thin, emaciated Chinese in a detention center and told the officers: 'These are the raw materials for your trial of courage.' Day after day the instructor taught them to how to cut off heads and bayonet living prisoners."

On the final day, we were taken out to the site of our trial. Twenty-four prisoners were squatting there with their hands tied behind their backs. They were blindfolded. A big hole had been dug—ten meters long, two meters wide, and more than three meters deep. The regimental commander, the battalion commanders, and the company commanders all took the seats arranged for them. Second Lieutenant Tanaka bowed to the regimental commander and reported, 'We shall now begin.' He ordered a soldier on fatigue duty to haul one of the prisoners to the edge of the pit; the prisoner was kicked when he resisted.

The soldiers finally dragged him over and forced him to his knees. Tanaka turned toward us and looked into each of our faces in turn. 'Heads should be cut off like this,' he said, unsheathing his army sword. He scooped water from a bucket with a dipper, then poured it over both sides of the blade. Swishing off the water, he raised his sword in a long arc. Standing behind the prisoner, Tanaka steadied himself, legs spread apart, and cut off the man's head with a shout, 'Yo!' The head flew more than a meter away. Blood spurted up in two fountains from the body and sprayed into the hole.

The scene was so appalling that I felt I couldn't breathe.

"But gradually, Tominaga Shozo learned to kill. And as he grew more adept at it, he no longer felt that his men's eyes were evil. For him, atrocities became routine, almost banal. Looking back on his experience, he wrote: 'We made them like this. Good sons, good daddies, good elder brothers at home were brought to the front to kill each other. Human beings turned into murdering demons. Everyone became a demon within three months."[14]

These "games and exercises" all have the hallmarks of systematic trauma bonding. It was clearly planned to overwhelm the recruits by forcing them to witness unimaginably cruel events, the unambiguous intent being clearly to shock and traumatize them. Besides shaking them loose from their moral bearings, it also had the effect of causing them to internalize the aggression they were witnessing. When you are forced to witness the ritualized slaughter of innocent people, it is too horrible to ignore; inevitably such conditioning would force the soldier to internalize—however unwillingly—the aggression he is witnessing, in order to survive psychologically.

By making the world of sadism his own, the soldier can survive it—all he has to do is internalize it, and then act it out, like the officers are telling him to do, and everybody around him is doing. If he is to survive in that world of total aggression, that is, he must internalize as much of the aggression as possible, by watching his superior officers in action and trying to imitate their behavior. A soldier in such a situation could quickly become a monster, because that is what people in such a situation do to survive. All that is required is to coerce the soldier into witnessing the atrocity, afterwards quickly ordering him to commit the same heinous act; soon he will become the monster that his officers want him to be. Some soldiers might understand what is happening to them, but are unlikely to speak up because of the extreme danger that would place them in. Historically, there have been soldiers that disobeyed their officers and refused to commit atrocities (by organizing rebellions, by killing themselves, or by voluntarily submitting to military execution) but although their individual cases are quite poignant—and can teach us much, incidentally—they are, numerically speaking, little more than exceptions to the rule.

Iris Chang at no point uses the expression 'trauma bonding'

in *The Rape of Nanking*, but the deliberate way in which Japanese recruits were carefully exposed to extreme cruelty, given some time to internalize the violence involved, and then quickly ordered to act out the same atrocity, is clearly a classic example of it. Criminal organizations and prison gangs do something similar: they insist that a recruit commit murder in order to bond him to the gang's ethos. (The drug cartels in Mexico and South America will go so far as to order a recruit to witness the killing of a friend, or even make the recruit kill the friend himself; in such a situation the resulting traumatic bonding is likely to be particularly strong.) Call it an extreme form of conditioning, if you will, but the psychological trauma of the soldier when exposed to extreme cruelty against civilians for the first time is beyond overwhelming. Furthermore, the way in which such traumatic violence can be used to bond people to various levels of aggression is too consistent to be a coincidence.

The ritualized nature of the conditioning is also notable: in his memoir quoted above, Tominaga Shozo writes that before the ritualized beheading ceremony a "regimental commander, the battalion commanders, and the company commanders all took the seats arranged for them," meaning that the beheading was organized like a kind of theater. That fact that so many officers were watching as their troops ritually beheaded innocent people must have greatly enhanced the desperate pressure to conform felt by the recruits.

The trauma bonding as described above may be a temporary state, one from which the individual can recover. Iris Chang surprises us, as she so often does, by demonstrating that people that have committed monstrous deeds can return to relative sanity once they are no longer under the discipline of a renegade army, terrorist group or military organization. Human evil is in human *behavior*, she is clearly telling us—at least in war—and not necessarily a permanent part of the person. A former soldier named Hakudo Nagatomi recalled the crimes he committed:

"I beheaded people, starved them to death, burned them, and buried them alive, over two hundred in all. It is terrible that I could turn into an animal and do these things. There are really no words to explain what I was doing. I was truly a devil." Furthermore, he said, he experienced no guilt at the time for the things he was doing.

But remorse eventually caught up with him.

"After almost sixty years of soul-searching, Nagatomi is a changed man," Chang writes. "A doctor in Japan, he has built a shrine of remorse in his waiting room. Patients can watch videotapes of his trial in Nanking and a full confession of his crimes. The gentle and hospitable demeanor of the doctor belies the horror of his past, making it almost impossible for one to imagine that he had once been a ruthless murderer."[15]

The long journey of Hakudo Nagatomi from total depravity, to trial and punishment as a war criminal, and finally to a decent and productive life, demonstrates vividly that no matter what crimes people have committed, redemption is possible. Hakudo's search for redemption was threefold: First, acknowledging the nature of the crimes committed; second, accepting punishment and trying to make some kind of amends; third, working for a world in which such crimes are less likely to occur. Dr. Hakudo Nagatomi succeeded in all three areas.

His extraordinary and productive remorse ironically takes us back to the second of the two questions posed earlier. We now see *how* the soldiers were prepared to act in a sadistic frenzy: they were conditioned by their officer corps, which traumatized them by forcing them to witness atrocities, ritualized beheadings, mutilation, mass rapes and various forms of torture; and then, after the troops had internalized huge amounts of that extreme aggression, the officers arranged for them to act out the same atrocities themselves. At that point the trauma bonding was complete, and their participation in the atrocities of Nanking proceeded.

The fact that this conditioning was so organized means that there was a strong consensus among the officer corps that they were supposed to be acting in this manner. The guilt of the top commanders is surely very great, but in the middle ranks of the officer corps there was also a consensus that troops should be encouraged to commit atrocities in Nanking; and for that reason, the entire officer corps must be held responsible for preparing the troops for their experiment in radical evil. In terms of moral and legal guilt, allegations about orders given by the top command are not as important as the fact that the Imperial Japanese Army behaved in a certain way, committing atrocities and acting with needless cruelty—that, and the fact that there was no organized effort within the officer corps to stop it. And after Nanking, it continued to behave with extraordinarily cruel ways throughout the Second World War.

In the case of Nanking, the barbarity of the attack on civilians was set up by the killing of POWs; and as it progressed, as in the killing and raping of civilians, nobody in authority intervened. A system was created, and it moved more or less inexorably toward its goal, which was a total descent into radical evil. This writer maintains that many people in such a system understand, on some level, what the system is doing, even if people are afraid to discuss it. It may be that others are unable to consciously comprehend what they are doing, because they are no longer capable of thinking rationally, or do not understand and cannot describe the aggressive emotions that drive their behavior.[16] The anomaly of Nanking, as many historians have remarked, is that its violence was so public—it seems to have been organized to be a kind of display, as though it were specifically designed to be an orgy of depravity and violence that China, along with the rest of the world, could not ignore. It began as systemic evil, of course, because it had its roots in a corrupt cultural and military system; but the way in which radical evil was acted out publicly in Nanking, as unbelieving journalists and foreign nationals watched in horror, is almost unique in the history of organized war crimes.

So we are left with the final question: *why* the Rape of Nanking? What did Imperial Japan have to gain by it?

Japan had *nothing* to gain by it, nothing at all; but the officers and leaders that acted it out were no longer thinking of their country. They no longer identified with Japan, but rather with the power of radical evil. Their intent was to participate in radical evil because it had, to them, become the highest good. It had become the most authentic of all experiences, which was to live beyond good and evil: that was where they were driven to go, whether it was good for Japan or not. To be sure, many of them had probably convinced themselves that the massacre at Nanking would frighten and demoralize the Chinese, but even the most perfunctory risk-assessment would quickly conclude that such atrocities would surely, on the contrary, stiffen China's will to fight back. So if Japan could not benefit from it, *why* the radical evil of Nanking?

Because evil has its own world, and they that are bonded to it no longer care for anything but that world. Radical evil exists— and far from being an emanation of the devil or a demonic magical spell, it already exists in all people, ready to be activated, implanted in all of us because of our descent from violent animals. The officer corps of the Imperial Japanese Army activated that aggression and violence in its most virulent forms by carefully, systematically conditioning troops through trauma bonding—by brutally beating them on a daily basis, then forcing them to watch and then participate in unthinkable atrocities, and in that manner systematically inducting them into the world of sadistic aggression known as radical evil.

That is the great lesson of the Rape of Nanking. Not only does the capacity for radical evil exist in all people, it can be activated through psychological trauma induced by witnessing—and then participating in—extreme human violence; and once bonded to that world of total aggression, the progression is always toward death and depravity. That is the *why* of the Rape of Nanking. To those under the influence of radical evil in Nanking, as those under its influence at Auschwitz, the depravity that it generated was its own reward and its own end.

7.

Iris Chang took all these things personally because that is the way she took everything. Yet the astonishing success of her book, *The Rape of Nanking: the Forgotten Holocaust of World War II*— published with great fanfare in the autumn of 1997—buoyed her during even the worst of times. America is a celebrity culture, and Iris became a celebrity overnight. She began almost immediately to receive honorary degrees, was invited to give lectures, and appeared on such TV shows as 'Good Morning, America,' 'Nightline,' and the 'NewsHour with Jim Lehrer'; the latter venue was the scene of one of Iris' most famous public media encounters, with Kunihiko Saito, Japanese Ambassador to the US, who was asked by Iris to publicly apologize, on behalf of the Japanese government, for past atrocities. (He declined.) She was profiled by the *New York Times* (a sure sign that she had caught the attention of the cultural elite) and then featured on the cover of the mass-circulation *Readers' Digest*. Hillary Clinton invited her to the White House, and the Organization of Chinese Americans voted her 'National Woman of the Year.' *The Atlantic Monthly*, the *Chicago Tribune*, *The Wall Street Journal* and (of course) the *New York Times* all featured ecstatic reviews of her book.

Iris participated in an excruciatingly lengthy book tour, involving 65 cities and lasting a year and a half. It was during this long, seemingly endless book tour that Iris Chang became a human rights activist as well as an author, using the tour to call for an apology for the Nanking atrocities by the modern Japanese government, and just compensation for those survivors still living. For doing this in such a bold and public way, Iris Chang became a major culture hero in China and throughout the Chinese Diaspora. She promoted her message through academic forums, lectures and multiple appearances on radio and TV in cities where she was conducting book-signings. She came into contact with hundreds of thousands of people doing this tour, not to mention the millions of people who saw her on TV or heard her being interviewed on National Public Radio. (This writer remembers her speaking on National Public Radio's 'All Things Considered'—the same drive-time, news program that would announce, just seven years later, the shocking and almost unbelievable news of her suicide.)

China had recently offered Korea a formal apology for atrocities committed against Koreans in World War Two; and many in China and the Chinese Diaspora believed that soon an apology would be forthcoming for atrocities in China—but it never arrived. However much the apology to Korea may have been motivated by the political clout of the large Korean community in Japan, to Chinese and Chinese-Americans it seemed unreasonable that the Japanese government would offer such an apology to Korea, only to pass over again the opportunity to apologize to China for the Nanking massacre. One big reason, of course, was that the Rape of Nanking had long since become a flashpoint for nationalists and ultranationalists in Japan, since the ultranationalists denied—despite massive historical evidence—that the massacre in Nanking had ever happened. Sadly, even today few people in the political class in Japan will talk about the Nanking massacre, if there is any way they can avoid it.

Conferences and forums were organized on the subject of *The Rape of Nanking: the Forgotten Holocaust of World War II*, beginning at Princeton, Harvard and Yale and then spreading thereafter to universities across the country, including many in California. Chang gave lectures during which she was almost mobbed by fans. Everywhere she sold books, because people wanted to be a part of the historical and academic movement for long-delayed justice for the survivors of the Rape of Nanking, a movement that Iris had initiated. Media heavyweights as well as well-known academics came under her spell, because of her formidable intelligence, the willowy beauty she had inherited from her mother, and a certain highly-focused inner conviction that could spellbind an audience. As often happens with public figures who bespeak a cause whose time has come, Iris aroused intense loyalties: a great many people fell in love with her as a modern Joan of Arc figure, thrilled by the fury she brought to her subject matter.

And always there was that uncanny attraction of a person who speaks for the dead whose suffering the world has tried to erase from historical memory. She was charismatic, more so than any scholar or activist who had been on the lecture circuit for many years; yet there were times when she seemed haunted and overwhelmed, rattling off with a kind of deadpan voice the horrors of Nanking as though detached and driven by them at the same time. Above all, Iris Chang was a thoroughly compelling and fascinating public figure—the first important Asian-American celebrity since Amy Tan, in fact—despite the fact that one always had the distinct impression that under her perfectly controlled exterior Iris Chang had her demons. The awards that she received were about evenly divided between those presented for what she had written, and those she received for the charismatic human-rights activism she now undertook.

The wider public was also becoming enamored by this young Chinese-American warrior whose weapons were words and whose dream was justice. Iris Chang had consciously—and sometimes unconsciously—created a public persona for herself as a spokeswoman for the dead of Nanking. The world had tried to forget them, but Iris Chang insisted in the most uncompromising manner that the world *must remember them;* and the fact that she was able to get the world to pay attention and to honor them, was a kind of a dream come true for many Chinese-Americans and Chinese-Canadians, not to mention those in China and in the Chinese Diaspora who had long felt shame that the dead of Nanking had not been properly honored. Iris Chang's immense appeal to the Chinese, and to the world at large, was simple and dramatic: the voices of Nanking had perished in the hell created by Imperial Japan; Iris Chang would now speak for them, not only as their spokeswoman but as an incarnation of their pain, and the outrage of survivors and their descendants.

Iris' mother was relieved, as was almost everybody around her, when she decided to write her next book on the history of the Chinese in America. *The Chinese in America: a Narrative History* did not achieve the commercial success of *The Rape of Nanking*, which seemed to surprise and demoralize the young author; but it is a very good book, in some ways her best book. In it she warned that the Chinese would never be completely accepted in America, and that racism would always be something that Americans needed to be aware of. During the period in which she was writing *The Chinese in America* she was still being invited to numerous places to lecture, but almost invariably she was expected to speak during Q & A on *The Rape of Nanking* and its attendant political fallout. When *The Chinese in America* was published, her publisher devised a long and difficult schedule for her book tour, apparently depending on her skills as a speaker to stimulate sales; once again she was launched on a travel and speaking tour that would go on for a long time. But now something unexpected began to happen: the people she met on this tour wanted to talk about *The Rape of Nanking*, not about *The Chinese in America*, the book that she was on tour to promote.

A great deal of this public fascination had to do with the manner in which Chang could elicit traumatic memory. There was something about Iris Chang that caused victims of every variety to speak about the unspeakable. There was a certain quality emanating from this poised young woman with the haunted eyes and the intense, exacting voice that caused people in audiences where she spoke to break down in tears. And not just for victims of Nanking. "Orphans, rape victims and Holocaust survivors all wanted to bare their souls to her," wrote Oliver August, a British author, "finally relieving themselves of agonies sometimes decades old. They felt encouraged by the passion that she brought to the sort of grievances few of them could tackle on their own. Chang cried when they cried. She was enraged even when they no longer were. It was unthinkable for her just to pass the paper tissues and wait until people had composed themselves again. Chang invited memories of atrocity and abuse with a seemingly limitless appetite."[17] This theme of victimization and trauma was something she should have turned away from, but a certain innate compassion wouldn't let her do so. She had a gift, she felt, for understanding and describing psychological trauma, and she found it compelling and even fascinating.

Chang had decided that her next book would be about the American survivors of the Bataan Death March. Her mother and her husband were both opposed to this choice, because it would once again plunge Iris into the world of radical evil, in the form of atrocities committed by the Imperial Japanese army. In her book about Iris, her mother Ying-Ying writes about her own fears regarding Iris' mental health, considered in light of both Iris' book tour schedule and her choice of subject matter for this proposed fourth book:

"In 2004, Iris focused her research on a group of American World War II POWs in preparation for the proposal for her next book. This was the story of the American 192nd tank battalion from the Midwest states of Wisconsin, Illinois, Ohio, and Kentucky. The 192nd was deployed to the Philippines in 1941.

They fought the Japanese and were subsequently captured by the Japanese Army. This tank battalion unit went through hell in the Philippines. There were some survivors, but many died from starvation, disease, and torture. In November 2003, Iris had visited and interviewed several of the battalion survivors in those states. Now she systematically interviewed and tape-recorded each one of them over the phone. This involved many hours of Q&A and was a long and tedious process."

"The stories of these surviving POWs were horrendous and excruciating beyond words. Iris said even her typist could not stop her tears while she was transcribing the recording tapes. This book project was certainly a dark subject and not good for her mental health, but Iris said she just could not turn her back on those veterans and let their stories be forgotten." And the sleep disturbance not only continued, but was getting worse. "Sometimes she worked late into the night. By the time that she went to bed, it was almost time for [her son Christopher] to wake up. It seemed that Iris was continuing to push herself to maintain the same productivity she'd had before Christopher was born. She did not realize that she was suffering constant sleep deprivation." Furthermore, since her typist could not stop crying while transcribing the recording tapes, Iris ended up typing up all the tapes—she endured the Death March interviews twice, first as an interviewer and secondly while typing them up.

Iris launched herself on another strenuous book tour that lasted from March 31 to May 6. Iris' mother writes in her book that the tour included "some twenty cities for thirty-five events. The most strenuous part of the trip was her zigzagging across the continent almost four times. Even a person in top physical and mental condition would have found this schedule highly stressful." For a person experiencing consistent sleep deprivation it would be emotionally impossible. In late April, Iris came back to make a speech at the San Francisco Commonwealth Club, at which time her mother noticed that she "looked extremely exhausted."

"In retrospect," her mother Ying-Ying wrote, "Shau-Jin and I felt that Iris had become preoccupied and somewhat absent-minded right after the April book tour. She looked tired and seemed to have lost her energy. This could have been due to the five-week, non-stop travel on the road, but she became exceedingly moody, more quiet and apprehensive than expected." Iris told her mother that while on the latest book tour for *The Chinese in America*, she was approached by a mysterious stranger who said in a threatening tone: "You would be safer if you joined us." Iris was extremely frightened and quickly walked away, but later couldn't get the incident out of her mind. What organization or group was he talking about? Was this the group that seemed to be working against her? Was he hinting that her life was in danger?

When Iris Chang came back from *The Chinese in America* book tour, in May 2004, people close to her noticed a distinct change. She was moody and distant, and definitely not her old high-energy, vivacious self. And there was something else: she spoke of evil forces of conspiracy that she believed were working against her. Family and friends dismissed it as a very tired, very sensitive writer's momentary slough of despair, to be quickly left behind as she rested and regained her old life-embracing energy. But she continued to have trouble sleeping, and the paranoid thoughts worsened.

At the same time that these mental and emotional changes were happening, Iris prepared to amplify the research for her next book on the Bataan Death March. Although those closest to her believed that the Death March was an extremely bad choice of subjects for Iris, particularly in her darkening frame of mind, backing away from the subject now seemed impossible to her. The interviews with survivors started in autumn of 2003, and had continued up to, and through, her book tour for *The Chinese in America*.

The long years of research into the Nanking massacre clearly appeared to have resulted in an extraordinary amount of secondary trauma, although Iris was able to work through it; but now, as Iris continued to conduct interviews with survivors of the Bataan Death March, the secondary trauma seemed to be much worse. Something in her personality was pulling Iris Chang back into the dark world of radical evil. She said it was because the survivors of the Death March were dying, and she had to get justice for them by writing a book about their experiences before they were all dead; but she simply did not notice, or chose to ignore, that she was running out of the high energy she had once drawn on. Whereas her high spirits and boundless supply of energy was previously enough to pull her through the long all-nighters without food or sleep, at the age of 36 she could no longer pull it off.

The stories of the Bataan Death March survivors seemed increasingly burdensome—and now, in the late spring and summer of 2004, she was listening to those stories in an increasingly troubled mood. The combination of secondary trauma and sleep disturbance would be too much even for the redoubtable Iris Chang, and both contributed to her paranoia. The Bataan Death March, when added to the turmoil in her mind and memory, would be too much for her to handle. Driving it all— both as a symptom and as a complicating factor adding to her acute distress—was her inability to sleep.

In the months before her breakdown, Iris seemed unaware that she was suffering from chronic and growing sleep deprivation—or perhaps she simply didn't want to think about it, since it was a cycle she could no longer control. People in such a situation may know intellectually that they're not getting enough sleep, but they don't sleep because they *can't* sleep, usually because there is something biological driving their wakefulness. When Iris arrived home on April 26 after four weeks on the last lap of her book tour, she was only home for a few minutes—then she had to rush off to give a speech at the Commonwealth Club in San Francisco. (It was as this point that her mother noticed that she looked "extremely exhausted.") Iris said she wanted to stay in a hotel in San Francisco, remarking that she needed to prepare herself for her speech the next day; but this may have been in part a way of concealing her inability to sleep from those closest to her.

Later, in May, Iris and her mother went out to a Mother's Day concert, but Iris' mood was withdrawn and troubled. On June 9 she invited her mother to visit, at which time Ying-Ying noticed that Iris' face "looked gray and very tired"; "[Iris] said that she had just finished the phone interviews with the tank battalion survivors and she wanted to take a nap. I was heartbroken. It was obvious that she had not gotten enough sleep." On June 12th she was awarded an honorary degree from California State University at Hayward; her mother Ying-Ying said it was the last time she saw her happy. On June 19, Ying-Ying again thought that her daughter "seemed preoccupied, almost obsessed" about something. On June 30, she again thought Iris looked "tired and unhappy," even sick.

Iris was scheduled to fly to Louisville to interview more Bataan Death March survivors on August 12. On August 11, a trusted nanny called both of Iris' parents to tell them that their daughter was sick; both rushed over to find Iris in "an exhausted and devastated state." It later became apparent that because of a breakdown in communication—the nanny spoke only Mandarin Chinese—Iris had been up without sleeping for the better part of four days, reading and working, and Brett, Iris' husband, had been unaware of it because of the language barrier. (He thought that she was sleeping during the day.) Her parents, along with the nanny, pleaded for Iris to cancel her trip, but she refused. The parents left; and when Ying-Ying came back the next morning, Iris claimed that she'd managed to sleep for a "couple of hours," and that she was fine.

Iris caught her plane to Louisville, Kentucky, and checked into a hotel. As usual, she was unable to sleep, so that night she tried to watch TV. About 2 AM on Friday, August 13, Iris called her parents to say that she had seen some very frightening pictures on the TV in her hotel room. According to her mother, Iris said that the pictures were of "horrible atrocities and ugly images of children torn apart by wars," not unlike the stories her parents had told her, when she was a child, of Japanese soldiers who had "sliced babies not just in half but in thirds and fourths" during the Rape of Nanking. And there was more. The hotel, Iris told her mother, had deliberately wired her room, and the terrifying pictures had been deliberately transmitted to the TV set by people who sought to frighten and threaten her. Furthermore, she was afraid to drink the water because she was afraid of being poisoned. Her delusional belief that the hotel was deliberately frightening her with violent images of "horrible atrocities," and her fear that the hotel water was poisoned, were clear signals that she had crossed a line. She had become acutely psychotic.

Later that morning one of the Death March survivors whom she hoped to interview arrived with his wife, who was a former nurse. At her suggestion, they took Iris to the Emergency Room of a local hospital, where she was transferred to the Psychiatric Unit. When her parents rushed to the hospital two days later, the doctors told them that Iris had possibly had a "brief reactive psychosis" as a result of the research she was doing. But they also suspected the onset of bipolar disorder.

8.

There were many incidents in the seemingly charmed life of Iris Chang that prefigured both her greatest triumphs and her ultimate tragedy.

When Iris was a child, both her mother Ying-Ying and father Shau-Jin liked to involve the children in discussing the events of the day around the dinner table, but there was a problem. "Iris had by far the most opinions, about anything and everything.

She was very talkative and often dominated the entire conversation. We sometimes needed to stop her to give [her brother] Michael a chance to talk. Because Iris spent most of her time talking at the dinner table, she ate very little or ate slowly. Sometimes everyone else had finished the meal, but she had not even started her main course, so concerned was she with finishing her train of thought." In adulthood her ideas continued to be distinctive and often brilliant, but to her friends it often seemed as though she was talking *at* them rather than *with* them. Her husband Brett would someday refer to this as her "attention-surplus disorder."

According to her mother, Iris would stay up reading when she was supposed to be sleeping. "We had a house rule that everyone should go to bed before midnight. We found that Iris had a difficult time getting up in the morning for school. Later we realized that she was still reading when she was supposed to be asleep." All of her life, Iris Chang preferred to work at night, but would also—after she was afflicted with dangerously high levels of sleep disorder—use this pattern to conceal how little sleep she was getting.

Iris attended the University High School (called Uni High by students) at the University of Illinois at Champaign-Urbana, where she was seen by many as aloof, and rather brusque to people whose ideas didn't challenge her. One high school teacher, Adele Suslick, described her drive "as a matter of being very focused, very focused, about what she had to accomplish," comparing her to a "bullet train." After her death Paula Kamen spoke with mutual friends about this tendency: "This was the beginning of a long dialogue I would have about Iris' habit of planning her life strategically, which some would see as positive (focused) and others as negative (calculating)." Suslick agreed that Iris was "very goal oriented. She always knew where she wanted to be. Nothing was done accidentally. She had thoughts about the outcomes and where they would put her."

Suslick also believes that Iris Chang thought of herself as a writer at a very early age, and lived according to how she had defined that role. "It's almost as if she programmed herself.... She defined the role, and then stepped into it." On one level this was admirable, but on another it betrayed a compulsive inflexibility, an inability to occasionally renegotiate her contract with an imagined destiny.

Suslick had an astounding interaction with Chang that reveals the extent of Iris' naiveté and ambition, as well as a certain youthful narcissism. Iris launched an on-campus campaign to revive her high school literary magazine, *Unique*. Adele Suslick was to be the faculty sponsor, while Iris was to co-edit. As the publication date for the magazine neared, Suslick checked the contents, and to her astonishment found that most of the contents were written by Iris! The editorial board read submissions anonymously, and had accepted many of them without realizing that they were to a great extent from one student. Suslick, of course, put the kibosh on Iris' plan; for one thing, she insisted that one of her longer contributions be published as 'anonymous.'

Suslick remembers asking, "Iris, is this a school magazine or is it your publication?"

The following year Iris got a new faculty sponsor for the magazine.

One high school teacher described her as "kind of spacey"; another classmate remembered her as "withdrawn"; and yet another student recalled her as difficult: "It sounds like a harsh word, I think, to say someone is 'difficult.' But some people kind of know when to speak their mind, and get along with people at the same time, be diplomatic. I would not say she was diplomatic." Many have recollections, as do many of her friends in college, that suggest that the young Iris Chang sometimes had difficulty recognizing—or even understanding—social cues; or (worse yet) was perhaps aware of them, but chose to ignore them.

In high school she did not hesitate to share with her contemporaries the interesting fact that she belonged to children's Mensa. (Mensa is an organization for people with genius-level IQs; Iris found that there was a children's division, had herself tested, and was asked to join.) Uni High was a university lab school—with students who were mainly children of faculty— which made it an eminently geeky school; but Iris at times seemed compelled to posture herself as a geekier-than-thou subset of one. It was no doubt for this reason that she was the victim of some intense bullying. Her friend Paula Kamen dates her solidarity with the underdog back to this experience of being bullied.

At the age of 15, Iris later told her mother, she sat down and wrote a life-plan in the form of goals. "To her astonishment, she said, by the end of the year, she had achieved everything she had set out to accomplish on her list—the grades, the extracurricular activities, the awards. She said it was as if the words themselves were possessed by magic." In college Iris was greatly impressed by *When Words Hurt: How to Keep Criticism from Undermining Your Self-Esteem*, a self-help book by Mary Lynne Heldmann. (Her mother Ying-Ying described its message as "picturing yourself achieving your goals in situations where you were in control.")

This rigid, rather schematic way of setting goals for oneself remained a major trait. Most of us have plans for our lives, but they remain open as we encounter different obstacles, and develop new values. Furthermore, our plans change as we encounter new experiences and learn to negotiate power-sharing with the people around us. Chang, on the other hand, would decide on a particular plan for her life, and would insistently keep whacking away at obstacles until she got what she wanted. When she wanted to find a safe place to live on the Champaign-Urbana campus, she joined a sorority. When she thought it was time to have a boyfriend, she went to a fraternity party and got herself a boyfriend, who later became her husband. When she thought it was time to be a Homecoming Queen, she ran for it, and was elected to the office of 'Princess' in the Homecoming Court.

When she decided to write for the *New York Times*, she called up a top editor in New York (while still in college) and got so many byline stories published on the front page of the *Times* that they pleaded with her to stop sending them copy. (The average journalism student would probably work a decade or so in the field before even thinking about submitting copy to the Newspaper of Record.)

Her aggressive, bulldozing manner offended and sometimes alarmed people, partly because she appeared to be unaware of it. In college, she went to a meeting of the school literary magazine, after which one of the attendees reported that she tried to 'take over' the meeting. Among other things, she reportedly asked the editor, "How can I get your job?" His answer has not survived, perhaps because he was too speechless to reply.

Her friends complained that her telephone calls, although extremely interesting, were also quite burdensome — so exhausting, in fact, that it took days to prepare for them, and days to recover. When friends articulated their problems, Iris had a thousand remedies for whatever ailed them, whether socially, intellectually, and emotionally, and would lay out her proposed solutions for two or three hours, without much inter-action with the person on the other end of the line. Then she would repeatedly and passionately articulate her own troubles and dilemmas, without necessarily waiting for, or soliciting, any response to them.

In other words, there was a passionate but slightly schizoid quality to her conversations, as though everything presented a problem that she was required to solve, rather than presenting an opportunity for friends to simply talk about the stresses of everyday life. And she also, some noticed, had a distinct tendency to pick friends who could teach her something, or model some particular skill or behavior that she wished to acquire. On the other hand, Iris had a great sense of humor, had a natural propensity for putting the problems of others into some unique and often hilarious perspective, and was a loyal friend.

It is said that when she was working as a young journalist she was able to write three stories in the time that most young reporters would take to write one. (She once complained to her mother that she was intensely frustrated because she couldn't write faster.) She would approach the editors with finished copy and say, "Do you have any more assignments?" That kind of ferocious energy gets things done, but it suggests a certain inner compulsivity, and has little to do with getting along with one's colleagues. Iris was simply operating at a higher energy level than everybody else, and because she was flying higher than anyone else, she incurred greater risks.

When interning at the *Chicago Tribune*, she was asked by an editor to call up a grieving family and get a quote about a recently deceased family member. Several tries had already been made, all unsuccessful: the surviving family members understandably didn't want to speak to the press. Her *Tribune* editor ordered her to call again, and get the quote no matter what.

Iris dialed the number, and handed the phone to the editor.

"You do it," she said.

The *Tribune* did not offer her a job at the end of her internship. While one applauds Iris' courageous willingness to stand up for her own values, most of us understand that dramatic, public acts of conscience have consequences, so that we must choose our battles. Iris, on the other hand, fully expected to be offered a job—and that was, in fact, a big part of Iris' problem. She wanted to be a warrior-woman, part of a progressive ideological and cultural minority who would do battle with injustice, but she also wanted to be rewarded for it, rather than punished by narrow-minded, insensitive bosses. This desire, to be a cultural and political firebrand on the one hand, and on the other to be successful, was a contradiction at the core of her personality.

Throughout college, in her sorority, in internships in the Associated Press and the Chicago Tribune, and then at John Hopkins (where she studied in a special writing program), Iris managed to rub a great many people the wrong way. She wasn't hateful or openly manipulative; she was simply very aggressive, she seemed to have a separate agenda, and she didn't care much about the feelings of the people around her. This was in part a recurring narcissistic trait, expressed most obstinately in her tendency to feel that other peoples' reactions and aspirations weren't as important as hers. "Once again," Paula Kamen writes, "Iris' outspokenness, individualism, and ultimate focus on the big picture turned off others as 'selfish.' And, to some extent, they were right. When one fixes on such high goals, relating to the community isn't necessarily the first priority."

It's an old story, actually. The noblest and most idealistic social-justice activists are often quite exploitive regarding the people closest to them. They don't necessarily believe that the people they offend are inferior; they just don't see them as being as important as the big picture they're fixated on.

To be sure, many of the people who didn't like Iris Chang were simply jealous. For example, at John Hopkins there were many faculty members who had been struggling for years to sell a book, whereas she, Iris Chang, had already snagged—at the tender age of twenty-three—her first book contract for *Thread of the Silkworm*; and she didn't think twice about letting both faculty and fellow students know about her good fortune. (Shades of telling her classmates in high school that she belonged to children's Mensa!) Some of Iris' friends, especially fellow *Chicago Tribune* intern Christie Parsons, suggested in various ways that Iris try to act "more normal' to get along with people. "And I felt frustrated with her a little bit as a friend because she wouldn't internalize," Christie said, "she wouldn't play by the rules."

Well, yes and no. She never played the short con well, or even tried; she was never one to put on the game face for office or academic politics, because she couldn't imagine being (or pretending to be) the kind of person who would engage in them. Partly it was class; she'd been raised in a privileged environment, so she didn't have to keep her enemies close; and a certain intellectual brilliance was not something she was inclined to hide. And since she often lacked the ability to factor into her game the prerogatives (and feelings) of the people around her, all too often she treated them in a remarkably shabby way.

Iris Chang was playing the game, all right, but for much different and higher stakes than everybody else. There was an urgency about her, a sense that she had to grab the brass ring a little sooner than everybody else. At the same time, she was going to do it her way, ready or not. That worried her friends, who feared that she couldn't achieve success so brazenly on her own terms.

Her friend Paula Kamen admired Iris because she was wildly, outrageously ambitious. But ambition can be a tricky thing. In America people tend to define success as money and power, a hopelessly short-sighted worldview that has crippled the lives of millions; whereas compassion, kindness and love of justice are what America really needs. In her literary career, Iris wanted to have both the power-and-money kind of success *and* to be a fearless literary rebel attacking injustice. Those are two very different things; sometimes they work together, and more often they don't. Iris never seemed completely aware of this dichotomy, so deeply had she internalized it, so her ambition—however muscular—always carried within it a profound contradiction. Furthermore, her genuinely high ideals, when combined with behavior that seemed aggressive and self-centered, sometimes made her a target for ridicule.

There was, in short, a part of Iris Chang who wanted to be like Clara Barton, who cared for the dead and dying on the battlefield; but another big part of her wanted to be admired, to make a lot of money, to be a celebrity in a celebrity culture, and to be the center of attention. It must be acknowledged, of course, that being a celebrity *did* help her promote her message about Nanking; but she increasingly enjoyed celebrity status for its own sake. The contradiction was always there; and as long as it was in balance, it was good for her and good for everybody who read her books. But it was always an unwieldy compound, and when it drifted out of balance the result was catastrophic.

In his essay "Terracotta Warrior," Eric J. Baker wrote that reading Iris Chang's emails, as included in her mother's book, made him see Iris Chang in a different light. "In e-mails written soon after [*The Rape of Nanking*] became a bestseller, Iris brags about how everyone praised her lecture or wanted her autograph or how she was the star in the room. Ying-Ying Chang cites these writings as examples of how her daughter was once happy, but Iris' unedited words read as slightly narcissistic. The younger Chang's husband of a decade and a half is almost a nonentity in the memoir, and Iris doesn't appear to have spent much time with him, given her endless world travels for research, interviews, and lectures."

"I do not imply that Iris comes off poorly in the memoir. Rather, she's even more fascinating for her burning self-determination and her frustration at not being able to single-handedly change the world. She was a warrior indeed, as her mother says, just not a selfless one." Baker adds that it was frustrating to him that Iris' parents had no realization that something was going terribly wrong when it seems so obvious in Ying-Ying's own narrative that it was. But this was an upper-middle-class Chinese-American family in which mental illness was not supposed to intrude.[18]

For many people, Iris' rough edges seemed to magically vanish when she became famous. "Ironically," Paula Kamen wrote, "now [that she was] mixing regularly in elite circles, Iris never fitted in better in her life. Hanging out with celebrities was natural for her. While author Amy Tan described Iris as 'in awe' at such events, I did not get the sense that Iris was intimidated. After all, she was with her kind. No one thought she was too ambitious; no one thought she was 'weird'; and no one was jealous—because they were as successful as she was." But that only fixed the world in which Iris moved, and did not address the inside demons that had long driven her. Paula Kamen: "It was now clear that although Iris had extraordinary talents as a writer and thinker from an early age, like a lot of 'sensitive types,' she lacked some of the most ordinary skills for picking up social cues and 'playing by the rules.' Usually marching to her own drummer, for better and for worse, she was always more advanced than peers and co-workers in some ways, and much less in others."[19]

At the Clinton White House Renaissance weekends in Hilton Head, South Carolina, she was a big hit. "Iris really wowed a lot of people because most of the people there at Renaissance Weekend were older," Brett told Paula Kamen. "They were in their forties and fifties, and they built up their careers over a period of time. And here's this woman who was thirty, and she looked like she was twenty-five. She was beautiful and articulate, and so they actually had her speaking at the closing speeches. They'd have a Nobel Prize winner, and a TV personality, and then Iris. She was a big hit. I mean her book was on the best-seller list almost that whole year."

She never learned to hold her tongue, it seems from all accounts. But sometimes even her most outspoken and politically incorrect statements could come across as calculated. Take the time she was invited to speak at a discussion session on racism at the Renaissance weekend. "When her turn came to testify about racism in her life, Brett recalled, 'Iris would always say, 'I've never experienced any racism in my life; I think this is silly. People should just move on and not worry about it.'"

But that doesn't quite add up. In fact this incident is typical of the seemingly unconscious way Iris Chang sought both notoriety and a niche for herself as an author. This was, remember, the author who wrote the seminal book of her generation on racism and Chinese-Americans (*The Chinese in America: a Narrative History*). This is the woman who perfectly described the compound of racism and McCarthyism that destroyed the career of Tsien Hsue-Shen in *Thread of the Silkworm*. This was the woman who wept over the atrocities committed against the people of Nanking because a generation of Japanese soldiers had been trained to regard the Chinese as subhuman. Why was she dismissing the power of racism here?

Perhaps she regarded her understanding of racism as sufficiently nuanced that she didn't care to discuss it publicly. And no doubt it was also because of a certain snobbery in Iris' personality, a perennial inability to address generalized challenges that might affect people not as privileged or as gifted as she was. But it seems also in some part to have been a signal to the cultural establishment (especially that section of it that gravitated to the Clintons) that although her message was sometimes radical, she could be counted on not to be personally 'difficult,' offering her own brand of enlightenment as long as it was in fashion and without threatening any fundamental paradigms of power.

9.

These personal traits shed some light on Iris Chang's reaction to the onset of mental illness. But they do not explain the illness itself. Ultimately her mother, Ying-Ying Chang, blamed her suicide on the psychoactive medications she was given by psychiatrists. There may indeed have been some mistakes—as we will see—in the medications she ultimately consumed; but even if the meds were uniformly bad for her that would not explain the breakdown in Louisville, Kentucky. What caused Iris Chang's breakdown?

The one recurring negative factor in Iris Chang's life, going all the way back to childhood and then re-emerging in college and young adulthood, was her profound, unremitting sleep disturbance, an inability to sleep that apparently got worse with every year. Evidently potentiating that same sleep deprivation, and making it much worse, was the secondary trauma she suffered writing *The Rape of Nanking*, and then researching the Bataan Death March. Being unable to rest for any sustained length of time must have made the impact of the horrible photos, reports and written accounts of atrocities that much harder to bear. And Chang was—by her own account—frequently bothered, on those occasions when she could get to sleep, by terrible nightmares relating to the atrocities she was writing about.

Finally, when she was doing the Death March interviews in 2003 and 2004, the sleep disturbance had reached a point at which it was interfering with every part of her life. In short, the secondary trauma and the sleep disturbance worked together in a destructive synergy to debilitate her mentally and physically. This led, on several occasions, to further episodes in which she stopped eating and sleeping, grew thin and weak, wept, and reported that her hair was falling out.

These were, in other words, repeated episodes in which Chang showed clear signs of being psychologically and physically debilitated; and this was made worse, over a period of time, by her ongoing exposure to interviews, photographs and written accounts of atrocities. The interviews for her proposed fourth book on the Bataan Death March, which she not only conducted but personally transcribed from recordings, were done at a time when she found it almost impossible to sleep—and the secondary trauma and the sleep disturbance unquestionably potentiated each other, and in so doing, contributed directly to her breakdown.

But at this point we must ask: what was driving the sleep disturbance? The reader will remember that Paula Kamen reported an episode of debilitation in the early 1990s, in which Isis complained that her hair was falling out, long before she had chosen the Nanking massacre as a subject for her second book. The exposure to the atrocities of the Japanese Imperial Army undoubtedly made her sleep disturbance worse, but it did not originally cause it. Unless she was secretly abusing amphetamines, all the evidence suggests a subtle but progressive form of mania associated with Type II bipolar disorder. Up to five percent of the population may suffer from this kind of bipolar disorder; it can gradually drift into Type I, at which point the symptoms become more noticeable, and the entire situation much more dangerous. People with Type II can present as extremely diligent, ambitious and drawing on an almost endless store of energy; this works wonderfully until the manic energy becomes too overwhelming, at which point the individual begins to slip into Type I bipolar, and ultimately experiences symptoms of psychosis. At that point, it is no longer 'bipolar disorder,' but 'bipolar disorder with psychotic features.'

When Iris became acutely delusional, there were really only a few things it could have been. Late onset of paranoid schizophrenia (very unlikely); an atypical form of schizoaffective disorder (perhaps); or the late onset of bipolar disorder. All the evidence—especially the extreme, long-term problems with sleep disturbance, going back more than a decade—points to late-onset bipolar. Why late onset, if some form of mania had been operative for so long? Because the symptoms weren't obvious until Iris was 36—then they became obvious in a terribly acute way, in the form of a psychotic paranoia that would eventually cause her to believe that even her husband and parents might be involved in a conspiracy against her.

The psychiatrists in Louisville suspected bipolar disorder, and Iris actually received the diagnosis in California some weeks before her suicide. But how can that be, when nobody seemed to see it before? It was a killer hiding in plain sight, it turns out, because of cultural (and probably class) reasons. The first person to write convincingly about this was Paula Kamen, Iris' friend, who wrote about it in her book *Seeking Iris Chang: Friendship, Ambition and the Loss of an Extraordinary Mind*. "It turns out that I, along with many others, [was] using a very 'Eurocentric' model in overlooking Iris' mania. That was the observation of Dr. Aruna Jha, a scholar and activist on the issue of Asian suicide based in Chicago. She explained to me that Asians' typical range of accepted behavior is much *narrower* than that of Caucasians. For a greater number of them, such 'reckless' behaviors of promiscuity or shoplifting would be unthinkable, even in the most unhinged states."

"'It would take another Asian or a very sensitive person to realize that [Iris] had gone past all the limits of what Asian human beings tolerate at this point,' Dr. Jha said. 'And even when white people do recognize extreme behaviors in Asian friends or co-workers, such as nonstop work for days, they may accept that as a normal characteristic of the Asian super-achiever or 'model minority.' She added that compounding inaccuracy of diagnosis, even for trained professionals, is an extreme lack of clinical research into nonwhite subjects and how they experience mental illness."

But even the Asian-Americans in Iris' orbit didn't really grasp the clinical implication of her behavior. Paula Kamen quotes Iris Chang Herrera, a California protégé of Iris Chang: "People knew that [Iris] needed to take a break. But at the same time we didn't really question it as much as we should because we just thought, 'Oh, she's a superwoman. She just keeps on going, doesn't stop.'" Not only did the stereotype of the super-achieving Asian-American serve in part to explain her manic behavior to some, the equally seductive—and equally dangerous—stereotype of the superwoman (the 'successful' working mom who is a perfect mother and wife, has ideal kids, a perfect career, and is in total control of every aspect of her life) also caused a great many people to accept her take-no-prisoners manner as simply a natural personal accoutrement of the 'successful' woman.

There was another exacerbating factor that Iris didn't often share with others, that had to do with the fertility drugs she took in 2001, as recounted by Paula Kamen in her book: "Brett said that she would have problems getting pregnant and then miscarry repeatedly. That process, along with weeks of infertility-drug treatment, shifted her hormones wildly, which can have an impact on destabilizing brain chemistry." Hormonal drugs can, in other words, deeply affect people with a predilection for mood disorders. Brett and Iris eventually had a child with a surrogate mother, a fact that Iris went to great lengths to conceal from her friends. "The mere weight of keeping secrets was a stressor in itself," writes Paula Kamen, adding: "Above all, Iris' very intentional 'cover up' of her use of a surrogate reveals the intense pressure that she felt to appear perfect. Again, it wasn't just coincidence that all her friends had this impression of her. She was *actively working* to produce this image."[20]

Some people hate the diagnosis 'bipolar disorder' because of the words 'manic' or 'mania,' which suggests a wild-eyed person running amuck. (Iris herself didn't like the diagnosis, and her mother Ying-Ying—who once accepted it—has retroactively decided that it was inaccurate.) But Type II can be extremely subtle. This writer once lived in a household with adults and several children, which included a young man of 20 or 21 years who was extremely active working as a DJ while attending classes at the local community college. He was often out most of the night, but he did manage to sleep a little, and his judgment wasn't bad; I was impressed by his often-verbalized opposition to the dangerous designer drugs he saw at the raves, clubs and parties where he worked. Full of little-kid enthusiasms, he nonetheless did his homework, never lost his car keys or other personal items, and often did errands for his mother. He was just a very active young man who was always on the run, like a lot of kids at that age. Then he went on tour for a week or so.

Shortly afterwards he turned up at the county-funded mental health facility where I worked as a counselor, diagnosed with Type II bipolar disorder. He had years before suffered several hypo-manic episodes, it seems, but had gone for a long time without meds, and now his mania had been drifting into the Type I range. When I got to work, his med sheets were all set up (he knew which meds he should be taking) and he had already gotten back on them. It was an amazing and humbling experience. How on earth could I, who had a fair amount of experience with clients who had bipolar disorder, have missed all the signs? The answer is that if they're sufficiently subtle anybody could miss them. The person with Type II bipolar disorder may not seem irrational, but on the contrary may seem intelligent, an energetic worker, quite conscientious, and perhaps a bit of a perfectionist.

The common denominator in most cases of mania associated with bipolar disorder is boundless energy, the natural concomitant of which is lack of sleep. People with mania simply don't *want* to sleep, and they don't think they have to. When they say they've been up for several days (as Iris Chang said to Amy Tan) they're likely to say it with a kind of perverse pride—and yes, the long hours of the average book tour *can* feed into Type II mania, and vice versa. After some time, however—as they get older—such people may start concealing how little they are sleeping, in order to keep from alarming friends, spouses and family members.

"A lack of sleep is one of the hallmark symptoms of mania," said Dr. Kay Redfield Jamison in an interview after Chang's death. "Typically, people start losing sleep, then stay up later and later each night. It has a terrible reverberating effect. The lack of sleep can exacerbate the illness and vice versa." In Jamison's book *An Unquiet Mind: a Memoir of Moods and Madness*, which is about her own struggles with bipolar disorder, she writes about the tremendous creative energy of even the milder forms of mania. "My manias, at least in their early and mild forms, were absolutely intoxicating states that gave rise to great personal pleasure, an incomparable flow of thoughts, and a ceaseless energy that allowed the translation of new ideas into papers and projects."[21] That could feel like a kind of superpower. Who would voluntarily give that up?

Particularly at risk are the early over-achievers, the youthful academic stars and professional luminaries who are struck down by the onset of mental illnesses—and in this population, it is late onset that is particularly difficult to treat. Likewise at risk are creative or humanitarian types who labor under a heavy sense of duty to some higher calling, but who feel shame for not discharging their duty perfectly. Iris Chang fitted into both these categories. She was ambitious, capable and an extremely successful author who also felt a sense of obligation to her parents; even more, she felt a sense of obligation to the millions of people in the Chinese Diaspora. Iris Chang also felt, it should be pointed out, a deeply personal obligation to the dead of Nanking, who had been silenced by death and whose voice she aspired to be.

Likewise she felt a duty to the survivors of the Bataan Death March, because they were dying off, she said, and she had to continue the interviews to win justice for them before they were all dead. This was an emotional orientation including both duty and ambition, in which duty to the survivors had gradually come to play a preponderant role—and it was precisely at this point where her almost superhuman energy began to fail her. And it was then, this writer maintains, that the influence of secondary trauma most likely became most acute. Before, during the research of the Nanking massacre, she was apparently able to use her nonstop reserves of energy to distance herself somewhat from the horrendous stories of atrocity. Now, as she both conducted and typed up the interviews with the Death March survivors, she would have less energy with which to distance herself from the violent and disturbing content.

When Paula Kamen interviewed Brett, Iris' husband, he at first played down the emotional effects of the depressing material associated with the Death March interviews. It was the last book tour, ending in May 2004, that triggered the big change in Iris, he said. On the other hand, he found the Death March material so depressing that he asked her to stop talking about it. "'She would interview those survivors, and just have one horrible story after another and just tell me. And I finally said, 'Look, I don't want to hear it anymore. If you want to write the book fine, but I don't want to hear the stories anymore.'"[22]

As we've seen, Iris ended up typing up the Death March transcriptions herself, because the typist she'd been using kept breaking down in tears while typing the stories. "Brett did concede that the Bataan book may have had an influence on depressing Iris because of how elderly and infirm her typical subjects were. She felt intense pressure to interview them as soon as possible, before they died; many of whom she had befriended had passed away within weeks of her meeting them, which was tough on Iris." Toward the end she probably felt shame for being unable to finish her book about them, and—in the heightened tendency to self-blame brought on by depression and paranoia— may have felt that she personally let them down.

Iris' closet friends verify that the atrocities that she wrote about affected her very deeply emotionally. The writer Barbara Masin, who was Iris' closest friend in the last ten years of her life, helped her with the translation of John Rabe's diaries, because of her fluency in German. Barbara could tell that Iris was upset by Rabe's accounts of the Nanking atrocities, because she often translated parts of the diaries to Iris directly. "[Iris] always got very distressed when she was dealing with atrocity-type situations. She took it very personally... for me it was you read it, and it's not nice stuff, but there's a part of yourself you can kind of shut off. You kill that part of you just to get through that material. And I don't think Iris ever did that. She really was viscerally as shocked for the last atrocity as for the first one."[23]

Iris told another friend, Li Wen Huang, about stresses relating to problems with her first book. "But there, she also suffered greatly with the darkness of the subject matter. As she had told reporters after the book's publication, Iris let Li Wen know that the grisly materials was having an effect on her, and interrupting her sleep. 'That's one of the things I noticed about Iris is that, especially when she was intent on writing a book, she would be pretty much an insomniac,' said Li Wen. 'She'd be really stressed out because she couldn't stop thinking about things.'" (Ironically, according to Paula Kamen, Li Wen had herself had some problems with depression, but was afraid to discuss it with Iris Chang because of the public image of 'perfection' she perceived Iris as having.)[24]

Iris' most important journalism mentor was the late Robert Reid, a greatly-admired professor of journalism at the University of Illinois. Reid had been in the newspaper business forever and was notoriously strict; he formed a powerful bond with Chang, since they were both idealists, and both liked to talk. Chang was very open with him regarding her concerns with the way her chosen subject matter was affecting her psychologically: "With remarkable openness, they discussed her emotional fallout from the dark topics she was researching in college and beyond," wrote Paula Kamen. "In media interviews before and after her death, he described an episode during which she had broken down in tears in front of his class while describing her experiences writing about a man who had died of AIDS. 'She put her head on the table and started sobbing,' he recalled in the January/February 1998 *Illinois Alumni* magazine. 'She sobbed for five minutes, Everybody sat respectfully, nobody was uncomfortable. Then she lifted her head up and began talking.'"

In that same issue of the alumni magazine, Reid added that she also called him for support when she was working on *The Rape of Nanking*, and "ended up crying for an hour on the phone. She said she didn't know how she could go on, knowing that human nature was capable of such cruelty. It took more than an hour, but she worked herself through it."[25]

Iris was also influenced by Dale Maharidge's concept of "method journalism," a form of immersing oneself emotionally so deeply in a particular human situation that there is no longer any boundaries between the writer and the people written about. Maharidge, who now teaches journalism at Columbia, once did a piece on homeless people, in which—rather like George Orwell in *Down and Out in London and Paris*—he spent five months living with homeless people under bridges and in hobo camps. In the same way, Iris also became emotionally connected to the suffering of the dead of Nanking, and the shame of people in the Chinese Diaspora because they'd not been honored properly. Interestingly, however, Maharidge made a conscious decision to distance himself from Chang as early as 1999; his conversations with her, he said, were exhausting him.

One of the former American POWs of the Second World War that Iris interviewed was Ray "Hap" Halloran, who lived in Menlo Park, not far from where Iris and Brett were living in the San Francisco Bay Area. 'Hap' had an interesting experience while chatting with Iris Chang that suggests her volatile state of mind at that time, as well as her emotional involvement with the people, living and dead, that she wrote about. Paula Kamen tells the story: "At one point, Hap, who is very staunch in his views, told Iris that her quest to get the Japanese government to officially apologize to China for the massacre at Nanking was futile. [Iris] became very upset. She retreated to the bathroom to collect herself, where she stayed for about twenty-five minutes." Five minutes in the bathroom to collect oneself would be about right; twenty-five minutes suggests that something in Iris' personality was going badly wrong.

It is likely that when Iris' moodiness and paranoid feelings began to escalate in the spring and summer of 2004, her ability to block out the horrors of the Death March interviews were greatly diminished. We know that even as paranoid fears were coming to dominate her thoughts in the summer of 2004, her sleep disturbance continued, and was in fact getting worse. That would make it even more difficult to block out nightmares, intrusive thoughts of violence and atrocities, and the anxiety associated with secondary or vicarious trauma. And as we know, one of the symptoms of secondary trauma, like that of mania, is sleep disturbance—and the two evidently worked together to make the already critical sleep deprivation worse. Furthermore, vicarious trauma also interferes somewhat with the ability to trust others, which could only add to the paranoia Iris felt.

Evidently Iris Chang's paranoia and secondary trauma potentiated each other, during the summer of 2004, in a dangerous and finally fatal synergy, ultimately culminating in the appalling delusional imagines she saw on the TV in the early hours of August 13, 2004, in Louisville, Kentucky—images of "horrible atrocities and ugly images of children torn apart by wars," exactly the kind of terrifying images of atrocity she had dealt with so extensively as an author.

10.

A kindly veteran, a retired Colonel who had been coordinating her interviews in Kentucky, came with his wife to Iris' hotel room early in the morning of 13 August, 2004, apparently in response to her panicked telephone call. He offered her some bottled water, but she refused it, convinced it might be poisoned. According to her husband Brett, Iris thought he might be a representative of the 'dark forces of conspiracy' that were persecuting her. She interpreted something he said as an indication that he might be in league with the mysterious stranger who told her, during her spring book tour, "You'd be better off being with us." Later, after her three-day hospitalization in Kentucky she would say, "They tried to recruit me, and I turned them down, and now they're out to get me."

She told Brett that the government was behind her hospitalization, because it didn't like what she was writing. This feeling was apparently the result of what she perceived as the government's gross indifference to the Bataan Death March survivors, and the well-known opposition of the State Department to further books being written about it, not to mention further advocacy for the survivors. Furthermore, there was a general feeling among the Chinese-American activists with whom she was in contact that they were being monitored by the government; many complained that their phones were being tapped. A few days before she left for Kentucky, Iris had seen the 2004 remake of "The Manchurian Candidate," which is about government brainwashing of a Gulf War veteran, and after her hospitalization started to feel that perhaps the government was trying to do something similar to her.

Back home in California, Brett threw himself into the effort to help Iris, writing a "Twenty-Point Plan to Make Iris Well." He set up a gym in the basement and began working out with her. But she became easily distracted, so easily that it was hard to stick to any plan. "There was always a crisis. When she was mentally ill, we'd start with a plan at the beginning of the day, a weekly plan, and by Monday at noon it would just be shot. Her mother would always call in a panic if something was going wrong."[26] (Iris' mother and father were now living in the same apartment complex as Brett and Iris.) It was about this time that Iris became very concerned about the Illuminati, a supposedly secret society that—according to many conspiracy theorists—was covertly controlling world events.

"For anybody who experiences mental illness for the first time, it's very hard to accept that it is your biology that is making it happen," said Dr. David Lo, former director of San Francisco Chinatown's Mental Health Center. "It's very hard to believe that there is something wrong with your mind... there is no way a family could sort out all the details, let alone their own feelings, because they're connected to the person. The onus is on us, as Western medical professionals, to be aware of cultural influences—and to be proactive in educating family members and the patient when there is a first encounter with mental illness."[27] There is a very, very powerful stigma attached to mental illness in Asian-American communities, causing many families to attempt to hide it until it results in hospitalization or suicide.

Furthermore, people who are just confronting the symptoms of mental illness are at greater risk for suicide, because they haven't had time to develop good coping mechanisms. In September, Iris made what Paula Kamen referred to in *Finding Iris Chang* as "a somewhat ambiguous suicide attempt"—I would call it a suicide gesture—when she reported taking multiple pills in a hotel room and washing it down with vodka. (She was taken to the hospital, where the doctors concluded that she'd only imagined taking the pills.) Still, the uncanny experience had the effect of putting her husband and parents on notice that suicide was definitely on her mind.

Among other things, Iris felt that she'd caused her son Christopher to be autistic by having him vaccinated. She'd had no such fears at the time of the actual vaccinations, but later feelings of self-blame became so strong that she became convinced that she was responsible for some symptoms that she interpreted as autism. This gradually became an obsession. Iris also felt that Christopher's life was in danger from the unknown forces that she felt were targeting her. Eventually Christopher was sent back east to live with Brett's parents, so that everybody could concentrate on helping Iris achieve some stability. During September and October, Iris became increasingly afraid that she was being monitored by the government.

Iris hated the way the psychoactive medication made her feel—she said it made her "groggy," and robbed her of the high energy which she had always cherished. (And it made her sleepy, which she also didn't like.) Sometimes she took the medication, but often she didn't. ("She had the perspective that she was more capable than these doctors for understanding what was going wrong," Brett told Paula Kamen.) And there was another thing that she had strong feelings about: she wanted to keep her condition a secret. Brett and her parents agreed to this, limiting information about her mental illness to a small group of people.

Meanwhile, they all began a desperate search for psychiatric help for Iris, a search that involved the usual demoralizing dead-ends and mind-boggling disappointments that any family with a mentally-ill member will quickly recognize. Psychiatrist 'A' listened for awhile before announcing that he was going on a month's vacation. Psychiatrist 'B' was mainly concerned with getting his co-pay. Psychiatrist 'C' seemed a good fit for Iris, meeting with her for psychotherapy three times a week; but after her suicide it became obvious that she had decided not to be truthful with him. In retrospect it seems she had, at a very early point, made up her mind to commit suicide; and what others perceived as an improvement in her mood was most likely her relief at making the decision to end her life.

Early in October, an unfortunate event occurred that would have a pivotal effect on Iris' thinking. Desperate to help her, her mother took her to a Stanford support group of people with bipolar disorder, but it backfired badly. The group was made up of psychiatric patients—a rather scruffy lot, it would seem—who were struggling with their illnesses, had not found the right meds and dosages to give them stability, and were hardly poster children for successful psychopharmacology. Iris denounced the participants as "Zombies," said she would never attend such a meeting again, announcing furthermore that she was stopping her meds immediately. (Brett called Dr. 'C' and asked if he would supply him with a list of successful professionals with bipolar disorder who took meds and lived stable lives, and he complied. But Iris refused to talk to any of them.)

What she apparently got from the unfortunate 'support group' experience was a conviction that she would rather be dead than bipolar. Indeed, it must have felt to her like the ultimate betrayal of her own biology: the incredible high energy that caused her high school teacher to see her as a "bullet train," now led to psychosis! In his classic book *Suicide*, sociologist Emile Durkheim suggested that suicide can be a radical rejection of a particular set of social and personal circumstances. If Iris couldn't live at the fever pitch that she previously had, if that same magical energy now led to psychosis, she may have felt that it wasn't worth living at all.

What is interesting is that the idea of recovery from her mental illness did not enter Iris' thinking at all—she simply wanted everything to go back to the way it was before her breakdown. That is regrettable, because if she'd accepted the challenge of recovery, she could have written the seminal book about Asian women and mental illness, a book that desperately needs to be written. But she'd already written one book that changed everything in the Chinese Diaspora; it would have been too much, perhaps, to ask for two.

After the bad experience of the 'support group,' Iris embarked on a series of hardball negotiations with Dr. 'C' regarding her medications, and he agreed to letting her lower the dosage of Risperdal that she was taking. At the same time, she unilaterally stopped taking Celexa, a very dangerous thing to do. Dr. "C" threatened to hospitalize her if she didn't resume taking it, but she'd already stopped for almost two weeks. After her suicide, her mother came to believe that psychoactive medication had caused her daughter to commit suicide, pointing out reputable studies that suggest that Asians have a lower threshold for both therapeutic *and* adverse effects of psychoactive medications. On the other hand, it is just as likely that Iris' habit of starting and stopping medication against medical advice—such as suddenly quitting the antidepressant Celexa for two weeks after attending the disastrous support group—was what was making her worse.

On October 21st Iris told her mother that she wanted to die, mentioning the unremitting nature of the psychological pain she was experiencing. That night she asked her father to help her organize photos for her archives; by October 25, family members became aware that she was visiting suicide and euthanasia websites online. On October 28, her mother Ying-Ying entered her house and examined Iris' computer, discovering that Iris had been browsing on the internet for the address of a sporting goods shop; she then went through Iris' purse and found a safety manual for gun owners. (After her death, Brett found that she had purchased the book *Final Exit*, by Derek Humphry, a book for people contemplating suicide that advises readers on guns to buy for "self-deliverance.") Residential treatment might have worked at that point, but Iris had already rejected it; a forced hospitalization might have bought everybody some time, but the frazzled, terrified family was incapable of such an aggressive intervention.

During that last week Iris refused to see her mother, or return her calls and emails; Ying-Ying left small gifts of flowers and food on her doorstep, but Iris shunned her. Iris seemed calm, however, and Brett hoped she was getting better. The following Monday, Iris went to a sporting goods store and purchased an antique pistol, one so old that only collectors would normally buy it—one that would not, in other words, require a background check. (She was apparently wary that there might be a record of her hospitalization in Kentucky that would prevent her from purchasing a gun.) That night Brett found her pacing around in the hallway, and suggested that she go to bed. She did—but during the early AM hours on Tuesday morning, she got up, left the house, drove her 1999 Oldsmobile west on Highway 17; about 25 miles from her home she parked on a remote turnoff.

It was there that she took her life. After placing the antique weapon she had recently purchased in her mouth, she pulled the trigger; the antique lead ball went through her hard palate and the left dural sinus, through the left cerebral and occipital lobes, finally breaking through the skull but coming to rest without exiting the scalp. In the nanosecond that it takes to pull a trigger, the beautiful mind and courageous life of Iris Chang was taken from the world.

Waking in the morning, her husband Brett discovered three suicide notes, the third one a revision of the second. These lines from the third one demonstrate how deeply her paranoia had worked its way into her worldview: *"There are aspects of my experience in Louisville that I will never understand. Deep down I suspect that you may have more answers about this than I do. I can never shake my belief that I was being recruited, and later persecuted, by forces more powerful than I could have imagined. Whether it was the CIA or some other organization I will never know. As long as I am alive, these forces will never stop hounding me...."*

11.

Why did Iris Chang write about human evil? For that matter, why do *any* of us write about violence, aggression and human evil? Because, this writer would say, there is a growing consensus that we must understand the dark side of human behavior if humankind is to survive its tumultuous adolescence. For that reason, writing about systemic evil can lift us up, because by telling the truth about it we are exposing—and thereby fighting—the self-destruction that threatens humankind. But there are also times when human brutality pulls us down, overwhelming us with what seems to be a limitless human capacity for cruelty and perversity.

What's the difference between the two emotional reactions? It probably depends almost entirely on whatever else is going on in the rest of our lives. There are times when we are too vulnerable to confront the abyss; and the better part of wisdom—forget about valor—is knowing when to step back. The world doesn't need more martyrs. The journalist who knows her or his own limits is the warrior for truth who lives to fight another day.

The brilliant historian and author Iris Chang was killed by mental illness, not writing about the Rape of Nanking or research into the Bataan Death March. But we must also acknowledge that the extreme violence of the material she worked with debilitated her physically and mentally, because she herself so often said so. Her research into the Bataan Death March, occurring in tandem with the onset of serious bipolar disorder, made her sleep disturbance worse; that added to her growing psychosis. Meanwhile, the testimony of the Death March survivors about the indifference of the US government to their plight fed into her growing paranoia. These were not the main reasons Iris Chang took her own life, but were definitely contributing factors in bringing her to the edge.

There is a strong tendency on the part of some to deny that the violence she explored in her writing could *ever* have contributed to her final debilitation. There are those publishers, editors and agents who insist that she was never affected by what she wrote about, perhaps because they were so intimately a part of it, and to some extent benefitted from it—yet when she became mentally ill, they were the first ones to suggest that Iris take a break from researching the Bataan Death March. Secondly, there are those who are deeply invested in the idea of Iris Chang as the ultimate "strong woman"—so strong that human emotions couldn't wound her. But isn't it time we retire this patriarchal idea as essentially false for both men and women, and instead embrace the fact that strength is often accompanied—and perhaps *should* be accompanied—by the usual human vulnerability?

For much of her life, Iris Chang had very effective defenses that allowed her to probe some of humankind's darkest secrets.

But her main defense seems to have been her soaring energy—the ability to stay up all night and work twice as hard as everybody else also made it possible for her to look fearlessly at human brutality and to write about it objectively. But when the limitless energy began to run out, and the same part of her biology that had produced such overwhelming vivacity began to produce depression and paranoid fears, that aspect of her defense system was lost. At that point the research into the Bataan Death March and her mental illness worked together in a destructive synergy to make her sleep disturbance worse; and that in turn contributed to the acuteness of her crisis as her illness caught up with her, and Type II became Type I mania, and then psychosis.

Iris Chang seemed the very personification of the talented and highly-motivated Asian-American who excels at everything. But what were the pressures she experienced, as she acted out a role that elicited both pride and jealousy from others? And more importantly, to what extent did stereotypical mainstream American thinking about Asians allow Iris Chang to conceal her illness in plain sight? We *expect* Asians to be academic stars, we *expect* Asians to work harder than other racial groups, and we *expect* them to be more successful, using the traditional metrics of money and power—and finally fame—to measure success. To what extent did the people around Iris Chang attribute her tendency to go without sleep and work herself into debilitation as simply another aspect of being an Asian-American woman in a hyper-competitive society? *To what extent did non-Asians perceive a symptom of mental illness as an Asian trait, and to what extent did other Asians make the same mistake?*

A book by Iris' mother Ying-Ying Chang, written some years after Iris' suicide, has been seen as an attempt to "resurrect Iris' reputation," as one headline puts it, the main purpose being to celebrate Iris' life and work; but with a subtext in the book's closing chapters that suggests that mental illness and suicide are a form of moral disgrace from which Ying-Ying is at pains to disabuse the reader. Most of the book is an excellent source of information about Iris' life and career; but the last part, in which Ying-Ying develops her theory about why Iris took her own life, is clearly speculative.

She denounces the diagnosis of bipolar disorder ("This kind of generalization implies that any person who is energetic and ambitious or a perfectionist would have or would develop bipolar disorder."). She attributes Iris' suicide entirely to the psychoactive medications she was given after hospitalization. ("Tragically, Iris was not given a chance to recover from her physical and mental exhaustion. She was immediately given an antipsychotic drug and then an antidepressant with side effects which could exacerbate her anxiety and mild depression.") If only Iris hadn't been given psych meds, she would have recovered. ("With rest and support, she would have been able to manage her problems, personal or professional, in a systematic and logical way.") In some interviews about the book, Ying-Ying seems to be saying that Iris really didn't have mental illness—that it was, in effect, all a big mistake.

The culture-based stigma regarding mental illness will be dealt with in time by Asian authors, filmmakers and artists. Somewhere out there is a great book or screenplay waiting to be written by an Asian woman or man who is in recovery from—or struggling with—mental illness. In the meantime, *all* of us who write about the dark side of human behavior can learn something from the story of Iris Chang. We must pace ourselves in all we write, but especially when we write about violence, brutality and war. The thing that causes the secondary or vicarious trauma may be different for all of us—with Iris Chang, toward the end, it was the *infirmity* of the American Death March survivors that distressed and haunted her.

When we write about difficult subjects, we must take care of ourselves—eat regularly, get enough sleep, discuss what we're writing with friends and colleagues. The idea that we can write about traumatizing events without some of it rubbing off on ourselves is an idea that was never true, and is even less true today. When our defenses are strong, we can sometimes look into the abyss; but when our defenses are down, we must have the prudence and the respect for ourselves and others to turn away until our defenses return.

Chapter Eight

Hiroshima, Mon Amour and the Dilemma of the Trauma-Bonded Lovers

1.

Hiroshima, Mon Amour (Hiroshima, My Love) was written by Marguerite Duras, directed by Alain Resnais, and released to the world in 1959. Today it is regarded as one of the greatest films of all time. It is an intensely shocking, intensely bittersweet story of lovers struggling with traumatic memories of two incidents that occurred in World War II: the destruction of Hiroshima by an American atom bomb on 6 August, 1945, and a violent incident at the end of the Nazi occupation of France. The film consists of the intimate and increasingly volatile conversations of the film's two traumatized lovers, a French woman and a Japanese man, and the flashbacks triggered by their words as they use their love affair as a cathartic medium for gaining some perspective on the memories that haunt and disorient them. By the end of the film the woman is able to let go of a traumatic memory that she'd previously used to keep a dead lover—her first love—alive in her mind and emotions.

Critic Dwight McDonald, who was not given to hyperbole, wrote of the film: "For the first time since Eisenstein, we have here a cinematic intelligence so quick, so subtle, so original, so at once passionate and sophisticated that it can be compared with Joyce, with Picasso, with Berg and Bartok and Stravinsky. The audience was extraordinarily quiet—no coughing, whispering, rustling of paper; a hypnotic trance. We were absorbed in the human experience flickering across the screen, attentive lest we miss a clue to the mystery... It was oddly like a religious service, and if someone had made a wisecrack it would have seemed not an irritation but a blasphemy."[1]

The uncanny power of *Hiroshima, Mon Amour* can be judged by the fact that although the film premiered at the Cannes Film Festival, it was shown separately from all the other films—the organizers of the festival were afraid of antagonizing the American government if it won the competition, as it probably would have.

Resnais departed from Marguerite Duras's screenplay at several points; so while this writer has consulted her script, my goal has been to reach an understanding of the film itself, based on repeated viewings of it. To facilitate that goal, I have concentrated only on those parts that advance the film's underlying subject matter, as I experience it. The film enters the unconscious mind as a kind of slow-motion explosion, a slow encroachment that gradually penetrates the waking and sleeping dreams of the viewer. Even before the film credits, one sees a heavy, silently rising, oval-shaped firestorm of an atomic bomb exploding, slowly filling the screen. But there is no sound of a detonation— only some rather haunting music, which continues through most of the film credits. The atonal nature of the music suggests not so much the physical proximity of the explosion, as its emotional after-effects.

Then, as the film begins, we see the naked upper torsos of two lovers, a man and a woman, passionately making love: we cannot see their faces nor can we see below their waists. Yet it is our impression that they are young and rather beautiful. The footage of the lovers—and the rest of the film as well—is shot in a lush, dreamy black-and-white, which is exactly the color scheme that people dream in.

All too soon, however, the ghostly gray imminence of the naked bodies gives way to an alarming, sandy iridescence in which the flesh of the lovers seems to be falling or burning away, becoming infirm, crumbling to the touch, and dirty with clinging sand or soil. The disturbing but still sensual lovers' caresses are accompanied by a second strange but beautiful musical theme (by the composer Giovanni Fusco). Although we cannot see the faces of the man and woman, we can hear their voices: the woman and the man are having a disagreement. The woman says she saw Hiroshima, but the man disagrees.

"You saw *nothing* in Hiroshima," says the man.

"I saw *everything,*" replies the woman. *"Everything."*

The two principal characters in the film are referred to in Duras's script simply as *She* and *He*. Their voices—as called for by the script—are "flat and calm, as if reciting"; both *She* and *He* speak in French, and the woman speaks in a way that is "calm, colorless, and incantatory." Now the camera cuts to slow, lingering shots of people in a Hiroshima hospital, as though encouraging us to view the same Hiroshima that the woman claims to have seen. There is pathos in the scene, because we quickly guess that the hospital patients are victims of the atom bomb that destroyed Hiroshima in 1945; but the patients do not seem to be unhappy, but rather seem calm and focused. This is just another day for them. They rest; some read books or look incuriously at the camera; they do not speak.

"The hospital, for instance, I saw it," the woman on the screen is saying. "I'm sure I did. There is a hospital in Hiroshima. How could I help seeing it?"

"You did not see the hospital in Hiroshima," the man replies firmly. "You saw nothing in Hiroshima."

Now the camera starts to move around the port city of Hiroshima, providing visual evidence for the things the woman says she saw. Although the flashbacks are often jarring, the overall pacing of the dialog—and indeed the film itself—is unhurried, uncanny and lyrical. Although everything in Hiroshima is modern, built-up after 1945, the slow exploration and skilled camera-work of cinematographer Sacha Vierny insinuates a certain haunted quality as it winds slowly through the streets of Hiroshima. The woman comments on what we are seeing of Hiroshima in a stream-of-consciousness voice-over, her jumbled words reflecting her jumbled thoughts.

She: "Four times at the museum in Hiroshima. I saw the people walking around. The people walk around, lost in thought, among the photographs, the reconstructions, for want of something else, among the photographs, the photographs, the reconstructions, for want of something else, the explanations, for want of something else. Four times at the museum in Hiroshima."

"I looked at the people. I myself looked thoughtfully at the iron. The burned iron. The broken iron, the iron made vulnerable as flesh. I saw the bouquet of bottle caps: who would have suspected that? Human skin floating, surviving, still in the bloom of its agony. Stones. Burned stones. Shattered stones. Anonymous heads of hair that the women of Hiroshima, when they awoke in the morning, discovered had fallen out."

He: "You saw nothing in Hiroshima. Nothing."

Behind their voices we now see archival footage of the dead, the dying and the mortally burned and wounded in Hiroshima after the blast on 6 August 1945, the day that America dropped the world's first atom bomb. At this point in the film there are several minutes—about twelve minutes, actually—of footage of Hiroshima after it had been flattened, instantly killing 70,000 to 80,000 people, most of them civilians. (A like number would die later of radiation poison.)

The footage shows not only crowds of traumatized and burned civilians streaming into the Ota River but also the interiors of hospitals and treatment centers where the injured and dying are being treated. Some of the footage appears to be well-done film reenactments rather than archival records of actual events. (This was done purposely by Resnais to suggest how easily the reality of Hiroshima can be obscured even while trying to convey it realistically.)

She: "The reconstructions have been made as authentically as possible. The films have been made as authentically as possible.

The illusion, it's quite simple, the illusion is so perfect that the tourists cry. One can always scoff, but what else can a tourist do, really, but cry? I've always wept over the fate of Hiroshima. Always."

He: "No. What would you have wept about?"

She: (As the footage of the dead and dying continue) "I saw the newsreels. On the second day, history tells, I'm not making it up, on the second day certain species of animals rose again from the depths of the earth and from the ashes. Dogs were photographed. For all eternity. I saw them. I *saw* the newsreels. I *saw* them. On the first day. On the second day. On the third day."

He: *(Interrupting her)*: "You saw nothing. Nothing."

We see footage of a dog with a leg missing. There are wounded and burned people, children screaming.

She: "...on the fifteenth day too. Hiroshima was blanketed with flowers. There were cornflowers and gladiolas everywhere, and morning glories and day lilies that rose again from the ashes with an extraordinary vigor, quite unheard of for flowers till then. I didn't make anything up."

He: "You made it *all* up."

"*Nothing,*" the woman says firmly. "Just as in love this illusion exists, this illusion of being able never to forget, so I was under the illusion that I would never forget Hiroshima."

A doctor, in one of the burn wards for victims of the blast, uses surgical forceps to gently open a woman's badly burnt eye, revealing that there is nothing left inside. She is blind, because there is no eye left. (This scene is clearly intended to momentarily overwhelm, or perhaps traumatize, the viewer.) But we, the omnipresent viewers of a film, continue to possess both sight and hearing. So we listen for clues, during the continued musings of our two beautiful, half-naked lovers in their hotel room—the voiceovers that clearly belong to them. As the woman speaks, we see survivors in the hospital: a blind girl; a girl looking in the mirror; a blind girl with deformed hands playing a musical instrument; a woman praying for her children.

She: "I also saw the survivors, and those who were in the wombs of the women of Hiroshima. I saw the patience, the innocence, the apparent meekness with which the temporary survivors of Hiroshima adapted themselves to a fate so unjust that the imagination, normally so fertile, cannot conceive it."

The camera cuts away from the sight of survivors, and back to the bodies of our lovers embracing. Both continue to speak in French. We now see that the woman is European, the man Asian; and his proprietary way of speaking about Hiroshima suggests he is Japanese, and probably from Hiroshima.

"Listen to me," the woman says softly. "Like you, I know what it is to forget."

"No, you don't know what it is to forget."

"Like you, I have a memory. I know what it is to forget."

"No," he says, "you are not endowed with memory."

"Like you," she continues with a kind of gentle insistence, "I too have tried with all my might not to forget. Like you, I forgot. Like you, I wanted to have an inconsolable memory, a memory of shadows and stone. For my part, I struggled with all my might, every day, against the horror of no longer understanding at all the reason for remembering. Like you, I forgot..."

We see a shot of the interior of a tour bus, in which a pretty young Japanese woman is addressing the passengers, educating the tourists—who paradoxically seem to be mostly Japanese—regarding the historical sites around Hiroshima. But the woman we hear next is the French-speaking European woman in a voice-over, to her lover. She speaks to him, but it seems that she is also speaking to Hiroshima.

She: "...Listen to me. I know something else. It will begin all over again. Two hundred thousand dead. Eighty thousand wounded. In nine seconds. These figures are official. It will begin all over again." As she speaks, the camera is once again moving slowly through Hiroshima, allowing us to see streets, bridges, covered lanes. Her thoughts become more confused, more irrational and increasingly sexualized: "I meet you. I remember you. Who are you? You destroy me. You're so good for me. How could I have known that this city was made to the size of love? How could I have known that you were made to the size of my body? You're great. How wonderful. You're great. How slow all of a sudden. And how sweet... more than you can know... you destroy me."

The voice-over comes not as dialog, but an unalloyed stream of consciousness, raw and unbidden and embarrassingly sexualized, because the words reflect not ideas but disorganized and highly conflicted emotions—which boldly suggest the traumatic memories that haunt the French-speaking woman, memories that contain a high degree of eroticism. But why does she address Hiroshima as though it were something in her past, something bad that she is remembering? She speaks in that way to Hiroshima because she finds it possible—convenient, one might say—to conflate horrifying memories in her past with the larger and more generalized suffering of Hiroshima. Many others have done this, and will continue to do it, because although Hiroshima is a tourist destination, it is also a destination for a certain kind of pilgrim.

The camera continues to move through the streets and byways of Hiroshima. There is something in Hiroshima that is connecting with a memory in the unnamed woman, a revenant of a dead love that she has both wrestled with and embraced for a long time. The next lines are a helpless litany:

"You destroy me. You're so good for me. You destroy me. You're so good for me." *(Pause)* "Plenty of time. Please. Take me. Deform me, make me ugly. Why not you? *Why not you in this city and in this night so like the others you can't tell the difference?*"

The witch's broom of the camera whisks us to the hotel room where our lovers have spent the night; we see the woman's face for the first time, turning with great tenderness toward the man in bed beside her. His skin is extraordinarily beautiful, she tells him (we now assume he is in fact Japanese, although he is speaking in French); we can see that the European woman is attractive, and that the man is likewise handsome. Both are probably in their early thirties. They are relaxed, two lovers enjoying a precious moments of post-coital pleasure in the night. A soft breeze pushes the curtains in the hotel room; and we hear a coughing sound from the night outside. The woman sleepily observes that it must be 4 AM—there's a man, she says, who walks by at 4 AM, who is always coughing.

"What are you doing in Hiroshima?" he asks her.

She is an actress in a film in production here, she tells him. She is appearing in a film about peace, since Hiroshima has become the capital of a new kind of peace tourism. People come here looking for some answer to the problem of war and human violence, as though the victims of war had the answers they seek.

The man shares the fact that his family perished when Hiroshima was destroyed. The viewer struggles for a moment to assimilate this fact.

"And before coming to Hiroshima, where were you?" he asks.

"In Paris."

"And before Paris?"

"Before Paris? ...I was at Nevers. *Ne-vers.*"

"Nevers?" he asks.

"It's in the providence of Nievre. You don't know it."

He senses that there is something about Nevers—and about her life—that she wants to conceal; and his intuition tells him that there may be a link between the thing she is hiding and her reason for being in Hiroshima.

"Why did you want to see Hiroshima?" he asks.

2.

She is played by the French actress Emmanuelle Riva; *He* is played by the late Japanese actor Eiji Okada. The viewer doesn't know the names of their characters, because they don't use names until the last scene, when they invent names for each other based on their traumatic memories. But there are many things we know about them already, simply by watching them and listening to what they say. They present in the opening scenes as upper middle-class, educated and cosmopolitan; they chat in a civilized and pleasant way; but from the beginning there is something about their interactions that is strange, problematical, and highly-charged emotionally.

They talk as though they already know each other, although it is clear from the dialog that they just met the day before. The film often switches from dialog to voice-over, usually of the woman's stream-of-conscious reveries. The woman tells the man that she *sees* Hiroshima, but the man repeatedly insists—not taunting her, but saying it quite firmly—that the woman does *not* see Hiroshima: that she is wrong, confused, mistaken or lying. That tells us immediately that something unusual is going on. But what exactly?

The extraordinary verbal sparring between the film's two principal characters probably reflects, among other things, the intense confusion of humanity still trying to come to terms emotionally, in the late 1950s, with the meaning of Hiroshima, Nagasaki and the atom bomb. Clearly humanity had a new weapon that could destroy entire cities in a single detonation—a full nuclear exchange could destroy entire countries; and in any nuclear war, enough radiation would be generated to kill most of the world's people. Russia and the US were already locked in a fierce arms race, and were rapidly stockpiling new nuclear weapons. All of this seemed at that time to have come upon humanity almost overnight, and people still didn't comprehend what this new thing meant.

Cognitively humankind had a general impression regarding the changes that the destruction of Hiroshima and Nagasaki had brought, but the nuclear arms race that emerged in the 1950s had a science-fiction quality that was counter-intuitive and alien-ating; the more you tried to get your head around it, the stranger and more frightening it became. Emotionally, people weren't even close to integrating it into their collective consciousness—in any case, the nuclear arms race was more like a bad dream or a bad movie than a political reality.

The verbal sparring of *She* and *He* is also reflective of a second and more personal dilemma. Millions of people had been psychologically traumatized by events associated with World War II, but on a personal level people still didn't quite under-stand what had happened to them, although many sensed changes in their own personalities. But for the Japanese man who lost his family in *Hiroshima, Mon Amour*, there was a special problem; he knew his family was gone, but to where? They had simply disappeared one day, and for him the wound was exacer-bated by the fact that there were no remains. The enormity of his psychic wound, shared with tens of millions of other survivors of World War II, is why he doggedly insists that the European woman cannot *see* Hiroshima.

But at times it seems as though he protests too much, so much so that we must ask if perhaps *he* is afraid to see Hiroshima— afraid, that is, to talk about what happened there on 6 August, 1945, or perhaps afraid to open up and talk about his military service in World War II. Does he fear that if they talk about Hiroshima it might cause them to destroy each other?

There's a moment when the verbal sparring stops, when the Japanese man begins to sense that the French woman has her own version of Hiroshima inside her mind and emotions, just as he does—a wound with different dimensions, but one equally pathogenic. That's when he starts trying to draw her out, to find out what ghosts are lacerating her. Historically, it seems that from time to time in the past she has engaged in brief love affairs where there's no commitment, not even a commitment to share one's first name. And there's something powerful and dangerous lurking behind the cosmopolitan, witty conversation that they're having, and he wants to find out what it is; and—because he may be able to help himself by so doing—he would like to help her if he can.

This could be his idea of redemption: losing one's family in Hiroshima would make one think about things like that, as would being in the Imperial Japanese Army. And we are never quite free of the feeling that in some absurd and unconscious way he is caught up in the role of being her 'host' in Hiroshima; that he has already guessed that she has come here to confront something terrible in her past. He may have encountered others—other women, one suspects—who have come to Hiroshima in the 1950s for similar reasons, to confront certain ghosts in their past, or simply to see—for reasons both personal and historical—what the aftermath of pure destruction looks like.

There's another powerful reason driving his desire to help her. Trauma can make people hypersexual; traumatized people have a way of spotting each other, like closeted homosexuals or religious minorities, and often experience an intense attraction to each other. The basis for this attraction is usually, in part, the unspoken hope that they can 'cure' each other, that one wounded person has the key to the other person's suffering, and can be a Messiah or a Christ-figure for the other. As the reader might have already guessed, it usually doesn't work. Hell hath no fury like the trauma-ridden individual who discovers that his or her charming lover, far from being the key to mental health and happiness, is a sociopath, an addict, a sexual cheat or a violent abuser. In other words, traumatized people who fall in love with each other frequently end up with the most frustrating and explosive kind of disappointment, because although the sex may be delicious in the short term, it can't exorcise traumatic memory—which is by definition a wound that doesn't heal, but can only be managed.

Traumatized people *do* sometimes enjoy sex of an almost

insupportable intensity with others who are similarly afflicted. But the relief is only in the sex itself—there is usually very little sustained relief before and after the sexual release. In *Hiroshima, Mon Amour*, the case is a little different. Both are very good talkers; the man welcomes the chance to exercise his command of the French language; and he clearly wants to hear the woman's back story, the simmering traumatic memory that brought her to Hiroshima and has now become too much to carry alone. Maybe the charming Japanese man is simply very curious; but most likely he sees a chance to experience some catharsis of his own by proximity to the woman as she struggles with her own traumatic memory. Do not men often do this, by experiencing their own emotional release through a woman's more deeply-felt emotions?

And *He* is sufficiently helpful—even if it is to a great extent for the passionate sex—and *She* so courageous in the way she opens herself up, that their collaboration begins at some point to make emotional sense. They look very good together on the screen, so much so that one might legitimately criticize the movie at this point for being an improbable fantasy. But in a sense all works of narrative art are fantasies; so the question becomes, is it a good fantasy? (That is, is it a compelling lie that also imparts an emotional truth?) Their romance is within the realm of the possible; such a brief affair *could* happen; and the intense inter-connectedness of *She* and *He* suggests an emotional logic so strong that—even when viewed in hindsight—there is a sense of inevitability, or fate, about everything that happens to them during their thirty-six or so hours of intense conversations and love-making.

3.

He is still sleeping in the morning, after their night together; *She* gets up and gets a cup of coffee, and stands looking at him. His hand trembles briefly. Suddenly, he is replaced for an instant by the image of another man in his death throes—his hand, too, is trembling. This is a flashback to something the French woman remembers, the violent death of her lover at the end of World War II. The flashback appears suddenly and is over quickly.

He gets up, they shower together, laughing. Afterwards they chat pleasantly together.

"What did Hiroshima mean for you, in France?" he asks.

"The end of the war," she says. "I mean, *really* the end. Amazement... at the idea that they had dared... amazement at the idea that they had succeeded. And then too, for us, the beginning of an unknown fear. And then, indifference. And also the fear of indifference..."

"Where were you?"

"I had just left Nevers. I was in Paris. In the street."

Watching her, he says: "That's a pretty French word, Nevers."

She: (abruptly, after a pause) "It's a word like any other. Like the city."

She turns suddenly away, with a brief tremor of agitation. Now the man knows for sure there is something important in her past, her youth in Nevers, before she came to Paris. They continue to chat, as he lights a cigarette. We imagine that he is perhaps making a mental note not to push her too much in the short term; but clearly he intends to find out what she is hiding.

She is now completely dressed, wearing a nurses uniform for the movie in which she is acting. "What do you do in life?" she wants to know.

"Architecture. And I'm involved in politics."

"Oh, so that's why you speak such good French."

"That's why. To read about the French revolution."

The film would never be so clumsy as to tell us precisely what kind of politics the man is involved in, but anybody who wished to read about the French Revolution would probably be a political and cultural progressive.

He: "What's the film you're appearing in?"

She: "A film about Peace. What else do you expect them to make in Hiroshima except a picture about Peace?"

A group of noisy cyclists go by outside.

"I'd like to see you again," he says.

"This time tomorrow I'll be on my way back to France."

"Is that true? You didn't tell me."

"It's true. There was no point in telling you."

There's one point he is curious about, and he wants to ask her before he forgets about it. "Tell me," he says, "do things like this… happen to you often?"

"Not very often. But it happens. I have a weakness for men." She pauses. "I have doubtful morals, you know." She laughs.

"What do you call having doubtful morals?"

"Being doubtful about the morals of others."

He laughs with great gusto. Afterwards he asks her again if she would consider staying in Hiroshima. But she dismisses the question, with another slight gesture of irritation.

They go out into the hotel corridor. The light in this hotel—in the hallways especially—seems to radiate a kind of soft languor, as though time has stopped. There is no staff visible, nor do we ever see any other guests. We notice again that the Emmanuelle Riva character is European, and the man played by the late Eiji Okada is Japanese, but speaks excellent French. The viewer sees that they are probably in their early thirties; they are supremely confident—or at least seem to be—and speak knowingly about the world and about their thoughts and feelings.

In what is perhaps a certain timeless tradition of certain married lovers, they seem to have arrived—without actually discussing their preferences in the matter—at an unspoken agreement not to share their names with each other. As we have already mentioned, Marguerite Duras's screenplay refers only to the woman as *She* and the man as *He*, this anonymity continuing until the last scene of the movie.

"Where are you going in France? To Nevers?"

That gets a slight reaction. "I don't ever go to Nevers any more."

"Not ever?"

This time she grimaces. "Not ever. (She senses that she is giving something away, but can't stop herself) In Nevers I was younger than I've ever been..."

"Young-in-Nevers."

"Yes. Young in Nevers. And then too, once, mad in Nevers."

They leave the corridor of the hotel, and are now standing outside in the sunlight, waiting for the woman's ride to the film location. She plunges on, throwing caution to the wind.

"You see," she says, "Nevers is the city in the world, and even the thing in the world, I dream about most often at night. And at the same time it's the thing I think about the least."

"What was your madness like at Nevers?"

"Madness is like intelligence, you know. You can't explain it. Just like intelligence. It comes on you, it fills you, and then you understand it. But when it goes away you can't understand it at all any longer."

"Were you full of hate?" he asks.

"That was what my madness was. I was mad with hate. I had the impression it would be possible to make a real career of hate. All I cared about was hate. Do you understand?"

"Yes."

"It's true. I suppose you must understand that too."

"Did it ever happen to you again?"

"No." (She almost whispers) "It's all over."

"During the war?"

"Right after it."

"Was that part of the difficulties of life in France after the war?"

"Yes, that's one way of putting it."

"When did you get over your madness?"

"It went away little by little," the woman says. "And then of course when I had children..."

He remarks again that he wishes he could spend a few days with her. She appears ready to accept, but remembers that she must leave Hiroshima the next morning. They continue their conversation; her taxi arrives; she leaves.

4.

Later that day, around 4 PM, we see the French woman resting, after shooting her scene in the antiwar film she's acting in. In fact, she's sleeping, lying on her side on the ground, resting her head on a crude pillow made of personal effects. The film crew has been shooting at Peace Square, or Hiroshima Peace Memorial Park, which is dedicated to the memory of those who died on 6 August, 1945. There is a crowd where they have been shooting, but the people in it are fundamentally indifferent—they are used to seeing films being shot in Hiroshima, especially peace films. *He*, the Japanese man that we recognize from the love-making hotel scenes, approaches the sleeping woman and intently watches her. She awakens, sees him, and is instantly alert.

"It was easy to find you in Hiroshima," he says.

She gets up, laughing; she is quite happy to see him. Two film technicians pass, carrying an enlarged photo from *The Children of Hiroshima* showing a mother and child in the ruins after the nuclear blast. Technicians also carry an enlarged photo of Albert Einstein, reminding us that Einstein's scientific theories made the atomic bomb possible.

The man touches the woman's face, in a gesture of extreme tenderness made erotic by our knowledge of their previous love-making.

"You give me a great desire to love," he says.

She is silent for a moment, looking at the ground. His words both disturb and challenge her.

She: "Always... chance love affairs... Me too."

He murmurs that it's different for him this time, in so doing acknowledging that he, too, engages in the occasional romantic adventure. He senses that she is concerned about the anonymous—and perhaps compulsive—nature of her chance love affairs, and wants very much to find out what drives her. Maybe, here in Hiroshima, she will be able to tell him.

Suddenly a parade of people carrying signs is marching toward them, a crowd scene in the movie that is being filmed. We can see that both of our principal characters want to get away from the crowd, away from the movie about Hiroshima being filmed in Hiroshima. The man begins to gently guide her out of the crowd. For a moment they get lost in the crowd, but quickly find each other.

He murmurs that he wants her to come with him.

"Are you afraid?" he asks.

"No," she says, smiling and shaking her head for emphasis.

When we see them next, they are entering the man's house. It is an unexceptional Japanese home, cramped by Western standards, but with many books. The light is soft, as it was in the hotel. The French woman stands a bit awkwardly in the front room, like a guest waiting to be told to sit down.

"Sit down," he suggests rather tentatively.

But she doesn't. Both remain standing. In her script Duras writes, *"We feel that eroticism is held in check by love, at least for the moment."* More likely eroticism is held in check by a certain reticence, since this is the house that the Japanese man shares with his wife; at the same time, there is a growing feeling that the French woman wants to reveal something important about the past, but is finding it difficult to do so.

The French woman asks about his wife.

"She's at Unzen, in the mountains," he says. "I'm alone."

"When is she coming back?"

"In a few days."

She: "What is your wife like?"

He: "Beautiful. I'm a man who is happy with his wife."

616

"So am I." she says. "I'm a woman who's happy with her husband." (They seem to have removed an invisible barrier—at the very least, neither of them is engaging in a retaliatory affair because of anger or dissatisfaction.) "Don't you work in the afternoon?"

"Yes. A lot. Mainly in the afternoon."

"The whole thing is stupid…"

The telephone rings, but he does not answer it.

"Is it because of me you're wasting your afternoon?" Since the previous line ("The whole thing is stupid") she has been unbuttoning her blouse.

It is not seductive, almost the act of a friend rather than a lover. The telephone continues to ring; the man makes no move to answer it. The couple make love, although—as in a Victorian novel—we are not exposed to even the first kisses, any of the following love-making, or even anything that suggests sexual intimacy. Instead there is a sense that this is simply a prelude to what is coming afterwards: a physical intimacy that facilitates, but does not define, the approaching emotional intimacy.

We see them after the love-making, lying on a mat. We notice the light is different, darker, closer to night. Their voices are low and soft, as though enjoying what Americans might call 'pillow-talk.' But these are not exactly endearments.

He: "Was he French, the man you loved during the war?"

She: "No… he wasn't French."

(There is a superimposed image of a German soldier crossing a square at Nevers. The room becomes darker.)

She: (Anticipating his question) "Yes. It was at Nevers. (Footage of her and the German soldier meeting secretly.) At first we met in barns. Then among the ruins. And then in rooms. Like anywhere else. (The light in the room grows even darker) And then he was dead."

(Footage of Nevers—Rivers, quays, poplar trees in the wind— but now they are blending into footage of Hiroshima.)

"I was eighteen and he was twenty-three," she says. More footage of Nevers, and of her at the age of 18, running to be with her lover. And then a shot of them entering an abandoned hut together. "Why talk of him rather than the others?"

"Why not?"

"No. Why?"

"Because of Nevers. I can only begin to know you, and among the many thousands of things in your life, I'm choosing Nevers."

She: (Insistently) "You have to tell me why."

(He stumbles, answering in a way that evades the intent of her question, but she doesn't believe him. So he tells the truth.)

He: "It was there, I seem to have understood, that you must have begun to be what you are today."

And it has everything to do with her love affair with a German soldier. How does the man guess how deeply these events affected her? Part of the reason must be because something terrible happened to him, too, with the loss of his family, a loss that he did not witness but which was all the more traumatizing for just that reason. He had no direct knowledge of what happened to his family on 6 August, 1945, but he filled and embroidered with his imagination the lacuna of ignorance regarding the likely details of his family's death.

The French woman's traumatic memory is more concrete, and at least is a story that she can tell, if she can only muster up the emotional strength to do so. His trauma, on the other hand, is the multiple unknowns of a family vaporized by a man-made instrument of war—one moment they are there, the next moment gone. Since he was deprived of concrete details, in an odd way it seems that the woman must tell her story for both of them.

She: (Shouting) "I want to leave here!"

But she clings to him, as though she wants him to help her, and he responds by embracing her. She still wants to tell the story of Nevers, but not here, not in his home. After a moment's pause we see them dressed and in the living room, where they again stand rather awkwardly. The lights are on: it is now night.

"All we can do now," he says, "is to kill the time left before you leave. Still sixteen hours before your plane leaves."

"That's a terribly long time…"

"No. You mustn't be afraid."

5.

It is now late evening in Hiroshima, but with some light still in the sky. They are in a café, a modern and "Americanized" café, but with a long bay window. The café is by one of the many rivers—or tributaries of the Ota River—that run through Hiroshima into the sea; and between the café and the river is a wide footpath in which pedestrians walk slowly, many of them seemingly already half-asleep. There are not many people out at night in Hiroshima. Our couple is toward the back of the café, talking softly but with great intensity. The woman is telling the story of what happened to her in Nevers in 1945; and as she does so, visual memories appear as flashbacks on the screen, in the same way that intrusive memories of the past will appear spontaneously in a person's mind. In Duras's script these flashbacks are not entirely sequential, and in Resnais's completed film only partially so; both script and film assume some knowledge of post-Second World War France. But the story itself is easy enough to understand, for it is a very old story.

France is occupied by the German armed forces during the Second World War. The woman is very young, and the politics of the war mean nothing to her. Instead she is focused entirely on her feelings for a young German soldier, with whom she is having a secret love affair—he's her first love, and they meet secretly in various hiding places around Nevers. They have a crazy plan to go together to Bavaria, in Germany, where they will marry and make a life together. She is to meet the German soldier at a quay on the Loire River (on the right bank of which Nevers is located) but as she runs excitedly to their rendezvous, someone takes a shot from the cover of a garden, mortally wounding the German soldier. *She*, the woman who is telling the story, stays with him as he dies, and stays with his dead body all night.

After the Liberation, the people of Never publicly take revenge on the woman by publicly shaving off her hair, a punishment often meted out to French women who were romantically involved with German soldiers during the Occupation. (In a voice-over she compares the shaving of hair to the hair "that the women of Hiroshima would find has fallen out in the morning.") Such punishment of women was frequent in post-war France, with women made scapegoats because of generalized guilt regarding widespread collaboration in all sectors of French society. Her father is compelled to close his pharmacy because of shame associated with his daughter's love affair with the German soldier; the woman's family hides her in their basement for the same reason. The disgraced twenty-year-old is in an emotionally traumatized state, grieving for her German lover and the loss of the life they planned together—she cannot get her desire for him out of her thoughts and feelings. Gradually she comes back to some kind of sanity, and her mother sends her away to Paris.

Two days after arriving in Paris, the woman hears about the atomic bomb being dropped on Hiroshima, Japan.

He: "When you are in the cellar, am I dead?

She: "You are dead... and..."

We see a flashback of her German lover dying on the quay. The woman explains that there was nothing to do with one's hands in the basement...

"Hands become useless in cellars," she says. "They scrape. They rub skin off... against the walls..." We see her bleeding hands in a flashback to the basement at Nevers; the same hands, at the café in Hiroshima, intact and beautiful. A flashback to Nevers: we see her lick blood off her hands. "That's all you can find to do, to make you feel better... and also to remember... I loved blood since I had tasted yours."

The woman addresses her Japanese lover sitting across from her in a café in Hiroshima as though he were her German lover who died in Nevers, banishing the passage of time by conflating the two men. The Japanese man not only accepts this but encourages it, because he understands the emotional logic of the role-playing. It allows her to confront the past through the present: she boldly addresses her Japanese lover in Hiroshima as though he were her German lover in France. She goes back repeatedly to the trauma of being locked in the basement of her parents' house—it is there that she realized how devastating the killing of her lover was, and how insanely and totally she misses him. Although he is dead—or perhaps *because* he is dead—she is flooded with desire for him, as though the intensity of her desire will keep him alive. And in a sense, it has—it has kept the memory of him alive all these years.

"Do you scream?" he asks her.

(A flashback to the room in Nevers.)

"Not in the beginning; no, I don't scream: I call you softly."

"But I'm dead."

"Nevertheless I call you. Even though you're dead. Then one day, I scream, I scream as loud as I can, like a deaf person would. That's when they put me in the cellar. To punish me."

"What do you scream?"

"Your German name. Only your name. I only have one memory left, your name."

(Flashback to Nevers.)

"I want you so badly I can't bear it anymore," she says. We understand that although she appears to be speaking to the Eiji Okada character, she is really speaking to her dead German lover.

"Are you afraid?" he asks

"I'm afraid. Everywhere. In the cellar. In my room."

"Of what?"

"Of not ever seeing you again. Ever, ever."

The man gives the woman more to drink. He senses that she is close to remembering all of it, and perhaps then being able to put it into some perspective, in a way that will make the memory less powerful, and as a consequence less harmful.

She: (suddenly) "Afterward, I don't remember any more. I don't remember any more…"

He: (helping her remember) These cellars are very old, and very damp, these Nevers cellars… you were saying…

"Yes. Full of saltpeter." There is a flashback to Nevers: she is biting the side of the wall, tasting the saltpeter.

"Sometimes a cat comes in and looks. It's not a mean cat. I don't remember any more."

(Flashback to Nevers: a cat comes into her cellar. They look at each other.)

"Afterwards, I don't remember any more," she says.

"How long?"

"Eternity."

There are increasing numbers of flashbacks that take us irresistibly back to Nevers, so that for a certain time we spend more time in Nevers than in the café in Hiroshima. There is an entire gamut of memories playing in the mind's eye of the woman, as she systematically identifies the memories in her voice-over.

"At night… my mother takes me down into the garden. She looks at my head. Every night she looks carefully at my head. She still doesn't dare come near me… It's at night that I can look at the square, so I look at it. It's enormous. (Gesturing) It curves in the middle."

(We see people's feet walking on the sidewalk outside the street-level window where she is confined in her cellar.)

"I think of you, but I don't talk about it anymore."

"Mad," he suggests.

"Madly in love with you. *(Pause.)* My hair is growing back. I can feel it every day, with my hand. I don't care. But nevertheless my hair is growing back..."

"Do you scream, before the cellar?"

"No. I'm numb."

(They sit cheek to cheek, until suddenly we see the flashback of the hair-cutting in Nevers. A group of men, with some women, gloatingly cut off her hair in the town square, punishing her for falling in love with a German soldier. It is noticeable that all of the hair-cutters, all of them, are smiling with unalloyed pleasure.)

"They shave my head carefully till they're finished. They think it's their duty to do a good job shaving the women's heads."

"Are you ashamed for them, my love?"

"No," she says. "You're dead—I'm much too busy suffering. All I hear is the sound of the scissors on my head. It makes me feel a little bit better about... your death... like... like, oh! I can't give you a better example, like my nails, the walls... for my anger."

(She clings to her lover in Hiroshima, interspersed with the flashbacks to Nevers. She is at that point where she can't quite control or stop the flashbacks from appearing in her mind when she talks about the past.)

She: "Oh! What pain. What pain in my heart! It's unbelievable. Everywhere in the city they're singing the *Marseillaise*. Night falls. My dead love is an enemy of France. Someone says she should be made to walk through the city. My father's drug store is closed because of the disgrace. I'm alone. Some of them laugh. At night I return home."

(We see a brief flashback of her mother embracing her, followed by a scene of her Japanese lover embracing her in Hiroshima.)

"And then," he says, "one day, my love, you come out of eternity."

(There is a flashback of her pacing the floor in her bedroom in Nevers.)

"Yes, it takes a long time. They told me it had taken a very long time. At six in the evening, the bells of the St. Etienne Cathedral ring, winter and summer. One day, it is true, I hear them. I remember having heard them before—before—when we were in love, when we were happy. I'm beginning to see. I remember having already seen before—before—when we were in love, when we were happy. I remember. I see the ink. I see the daylight. I see my life. Your death. My life that goes on. Your death that goes on."

Continuing to remember it: "And that it took the shadows longer now to reach the corners of the room. And that it took the shadows longer now to reach the corners of the cellar walls. About half past six. Winter is over."

(There's a flashback of her room—and the cellar—at Nevers, then back to Hiroshima.)

"Oh! It's horrible—I'm beginning to remember you less clearly. (He holds her glass up and makes her drink from it.) ...I'm beginning to forget you. I tremble at the thought of having forgotten so much love." (Again he bids her to drink.) We were supposed to meet at noon on the quays of the Loire. I was going to leave with him. When I arrived at noon on the quay of the Loire, he wasn't quite dead yet. Someone had fired on him from a garden. (We see a flashback of an enclosed garden about the quay where they were supposed to meet.) I stayed near his body all that day and then all the next night."

"The next morning they came to pick him up and they put him in a truck. It was that night Nevers was liberated. The bells of St. Etienne were ringing, ringing... Little by little he grew cold beneath me. Oh! How long it took him to die! When? I'm not quite sure. I was lying on top of him... yes... the moment of his death actually escaped me, because... because even at that very moment, and even afterward, yes, even afterward, I can say that

I couldn't feel the slightest difference between this dead body and mine. All I could find between this body and mine were obvious similarities, do you understand? (Shouting.) He was my first love!..."

The Japanese man slaps her. She seems to understand, and that tells us that she was becoming hysterical, and that she understands his action. She is still in her memories, except that now they come to her as flashbacks of concrete events rather than runaway emotions.

She: "And then one day... I had screamed again. So they put me back in the cellar. *(Pause.)* I think then is when I got over my hate. I don't scream any more. I'm becoming reasonable. They say, 'She's becoming reasonable.' *(Pause.)* One night, a holiday, they let me go out." (A flashback of the town square at night in Nevers.) "Not long after that my mother tells me I have to leave for Paris, by night. She gives me some money. I leave for Paris, on a bicycle, at night. It's summer. The nights are warm. When I reach Paris two days later the name of Hiroshima is in all the newspapers. My hair is now a decent length. I'm in the street with the people."

In the Hiroshima café, someone plays a record on the juke box, a record of music of the French bal-musette style. Popular in post-war France, bal-musette was an intense kind of dance expressed in small or constricted spaces. It suggests the problem faced by the trauma-bonded lovers: how do they engage in their unruly dance without detonating the explosive *denouement* threatened by the uncontrollable nature of their memories... how do they remove the overhanging threat of past violence repeatedly intruding into and finally blowing up in the present moment?

She: (as if waking up) "Fourteen years have passed!"

(He gives her another drink.)

"I don't even remember his hands very well," she says. "The pain, I still remember the pain a little."

"Tonight?"

"Yes, tonight, I remember. But one day I won't remember it any more. Not at all. Nothing."

The café is closing. *He* and *she* get up and prepare to walk out into the night; a gentle breeze is blowing off the sea. The French woman is now quite calm, seemingly resigned. We notice that already she has referred once to her German lover in the third person, rather than confronting him in the person of her Japanese lover. She is back in the present moment. (In the script Duras writes: *They are emerging from their Nevers tunnel.*) She is detaching from her memories, and they're beginning the process of trying to detach from each other.

"Does your husband know of this?"

"No."

"Then I'm the only one who does?"

"Yes."

He takes her in his arms in a fierce hug. "I'm the only one who knows. No one else?"

She: *(closing her eyes)* "Don't say any more." Desire overtakes her. She caresses his lips gently with her fingers. "How good it is to be with someone, sometimes."

"Yes."

"I'd like to live through that moment again," she says. "That incomparable moment."

He is waxing philosophical now, thinking about his own struggles with memory. "In a few years, when I'll have forgotten you, and when other such adventures, from sheer habit, will happen to me, I'll remember you as the symbol of love's forget-fulness. I'll think of this adventure as of the horror of oblivion. I already know it."

People enter the café. She glances at them, away from her lover. "Doesn't anything ever stop at night, in Hiroshima?"

"No, it never stops in Hiroshima."

She: "I love that... cities where there are always people awake, day or night..."

Duras writes in the script: *The late but ineluctable hour when the cafés close is fast approaching. They both close their eyes, as if seized by a feeling of modesty. The well-ordered world has thrown them out, for their adventure has no place in it. No use fighting. She suddenly understands this.*

They leave the café together, and are now standing outside.

"It's sometimes necessary to keep from thinking about these difficulties the world makes," she says. "If we didn't we'd suffocate." A last light goes out in the café. "Go away, leave me," she says unexpectedly.

(He starts to leave, but then looks up at the black sky.)

"It isn't daylight yet..." he says.

"No," she says." There's a long pause. "Probably... we'll die without ever seeing each other again."

"Yes, probably." Another long pause. "Unless, perhaps, someday, a war..."

She: *(softly)* "Yes, a war..."

6.

Watching this film in a theater in the early 1960s, this last line, so filled with longing and yet so terrifying, would typically elicit a sharp intake of breath from viewers, followed by rueful laughter. It was a great line, and a great insight by Marguerite Duras: that her two characters openly wonder if only war could rescue them, wonder if only war can give them back the context in which their rampant emotions belong, and bring them back together again. *Does not the victim of traumatic memory seek to go back to the time and place of the original trauma?* Did not war bring *He* and *She* together in Hiroshima, and was not war interwoven into every thought and feeling throughout their amatory adventure? In fact the Second World War—and the traumatic memory left in its wake—is the film's true subject, and in many ways its main character: and that, finally, is the reason why it makes such emotional sense that the two principle characters remain unnamed. The war is still so big, even after it is over, that people traumatized by its brutality haven't been able to completely reclaim their identifies as existing independently of the recent carnage.

The sense of wounded people haunted by past violence is well served by the film's use of Hiroshima at night; the city itself again becomes a character during the last thirty minutes of the film. After parting from her Japanese lover, our French protagonist— at this point in the film, after seeing so many of her memories in the form of flashbacks, it is accurate to think of her as a protagonist—walks slowly back to her hotel room along the river, perhaps one of the same tributaries of the Ota River into whose water burning men, women and children flung themselves on that terrible day of 6 August, 1945. In *Hiroshima, Mon Amour* we see people sitting quietly by the river in the evening, and well into the night; they do not talk, and rarely move. When they *do* move, it is with the great lassitude of people already half asleep, as though the scenes of the river are themselves part of their dreaming.

After midnight in Hiroshima, the few pedestrians likewise walk slowly in the gray neon-lit light. It seems a kind of indirect comment on what has happened to Japan generally, and Hiroshima specifically: these ghost figures in the night resemble neither conspirators nor heroes, and certainly not assassins or victims; instead they remind us of sleepwalkers. Hiroshima had, by the late 1950s, rather desperately cast itself as a capital of peace tourism, a destination especially tailored for tourists seeking to contemplate or celebrate antiwar sentiment. The city boasted a Hiroshima Peace Memorial Museum (alluded to in the opening scenes), the Peace Memorial Park, the Children's Peace Monument and the Hiroshima National Peace Memorial Hall for the Atomic Bomb Victims. One senses, considering the efforts of the locals to encourage peace tourism, that it would not have seemed particularly unusual in Hiroshima at that time if European visitors were seen wandering about late at night absorbed in intense private conversations or struggling with private thoughts.

And Hiroshima apparently *did* stay open all night then, with commercial neon signs providing the main light. It is well after midnight now, and the walkway by the river on which our lovers had formerly tarried is now nearly deserted; and when lit by the omnipresent neon the walkway, the river, and the cafés could be a small town anywhere at night, the streets deserted, the neon light pulsing softly, the heat of the summer night fading into coolness. On this particular street by this particular river in Hiroshima a slight breeze blows, touching the hair and faces of the few night people abroad. The atmosphere is one of magic, of a great and almost insupportable tenderness, and of a place that is irrevocably haunted.

One wonders, were there twentieth-century seers who could discern the message in the neon-light at night, in the same manner that certain poets discerned nineteenth-century secrets in the Celtic Twilight? In *Hiroshima, Mon Amor* the neon lights *are* the twilight, and the dead of night is precisely the right time and place for the desperate convolutions of our two main characters, who—having conjured up enough remembrances of times past to keep them occupied for decades—must now wrestle into some semblance of order the tumultuous ghosts they have summoned forth.

By this time it should be clear to even the most phlegmatic viewer that the film, if for no other reason than its subject matter, is a work of uncanny power. That doesn't mean that there aren't big aesthetic mistakes and occasional narrative lapses: at times the film's makers get lost in the predictable French pursuit of personal conceits, as when our Japanese architect tells his lover that he will someday consider their adventure as "the horror of oblivion." It would have been much better, and more to the point, if he'd simply acknowledged that he was afraid of forgetting her, perhaps in the same way that she was afraid of forgetting her dead German lover. And certain things in the back story of the characters are not made explicit in the film.

For example, the filmmakers are on record as publicly insisting that some filmed footage of Hiroshima in the early part of the film, footage that appears to be archival but it actually re-enacted documentary footage—not of dying people but of actors *playing* dying people—should be thought of as footage from the Hiroshima peace film in which the character of the French woman appears as an actress. But that connection is never made clear, although it could have been done quite simply. Despite the film's awesome power, there are times when the filmmakers care more about their own sensibilities than about the film they are creating.

But there are many seemingly insignificant details that do have great power. For example, in the beginning of *Hiroshima, Mon Amour* the two principals laugh in an overdone and exaggerated way at each others' small jokes, as a way of signaling that sexual escapades are a familiar game to them, that in such amorous adventures they operate out of a script already committed to memory; it is not often that one sees the visual grammar of film art used so economically and so well. Another important detail comes in the very early part of the film, as the French actress is looking at her sleeping Japanese lover, and for a brief moment sees her dying German lover. This prefigures the later use of flashbacks as the Emmanuelle Riva character begins to unpack her traumatic memories from Nevers, France. Flashbacks, we know, are an established film technique to reveal the back story of a character, often to explain motivation. But flashbacks are also a psychological phenomenon in which intrusive thoughts, images and feelings from the past invade the present moment in unbidden and unexpected ways.

In *Hiroshima, Mon Amour* flashbacks occur according to both definitions of the word. The French woman—the character on whom the film focuses—experiences intrusive memories that cause her to behave in a certain way (that is, she has brief love affairs, the excitement and danger of which helps her to keep memories of her first love alive); but the filmmakers also consciously use flashbacks as a film technique. This has caused some film critics to write that the film is 'non-linear.' That isn't quite the case, however—the story that is occurring in post-war Hiroshima in the late 1950s is quite linear, with a definite beginning, middle and end; it is the story of Nevers in 1945 told by the flashbacks that is non-linear, because memory itself is often chaotic and is typically aroused by specific but unrelated stimuli. (See Proust's *Recherche du Temps Perdu*, the preferred translation of which is now *In Search of Lost Time*.)

The flashbacks in this film are instructive: it is my contention that this is exactly the way traumatic memory operates, at the point when it becomes problematical in an individual's life and behavior. Often it isn't so much a matter of experiencing flash-backs, a reliving of actual events, as a reliving of crippling *emotions* associated with those past events, the exact cause of which may not always be obvious. Complicating this process, emotional orientations rooted in past events *change* to accom-modate emotional preoccupations of the present. Even though the story told by the flashbacks on *Hiroshima, Mon Amour* is not linear, the viewer has no problem using the visual and emotional evidence these flashbacks provide to arrive at a narrative of the events that occurred in Nevers, France, in 1945. From that, we may conclude that humans are not only story-telling creatures, but also that their stories are linear even when memory isn't. That is seemingly one role of narrative art—transforming the chaotic memories of the past into coherent stories that make sense in the present.

Alain Resnais made *Hiroshima, Mon Amour* after he made *Night and Fog*, which is a documentary about the Nazi Holocaust.

I'm not a great fan of the latter film, because I think the reality of the Holocaust can be best understood through the thoughts, emotions and behavior of Germans and Jews who have been compelled by history to live out its traumatic after-effects. Evil is not outside people, it is inside us before we act on it. Hell, as Sartre put it, is other people—but other people are also the closest we get to heaven. Sorting out the exact relativity between the two can come only from detailed interrogations of human behavior, including the relativity between our memories, our goals and our behavior. *Hiroshima, Mon Amour* does that in an unprecedented way. It also lets us examine the relationship between aggression and traumatic memory in a way that is rare in film art.

7.

She now walks quickly toward her hotel room, our French actress, in the dead of night. For the moment she is alone. Something stops her from entering her room; so instead she paces in the hallway and walks on the stairs, then returns to her room and opens the door. (Again, as before, we see nobody in the hotel, neither staff nor other guests. It appears to be empty, abandoned.) Once inside her hotel room, she goes to the basin in the room's small bathroom, and looks at her own image in the mirror. She splashes water on her face.

Looking at herself in the mirror, she talks to her German lover:

"You were not yet quite dead. I told our story. I was unfaithful to you tonight with this stranger. I told our story. It was, you see, a story that could be told. For fourteen years I hadn't found… the taste of an impossible love again. Since Nevers. Look how I'm forgetting you… Look how I've forgotten you. *Look at me.*"

Through the window we see Hiroshima at night. She looks sharply at herself in the mirror, her face still wet; then she closes her eyes. Having confessed her "betrayal" to her German lover, she quickly exits the hotel room.

8.

Apocalyptic historical events that cause psychological damage to millions of people—war, genocide and brutal dictatorships—are different from other experiences, as are the traumatic memories arising from them. Most experiences stay in the past; but traumatic memory often defies time and space to influence how we act in the present. And when trauma occurs because of human aggression, we are forced to identify with the world of the aggressor, and then to internalize his aggression—these are the things we do to survive.

All too often we then act out the internalized aggression against others, or against ourselves. Trauma is the medium by which aggression becomes a part of our personalities, frozen in our memories, demanding to be acted out in ever-changing new ways against others, and against ourselves. We all sense that this happens sometimes, yet this bonding to aggression is a terrifying overthrowing of our human ability to think clearly, to engage in rational risk assessment, and to make rational decisions. We *think* we make decisions rationally; but the problem with internalized aggression, acquired from the aggression we ourselves have endured, is that it so often bypasses our conscious decision-making, and ends up driving destructive behavior that is fundamentally irrational and dangerous.

The Japanese man in *Hiroshima, Mon Amour* has his aggression—and his feelings arising from the destruction of Hiroshima—well under control, a fact that is never explained in the film, but which may be because he is burnt out emotionally; or because he—like many other men—has simply put his dangerous emotions on lock-down. But regardless of how he manages his emotions, his awareness of Hiroshima is clearly always with him. Although he was not in Hiroshima on 6 August, 1945, he lost his family there on that day: and it is therefore, despite his seeming stability, a wound that will not heal. We know this because of the manner in which he identifies with the traumatic memory of his French lover. They have a division of labor in which she will deal directly with the demons from her past, and he will deal with his demons through the catharsis that she provides for both of them. This is not unusual when traumatized people fall in love, although there is always a great danger involved in that situation, because people struggling with traumatic memory tend to want the impossible from each other.

The enormity of the Japanese man's psychic wound, which he shares with millions of other men around the world, is the reason why he doggedly insists that the European woman cannot *see* Hiroshima; but when she insists that she does, he begins to realize that she has a wound similar to his. Why are traumatized people so often drawn to others who are likewise traumatized? Because they are citizens of the same emotional country; they are aware of extremes in the human mind and emotions that other people do not suspect. And it is when the woman challenges him—tells him that she, too, struggles with memories of the terrible things that people do—that he realizes how deeply connected they really are.

The film is about two people with wounds that will not heal, and the way they seek to use each other to comprehend the nature and extent of their separate traumatic afflictions. But the woman is much more capable of talking about her emotions than he is; she can be an excellent resource for him in the present moment, monitoring certain emotional realities in their love relationship. He, on the other hand, can be a referee helping her avoid emotional extremes, and likewise helping her cope with her memories when the past threatens to overrun the present. In this way they use each other to understand themselves.

But they are also trying to relate their personal wounds to the momentous historical events that have so consummately smashed and rearranged their lives, along with millions of others hurt by the Second World War. When the aggression is too big, when it involves a cast of millions, it becomes overwhelming, and we are just as likely to feel despair—or nothing at all—as sorrow or pain. When aggression is too big, it can bond people to nihilism, and to death. This can happen because such large, impersonal tragedies of war, genocide and nuclear weapons rob the individual of all power—the suffering of the individual is subsumed too quickly into the larger tragedy, almost making a person feel that his or her own personhood no longer exists.

We can use words to describe our personal pain, and accurately determine how it influences us as individual people; but there are no words that can describe the mass suffering of Hiroshima, no words that can really describe the suffering caused by the Holocaust, and no words for the Second World War. Our two lovers seek to reduce these huge, impersonal engines of suffering to the tangible experiences of two individuals making love in the night, the better to understand how and why and to what extent they were wounded. And like most of us, they begin with their own emotions and predicaments. They try to respond to an overwhelming *impersonal* tragedy with *personal* emotions and experiences.

Why do they use sexuality as a way to solve this problem? Partly because of the hyper-sexuality of the traumatized, as we have already pointed out; but also because people so afflicted often use sex as a drug, a sedative for emotional pain. In such a way traumatized people often become bonded—addicted—to other people with the same problem, in the same way that they are bonded or addicted to the aggression that originally traumatized them. Despite the wonderful sex, in the long run such couples can become abusive to each other, in extreme cases ending in homicide, with the man (as it usually happens) killing the woman.

But even if trauma-bonded couples do not have the ability to heal each other, could they not at long last—at the very least— *help* each other? Yes, although such a venture is quite often a disaster, it does sometimes turn out well, depending on the level of cultural literacy, relative emotional maturity, goodwill, capacity for introspection, and—above all—the social skills of the individuals involved. That is what seems to be happening in this film, although such a happy resolution is so rare that at times it seems like a dream, but a dream of mythic proportions: *two lovers, lovers that are also strangers, seek through their interactions to embody the answer to the riddle that war has caused their lives to become.*

The dilemma of war victims is that although their pain is real, the causes of their wounds are impossible to rationally explain and understand, because words usually can't embody the meaning of the immense historical events that have injured them. Only when they find a *personal* answer to the psychological trauma caused by an *impersonal* history will they be able to put their pain into perspective.

The Emmanuelle Riva character challenges Hiroshima to hurt her, deform her, to remake her as ugly as war itself. *Why does the woman talk about Hiroshima as though it were an abusive lover?* Why does she first implore Hiroshima to leave her alone, and then to hurt her? Because of the conflicted and histrionic manner in which traumatic memory often operates. On one level, people want to get rid of traumatic memories of human violence, and the bad behavior and emotional paralysis it causes; at the same time, such memories may contain a foundational energy that—rightly or wrongly—drives their personalities, even though that energy is experienced in the form of aggressive emotional orientations.

Above all, it is very difficult to get rid of the human aggression internalized at the time of trauma, because so much of the traumatic memory *consists* of aggression. The person who would leave that memory behind must deconstruct the aggression ensconced in it, but when and if the aggression is deconstructed, it robs the traumatic memory of its previously charismatic nature. That is the path that our French actress takes when she is finally able to talk about what happened to her in Nevers, after so many years of silence.

Can we excise such fundamental, defining memories without disrupting our personalities? The woman in *Hiroshima, Mon Amour* witnessed the killing of her German lover at the end of World War II. She is completely conflicted about the memory. She knows she must somehow let it go, because it is bad for her: it memorializes and keeps alive the violence that killed the young German soldier, and that he probably represented and acted upon himself. At the same time, if she lets it go she will be killing her lover, whose memory—because he was her first love—has animated her life and given it a core meaning, however destructive that meaning has become.

Arguably, the very pain associated with the memory of her lover has made it harder for her to let it go, with all that this highly-sexualized private obsession has meant to her. But it is for precisely that reason—to let that traumatic memory go—that she has come to Hiroshima, although she may not be fully conscious of that fact. Is not Hiroshima a favorite destination of the peace tourist for just that reason? Does she not seek a personal solution, however conditionally, by identifying her pain with the pain of those that suffered and died in Hiroshima?

9.

The French actress sits in the waiting room of the Hiroshima railroad station. Why is she here? She has no baggage with her; she seems utterly distracted. An elderly Japanese woman sits next to her. Clearly some time has elapsed, although not more than perhaps fifteen or twenty minutes. The French woman continues her interior monolog, as she continues, in a slightly different way, to simultaneously experience her memories of Nevers. The flashbacks are slightly out of sync with her voice-over, and we realize that she is beginning to let her memories go.

"Nevers, that I'd forgotten, I'd like to see you again tonight," she is saying to herself in a voice-over, and speaking sometimes to, and sometimes of, the German soldier who was her first love. "Every night for months on end I set you on fire, while my body was aflame with his memory." As the ruminative voice-over continues, the Japanese architect, her lover, comes in and sits on the bench in the railroad station, on the other side of the old woman, without looking at either of them. "While my body is still on fire with your memory, I would like to see Nevers again… the Loire."

There's a long, beautiful shot of poplar trees by the Loire River.

We're beginning to see that she has long been haunted not just by traumatic memory, but by an entire myth-system that she has created about herself, a myth-system that both threatens and gives coherence to her life, constituting a dramatic back story that any actress would appreciate. There is something endlessly seductive about a dead lover; and her story is all the more powerful because she was there as he died, lying on his dying body listening to his last breaths. She has internalized this primal horror so deeply that it has become a part of her personality—it would be accurate to say that she *identifies* with the shooting, and death, of her lover as the central and most influential event of her life.

"Lovely popular trees of Nievre, I offer you to oblivion," she says to herself and her memory in a voice-over. "Three-penny story, I bequeath you to oblivion. One night without you and I waited for daylight to free me." There is a shot of some ruins at Nevers, a place where she and her German lover met. "One day without his eyes was enough to kill her. Little girl of Nevers— shameless child of Nevers. One day without his hands and she thinks how sad it is to love. Silly little girl—who dies of love at Nevers. Little girl with shaven head, I bequeath you to oblivion."

There are more footage of Nevers, while the loudspeaker at the Hiroshima railroad station blares dully: *"Hiroshima!*

Hiroshima!"

10.

Both the French woman and her Japanese architect have difficulty loving: that is a pivotal reality in their lives. They have brief
sexual adventures that simulate, through their intensity, a world
in which love seems natural and easy. But that is an illusion: love
is never particularly easy, although even the most difficult love
can be unexpectedly invigorating. Although different for each of
these two people, their brief affair has revealed an emotional
fault-line in their lives. The woman needs her occasional memory
of a murdered lover to feel alive, memories which she acts out in
brief affairs; the man also needs his occasional adventures for
reasons of which he is himself probably not completely aware.
The fact that he brings his lover back to the house he shares with
his wife suggests, at the very least, either a need to take risks or
a disregard for social proprieties.

Again: traumatized people frequently make messiahs out of
their lovers, but when they discover that those same messiahs
are train wrecks like themselves, the reaction is often violent fury
directed at themselves, the world, and the unfortunate lover.
Therefore, we suggest again that *Hiroshima, Mon Amour* is to
some extent an unrealistic fantasy. There are very few people one
meets in the course of a one-night stand that have the patience
and psychological intuition of the Japanese man in the film. But
such people do exist; and furthermore, the woman has a very
high degree of introspective curiosity about her own emotions,
and understands very well—almost too well, in fact—what is
happening in her interior life. (That, by itself, makes her excep-
tional.) She realizes, almost from the beginning of the film, that
she must completely renegotiate—and to some extent get rid
of—the traumatic memory of her German lover. It is time for her
to take action against that problem, even though she feels a
terrible sense of disloyalty in doing so.

She can keep the narrative of what happened at Nevers—indeed, how could she repress such a memory?—but must let go of the aggression she internalized when her lover was shot, because she has too often turned the fatal aggression of war on herself. That is why she tells the Japanese architect about it, admitting something she has told no one but him. She would only tell someone about it, it seems certain, if she was getting ready to deconstruct the entire traumatic memory, including the aggression at its heart. She has taken the first huge step by telling another human being about what happened to her. Now it is no longer a secret, and is therefore much less able to hurt her.

11.

She is inside her hotel room leaning back against the door. There is a knock on the door. She opens it to find her Japanese lover.

"It was impossible not to come," he says.

He stands looking at her, worried and distracted. They are both standing in her hotel room, back where they first made love, where their love affair began. They must find some formula by which to understand what has happened to them over the past thirty-six hours, in order to understand what the future holds. Dawn has arrived, and the pale light comes in through the window.

"I'll forget you! I'm forgetting you already! Look how I'm forgetting you! Look at me!"

Her eyes are wide with excitement and the proximity of the right words to explain her emotions in some definitive way. *She has succeeded in drowning him in universal oblivion*, Duras writes in the script. *And that is a source of amazement to her.*

"Hi-ro-shi-ma," she says, explaining the miracle that has occurred. "Hi-ro-shi-ma. That's your name…"

"Yes. That's my name. Yes. Your name is Nevers. Nevers in France."

And at this point, the film ends.

12.

It is here, in the so-called city of peace, that the traumatic memory has been externalized, disembodied, and here most of the internalized aggression will remain. *She*, the character played beautifully by Emmanuelle Riva, has identified her personal sorrow with the cumulative horrors of the Second World War, for which Hiroshima has become a representative, a symbol, a metaphor and to some extent an emotional proxy. Hiroshima is the name by which she will remember her German lover, her first love, and also her Japanese lover. It is not quite an exorcism; it is not that she sought to replace tragic memories with a larger tragedy; but that she allowed Hiroshima and the two lovers *to become the same thing*, so that now, when she feels the sorrow of her first love's death, she feels it as part of the world's larger tragedy, which the gratuitous brutality of Hiroshima is both a terrifying but very tangible representative. It doesn't completely banish the pain, but it helps her make sense out of the pain that remains, by making her a part of humanity that is determined to survive the affects of this most disastrous of wars—and that fact alone makes her a stakeholder, this writer would argue, in the creation of a better world.

She will remember what she must, and forget what she no longer needs. Working with others for a better world would help her put the two in perspective. She will remember enough, and forget enough, so that traumatic memory from the past no longer dominates her present. And she may have learned (and accepted) the reality that good people forget past lovers and spouses, and for good reason: memories with insupportable, overwhelming pain are just as toxic as remembering nothing. In any case, only the great loves of literature, myth and film art outlast the average life expectancy. Sometimes one must forget the past to appreciate the present.

She, the actress played by Emmanuelle Riva, will probably be smart enough to figure out that it was this traumatic memory—

and the internalized violence of her German lover's killing—that was preventing her from enjoying life's simple pleasures, and making an emotional rather than a merely social commitment to her marriage; and in time she may understand also that it was this same traumatic memory, and a desperate attempt to keep her German lover alive, that drove her sexual adventures, and the sexual attraction between herself and the Japanese architect.

On the other hand, she unhesitatingly accepts the Japanese architect's help during the complicated and frequently bewildering histrionics that beset them over their day and a half together. In fact she honors him by giving him the name of the place where his family died—*Hiroshima*—which is the name of the larger trauma that she has allowed to subsume her own. Hiroshima has come, in that usage, to represent the war that battered both of them. On another level, one might say, it is also the name of the actual, physical place where she came to be reborn, and has to some extent succeeded in doing so.

The Japanese man also acknowledges what their relationship has really been about, a coming to terms with the past. He unhesitatingly accepts her conflation of Hiroshima with her personal trauma. He has found relief from his own demons by helping her confront hers; and although her experiences in Nevers will always to some extent haunt her, we have good reason to believe that it will no longer intrude so violently into her thoughts and feelings.

Our reason for this optimism is her decision to tell her secret to her Japanese lover, a secret she hadn't even been able to tell her husband. By telling her Japanese lover about Nevers she robbed it of its power; by conflating it with a much larger historical tragedy, she accepts herself as a part of humanity traumatized by the horrors of war. Her bad memories are no longer the most powerful thing in her life; her past, in other words, no longer controls her present. Therefore it isn't strong enough to control her future.

Is it possible that the French actress will stay in Hiroshima? Marguerite Duras, when asked this question, waxed agnostic on the future of her fascinating character. *This* writer, on the other hand, doubts that the French actress played with such consummate skill by Emmanuelle Riva would get stuck in Hiroshima. She has begun the deconstruction of her traumatic memory, which in her mind now represents the pain of all war. But because she has objectified her trauma by associating it with a tragic city—the place where her Japanese lover lost his family—she is likely to leave it behind, and go back to France to a better life. I see her as waiting two or three days in Hiroshima, striving to integrate into her personality the complicated things that have transpired. Then she would leave: after all, she's already mentioned her children as part of her own maturation process: so this writer finds it highly unlikely that she would abandon them. Rather she is more likely to return to her suburb of Paris, and to her children, as a different and better person.

She is smarter than many war survivors, and luckier. The reality is that *human aggression impacts the human personality more powerfully than anything else.* The psychological trauma of war, rape and physical abuse is different than trauma arising from the tornado, the earthquake and the house fire. Traumatic memory secondary to human violence and aggression is different from other memories, just as it is different from other traumata. *Hiroshima, Mon Amour* is a case study of the personal devastation that is caused when war-scarred people carry lacerating images and emotions of past violence that regularly intrude into the present. It is also a case study of the way people turn aggressive emotional orientations against themselves.

Besides the inevitable survival guilt—and sheer fury at humankind for the gratuitous cruelty of war—the French woman in *Hiroshima, Mon Amour* has internalized a staggering amount of aggression, which she has turned on herself mercilessly over the years, as the memory of the lost lover's violent death invaded her thoughts, driving her to high-risk behavior in an effort to keep him alive in her memory; but by so doing, she also created an emotional alienation that made it nearly impossible for her to love in the present moment. Worst of all, it made her a prisoner of her past, rather than the protagonist of her own story in the present moment. All of these things were made many times stronger because she had never told anyone about these experiences, but instead kept them a secret.

Does this mean that traumatic memory is more powerful than love, and other benign emotions? Yes, in the short term, it does mean that, because in the short run aggression affects the human personality more powerfully than love. ("The evil that men do lives after them; the good is oft interred with their bones.") Of course, this book is all about devising strategies for *defeating* the traumatic memory that arises out of the "evil that men do"—but overcoming the effects of a violent, traumatizing event takes longer than the duration of the event itself. This fact is very important to the future of humanity, since it is well known to sociopaths, politicians and generals who intuitively understand that they can achieve control over people very quickly by traumatizing them, and that it will take their victims much longer to deconstruct the after-effects of that violence.

How did the French woman who is at the center of *Hiroshima, Mon Amour* manage to deconstruct such a powerful traumatic memory? By finding someone with whom she could talk about it, someone who offered her emotional support while she confronted the memories—the images and feelings—their words inevitably triggered. Above all, she is ready to let the memories go, despite her tremendous ambivalence about symbolically letting her German lover "die." But she doesn't relish victim status, she wants to be strong, and is tired of carrying both this traumatic memory and the aggression she internalized in 1945 at Nevers. Furthermore, she is dedicated to the idea of world peace, which we know because of her role in a film about peace.

Her Japanese lover helps her at every step, engaging in provocative questions, guiding their discussion, engaging in some very tough role-playing, and in general providing emotional support for the deconstruction of traumatic memory and internalized violence she no longer wants. Most lovers—indeed, most friends and spouses, and most psychotherapists as well—are not that sensitive, that thoughtful, or that steadfast. *Hiroshima, Mon Amour* is not reality, certainly not 'real life,' but rather images on a screen that tell a story. But the film convinces us that such a profound emotional rebirth *could* happen, and suggests the way it might occur, and suggests as well the great power of such a process.

13.

Between 70,000 and 80,000 residents of Hiroshima died in the blast from the atom bomb, and about the same number died of the lingering effects of radiation poisoning and wounds generally; the survivors helped to rebuild the city, with a great deal of help from the international community, including the Americans. Among other things, the people of Hiroshima—and of post-war Japan generally—became enthusiastic baseball fans. In Hiroshima a compact but beautiful new baseball stadium was built in the late 1950s; Hiroshima's baseball team struggled for a few years, but soon became competitive throughout Japan. They are called—delightfully, for those of us who prefer the anti-heroic sensibility—the 'Hiroshima Carp.' (One imagines an American-style fan yelling, "C'mon, you damn carp, let's get some runners on base!")

Emmanuelle Riva's character in *Hiroshima, Mon Amour* ends up experiencing her traumatic memory as part of the larger trauma of World War II, which is an important step in her recovery, all of which comes about because of her decision to talk about her memories; above all, it helps her put her traumatic memory into perspective, and allows her to work with others for peace. But there is a subtle danger involved. When one's personal tragedy is subsumed into a larger historical tragedy, it becomes tempting to think of it as a kind of impersonal natural disaster, rather than the result of human evil. That's a dangerous tendency because systemic evil has an effect on the emotions of everybody involved. To think of it as an impersonal force creates the clear and present danger of a subtle internalization of the systemic evil itself.

There is, let us say it again, a discernible tendency to regard large, impersonal forms of human aggression as a *force majeure* rather than a discoverable process of human evil. That, in turn, leads to a sense that evil is simply another part of life. But evil *isn't* just another part of life, nor is it inevitable, but the result of discrete human choices—to think otherwise is to be complicit with it. An entire generation of Japanese men internalized profoundly patriarchal and racist ideas, which caused Japan to invade and brutally occupy several Asian countries, and to bomb Pearl Harbor—but the war started by Japan in Asia ultimately become a form of evil in which America became complicit. How this happened needs to be explained.

Was the nuclear bombing of Hiroshima systemic evil? Yes, of course it was; but it began as a malevolent Japanese cultural system with philosophical roots deep in the warrior code, and the brutality inherent in that code. The fanaticism inherent in it, as well as certain decisions made by the Japanese leadership, caused the Americans to believe that only a nuclear weapon could prevent a last-ditch effort to defend the Japanese Islands, despite the demonstrable fact that Japan had lost the war. This led to the American decision to drop an atom bomb on Hiroshima and Nagasaki, without first exploding a nuclear device in an unpopulated area as a way of demonstrating the weapon's power to the Japanese.

The atom bomb in Hiroshima and Nagasaki was perceived by the Americans as a lesser evil, because it was aimed at stopping a brutal military machine, and it succeeded in doing that. If you were a POW held by the Japanese, you would unquestionably have been overjoyed to hear of the destruction of Hiroshima, because ending the war quickly would mean freedom from torture and ill-treatment generally. On the other hand, nobody — not then, not now — can say it is justifiable to incinerate tens of thousands of small children, and cause tens of thousands more to die from the lingering effects of radiation sickness, as part of a war strategy. At the very least one must acknowledge it as a horrible tragedy — to believe otherwise would be monstrous.

The point is: the use of the atom bomb on Hiroshima was the last act of a long process of discoverable human evil that began with Japan's occupation of Manchuria in the early 1930s. The Imperial Japanese Army attacked other countries cruelly and without provocation, especially China; but even as the Americans defeated the Imperial Japanese Army militarily, they added to the evil already in play. I say again, the Americans should have exploded a nuclear device in an uninhabited area to demonstrate the power of their new weapon; instead, they destroyed Hiroshima and Nagasaki. Today, the existence of nuclear weapons means we must learn ways to negotiate win-win solutions to most human conflicts. Struggling to achieve that, and exposing the evils of unnecessary war, is the best way to redeem the suffering of Hiroshima.

The French-speaking actress in *Hiroshima, Mon Amour* knew that she needed to make a personal change, a change in her personality, and she comes as a pilgrim to Hiroshima to accomplish that. There she finds a sympathetic person who has also suffered a great loss, who himself obtains relief by helping her face her traumatic memories. People are not often that lucky in finding a sympathetic ear; yet one sometimes does, and it is worth noting that the underlying dynamic of *Hiroshima, Mon Amour* is the same as the dynamic for recovery from traumatic memory: to talk about the memory with somebody who is both empathic and sympathetic, while trying to neutralize the internalized aggression that negatively affects behavior. Specifically, in addition to talking about the traumatizing events, one should follow it up with some kind of socially-beneficial activity—in the case of the Emmanuelle Riva character, that meant making antiwar films. (Taken together, these two things are recognizably an example of the 'recovery dualism' that this book advocates.)

What we feel with increasing intensity in the 21st century is a consensus that wars as they were waged in the past no longer work as a way of resolving problems. This is partly because the weapons for those wars have changed—they are increasingly weapons that harm the innocent, because by their very nature they kill mainly civilians. Who gains from killing innocent people? There is also a growing if partly unconscious sense that patriarchy, the unconscious emotional orientation that lies behind much war, is no longer a viable approach to modern life. People are beginning to reject the zero-sum perception of life's conflicts, and are instead searching for win-win solutions, however conditional many of them may be, solutions that at the very least allow us to minimize—or if possible, avoid—violence. The personal task of individuals is to deconstruct the violence they have internalized; society's responsibility is to embrace and enforce universal human rights.

Only human beings that have arrived at a consensus, working together *en masse*, can insist that universal rights be respected and implemented. If such efforts aren't successful, there is a good chance humanity will destroy itself, either through nuclear weapons or man-made destruction of the environment. Working for peace can be difficult, of course—individual manifestations of the spirit of peace are often naïve, self-congratulatory, ill-informed or pretentious. (Think how ineffective the hundreds of first-rate antiwar films and books have been in getting governments to stop fighting unnecessary wars.) Yet a consensus is building that unnecessary war is an abomination, a refuge for cowards and ambitious extremists.

Of course, if a war is forced on a people by an armed enemy, they must fight it—for example, the US intervention in Afghanistan was necessary, because the Taliban gave Al Qaeda a base from which to attack innocent Americans on 9/11. But it is painfully clear that the Iraq War, as waged by President George Bush, was completely unnecessary, because the Iraqis never attacked us. And Americans knew it then, even as the Bush administration lied, and even as America's corporate media repeated the lies told by the government. Why do we put up with this? Are we not complicit in evil when we knowingly go along with unnecessary wars?

Wars, genocide and dictatorships create psychological trauma from which it is difficult for human beings to recover. An important part of this process is the internalization by victims of the aggression they endure or witness. If this internalized aggression is not deconstructed, the individuals involved are likely to continue the cycle of violence. Recovery from traumatic memories means deconstructing the aggression one has internalized during the violent events that caused those memories. Only in that way can aggression be managed.

Individuals that have been traumatized can also achieve a level of catharsis from helping other people deal with their traumatic memory—the character of the Japanese architect in *Hiroshima, Mon Amour* demonstrates that clearly—and his lover, the French actress, also does what is necessary to move past the ghosts of her past, and heal herself. Again: these steps roughly correlate to the 'recovery dualism' this book recommends... *First*, the French actress played by Emmanuelle Riva talks about her traumatic memory, which she had previously kept secret, and in talking about it robs it of its malevolent power. *Second*, she engages in a socially-beneficial activity by making antiwar movies and documentaries.

She was once a very young girl who loved a German soldier, and saw him killed in the last days of World War II. Over time the traumatic memory of his death became a way of keeping him alive. *He,* her Japanese lover, knew that the only way she could get over this traumatic memory would be to talk about it. By doing so, she deconstructs her internalized aggression at the same times that she lets go of her traumatic memories; ultimately she identifies with the suffering of Hiroshima as a way of comprehending the power of aggression that has become systemic evil. Although she may never completely forget what happened to her long ago, it seems undeniable that she has deconstructed the worst parts of her traumatic memory, while remaining willing and able to honor the wild dreams and emotions she felt as a teenage girl caught up in the most destructive war in history.

Chapter Nine

Why the Trauma of the Holocaust Still Haunts Us, and How it is Leading to Religious War

1.

It was the 1960s in San Francisco, and almost everyone thought of themselves as cultural and political progressives. My young wife and I didn't want to send our children to any regular school, public or private, and there were a lot of non-traditional schools, including Waldorf Schools, open classrooms and educational experiments of every description; but we decided on a private but affordable school that was based on a multicultural model, a school that taught mainly in English, but also did language instruction. The four languages they taught were Cantonese, Hebrew, Spanish and Swahili; for us the core language instruction would be Hebrew, since my wife was Jewish. (You got lowered tuition under certain conditions, and we qualified for that.) We signed up our son for pre-school and our daughter in the equivalent of kindergarten, as I remember; and since it was in part funded by a local Jewish Social Service agency, and was located on the grounds of a former Jewish orphanage, it had very good and well-attended Hebrew-language instruction. It was, in everything but name, a Hebrew school that also taught a smattering of other languages.

The school got its Hebrew-language teaching materials from the American publisher of such materials, which I later learned was owned and managed by right-wing Zionists. I didn't pay much attention to it at first. Most of the Hebrew was taught at this school by an individual who had lived in Israel, and had perhaps been born there—he had a thick accent, and clearly hadn't learned English as a first language. He seemed like an efficient but businesslike young man, with nothing extraordinary about his personality one way or the other. Later on there were other teachers, all of them rather uncommunicative. My guess is that they weren't getting paid that much. They weren't particularly interested in talking to parents, either.

My wife and I thought of Hebrew-language instruction as a great opportunity for our two children to learn a second language early in life; an added incentive was that some kids received scholarships that made it quite inexpensive. (I can't remember whether this scholarship was offered for all kids learning languages, or wholly or mainly for the Hebrew students.) The school also taught some Jewish history and culture, all from a secular point of view. I was reading Yiddish authors in translation, and often found myself wondering why the children were being taught Hebrew instead of Yiddish, since Yiddish had, after all, a much larger literature than Hebrew. What I kept hearing from people in the school was that Yiddish was a "dead language," whereas Hebrew was the language of a vibrant young country that was increasingly influential in the world.

I remember that my wife hadn't liked the Israelis she'd met, and I distinctly remember her saying that she found them "arrogant," and not to be trusted. As for myself, I simply accepted all the things that Americans were being told at that time about Israel, beginning with the idea that Israel was "a land without people, for a people without a land." Founding a new country seemed an incredible accomplishment, all the more compelling since it had been brought about in large part by refugees from the world's worst genocide.

I came from a progressive middle-western tradition that began in nineteenth-century Kansas with my great-grandfather, a vigorous Democratic legislator who cooperated with the populists and fought the eastern banks on behalf of the farmers. My grandfather and his many siblings were stalwart supporters of the New Deal, and both my parents were liberal Democrats who pulled themselves up from the rock-bottom poverty of the Depression. They were fanatical believers in education, which they saw as the key to a better life, and a better world; my father, amazingly, earned a Ph.D. at Kansas University at Lawrence attending mainly night classes. My mother was a gifted composer and piano teacher who held piano recitals every couple of months at our house, with catered refreshments afterwards.

My wife, the scion of progressive German Jews, greatly admired my parents and held them up as examples of what Christians ought to be. She was more than willing to raise our children as Episcopalians—odd, given her identification with German-Jewish culture—but I insisted that they ought to have some idea of the Jewish part of themselves. They would get most of their Jewish values by osmosis, through the attitudes and ideas of their mother; still, I thought it a sound idea for the kids to have some practical Jewish education to put it all into historical perspective. So the Hebrew instruction continued apace at the multicultural school, along with all the other kinds of instruction offered there.

The problem arose when my daughter, a bright and very savvy child, showed me some of the school's Hebrew-language instructional materials. One book featured cartoons and illustrations of scowling, hook-nosed Arabs engaged in plotting mayhem against Israeli Jews. Another—this one was actually on the cover of one of the Hebrew-language booklets—showed an equally hideous Arab throwing a bomb into the United Nations. (The bomb was one of those round jobs with a lit fuse, like nineteenth-century newspapers used to show anarchists throwing.) Apparently the main occupation of Arabs was throwing bombs and scowling threateningly, and their main feature was their huge hook noses. My daughter was delighted to show me this exercise in stereotyping, partly because she lived for any opportunity to challenge the adults; but also because she never doubted for a moment that there were better Hebrew books out there, and that I could get some for her class. She was simply alerting us to the inappropriateness of the current books, so that the responsible adults could find better ones.

"Daddy, look, that's racism, isn't it?" she asked triumphantly, pointing to an illustration of a threatening, hook-nosed Arab.

What I didn't know at that time was that she and the other children were discussing this dire situation among themselves; and some of the others were even starting to talk to *their* parents. One must remember that these were precocious children whose parents thought of themselves as progressives, liberals and radicals, and many of them were in the arts; and here we were, smack dab in the middle of the 1960s. The kids listened to their parents, and in objecting to the racism in the Hebrew books they accurately reflected the political and cultural values their progressive parents had taught them.

"Yes," I said," these cartoons are without question racist. It's statistically impossible that all Arabs could look so hideous, harbor such evil intentions, or have such large noses. Clearly, by disseminating such a cartoon in a Hebrew-language book, the people who created these materials sought to create negative thoughts and feelings about Arabs, and to suggest that they are all fundamentally violent."

"They're making people hate Arabs," my daughter said. It was open and shut to her. "Why do they always show Arabs doing bad things in this book?"

"Probably because they want to make people afraid of Arabs, so they'll be prepared to fight them."

"Why?"

I explained what little I knew about the problems faced by the Israelis, but my daughter wasn't having any of it: "Some of the Arabs may be bad, Daddy, but not all of them. That's what you told us: that there's good and bad in every group. So why do they *always* show Arabs as bad?"

My daughter was awash with glee, in the manner of precocious children of all times and places who are able to confound
their parents regarding something important. Also she didn't, for
a moment, see why the persecution of Jews should justify racism
against Arabs. "Aren't they doing to the Arabs what the Bad
Guys did to them?"

I had no idea that most of these "Arabs" —whom we today call
"Palestinians"—had actually, many of them, become refugees
when they were systematically driven out of their villages, farms
and neighborhoods by the Zionist founders of Israel. That would
not become known until the 1980s, when the Israelis opened up
their military archives and the New Historians began to write
about it. And it would continue to be vehemently denied by
Jewish leaders, except in Israel, where everybody knew the truth.

My wife remarked that the racism in the Hebrew-language
instructional materials served mainly to confirm what she had
always felt about Israelis. As for myself, I tried to find out more
about the language materials. Very shortly after this first
discussion, I sat down and went through all the booklets the kids
were using. They were filled with the most racist kind of propaganda imaginable. I would find out decades later, speaking to a
well-known Jewish author and activist who was a source for a
story I was writing, that these Hebrew-language materials were
widely acknowledged to be outrageously biased against Arabs
and Palestinians; but they had never been challenged publicly,
apparently because everybody was afraid to talk about it. (That
is, Jews were afraid of being called self-hating Jews, and non-
Jews were afraid of being called anti-Semites.)

And there was something else. These Hebrew instructional
booklets encouraged the children reading them to *write a letter to
an Israeli soldier*, praising him for his bravery on behalf of Jews
everywhere. The publishers would even deliver the letter. But
why a soldier? Why not a dentist, a farmer or somebody's grandparents? Or a writer, a poet or a musician in the Israeli

Philharmonic Symphony? Best of all: why not have children studying Hebrew write *to other children* living in Israel? That seemed like a much saner approach than haranguing kids to write a letter to an Israeli soldier, with whom they had nothing in common. In fact, everything in these Hebrew-language booklets seemed to be nothing more than a particularly transparent form of ideological indoctrination, with a heavy dose of militarism; and—worst of all—the most blatant kind of anti-Arab racism. It was all the more reprehensible, I thought, since it was aimed at children, and was supposed to be part of a classroom teaching experience in a multicultural school.

What was immediately noticeable was my daughter's touching tendency to repeat exactly the same things—often using the same phrases—her mother and I had taught her regarding racial and religious stereotyping. But as far as my daughter was concerned, the question always came back to this: Why was the Hebrew school using racist instructional materials, and when would we get materials without hateful cartoons of buffoonish Arabs, and without the noxious right-wing ideological hard-sell? In the meantime, there had been a mini-revolt at the school. Children using the Hebrew-language materials were rebelling against the painfully obvious bigotry in the text and graphics of the instructional materials. The kids knew what was being dished out to them, and they were mad as hell about it. It was the parents, teachers and administrators who were befuddled and unsure what to do about it.

2.

I went out of my way to talk to other parents about the anti-Arab racism in the Hebrew-language instructional material, but they seemed oddly evasive. Anybody who has had this experience will know the uncanny vibes that immediately manifest themselves when anybody tries to talk about Israeli racism. Even allowing for some subjectivity on my part, it was obvious, almost from the beginning, that the subject made everybody uncomfortable, and that I was to some extent seen as "causing trouble" by bringing it up. The Jewish parents at first agreed with me that the cartoons and graphics were racist; it was sad, they said, but look at what the Israelis were going through. After all, they had never done anything bad to the Arabs, and the Arabs attacked the Israelis solely because they hated Jews. Considering that, the racist illustrations, while not admirable, were at least understandable, the Jewish parents seemed to be saying. These conversations were accompanied by a distinct undertone of resentment that I had brought it up at all, and continued to bring it up.

It wasn't going to go away by itself, I thought, any more than concerns about fascism and Stalinism had gone away in preceding generations; and sure enough, most of the parents now began to internalize (or "contextualize," as they might have said) the racism of the instructional Hebrew booklets, through the expedient of a thousand and one rationalizations for it. Now I was starting to hear the parents and teachers say things like, "Yes, of course it's bad, but since when was the world fair? Isn't fighting segregation in the American south and stopping the Vietnam War more important, because they're so much more immediate? Isn't it likely that the Israelis themselves will come to terms with their own racism someday?" And so on.

The Hebrew-language materials were cheesy and biased against Arabs, I kept hearing from parents, but what choice did any of us have? "We're lucky to be getting language instruction so cheaply," I heard from many parents, including those whose children were receiving instruction in other languages. (I have to admit that the same thought occurred to me.) But why had my wife and I wanted our two children to learn Hebrew in the first place? Because we wanted to open up to them the world beyond our little neighborhood in San Francisco (Potrero Hill), but at the same time we wanted them to envision a world based on what we would today call universal human rights. Yet here we were, sending our kids to a so-called multicultural school, where they were being indoctrinated with what seemed like an almost medieval form of ethnic hatred. Putting up with that, it seemed, was the price we had to pay to stay in the school. (After all, we couldn't expect our kids to suddenly start studying Cantonese, after making a good start on Hebrew.) Furthermore, a great many people I respected made weird excuses for the instructional materials, for reasons that didn't make sense to me.

I gradually became aware that the other parents didn't want to think about the Hebrew books, and at a certain point they politely refused to talk to me about it. The demonstrable racism of these Hebrew instructional booklets was different than any other form of racism, it seemed, and for that reason had to be justified with complicated excuses and explanations—in other words, denied. It was about this time that uncritical American supporters of Israel began to call anybody who was critical of Israel anti-Semites. (This may have been one reason why the parents didn't want to talk about the racism of the Hebrew books, that they didn't want to be denounced publicly as self-hating Jews or anti-Semites.) Compared to the fate of being stigmatized in that manner, racism against a bunch of Arabs didn't seem so bad.

It was different with the kids. They continued to be offended by the Hebrew books—they could see exactly what the materials were trying to do, which was to indoctrinate them with a really dumb racist ideology, which they didn't like. (Why? Because it was radically contrary to the values they had learned from their parents—or at least, the values their parents had verbally espoused).

So, I took it up with a couple of the people in the administration of the school. They seemed a shadowy bunch, not because they consciously kept a low profile, but because—like so many other things in the sixties—they were making everything up as they went along, with the school seemingly lurching along from one carefully-cultivated donor to the next. Such policies as they had arose from intense ad hoc discussions among whoever happened to be on staff at the time; people came and went.

Finally I got an interview with a woman whose face I cannot recall, almost surely because I have since repressed it; but I remember well the nature of our discussion about the Hebrew-language teaching materials. "Yes, some of the pictures and text are undeniably racist, from our middle-class American point of view," she began. "But the Israelis, you know, don't have the luxury of being nice to their adversaries. It's not like in America, where the whites are in a large majority, and are therefore in a position to make significant concessions. In Israel, the Jews are a small minority in the Middle East, surrounded by hundreds of millions of Arabs, who are already on record as wanting to push them into the sea. The Arabs hate Jews, and would gladly wipe them out if they could. So it's understandable that the Israelis would portray them as less than friendly."

It occurred to me that if the Israelis were surrounded by millions of Arabs, they might wish, eventually, to integrate themselves into that part of the world; and I couldn't see how this kind of cartoonish bigotry against Arabs could help them lay the groundwork for that. "The Arabs aren't portrayed as less than friendly," I said, "they're portrayed as violently evil, people who are almost exclusively engaged in scowling, throwing bombs and lurking about in the shadows waiting to kill Jews."

"Don't they, to some extent?"

"Some, maybe," I said, remembering how I had taught my children not to generalize about an entire group. "But I don't believe all Arabs could be that evil. Besides, isn't it possible that the Israelis may have been less than friendly to them?"

She bristled. "What? Israeli Jews never did anything to the Arabs. The Arabs are poor and backward. After all, didn't most of them leave Palestine at the first opportunity, when the Jews set up the state of Israel?"

"Well," I said, "I don't know the history. But I know racism when I see it, and it is invariably contemptible, and indicative of unresolved emotional conflicts in the personalities of those that disseminate it. There's always a kernel of truth in stereotypes, but only a kernel. Do you think Jews should put up with pictures that portray them as having huge hook noses, throwing bombs and hurting people?" (I was especially appalled by the hook noses, since they looked so much like anti-Semitic newspaper cartoons from Europe in the 1930s.) "Someday the Israelis will want to make peace, if they have any sense, and integrate themselves into the rest of the Middle East. This kind of hatred and venom surely isn't going to make it any easier. How can the Israelis have peace someday, when they disseminate these kinds of inflammatory gutter images in their Hebrew books?"

At this point she drew herself up. Here it comes, I thought, even though I didn't yet know what was coming. "Surely you must be aware that Jews have suffered the most devastating genocide in human history. I refer to the Holocaust."

"I know what the Holocaust is."

"You must realize that Jews have been persecuted forever in Europe, and the Holocaust was the tipping point." Now she began to talk at length about the Holocaust, and what it meant to her, and what it meant to the world, and what it ought to mean to me. I can't remember all that she said, but it was mainly about the power of the Holocaust; and the gist of it was that the Holocaust had changed everything, and now everything we thought about right and wrong had to change.

We now had to do things that may have seemed wrong before, but now that the Holocaust had happened, we had to do those wrong things anyway. "Jews had to find a way to protect themselves, and having their own country was the only way to do it. The creation of the state of Israel was a historical necessity. Yes, I'm sure people get hurt in such a process, I'm sure there have been excesses throughout this historical process, and still are—but Jews *have the right to defend themselves,* don't you see?" In her tone was absolute moral certainty. "They have done wonders with the land, too."

"But these Hebrew booklets studied by the kids are still full of racist propaganda."

She sighed. "It's inevitable that such feelings would be present so soon after the founding of a new country, particularly when you consider how much opposition there's been. I'm sure that the more extreme feelings will fade after awhile."

Even then I knew that racism and religious bigotry are like an addiction, and that addictions always get worse unless confronted directly. And even then, although I was young and somewhat immature, I knew that what you had to do with racism was simply not cooperate with it, despite all the mitigating circumstances that might be trotted out to justify or explain it. That was what briefly living in the south as a teenager had taught me.

"What if these more extreme feelings *don't* fade after awhile?"

Now she was starting to get impatient. For her, the conversation was already over, now that she had made her main points. My role was to understand the emotional verisimilitude of what she was saying, agree respectfully, and go away. "That's up to the Israelis themselves," she said firmly. "If you don't share the same dangers and problems of the Israelis, you can't judge them. Anyway, who knows *what* the future will bring?"

"Can't we look for better instructional materials, materials that don't portray Arabs in almost exactly the way that people in Europe used to portray Jews?"

"We have to use those particular materials, because the company that produces them is the only Hebrew-language publisher in the USA."

That thought alone was terrifying. I had a sudden vision of tens of thousands of kids studying these booklets, and internalizing the racism that they contained. "Look, I just don't like my kids using these materials."

"Do you want to withdraw your children from the Hebrew class?" she asked after a pause.

I asked to talk with my children about it again; but my daughter felt strongly that it was simply a case of finding Hebrew-language materials without racism. Except for the lousy instructional materials, the kids were enjoying learning Hebrew—along with the smattering of other languages the school taught—and they had made a lot of friends in the multicultural school.

What to do?

The people in the administration at the school, at least those that I talked to—as well as almost all of the other parents—now began to bring up the Holocaust every time I pointed out the undeniable racism in the Hebrew instructional materials; the idea that I kept hearing was that Jews had been persecuted more than any other group, so they had to take extraordinary measures. Although the Israelis weren't crazy about Arabs, they said, such racism was understandable, or perhaps even necessary, in the short run. It seemed that the Holocaust was a kind of emotional and social kryptonite that had completely turned the world's understanding of morality upside down. No longer was there such a thing as right and wrong, at least where the thought, speech and behavior of Israelis was concerned. Because of the Holocaust, you had to support the Israeli state, no matter what it—or its proxies—did or said, even when they were clearly wrong.

If the Holocaust had *that* kind of power, it seemed to me, it could be used to inspire hatred of *anybody*, and not just Arabs.

I quickly learned that the Holocaust was still going on, in the form of a traumatic memory, and that it was a profound emotional and social force; and I also discovered that it was kept alive by people who wished to use it to enhance their personal or political power, usually by suppressing discussion. Most of all it gave people the right to exist beyond good and evil, beyond the normal moral reference points. References to the trauma of the Holocaust had to be invoked whenever the Israeli state did something violent, or when those violent things had to be rationalized. The lady I talked to at the multicultural school was clearly under the influence of it; I could tell by the way her voice dropped and her eyes widened when she talked about it, and she always talked about it when she was trying to justify the racism in the Hebrew instructional materials. It was like a drug, this shared traumatic memory, which could make people say that black was white, that right was wrong and up was down; specifically, in this case, it could justify racism because the Israeli state said it was necessary to do so.

I knew that this particular drug had to be terribly addictive, no matter how much you tried to rationalize it; and I thought my kids were spot-on right to challenge it, when it appeared in their instructional materials. As for the adults, there was something grievously off-balanced and skewed and just plain wrong in the thinking of just about every person I talked to about it. There was a tremendous tendency to justify racism when Jews did it, even when it was clearly despicable. Yet when my kids, especially my daughter, complained about it, I couldn't seem to do anything to change the situation myself. This odd inability to think, speak or act also appeared to drive the attitude of the school's administration: it was sad, the racism in the Hebrew books, but they couldn't do anything about it. And after all, when you got right down to it, the Arabs *were* a little backward, weren't they?

Now I wish more than anything that I'd simply taken my kids out of the school, and gone public to all the other parents about why I was doing so. I think maybe I would have done that, eventually; but I'll never know for sure, because the problem was resolved for all of us in a manner nobody would have anticipated.

3.

The problem was resolved by the implosion of the school, brought about by a sensational but somewhat pitiful sex scandal that shook San Francisco to its foundations. A well-known, married San Francisco Supervisor was found to have been having a torrid affair with an equally well-known woman involved with the Jewish organizations that funded the school. Furthermore, the two lovebirds had been meeting on the mainly abandoned grounds of the Jewish orphanage, where the multicultural school was located; and the kids attending the school, it turned out, had known about their supposedly secret get-togethers long before the parents and administrators did. (As I said, the kids were a precocious bunch.)

There were public charges and counter-charges from the stricken and infuriated adulterers, who had declared war on each other; the married Supervisor hinted darkly that his lover had been unduly influenced by, and perhaps sleeping with, a "progressive Arab" man (I'm not making this up), since apparently that was the most damaging thing he could think of to say publicly about her; and the whole ridiculous, ugly mess ended up on the front page of the *San Francisco Chronicle*.

There had been other problems with the school, but this was apparently the final straw. The school announced that it was sorry it was closing, but that it would certainly notify us when and if it re-opened. Our little family's experiment with multicultural education and language instruction was finished, terminated, kaput, *verschimmelt*.

The experience also taught me, for the first but not the last time, about the power of the Holocaust, the power of traumatic privilege, and the power of systemic evil. Most terrifying was the manner in which people used the Holocaust to justify evil, to virtually guarantee that the circumstances that first created the Holocaust—nationalism, patriarchy, racism and militarism—would be replicated and acted out in new venues. What I was learning was that those who were most traumatized and disoriented by a shared memory of the Nazi Holocaust were often the most likely to identify with the negative social dynamics that had caused it.

It is perhaps this same dangerous psychological tendency that causes the West to stand by, as it stands by today, while the Israelis continue to conduct their slow and tortuous ethnic cleansing of the Palestinian people, whose main crime is to have the wrong religion and to belong to the wrong ethnic group; although the West sees the horror of it, it refuses to act. Perhaps it is the same moral distortion that allows Americans to accept the fact that a large plurality—some say a majority—of their elected legislators in Congress receive money to vote as the Prime Minister of Israel wants them to. It is an odd and malignant kind of moral autism that grips all Western societies, and particularly America: those who see corruption most clearly are often those most likely to make excuses for it. Having nothing to lose, the children at the multicultural school in San Francisco saw evil, and rebelled against it. In so doing, they raised a troubling question: if children could see evil and rebel against it, and their much more educated parents couldn't, what exactly is the good of education?

What few of us really understood was that we'd run smack up against one of the most powerful and dangerous ideological systems of the last half of the 20th century, which was Zionism, and the religious nationalism released by it. (Granted, it happened to be a particularly right-wing form of Zionism, but that was the only form that these children were likely to encounter, at least in their Hebrew instruction.) Secondly, we were witnessing—and to some extent participating in—the systematic corruption of the Jewish people, a corruption that continues today. Third, we were witnessing a major corruption of American thought and sensibilities, by the dissemination of an anti-Arab fantasy that would someday contribute to the most loathsome kinds of Islamophobia, religious nationalism and gutter racism. I would not know the true malignance of this until much later, when—with a different partner—I became the parent of a Muslim daughter.

Fourth, we were seeing the opening rounds of the degradation of American religion generally—social-justice Catholicism would be swamped by Republican bishops, liberal mainstream Protestants would be overwhelmed by right-wing evangelicals, and the G-d of the Torah would be replaced in many Jewish sensibilities by the worship of the Israeli state. Finally, we were experiencing the fallout from the West's unwillingness to unpack the causes of the Holocaust, and grapple meaningfully with the violent contradictions within Christianity that caused anti-Semitism to arise in the first place.

But for those young students of Hebrew, sorting it all out was a lot easier. They knew that the racist pictures and texts they'd been given were stupid and wrong, and they responded by protesting against them. It was the exact opposite of their parents' moral paralysis, in which I include my own. The children instantly understood what was wrong with Israel and they courageously objected to it, even as the world of the adults continued to invent new and ever more pathological forms of denial.

4.

Today, many decades after the 1960s, the most effective political and cultural force in America is the overlapping systems of influence and control set up by the Israel Lobby (although the gun lobby comes close). The Israel Lobby is a generic term referring to disparate people and institutions that are convinced that Americans should never be allowed to publicly criticize the government of Israel, even when—or especially when—it makes mistakes or does bad things, despite the fact that America gives more foreign-aid money to Israel than any other country in the world. It is with these things in mind that members of the Israel Lobby conduct extensive policing of public discussion of everything having to do with Israel.

Especially prominent in 'The Lobby' are the leaders of three important organizations—the Anti-Defamation League, the American Jewish Committee and the Simon Wiesenthal Center; the Lobby's most well-known public figures have been Abraham Foxman, Director of the ADL, and Alan Dershowitz, a self-promoting American attorney, professor lawyer and political commentator. (The reader will remember Dershowitz as being the main leader of the forces responsible for preventing Norman Finkelstein from receiving tenure at DePaul University.) They are backed up by an even larger contingent of right-wing Christian evangelicals, who constitute the most active—and culturally backward—constituency in the Republican Party, many of whom believe that a religious war in Israel/Palestine is God's will, and a very good thing because it would bring about the Second Coming of Christ.

All of the above-mentioned people and organizations have one thing in common: they attack American critics of the Israeli state, usually by calling them anti-Semites or self-hating Jews. Their goal is to prevent such critics from getting tenure in academia, to ruin their reputations and drive them from their jobs, and if possible to make them unemployable. And although they do this by calling them anti-Semites and self-hating Jews, the huge majority of Israel's critics are neither, but are instead sincere advocates for social justice who don't want American tax dollars spent on torture, murder and collective punishment of anyone, whether Jews, Palestinians or anyone else.

In Congress the American-Israeli Public Affairs Committee (AIPAC) does pretty much the same thing, with one major difference: they have at their disposal immense amounts of money. Currently a very high percentage of elected politicians in Congress receive money from AIPAC to vote as the current

Prime Minister of Israel wants them to, at least on issues having to do with the perceived interests of Israel's current Likud government. There's nothing illegal about it—it's called 'bundling,' and is basically a form of legal bribery. But it's rather odd, not to mention unprecedented, that close to a majority of the legislative branch of America now receive money to vote as the Prime Minister of a foreign country wants them to. From the point of view of American sovereignty, not to mention political morality, it's an unacceptable situation. And 'the Lobby' isn't just retailing access—you have to vote exactly as the Israel Lobby tells you to on issues involving the Middle East, or your money is cut off.

But *why* do people and organizations in the Israel Lobby behave in this manner, and *why* do so many supposedly free Americans follow their dictates? Why do so many people who say they love Israel embrace doctrines that ensure Israel's eventual destruction? Why do they cooperate in suppressing criticism of the Israeli state, when everybody knows that self-criticism and robust debate are necessary to the health of the state, *any* state? And why do so many people feel constrained to think, speak and act according to the dictates of a Lobby that is often irrational? They do so partly because they are afraid not to. But they do so also because people are struggling with a shared traumatic memory of the Nazi Holocaust, in the process internalizing so much of its evil that it radically affects their thoughts, emotions and behavior.

Some institutions, especially the Simon Wiesenthal Center in Los Angeles, actually insist that identification with the victims of the Holocaust should be the basis of Jewish identity, rather than identifying with those who tried to *stop* the Holocaust. In my book *The Death of Judeo-Christianity: Religious Aggression and Systemic Evil in the Modern World*, I call attention to the extreme danger of this approach: "To live in the same world in which the Holocaust occurred, the Wiesenthal Center is saying, you must accept it both as history's biggest crime and the most important determinant of Jewish identity. But that is a mistaken strategy, because that gives too much power to the Holocaust. You cannot base *identity* on the Holocaust without internalizing its *aggression*, because you cannot take in one without the other." This creates a *trauma bond*, which bonds the victim not to the aggressor, but to his aggression. This trauma bonding is why so many victims appear to imitate and act out the kind of aggression with which they were once victimized. In other words, the abused child grows up to be an abuser.

It is this internalization of Holocaust aggression—and identification with it—that one meets at every point in the Israel Lobby, and in the people who follow its cultural and political dictates, even when those dictates are bad for Israelis, Palestinians and Americans alike. Managing traumatic memory of the Holocaust also means managing the internalized aggression that inevitably accompanies it. That is not to say that all people who uncritically support the Israeli state are affected by multigenerational trauma, nor are all the Christians and Jews who obediently do its bidding. The trauma associated with the Nazi Holocaust often affects people who have no connection whatsoever to Europe, or the historical period when the Holocaust occurred; and that is, for the most part, because the Holocaust confronts people with the problem of systemic evil in a manner they are unable to assimilate, either emotionally or intellectually. Modern people—especially those of the educated middle classes—are so unused to confronting the omnipresence of evil that simply *trying* to do so can be traumatizing, because modernity has no philosophy, no theology, and no explanation whatsoever, that can explain why aggression and evil are so powerful in human affairs. And while institutional religion tries to identify evil, it usually can't stop it—and when the evil is systemic, religion often makes it worse.

Acknowledging the existence of evil often leads people to

realize—including a great many people that are horrified by this realization—that evil can be more powerful than good, and usually is, at least in the short term. This realization is by itself quite disorienting, because it goes against what enlightened people have believed for the last three centuries. It is not based on mere philosophical speculations, but arises as the result of excruciating psychological upheavals in which people discover that the world they once knew no longer exists. This process creates an anxiety so profound that the only way some people can suppress it is to create an imaginary system in which delusions replace unpredictable realities, and the reactions of other people must be endlessly manipulated through a kind of emotional totalitarianism. (That is, the manipulation of negative emotions— especially fear, guilt, aggression and shame—can be used to make people avoid taboo subjects, and in so doing encourage them to suppress thoughts about those same taboo subjects.)

This is a big part of the cultural and psychological system that the Israel Lobby has set up in America, but there is another component to it, one that is hidden. At a very deep level, uncritical supporters of the Israeli state themselves suffer from a gnawing fear that Israel is not the perfect place that the Lobby says it is; that in fact it has, from its very beginning, practiced a form of systemic evil; and to control their suppressed fears, these erstwhile Zionists must strive to control what everybody else thinks and feels about it, often by ritually punishing unrepentant American critics of Israel in conspicuous, public and sometimes surreal ways.

That brings up the phenomenon of *ex post facto* scapegoating, an expedient widely practiced by visionaries when their shimmering dreams turn into nightmares; consider, for example, the pathologies associated with Stalinism. Why were there show trials, assassinations, people sent by the millions to the gulag? Because Communism could not deliver on its promises: therefore scapegoats had to be found, blamed and punished. In the case of

Israel, the ideals of generations of liberals, social democrats and socialists regarding a Jewish state have collapsed or been mainly abandoned; so someone, or some group of people, must be blamed and punished for this failure. Thus the suppressed fury at Israel's moral collapse is seamlessly displaced onto the critics who document that same collapse. This may partially explain the over-the-top, buffoonish nature of the accusations hurled by the Israel Lobby at those who criticize the current government of Israel: that critics are secret crypto-fascists; that they long for the destruction of Israel; that they are planning another Holocaust; and so forth.

If you're still wondering why people in the Israel Lobby behave as they do, consider also the following dynamics from the point of view of a Holocaust survivor, or someone who lost family members in the Holocaust. Where was God at the moment of greatest peril to his people, when 10,000 Jews were being asphyxiated every day in the gas chambers at Auschwitz-Birkenau? God was not there for his people when they needed him—no, God was nowhere to be found. Likewise the secular faith in liberal, social democratic and progressive ideas embraced by secular Jews since the Enlightenment: all of them made not the slightest difference once the *Endloesung*, the Final Solution, was in place. The result was a largely unconscious loss of faith in God, in liberal democracy, and in any solution to political problems except military force. Many survivors ended up believing—unconsciously more than consciously—that those who survive in this world can do so only by hurting others. They believed this mainly because they internalized the aggression Christians had been practicing against them for centuries, which culminated in the Holocaust.

But what institution could act out all this internalized aggression? The Israeli state could. But could it protect Jews, as God and social democracy had failed to do? Yes, by ethnically cleansing Palestinians and taking their property. Of course, that made endless war in the Middle East inevitable, but who cares? What power! What a feeling! For the first time in history, Jews had power! This led to a process in which worship of the Israeli state slowly replaced a Torah-based God, replacing also the secular belief in progressive political solutions. People who increasingly saw God as little more than an ancient metaphor could now worship something far more concrete: the Israeli state's victorious army, its vast propaganda initiatives, not to mention its interrogation centers and its 200 to 400 nuclear weapons—all the furnishings of a successful theocratic state!

And instead of feeling close to a mainly absent and intangible God, Jewish survivors of the Holocaust could now experience tumultuous feelings of religious nationalism, the strongest and most dangerous force on the planet. Indeed, religious nationalism constitutes the central dynamic of Zionism, and is the main animating force behind the US Israel Lobby. Religious nationalism *feels* like God, because it is so powerful—and considering what Jews have gone through in the past, certainly Jews need power in order to protect themselves. But what Israeli Jews have done to the Palestinians, beginning in 1948, and what they continue to do to anybody defined by the Israeli state as an enemy, is the wrong *kind* of power. In the Occupied Palestinian Territories, they have embraced a form of systemic evil, the addictive nature of which only a few are now beginning to comprehend. The Israeli political class has internalized the aggression of the European anti-Semites, aided by the almost daily references to the Holocaust by Israeli media and right-wing politicians—starting with Netanyahu himself—the social outcome being that they now hate the Palestinians in much the same way as the anti-Semites in Europe once hated Jews.

But if Jews struggle with aggression that they cannot acknowledge, so do Christians in Europe and America wrestle with a shame that dares not speak its name. After all, it was Christians who carried out the Holocaust, which was but the final act in a thousand years of Christian anti-Semitism. If Christians thought too much about this last fact, it might occur to some of them that Christianity has been, and is, by its own standards, a failed religion. Thus the built-in incentive to declare the Israeli project a smashing success: an unacknowledged guilt so powerful that Christians will give the Israelis anything they want. For along with the guilt is a generalized fear of being publicly vilified as anti-Semites, which Zionists quickly learned to do to get what they wanted. Thus anything having to do with Israel/Palestine is hedged about with elaborate taboos, for Christians as well as Jews, to the extent that Americans dare not talk publicly, or even think privately, about the moral and political implications of impunity for Israel's crimes and misdemeanors.

All of which should help us understand why Israel must be represented as perfect by the Israel Lobby, and why, according to the Lobby in America, Israel must never be criticized. The Nazi Holocaust must be morally repudiated, and its traumatic memory suppressed—but not in a way that would require anybody to do anything, or make any big changes; so only a Holy State, a perfect state, an exalted and utopian state thousands of miles away (that is to say, an *imaginary* state) could in a quick and efficient manner redeem the shame of Christians, and help to suppress the anger and internalized aggression of Jews. If the Nazi madness was pure evil, the Israeli state must now be perceived as wholly and perfectly wonderful; only the most transcendent and eternally perfect State could help people repress the traumatic memory of the six million dead in Europe, and in so doing suppress all thought of the human evil in the present moment. (Because if the Holy State is perfect, Christians and Jews that uncritically support it are likewise perfect, and need not make any changes or do anything.)

The result of this malignant, self-exculpatory fantasy is a wholly dysfunctional system in which legislators are paid to sign off on proclamations they don't really believe, Christians and Jews are obligated to do obeisance to flagrantly mediocre leaders, and intellectuals are browbeat into pretending that they love Israel when most of them secretly wish that the state of Israel and its power-hungry supporters would go away.

Of course, it isn't as though Western civilization has not seen fanatical, power-obsessed lobbies before. As George Orwell documented in the 1940s, the intellectual classes of Britain and Europe were obsessed for a time by the Soviet Union, which Orwell understood to be a covert form of power worship. But the Communists in the US were never strong institutionally, being confined mainly to a following among creative intellectuals and a handful of trade unionists. The Israel Lobby, on the other hand, possesses enormous wealth from its billionaire donors, and its influence is very strong at every level of institutional life in America; furthermore, as pointed out before, its evangelical Christian followers constitute the most dynamic—if bigoted and culturally backward—constituency in the Republican Party.

The conviction that Israel cannot be criticized isn't just the fancy of a few highly-paid fanatics in the Israel Lobby, although they define fanaticism in our time; they are probably, at this point, supported by a majority of the American people, who have their own pathetic middlebrow reasons for wanting to believe that Israel is perfect. (If Israel is perfect, that's one less thing to worry about in the Middle East, and one doesn't have to think about why Christianity obsessively oppressed Jews for a thousand years.)

But the fact that irrational and profoundly immoral beliefs and behavior have a great following doesn't make those beliefs and behaviors right. The traumas of the 20th century have driven millions of intelligent, capable people into active psychological pathologies, which they experience as ideological realities. The Israeli/Palestinian conflict is not about politics, nor religion, nor even geo-politics. It is about pathology; and ultimately it is about systemic evil. The evil of the Holocaust, like the traumatic memory it generates, is by definition a wound that will never heal; it cannot be suppressed, but only acknowledged and managed. And the only way to really manage it is to deconstruct the trauma bond—the emotional bondage to aggression as the supreme arbiter of history—at its heart. But the neo-Zionists who believe that nobody in the US should be allowed to criticize Israel are completely bonded to the aggression used by the Israeli state, which is aimed not just at Palestinians, but increasingly against international law and the entire concept of universal human rights. (Universal human rights are rights for *everybody*, not *everybody except Palestinians*.)

In the meantime, the real state of Israel (not the fantasy that Americans are encouraged to believe in) keeps moving to the right, the politicians of American and Israel continue to lie about what is really happening, and the use of targeted assassinations, internment without trial, mass use of torture and collective punishment of Palestinians continues. What the state of Israel really needs is what every state needs, which is educated critics denouncing what is wrong about it and supporting what is right, and working to confront injustices and correct them.

But the message of the Israel Lobby, like so much American cultural and political expression, is not about reality, but about an apocalyptic idea of perfection that its *apparatchiki* must ram down everybody's throat in order to suppress their own trauma—in this case, the traumatic memory of the Holocaust, and the creeping doubts about the real nature of the Holy State begotten by its horrors. Israel is not an alternative to the Holocaust, but a continuation of precisely those elements—nationalism, patriarchy, racism and militarism—that caused the Holocaust to happen in the first place. For those reasons it has now become the potential detonator for a world-wide religious war.

5.

Moshe Dayan, the famous general who led Israeli troops in the 1956 Suez War and the Six-Day War of 1967, actually argued long and openly that Israel should follow a "detonator" strategy. "When someone wishes to force on us things which are detrimental to our existence," Dayan said, "there will be an explosion which will shake up wide areas, and realizing this, such elements in the international system will do their utmost to prevent damage to us." In other words, Israel reserves the right to destabilize the Middle East whenever they want to, in order to coerce support from the rest of the world. Interestingly, Dayan, an outspoken and garrulous individual, acknowledged rather proudly that this was not a "constructive thesis," but rather a destructive one. So why should Israel behave in this way, and why should other countries go along with it?

Because of the Holocaust, Dayan and others in Israel typically argued, the Jewish state must now do whatever was necessary to make sure Jews were never hurt again. This meant that sometimes the Israeli state would be obligated to hurt innocent people, because that, they felt, was necessary for the survival of the Jews. Because of the profound traumatic memory that drove this thinking, people were unable to see the harm this would bring to Israel itself—they failed to see that they were, in effect, picking a fight with the rest of the world. Of course, if the international community criticized them, they could always say that it was just because everybody hated Jews, that the world was anti-Semitic—but how exactly did that kind of name-calling benefit Israel?

"It is a thesis," Dayan said in typically colorful language, that Israel "should be a kind of biting beast, capable of developing a crisis beyond our borders. If anyone tries to harm us, the explosion will do damage to others too."

Mess with us, and we'll throw a wrench into the geopolitical machinery, Dayan was saying, and he was saying so rather openly. This polity is roughly comparable to responding to a criminal attack by beating up the first pedestrian that walks by one's house. To respond in that way is not proportional to the original offence, not does it give any thought to Israel's ultimate integration into the region; on the contrary, it seems calculated to make everybody Israel's enemy. Dayan's argument—that Israel reserves the right to destabilize other countries whenever it wants to—is pure arrogance; sadly, nobody had the courage in the US to point this out, or the problems this could ultimately create, for America, the world, and the Israelis themselves.

As time went on, the "detonator thesis" increasingly came to mean the willingness of elements in Israel's political class not merely to destabilize the region, but in certain situations to start wars affecting the rest of the world. This has not gone unnoticed by American observers. In 25 September 2012, American journalist Patrick Tyler argued in the *Los Angeles Times* that the US should be resisting Israel's "detonator strategy," implying that Israel needed to retire gratuitous militarism in exchange for negotiation and compromise. Israel might have the power to destabilize the region—or even blow up the world, with its nuclear weapons—but again, how exactly does that serve Israel's interests?

And why should the world give a single small country in the Middle East the option to disrupt world peace whenever it wants to? Of course, the world shouldn't give *any* country that option, but regarding the Israel Lobby in America, it should be remembered that political life in the US is increasingly run like a casino. At this point, the pro-Likud billionaire political donors of the Israel Lobby are so ensconced in American public life, and the flow of money from them to bought-and-paid-for legislators in the US Congress so substantial, that it is very hard to stop them. Therefore it is up to the prophetic intellectual, working alone and without support, to sound the alarm and tell the truth as he finds it.

That truth is as follows:

Israel is potentially a detonator of a world-wide religious war. This could happen not just because of Netanyahu's warlike policies, but for another reason of which most Americans are blissfully unaware. A growing number of religious fanatics in Israel, now including many Jewish members of the Knesset, Israel's Parliament, are determined to destroy the Al-Asqa Mosque in Jerusalem. The Al-Aqsa Mosque—besides being a beautiful seventh-century house of worship—happens to be the third-most holy site in all of Islam, at least to most Sunni Muslims. The Jewish terrorists are being supported, financially and logistically, not only by billionaire political donors, but also by a large contingent of Christian fundamentalists and evangelicals in the US, who believe a religious war between Islam and the West could bring about the Second Coming of Christ.

The millions of innocent people that could die in such a religious conflagration is of no concern whatsoever to these Jewish and Christian fanatics, because they believe such a horrifying religious war to be the will of God. These are seemingly rational people who nonetheless operate under the delusion that they can summon up the Apocalypse by inciting an international religious war. The emphasis on destroying the Al-Aqsa Mosque to bring about the End Time is particularly strong among the premillennial dispensationalist Christian evangelicals who give money to the Jewish extremists. The evangelicals—the vast majority of which are from the American hinterlands—believe the resulting chaos will cause the Second Coming of Christ; for Jewish extremists, it means the arrival of the long-overdue Messiah. Both groups are delusional and quite dangerous, but for different political reasons have gotten into positions of power in their two respective countries.

6.

The contested area mentioned above is on a level esplanade in

Jerusalem known to Jews as the Temple Mount, and by Muslims as the Haram al-Sharif, or Noble Sanctuary. It has long been believed by religious Jews to have been the site of the Second Temple of the ancient Hebrew-speaking people. After the destruction of the Second Temple in 70 CE, the site was abandoned until the 7th century, at which time two important Muslim structures were constructed by the Umayyad Caliphs in 637. Those two structures were the Al-Aqsa Mosque and the Dome of the Rock, which have heretofore occupied that space. (A third but somewhat unimportant building, the Chain of the Rock, also sits on the Haram al-Sharif.) The Al-Aqsa Mosque, the most important of the structures, has been in continuous use as a Muslim house of worship since the Crusades. Although technically under the control of Jordan since 1967, it is in practice maintained by the Muslim community of Jerusalem.

There are a growing number of religious Jews in Israel, and right-wing Christian evangelicals in the US, who wish to destroy the Al-Aqsa Mosque, so that Jews can *build a Third Temple on its ruins*. (Needless to say, these extremists believe this to be God's will.) Of course, the burning or blowing up of the Al-Aqsa Mosque—besides destroying one of the world's most beautiful and historically important houses of worship—would be a terribly wonton act of aggression against the Muslims that revere it, both in Israel and in Muslim-majority countries around the world. But igniting a worldwide religious conflict is precisely the outcome sought by the religious fanatics involved in this madness.

On January 26, 1984, Palestinian guards near the Al-Aqsa Mosque detained two Jewish extremists bearing high explosives. Further investigation by the Israeli government revealed a powerful and rather far-flung underground movement dedicated to blowing up either Al-Aqsa or the Dome of the Rock, or both. (One aspect of the plot involved an Israeli pilot seizing a plane and bombing the Temple Mount.) According to Charles

Kimball in *When Religious Becomes Evil*, there have been some *twelve attempts* to blow up the Al-Aqsa Mosque and the Dome of the Rock by different bands of Jewish extremists. Success in this venture would almost surely set off a religious war, first in the Middle East and then elsewhere. For those reasons—and for certain religious reasons associated with Orthodox Judaism— past governments of Israel have prohibited Jews from entering the esplanade around the Al-Aqsa Mosque.

These days, however, as Israel continues its precipitous slide to the extreme right, government parties actually *encourage* Jews to go to the Temple Mount, in order to engage in violent confrontations with Muslim worshippers, often shoving their way into the Mosque and starting fights with Muslim worshippers. And it isn't just the right-wing settlers who go there: some of the most active members of Israel's Knesset, or Parliament, go there specifically to provoke Muslim worshippers. Demonstrating Jewish "sovereignty" over the Mosque in this juvenile fashion has become a kind of ritual by which Jewish nationalists demonstrate their bone fides to the voters—those of the governing Likud party, the Jewish Home party, and the religious parties alike.

What is pivotal in these provocations is the participation of governmental figures. MKs and ministers in the Likud government that have done so include Miri Regev (Likud); the Housing Minister Uri Ariel (the Jewish Home party); Deputy Foreign Minister Zeev Elkin (Likud); and especially Moshe Feiglin (Likud), who goes to the Temple Mount or Haram al-Sharif regularly, and has been detained by police more than once for getting in fights or participating in various kinds of provocations. Also going often to the Al-Aqsa Mosque are Defense Minister Danny Danon (Likud) and Knesset members Shuli Moalem and Ayelet Shaked, both of whom are from the neo-fascist Jewish Home party.

Why on earth, one might ask, do so many government figures

go to the Al-Aqsa Mosque, and encourage others to go there, in order to provoke Muslim worshippers? When asked by journalists most say they're just there "to pray at the Temple Mount." Others avow that it is important "to have sovereignty over the Temple Mount." But why sovereignty? Why is sovereignty over a couple of historic mosques so important? There seem to be two answers. The first reason, given by a numerically small but growing contingent of Israeli Jews, is the fanatical religious one: that the ruins of the Second Temple lie beneath the Temple Mount, so Al-Aqsa Mosque and the Dome of the Rock must be destroyed so that a wholly imaginary [Third] Temple can be built it their place. The second reason—the one that apparently motivates most of the politicians—is simply that it has the capacity to cause maximum pain, anxiety and humiliation to Palestinians and to Muslims everywhere, and is therefore a good thing for that reason alone.

The Likud party knows that those Jews that seek to destroy the Al-Aqsa Mosque are delusional fanatics, but Likud also knows that many Jewish voters are turning to the Jewish Home party and the religious parties, both to Likud's right, and some even to the Labor party, on Likud's left. And they are also aware that an increasing number of their own supporters want to see the historic Muslim structures destroyed simply to cause the Palestinians pain and humiliation. At a certain point, the argument for right-wing Jewish nationalism overlaps with that of Israel's religious fanatics. If Israel is the homeland of the Jews, and they can do anything they want in it, why *not* destroy the Al-Aqsa Mosque, just to cause maximum pain and suffering to the Palestinians? Some, in fact, seem to see destroying the Al-Aqsa Mosque as central to establishing Israel's sovereignty over Jerusalem. And some see it as central to Jewish identity.

As far as this writer can determine, the incursions at Al-Aqsa became much more than a nuisance in 2009, when they became a logistical problem for Muslim clergy. At that time Israeli police began to prevent worshippers from entering Al-Aqsa Mosque so regularly that a nearby Mosque, the Mohammad al-Fitih Mosque in the Ras al-moud neighborhood of East Jerusalem, was expanded to accommodate Muslim worshippers. (In May 13 of 2013, for reasons unknown, the Israelis demolished that part of the Muhammad Al-Fatih Mosque in East Jerusalem that had been expanded. Those who had been going to Al-Fatih in East Jerusalem, in the process avoiding Al-Aqsa, now had no choice but to resume attendance at the increasingly embattled Al-Aqsa.)

In 2011, the time I began this research, there were, in Israel, only 137 sites that were protected religious sites; and every single one was Jewish. (This fact was mentioned by the State Department's International Religious Freedom Report as early as 2009.) All the other religious sites in Israel/Palestine (of which there are hundreds) fall under the category of "Special Antiquities Sites"—sometimes also referred to as "heritage sites"—which in practice are sites that receive no protection whatsoever from the Israeli government. Israel's Muslim cemeteries have been allowed to fade into disuse, and many are destroyed when the government thinks it can get away with it.

The 900-year-old Hittin mosque built by Saladin in the Galilee region has been deliberately fenced off and allowed to go to ruin; Muslims are not allowed to worship there, or assume any responsibility for its upkeep. According to Bethlehem-based journalist Jonathan Cook, some mosques are used by rural Jewish communities as animal sheds. "And yet more," he writes, "have been converted into discos, bars or nightclubs, including the Dahir al-Umar mosque—now the Dona Rosa restaurant—in the former Palestinian village of Ayn Hawd."

Meron Benvenisti, a former Deputy Mayor of Jerusalem who wrote *Sacred Landscape: Buried History of the Holy Land Since 1948*, has repeatedly pointed out that Muslim groups, contrary to the blatant lies often put out by the Israeli government and the US Israel Lobby, pleaded over the years to be allowed to officially refurbish and keep up their sacred sites and cemeteries, but were never allowed to do so. Many important Islamic sites, he has written, have been "turned into dumps, parking lots, roads and construction sites."

Ominously, the Israeli government has recently recognized Ibrahimi and Bilal Bin Abi Rabah Mosques as "heritage sites," which means—in the context of Israel's oppression of Palestinians—that they are *not* protected as religious sites, since Israel refuses to protect any religious sites except Jewish ones. Again: in practice this means that the Israeli government is likely to sell off, close or develop the sites, just as they are doing with Mamilla Cemetery (and many other sacred sites, as Meron Benvenisti has documented) which appears on the so-called 'heritage list,' but are denied protection as a religious site. (The interested reader is referred to my investigative article on Mamilla Cemetery, "Israel's War against the Dead.")

The Muslim leadership within Israel appealed the desecration of Mamilla Cemetery to the UN organization for Education, Science and Culture (UNESCO), to which Israel's Deputy Foreign Minister Danny Ayalon replied by freezing relations with UNESCO. After a period of time, talks resumed, but the Israelis made it clear that the Israeli state would do whatever they wished with Islamic and Christian sites. The existence of a 'heritage list' seems mainly a duplicitous instrument to reassure the international community that these sites will be protected, whereas the opposite is true. There is little religious liberty in Israel, since Muslims are discouraged or prevented from maintaining and using a great many of their own historic houses of worship by government policy. (Christian Palestinians have limited rights along those lines, but their churches also face attacks by right-wing Jewish settlers in the West Bank, who have a habit of putting threatening graffiti messages on them.)

On a tour of East Jerusalem in late summer 2010, activist and author Phillip Weiss wrote on his website *Mondoweiss*:

Maybe the most pitiable sight I saw yesterday, inside the West Bank but close to the north Jerusalem colonies of Ramot and Ramat Shlomo, [was] the hilltop tomb of the prophet Samuel, which is worshiped by Jews and Muslims. The tomb is both a mosque with a minaret and a Jewish place of worship. Well when we visited, busloads of Jewish schoolchildren were arriving and Israeli soldiers were in the tomb davening and Hasidic boys were descending, too.

But next door it was a different story:

The door is chained, pigeons fly into the outer rooms, the Palestinian who runs a store there told us that the authorities had shut down the minaret. There are no Palestinian worshipers.

Weiss points out that this is an Israeli National Park in the West Bank, which is supposedly Palestinian land and supposedly—if there were actually ever to be a two-state solution—the future site of a Palestinian state. But being under the authority of the Israeli army, the Jewish site is protected as a religious site, whereas the Muslim worship facility next to the tomb of the prophet Samuel has been deliberately closed down. But this is only the beginning. For the last few years there have been increasingly violent attempts by right-wing Jewish settlers to establish the same "sovereignty" over Palestinian churches and mosques that they seek over the Al-Aqsa Mosque. In reality this is simply a movement of right-wing Jews that aims at humiliating Palestinians, both Muslims and Christians, while generating a feeling of personal insecurity. This often consists of right-wing Jews barging into Christian or Muslims houses of worship, without notice and at odd hours, to perform rituals.

In 2009, a pattern began to emerge regarding incursions at the Al-Aqsa Mosque. Right-wing settlers would suddenly rush into the area around the Mosque, and attack worshippers. Other times they would rush into the Mosque itself, in order to conduct

Jewish prayers and rituals. The Muslim authorities would put out a call for help, and young men would rush on foot to the site from East Jerusalem, and a pitched battle would result.

By 2010 right-wing politicians in Israel were starting to demand as *Israeli policy* that Jews be allowed to pray near, or in, the Al-Aqsa Mosque. The Israeli Police would sometimes try to stop the right-wing Jewish settlers, but in the ensuing melees tended to arrest only Palestinians. It was unclear at that time exactly what the right-wing settlers were trying to accomplish, partly because the media of Israel put the entire subject under blackout. To the extent that there was any discussion of it, it was suggested that Jews should be allowed to pray in or near the Al-Aqsa Mosque because it was the Temple Mount—that is, the supposed site of the Second Temple in Jerusalem before 70 CE. It was common even for liberals and people on the Left to say,

"Well, that's not so bad—what's wrong with letting Jews pray there? Maybe we could set up a regular time... twice a week, say... when Jews can pray on the esplanade."

That ignored the fact that there are already many, many places throughout Israel where Jews can pray, and not nearly as many where Muslims can pray—and the Al-Aqsa Mosque is arguably the most important historically to Muslims in Jerusalem, as well as in the Middle East, not to mention the fact that it is the third-most holy site in all of Islam. What would Israeli Jews say if Muslims tried to force their way into a Jewish synagogue in West Jerusalem to pray? Any Palestinian Muslim trying to do that would probably be shot dead at the doorway, and his wife and children subjected to rough interrogation as terrorists. When discussion regarding Al-Aqsa does manage to get into the newspapers—in Israel or the US—it is rarely mentioned that many leaders of this movement wish to assert their "sovereignty" over the Al-Aqsa Mosque in order to burn it down or blow it up.

In the minds of these fanatics, religious war isn't simply one of many possible outcomes of such an act, *but the outcome they are seeking.* Of course, the short-term object of the right-wing politicians is to humiliate local Palestinians for their own political reasons. But the plot by fanatics also seems quite transparently to be about inciting worldwide religious conflict, and causing the most widespread destruction possible to Israelis, Palestinians, Americans and the world at large. As I have repeatedly tried to point out in this book, shared traumatic memory and the aggression at its heart does not care who gets hurt, or why—it only wants a body count.

Why would Jewish extremists seek to ignite a worldwide religious war, and why would officials in Israel's government encourage them in this murderous endeavor? On a very deep and unspoken level, I believe both are motivated by a desire to punish the world for letting the Holocaust happen—such is the power of traumatic memory in Israel. Although I believe that not all of the fanatics are conscious of this underlying pathology, they have gone repeatedly on the record as seeking a "final conflict" with Islam. As hideous as this eventuality would be, right-wing politicians in Israel have discovered that systematically humiliating and inciting Palestinians has become such an irresistible temptation that the movement for control of the Al-Aqsa Mosque, along with the childish fantasy of building a magical Third Temple on its ruins, has now become a pet project of the Israeli Knesset.

The destruction of the Al-Aqsa Mosque would no doubt receive much impassioned American support from the right-wing evangelicals in the US Republican party, who approve of religious war—at least in part—because they believe such an apocalyptic worldwide conflict would kick off the End Time and the Second Coming of Christ. Other right-wing evangelicals believe that defeating Islam could lead to the wholesale conversion of the world to their unpleasant brand of Christianity. Others will simply see it as a wonderful opportunity to kill, humiliate and torment Muslims in the developing world, and to some extent in America as well—and in the resulting chaos they may call for US Muslims to be subjected to various kinds of legal discrimination. Certain elements of the far right in the US—including some right-wing evangelical Christians—will try to mainstream the idea of putting American Muslims in detention camps.

In 2010 the leader of Israeli's Islamic Movement, Sheikh Raed Salah, had begun to organize protests in East Jerusalem against the increasing tempo of the Jewish incursions into the Al-Aqsa Mosque; the Israelis responded by arresting him. After Raed Salah was arrested, a group of Jewish extremists close to the fascist Kach party, the once-banned followers of which are now a disciplined force in the Knesset, staged a march aimed at destroying the headquarters of the Islamic Movement at Umm al-Fahm. A group of Palestinian protesters stopped them from doing that, although several—including two Palestinian members of the Knesset—were shot with rubber bullets; furthermore, Sheikh Raed Salah's incarceration attracted attention from the international community, and made people aware, because of the attack on Umm al-Fahm, of the resurgence of Israeli fascism. This fascist resurgence shows no signs of abating.

In late 2010 Jewish settlers were increasingly entering Palestinian mosques and churches throughout the West Bank, sometimes to display flags, write graffiti, or conduct religious rituals. On December 16, 2010, at 4 AM, a group of right-wing settlers entered the Beit Ommar Mosque, an eight-hundred-year-old structure that is the spiritual and cultural center of the 17,000 Palestinians in Beit Ommar. Ominously, they were accompanied by a group of Israeli soldiers. After waking up the caretaker, the Israeli soldiers and right-wing settlers informed him—and the other Palestinians present—that they were going to partition the Mosque and conduct their own worship services there three times a week. This was not simply a one-time incursion of racist settlers seeking to humiliate Palestinians; they were accompanied by troops, and that means that they almost surely had political protection from top levels of government. Similar events occurred throughout the West Bank, where settlers accompanied by troops asserted their right to conduct Jewish religious rituals and Jewish services in Palestinian mosques and churches.

The attacks on Al-Aqsa Mosque continued throughout 2011, the main difference being that the extremists now had much more support from right-wing politicians. This meant that increasingly members of the Knesset—and sometimes government ministers—appeared with settlers demanding more "sovereignty" over the al-Haram al-Sharif, the esplanade upon which both the Mosque and the Dome of the Rock sit. For example, on May 18, 2012, a group of 24 settlers showed up with several Members of the Israeli Knesset, and at least one Israeli government minister, to "inspect" the area outside of the Mosque. They were accompanied by heavily-armed troops. A spokesperson for the Al-Aqsa Foundation for Endowment and Heritage was warned that since the forty-fifth anniversary of the unification of Jerusalem was underway, many more such incursions were likely—and indeed, they occurred as feared.

The Israelis apparently began to feel that the defense of the Al-Aqsa Mosque by Muslims was somehow tied to Palestinian resistance, to the slow ethnic cleansing being carried out by Israeli forces on East Jerusalem. Perhaps as a result, the police gradually began to favor the right-wing settlers more openly. By October 2012, after acrimonious debate in the Knesset, the police announced they would no longer ban Jewish settlers from forcing their way into the Al-Aqsa Mosque. Although the Israeli media tried to subject the news to a blackout, it gradually became known throughout Israel (and Muslim-majority countries throughout the world) that right-wing politicians in the Knesset had begun to speak openly of working with extremists that openly sought the destruction of the Al-Aqsa Mosque.

Here's a typical story from Palestinian media:

> On Tuesday 2nd October, since the early hours of the morning, Likud member Moshe Feiglin, escorted by 50 settlers performed their religious rituals, under the protection of the Israeli forces. Al-Aqsa Association for Waqf and Heritage reported that another group of 30 settlers entered to the mosque through Bab al-Magharbeh, and roamed in its yards. Israeli forces arrested four Palestinian Journalists, a TV photographer and a girl from inside al-Aqsa mosque. Dozens of Special Forces spread out in the mosque and forced Muslims, whose ages are less than 45, to go out of the mosque.
>
> On Wednesday an Israeli court appeared to support the efforts of these violent extremists. A Jerusalem Magistrate's Court judge said Wednesday that the police should allow Jews to pray on the Temple Mount—an exceptional remark given that the High Court of Justice has ruled that policy on the Temple Mount is the sole purview of the police.

As the conflicts around Al-Aqsa continued through 2012 and progressed on into 2013, Palestinians began to wonder, also, if the political groupings and politicians that supported the settler incursions weren't also trying to incite a Third Intifada. (The Second Intifada had been caused by Ariel Sharon's visit to the Al-Aqsa Mosque with Israeli officials and army officers, and it has often been called the Al-Aqsa Intifada.) But since the Second Intifada, Palestinians had developed a new instrument of struggle against the Israeli state, this one a nonviolent but extremely effective one: the movement for Boycott, Divestment and Sanctions (BDS) on behalf of the global struggle for Palestinian rights. It was the strategic use of these economic movements that had toppled South Africa's brutal apartheid regime, and Palestinians had taken up the same tactics, and the same strategy, for bringing down apartheid in Israel/Palestine. So Palestinians were not as anxious, this time, to go into the streets with stones against tanks and machine guns. They had found another method of struggle.

In 2013 various provocations and attacks against the Al-Aqsa Mosque continued. A couple of Republican congressmen from the US, clearly angling for evangelical votes, took a staged walk around the Temple Mount with some people from the Temple Institute, one of the groups agitating for Jewish 'sovereignty' over Al-Aqsa Mosque. Shortly afterwards a US group called the "Friends of LIBI" also began to release statements inciting Jews to take over the Temple Mount. (This supposedly American group turned out to be a quasi-official Israel group reportedly started by none other than David Ben-Gurion.) Right-wing US evangelicals were increasingly supportive of the attacks on Al-Aqsa—not only do they want a religious war, many are positively ecstatic about that possibility, since so many of them think that will bring on the End Time and the Second Coming of Christ.

King David's Tomb in the West Bank was supposedly under the 'protection' of the Israeli Antiquities Authority, which means no protection at all. Therefore, in the summer of 2013, Jewish extremists entered the Tomb, and proceeded to destroy all evidence of Muslim influence. The vandals did this by smashing tiles created in the 17th century by Muslim artists under the Ottoman Empire. (The Tomb was used as a mosque during that century; the smashed tiles were similar to those seen at the Dome of the Rock on Temple Mount.) The various administrators in charge of the Israeli Antiquities Authority pretended to be shocked, shocked that someone would do such a thing; but to nobody's surprise, the same vandals returned two weeks later and finished the job.

Haaretz, a liberal Israeli newspaper, put it this way: "A serious act of vandalism, a string of coincidences, and a decision by the Israel Antiquities Authority have combined to change the character of King David's Tomb on Mt. Zion from a Muslim site into a synagogue." The Antiquities Authority rationalized their decision not to reconstruct the tiles by saying they were "protecting the walls" behind the tiles, rather than the tiles themselves. Actually it should be viewed as one more part of a major effort by right-wing settlers and their friends in the government to 'Judaize' sites that ought, by rights, to belong to all three Abrahamic faith communities, and to humankind in general.

In May of 2013 the 'Friends of Al-Aqsa,' a caretaker group that includes Muslims from many countries, reported the following incidents, all of which are sadly typical of what Mosque caretakers would experience throughout the summer. The situation this report describes would continue through the autumn of 2014:

> The blessed Al-Aqsa sanctuary has come under relentless and vicious Israeli attacks this week in a series of escalated incidents. Israeli violations come as Israel continues to deny access to the sanctuary to all Palestinian women and men under 50. Israeli forces regularly deploy heavy handed tactics to terrorize Palestinians wishing to enter the sanctuary. Also on Tuesday, a group of around 40 Jewish settlers stormed the Al-Aqsa sanctuary through the Moroccan Gate. The settlers toured the compound escorted by Israeli police officers to commemorate the eve of Jerusalem Day, a national holiday in Israel celebrating the occupation of East Jerusalem.
>
> Furthermore, Israeli forces once again showcased their penchant for brutality by clashing with Palestinian women trying to access the mosque. The soldiers verbally insulted the women and pushed them with one woman taken to hospital for treatment.
>
> The Al-Aqsa sanctuary was attacked on Wednesday when a group of over 100 settlers accompanied by Israeli forces entered the Al-Aqsa sanctuary, through the Moroccan Gate, for the second

consecutive day. The settlers toured the compound escorted by Israeli police officers to commemorate Jerusalem Day, a national holiday in Israel celebrating the occupation of East Jerusalem and implementing of racist laws.

On Thursday, a provocative procession was held by extremist settlers who marched in Jerusalem chanting 'Death to Arabs' and 'Jerusalem is ours'. The settlers also attacked dozens of Palestinians, Palestinian shops and property, and called for the expulsion of Arabs and Palestinians from the city. A counter-demonstration saw Israel police deploy their usual heavy-handed tactics as they attacked Palestinian protestors and reporters with 21 Palestinians being kidnapped.

But these are not merely wild mobs gathering spontaneously. As the 'Friends of Al-Aqsa Mosque' reports, they have their friends in the Knesset, the Israeli parliament:

Hard-line Knesset members have renewed their calls for violating and attacking the Al-Aqsa sanctuary. Naftali Bennett, Israel's minister of religion and leader of the extremist settler 'Jewish Home' party, is seeking to amend the law in order to allow Jews to pray at the blessed Al-Aqsa sanctuary. Speaking to a parliamentary committee, ministry director Elhanan Glat said 'We would like to ensure that Jews who want to pray there can do so.' And of course, those Jews would invariably want to pray inside the Al-Aqsa Mosque, as a means of ultimately declaring sovereignty over it; the destruction of the Mosque, sought by so many, would not be long in coming.

Bennett is being backed by another notorious hardliner Moshe Feiglin, an MP from the radical rightwing of Prime Minister Benjamin Netanyahu's ruling Likud party, who said "How can we accept the fact that Jews don't have the right to pray at the place which is most sacred to them?"

The 'Friends of the Al-Aqsa Mosque' summed up their increasingly dire situation thusly:

> We are currently witnessing a severe escalation of attacks on the blessed sanctuary. Israeli MPs, illegal settlers and Zionist tourists now violate the sanctity of the Al-Aqsa sanctuary on a daily basis, safe in the knowledge that their actions will not be contested and that they will enjoy the security of occupying Israeli forces.
>
> As the international community has been silent throughout Israel's frequent violations, this gives Israel confidence that when it proceeds with the destruction of the Al-Aqsa sanctuary, it will have nothing to fear by way of reprisal from the international community. The international community must wake up from its slumber of complicity in silence and take meaningful and effective steps to pressure Israel into respecting the Palestinian heritage within the Holy Al-Aqsa sanctuary.

7.

There was from the beginning a press blackout in Israel regarding events occurring at Al-Aqsa and the Temple Mount, although the blackout hasn't always been successful. The astonishing thing, however, was that American newspapers, starting with the *New York Times* and *Washington Post*, have likewise adopted a blackout on the entire subject matter. One can understand why Israeli authorities might want to suppress news about the Al-Aqsa Mosque, however wrong that suppression would be. But there is no reason whatsoever why American newspapers should not report on such events, except fear of the Israel Lobby. The struggle over the Al-Aqsa Mosque—as well as other Muslim religious sites in Israel/Palestine—are absolutely pivotal to world peace, but daily journalism in America refuses to report on it.

There is really no rational reason why Israeli Jews, who already have so many beautiful places to worship in the state of Israel, should want to destroy a historic mosque in Jerusalem, or cooperate with those that do, especially since the Israeli government has partially dismantled the only other mosque in East Jerusalem. Nor is there any rational reason why Israelis should want a religious war. The inevitable conclusion one reaches is that Israel's current leaders, and the constituencies that elect them, are no longer rational actors on the world's stage. Furthermore, they are likely to become increasingly irrational, as long as there are no "countervailing forces," as the sociologists like to say, that can stop them.

Instead of a refuge for Jews, the state of Israel has created a theater for ongoing, permanent psychological trauma, first from a shared traumatic memory of the Holocaust, and secondly from the successive wars made inevitable by the ethnic cleansing of the Palestinians. Israeli Jews have internalized the aggression at the heart of these successive traumatic memories, and are now prepared to act that aggression out against the Palestinians, and against the world. A religious war would almost surely set the stage for the destruction of Israel, but internalized aggression of this magnitude doesn't care who or what it kills. It simply wants the biggest body count possible.

The underlying motive for destroying the Al-Aqsa Mosque is aggression: it is the single and most effective way for Israeli Jews to impose the maximum amount of pain and humiliation on Muslims everywhere. The Palestinians—and to some extent the world's one and one half billion Muslims—are mainly poor and often live in tribal societies, but they have the collective memory of a great imperial culture. Therefore the goal is to generate the maximum agony and humiliation among Palestinians and Muslims generally, and the best way to do this is to attack and destroy their cultural artifacts. That is, of course, completely unnecessary, not to mention gratuitously sadistic, but the Israeli political class no longer cares about what is good or necessary. They have internalized so much aggression, and spent so much time acting it out, that they can think only about hurting the

'Other,' the perceived enemy identified by the almighty state. That is the only thing that makes sense to them, in the same way that the only activity that makes sense to a heroin addict is to get more heroin.

It is exactly the same reason why Christians in Europe burned down Jewish homes and houses of worship during Easter Week, in the long centuries in which such things were practiced. Israeli Jews are now doing to Palestinians what the Christians did to them in Europe—and that was always the true purpose and psychological subtext of Zionism, the creation of a warrior culture that could erase the shame of European anti-Semitism through redemptive violence. The Israeli political class's bond to aggression is so powerful that it will most likely cause it to destroy Israel. And it will do this in ways that are so stupid that they will astound the rest of the world, which will not understand why the right-wing politicians and their allies in the religious parties are behaving so irrationally and self-destructively.

Educated, liberal people don't understand religious fanaticism because they don't think that way—emotionally, they are in a different universe. Therefore they don't believe that highly-organized fanatics are dangerous, because they can't imagine the world in which fanatics live. This was why American liberals didn't understand the power of AM Hate Radio in the US, because they saw the talk show 'hosts' as smutty, low-brow, hate-mongering and uneducated neo-fascists whom it was impossible to take seriously. (Just as educated Tutsis couldn't take seriously the Hutu Power organizers who flourished on Rwandan radio long before the genocide.) But they should have, because AM Hate Radio in the US created the groundwork for Fox News, and Fox News has created a new, neo-fascist language for the hard right, a coherent, consistently hateful rhetoric of racial and religious division that increasingly holds sway over the Republican Party base. The right-wing fanaticism of AM Hate Radio and Fox News changed America, and thus the world; and liberals had no idea why or how this was happening, because they cannot imagine the mental universe in which such fanaticism occurs.

If the Al-Aqsa Mosque were destroyed, the US State Department would emit the usual sanctimonious squeaks and murmurings, but they would continue to give the Israelis more money than any other country, and they will never vote to censure them in the UN. The religiously-motivated terrorists in the Muslim-majority countries will know whom to attack. They will attack the Israelis, but they will also attack America, however much they may like American popular culture. The resulting religious war could last for much of the 21st century. As someone who has both a Jewish daughter and a Muslim one, I say that this is a terrible future for the mind to grasp. But as a prophetic intellectual as well as a public one, it is my work to warn the reader of what is likely to happen. You will never get this kind of discussion from the American media, nor will you get even a hint of the danger from the corrupt American intellectual and political classes. Their job is to tell you the story that you want to hear, so that you will pay money for it.

Many people say, "How can people who were such victims before, turn around and victimize others in such a brutal way?" This reflects the sentimentalized, Disney version of the world that most Americans wish to inhabit. It is precisely those who have been oppressed that are most likely to oppress others: *people internalize the aggression they endure, and act out that aggression against others, and against themselves.* A few do not act on their shared traumatic memory, and instead learn from it: they become the spiritual teachers of humankind. But a strong plurality—and in Israel a majority—are only too happy to become oppressors; and the desperate sadism of their oppression may not stop until the world stops it.

But this is a book about people who escape from traumatic

memory, and break free of its terrible proclivity for bonding people to aggression as a way of life. You may be one of those people, someone overwhelmed by the traumatic memory of the Holocaust or the systemic evil of the Israeli occupation, or by the terrifying reality of systemic evil generally. If so, this is your time to change, following the suggestions in this book. *The only way to defeat the Holocaust is to work for a better world, and in the Middle East that means justice and security for Jews and Palestinians alike.* That is exactly what the heroic young Jews of 'A Jewish Voice for Peace,' 'Not in Our Name' and 'Open Hillel' are doing all over America. It is also what progressive Christian groups like the Israel/Palestine Mission Group of the Presbyterian Church are doing. Despite vicious attacks by the Israel Lobby, the people in these groups have broken free of the Lobby's use of traumatic memory, and chosen lives dedicated to creating a better world.

8.

Larry ("Go-Go") Gagosian, the art dealer who owns the Gagosian Gallery in New York, did a stint when very young at the William Morris Agency in Los Angeles (as Michael Ovitz's secretary) but found his real niche in the 'art business' by selling quality posters to students at UCLA. He began to open art galleries around the world (he has three spaces in New York City), at first leaning heavily on retrospectives of modern artists (Rauschenberg, Lichtenstein, de Kooning) but then developing a strategy of buying and selling art pieces for quick turnover and maximum profit. (Partly by pre-arrangement, one suspects.) Gagosian works his highly profitable inside game with a coterie of fabulously wealthy collectors such as Charles Saatchi, Samuel Newhouse, David Geffen and many others. Gagosian is often considered the world's top art dealer, but also represents the total submergence of painting and photography in the values of monopoly capitalism, which has changed the nature of art in a variety of ways. One of those ways has been to encourage oversized, installation-type art in big, supermarket-like spaces.

Thus it did not surprise New Yorkers when the Gagosian Gallery in the Chelsea district featured the haunting work—in 2010—of the German painter Anselm Kiefer. It was Kiefer's first show in eight years, and probably his best. It was disturbingly entitled *Next Year in Jerusalem* (written in both English and Hebrew) which is the phrase that is repeated at Seder during the Jewish Passover. Originally understood as a religious metaphor, the phrase can now be seen as having an unsettling subtext, since Jews now control the government of Jerusalem, and the Likud government of Israel claims Jerusalem as belonging entirely to the Jewish state (despite the Palestinian Arabs that live in East Jerusalem). So the metaphor has, in a sense, been realized in history: instead of 'Next Year in Jerusalem,' it is now '*This* Year in Jerusalem,' which increasingly includes the troubling and unnecessarily provocative attacks on the Al-Aqsa Mosque summarized above.

But this phrase, 'Next Year in Jerusalem,' was never meant to be physically acted out. It was never a call for Jews to depart *physically* for Jerusalem, but a liturgical and metaphorical challenge to Jews to seek a better life for themselves, and a more just world generally. Jerusalem was the spiritual goal, a beautiful city as an ideal of what life could be. What happens when you dream with your eyes open, and transform what was intended to be a religious metaphor into a theocratic state? Kiefer's entire show seeks to evoke the systemic evil of the Third Reich generally, and the Nazi Holocaust in particular. But the show also clearly suggests that the Holocaust, or something in the Holocaust, is now in Jerusalem—or at the very least, heading in the direction of Jerusalem. (One imagines an irreverent paraphrase of Yeats: *What rough beast, its time come round at last, slouches toward Jerusalem to be born...*)

During the show (on December 18, 2010, the show's last day) occurred a disturbing but otherwise quite revealing incident that illuminated Kiefer's thesis more concretely than anyone could have planned or even imagined. This incident occurred when four people wearing black T-shirts with the show's title *Next Year in Jerusalem* on them (in English, Arabic and Hebrew) were violently removed from the gallery. (On the back of the T-Shirts was "US Boat to Gaza" and underneath that "The Audacity of Hope.")

The New Yorker covered the Kiefer show, and commented on the incident:

"Quietly moving through the Anselm Kiefer show at the Gagosian gallery on its final afternoon were eight people wearing black T-shirts that bore the show's portentous title— *Next Year in Jerusalem*—in English, Hebrew, and Arabic. They didn't speak unless spoken to; they took pictures of themselves standing before some equally portentous works of Holocaust-evoking art. (Everyone was taking pictures; the catalogue cost a hundred dollars.) Only if approached did one of the group explain that they were part of an organization called U.S. Boat to Gaza, which plans to sponsor a ship in the next flotilla to sail against the Israeli blockade."

"Half of the group had left, and they were reduced to four by the time that gallery representatives asked them to leave, unimpressed by their claims to be extending the discussion that Kiefer had begun. Morality. Guilt. Jewish tragedy, past and present. ("This is private property," a gallerista in towering heels shot back. "We're here to sell art.") A call to the police was threatened. In response, the activists put on their jackets— covering the offending Passover phrase, even while complaining that it had not, to their knowledge, been copyrighted—and asked if they might stay. Without reply, the representatives walked away."

Several people had approached them to ask about the words on their T-Shirts. One of those was a German-American woman named Ingrid Homberg. *The New Yorker* reported that Homberg "had gone to Gagosian that day to lift her spirits. A delicate blonde woman in her late fifties, she grew up in Germany—she is roughly of Kiefer's generation—but never felt that she belonged there; she moved to New York with her young daughter in 1980, and the city has proved a much happier fit. In recent years, however, she has been ill (fibromyalgia, arthritis) and suffers frequent pain. Still, she was immediately buoyed by Kiefer's magisterial landscapes, in which massive wings overhead suggest the judgment of God. The gallery was filled with such disturbing images. She had earlier noticed the people in the T-shirts, and now she approached them, hoping to discuss the feelings that the artist's work provoked."

"But there was no discussion. Two police officers arrived just a moment after Homberg did, and ordered the group out. Including Homberg. She said that she had no reason to leave. She asked one of the officers— 'Young man,' she addressed him, and he did look very young—why they did not allow the group to speak. And that was it. His partner grabbed her by the arm and began to pull her out. The force of the motion caused her to lose her balance; she fell. And the Gagosian's chamber of artful horrors came to appalling life, as crowds of gallery goers, on a busy Saturday afternoon, watched a police officer drag a frail and terrified woman, howling with pain, across the floor of two long rooms to the doorway."

"Many people might have assumed that her cries were part of a staged scene, since the protesters were shepherded out behind her, loudly bemoaning their deprivation of freedom of speech. But on the street, Homberg pulled off her coat and rolled up her sleeve to reveal an arm thickly blotched black and blue. The officer, she explained, had not merely grabbed her arm—thin enough, and easy to grab—but had strongly pressed his fingers into the upper inner muscle as he dragged her. The result, she said, was agony."

The *New Yorker* writer plays the story partly for laughs (the protesters "loudly bemoaning their deprivation of freedom of speech"), probably because it would be awkward for that writer to examine in any detail why and how one of the City's prime art venues could be so complicit in censorship. Nor would the *New Yorker* be likely to acknowledge the extent to which neo-Zionism has become the unspoken litmus test of a great many elements of the cultural establishment in New York in 2014, in the same way that Left ideas were the litmus test for many intellectuals during the Popular Front period of the late 1930s.

"A sympathetic bystander informed the officers that they had made a mistake: the sobbing woman was not with the group and no one had ordered her out of the gallery. They [the officers] replied that *they* had ordered her out, and she had not complied; therefore, no mistake was made. Homberg asked to speak to someone from the gallery, but her request, when relayed, was met with conspicuous disinterest. A Gagosian representative has since expressed regret that anyone was hurt during the 'unfortunate disturbance.' The New York Police Department, however, insists that Homberg was merely 'escorted' from the gallery, and denies that she was dragged or mistreated in any way."

"As she was bundled off for medical attention following the incident, Homberg continued to cry. She was upset, she said, because of the terrible pain, because of the shock, and because she had not been able to finish looking at the exhibition. The service of a car was offered by one of the protestors, who had somehow found time to change into a T-shirt that read 'Greed Kills.'" Homberg was then driven to the emergency ward of a nearby hospital.

The Gagosian Gallery in New York may exist only to "sell art," as the stiletto-shod gallerista proclaimed, but the incident related above succeeded in making painfully clear the meaning of Anselm Kiefer's show *Next Year in Jerusalem*. Something terrible happened in Europe, and it is now in Jerusalem. Any Germans, any Jews—any *people*—who criticize or raise questions about the government of Israel, however inoffensively or thoughtfully, will be suppressed, with as much physical brutality as possible. Anselm Kiefer's premise is vindicated. The traumatic memory of the Holocaust is in Jerusalem; and soon—next year in Jerusalem, or perhaps a few years after that—it will be acted out. The religious war detonated by Israel will be a continuation of what began in Europe, the Holocaust by different means.

Notes/References

Chapter One

1. Of course, victims of natural disasters often suffer psychological trauma, and are often haunted by terrible thoughts, feelings and dreams afterwards. But there are differences between that and trauma secondary to human violence. Although there is some disagreement on this issue, there is a general consensus that psychological trauma because of natural disasters affects a smaller population than trauma as a result of man-made disasters and crimes. Natural disasters are blame-free, and in their aftermath families and communities can pull together in ways that are therapeutic in terms of overcoming psychological after-effects. People that are psychologically traumatized by human violence, on the other hand, tend to experience a generalized loss of trust in other people, and find it harder to make simple social contracts. And—as this book argues—human violence changes victims, making them more aggressive.

2. Lawrence Swaim, *Trauma Bond: An Inquiry into the Nature of Evil* (Winchester UK and Washington USA: Psyche Books 2013), 120-240.

Chapter Two

1. Stephen Holden, "Is This a Man Who Sheds Light, or Simply Sets Fires?" *The New York Times*, February 11, 2010, Movies. Holden takes the approach almost all writers about Finkelstein take, which is to comment on the fact that his ideas are extremely controversial, which is essentially irrelevant. The real question is, or should be: is he telling the truth? If so, why are so many people attacking him?

2. Fossion, Pierre; Rejas, Mari-Carmen; Servais, Laurent; Pelc, Isy; Hirsche Siegi, "Family Approach with Grandchildren of Holocaust Survivors," *American Journal of Psychotherapy*, Vol.

57, No. 4, January 1, 2003.

3. Noam Chomsky, *Understanding Power* (New York: The New Press, 2002), pp. 244-248

4. Jabotinsky, whose ideas predominate in today's Israeli political class, modeled his political groups on Italian fascism, and actually sent some of his people to Italy to observe and copy the Italian fascists.

5. http://web.ceu.hu/jewishstudies/pdf/01_kwiet.pdf; see also ^ "RAUL HILBERG - IS THERE A NEW ANTI-SEMITISM? A CONVERSATION WITH RAUL HILBERG - LOGOS 6.1-2 WINTER-SPRING 2007". Logosjournal.com. http://www. logosjournal.com/issue_6.1-2/hilberg.htm. Retrieved 2011-01-06.

6. This writer is increasingly concerned about the Jewish and Christian extremists that are dedicated to destroying the Al-Aqsa Mosque in Jerusalem, which is the third-most holy site in Islam. This volatile situation is dealt with in detail in the last chapter of this book.

7. Throughout this chapter I quote from, and refer to, the Second Edition, which contains added material about the confrontation with the Swiss banks and the demands made against them for money. By 2000 Finkelstein had written four books, beginning with his Princeton thesis, entitled *From the Jewish Question to the Jewish State: An Essay on the Theory of Zionism*. It is in the library of Princeton University. In 1995 he published *Image and Reality in the Israel-Palestine Conflict*. In 1996 he published *The Rise and Fall of Palestine: A Personal Account of the Intifada Years*, and in 1998 with Ruth Bettina Birn came *A Nation on Trial: The Goldhagen Thesis and Historical Truth*.

8. Indeed, many Jewish leaders sought to posture themselves as anti-Communists, led by the Anti-Defamation League, which cravenly turned over names of suspected Jewish Communists to the FBI.

9. Kurt Vonnegut, *Mother Night* (New York: Dell Publishing, 1961), 32.

10. Norman Finkelstein, *The Holocaust Industry: Reflections on the Exploitation of Jewish Suffering* (New York: Verso, Second Edition, 2003), 29-31.

11. Ibid., 30, ftn.

12. In two years the National Museum of African American History and Culture, designed by architect David Adjaye, will go up on the mall in Washington, D.C. It is a great accomplishment, but it is not the same as a museum about slavery, segregation and racism.

13. The founding brothers of America were painfully aware of the existence of evil, which is why they paid so much attention to the dangers of "the mob." They proposed to handle this danger through a separation of political powers, and through the balancing-out of disparate interests, an expedient that has been surprising effective. What is interesting to this writer is that although the founders tended to be theologically liberal, they were intensely aware of the existence and prominence of human evil. Modern religious believers who are theologically liberal tend to dance around the question of human evil, never quite acknowledging it, but never denying it either. Needless to say, they rarely know how to combat evil.

14. Norman Finkelstein, *The Holocaust Industry: Reflections on the Exploitation of Jewish Suffering* (New York: Verso, Second Edition, 2003), 86.

15. Ibid., 81-87.

16. Ibid., 90.

17. Tom Bower, *Nazi Gold: The Full Story of the Fifty-Year Swiss-Nazi Conspiracy to Steal Billions from Europe's Jews and Holocaust Survivors* (New York: HarperCollins Publishers, Inc., 1997), ix.

18. Norman G. Finkelstein, *The Holocaust Industry* (New York:

Verso, Second Edition, 2003), pp. 93-94.

19. Tom Bower, *Nazi Gold: The Full Story of the Fifty-Year Swiss-Nazi Conspiracy to Steal Billions from Europe's Jews and Holocaust Survivors* (New York: Verso, Second Edition, 2003), ix.

20. Norman G. Finkelstein, *The Holocaust Industry* (New York: Verso, Second Edition, 2003), pp. 99.

21. In 2005 former President Bill Clinton created the Clinton Global Initiative (CGI), a charitable organization of the Clinton family. Edgar Bronfman, Sr., is listed as an advisor on one or more of the four advisory boards, as is "Senator Barack Obama."

22. Norman Finkelstein, *The Holocaust Industry: Reflections on the Exploitation of Jewish Suffering* (New York: Verso, Second Edition, 2003), 91.

23. Ibid., 100.

24. Ibid., 130.

25. Ibid., 131.

26. I have two degrees that I earned through independent study, a BA from Goddard and an MA from Antioch College. But to graduate in independent study, I had to recruit my own degree committee from various academics. More than one academic *macher* told me that for him to serve on my degree committee I would have to do research in his area of academic interest, and share the results with him. I am happy to report that the majority, however, made no such request.

27. March 22, 2007, "Memorandum to the University Board on Tenure and Promotion," From Chuck Suchar, Dean, College of Arts and Sciences. Peter N. Kistein, Blog A.

28. "Joint Statement of Norman Finkelstein and DePaul University on their tenure controversy and its resolution." DePaul University, September 5, 2007.

29. The Associated Press (September 5, 2007). "Embattled US

professor who accused Jews of using Holocaust to stifle criticism agrees to resign". The International Herald Tribune. http://www.iht.com/articles/ap/2007/09/05/amer ica/NA-GEN-US-Controversial-Professor.php.

30. He died December 21, 2013, in New York.

Chapter Three

1. Eric Lomax, *The Railway Man: A POW's Searing Account of War, Brutality and Forgiveness* (New York: W.W. Norton & Company, Inc., First American Edition, 1995).

2. Jacobo Timerman, *Prisoner Without a Name, Cell Without a Number* (New York: Alfred A. Knopf, 1981), 33.

Chapter Four

1. Tim O'Brien, *The Things They Carried* (Boston: Houghton Mifflin, 1990), 1-36.

2. The Viet Cong and NVA used sappers as commandos. They were extremely bold, but sustained very high casualty rates. There is some evidence that the use of sappers was one of the most effective initiatives of the Viet Cong and NVA. Many historians believe that the successful sapper attack on Firebase Mary Ann in 1971, in which 30 US soldiers died and over 80 were wounded, was the most humiliating defeat of the US in Vietnam.

3. http://www.vietnam.ttu.edu/virtualarchive/redirects/sym posium2005.htm. Fred Whitehurst's remarks were made in a National Public Radio interview. They are also quoted in the Teachers' Guide to *Last Night I Dreamed of Peace*.

4. Michael Specter, "Partial Recall," *The New Yorker*, 19 May 2014, 38.

5. I am aware of the similarity of this common-sense argument to the 'just war' theory association with Roman Catholicism. But Roman Catholics have certain criteria for a war to be considered just, and my fundamentally secular criteria

would be different than theirs. Nonetheless, the belief that a war must meet certain criteria before one participates in it is a fundamentally sound precept for secular and religious people alike.

6. Why doesn't the US government encourage reconciliation with the Vietnamese, considering how healthy that would be for all concerned? A variety of reasons are usually given, including the fact that the Vietnamese brutally tortured our captured airmen. On the other hand, the carpet-bombing of rural Vietnam was an even greater brutality. The dominant reason that the US doesn't seek reconciliation with the Vietnamese seems to be that powerful elements of the US political establishment simply can't forgive the Vietnamese for defeating the US. That is typical patriarchy—the same national security elite that got us into an unwinnable and unnecessary war, becomes enraged and punitive when the inevitable occurs, and the other side wins.

Chapter Five

1. Morris Fraser, *Children in Conflict* (New York: Basic Books, 1973), viii-ix.
2. Padriag O'Malley, *The Uncivil Wars: Ireland Today* (Boston: Houghton Mifflin Company, 1983), 10, 15.
3. Morris Fraser, *Children in Conflict* (New York: Basic Books, 1973), xi-xii.
4. Ibid., viii.
5. The FV603 Saracen was an armored personnel carrier widely used by the British in Northern Ireland during 'the Troubles.'
6. Morris Fraser, *Children in Conflict* (New York: Basic Books, 1973), xi.
7. Fenians were fighters against British rule in Ireland, most of whom believed that 'physical force'—that is, violence—was necessary to remove the British from Ireland. Almost as soon as it appeared in nineteenth-century newspapers, the word

'Fenian' became a favorite insult hurled by the British Establishment, sometimes used in a dismissive way not only to insult the unruly Irish, but also to denounce trade unionists and others who somehow threatened, or seemed likely to threaten, the customary power relations of British life.

8. 'Ulster' is used universally in the press and by many scholars and writers as a synonym for 'Northern Ireland'; the two may be used interchangeably.

9. Peter Taylor, *Behind the Mask: The IRA and Sinn Fein* (New York: TV Books, Inc., 1999), 40-41.

10. Ibid., 44.

11. Irish Travelers, an itinerant group originating a thousand years ago in Ireland, are often called Pavee, tinkers or Gypies, but are actually ethnically distinct from the Romani people. They speak different versions of *cant,* an ancient Irish language, the most well-known dialect being *Shelta.* Right-wing elements within the Ulster Unionist Party often denounced the Irish Travelers' sites, or camps.

12. This occurred in ways very similar to the so-called 'race riots' in early twentieth-century America, in which it was usually white mobs that entered and attacked Black neighborhoods. This changed with the Watts uprising in 1965, in which Blacks burned cars and buildings and looted stores in their own neighborhoods, then fought off police and firefighters trying to restore order. This set a pattern for subsequent disturbances in the US.

13. Gerry Adams, *Politics of Irish Freedom* (Dingle, Count Kerry: Brandon Book Publishers, Ltd., 1986) 12, 17. First encountered by this writer in Richard English, *Armed Struggle: The History of the IRA* (Oxford New York: Oxford University Press, 2003), 92.

14. Peter Taylor, *Behind the Mask: The IRA and Sinn Fein* (New York: TV Books, Inc., 1999), 60.

15. Richard English, *Armed Struggle: The History of the IRA* (Oxford New York: Oxford University Press, 2003), 98.

16. Militant Protestants who want Northern Ireland to continue its connection to Britain. The world 'loyalist' is used as a synonym for 'unionist' by many authors writing about Northern Ireland, but rightly or wrongly it has developed certain connotations of violence. Many unionists would prefer not to be called loyalists.

17. Peter Taylor, *Behind the Mask: The IRA and Sinn Fein* (New York: TV books, 1997), 131-132.

18. http://en.wikipedia.org/wiki/Little_Armalite

19. Peter Taylor, *Behind the Mask: The IRA and Sinn Fein* (New York: TV books, 1997), 127.

20. Ibid., 133.

21. Ibid., 133-134.

22. Ibid., 134.

23. Ibid., 250-251.

24. Mairead Corrigan Miguire was the aunt of three children who were run over by a car driven by an IRA man who had just been fatally shot by British troops. She and Betty Williams, both Catholic women, formed a nonsectarian peace organization made up of both Protestant and Catholic women pleading for peace between Republicans and loyalists. Maguire and Williams jointly received the Nobel Prize for 1977.

25. O'Malley's interview with Mairead Corrigan Maguire, Peace House, Lisburn Road, Belfast, which occurred on 29 December 1981. Padraig O'Malley, *The Uncivil Wars: Ireland Today* (Boston: Houghton-Miflin, 1983), 267-68.

26. Ibid, 6.

27. Conor Cruise O'Brien, *States of Ireland* (New York: Vintage Books, 1972), 317-18.

28. Adams put it this way in his book *A Farther Shore*, 356: "The inclusion of a clause limiting the life of the union to the will

of a majority in the northern state was a bit like a partner in a relationship saying that the relationship is over, but that she or he had to wait until the children have grown up." Or, on the other hand, the disaffected partner might decide to dwell in the Old Manse indefinitely.

Chapter Six

1. *Hasbara* is a Hebrew word that translates literally as 'explaining,' or sometimes as 'public diplomacy,' but has come to be used sarcastically by both Palestinians and left-wing Israelis to mean 'propaganda.' It very often comes down to the Israeli state rationalizing something illegal, violent or unpleasant it has done.

2. The correct term for an indigenous, Arabic-speaking person living in Israel, or the Occupied Palestinian Territories, is *Palestinian*. Many Israelis refuse to call them Palestinians, because they think that means recognizing—and hence encouraging—their right to self-determination. The word *Palestinian* became standard usage outside of Israel a long time before it became permissible to use it in Israel. Noam Chayut uses the word *Arab* and *Arabs* when describing Palestinians because the conservative Israeli Jews in his book often tend to see them (and to refer to them) in that way—as part of an undifferentiated Arab mass.

3. The Nihal, or Nihal Brigade, was an early Zionist organization originally devised for agricultural development and self-defense. After the war in Lebanon, the Nihal Infantry Brigade was organized out of it. It is noted for good morale and a high level of internal organization.

4. 'Breaking the Silence' is an organization of former Israeli Defense Force (IDF) soldiers who publish memoirs and hold public meetings to testify to the violations of human rights by Israel in the Occupied Palestinian Territories. When its speakers first began to appear on campuses in the US,

uncritical American supporters of Israel's Likud government referred to them as 'anti-Semitic,' but since 'Breaking the Silence' is exclusively made up of Jewish Israeli ex-soldiers, that particular accusation got little traction.

5. Qalandiya Checkpoint is a military checkpoint between Ramallah and Jerusalem. Palestinians must pass through it to go to work, to seek medical assistance, or anything else that requires them leaving their city. Qalandiya is sometimes spelled *Kalandia*.

6. This is part of the general political line of conservatives in Israel, especially those that support the Likud party and the religious parties to its right. One can see the propaganda benefit to the Likudniks: if *everybody* outside Israel is anti-Semitic, the Likudniks in government can do anything they want, and are no longer bound by law or morality. Did Yoav Shamir know the answer that he was likely to receive when he queried this particular journalist? Probably; but it is still representative of the way many feel in Israel.

7. Peter Novick, *The Holocaust in American Life* (Boston and New York: A Mariner Book: Houghton Mifflin Company, 2000), 160.

8. Hajo G. Meyer, *The End of Judaism* (The Netherlands: Oscar van Gelderen, 2010), 122.

9. *Shahid* or *Shaheed* comes from a Qur'anic word meaning 'witness,' but has come popularly to refer to martyrdom in a good cause. Interestingly, variations of this Qur'an-based word are also used by Hindus, Sikhs and Arab Christians, with the same meaning. For example, the Sikh martyr of the Indian independence movement Bhagat Singh is often referred to as Shaheed Bhagat Singh; the popular 1965 Hindu movie about his life is entitled *Shaheed*. The word is sometimes confused with *Shahada*, which is simply the Muslim declaration of faith in one God, and in Muhammad as God's messenger.

10. Barbed wire in coils.

11. Noam Chayut, *The Girl Who Stole My Holocaust* (London and New York: Verso 2013), 13-63.

12. The second intifada started in September 2000, and is generally thought of as ending around February 2005, at the time of the Sharm el-Scheikh Summit.

13. On the day that I fished writing this section, came word that an elderly man was crushed to death at the Ephraim/Taybeh checkpoint, in the West Bank.

Chapter Seven

1. Joseph Commins, *The World's Bloodiest History* (Beverly MA: Fair Winds Press, 2009), 149.

2. Iris Chang, *The Rape of Nanking: The Forgotten Holocaust of World War II* (New York: Penguin Books, 1998), 7.

3. Paula Kamen, "How Iris Chang Became a Verb" http://www.salon.com/2004/11/30/iris_chang/

4. Ying-Ying Chang, *The Woman Who Could Not Forget: Iris Chang Before and Beyond The Rape of Nanking* (New York: Pegasus Books, 2011), 162-63.

5. Ibid., 163.

6. This photo appears in Ying-Ying Chang's book about her daughter; the text accompanying it indicates that it was taken at the Cupertino event. A similar photo—probably also taken at the Cupertino conference—appeared in the *San Jose Mercury News* on November 3, 1996, with a long story about Iris. After the appearance of this story and photo Iris Chang became extremely well known in the large Chinese-American community of the San Francisco Bay Area. There were several photos taken of Iris Chang standing next to photographs of atrocities in Nanking, clearly signaling the proximity she sought to the suffering of the victims.

7. Iris Chang, *The Rape of Nanking: The Forgotten Holocaust of World War II* (New York: Penguin Books, 1998), 83-104.

8. Ying-Ying Chang, *The Woman Who Could Not Forget: Iris Chang Before and Beyond The Rape of Nanking* (New York: Pegasus Books, 2011), 199.

9. Iris Chang, *The Rape of Nanking: The Forgotten Holocaust of World War II* (New York: Penguin Books, 1998), 14, 200.

10. Paula Kamen, *Finding Iris Chang: Friendship, Ambition and the Loss of an Extraordinary Mind* (Philadelphia: DeCapo Press, 2007), 274

11. Oliver August, "Iris Chang: Her Friends Used to Worry About her," *London Time*, 26 March 2005.

12. Iris Chang, *The Rape of Nanking: The Forgotten Holocaust of World War II* (New York: Penguin Books, 1998), 27.

13. Ibid., 219

14. Ibid., 57-58.

15. Ibid., 54-59.

16. It was to make people aware of that, and of their responsibilities to humanity, that the Nuremburg Trials determined that 'following orders' is not an acceptable legal defense when used by war criminals. This same concept was similarly adopted by the Nanking War Crimes Tribunal and the International Military Tribunal of the Far East.

17. Oliver August, "Iris Chang: Her Friends Used to Worry About Her," *London Times*, 26 March 2005.

18. http://purefilmcreative.com/baker-street/terracotta-warrior.html

19. Paula Kamen, *Finding Iris Chang: Friendship, Ambition and the Loss of an Extraordinary Mind* (Philadelphia: DeCapo Press, 2007), 210-11.

20. Ibid., 268.

21. Kay Redfield Jamison, *An Unquiet Mind: A Memoir of Moods and Madness* (New York: Vintage Books, 1996), 5-6.

22. Paula Kamen, *Finding Iris Chang: Friendship, Ambition, and the Loss of an Extraordinary Mind* (Philadelphia: DeCapo Press, 2007), 194-95.

23. Ibid., 134.

24. At least two other close friends declined to talk with Iris about their personal and psychological problems because they thought her "too perfect."

25. Ibid., 111.

26. Paula Kamen, *Finding Iris Chang: Friendship, Ambition, and the Loss of an Extraordinary Mind* (Philadelphia: DeCapo Press, 2007), 181.

27. http://www.sfgate.com/health/article/Historian-Iris-Chang-won-many-battles-The-war-2679354.php#page-14. Dr. Lo's comment appears in Heidi Benson's powerful account of Iris Chang's last weeks.

Chapter Eight

1. Dwight McDonald, *Dwight McDonald on Movies* (Englewood Cliffs, N.J.: Prentice-Hall, Inc., 1969) 367.

**PSYCHE
BOOKS**

The study of the mind: interactions, behaviours, functions.
Developing and learning our understanding of self. Psyche
Books cover all aspects of psychology and matters relating to
the head.